D1000120

China
a country study

Federal Research Division
Library of Congress
Edited by
Robert L. Worden,
Andrea Matles Savada,
and Ronald E. Dolan
Research Completed
July 1987

On the cover: The artist's pen-and-ink rendering of a cast-bronze horse, chariot, and driver of the Eastern Han dynasty (A.D. 25-220) reveals the dual sense of vitality and passivity often found in Chinese art.

Fourth Edition, First Printing, 1988.

Library of Congress Cataloging in Publication Data

China, a country study.

(DA pam; 550-60)
"Research completed September 1987."
Bibliography: p. 637.
Includes index.
Supt. of Docs. no. : LC D101.22:60/987
1. China. I. Worden, Robert L., 1945- . II. Savada, Andrea Matles, 1950- . III. Dolan, Ronald E., 1939- IV. Library of Congress. Federal Research Division. V. Series.

DS706.C489 1988 951 87-600493

Headquarters, Department of the Army
DA Pam 550-60
Supersedes 1981 edition

For Sale by the Superintendent of Documents, U.S. Government Printing Office
Washington, D.C. 20402

Foreword

This volume is one in a continuing series of books now being prepared by the Federal Research Division of the Library of Congress under the Country Studies—Area Handbook Program. The last page of this book lists the other published studies.

Most books in the series deal with a particular foreign country, describing and analyzing its political, economic, social, and national security systems and institutions, and examining the interrelationships of those systems and the ways they are shaped by cultural factors. Each study is written by a multidisciplinary team of social scientists. The authors seek to provide a basic understanding of the observed society, striving for a dynamic rather than a static portrayal. Particular attention is devoted to the people who make up the society, their origins, dominant beliefs and values, their common interests and the issues on which they are divided, the nature and extent of their involvement with national institutions, and their attitudes toward each other and toward their social system and political order.

The books represent the analysis of the authors and should not be construed as an expression of an official United States government position, policy, or decision. The authors have sought to adhere to accepted standards of scholarly objectivity. Corrections, additions, and suggestions for changes from readers will be welcomed for use in future editions.

The Chief
Federal Research Division
Library of Congress
Washington, D.C. 20540

Acknowledgments

The authors wish to acknowledge their use and adaptation of several chapters from the 1981 edition of *China: A Country Study*, edited by Frederica M. Bunge and Rinn-Sup Shinn. In particular, substantial parts of the following chapters were incorporated by the authors of the new edition: Martin Weil's "Physical Environment and Population," Joel N. Glassman's "Education and Culture," Thomas R. Gottschang's "Industry" and "Trade and Transportation," Rinn-Sup Shinn's "Party and Government," and David G. Barlow and Daniel W. Wagner's "Public Order and Internal Security."

The authors also are indebted to a number of individuals in the United States government and in international, diplomatic, and private organizations who gave of their time and special knowledge on Chinese affairs to provide research data and perspective. Those who were particularly helpful were Judith Banister of the United States Bureau of the Census; Paul Schroeder of the Map Library, Department of State; Edward P. Parris of the Department of Defense; Chi Wang of the Asian Division, Library of Congress; and Constance A. Johnson of the Far Eastern Law Library, Library of Congress. The photographs that illustrate this study were generously contributed by a variety of individuals and public and private organizations. All have been credited in the captions. In particular, Liu Haiming of the Embassy of the People's Republic of China assisted in making available numerous photographs on diverse subjects. None of the aforementioned individuals or their organizations, however, are responsible for the contents of the book.

The authors also wish to express their appreciation to members of the staff of the Federal Research Division, Library of Congress, who contributed to the preparation of the book. Foremost among these was Barbara L. Dash, who meticulously reviewed the text. Without her assistance the entire effort would not have been as complete and as finely tuned as it has come to be. Ms. Dash was assisted in editing by Glenn E. Curtis and Martha E. Hopkins, who also managed production of the book. Mervin J. Shello and Ly H. Burnham examined specialized and technical sections of the manuscript, and Carolina E. Forrester reviewed textual references to China's geography and scrutinized the maps that appear in this volume. David P. Cabitto, Sandra K. Cotugno, and Kimberly Lord provided copious graphic arts support. Tracy M. Henry assisted on numerous phases of the book, including wordprocessing of chapter texts, formatting and typing much of the tabular data, and proofreading. Alberta Jones King, Barbara Edgerton, and Izella Watson diligently provided wordprocessing. Richard F. Nyrop reviewed all parts of the book and made valuable suggestions throughout its development.

Others who contributed to this edition were Paulette A. Marshall, who designed the cover and chapter illustrations; Teresa E. Kamp, who prepared several of the maps; and Margaret Varghese of Editorial Experts, who compiled the index. Andrea T. Merrill made a very important contribution to the overall consistency and quality of the book in performing the final, prepublication review. Also, the late John G. Early, head of the Printing and Processing Section, Library of Congress, was instrumental in establishing procedures for typesetting the final text. Peggy F. Pixley, of the same section, directed the actual typesetting, which was accomplished by Diann Johnson.

Contents

Page

Foreword iii

Acknowledgments v

Preface xvii

Country Profile xxi

Introduction xxxi

Chapter 1. Historical Setting 1
Rinn-Sup Shinn and Robert L. Worden

THE ANCIENT DYNASTIES 5
- The Dawn of History 5
- The Zhou Period 6
- The Hundred Schools of Thought 7

THE IMPERIAL ERA 11
- The First Imperial Period 11
- Era of Disunity 13
- Restoration of Empire 13
- Mongolian Interlude 16
- The Chinese Regain Power 18
- The Rise of the Manchus 18

EMERGENCE OF MODERN CHINA 21
- The Western Powers Arrive 21
- The Opium War, 1839-42 22
- The Taiping Rebellion, 1851-64 23
- The Self-Strengthening Movement 24
- The Hundred Days' Reform and the Aftermath 28
- The Republican Revolution of 1911 29

REPUBLICAN CHINA 30
- Nationalism and Communism 31
- Anti-Japanese War 36
- Return to Civil War 38

THE PEOPLE'S REPUBLIC OF CHINA 39
- The Transition to Socialism, 1953-57 41
- The Great Leap Forward, 1958-60 43
- Readjustment and Recovery, 1961-65 46
- The Cultural Revolution Decade, 1966-76 47
- The Post-Mao Period, 1976-78 53
- China and the Four Modernizations, 1979-82 54

Chapter 2. Physical Environment and Population 59
Michael L. Waddle
PHYSICAL ENVIRONMENT 62
Boundaries 64
Terrain and Drainage 65
Climate 71
Wildlife 71
POPULATION 72
The Data Base 72
Mortality and Fertility 74
Population Control Programs 75
Density and Distribution 78
Migration 78
Minority Nationalities 84
Policy 87
Labor Force 88
Health Care 90
Chapter 3. The Social System 97
Donald R. DeGlopper
ETHNIC BOUNDARIES 99
HAN DIVERSITY AND UNITY 101
TRADITIONAL SOCIETY AND CULTURE 103
Diffusion of Values 105
The Confucian Legacy 105
Traditional Social Structure 106
The Examination System 107
Social Stratification 108
Stratification and Families 109
Social Mobility 110
SOCIAL CHANGE 112
DIFFERENTIATION 114
The Work Place 114
Communist Party Membership 116
Urban-Rural Distinctions 117
Regional Distinctions 118
COMMON PATTERNS 119
Work Units 120
Wages and Benefits 121
Informal Mechanisms of Exchange 122
RURAL SOCIETY 124
Collectivization and Class Status 124
Decollectivization 125

The Role of the Household 126
Consequences of Rural Reform 127
Regulations and Favors 128
Family and Household 130
Marriage 132
Community Structure 133
URBAN SOCIETY 134
Distinctive Features 134
Housing 136
Families and Marriage 138
Providing for the Next Generation 139
Opportunities and Competition 140
Examinations, Hereditary Transmission of Jobs, and Connections 142
WOMEN 143
RELIGION 145
TRENDS AND TENSIONS 147
Chapter 4. Education and Culture 151
Andrea Matles Savada and Ronald E. Dolan
EDUCATION POLICY 154
THE EDUCATION SYSTEM 156
New Directions 156
Compulsory Education Law 157
Key Schools 159
PRIMARY EDUCATION 160
Primary Schools 160
Preschool Education 162
Special Education 163
SECONDARY EDUCATION 163
Middle Schools 163
Vocational and Technical Schools 164
HIGHER EDUCATION 166
Background 166
Modernization Goals in the 1980s 168
Entrance Examinations and Admission Criteria 169
Changes in Enrollment and Assignment Policies 171
Scholarship and Loan System 173
Study Abroad 173
Educational Investment 174
TEACHERS 176
ADULT EDUCATION 177
Role in Modernization 177
Alternative Forms 177
Literacy and Language Reform 179

POLICY TOWARD INTELLECTUALS 180
Background 180
Post-Mao Development 182
CULTURE AND THE ARTS 185
Traditional Literature 185
Modern Prose 188
Literature in the Post-Mao Period 189
Traditional Arts 190
Contemporary Performing Arts 195
Publishing 198

Chapter 5. Economic Context 205
Thomas R. Gottschang

GENERAL NATURE OF THE ECONOMY 210
ECONOMIC POLICIES, 1949-80 213
Recovery from War, 1949-52 213
The First Five-Year Plan, 1953-57 215
The Great Leap Forward, 1958-60 216
Readjustment and Recovery: "Agriculture First," 1961-65 218
Events During the Cultural Revolution, 1966-76 220
The Post-Mao Interlude, 1976-78 222
Reform of the Economic System, Beginning in 1979 .. 223
STRUCTURE AND OPERATION OF THE ECONOMY 228
Roles of the Government and the Party 228
The Two Major Sectors: Agriculture and Industry ... 231
Other Important Sectors 236
Planning 238
The Budget 242
The Banking System 243
Prices 246
LIVING STANDARDS 250
Progress since 1949 250
Food 251
Clothing 252
Consumer Goods 254
Housing 254
Income Distribution 255
POTENTIAL FOR ACHIEVING NATIONAL GOALS 260

Chapter 6. Agriculture 265
Frederick W. Crook

RESOURCES ENDOWMENT 268

AGRICULTURAL POLICIES 271
The 1950s 271
Importance of Agriculture Recognized 273
Recovery 274
Post-Mao Policies 275
PLANNING AND ORGANIZATION 278
OPERATIONAL METHODS AND INPUTS 281
Cropping Patterns 281
Fertilizer 281
Mechanization 282
Water Conservancy 284
Pest Control 284
Seed Varieties 285
Agricultural Science 285
PRODUCTION 286
Crops 286
Animal Husbandry 291
Forestry 292
Fishery 292
Sideline Production 292
AGRICULTURAL TRADE 294

Chapter 7. Industry 299
Michael L. Waddle

TRENDS IN INDUSTRIAL PRODUCTION 302
ORGANIZATION 305
GEOGRAPHICAL DISTRIBUTION OF INDUSTRY 305
LEVEL OF TECHNOLOGY 306
SUPPLIES OF INDUSTRIAL RESOURCES 308
Capital 308
Labor 309
Raw Materials 309
Energy 310
MANUFACTURING 310
Iron and Steel 310
Machine Building 313
Chemicals 317
Building Materials 318
Paper 319
Textiles 320
Food Processing 321
Other Consumer Goods 322
CONSTRUCTION 322
Housing Construction 322
Capital Construction 323

MINING 324
Coal 324
Iron Ore 324
Other Minerals and Metals 325
ENERGY 326
Oil and Natural Gas 326
Electric and Nuclear Power 328
RURAL INDUSTRY 331
DEFENSE INDUSTRY 332

Chapter 8. Trade and Transportation 335
Roxane D.V. Sismanidis and Ernestine H. Wang

INTERNAL TRADE AND DISTRIBUTION 337
Agriculture 337
Industry 340
Lateral Economic Cooperation 342
Retail Sales 343
FOREIGN TRADE 344
History of Chinese Foreign Trade 344
Trade Policy in the 1980s 347
Organization of Foreign Trade 349
Composition of Foreign Trade 352
Trading Partners 353
Tourism 354
TRANSPORTATION 354
Railroads 357
Subways 358
Highways and Roads 360
Bridges 361
Inland Waterways 361
Maritime Shipping 362
Civil Aviation 363
POSTAL SERVICES 364
TELECOMMUNICATIONS 365
Historical Development 365
Telecommunication Services 366

Chapter 9. Science and Technology 371
Donald R. DeGlopper

HISTORICAL DEVELOPMENT OF SCIENCE AND TECHNOLOGY POLICY 374
Pre-1949 Patterns 374
Soviet Influence in the 1950s 377
"Reds" Versus "Experts" in the 1950s and 1960s ... 379
Rehabilitation and Rethinking, 1977–84 382

SCIENCE AND TECHNOLOGY IN THE 1980s 386
The Supply of Skilled Manpower 386
Research Institutes 387
National Organization and Administration 387
Integration of Administrative Systems 393
International Ties 395
THE REFORM PROGRAM 397
Shortcomings of the Science and Technology System 397
The Program 398
TECHNOLOGY TRANSFER 403
Policy 403
Modes of Transfer 403
Linking Technology and Economics 404

Chapter 10. Party and Government 407
Marcia R. Ristaino

CHINESE COMMUNIST PARTY 411
Party Constitution 411
National Party Congresses 412
Central Committee and Political Bureau 413
Secretariat 415
Central Military Commission 415
Other Party Organs 416
Membership 417
Mass Organizations 418
THE GOVERNMENT 421
Constitutional Framework 421
The National People's Congress 424
The State Council 426
The Judiciary 427
Local Administration 428
The Cadre System 434
THE MEDIA 437

Chapter 11. The Political Process 443
Marcia R. Ristaino

POLITICAL REALIGNMENTS AT THE PARTY CENTER 447
Deng Xiaoping Consolidates Power 447
Institutionalizing Collective Leadership 450
A Successor Generation 452

THE FIRST WAVE OF REFORM, 1979-84 453
The Opening Up Policy and Reform in the Countryside 454
Rectification and Reform 456
THE SECOND WAVE OF REFORM, 1984-86 458
The Repercussions of Urban Reform 458
The Decentralization of Power 459
THE THIRD WAVE OF REFORM, BEGINNING IN 1986 460
Political Reform 460
Resistance and the Campaign Against Bourgeois Liberalization 461
THE POLITICS OF MODERNIZATION 462
The Components of Reform 463
Competing Bureaucratic Interests 463
Deng Xiaoping's Seminal Role 465
MARXISM-LENINISM-MAO ZEDONG THOUGHT RE-THOUGHT 465
The Role of Ideology 466
Ideology and the Socialist Man 468
Ideology and Social Change 468
Chapter 12. Foreign Relations 471
Elizabeth E. Green
EVOLUTION OF FOREIGN POLICY 475
Historical Legacy and Worldview 475
Nationalism 476
The Influence of Ideology 478
Decision Making and Implementation 481
AN OVERVIEW OF CHINA'S FOREIGN RELATIONS ... 488
Sino-Soviet Relations 488
Sino-American Relations 492
Relations with the Third World 495
Relations with the Developed World 498
China's Role in International Organizations 501
Chapter 13. Criminal Justice and Public Security 505
Ronald E. Dolan
THE LEGAL SYSTEM 508
Imperial China 508
The Republican Period 509
Developments after 1949 509
Return to Socialist Legality 517

COURT STRUCTURE AND PROCESS 522
LAW ENFORCEMENT 525
Historical Background 525
Public Security Forces 529
Grass-Roots Organizations 534
THE PENAL SYSTEM 537

Chapter 14. National Defense 541
Roxane D.V. Sismanidis

HISTORICAL DEVELOPMENT, 1927–79 545
From the Founding of the People's Liberation Army to the Korean War 545
Military Modernization in the 1950s and 1960s 547
The People's Liberation Army in the Cultural Revolution 549
Military Modernization in the 1970s 551
MILITARY MODERNIZATION 553
Civil-Military Relations 555
Political Role of the People's Liberation Army 555
Military Organization 557
Doctrine, Strategy, and Tactics 562
Education and Training 564
Personnel 565
Defense Industry and the Economic Role of the People's Liberation Army 568
PERCEPTION OF THREAT 575
The Soviet Union 576
Vietnam 577
India 578
South China Sea 579
Taiwan 579
FOREIGN MILITARY COOPERATION 579
FORCE STRUCTURE 582
Ground Forces 582
Air Force 583
Navy 585
Nuclear Forces 587
Paramilitary Forces 590
ACCOMPLISHMENTS AND PROSPECTS 593

Appendix A. Tables 595

Appendix B. Chronology and Lists 617

Appendix C. The People's Liberation Army at a Glance 633

Bibliography 637

Glossary 699

Index 709

List of Figures

1 China, 1988 xxx
2 The Chinese Empire, circa 220 B.C., A.D. 700, 1580, and 1775 12
3 China-Soviet Union Border Area 66
4 Topography and Drainage 70
5 Population Density, 1982 79
6 Distribution of Major Minority Nationalities 85
7 Gross National Product and Major Economic Sectors, 1952-86 212
8 Agricultural Regions, 1987 269
9 Per Capita Gross Value of Agricultural Output (GVAO) and Crop Production, 1952-83 276
10 Composition of Agricultural Exports and Imports, 1985 296
11 Major Industrial Facilities, 1987 307
12 Steel Production and Capacity, 1948-86 314
13 Coal Reserves and Major Mining Areas, 1987 325
14 Major Oil Basins and Oil Fields, 1987 329
15 Railroads and Major Air and Sea Ports, 1987 355
16 Principal Improved Inland Waterways, 1987 363
17 Organization of the Science and Technology Establishment 389
18 Organization of the Chinese Communist Party, 1987 414
19 The Structure of the Government, 1987 428
20 Organization of the People's Courts and People's Procuratorates, 1987 524
21 Organization of the Public Security System, 1987 530
22 Organization of the Military Establishment, 1987 558
23 Military Regions and Fleet Commands, 1986 563

Preface

China in the 1980s was a nation rapidly modernizing as its leadership implemented sweeping reforms in the economic, social, and political sectors and adopted a policy of opening up to the outside world. The scale and pace of China's comprehensive modernization program have necessitated this new and updated edition of *China: A Country Study*, which supersedes the third edition published in 1981 under the same title. Much of what was reported in 1981 has been overtaken by events. Sources of information in the new edition have included scholarly journals and monographs, official reports of governments and international organizations, foreign and domestic media reports, numerous periodicals, and, significantly, the increasingly available and accurate Chinese government statistical reports and analyses. Bibliographic essays calling attention to useful sources of further reading appear at the end of each chapter.

The aim of the authors has been to present an understanding of China in a period of transition and modernization against the backdrop of both a long and illustrious historical heritage and twentieth-century political turmoil. As an aid to readers seeking an understanding of the broad framework of China's long history, a chronology of dynasties is provided (see table A). Increasingly reliable information about all sectors of Chinese society became available in the 1980s—emanating from scholars and technical experts, both Chinese and foreign—aiding the authors of this volume in presenting what is hoped is a clear and thoughtful analysis. Nevertheless, gaps in data and inconsistent reporting have required the authors to make interpretations and conclusions, some of which must be regarded as highly tentative. Both old questions and new developments need additional investigation by interested observers of Chinese affairs.

With certain minor exceptions, Chinese personal names and place-names in this study are represented according to the pinyin system of romanization. For those familiar with the Wade-Giles system of romanization, once commonly used in Western-language publications on Chinese subjects and still used in whole or in part by some, conversions are provided for pinyin, Wade-Giles, and conventional ("post office") spellings of major place-names (see table 2, table 3, Appendix A). The standard spellings provided by the United States Board on Geographic Names are used throughout the book. Exceptions were made for the names of well-known historical figures like Confucius and Sun Yat-sen and certain place-names, such as Hong Kong and Macao, to coincide with official usage in English-language publications of the government of the People's Republic of China. It should be noted too that in the text and on maps some generic parts of Chinese geographic names have been retained in following Chinese official usage in foreign-language publications. Thus *jiang* and *he* (river), *hai* (sea), *wan* (bay), and *shan* and *ling* (mountain) have been used, but the English terms have been retained for island, plateau, basin, plain, desert, province, autonomous region, and special municipality.

Measurements are given in the metric system; a table is provided to assist those readers who wish to convert between metric and non-metric systems (see table 1, Appendix A). A glossary and bibliography also are included at the back of the book.

Organizational names are spelled out to avoid confusing those reading about China for the first time. Thus, there are the National Party Congress (of the Chinese Communist Party) and the National People's Congress (the legislature), rather than the acronym NPC. Some longer or more complicated names appear in acronym form after being spelled out in their first use in each chapter.

Table A. Chronology of Chinese Dynasties

Dates	Dynasty
ca. 21st–16th century B.C.	Xia
1700–1027 B.C.	Shang
1027–771 B.C.	Western Zhou
770–221 B.C.	Eastern Zhou
770–476 B.C.	Spring and Autumn period
475–221 B.C.	Warring States period
221–207 B.C.	Qin
206 B.C.–A.D. 9	Western Han
A.D. 9–24	Xin (Wang Mang interregnum)
A.D. 25–220	Eastern Han
A.D. 220–280	Three Kingdoms (San Guo)
220–265	Wei
221–263	Shu
229–280	Wu
A.D. 265–316	Western Jin
A.D. 317–420	Eastern Jin
A.D. 420–588	Southern and Northern Dynasties
420–588	Southern Dynasties
420–478	Song
479–501	Qi
502–556	Liang
557–588	Chen
386–588	Northern Dynasties
386–533	Northern Wei
534–549	Eastern Wei
535–557	Western Wei
550–577	Northern Qi
557–588	Northern Zhou
A.D. 581–617	Sui
A.D. 618–907	Tang
A.D. 907–960	Five Dynasties
A.D. 907–979	Ten Kingdoms
916–1125	Liao

Table A.—Cont.

Dates	Dynasty
960–1279	Song
960–1127	Northern Song
1127–1279	Southern Song
1038–1227	Western Xia
1115–1234	Jin
1279–1368	Yuan
1368–1644	Ming
1644–1911	Qing

Source: Based on information from China Handbook Editorial Committee, *China Handbook Series: History* (trans., Dun J. Li), Beijing, 1982, 188–89; and Shao Chang Lee, "China's Cultural Development" (wall chart), East Lansing, 1964.

Country Profile

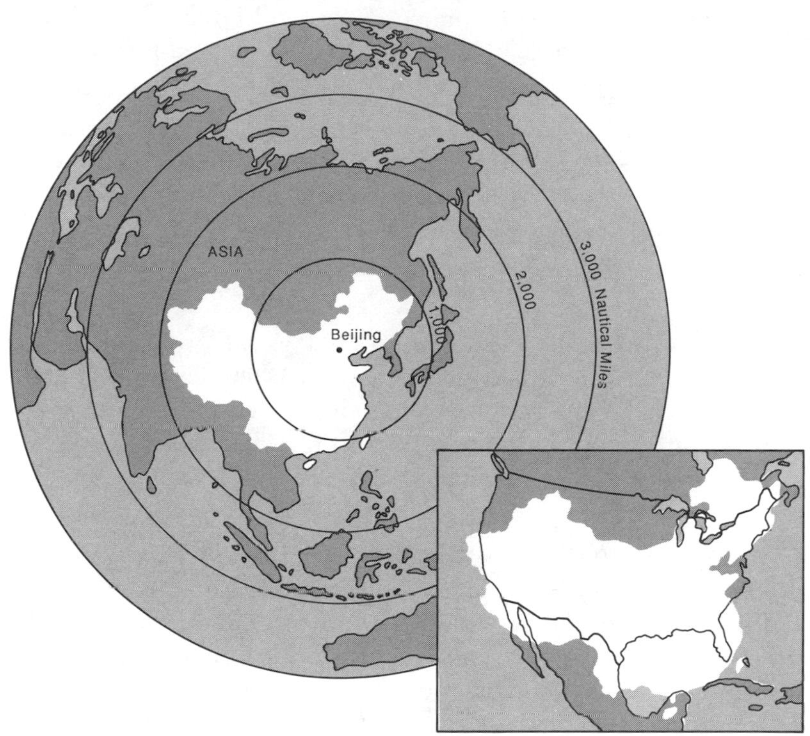

Country

Formal Name: People's Republic of China.

Short Form: China.

Term for Citizens: Chinese.

Capital: Beijing.

Geography

Size: Area about 9.6 million square kilometers; east to west distance about 5,000 kilometers, from the Heilong Jiang (Amur River) to Pamir Mountains in Central Asia; north to south distance approximately 4,050 kilometers, from Heilongjiang Province to Hainan Island in south, and another 1,450 kilometers further south to Zengmu Shoal, territorial claim off north coast of Malaysia.

Topography: Main topographic features include Qing-Zang (Qinghai-Tibet) Plateau 4,000 meters above sea level and Kunlun, Qin Ling, and Greater Hinggan ranges. Longest of country's numerous rivers, Chang Jiang (Yangtze River) and Huang He (Yellow River), extend for some 6,300 and 5,400 kilometers, respectively.

Climate: Most of country in temperate belt. Complex climatic patterns ranging from cold-temperate north to tropical south. Precipitation varies regionally; temperatures range from minus 30°C in north in January to 28°C in south in July. Alternating wet monsoon in summer, dry monsoon in winter.

Society

Population: 1982 census reported total population of 1,008,180,738; official estimate at end of 1986 nearly 1.1 billion with 1.4 percent annual rate of increase. Urban population officially estimated at 382 million by end of 1985, or 37 percent of total. About 94 percent of population lives on approximately 36 percent of land.

Education: In 1985, about 96 percent of primary-school-age children attended school as compared with about 20 percent before 1949. About 136 million students enrolled in more than 832,000 primary schools. Secondary-level middle schools divided into junior and senior stages; majority of schools at lower level. About 48.6 million students attended some 104,800 secondary-level institutions. Technical education emphasized. Intense competition for admission to more than 1,000 colleges and universities; about 1.7 million students in various higher educational institutions. Beijing and Qinghua universities and more than 100 other key universities most sought after by college entrants.

Ethnic Minorities: As of 1987 China recognized 55 minority nationalities, numbering about 70 million persons, concentrated in northwest and southwest. Not largest, but most important politically, Tibetans (Zang nationality) and various Turkic-speaking groups constituted majorities in Xizang (Tibet) and Xinjiang-Uygur autonomous regions, respectively.

Health: Level of health and medical care improving. System of national, provincial-level, and local facilities in urban and rural areas plus network of industrial and state-enterprise hospitals. Traditional and Western medicine both practiced. Average life expectancy of sixty-nine years in 1985. Many once-widespread epidemic diseases now under control or eradicated.

Economy

Salient Features: Economic system in transition, cautiously moving away from Soviet-style central planning and gradually adopting market economy mechanisms and reduced government role. Industry, largely based on state and collective ownership, marked by increasing technological advancements and productivity. China's people's communes (see Glossary) largely eliminated by 1984—after more than twenty-five years—and responsibility system (see Glossary) of production introduced in agricultural sector. Private ownership of production assets legal, although major nonagricultural and industrial facilities still state owned and centrally planned. Restraints on foreign trade relaxed and joint ventures encouraged.

Industry: In 1985 employed about 17 percent of labor force but produced more than 43 percent of gross national product (GNP). Fastest growing sector; average annual growth of 11 percent from 1952 to 1985. Wide range of technological levels; many small handicraft units; many enterprises using machinery installed or designed in 1950s and 1960s; significant number of big, up-to-date plants, including textile mills, steel mills, chemical fertilizer plants, and petrochemical facilities but also burgeoning light industries producing consumer goods. Produced most kinds of products made by industrialized nations but limited quantities of high-technology items. Technology transfer by importing whole plants, equipment, and designs an important means of progress. Major industrial centers in Liaoning Province, Beijing-Tianjin-Tangshan area, Shanghai, and Wuhan. Mineral resources included huge reserves of iron ore; adequate to abundant supplies of nearly all other industrial minerals. Outdated mining and ore processing technologies gradually being replaced with modern techniques.

Agriculture: In 1985 employed about 63 percent of labor force; proportion of GNP about 29 percent. Low worker productivity because of scanty supplies of agricultural machinery and other modern inputs. Most agricultural processes still performed by hand. Very small arable land area (just above 10 percent of total area, as compared with 22 percent in United States) in relation to size of country and population. Intensive use of land; all fields produce at least one crop a year; wherever conditions permit, two or even three crops grown annually, especially in south. Grain most important product, including rice, wheat, corn, sorghum, barley, and millet. Other important crops include cotton, jute, oilseeds, sugarcane, and sugar beets. Eggs a major product. Pork production has increased steadily; poultry and pigs raised on family plots. Other livestock relatively limited in numbers, except for sheep and goats, grazed in large herds on grasslands of Nei Monggol Autonomous Region (Inner Mongolia) and northwest. Substantial marine and freshwater fishery. Timber resources mainly located in northeast and southwest; much of country deforested centuries ago. Wide variety of fruits and vegetables grown.

Energy Sources: Self-sufficient in all energy forms; coal and petroleum exported since early 1970s. Coal reserves among world's largest; mining technology inadequately developed but improving in late 1980s. Petroleum reserves very large but of varying quality and in disparate locations. Suspected oil deposits in northwest and offshore tracts believed to be among world's largest; exploration and extraction limited by scarcity of equipment and trained personnel; twenty-seven contracts for joint offshore exploration and production by Japanese and Western oil companies signed by 1982, but by late 1980s only handful of wells producing. Substantial natural gas reserves in north, northwest, and offshore. Hydroelectric potential greatest in world, sixth largest in capacity; very large hydroelectric projects under construction, others in planning stage. Thermal power, mostly coal fired, produced approximately 68 percent of generating capacity in 1985; expected to increase to 72 percent by 1990. Emphasis on thermal power in late 1980s seen by policy makers as quick, short-term solution to energy needs; hydroelectric power seen as long-term solution. Petroleum production growth to continue in order to meet needs of nationwide mechanization and provide important foreign exchange but domestic use to be restricted as much as possible.

Foreign Trade: Small by international standards but growing rapidly in size and importance, represented 20 percent of GNP in 1985. Trade controlled by Ministry of Foreign Economic Relations and Trade and subordinate units and by Bank of China, foreign exchange arm of central bank. Substantial decentralization and increased flexibility in foreign trade operations since late 1970s. Textiles leading export category. Other important exports included petroleum and foodstuffs. Leading imports included machinery, transport equipment, manufactured goods, and chemicals. Japan dominant trading partner, accounting for 28.9 percent of imports and 15.2 percent of exports in 1986. Hong Kong leading market for exports (31.6 percent) but source of only 13 percent of imports. In 1979 United States became China's second largest source of imports and in 1986 was third largest overall trade partner. Western Europe, particularly Federal Republic of Germany, also major trading partner. Tourism encouraged and growing.

Transportation and Communications

Railroads: Basis of transportation system. About 52,000 kilometers of track in operation. Only 18 percent double tracked in 1984 and some important lines lacking modern equipment. Ninety percent of locomotives steam engines in 1979; but by mid-1980s production of diesel and electric models growing rapidly. Freight cars numbered 280,000, passenger cars numbered 20,000 in 1985. Railroads efficient within limits of track system. Expansion and improvement progressing in 1987.

Roads: About 962,800 kilometers in 1986; about 80 percent surfaced. Importance of highways and motor vehicles growing but bicycles and animal carts still much in evidence throughout country.

Inland Waterways: About 136,000 kilometers of navigable rivers, streams, lakes, and canals carried 44 percent of freight traffic in 1986, only slightly less than railroads. Rapid growth. Principal system Chang Jiang and its tributaries in central and east China; major freight artery. Secondary system Zhu Jiang (Pearl River) and its tributaries in south.

Maritime Shipping: Rapidly growing merchant fleet; 600 vessels of various kinds in 1984, total cargo capacity over 16 million tons. Major ports include Shanghai, Dalian, Qinhuangdao, Qingdao, Tianjin, and Huangpu. Rapid modernization of port facilities.

Civil Aviation: About 228,000 kilometers of domestic routes; about 94,000 kilometers of international routes in 1987. State airline General Administration of Civil Aviation of China known as CAAC. Regional airlines established in mid-1980s. Small but growing share of total freight and passenger traffic; important link to remote areas and foreign countries. In 1987 fleet included American-made Boeing 707, 737, 747, and 767 and McDonnell-Douglas MD–82 jetliners as well as other American, British, Soviet, West German, and domestic aircraft. Beijing International Airport completed in 1980.

Telecommunications: Diversified system linked all parts of country by telephone, telegraph, radio, and television. Marked improvements by mid-1980s with influx of foreign technology and increased domestic production capabilities. International and long-distance telephone links by cable and satellite of high quality. Telegraph, facsimile, and telex all in use. International satellite ground stations in Beijing and Shanghai; domestic satellite communication network operational in 1986. Over 160 radio stations by mid-1980s; transistorized radio receivers common. Vast wired broadcasting system including over 2,600 stations carrying radio transmissions into all rural units and many urban areas. Television system grew rapidly in 1980s; 90 television stations and 80 million sets.

Science and Technology: One of Four Modernizations, its high-speed development declared essential to all national economic development by Deng Xiaoping. Major breakthroughs in nuclear weapons, satellite launching and recovery, superconductivity, high-yield hybrid rice. Policy formulation at top levels puts emphasis on application of science to industry and foreign technology transfer.

Government and Politics

Party and Government: A unitary and "socialist state of the dictatorship of the proletariat," based on Marxism-Leninism-Mao Zedong Thought, led by 46-million-member Chinese Communist Party (CCP). Political processes guided by party and state constitutions, both promulgated in 1982; constitutions stress principle of democratic centralism (see Glossary), under which representative organs of both party and state are elected by lower bodies and they in turn elect their administrative arms at corresponding levels. Within representative and executive bodies minority must abide by decisions of majority; lower bodies obey orders of higher level organs. In theory, National Party Congress highest organ of power of party, but real power lies in Political Bureau of CCP Central Committee and, still more, in select Standing Committee of Political Bureau. National People's Congress highest government organ of state power; ratifies CCP-approved policies and programs. Reforms implemented in early 1980s allowed more serious review and deliberations concerning government programs in National People's Congress. State Council serves as equivalent of cabinet; key members also hold positions in important party organs.

Administrative Divisions: Divided into three tiers. In 1987 twenty-nine provincial-level units comprise twenty-one provinces, five autonomous regions, and three centrally governed special municipalities; middle tier consists of autonomous prefectures, counties, autonomous counties, cities, and municipal districts; and basic level comprises townships, and villages.

Judicial System: Four-level court system. Supreme People's Court in Beijing; higher people's courts in provinces, autonomous regions, and special municipalities; intermediate people's courts at prefecture level and also in parts of provinces, autonomous regions, and special municipalities; basic people's courts in counties, towns, and municipal districts. Special courts handle matters affecting military, railroad transportation, water transportation, and forestry. Court system paralleled by hierarchy of prosecuting organs called people's procuratorates; at apex stands Supreme People's Procuratorate.

Foreign Affairs: As of late 1980s, China pursued independent foreign policy and sought friendly relations and trade with many countries despite political differences. China regards itself as developing country and member of Third World. China, however, has close cooperative relations, including economic, technological, political, and limited military cooperation, with United States, Japan, and other industrially developed nations. Earlier strains in Chinese relations with Soviet Union, long considered by Beijing as main threat of war, somewhat ameliorated by late 1980s but still fell short of full normalization.

National Security

Armed Forces: In 1987 combined strength of combat support units of People's Liberation Army (PLA) just under 3 million. Ground forces estimated at 2.1 million, world's largest standing army. Air Force estimated at 390,000. Navy estimated at 350,000, including those assigned to Naval Air Force, Coastal Defense Forces, and Marine Corps. Strategic Missile Force estimated at 100,000.

Combat Units and Major Equipment: In 1987 ground forces consisted of 35 main-force armies comprising 118 infantry divisions, 13 armored divisions, and 33 artillery and antiaircraft divisions; 73 regional-force divisions, about 70 main- and regional-force independent combat and combat support regiments. Major weapons systems included Type 34, Type 59, and Type 69 main battle tanks, Type 62 and Type 63 light battle tanks; various caliber howitzers and guns and antiaircraft artillery. Air Force equipment included nearly 5,200 combat aircraft. Navy equipment included 5 nuclear-powered submarines (3 attack and 2 ballistic missile launching), 110 diesel attack submarines, 46 major surface combatants (destroyers and frigates), 877 fast-attack craft (armed with guns, missiles, or torpedoes), nearly 900 other combatant and support ships and boats, and 780 Naval Air Force combat aircraft. Strategic Missile Force included 50 medium-range ballistic missiles (range of 650 nautical miles), 60 intermediate-range ballistic missiles (range of 1,620 nautical miles), 4 limited-range intercontinental ballistic missiles (range of 3,780 nautical miles), and 2 full-range intercontinental ballistic missiles (range of 8,100 nautical miles).

Military Budget: Officially announced for 1987 at ¥20.4 billion (for value of the yuan—see Glossary). Western analysts believe defense spending roughly double announced budget, or about 4 percent of GNP.

Police Agencies and Paramilitary Forces: Police organized under Ministry of Public Security. People's Armed Police Force, primarily demobilized PLA troops estimated at 600,000. Supported by grass-roots party, government, and neighborhood organizations. Armed militia estimated at 4.3 million; ordinary, unarmed militia estimated at 6 million.

Figure 1. China, 1988

Introduction

REFORM—DUBBED CHINA'S "SECOND REVOLUTION"—was one of the most common terms in China's political vocabulary in the 1980s. Reform of the Chinese Communist Party and its political activities, reform of government organization, reform of the economy, military reforms, cultural and artistic reforms, indeed, China's post-Mao Zedong leaders called for reform of every part of Chinese society. The leaders of the People's Republic of China saw reform as the way to realize the broad goal of the Four Modernizations (announced by Premier Zhou Enlai in 1975: the modernization of industry, agriculture, science and technology, and national defense) and to bring China into the community of advanced industrial nations by the start of the new millennium. The reform movement had antecedents in Chinese history in the Han (206 B.C.-A.D. 220), Song (960–1279), and Qing (1644–1911) dynasties, when concerted efforts were made to bring about fundamental changes in administrative methods while keeping the overall institutional framework intact. Thus, the reform movement of the 1980s—which has been attributed largely to the insights and determination of Deng Xiaoping, the most important figure in the post-Mao Zedong leadership—took its place in the broad spectrum of Chinese history. As with previous reform movements, history will measure this one's success.

Late twentieth-century Chinese society has developed out of some 3,300 years of recorded history and, as archaeological finds indicate, several millennia of prehistoric civilization. For thousands of years, the Middle Kingdom (Zhongguo—the Chinese name for China) was marked by organizational and cultural continuity, which were reaffirmed in a cyclic rise, flourishing, and decline of imperial dynasties. Short-lived, vibrant, but often tyrannical dynasties frequently were followed by long periods of stability and benevolent rule that were built on the best features of the preceding era and that discarded or modified more authoritarian ideas. An ethical system of relations—governed by rules of propriety attributed to the School of Literati (also known as the Confucian school)—carefully defined each person's place in society. In this system, harmony of social relations rather than the rights of the individual was the ideal. The highest social status was held by scholar-officials, the literati who provided the interpretations needed for maintaining harmony in a slowly evolving world. Hard-working farmers, the providers of sustenance to society, also occupied an important place in the societal structure.

China's development was influenced by the alien peoples on the frontiers of Chinese civilization, who were sinicized into the Chinese polity (see fig. 1, frontispiece). Occasionally, groups arose among alien border peoples that were strong enough to conquer China itself. These groups established their own dynasties, only to be absorbed into an age-old system of governance. The importation of Buddhism, too, in the first century A.D. and its gradual assimilation had a fundamental impact on China. Early contacts with the premodern Western world brought a variety of exchanges. The Chinese contributed silk, printing, gunpowder, and porcelain. Staple foodstuffs from Africa and the Americas were assimilated by China, as was the Western-style chair. In later centuries, Chinese scholars studied Western astronomy, mathematics, and other branches of science. Westerners arrived in China in the nineteenth century, during the decline of the Qing dynasty, in search of trade and colonial empires. Through force of arms the Westerners imposed unequal treaties compelling China to accept humiliating compromises to its traditional system of society and government.

China reacted to intrusions from the West—and from a newly modernized Japan (to which China lost a war in 1895)—in a variety of ways, sometimes maintaining the traditional status quo, adapting Western functions to Chinese substance, or rejecting Chinese tradition in favor of Western substance and form. As the Qing dynasty declined, reforms came too late and did too little. The unsuccessful reform efforts were followed by revolution. Still burdened with the legacy of thousands of years of imperial rule and nearly a century of humiliations at foreign hands, China saw the establishment of a republic in 1911. But warlord rule and civil war continued for nearly forty more years, accompanied in 1937–45 by war with Japan.

The Chinese civil war of 1945–49 was won by the Chinese Communist Party, the current ruling party of China, led by its chairman and chief ideologist, Mao Zedong. The Communists moved quickly to consolidate their victory and integrate all Chinese society into a People's Republic. Except for the island of Taiwan (which became the home of the exiled Guomindang under Chiang Kai-shek and his successors), the new government unified the nation and achieved a stability China had not experienced for generations. Eagerness on the part of some Communist leaders to achieve even faster results engendered the Great Leap Forward (1958–60), a program that attempted rapid economic modernization but proved disastrous. Political reaction to the Great Leap Forward brought only a temporary respite before a counterreaction occurred in the form of the Cultural Revolution (1966–76), a period of radical experimentation and political chaos that brought the educational system to a halt and severely disrupted attempts at rational economic planning. When Mao Zedong died in 1976, the Cultural Revolution era effectively came to an end.

Eager to make up for lost time and wasted resources, China's leaders initiated China's "second revolution"—a comprehensive economic modernization and organizational reform program. Deng Xiaoping and his associates mobilized the Chinese people in new ways to make China a world power. Starting with the Third Plenum of the Chinese Communist Party's Eleventh National Party Congress in December 1978, Deng reaffirmed the aims of the Four Modernizations, placing economic progress above the Maoist goals of class struggle and permanent revolution. Profit incentives and bonuses took the place of ideological slogans and red banners as China's leaders experimented with ways to modernize the economy. Mao's legendary people's communes were dismantled and replaced by a responsibility system, in which peasant households were given greater decision-making power over agricultural production and distribution. Farm families were allowed to lease land and grow crops of their own choosing. In the urban sector, factory managers were granted the flexibility to negotiate with both domestic and foreign counterparts over matters that previously had been handled by central planners in Beijing. Exploitation of China's rich natural resources advanced significantly in the late 1970s and throughout the 1980s. As China's industrial sector advanced, there was increasing movement of the population to urban areas. China's population itself had surpassed 1 billion people by 1982 and was experiencing an annual rate of increase of 1.4 percent. As in times past, foreign specialists were invited to assist in the modernization process, and joint ventures with foreign capitalists and multinational conglomerates proliferated. Increasing numbers of Chinese students went abroad to pursue advanced degrees in a wide range of scientific and technical fields.

All this change was not without cost—both political and monetary. Efforts at fundamental transformation of economic, governmental, and political organizations caused discontent among some people and in some institutions and were resisted by those who clung to the "iron rice bowl" of guaranteed lifetime job tenure. Beijing's reform leaders made repeated calls for party members and government bureaucrats to reform their "ossified thinking" and to adopt modern methods. Older and inappropriately trained bureaucrats retired in great numbers as a younger and more technically oriented generation took over. In the ongoing debate between those who emphasized ideological correctness and those who stressed the need for technical competence—"reds" versus "experts"—the technocrats again emerged predominant. But developing and successfully applying technological expertise—the very essence of the Four Modernizations—cost vast sums of money and required special effort on the part of the Chinese people. In a rejection of the time-honored concept of "self-reliance," China entered into the milieu of international bank loans, joint ventures, and a whole panoply of once-abhorred capitalist economic practices.

As politics and the economy continued to respond to and change each other, China's reformers had to balance contending forces within and against their reform efforts while maintaining the momentum of the Four Modernizations program. In doing so, Deng Xiaoping and his associates were faced with several unenviable tasks. One was to create unity and support for the scope and pace of the reform program among party members. There was also a necessity to deliver material results to the broad masses of people amid economic experiments and mounting inflation. Failure to achieve these balances and to make mid-course corrections could prove disastrous for the reform leadership.

A sound ideological basis was needed to ensure the support of the party for the reform program. Deng's political idioms, such as "seeking truth from facts" and "socialism with Chinese characteristics," were reminiscent of reformist formulations of centuries past and had underlying practical ramifications. The supporters of Deng held that theory and practice must be fully integrated if success is to be hoped for, and they articulated the position that the Marxist-Leninist creed is not only valid but is adaptable to China's special—if not unique—situation. The ideological conviction that China was still in the "initial stage of socialism"—a viewpoint reaffirmed at the Thirteenth National Party Congress in October and November 1987—provided a still broader ideological basis for continuing the development of the Deng's reform program in the late 1980s and early 1990s. This ideological pronouncement also emphasized reformers' fundamental tenet that since the end of the "period of socialist transformation" (turning over private ownership of the means of production to the state) in 1956, there had been numerous "leftist" errors made in the party's ideological line. Mistakes such as the Great Leap Forward and the Cultural Revolution had produced setbacks in achieving "socialist modernization" and had kept China from emerging from the initial stage of socialism. It was, perhaps, the very failure of these leftist campaigns that had paved the way for the reforms of the 1980s.

Political confrontation over the reforms was pervasive and, to many foreign observers, confusing. In simplistic terms, the "conservatives" in the reform debate were members of the post-Mao "left," while the "liberals" were the pro-Deng "right." Being conservative in China in the 1980s variously meant adhering to the less radical aspects of Maoist orthodoxy (not all of which had been discredited) or accepting the goals of reform but rejecting the pace, scope, or certain methods of the Deng program. Thus, there were both conservative opponents to reform and conservative reformers. While many reform opponents had been swept away into "retirement," conservative reformers until the late 1980s served as members of China's highest ruling body and locus of power, the Standing Committee of the party's Political Bureau. Such leaders as Standing Committee member Chen Yun, one of the principal architects of economic reform, objected to the "bourgeois liberalization" of the modernization process that came with infusions of foreign, especially Western, culture. In the conservative reform view, the application of Chinese values to Western technology (reminiscent of the traditional *tiyong* [substance versus form] formulation evoked in the late-nineteenth-century reform period) would serve the People's Republic in good stead.

In the 1980s China's intellectuals and students frequently tested the limits of official tolerance in calls for freer artistic and literary expression, demands for more democratic processes, and even criticisms of the party. These confrontations reached their apex in late 1986, when thousands of students throughout the nation took to the streets to make their views known. In the resulting crackdown, some prominent intellectuals were demoted or expelled from the party. Even its highest official was not invulnerable: General Secretary Hu Yaobang was demoted in January 1987 for having dealt unsuccessfully with public activism and criticism of the party. Hu's ouster paved the way for the chief implementer of the Deng reforms, Zhao Ziyang, premier of the State Council, to assume command of the party and more firmly establish Deng's ideology as the status quo of reform. At the time of the writing of this book, it remained to be seen what degree of success the conservative reform elements would have in effecting a compromise, having placed their own representatives in the Political Bureau Standing Committee and the State Council's highest offices in late 1987.

Self-proclaimed successes of the reforms of the 1980s included improvements in both rural and urban life, adjustment of the structures of ownership, diversification of methods of operation, and introduction of more people into the decision-making process. As market mechanisms became an important part of the newly reformed planning system, products circulated more freely and the commodity market was rapidly improved. The government sought to rationalize prices, revamp the wage structure, and reform the financial and taxation systems. The policy of opening up to the outside world (the Chinese eschew the term *open door*, with its legacy of imperialist impositions) brought a significant expansion of economic, technological, and trade relations with other countries. Reforms of the scientific, technological, and educational institutions rounded out the successes of the Deng-inspired reforms. For the first time in modern Chinese history, the reforms also were being placed on the firm basis of a rational body of law and a carefully codified judicial system. Although reform and liberalization left the once more-strictly regimented society open to abuses, the new system of laws and judicial organizations continued to foster the stable domestic environment and favorable investment climate that China needed to realize its modernization goals.

Amid these successes, the authorities admitted that there were difficulties in attempting simultaneously to change the basic economic structure and to avoid the disruptions and declines in production that had marked the ill-conceived "leftist experiments" of the previous thirty years. China's size and increasing economic development rendered central economic planning ineffective, and the absence of markets and a modern banking system left the central authorities few tools with which to manage the economy. A realistic pricing system that reflected accurately levels of supply and demand and the value of scarce resources had yet to be implemented. The tremendous pent-up demand for consumer goods and the lack of effective controls on investment and capital grants to local factories unleashed inflationary pressures that the government found difficult to contain. Efforts to transform lethargic state factories into efficient enterprises responsible for their own profits and losses were hampered by shortages of qualified managers and by the lack of both a legal framework for contracts and a consistent and predictable taxation system. The goals of economic reform were clear, but their implementation was slowed by practical and political obstacles. National leaders responded by reaffirming support for reform in general terms and by publicizing the successes of those cities that had been permitted to experiment with managerial responsibility, markets for raw materials, and fundraising through the sale of corporate bonds.

National security has been a key determinant of Chinese planning since 1949. Although national defense has been the lowest priority of the Four Modernizations, it has not been neglected. China has had a perennial concern with being surrounded by enemies—the Soviets to the north and west, the Vietnamese to the south, and the Indians to the southwest—and has sought increasingly to project itself as a regional power. In response to this concern and power projection, in the 1980s China moved to augment "people's war" tactics with combined-arms tactics; to develop intercontinental ballistic missiles, nuclear submarines, and other strategic forces; and to acquire sophisticated foreign technologies with military applications. In the international arena, China in the 1980s increasingly used improved bilateral relations and a variety of international forums to project its "independent foreign policy of peace" while opening up to the outside world.

March 8, 1988

* * *

After the manuscript for this book was completed in the summer of 1987, several momentous events took place in China. Some were alluded to as imminent in the various chapters of the book. From October 25 to November 1, 1987, the Chinese Communist Party held its Thirteenth National Party Congress. Dozens of veteran party leaders retired from active front-line positions. Not least among the changes was the alteration of the Standing Committee of the party Political Bureau—the very apex of power in China—both in personnel and in stated purpose. Deng Xiaoping, Chen Yun, and Li Xiannian stepped down, and Hu Yaobang's demotion to mere Political Bureau membership was confirmed. Only one incumbent—Zhao Ziyang—was left on the Standing Committee. In place of the party elders and Hu Yaobang, a group of mostly younger, more technologically oriented individuals were seated. The Political Bureau's Standing Committee comprised Deng's protégé, sixty-eight-year-old Zhao Ziyang (who relinquished his position as head of government to become general secretary of the party); Li Peng, a sixty-year-old, Soviet-educated engineer, who became acting premier of the State Council in Zhao's place (he was confirmed as premier in spring 1988); Qiao Shi, a sixty-four-year-old expert in party affairs, government administration, and legal matters; Hu Qili, a fifty-eight-year-old party Secretariat member in charge of ideological education, theoretical research, and propaganda; and veteran economic planner and conservative reform architect Yao Yilin, the new party elder at age seventy-one. In regard to function, the Political Bureau no longer was conceived of as a group of influential individuals but as a consensual decision-making organization. The party constitution was amended to make the party Secretariat a staff arm of the Political Bureau and its Standing Committee, rather than the somewhat autonomous body it had been since 1982. By mid-1988 the Chinese Communist Party had announced that its increasingly well educated membership had risen to 47 million, an all-time high.

The retirees were not left without a voice. Deng, eighty-three and still China's de facto leader, retained his positions as chairman of the party and state Central Military Commissions, the latter of which designated him as commander-in-chief of the Chinese armed forces. (Zhao Ziyang was appointed first vice chairman of the party and state Central Military Commissions, giving him military credentials and paving the way for him to succeed Deng.) Eighty-two-year-old Chen Yun gave up his position as first secretary of the party Central Commission for Discipline Inspection but replaced Deng as chairman of the party's Central Advisory Commission, a significant forum for party elders. Li Xiannian who relinquished his position as head of state, or president, to another party elder—eighty-one-year-old Yang Shangkun—to become chairman of the Seventh Chinese People's Political Consultative Conference in spring 1988, was left without a leading party position. Hu Yaobang, far from being totally disgraced after his January 1987 debacle, retained membership on the Political Bureau and enjoyed a fair amount of popular support at the Thirteenth National Party Congress and afterward.

Below the national level, numerous leadership changes also took place following the Thirteenth National Party Congress. More than 600 younger and better educated leaders of provincial-level congresses and governments had been elected in China's twenty-nine provinces, autonomous regions, and special municipalities.

The Seventh National People's Congress was held from March 25 to April 13, 1988. This congress, along with the Seventh Chinese People's Political Consultative Conference, held from March 24 to April 10, 1988, was marked by a new openness and tolerance of debate and dissent. The opening ceremony of the National People's Congress was televised live, and meetings and panel discussions were recorded and broadcast the same day. Chinese and foreign journalists were permitted to attend the panel discussions and question the deputies in press conferences. Dissenting statements and dissenting votes were widely publicized in the domestic press. A spirit of reform prevailed as laws and constitutional amendments were ratified to legitimize private business and land sales and to encourage foreign investment. The State Council was restructured and streamlined. Fourteen ministries and commissions were dissolved and ten new ones—the State Planning Commission and ministries of personnel, labor, materials, transportation, energy, construction, aeronautics and astronautics industry, water resources, and machine building and electronics industry—were established. Many of the ministries that were dissolved were converted into business enterprises responsible for their own profits and losses.

Li Peng was elected premier of the State Council, as expected, and Yao Yilin and fifty-nine-year-old financial expert Tian Jiyun were re-elected as vice premiers. Sixty-six-year-old former Minister of Foreign Affairs Wu Xueqian also was elected vice premier. State councillors, all technocrats chosen for their professional expertise, were reduced in number from eleven to nine. All state councillors except Beijing mayor Chen Xitong and Secretary General of the State Council Chen Junsheng served concurrently as heads of national-level commissions or ministries. Although seven of the nine were new state councillors, only Li Guixian, the newly appointed governor of the People's Bank of China, was new to national politics. In a move that seemed to bode well for reform efforts, longtime Deng ally and political moderate Wan Li was selected to replace Peng Zhen as chairman of the Standing Committee of the Seventh National People's Congress. The conservative Peng had been considered instrumental in blocking or delaying many important pieces of reformist legislation. It also was decided at the Seventh National People's Congress to elevate Hainan Island, formerly part of Guangdong Province, to provincial status and to designate it as a special economic zone.

In September and October 1987 and again in March 1988, riots erupted in the streets of Lhasa, the capital of Xizang Autonomous Region (Tibet). Calls for "independence for Tibet" and expressions of support for the exiled spiritual leader, the Dalai Lama, were made amid violence that claimed the lives of at least six people in 1987 and at least nine more (including policemen) in 1988. Many more were reported to have been badly injured. Although Chinese authorities condemned the riots, their initial response was restrained in comparison with actions they had taken against earlier anti-Chinese demonstrations in Xizang. In addition, the authorities accompanied their censure of the Lhasa riots with a plethora of publicity on advances made by the inhabitants of Xizang in recent years and a lifting of travel restrictions on foreign correspondents. The March 1988 rioting spread to neighboring Qinghai Province, where there is a sizable Tibetan (Zang) minority. This time the authorities resorted to sterner measures, such as military force and numerous arrests, but only after offering lenient treatment to rioters who turned themselves in voluntarily. By mid-1988, it appeared that both the Dalai Lama, concerned that violence and bloodshed in his homeland was out of control, and the Chinese government, worried about instability in a strategic border area, were displaying greater flexibility in their respective positions.

The January 1988 death of Taiwan's leader, Chiang Ching-kuo, brought expressions of sympathy from Zhao Ziyang and other Chinese Communist Party leaders and renewed calls for the reunification of China under the slogan "one country, two systems." Implicit in the mainland's discussion of the transfer of power to a new generation of leaders—Taiwan-born Li Teng-hui succeeded Chiang—was regret that the opportunity had been lost for reaching a rapprochement with the last ruling member of the Chiang family. Beijing appealed to the patriotism of the people in Taiwan and called for unity with the mainland but, at the same time, kept a close watch for any sentiments that might lead to independence for Taiwan.

In foreign affairs, Beijing continued to balance its concern for security with its desire for an independent foreign policy. China reacted cautiously to the signing of a nuclear arms treaty by the Soviet Union and the United States and refused to hold its own summit with Soviet leader Mikhail Gorbachev. Despite a lessening of tensions between Beijing and Moscow and greatly improved Chinese relations with the governments and ruling parties throughout Eastern Europe, China continued to insist that the Soviet Union would have to end its support for Vietnamese occupation of Cambodia, withdraw all of its troops from Afghanistan, and significantly reduce Soviet forces deployed on the Sino-Soviet border and in the Mongolian People's Republic before relations between the Chinese and Soviet governments and parties could improve. By mid-1988 there were indications that the Soviet Union was taking steps to remove these "three obstacles" to improved Sino-Soviet relations. As early as the fall of 1986, the Soviet Union announced the pullback of a significant number of troops from Mongolia and the Sino-Soviet border. In May 1988 Moscow began withdrawing troops from Afghanistan with the goal of evacuating its forces from that country by early 1989. But China remained skeptical of Vietnamese government announcements that it would withdraw 50,000 troops from Cambodia by the end of 1988, and China's leaders continued to pressure the Soviet Union to exert more influence on Vietnam to secure an early withdrawal of all Vietnamese troops from Cambodia. Already strained Sino-Vietnamese relations were exacerbated when Chinese and Vietnamese naval forces clashed in March 1988 over several small islands in the strategically located Nansha (Spratly) archipelago.

In Sino-American relations, disputes over trade and technology transfer in 1987 were further clouded by United States concern over reported Chinese Silkworm shore-to-ship missile sales to Iran, sales of Dongfeng-3 intermediate-range missiles to Saudi Arabia, and disclosures that Israel allegedly assisted China in the development of the missile system later sold to the Saudis. Another concern was China's protest over an October 1987 United States Senate resolution on the "Tibetan question" that focused on alleged human rights violations in Xizang. A visit to Washington, by then Minister of Foreign Affairs Wu Xueqian in March 1988, however, had salutary effects on bilateral relations: China made assurances that it would cease Silkworm missile sales to Iran and the United States pledged to continue to make desired technologies available to China. The perennial Taiwan issue and problems in Xizang apparently were subsumed by larger national interests.

In February 1988 Beijing China achieved its long-sought goal of establishing diplomatic relations with Uruguay, one of the few nations that still had state-to-state ties with Taipei. With this accomplishment China increased its diplomatic exchanges to 134 countries, while Taiwan's official representations were reduced to 22.

The dynamism of China's domestic activities and international relations will continue as the new millennium approaches. Developments in the all-encompassing reform program and their resulting impact on Chinese society, particularly the efforts of China's leaders to bring increasing prosperity to the more than 1 billion Chinese people, and China's growing participation and influence in the international community will remain of interest to observers throughout the world.

July 15, 1988

Robert L. Worden,
Andrea Matles Savada,
and Ronald E. Dolan

Chapter 1. Historical Setting

This artist's conception of a human-shaped bronze wheel pin from the Western Zhou dynasty (1027–771 B.C.) shows not only the high level of ornamentation common for functional items, but also the style of dress of the period.

THE HISTORY OF CHINA, as documented in ancient writings, dates back some 3,300 years. Modern archaeological studies provide evidence of still more ancient origins in a culture that flourished between 2500 and 2000 B.C. in what is now central China and the lower Huang He (Yellow River) Valley of north China. Centuries of migration, amalgamation, and development brought about a distinctive system of writing, philosophy, art, and political organization that came to be recognized as Chinese civilization. What makes the civilization unique in world history is its continuity through over 4,000 years to the present century.

The Chinese have developed a strong sense of their real and mythological origins and have kept voluminous records since very early times. It is largely as a result of these records that knowledge concerning the ancient past, not only of China but also of its neighbors, has survived.

Chinese history, until the twentieth century, was written mostly by members of the ruling scholar-official class and was meant to provide the ruler with precedents to guide or justify his policies. These accounts focused on dynastic politics and colorful court histories and included developments among the commoners only as backdrops. The historians described a Chinese political pattern of dynasties, one following another in a cycle of ascent, achievement, decay, and rebirth under a new family.

Of the consistent traits identified by independent historians, a salient one has been the capacity of the Chinese to absorb the people of surrounding areas into their own civilization. Their success can be attributed to the superiority of their ideographic written language, their technology, and their political institutions; the refinement of their artistic and intellectual creativity; and the sheer weight of their numbers. The process of assimilation continued over the centuries through conquest and colonization until what is now known as China Proper was brought under unified rule. The Chinese also left an enduring mark on people beyond their borders, especially the Koreans, Japanese, and Vietnamese.

Another recurrent historical theme has been the unceasing struggle of the sedentary Chinese against the threat posed to their safety and way of life by non-Chinese peoples on the margins of their territory in the north, northeast, and northwest. In the thirteenth century, the Mongols from the northern steppes became the first alien people to conquer all China. Although not as culturally developed as the Chinese, they left an imprint on Chinese civilization. They also heightened Chinese perceptions of threat from the north. China came under alien rule for the second time in the mid-seventeenth century; the conquerors—the Manchus—came again from the north and northeast.

For centuries virtually all the foreigners that Chinese rulers saw came from the less developed societies along their land borders. This circumstance conditioned the Chinese view of the outside world. The Chinese saw their domain as the self-sufficient center of the universe and derived from this image the traditional (and still used) Chinese name for their country—Zhongguo, literally, Middle Kingdom or Central Nation. China saw itself surrounded on all sides by so-called barbarian peoples whose cultures were demonstrably inferior by Chinese standards.

This China-centered ("sinocentric") view of the world was still undisturbed in the nineteenth century, at the time of the first serious confrontation with the West. China had taken it for granted that its relations with Europeans would be conducted according to the tributary system that had evolved over the centuries between the emperor and representatives of the lesser states on China's borders as well as between the emperor and some earlier European visitors. But by the mid-nineteenth century, humiliated militarily by superior Western weaponry and technology and faced with imminent territorial dismemberment, China began to reassess its position with respect to Western civilization. By 1911 the two-millennia-old dynastic system of imperial government was brought down by its inability to make this adjustment successfully.

Because of its length and complexity, the history of the Middle Kingdom lends itself to varied interpretation. After the communist takeover in 1949, historians in mainland China wrote their own version of the past—a history of China built on a Marxist model of progression from primitive communism to slavery, feudalism, capitalism, and finally socialism. The events of history came to be presented as a function of the class struggle. Historiography became subordinated to proletarian politics fashioned and directed by the Chinese Communist Party. A series of thought-reform and anti-rightist campaigns were directed against intellectuals in the arts, sciences, and academic community. The Cultural Revolution (1966–76) further altered the objectivity of historians. In the years after the death of Mao Zedong in 1976, however, interest grew within the party, and outside it as well, in restoring the integrity of historical inquiry. This trend was consistent with the party's commitment to "seeking truth from facts." As a result, historians and social scientists raised probing questions concerning the state of historiography in China. Their investigations included not only historical study of traditional China but penetrating inquiries into modern Chinese history and the history of the Chinese Communist Party.

In post-Mao China, the discipline of historiography has not been separated from politics, although a much greater range of historical topics has been discussed. Figures from Confucius—who was bitterly excoriated for his "feudal" outlook by Cultural Revolution-era historians—to Mao himself have been evaluated with increasing flexibility. Among the criticisms made by Chinese social scientists is that Maoist-era historiography distorted Marxist and Leninist interpretations. This meant that considerable revision of historical texts was in order in the 1980s, although no substantive change away from the conventional Marxist approach was likely. Historical institutes were restored within the Chinese Academy of Social Sciences, and a growing corps of trained historians, in institutes and academia alike, returned to their work with the blessing of the Chinese Communist Party. This in itself was a potentially significant development.

The Ancient Dynasties

Chinese civilization, as described in mythology, begins with Pangu, the creator of the universe, and a succession of legendary sage-emperors and culture heroes who taught the ancient Chinese to communicate and to find sustenance, clothing, and shelter. The first prehistoric dynasty is said to be Xia, from about the twenty-first to the sixteenth century B.C. Until scientific excavations were made at early bronze-age sites at Anyang, Henan Province, in 1928, it was difficult to separate myth from reality in regard to the Xia. But since then, and especially in the 1960s and 1970s, archaeologists have uncovered urban sites, bronze implements, and tombs that point to the existence of Xia civilization in the same locations cited in ancient Chinese historical texts. At minimum, the Xia period marked an evolutionary stage between the late neolithic cultures and the Chinese urban civilization typical of the Shang dynasty.

The Dawn of History

Thousands of archaeological finds in the Huang He Valley—the apparent cradle of Chinese civilization—provide evidence about the Shang dynasty, which endured roughly from 1700 to 1027 B.C. The Shang dynasty (also called the Yin dynasty in its later stages) is believed to have been founded by a rebel leader who overthrew the last Xia ruler. Its civilization was based on agriculture, augmented by hunting and animal husbandry. Two important events of the period were the development of a writing system, as revealed in archaic Chinese inscriptions found on tortoise shells and flat cattle bones (commonly called oracle bones), and the use of bronze metallurgy. A number of ceremonial bronze vessels with inscriptions date from the Shang period; the workmanship on the bronzes attests to a high level of civilization.

A line of hereditary Shang kings ruled over much of northern China, and Shang troops fought frequent wars with neighboring settlements and nomadic herdsmen from the inner Asian steppes. The capitals, one of which was at the site of the modern city of Anyang, were centers of glittering court life. Court rituals to propitiate spirits and to honor sacred ancestors were highly developed. In addition to his secular position, the king was the head of the ancestor- and spirit-worship cult. Evidence from the royal tombs indicates that royal personages were buried with articles of value, presumably for use in the afterlife. Perhaps for the same reason, hundreds of commoners, who may have been slaves, were buried alive with the royal corpse.

The Zhou Period

The last Shang ruler, a despot according to standard Chinese accounts, was overthrown by a chieftain of a frontier tribe called Zhou, which had settled in the Wei Valley in modern Shaanxi Province. The Zhou dynasty had its capital at Hao, near the city of Xi'an, or Chang'an, as it was known in its heyday in the imperial period. Sharing the language and culture of the Shang, the early Zhou rulers, through conquest and colonization, gradually sinicized, that is, extended Shang culture through much of China Proper (see Glossary) north of the Chang Jiang (Yangtze River). The Zhou dynasty lasted longer than any other, from 1027 to 221 B.C. It was philosophers of this period who first enunciated the doctrine of the "mandate of heaven" (*tianming*), the notion that the ruler (the "son of heaven") governed by divine right but that his dethronement would prove that he had lost the mandate. The doctrine explained and justified the demise of the two earlier dynasties and at the same time supported the legitimacy of present and future rulers.

The term *feudal* has often been applied to the Zhou period because the Zhou's early decentralized rule invites comparison with medieval rule in Europe. At most, however, the early Zhou system was proto-feudal, being a more sophisticated version of earlier tribal organization, in which effective control depended more on familial ties than on feudal legal bonds. Whatever feudal elements there may have been decreased as time went on. The Zhou amalgam of city-states became progressively centralized and established increasingly impersonal political and economic institutions. These developments, which probably occurred in the latter Zhou period, were manifested in greater central control over local governments and a more routinized agricultural taxation.

In 771 B.C. the Zhou court was sacked, and its king was killed by invading barbarians who were allied with rebel lords. The capital was moved eastward to Luoyang in present-day Henan Province. Because of this shift, historians divide the Zhou era into Western Zhou (1027–771 B.C.) and Eastern Zhou (770–221 B.C.). With the royal line broken, the power of the Zhou court gradually diminished; the fragmentation of the kingdom accelerated. Eastern Zhou divides into two subperiods. The first, from 770 to 476 B.C., is called the Spring and Autumn Period, after a famous historical chronicle of the time; the second is known as the Warring States Period (475–221 B.C.).

The Hundred Schools of Thought

The Spring and Autumn and Warring States periods, though marked by disunity and civil strife, witnessed an unprecedented era of cultural prosperity—the "golden age" of China. The atmosphere of reform and new ideas was attributed to the struggle for survival among warring regional lords who competed in building strong and loyal armies and in increasing economic production to ensure a broader base for tax collection. To effect these economic, military, and cultural developments, the regional lords needed ever-increasing numbers of skilled, literate officials and teachers, the recruitment of whom was based on merit. Also during this time, commerce was stimulated through the introduction of coinage and technological improvements. Iron came into general use, making possible not only the forging of weapons of war but also the manufacture of farm implements. Public works on a grand scale—such as flood control, irrigation projects, and canal digging—were executed. Enormous walls were built around cities and along the broad stretches of the northern frontier.

So many different philosophies developed during the late Spring and Autumn and early Warring States periods that the era is often known as that of the Hundred Schools of Thought. From the Hundred Schools of Thought came many of the great classical writings on which Chinese practices were to be based for the next two and one-half millennia. Many of the thinkers were itinerant intellectuals who, besides teaching their disciples, were employed as advisers to one or another of the various state rulers on the methods of government, war, and diplomacy.

The body of thought that had the most enduring effect on subsequent Chinese life was that of the School of Literati (*ru*), often called the Confucian school in the West. The written legacy of the School of Literati is embodied in the Confucian Classics, which were to become the basis for the order of traditional society. Confucius (551-479 B.C.), also called Kong Zi, or Master Kong, looked to the early days of Zhou rule for an ideal social and political order. He believed that the only way such a system could be made to work properly was for each person to act according to prescribed relationships. "Let the ruler be a ruler and the subject a subject," he said, but he added that to rule properly a king must be virtuous. To Confucius, the functions of government and social stratification were facts of life to be sustained by ethical values. His ideal was the *junzi* (ruler's son), which came to mean *gentleman* in the sense of a cultivated or superior man.

Mencius (372-289 B.C.), or Meng Zi, was a Confucian disciple who made major contributions to the humanism of Confucian thought. Mencius declared that man was by nature good. He expostulated the idea that a ruler could not govern without the people's tacit consent and that the penalty for unpopular, despotic rule was the loss of the "mandate of heaven."

The effect of the combined work of Confucius, the codifier and interpreter of a system of relationships based on ethical behavior, and Mencius, the synthesizer and developer of applied Confucian thought, was to provide traditional Chinese society with a comprehensive framework on which to order virtually every aspect of life (see Traditional Society and Culture, ch. 3; Culture and the Arts, ch. 4).

There were to be accretions to the corpus of Confucian thought, both immediately and over the millennia, and from within and outside the Confucian school. Interpretations made to suit or influence contemporary society made Confucianism dynamic while preserving a fundamental system of model behavior based on ancient texts.

Diametrically opposed to Mencius, for example, was the interpretation of Xun Zi (ca. 300-237 B.C.), another Confucian follower. Xun Zi preached that man is innately selfish and evil and that goodness is attainable only through education and conduct befitting one's status. He also argued that the best government is one based on authoritarian control, not ethical or moral persuasion.

Xun Zi's unsentimental and authoritarian inclinations were developed into the doctrine embodied in the School of Law (*fa*), or Legalism. The doctrine was formulated by Han Fei

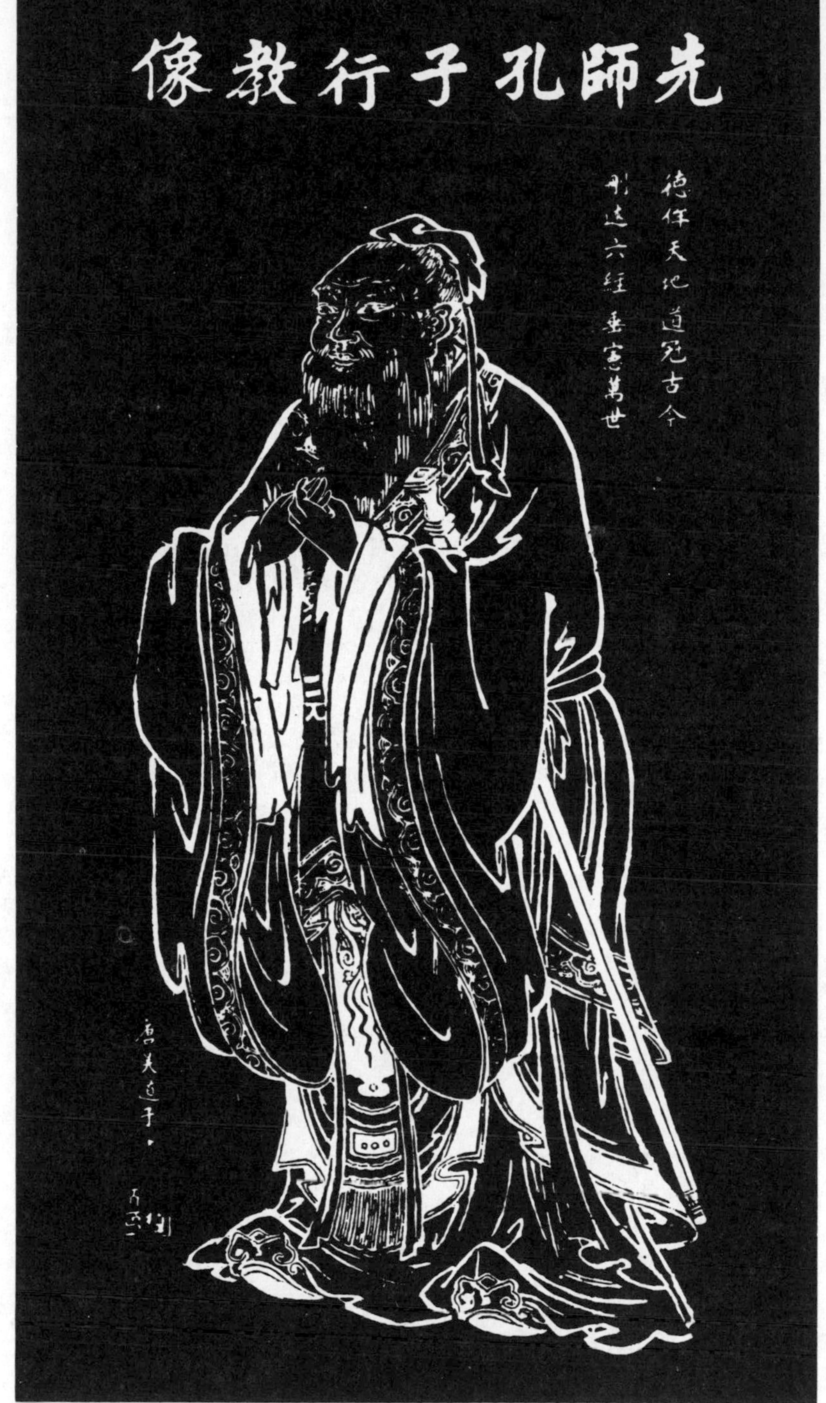

Confucius
Courtesy Library of Congress

(d. 233 B.C.) and Li Si (d. 208 B.C.), who maintained that human nature was incorrigibly selfish and therefore the only way to preserve the social order was to impose discipline from above and to enforce laws strictly. The Legalists exalted the state and sought its prosperity and martial prowess above the welfare of the common people. Legalism became the philosophic basis for the imperial form of government. When the most practical and useful aspects of Confucianism and Legalism were synthesized in the Han period (206 B.C.–A.D. 220), a system of governance came into existence that was to survive largely intact until the late nineteenth century. Taoism (or Daoism in pinyin), the second most important stream of Chinese thought, also developed during the Zhou period. Its formulation is attributed to the legendary sage Lao Zi (Old Master), said to predate Confucius, and Zhuang Zi (369–286 B.C.). The focus of Taoism is the individual in nature rather than the individual in society. It holds that the goal of life for each individual is to find one's own personal adjustment to the rhythm of the natural (and supernatural) world, to follow the Way (*dao*) of the universe. In many ways the opposite of rigid Confucian moralism, Taoism served many of its adherents as a complement to their ordered daily lives. A scholar on duty as an official would usually follow Confucian teachings but at leisure or in retirement might seek harmony with nature as a Taoist recluse.

Another strain of thought dating to the Warring States Period is the school of *yin-yang* and the five elements. The theories of this school attempted to explain the universe in terms of basic forces in nature, the complementary agents of *yin* (dark, cold, female, negative) and *yang* (light, hot, male, positive) and the five elements (water, fire, wood, metal, and earth). In later periods these theories came to have importance both in philosophy and in popular belief.

Still another school of thought was based on the doctrine of Mo Zi (470–391 B.C.?), or Mo Di. Mo Zi believed that "all men are equal before God" and that mankind should follow heaven by practicing universal love. Advocating that all action must be utilitarian, Mo Zi condemned the Confucian emphasis on ritual and music. He regarded warfare as wasteful and advocated pacificism. Mo Zi also believed that unity of thought and action were necessary to achieve social goals. He maintained that the people should obey their leaders and that the leaders should follow the will of heaven. Although Moism failed to establish itself as a major school of thought, its views are said to be "strongly echoed" in Legalist thought. In general, the teachings of Mo Zi left an indelible impression on the Chinese mind.

The Imperial Era

The First Imperial Period

Much of what came to constitute China Proper was unified for the first time in 221 B.C. (see fig. 2). In that year the western frontier state of Qin, the most aggressive of the Warring States, subjugated the last of its rival states. (*Qin* in Wade-Giles romanization is *Ch'in*, from which the English *China* probably derived.) Once the king of Qin consolidated his power, he took the title *Shi Huangdi* (First Emperor), a formulation previously reserved for deities and the mythological sage-emperors, and imposed Qin's centralized, nonhereditary bureaucratic system on his new empire. In subjugating the six other major states of Eastern Zhou, the Qin kings had relied heavily on Legalist scholar-advisers. Centralization, achieved by ruthless methods, was focused on standardizing legal codes and bureaucratic procedures, the forms of writing and coinage, and the pattern of thought and scholarship. To silence criticism of imperial rule, the kings banished or put to death many dissenting Confucian scholars and confiscated and burned their books. Qin aggrandizement was aided by frequent military expeditions pushing forward the frontiers in the north and south. To fend off barbarian intrusion, the fortification walls built by the various warring states were connected to make a 5,000-kilometer-long wall. (What is commonly referred to as the Great Wall is actually four great walls rebuilt or extended during the Western Han, Sui, Jin, and Ming periods, rather than a single, continuous wall.) At its extremities, the Great Wall reaches from northeastern Heilongjiang Province to northwestern Gansu. A number of public works projects were also undertaken to consolidate and strengthen imperial rule. These activities required enormous levies of manpower and resources, not to mention repressive measures. Revolts broke out as soon as the first Qin emperor died in 210 B.C. His dynasty was extinguished less than twenty years after its triumph. The imperial system initiated during the Qin dynasty, however, set a pattern that was developed over the next two millennia.

After a short civil war, a new dynasty, called Han (206 B.C.–A.D. 220), emerged with its capital at Chang'an. The new empire retained much of the Qin administrative structure but retreated a bit from centralized rule by establishing vassal principalities in some areas for the sake of political convenience. The Han rulers modified some of the harsher aspects of the previous dynasty; Confucian ideals of government, out of favor during the Qin period, were adopted as the creed of the Han empire, and Confucian scholars gained prominent status as the core of the civil service. A civil

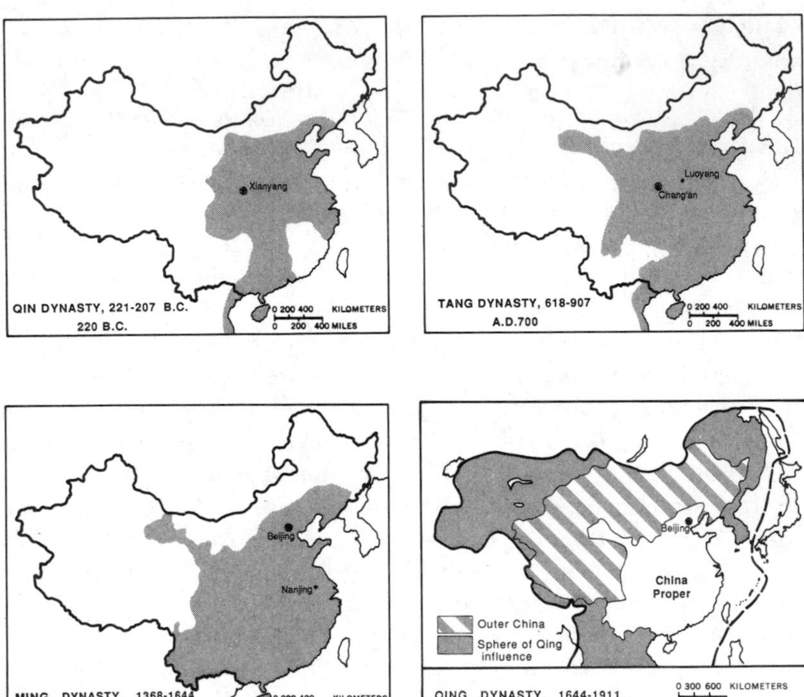

Source: Based on information from Chiao-min Hsieh *Atlas of China*, New York, 1973, 225, 238, 247, and 249.

Figure 2. The Chinese Empire, circa 220 B.C., A.D. 700, 1580, and 1775

service examination system also was initiated. Intellectual, literary, and artistic endeavors revived and flourished. The Han period produced China's most famous historian, Sima Qian (145–87 B.C.?), whose *Shiji* (Historical Records) provides a detailed chronicle from the time of a legendary Xia emperor to that of the Han emperor Wu Di (141–87 B.C.). Technological advances also marked this period. Two of the great Chinese inventions, paper and porcelain, date from Han times.

The Han dynasty, after which the members of the ethnic majority in China, the "people of Han," are named, was notable also for its military prowess. The empire expanded westward as far as the rim of the Tarim Basin (in modern Xinjiang-Uygur Autonomous Region), making possible relatively secure caravan traffic across Central Asia to Antioch, Baghdad, and Alexandria. The paths of caravan traffic are often called the "silk route" because the route was used to export Chinese silk to the Roman Empire. Chinese armies also invaded and annexed parts of northern Vietnam and northern Korea toward the end of the second century B.C. Han control of peripheral regions was generally insecure, however. To ensure peace with non-Chinese local powers, the Han court developed a mutually beneficial "tributary system." Non-Chinese states were allowed to remain autonomous in exchange for symbolic acceptance of Han overlordship. Tributary ties were confirmed and strengthened through intermarriages at the ruling level and periodic exchanges of gifts and goods.

After 200 years, Han rule was interrupted briefly (in A.D. 9–24 by Wang Mang, a reformer) and then restored for another 200 years. The Han rulers, however, were unable to adjust to what centralization had wrought: a growing population, increasing wealth and resultant financial difficulties and rivalries, and ever-more complex political institutions. Riddled with the corruption characteristic of the dynastic cycle, by A.D. 220 the Han empire collapsed.

Era of Disunity

The collapse of the Han dynasty was followed by nearly four centuries of rule by warlords. The age of civil wars and disunity began with the era of the Three Kingdoms (Wei, Shu, and Wu, which had overlapping reigns during the period A.D. 220–80). In later times, fiction and drama greatly romanticized the reputed chivalry of this period. Unity was restored briefly in the early years of the Jin dynasty (A.D. 265–420), but the Jin could not long contain the invasions of the nomadic peoples. In A.D. 317 the Jin court was forced to flee from Luoyang and reestablished itself at Nanjing to the south. The transfer of the capital coincided with China's political fragmentation into a succession of dynasties that was to last from A.D. 304 to 589. During this period the process of sinicization accelerated among the non-Chinese arrivals in the north and among the aboriginal tribesmen in the south. This process was also accompanied by the increasing popularity of Buddhism (introduced into China in the first century A.D.) in both north and south China. Despite the political disunity of the times, there were notable technological advances. The invention of gunpowder (at that time for use only in fireworks) and the wheelbarrow is believed to date from the sixth or seventh century. Advances in medicine, astronomy, and cartography are also noted by historians.

Restoration of Empire

China was reunified in A.D. 589 by the short-lived Sui dynasty (A.D. 581–617), which has often been compared to the earlier Qin dynasty in tenure and the ruthlessness of its accomplishments. The Sui dynasty's early demise was attributed to the government's tyrannical demands on the people, who bore the crushing burden of taxes and compulsory labor. These resources were overstrained in the completion of the Grand Canal—a monumental engineering feat—and in the undertaking of other construction projects, including the reconstruction of the Great Wall. Weakened by costly and disastrous military campaigns against Korea in the early seventh century, the dynasty disintegrated through a combination of popular revolts, disloyalty, and assassination.

The Tang dynasty (A.D. 618–907), with its capital at Chang'an, is regarded by historians as a high point in Chinese civilization—equal, or even superior, to the Han period. Its territory, acquired through the military exploits of its early rulers, was greater than that of the Han. Stimulated by contact with India and the Middle East, the empire saw a flowering of creativity in many fields. Buddhism, originating in India around the time of Confucius, flourished during the Tang period, becoming thoroughly sinicized and a permanent part of Chinese traditional culture. Block printing was invented, making the written word available to vastly greater audiences. The Tang period was the golden age of literature and art (see Culture and the Arts, ch. 4). A government system supported by a large class of Confucian literati selected through civil service examinations was perfected under Tang rule. This competitive procedure was designed to draw the best talents into government. But perhaps an even greater consideration for the Tang rulers, aware that imperial dependence on powerful aristocratic families and warlords would have destabilizing consequences, was to create a body of career officials having no autonomous territorial or functional power base. As it turned out, these scholar-officials acquired status in their local communities, family ties, and shared values that connected them to the imperial court. From Tang times until the closing days of the Qing empire in 1911, scholar-officials functioned often as intermediaries between the grass-roots level and the government.

By the middle of the eighth century A.D., Tang power had ebbed. Domestic economic instability and military defeat in 751 by Arabs at Talas, in Central Asia, marked the beginning of five centuries of steady military decline for the Chinese empire. Misrule, court intrigues, economic exploitation, and popular rebellions weakened the empire, making it possible for northern invaders to terminate the dynasty in 907. The next half-century saw the fragmentation of China into five northern dynasties and ten southern kingdoms. But in 960 a new power, Song (960–1279), reunified

Partially excavated terra-cotta figures unearthed during the 1970s at the tomb of China's first emperor, Shi Huangdi, near Xi'an. Chinese archaeologists discovered over 9,000 warriors, horses, chariots, and associated artifacts in the tomb.
Courtesy China Pictorial

most of China Proper. The Song period divides into two phases: Northern Song (960–1127) and Southern Song (1127–1279). The division was caused by the forced abandonment of north China in 1127 by the Song court, which could not push back the nomadic invaders.

The founders of the Song dynasty built an effective centralized bureaucracy staffed with civilian scholar-officials. Regional military governors and their supporters were replaced by centrally appointed officials. This system of civilian rule led to a greater concentration of power in the emperor and his palace bureaucracy than had been achieved in the previous dynasties.

The Song dynasty is notable for the development of cities not only for administrative purposes but also as centers of trade, industry, and maritime commerce. The landed scholar-officials, sometimes collectively referred to as the gentry, lived in the provincial centers alongside the shopkeepers, artisans, and merchants. A new group of wealthy commoners—the mercantile class—arose as printing and education spread, private trade grew, and a market economy began to link the coastal provinces and the interior. Landholding and government employment were no longer the only means of gaining wealth and prestige.

Culturally, the Song refined many of the developments of the previous centuries. Included in these refinements were not only the Tang ideal of the universal man, who combined the qualities of scholar, poet, painter, and statesman, but also historical writings, painting, calligraphy, and hard-glazed porcelain. Song intellectuals sought answers to all philosophical and political questions in the Confucian Classics. This renewed interest in the Confucian ideals and society of ancient times coincided with the decline of Buddhism, which the Chinese regarded as foreign and offering few practical guidelines for the solution of political and other mundane problems.

The Song Neo-Confucian philosophers, finding a certain purity in the originality of the ancient classical texts, wrote commentaries on them. The most influential of these philosophers was Zhu Xi (1130–1200), whose synthesis of Confucian thought and Buddhist, Taoist, and other ideas became the official imperial ideology from late Song times to the late nineteenth century. As incorporated into the examination system, Zhu Xi's philosophy evolved into a rigid official creed, which stressed the one-sided obligations of obedience and compliance of subject to ruler, child to father, wife to husband, and younger brother to elder brother. The effect was to inhibit the societal development of premodern China, resulting both in many generations of political, social, and spiritual stability and in a slowness of cultural and institutional change up to the nineteenth century (see Traditional Society and Culture, ch. 3). Neo-Confucian doctrines also came to play the dominant role in the intellectual life of Korea, Vietnam, and Japan.

Mongolian Interlude

By the mid-thirteenth century, the Mongols had subjugated north China, Korea, and the Muslim kingdoms of Central Asia and had twice penetrated Europe. With the resources of his vast empire, Kublai Khan (1215–94), a grandson of Genghis Khan (1167?–1227) and the supreme leader of all Mongol tribes, began his drive against the Southern Song. Even before the extinction of the Song dynasty, Kublai Khan had established the first alien dynasty to rule all China—the Yuan (1279–1368).

Although the Mongols sought to govern China through traditional institutions, using Chinese (Han) bureaucrats, they were not up to the task. The Han were discriminated against socially and politically. All important central and regional posts were monopolized by Mongols, who also preferred employing non-Chinese from other parts of the Mongol domain—Central Asia, the Middle East, and even Europe—in those positions for which no Mongol could be found. Chinese were more often employed in non-Chinese regions of the empire.

As in other periods of alien dynastic rule of China, a rich cultural diversity developed during the Yuan dynasty. The major cultural achievements were the development of drama and the novel and the increased use of the written vernacular. The Mongols' extensive West Asian and European contacts produced a fair amount of cultural exchange. Western musical instruments were introduced to enrich the Chinese performing arts. From this period dates the conversion to Islam, by Muslims of Central Asia, of growing numbers of Chinese in the northwest and southwest. Nestorianism and Roman Catholicism also enjoyed a period of toleration. Lamaism (Tibetan Buddhism) flourished, although native Taoism endured Mongol persecutions. Confucian governmental practices and examinations based on the Classics, which had fallen into disuse in north China during the period of disunity, were reinstated by the Mongols in the hope of maintaining order over Han society. Advances were realized in the fields of travel literature, cartography and geography, and scientific education. Certain key Chinese innovations, such as printing techniques, porcelain production, playing cards, and medical literature, were introduced in Europe, while the production of thin glass and cloisonné became popular in China. The first records of travel by Westerners date from this time. The most famous traveler of the period was the Venetian Marco Polo, whose account of his trip to "Cambaluc," the Great Khan's capital (now Beijing), and of life there astounded the people of Europe. The Mongols undertook extensive public works. Road and water communications were reorganized and improved. To provide against possible famines, granaries were ordered built throughout the empire. The city of Beijing was rebuilt with new palace grounds that included artificial lakes, hills and mountains, and parks. During the Yuan period, Beijing became the terminus of the Grand Canal, which was completely renovated. These commercially oriented improvements encouraged overland as well as maritime commerce throughout Asia and facilitated the first direct Chinese contacts with Europe. Chinese and Mongol travelers to the West were able to provide assistance in such areas as hydraulic engineering, while bringing back to the Middle Kingdom new scientific discoveries and architectural innovations. Contacts with the West also brought the introduction to China of a major new food crop—sorghum—along with other foreign food products and methods of preparation.

The Chinese Regain Power

Rivalry among the Mongol imperial heirs, natural disasters, and numerous peasant uprisings led to the collapse of the Yuan dynasty. The Ming dynasty (1368–1644) was founded by a Han Chinese peasant and former Buddhist monk turned rebel army leader. Having its capital first at Nanjing (which means Southern Capital) and later at Beijing (Northern Capital), the Ming reached the zenith of power during the first quarter of the fifteenth century. The Chinese armies reconquered Annam, as northern Vietnam was then known, in Southeast Asia and kept back the Mongols, while the Chinese fleet sailed the China seas and the Indian Ocean, cruising as far as the east coast of Africa. The maritime Asian nations sent envoys with tribute for the Chinese emperor. Internally, the Grand Canal was expanded to its farthest limits and proved to be a stimulus to domestic trade.

The Ming maritime expeditions stopped rather suddenly after 1433, the date of the last voyage. Historians have given as one of the reasons the great expense of large-scale expeditions at a time of preoccupation with northern defenses against the Mongols. Opposition at court also may have been a contributing factor, as conservative officials found the concept of expansion and commercial ventures alien to Chinese ideas of government. Pressure from the powerful Neo-Confucian bureaucracy led to a revival of strict agrarian-centered society. The stability of the Ming dynasty, which was without major disruptions of the population (then around 100 million), economy, arts, society, or politics, promoted a belief among the Chinese that they had achieved the most satisfactory civilization on earth and that nothing foreign was needed or welcome.

Long wars with the Mongols, incursions by the Japanese into Korea, and harassment of Chinese coastal cities by the Japanese in the sixteenth century weakened Ming rule, which became, as earlier Chinese dynasties had, ripe for an alien takeover. In 1644 the Manchus took Beijing from the north and became masters of north China, establishing the last imperial dynasty, the Qing (1644–1911).

The Rise of the Manchus

Although the Manchus were not Han Chinese and were strongly resisted, especially in the south, they had assimilated a great deal of Chinese culture before conquering China Proper. Realizing that to dominate the empire they would have to do things the Chinese way, the Manchus retained many institutions of Ming and earlier

Ming dynasty stone guardians near an inner section of the Great Wall northwest of Beijing
Courtesy Robert L. Worden

The Great Wall at Badaling, northwest of Beijing. The strategic section of the wall, known as the "key to the gate to Beijing" was built during the Ming dynasty.
Courtesy Beijing Slide Studio

Chinese derivation. They continued the Confucian court practices and temple rituals, over which the emperors had traditionally presided.

The Manchus continued the Confucian civil service system. Although Chinese were barred from the highest offices, Chinese officials predominated over Manchu officeholders outside the capital, except in military positions. The Neo-Confucian philosophy, emphasizing the obedience of subject to ruler, was enforced as the state creed. The Manchu emperors also supported Chinese literary and historical projects of enormous scope; the survival of much of China's ancient literature is attributed to these projects.

Ever suspicious of Han Chinese, the Qing rulers put into effect measures aimed at preventing the absorption of the Manchus into the dominant Han Chinese population. Han Chinese were prohibited from migrating into the Manchu homeland, and Manchus were forbidden to engage in trade or manual labor. Intermarriage between the two groups was forbidden. In many government positions a system of dual appointments was used—the Chinese appointee was required to do the substantive work and the Manchu to ensure Han loyalty to Qing rule.

The Qing regime was determined to protect itself not only from internal rebellion but also from foreign invasion. After China Proper had been subdued, the Manchus conquered Outer Mongolia (now the Mongolian People's Republic) in the late seventeenth century. In the eighteenth century, they gained control of Central Asia as far as the Pamir Mountains and established a protectorate over the area commonly known in the West as Tibet, but which the Chinese call Xizang. The Qing thus became the first dynasty to eliminate successfully all danger to China Proper from across its land borders. Under Manchu rule the empire grew to include a larger area than before or since; Taiwan, the last outpost of anti-Manchu resistance, was also incorporated into China for the first time. In addition, Qing emperors received tribute from the various border states.

The chief threat to China's integrity did not come overland, as it had so often in the past, but by sea, reaching the southern coastal area first. Western traders, missionaries, and soldiers of fortune began to arrive in large numbers even before the Qing, in the sixteenth century. The empire's inability to evaluate correctly the nature of the new challenge or to respond flexibly to it resulted in the demise of the Qing and the collapse of the entire millennia-old framework of dynastic rule.

Emergence of Modern China

The success of the Qing dynasty in maintaining the old order proved a liability when the empire was confronted with growing challenges from seafaring Western powers. The centuries of peace and self-satisfaction dating back to Ming times had encouraged little change in the attitudes of the ruling elite. The imperial Neo-Confucian scholars accepted as axiomatic the cultural superiority of Chinese civilization and the position of the empire at the hub of their perceived world. To question this assumption, to suggest innovation, or to promote the adoption of foreign ideas was viewed as tantamount to heresy. Imperial purges dealt severely with those who deviated from orthodoxy.

By the nineteenth century, China was experiencing growing internal pressures of economic origin. By the start of the century, there were over 300 million Chinese, but there was no industry or trade of sufficient scope to absorb the surplus labor. Moreover, the scarcity of land led to widespread rural discontent and a breakdown in law and order. The weakening through corruption of the bureaucratic and military systems and mounting urban pauperism also contributed to these disturbances. Localized revolts erupted in various parts of the empire in the early nineteenth century. Secret societies, such as the White Lotus sect in the north and the Triad Society in the south, gained ground, combining anti-Manchu subversion with banditry.

The Western Powers Arrive

As elsewhere in Asia, in China the Portuguese were the pioneers, establishing a foothold at Macao (Aomen in pinyin), from which they monopolized foreign trade at the Chinese port of Guangzhou (Canton). Soon the Spanish arrived, followed by the British and the French. Trade between China and the West was carried on in the guise of tribute: foreigners were obliged to follow the elaborate, centuries-old ritual imposed on envoys from China's tributary states. There was no conception at the imperial court that the Europeans would expect or deserve to be treated as cultural or political equals. The sole exception was Russia, the most powerful inland neighbor.

The Manchus were sensitive to the need for security along the northern land frontier and therefore were prepared to be realistic in dealing with Russia. The Treaty of Nerchinsk (1689) with the Russians, drafted to bring to an end a series of border incidents and to establish a border between Siberia and Manchuria (northeast China) along the Heilong Jiang (Amur River), was China's first bilateral agreement with a European power. In 1727 the Treaty of Kiakhta delimited the remainder of the eastern portion of the Sino-Russian border. Western diplomatic efforts to expand trade on equal terms were rebuffed, the official Chinese assumption being that the empire was not in need of foreign—and thus inferior—products. Despite this attitude, trade flourished, even though after 1760 all foreign trade was confined to Guangzhou, where the foreign traders had to limit their dealings to a dozen officially licensed Chinese merchant firms.

Trade was not the sole basis of contact with the West. Since the thirteenth century, Roman Catholic missionaries had been attempting to establish their church in China. Although by 1800 only a few hundred thousand Chinese had been converted, the missionaries—mostly Jesuits—contributed greatly to Chinese knowledge in such fields as cannon casting, calendar making, geography, mathematics, cartography, music, art, and architecture. The Jesuits were especially adept at fitting Christianity into a Chinese framework and were condemned by a papal decision in 1704 for having tolerated the continuance of Confucian ancestor rites among Christian converts. The papal decision quickly weakened the Christian movement, which it proscribed as heterodox and disloyal.

The Opium War, 1839–42

During the eighteenth century, the market in Europe and America for tea, a new drink in the West, expanded greatly. Additionally, there was a continuing demand for Chinese silk and porcelain. But China, still in its preindustrial stage, wanted little that the West had to offer, causing the Westerners, mostly British, to incur an unfavorable balance of trade. To remedy the situation, the foreigners developed a third-party trade, exchanging their merchandise in India and Southeast Asia for raw materials and semiprocessed goods, which found a ready market in Guangzhou. By the early nineteenth century, raw cotton and opium from India had become the staple British imports into China, in spite of the fact that opium was prohibited entry by imperial decree. The opium traffic was made possible through the connivance of profit-seeking merchants and a corrupt bureaucracy.

In 1839 the Qing government, after a decade of unsuccessful anti-opium campaigns, adopted drastic prohibitory laws against the opium trade. The emperor dispatched a commissioner, Lin Zexu (1785–1850), to Guangzhou to suppress illicit opium traffic. Lin seized illegal stocks of opium owned by Chinese dealers and then detained the entire foreign community and confiscated and destroyed some 20,000 chests of illicit British opium. The British retaliated with a punitive expedition, thus initiating the first Anglo-Chinese war, better known as the Opium War (1839–42). Unprepared for war and grossly underestimating the capabilities of the enemy, the Chinese were disastrously defeated, and their image of their own imperial power was tarnished beyond repair. The Treaty of Nanjing (1842), signed on board a British warship by two Manchu imperial commissioners and the British plenipotentiary, was the first of a series of agreements with the Western trading nations later called by the Chinese the "unequal treaties." Under the Treaty of Nanjing, China ceded the island of Hong Kong (Xianggang in pinyin) to the British; abolished the licensed monopoly system of trade; opened 5 ports to British residence and foreign trade; limited the tariff on trade to 5 percent ad valorem; granted British nationals extraterritoriality (exemption from Chinese laws); and paid a large indemnity. In addition, Britain was to have most-favored-nation treatment, that is, it would receive whatever trading concessions the Chinese granted other powers then or later. The Treaty of Nanjing set the scope and character of an unequal relationship for the ensuing century of what the Chinese would call "national humiliations." The treaty was followed by other incursions, wars, and treaties that granted new concessions and added new privileges for the foreigners.

The Taiping Rebellion, 1851–64

During the mid-nineteenth century, China's problems were compounded by natural calamities of unprecedented proportions, including droughts, famines, and floods. Government neglect of public works was in part responsible for this and other disasters, and the Qing administration did little to relieve the widespread misery caused by them. Economic tensions, military defeats at Western hands, and anti-Manchu sentiments all combined to produce widespread unrest, especially in the south. South China had been the last area to yield to the Qing conquerors and the first to be exposed to Western influence. It provided a likely setting for the largest uprising in modern Chinese history—the Taiping Rebellion.

The Taiping rebels were led by Hong Xiuquan (1814–64), a village teacher and unsuccessful imperial examination candidate. Hong formulated an eclectic ideology combining the ideals of pre-Confucian utopianism with Protestant beliefs. He soon had a following in the thousands who were heavily anti-Manchu and anti-establishment. Hong's followers formed a military organization to protect against bandits and recruited troops not only among believers but also from among other armed peasant groups and secret societies. In 1851 Hong Xiuquan and others launched an uprising in Guizhou Province. Hong proclaimed the Heavenly Kingdom of Great Peace (Taiping Tianguo, or Taiping for short) with himself as king. The new order was to reconstitute a legendary ancient state in which the peasantry owned and tilled the land in common; slavery, concubinage, arranged marriage, opium smoking, footbinding, judicial torture, and the worship of idols were all to be eliminated. The Taiping tolerance of the esoteric rituals and quasi-religious societies of south China—themselves a threat to Qing stability—and their relentless attacks on Confucianism—still widely accepted as the moral foundation of Chinese behavior—contributed to the ultimate defeat of the rebellion. Its advocacy of radical social reforms alienated the Han Chinese scholar-gentry class. The Taiping army, although it had captured Nanjing and driven as far north as Tianjin, failed to establish stable base areas. The movement's leaders found themselves in a net of internal feuds, defections, and corruption. Additionally, British and French forces, being more willing to deal with the weak Qing administration than contend with the uncertainties of a Taiping regime, came to the assistance of the imperial army. Before the Chinese army succeeded in crushing the revolt, however, 14 years had passed, and well over 30 million people were reported killed.

To defeat the rebellion, the Qing court needed, besides Western help, an army stronger and more popular than the demoralized imperial forces. In 1860 scholar-official Zeng Guofan (1811–72), from Hunan Province, was appointed imperial commissioner and governor-general of the Taiping-controlled territories and placed in command of the war against the rebels. Zeng's Hunan army, created and paid for by local taxes, became a powerful new fighting force under the command of eminent scholar-generals. Zeng's success gave new power to an emerging Han Chinese elite and eroded Qing authority. Simultaneous uprisings in north China (the Nian Rebellion) and southwest China (the Muslim Rebellion) further demonstrated Qing weakness.

The Self-Strengthening Movement

The rude realities of the Opium War, the unequal treaties, and the mid-century mass uprisings caused Qing courtiers and officials to recognize the need to strengthen China. Chinese scholars and officials had been examining and translating "Western learning" since the 1840s. Under the direction of modern-thinking Han officials, Western science and languages were studied, special schools were opened in the larger cities, and arsenals, factories, and shipyards were established according to Western models. Western

Ceremonial bronze tortoise incense burner known as Pei Xi, a mythological river god, Hall of Supreme Harmony, Forbidden City, Beijing
Courtesy Beijing Slide Studio

diplomatic practices were adopted by the Qing, and students were sent abroad by the government and on individual or community initiative in the hope that national regeneration could be achieved through the application of Western practical methods.

Amid these activities came an attempt to arrest the dynastic decline by restoring the traditional order. The effort was known as the Tongzhi Restoration, named for the Tongzhi Emperor (1862–74), and was engineered by the young emperor's mother, the Empress Dowager Ci Xi (1835–1908). The restoration, however, which applied "practical knowledge" while reaffirming the old mentality, was not a genuine program of modernization.

The effort to graft Western technology onto Chinese institutions became known as the Self-Strengthening Movement. The movement was championed by scholar-generals like Li Hongzhang (1823–1901) and Zuo Zongtang (1812–85), who had fought with the government forces in the Taiping Rebellion. From 1861 to 1894, leaders such as these, now turned scholar-administrators, were responsible for establishing modern institutions, developing basic industries, communications, and transportation, and modernizing the military. But despite its leaders' accomplishments, the Self-Strengthening Movement did not recognize the significance of the political institutions and social theories that had fostered Western advances and innovations. This weakness led to the movement's failure. Modernization during this period would have been difficult under the best of circumstances. The bureaucracy was still deeply influenced by Neo-Confucian orthodoxy. Chinese society was still reeling from the ravages of the Taiping and other rebellions, and foreign encroachments continued to threaten the integrity of China.

The first step in the foreign powers' effort to carve up the empire was taken by Russia, which had been expanding into Central Asia. By the 1850s, tsarist troops also had invaded the Heilong Jiang watershed of Manchuria, from which their countrymen had been ejected under the Treaty of Nerchinsk. The Russians used the superior knowledge of China they had acquired through their century-long residence in Beijing to further their aggrandizement. In 1860 Russian diplomats secured the secession of all of Manchuria north of the Heilong Jiang and east of the Wusuli Jiang (Ussuri River). Foreign encroachments increased after 1860 by means of a series of treaties imposed on China on one pretext or another. The foreign stranglehold on the vital sectors of the Chinese economy was reinforced through a lengthening list of concessions. Foreign settlements in the treaty ports became extraterritorial—sovereign pockets of territories over which China had no jurisdiction. The safety of these foreign settlements was ensured by the menacing presence of warships and gunboats.

At this time the foreign powers also took over the peripheral states that had acknowledged Chinese suzerainty and given tribute to the emperor. France colonized Cochin China, as southern Vietnam was then called, and by 1864 established a protectorate over Cambodia. Following a victorious war against China in 1884–85, France also took Annam. Britain gained control over Burma. Russia penetrated into Chinese Turkestan (modern-day Xinjiang-Uygur Autonomous Region). Japan, having emerged from its century-and-a-half-long seclusion and having gone through its own modernization movement, defeated China in the war of 1894–95. The Treaty of Shimonoseki forced China to cede Taiwan and the Penghu Islands to Japan, pay a huge indemnity, permit the establishment of Japanese industries in four treaty ports, and recognize Japanese hegemony over Korea. In 1898 the British acquired a ninety-nine-year lease over the so-called New Territories of Kowloon (Jiulong in pinyin), which increased the size of their Hong Kong colony. Britain, Japan, Russia, Germany, France, and Belgium each gained spheres of influence in China. The United States, which had not acquired any territorial cessions, proposed in 1899 that there be an "open door" policy in China, whereby all foreign countries

A Ming dynasty marble huabiao *or ornamental column, just inside the Tiananmen Gate in Beijing incorporates a dragon in half relief and is crested with a dragon resting in a lotus flower. The crosspieces are stylized clouds.*
Courtesy Robert L. Worden

Empress Dowager Ci Xi's throne in the Palace of Gathering Excellence, Palace Museum, Beijing
Courtesy Beijing Slide Studio

would have equal duties and privileges in all treaty ports within and outside the various spheres of influence. All but Russia agreed to the United States overture.

The Hundred Days' Reform and the Aftermath

In the 103 days from June 11 to September 21, 1898, the Qing emperor, Guangxu (1875–1908), ordered a series of reforms aimed at making sweeping social and institutional changes. This effort reflected the thinking of a group of progressive scholar-reformers who had impressed the court with the urgency of making innovations for the nation's survival. Influenced by the Japanese success with modernization, the reformers declared that China needed more than "self-strengthening" and that innovation must be accompanied by institutional and ideological change.

The imperial edicts for reform covered a broad range of subjects, including stamping out corruption and remaking, among other things, the academic and civil-service examination systems, legal system, governmental structure, defense establishment, and postal services. The edicts attempted to modernize agriculture, medicine, and mining and to promote practical studies instead of Neo-Confucian orthodoxy. The court also planned to send students abroad for firsthand observation and technical studies. All these changes were to be brought about under a de facto constitutional monarchy.

Opposition to the reform was intense among the conservative ruling elite, especially the Manchus, who, in condemning the announced reform as too radical, proposed instead a more moderate and gradualist course of change. Supported by ultraconservatives and with the tacit support of the political opportunist Yuan Shikai (1859–1916), Empress Dowager Ci Xi engineered a coup d'état on September 21, 1898, forcing the young reform-minded Guangxu into seclusion. Ci Xi took over the government as regent. The Hundred Days' Reform ended with the rescindment of the new edicts and the execution of six of the reform's chief advocates. The two principal leaders, Kang Youwei (1858–1927) and Liang Qichao (1873–1929), fled abroad to found the Baohuang Hui (Protect the Emperor Society) and to work, unsuccessfully, for a constitutional monarchy in China.

The conservatives then gave clandestine backing to the antiforeign and anti-Christian movement of secret societies known as Yihetuan (Society of Righteousness and Harmony). The movement has been better known in the West as the Boxers (from an earlier name—Yihequan, Righteousness and Harmony Boxers). In 1900 Boxer bands spread over the north China countryside, burning missionary facilities and killing Chinese Christians. Finally, in June 1900, the Boxers besieged the foreign concessions in Beijing and Tianjin, an action that provoked an allied relief expedition by the offended nations. The Qing declared war against the invaders, who easily crushed their opposition and occupied north China. Under the Protocol of 1901, the court was made to consent to the execution of ten high officials and the punishment of hundreds of others, expansion of the Legation Quarter, payment of war reparations, stationing of foreign troops in China, and razing of some Chinese fortifications.

In the decade that followed, the court belatedly put into effect some reform measures. These included the abolition of the moribund Confucian-based examination, educational and military modernization patterned after the model of Japan, and an experiment, if half-hearted, in constitutional and parliamentary government (see The Examination System, ch. 3). The suddenness and ambitiousness of the reform effort actually hindered its success. One effect, to be felt for decades to come, was the establishment of new armies, which, in turn, gave rise to warlordism.

The Republican Revolution of 1911

Failure of reform from the top and the fiasco of the Boxer Uprising convinced many Chinese that the only real solution lay in outright revolution, in sweeping away the old order and erecting a new one patterned preferably after the example of Japan. The revolutionary leader was Sun Yat-sen (Sun Yixian in pinyin, 1866–1925), a republican and anti-Qing activist who became increasingly popular among the overseas Chinese (see Glossary) and Chinese students abroad, especially in Japan. In 1905 Sun founded the Tongmeng Hui (United League) in Tokyo with Huang Xing (1874–1916), a popular leader of the Chinese revolutionary movement in Japan, as his deputy. This movement, generously supported by overseas Chinese funds, also gained political support with regional military officers and some of the reformers who had fled China after the Hundred Days' Reform. Sun's political philosophy was conceptualized in 1897, first enunciated in Tokyo in 1905, and modified through the early 1920s. It centered on the Three Principles of the People (*san min zhuyi*): "nationalism, democracy, and people's livelihood." The principle of nationalism called for overthrowing the Manchus and ending foreign hegemony over China. The second principle, democracy, was used to describe Sun's goal of a popularly elected republican form of government. People's livelihood, often referred to as socialism, was aimed at helping the common people through regulation of the ownership of the means of production and land.

The republican revolution broke out on October 10, 1911, in Wuchang, the capital of Hubei Province, among discontented modernized army units whose anti-Qing plot had been uncovered. It had been preceded by numerous abortive uprisings and organized protests inside China. The revolt quickly spread to neighboring cities, and Tongmeng Hui members throughout the country rose in immediate support of the Wuchang revolutionary forces. By late November, fifteen of the twenty-four provinces had declared their independence of the Qing empire. A month later, Sun Yat-sen returned to China from the United States, where he had been raising funds among overseas Chinese and American sympathizers. On January 1, 1912, Sun was inaugurated in Nanjing as the provisional president of the new Chinese republic. But power in Beijing already had passed to the commander-in-chief of the imperial army, Yuan Shikai, the strongest regional military leader at the time. To prevent civil war and possible foreign intervention from undermining the infant republic, Sun agreed to Yuan's demand that China be united under a Beijing government headed by Yuan. On February 12, 1912, the last Manchu emperor, the child Puyi, abdicated. On March 10, in Beijing, Yuan Shikai was sworn in as provisional president of the Republic of China.

Republican China

The republic that Sun Yat-sen and his associates envisioned evolved slowly. The revolutionists lacked an army, and the power of Yuan Shikai began to outstrip that of parliament. Yuan revised the constitution at will and became dictatorial. In August 1912 a new political party was founded by Song Jiaoren (1882–1913), one of Sun's associates. The party, the Guomindang (Kuomintang or KMT—the National People's Party, frequently referred to as the Nationalist Party), was an amalgamation of small political groups, including Sun's Tongmeng Hui. In the national elections held in February 1913 for the new bicameral parliament, Song campaigned against the Yuan administration, and his party won a majority of seats. Yuan had Song assassinated in March; he had already arranged the assassination of several pro-revolutionist generals. Animosity toward Yuan grew. In the summer of 1913 seven southern provinces rebelled against Yuan. When the rebellion was suppressed, Sun and other instigators fled to Japan. In October 1913 an intimidated parliament formally elected Yuan president of the Republic of China, and the major powers extended recognition to his government. To achieve international recognition, Yuan

A pavilion at the Yeheyuan (Summer Palace), Beijing
Courtesy Rinn-Sup Shinn

Shikai had to agree to autonomy for Outer Mongolia and Xizang. China was still to be suzerain, but it would have to allow Russia a free hand in Outer Mongolia and Britain continuance of its influence in Xizang.

In November Yuan Shikai, legally president, ordered the Guomindang dissolved and its members removed from parliament. Within a few months, he suspended parliament and the provincial assemblies and forced the promulgation of a new constitution, which, in effect, made him president for life. Yuan's ambitions still were not satisfied, and, by the end of 1915, it was announced that he would reestablish the monarchy. Widespread rebellions ensued, and numerous provinces declared independence. With opposition at every quarter and the nation breaking up into warlord factions, Yuan Shikai died of natural causes in June 1916, deserted by his lieutenants.

Nationalism and Communism

After Yuan Shikai's death, shifting alliances of regional warlords fought for control of the Beijing government. The nation also was threatened from without by the Japanese. When World War I broke out in 1914, Japan fought on the Allied side and seized German holdings in Shandong Province. In 1915 the Japanese set before the warlord government in Beijing the so-called Twenty-One

Demands, which would have made China a Japanese protectorate. The Beijing government rejected some of these demands but yielded to the Japanese insistence on keeping the Shandong territory already in its possession. Beijing also recognized Tokyo's authority over southern Manchuria and eastern Inner Mongolia. In 1917, in secret communiqués, Britain, France, and Italy assented to the Japanese claim in exchange for Japan's naval action against Germany.

In 1917 China declared war on Germany in the hope of recovering its lost province, then under Japanese control. But in 1918 the Beijing government signed a secret deal with Japan accepting the latter's claim to Shandong. When the Paris peace conference of 1919 confirmed the Japanese claim to Shandong and Beijing's sell-out became public, internal reaction was shattering. On May 4, 1919, there were massive student demonstrations against the Beijing government and Japan. The political fervor, student activism, and iconoclastic and reformist intellectual currents set in motion by the patriotic student protest developed into a national awakening known as the May Fourth Movement. The intellectual milieu in which the May Fourth Movement developed was known as the New Culture Movement and occupied the period from 1917 to 1923. The student demonstrations of May 4, 1919 were the high point of the New Culture Movement, and the terms are often used synonymously. Students returned from abroad advocating social and political theories ranging from complete Westernization of China to the socialism that one day would be adopted by China's communist rulers.

Opposing the Warlords

The May Fourth Movement helped to rekindle the then-fading cause of republican revolution. In 1917 Sun Yat-sen had become commander-in-chief of a rival military government in Guangzhou in collaboration with southern warlords. In October 1919 Sun reestablished the Guomindang to counter the government in Beijing. The latter, under a succession of warlords, still maintained its facade of legitimacy and its relations with the West. By 1921 Sun had become president of the southern government. He spent his remaining years trying to consolidate his regime and achieve unity with the north. His efforts to obtain aid from the Western democracies were ignored, however, and in 1921 he turned to the Soviet Union, which had recently achieved its own revolution. The Soviets sought to befriend the Chinese revolutionists by offering scathing attacks on "Western imperialism." But for political expediency, the Soviet leadership initiated a dual policy of support for both Sun and the newly established Chinese Communist

Party (CCP). The Soviets hoped for consolidation but were prepared for either side to emerge victorious. In this way the struggle for power in China began between the Nationalists and the Communists. In 1922 the Guomindang-warlord alliance in Guangzhou was ruptured, and Sun fled to Shanghai. By then Sun saw the need to seek Soviet support for his cause. In 1923 a joint statement by Sun and a Soviet representative in Shanghai pledged Soviet assistance for China's national unification. Soviet advisers—the most prominent of whom was an agent of the Comintern (see Glossary), Mikhail Borodin—began to arrive in China in 1923 to aid in the reorganization and consolidation of the Guomindang along the lines of the Communist Party of the Soviet Union. The CCP was under Comintern instructions to cooperate with the Guomindang, and its members were encouraged to join while maintaining their party identities. The CCP was still small at the time, having a membership of 300 in 1922 and only 1,500 by 1925. The Guomindang in 1922 already had 150,000 members.

Soviet advisers also helped the Nationalists set up a political institute to train propagandists in mass mobilization techniques and in 1923 sent Chiang Kai-shek (Jiang Jieshi in pinyin), one of Sun's lieutenants from Tongmeng Hui days, for several months' military and political study in Moscow. After Chiang's return in late 1923, he participated in the establishment of the Whampoa (Huangpu in pinyin) Military Academy outside Guangzhou, which was the seat of government under the Guomindang-CCP alliance. In 1924 Chiang became head of the academy and began the rise to prominence that would make him Sun's successor as head of the Guomindang and the unifier of all China under the right-wing nationalist government.

Sun Yat-sen died of cancer in Beijing in March 1925, but the Nationalist movement he had helped to initiate was gaining momentum. During the summer of 1925, Chiang, as commander-in-chief of the National Revolutionary Army, set out on the long-delayed Northern Expedition against the northern warlords. Within nine months, half of China had been conquered. By 1926, however, the Guomindang had divided into left- and right-wing factions, and the Communist bloc within it was also growing. In March 1926, after thwarting a kidnapping attempt against him, Chiang abruptly dismissed his Soviet advisers, imposed restrictions on CCP members' participation in the top leadership, and emerged as the preeminent Guomindang leader. The Soviet Union, still hoping to prevent a split between Chiang and the CCP, ordered Communist underground activities to facilitate the Northern Expedition, which was finally launched by Chiang from Guangzhou in July 1926.

In early 1927 the Guomindang-CCP rivalry led to a split in the revolutionary ranks. The CCP and the left wing of the Guomindang had decided to move the seat of the Nationalist government from Guangzhou to Wuhan. But Chiang, whose Northern Expedition was proving successful, set his forces to destroying the Shanghai CCP apparatus and established an anti-Communist government at Nanjing in April 1927. There now were three capitals in China: the internationally recognized warlord regime in Beijing; the Communist and left-wing Guomindang regime at Wuhan; and the right-wing civilian-military regime at Nanjing, which would remain the Nationalist capital for the next decade.

The Comintern cause appeared bankrupt. A new policy was instituted calling on the CCP to foment armed insurrections in both urban and rural areas in preparation for an expected rising tide of revolution. Unsuccessful attempts were made by Communists to take cities such as Nanchang, Changsha, Shantou, and Guangzhou, and an armed rural insurrection, known as the Autumn Harvest Uprising, was staged by peasants in Hunan Province. The insurrection was led by Mao Zedong (1893–1976), who would later become chairman of the CCP and head of state of the People's Republic of China. Mao was of peasant origins and was one of the founders of the CCP.

But in mid-1927 the CCP was at a low ebb. The Communists had been expelled from Wuhan by their left-wing Guomindang allies, who in turn were toppled by a military regime. By 1928 all of China was at least nominally under Chiang's control, and the Nanjing government received prompt international recognition as the sole legitimate government of China. The Nationalist government announced that in conformity with Sun Yat-sen's formula for the three stages of revolution—military unification, political tutelage, and constitutional democracy—China had reached the end of the first phase and would embark on the second, which would be under Guomindang direction.

Consolidation under the Guomindang

The decade of 1928–37 was one of consolidation and accomplishment by the Guomindang. Some of the harsh aspects of foreign concessions and privileges in China were moderated through diplomacy. The government acted energetically to modernize the legal and penal systems, stabilize prices, amortize debts, reform the banking and currency systems, build railroads and highways, improve public health facilities, legislate against traffic in narcotics, and augment industrial and agricultural production. Great strides also were made in education and, in an effort to help unify

The mausoleum of Sun Yat-sen in Nanjing
Courtesy Xinhua News Agency

Chinese society, in a program to popularize the national language and overcome dialectal variations. The widespread establishment of communications facilities further encouraged a sense of unity and pride among the people.

Rise of the Communists

There were forces at work during this period of progress that would eventually undermine the Chiang Kai-shek government. The first was the gradual rise of the Communists.

Mao Zedong, who had become a Marxist at the time of the emergence of the May Fourth Movement (he was working as a librarian at Beijing University), had boundless faith in the revolutionary potential of the peasantry. He advocated that revolution in China focus on them rather than on the urban proletariat, as prescribed by orthodox Marxist-Leninist theoreticians. Despite the failure of the Autumn Harvest Uprising of 1927, Mao continued to work among the peasants of Hunan Province. Without waiting for the sanction of the CCP center, then in Shanghai, he began establishing peasant-based soviets (Communist-run local governments) along the border between Hunan and Jiangxi provinces. In collaboration with military commander Zhu De (1886–1976), Mao turned the local peasants into a politicized guerrilla force. By the winter of 1927–28, the combined "peasants' and workers'" army had some 10,000 troops.

Mao's prestige rose steadily after the failure of the Comintern-directed urban insurrections. In late 1931 he was able to proclaim the establishment of the Chinese Soviet Republic under his chairmanship in Ruijin, Jiangxi Province. The Soviet-oriented CCP Political Bureau came to Ruijin at Mao's invitation with the intent of dismantling his apparatus. But, although he had yet to gain membership in the Political Bureau, Mao dominated the proceedings.

In the early 1930s, amid continued Political Bureau opposition to his military and agrarian policies and the deadly annihilation campaigns being waged against the Red Army by Chiang Kai-shek's forces, Mao's control of the Chinese Communist movement increased. The epic Long March of his Red Army and its supporters, which began in October 1934, would ensure his place in history. Forced to evacuate their camps and homes, Communist soldiers and government and party leaders and functionaries numbering about 100,000 (including only 35 women, the spouses of high leaders) set out on a circuitous retreat of some 12,500 kilometers through 11 provinces, 18 mountain ranges, and 24 rivers in southwest and northwest China. During the Long March, Mao finally gained unchallenged command of the CCP, ousting his rivals and reasserting guerrilla strategy. As a final destination, he selected southern Shaanxi Province, where some 8,000 survivors of the original group from Jiangxi Province (joined by some 22,000 from other areas) arrived in October 1935. The Communists set up their headquarters at Yan'an, where the movement would grow rapidly for the next ten years. Contributing to this growth would be a combination of internal and external circumstances, of which aggression by the Japanese was perhaps the most significant. Conflict with Japan, which would continue from the 1930s to the end of World War II, was the other force (besides the Communists themselves) that would undermine the Nationalist government.

Anti-Japanese War

Few Chinese had any illusions about Japanese designs on China. Hungry for raw materials and pressed by a growing population, Japan initiated the seizure of Manchuria in September 1931 and established ex-Qing emperor Puyi as head of the puppet regime of Manchukuo in 1932. The loss of Manchuria, and its vast potential for industrial development and war industries, was a blow to the Nationalist economy. The League of Nations, established at the end of World War I, was unable to act in the face of the Japanese defiance. The Japanese began to push from south of the Great Wall into northern China and into the coastal provinces. Chinese fury against Japan was predictable, but anger was also directed against the Guomindang government, which at the time was more preoccupied with anti-Communist extermination campaigns than with resisting the Japanese invaders. The importance of "internal unity before external danger" was forcefully brought home in December 1936, when Nationalist troops (who had been ousted from Manchuria by the Japanese) mutinied at Xi'an. The mutineers forcibly detained Chiang Kai-shek for several days until he agreed to cease hostilities against the Communist forces in northwest China and to assign Communist units combat duties in designated anti-Japanese front areas.

The Chinese resistance stiffened after July 7, 1937, when a clash occurred between Chinese and Japanese troops outside Beijing (then renamed Beiping) near the Marco Polo Bridge. This skirmish not only marked the beginning of open, though undeclared, war between China and Japan but also hastened the formal announcement of the second Guomindang-CCP united front against Japan. The collaboration took place with salutary effects for the beleaguered CCP. The distrust between the two parties, however, was scarcely veiled. The uneasy alliance began to break down after late 1938, despite Japan's steady territorial gains in northern China, the coastal regions, and the rich Chang Jiang Valley in central China. After 1940, conflicts between the Nationalists and Communists became more frequent in the areas not under Japanese control. The Communists expanded their influence wherever opportunities presented themselves through mass organizations, administrative reforms, and the land- and tax-reform measures favoring the peasants—while the Nationalists attempted to neutralize the spread of Communist influence.

At Yan'an and elsewhere in the "liberated areas," Mao was able to adapt Marxism-Leninism to Chinese conditions. He taught party cadres to lead the masses by living and working with them, eating their food, and thinking their thoughts. The Red Army fostered an image of conducting guerrilla warfare in defense of the people. Communist troops adapted to changing wartime conditions and became a seasoned fighting force. Mao also began preparing for the establishment of a new China. In 1940 he outlined the program of the Chinese Communists for an eventual seizure of power. His teachings became the central tenets of the CCP doctrine that came to be formalized as Mao Zedong Thought. With skillful organizational and propaganda work, the Communists increased party membership from 100,000 in 1937 to 1.2 million by 1945.

In 1945 China emerged from the war nominally a great military power but actually a nation economically prostrate and on the verge of all-out civil war. The economy deteriorated, sapped by the military demands of foreign war and internal strife, by spiraling inflation, and by Nationalist profiteering, speculation, and hoarding. Starvation came in the wake of the war, and millions were rendered homeless by floods and the unsettled conditions in many parts of the country. The situation was further complicated by an Allied agreement at the Yalta Conference in February 1945 that brought Soviet troops into Manchuria to hasten the termination of war against Japan. Although the Chinese had not been present at Yalta, they had been consulted; they had agreed to have the Soviets enter the war in the belief that the Soviet Union would deal only with the Nationalist government. After the war, the Soviet Union, as part of the Yalta agreement, dismantled and removed more than half the industrial equipment left there by the Japanese. The Soviet presence in northeast China enabled the Communists to move in long enough to arm themselves with the equipment surrendered by the withdrawing Japanese army. The problems of rehabilitating the formerly Japanese-occupied areas and of reconstructing the nation from the ravages of a protracted war were staggering, to say the least.

Return to Civil War

During World War II, the United States emerged as a major actor in Chinese affairs. As an ally it embarked in late 1941 on a program of massive military and financial aid to the hard-pressed Nationalist government. In January 1943 the United States and Britain led the way in revising their treaties with China, bringing to an end a century of unequal treaty relations. Within a few months, a new agreement was signed between the United States and China for the stationing of American troops in China for the common war effort against Japan. In December 1943 the Chinese exclusion acts of the 1880s and subsequent laws enacted by the United States Congress to restrict Chinese immigration into the United States were repealed.

The wartime policy of the United States was initially to help China become a strong ally and a stabilizing force in postwar East Asia. As the conflict between the Nationalists and the Communists intensified, however, the United States sought unsuccessfully to reconcile the rival forces for a more effective anti-Japanese war effort. Toward the end of the war, United States Marines were used to hold Beiping and Tianjin against a possible Soviet incursion, and logistic support was given to Nationalist forces in north and northeast China.

Through the mediatory influence of the United States a military truce was arranged in January 1946, but battles between

Nationalists and Communists soon resumed. Realizing that American efforts short of large-scale armed intervention could not stop the war, the United States withdrew the American mission, headed by General George C. Marshall, in early 1947. The civil war, in which the United States aided the Nationalists with massive economic loans but no military support, became more widespread. Battles raged not only for territories but also for the allegiance of cross sections of the population.

Belatedly, the Nationalist government sought to enlist popular support through internal reforms. The effort was in vain, however, because of the rampant corruption in government and the accompanying political and economic chaos. By late 1948 the Nationalist position was bleak. The demoralized and undisciplined Nationalist troops proved no match for the People's Liberation Army (PLA). The Communists were well established in the north and northeast. Although the Nationalists had an advantage in numbers of men and weapons, controlled a much larger territory and population than their adversaries, and enjoyed considerable international support, they were exhausted by the long war with Japan and the attendant internal responsibilities. In January 1949 Beiping was taken by the Communists without a fight, and its name was changed back to Beijing. Between April and November, major cities passed from Guomindang to Communist control with minimal resistance. In most cases the surrounding countryside and small towns had come under Communist influence long before the cities. After Chiang Kai-shek and a few hundred thousand Nationalist troops fled from the mainland to the island of Taiwan, there remained only isolated pockets of resistance. In December 1949 Chiang proclaimed Taipei, Taiwan, the temporary capital of China.

The People's Republic of China

On October 1, 1949, the People's Republic of China was formally established, with its national capital at Beijing. "The Chinese people have stood up!" declared Mao as he announced the creation of a "people's democratic dictatorship." The *people* were defined as a coalition of four social classes: the workers, the peasants, the petite bourgeoisie, and the national-capitalists. The four classes were to be led by the CCP, as the vanguard of the working class. At that time the CCP claimed a membership of 4.5 million, of which members of peasant origin accounted for nearly 90 percent. The party was under Mao's chairmanship, and the government was headed by Zhou Enlai (1898–1976) as premier of the State Administrative Council (the predecessor of the State Council).

The Soviet Union recognized the People's Republic on October 2, 1949. Earlier in the year, Mao had proclaimed his policy of "leaning to one side" as a commitment to the socialist bloc. In February 1950, after months of hard bargaining, China and the Soviet Union signed the Treaty of Friendship, Alliance, and Mutual Assistance, valid until 1980. The pact also was intended to counter Japan or any power's joining Japan for the purpose of aggression.

For the first time in decades a Chinese government was met with peace, instead of massive military opposition, within its territory. The new leadership was highly disciplined and, having a decade of wartime administrative experience to draw on, was able to embark on a program of national integration and reform. In the first year of Communist administration, moderate social and economic policies were implemented with skill and effectiveness. The leadership realized that the overwhelming and multitudinous task of economic reconstruction and achievement of political and social stability required the goodwill and cooperation of all classes of people. Results were impressive by any standard, and popular support was widespread.

By 1950 international recognition of the Communist government had increased considerably, but it was slowed by China's involvement in the Korean War. In October 1950, sensing a threat to the industrial heartland in northeast China from the advancing United Nations (UN) forces in the Democratic People's Republic of Korea (North Korea), units of the PLA—calling themselves the Chinese People's Volunteers—crossed the Yalü Jiang River into North Korea in response to a North Korean request for aid. Almost simultaneously the PLA forces also marched into Xizang to reassert Chinese sovereignty over a region that had been in effect independent of Chinese rule since the fall of the Qing dynasty in 1911. In 1951 the UN declared China to be an aggressor in Korea and sanctioned a global embargo on the shipment of arms and war matériel to China. This step foreclosed for the time being any possibility that the People's Republic might replace Nationalist China (on Taiwan) as a member of the UN and as a veto-holding member of the UN Security Council.

After China entered the Korean War, the initial moderation in Chinese domestic policies gave way to a massive campaign against the "enemies of the state," actual and potential. These enemies consisted of "war criminals, traitors, bureaucratic capitalists, and counterrevolutionaries." The campaign was combined with party-sponsored trials attended by huge numbers of people. The major targets in this drive were foreigners and Christian missionaries who were branded as United States agents at these mass trials. The 1951–52 drive against political enemies was accompanied by land reform, which had actually begun under the Agrarian Reform Law of June 28, 1950. The redistribution of land was accelerated, and a class struggle (see Glossary) against landlords and wealthy peasants was launched. An ideological reform campaign requiring self-criticisms and public confessions by university faculty members, scientists, and other professional workers was given wide publicity. Artists and writers were soon the objects of similar treatment for failing to heed Mao's dictum that culture and literature must reflect the class interest of the working people, led by the CCP. These campaigns were accompanied in 1951 and 1952 by the *san fan* ("three anti") and *wu fan* ("five anti") movements. The former was directed ostensibly against the evils of "corruption, waste, and bureaucratism"; its real aim was to eliminate incompetent and politically unreliable public officials and to bring about an efficient, disciplined, and responsive bureaucratic system. The *wu fan* movement aimed at eliminating recalcitrant and corrupt businessmen and industrialists, who were in effect the targets of the CCP's condemnation of "tax evasion, bribery, cheating in government contracts, thefts of economic intelligence, and stealing of state assets." In the course of this campaign the party claimed to have uncovered a well-organized attempt by businessmen and industrialists to corrupt party and government officials. This charge was enlarged into an assault on the bourgeoisie as a whole. The number of people affected by the various punitive or reform campaigns was estimated in the millions.

The Transition to Socialism, 1953–57

The period of officially designated "transition to socialism" corresponded to China's First Five-Year Plan (1953–57). The period was characterized by efforts to achieve industrialization, collectivization of agriculture, and political centralization.

The First Five-Year Plan stressed the development of heavy industry on the Soviet model. Soviet economic and technical assistance was expected to play a significant part in the implementation of the plan, and technical agreements were signed with the Soviets in 1953 and 1954. For the purpose of economic planning, the first modern census was taken in 1953; the population of mainland China was shown to be 583 million, a figure far greater than had been anticipated.

Among China's most pressing needs in the early 1950s were food for its burgeoning population, domestic capital for investment, and purchase of Soviet-supplied technology, capital equipment, and military hardware. To satisfy these needs, the government began to collectivize agriculture. Despite internal disagreement as to the speed of collectivization, which at least for the time being was resolved in Mao's favor, preliminary collectivization was 90 percent completed by the end of 1956. In addition, the government nationalized banking, industry, and trade. Private enterprise in mainland China was virtually abolished.

Major political developments included the centralization of party and government administration. Elections were held in 1953 for delegates to the First National People's Congress, China's national legislature, which met in 1954. The congress promulgated the state constitution of 1954 and formally elected Mao chairman (or president) of the People's Republic; it elected Liu Shaoqi (1898–1969) chairman of the Standing Committee of the National People's Congress and named Zhou Enlai premier of the new State Council.

In the midst of these major governmental changes, and helping to precipitate them, was a power struggle within the CCP leading to the 1954 purge of Political Bureau member Gao Gang and Party Organization Department head Rao Shushi, who were accused of illicitly trying to seize control of the party.

The process of national integration also was characterized by improvements in party organization under the administrative direction of the secretary general of the party, Deng Xiaoping (who served concurrently as vice premier of the State Council). There was a marked emphasis on recruiting intellectuals, who by 1956 constituted nearly 12 percent of the party's 10.8 million members. Peasant membership had decreased to 69 percent, while there was an increasing number of "experts" (see Glossary), who were needed for the party and governmental infrastructures, in the party ranks.

As part of the effort to encourage the participation of intellectuals in the new regime, in mid-1956 there began an official effort to liberalize the political climate (see Policy Toward Intellectuals, ch. 4). Cultural and intellectual figures were encouraged to speak their minds on the state of CCP rule and programs. Mao personally took the lead in the movement, which was launched under the classical slogan "Let a hundred flowers bloom, let the hundred schools of thought contend." At first the party's repeated invitation to air constructive views freely and openly was met with caution. By mid-1957, however, the movement unexpectedly mounted, bringing denunciation and criticism against the party in general and the excesses of its cadres in particular. Startled and embarrassed, leaders turned on the critics as "bourgeois rightists" and launched the Anti-Rightist Campaign. The Hundred Flowers Campaign (see Glossary),

Zhou Enlai, Liu Shaoqi, Zhu De, and Mao Zedong in 1957
Courtesy China Pictorial

sometimes called the Double Hundred Campaign, apparently had a sobering effect on the CCP leadership.

The Great Leap Forward, 1958–60

The antirightist drive was followed by a militant approach toward economic development. In 1958 the CCP launched the Great Leap Forward campaign under the new "General Line for Socialist Construction." The Great Leap Forward was aimed at accomplishing the economic and technical development of the country at a vastly faster pace and with greater results. The shift to the left that the new "General Line" represented was brought on by a combination of domestic and external factors. Although the party leaders appeared generally satisfied with the accomplishments of the First Five-Year Plan, they—Mao and his fellow radicals in particular—believed that more could be achieved in the Second Five-Year Plan (1958–62) if the people could be ideologically aroused and if domestic resources could be utilized more efficiently for the simultaneous development of industry and agriculture. These assumptions led the party to an intensified mobilization of the peasantry and mass organizations, stepped-up ideological guidance and indoctrination of technical experts, and efforts to build a more responsive political system. The last of these undertakings was to be accomplished through a new *xiafang* (down to the countryside) movement, under which cadres inside and outside the party would be sent to factories, communes, mines, and public works projects for manual labor and firsthand familiarization with grass-roots conditions. Although evidence is sketchy, Mao's decision to embark on the Great Leap Forward was based in part on his uncertainty about the Soviet policy of economic, financial, and technical assistance to China. That policy, in Mao's view, not only fell far short of his expectations and needs but also made him wary of the political and economic dependence in which China might find itself (see Sino-Soviet Relations, ch. 12).

The Great Leap Forward centered on a new socioeconomic and political system created in the countryside and in a few urban areas—the people's communes (see Glossary). By the fall of 1958, some 750,000 agricultural producers' cooperatives, now designated as production brigades, had been amalgamated into about 23,500 communes, each averaging 5,000 households, or 22,000 people. The individual commune was placed in control of all the means of production and was to operate as the sole accounting unit; it was subdivided into production brigades (generally coterminous with traditional villages) and production teams. Each commune was planned as a self-supporting community for agriculture, small-scale local industry (for example, the famous backyard pig-iron furnaces), schooling, marketing, administration, and local security (maintained by militia organizations). Organized along paramilitary and laborsaving lines, the commune had communal kitchens, mess halls, and nurseries. In a way, the people's communes constituted a fundamental attack on the institution of the family, especially in a few model areas where radical experiments in communal living—large dormitories in place of the traditional nuclear-family housing—occurred. (These were quickly dropped.) The system also was based on the assumption that it would release additional manpower for such major projects as irrigation works and hydroelectric dams, which were seen as integral parts of the plan for the simultaneous development of industry and agriculture (see Agricultural Policies, ch. 6).

The Great Leap Forward was an economic failure. In early 1959, amid signs of rising popular restiveness, the CCP admitted that the favorable production report for 1958 had been exaggerated. Among the Great Leap Forward's economic consequences were a shortage of food (in which natural disasters also played a part); shortages of raw materials for industry; overproduction of poor-quality goods; deterioration of industrial plants through mismanagement; and exhaustion and demoralization of the peasantry and of the intellectuals, not to mention the party and government cadres at all levels. Throughout 1959 efforts to modify the administration of the communes got under way; these were intended partly to restore some material incentives to the production brigades and teams, partly to decentralize control, and partly to house families that had been reunited as household units.

Political consequences were not inconsiderable. In April 1959 Mao, who bore the chief responsibility for the Great Leap Forward fiasco, stepped down from his position as chairman of the People's Republic. The National People's Congress elected Liu Shaoqi as Mao's successor, though Mao remained chairman of the CCP. Moreover, Mao's Great Leap Forward policy came under open criticism at a party conference at Lushan, Jiangxi Province. The attack was led by Minister of National Defense Peng Dehuai, who had become troubled by the potentially adverse effect Mao's policies would have on the modernization of the armed forces. Peng argued that "putting politics in command" was no substitute for economic laws and realistic economic policy; unnamed party leaders were also admonished for trying to "jump into communism in one step." After the Lushan showdown, Peng Dehuai, who allegedly had been encouraged by Soviet leader Nikita Khrushchev to oppose Mao, was deposed. Peng was replaced by Lin Biao, a radical and opportunist Maoist. The new defense minister initiated a systematic purge of Peng's supporters from the military.

Militancy on the domestic front was echoed in external policies (see Evolution of Foreign Policy, ch. 12). The "soft" foreign policy based on the Five Principles of Peaceful Coexistence (see Glossary) to which China had subscribed in the mid-1950s gave way to a "hard" line in 1958. From August through October of that year, the Chinese resumed a massive artillery bombardment of the Nationalist-held offshore islands of Jinmen (Chin-men in Wade-Giles, but often referred to as Kinmen or Quemoy) and Mazu (Ma-tsu in Wade Giles). This was accompanied by an aggressive propaganda assault on the United States and a declaration of intent to "liberate" Taiwan.

Chinese control over Xizang had been reasserted in 1950. The socialist revolution that took place thereafter increasingly became a process of sinicization for the Tibetans. Tension culminated in a revolt in 1958–59 and the flight to India by the Dalai Lama, the Tibetans' spiritual and de facto temporal leader. Relations with India—where sympathy for the rebels was aroused—deteriorated as thousands of Tibetan refugees crossed the Indian border. There were several border incidents in 1959, and a brief Sino-Indian border war erupted in October 1962 as China laid claim to Aksai Chin, nearly 103,600 square kilometers of territory that India regarded as its own (see Physical Environment, ch. 2). The Soviet Union gave India its moral support in the dispute, thus contributing to the growing tension between Beijing and Moscow.

The Sino-Soviet dispute of the late 1950s was the most important development in Chinese foreign relations. The Soviet Union had been China's principal benefactor and ally, but relations between the two were cooling. The Soviet agreement in late 1957 to help China produce its own nuclear weapons and missiles was terminated by mid-1959 (see Defense Industry and the Economic Role of the People's Liberation Army, ch. 14). From that point until the mid-1960s, the Soviets recalled all of their technicians and advisers from China and reduced or canceled economic and technical aid to China. The discord was occasioned by several factors. The two countries differed in their interpretation of the nature of "peaceful coexistence." The Chinese took a more militant and unyielding position on the issue of anti-imperialist struggle, but the Soviets were unwilling, for example, to give their support on the Taiwan question. In addition, the two communist powers disagreed on doctrinal matters. The Chinese accused the Soviets of "revisionism"; the latter countered with charges of "dogmatism." Rivalry within the international communist movement also exacerbated Sino-Soviet relations. An additional complication was the history of suspicion each side had toward the other, especially the Chinese, who had lost a substantial part of territory to tsarist Russia in the mid-nineteenth century. Whatever the causes of the dispute, the Soviet suspension of aid was a blow to the Chinese scheme for developing industrial and high-level (including nuclear) technology.

Readjustment and Recovery, 1961–65

In 1961 the political tide at home began to swing to the right, as evidenced by the ascendancy of a more moderate leadership. In an effort to stabilize the economic front, for example, the party—still under Mao's titular leadership but under the dominant influence of Liu Shaoqi, Deng Xiaoping, Chen Yun, Peng Zhen, Bo Yibo, and others—initiated a series of corrective measures. Among these measures was the reorganization of the commune system, with the result that production brigades and teams had more say in their own administrative and economic planning. To gain more effective control from the center, the CCP reestablished its six regional bureaus and initiated steps aimed at tightening party discipline and encouraging the leading party cadres to develop populist-style leadership at all levels. The efforts were prompted by the party's realization that the arrogance of party and government functionaries had engendered only public apathy. On the industrial front, much emphasis was now placed on realistic and efficient planning; ideological fervor and mass movements were no longer the controlling themes of industrial management. Production authority was restored to factory managers. Another notable emphasis after 1961 was the party's greater interest in strengthening the defense and internal security establishment. By early 1965 the country was well on its way to recovery under the direction of the party apparatus, or, to be more specific, the Central Committee's Secretariat headed by Secretary General Deng Xiaoping.

The Cultural Revolution Decade, 1966–76

In the early 1960s, Mao was on the political sidelines and in semi-seclusion. By 1962, however, he began an offensive to purify the party, having grown increasingly uneasy about what he believed were the creeping "capitalist" and antisocialist tendencies in the country. As a hardened veteran revolutionary who had overcome the severest adversities, Mao continued to believe that the material incentives that had been restored to the peasants and others were corrupting the masses and were counterrevolutionary.

To arrest the so-called capitalist trend, Mao launched the Socialist Education Movement (1962–65; see Glossary), in which the primary emphasis was on restoring ideological purity, reinfusing revolutionary fervor into the party and government bureaucracies, and intensifying class struggle. There were internal disagreements, however, not on the aim of the movement but on the methods of carrying it out. Opposition came mainly from the moderates represented by Liu Shaoqi and Deng Xiaoping, who were unsympathetic to Mao's policies. The Socialist Education Movement was soon paired with another Mao campaign, the theme of which was "to learn from the People's Liberation Army." Minister of National Defense Lin Biao's rise to the center of power was increasingly conspicuous. It was accompanied by his call on the PLA and the CCP to accentuate Maoist thought as the guiding principle for the Socialist Education Movement and for all revolutionary undertakings in China.

In connection with the Socialist Education Movement, a thorough reform of the school system, which had been planned earlier to coincide with the Great Leap Forward, went into effect. The reform was intended as a work-study program—a new *xiafang* movement—in which schooling was slated to accommodate the work schedule of communes and factories. It had the dual purpose of providing mass education less expensively than previously and of re-educating intellectuals and scholars to accept the need for their own participation in manual labor. The drafting of intellectuals for manual labor was part of the party's rectification campaign, publicized through the mass media as an effort to remove "bourgeois" influences from professional workers—particularly, their tendency to have greater regard for their own specialized fields than for the goals of the party. Official propaganda accused them of being more concerned with having "expertise" than being "red" (see Glossary).

The Militant Phase, 1966–68

By mid-1965 Mao had gradually but systematically regained control of the party with the support of Lin Biao, Jiang Qing (Mao's fourth wife), and Chen Boda, a leading theoretician. In late 1965 a leading member of Mao's "Shanghai Mafia," Yao Wenyuan, wrote a thinly veiled attack on the deputy mayor of Beijing, Wu Han. In the next six months, under the guise of upholding ideological purity, Mao and his supporters purged or attacked a wide variety of public figures, including State Chairman Liu Shaoqi and other party and state leaders. By mid-1966 Mao's campaign had erupted into what came to be known as the Great Proletarian Cultural Revolution, the first mass action to have emerged against the CCP apparatus itself.

Considerable intraparty opposition to the Cultural Revolution was evident. On the one side was the Mao-Lin Biao group, supported by the PLA; on the other side was a faction led by Liu Shaoqi and Deng Xiaoping, which had its strength in the regular party machine. Premier Zhou Enlai, while remaining personally loyal to Mao, tried to mediate or to reconcile the two factions.

Mao felt that he could no longer depend on the formal party organization, convinced that it had been permeated with the "capitalist" and bourgeois obstructionists. He turned to Lin Biao and the PLA to counteract the influence of those who were allegedly " 'left' in form but 'right' in essence." The PLA was widely extolled as a "great school" for the training of a new generation of revolutionary fighters and leaders. Maoists also turned to middle-school students for political demonstrations on their behalf. These students, joined also by some university students, came to be known as the Red Guards (see Glossary). Millions of Red Guards were encouraged by the Cultural Revolution group to become a "shock force" and to "bombard" with criticism both the regular party headquarters in Beijing and those at the regional and provincial levels. Red Guard activities were promoted as a reflection of Mao's policy of rekindling revolutionary enthusiasm and destroying "outdated," "counterrevolutionary" symbols and values. Mao's ideas, popularized in the *Quotations from Chairman Mao,* became the standard by which all revolutionary efforts were to be judged. The "four big rights"—speaking out freely, airing views fully, holding great debates, and writing big-character posters (see Glossary)—became an important factor in encouraging Mao's youthful followers to criticize his intraparty rivals. The "four big rights" became such a major feature during the period that they were later institutionalized in the state constitution of 1975 (see Constitutional Framework, ch. 10). The result of the unfettered criticism of established organs of control by China's exuberant youth was massive civil disorder, punctuated also by clashes among rival Red Guard gangs and between the gangs and local security authorities. The party organization was shattered from top to bottom. (The Central Committee's Secretariat ceased functioning in late 1966.) The resources of the public security organs were severely strained. Faced with imminent anarchy, the PLA—the only organization whose ranks for the most part had not been radicalized by Red Guard-style activities—emerged as the principal guarantor of law and order and the de facto political authority. And, although the PLA was under Mao's rallying call to "support the left," PLA regional military commanders ordered their forces to restrain the leftist radicals, thus restoring order throughout much of China. The PLA also was responsible for the appearance in early 1967 of the revolutionary committees, a new form of local control that replaced local party committees and administrative bodies. The revolutionary committees were staffed with Cultural Revolution activists, trusted cadres, and military commanders, the latter frequently holding the greatest power.

The radical tide receded somewhat beginning in late 1967, but it was not until after mid-1968 that Mao came to realize the uselessness of further revolutionary violence. Liu Shaoqi, Deng Xiaoping, and their fellow "revisionists" and "capitalist roaders" had been purged from public life by early 1967, and the Maoist group had since been in full command of the political scene.

Viewed in larger perspective, the need for domestic calm and stability was occasioned perhaps even more by pressures emanating from outside China. The Chinese were alarmed in 1966–68 by steady Soviet military buildups along their common border. The Soviet invasion of Czechoslovakia in 1968 heightened Chinese apprehensions. In March 1969 Chinese and Soviet troops clashed on Zhenbao Island (known to the Soviets as Damanskiy Island) in the disputed Wusuli Jiang (Ussuri River) border area. The tension on the border had a sobering effect on the fractious Chinese political scene and provided the regime with a new and unifying rallying call (see The Soviet Union, ch. 14).

The Ninth National Party Congress to the Demise of Lin Biao, 1969–71

The activist phase of the Cultural Revolution—considered to be the first in a series of cultural revolutions—was brought to an end in April 1969. This end was formally signaled at the CCP's Ninth National Party Congress, which convened under the dominance of the Maoist group. Mao was confirmed as the supreme leader. Lin Biao was promoted to the post of CCP vice chairman and was named as Mao's successor. Others who had risen to power by means of Cultural Revolution machinations were rewarded with positions on the Political Bureau; a significant number of military commanders were appointed to the Central Committee. The party congress also marked the rising influence of two opposing forces, Mao's wife, Jiang Qing, and Premier Zhou Enlai.

The general emphasis after 1969 was on reconstruction through rebuilding of the party, economic stabilization, and greater sensitivity to foreign affairs. Pragmatism gained momentum as a central theme of the years following the Ninth National Party Congress, but this tendency was paralleled by efforts of the radical group to reassert itself. The radical group—Kang Sheng, Xie Fuzhi, Jiang Qing, Zhang Chunqiao, Yao Wenyuan, and Wang Hongwen—no longer had Mao's unqualified support. By 1970 Mao viewed his role more as that of the supreme elder statesman than of an activist in the policy-making process. This was probably the result as much of his declining health as of his view that a stabilizing influence should be brought to bear on a divided nation. As Mao saw it, China needed both pragmatism and revolutionary enthusiasm, each acting as a check on the other. Factional infighting would continue unabated through the mid-1970s, although an uneasy coexistence was maintained while Mao was alive.

The rebuilding of the CCP got under way in 1969. The process was difficult, however, given the pervasiveness of factional tensions and the discord carried over from the Cultural Revolution years. Differences persisted among the military, the party, and left-dominated mass organizations over a wide range of policy issues, to say nothing of the radical-moderate rivalry. It was not until December 1970 that a party committee could be reestablished at the provincial level. In political reconstruction two developments were noteworthy. As the only institution of power for the most part left unscathed by the Cultural Revolution, the PLA was particularly important in the politics of transition and reconstruction. The PLA was, however, not a homogeneous body. In 1970–71 Zhou Enlai was able to forge a centrist-rightist alliance with a group of

PLA regional military commanders who had taken exception to certain of Lin Biao's policies. This coalition paved the way for a more moderate party and government leadership in the late 1970s and 1980s (see The First Wave of Reform, 1979–84, ch. 11).

The PLA was divided largely on policy issues. On one side of the infighting was the Lin Biao faction, which continued to exhort the need for "politics in command" and for an unremitting struggle against both the Soviet Union and the United States. On the other side was a majority of the regional military commanders, who had become concerned about the effect Lin Biao's political ambitions would have on military modernization and economic development. These commanders' views generally were in tune with the positions taken by Zhou Enlai and his moderate associates. Specifically, the moderate groups within the civilian bureaucracy and the armed forces spoke for more material incentives for the peasantry, efficient economic planning, and a thorough reassessment of the Cultural Revolution. They also advocated improved relations with the West in general and the United States in particular—if for no other reason than to counter the perceived expansionist aims of the Soviet Union. Generally, the radicals' objection notwithstanding, the Chinese political tide shifted steadily toward the right of center. Among the notable achievements of the early 1970s was China's decision to seek rapprochement with the United States, as dramatized by President Richard M. Nixon's visit in February 1972. In September 1972 diplomatic relations were established with Japan.

Without question, the turning point in the decade of the Cultural Revolution was Lin Biao's abortive coup attempt and his subsequent death in a plane crash as he fled China in September 1971. The immediate consequence was a steady erosion of the fundamentalist influence of the left-wing radicals. Lin Biao's closest supporters were purged systematically. Efforts to depoliticize and promote professionalism were intensified within the PLA. These were also accompanied by the rehabilitation (see Glossary) of those persons who had been persecuted or fallen into disgrace in 1966–68.

End of the Era of Mao Zedong, 1972–76

Among the most prominent of those rehabilitated was Deng Xiaoping, who was reinstated as a vice premier in April 1973, ostensibly under the aegis of Premier Zhou Enlai but certainly with the concurrence of Mao Zedong. Together, Zhou Enlai and Deng Xiaoping came to exert strong influence. Their moderate line favoring modernization of all sectors of the economy was formally confirmed at the Tenth National Party Congress in August 1973, at which time Deng Xiaoping was made a member of the party's Central Committee (but not yet of the Political Bureau).

The radical camp fought back by building an armed urban militia, but its mass base of support was limited to Shanghai and parts of northeastern China—hardly sufficient to arrest what it denounced as "revisionist" and "capitalist" tendencies. In January 1975 Zhou Enlai, speaking before the Fourth National People's Congress, outlined a program of what has come to be known as the Four Modernizations (see Glossary) for the four sectors of agriculture, industry, national defense, and science and technology (see Economic Policies, 1949–80, ch. 5). This program would be reaffirmed at the Eleventh National Party Congress, which convened in August 1977. Also in January 1975, Deng Xiaoping's position was solidified by his election as a vice chairman of the CCP and as a member of the Political Bureau and its Standing Committee. Deng also was installed as China's first civilian chief of the PLA General Staff Department.

The year 1976 saw the deaths of the three most senior officials in the CCP and the state apparatus: Zhou Enlai in January, Zhu De (then chairman of the Standing Committee of the National People's Congress and de jure head of state) in July, and Mao Zedong in September. In April of the same year, masses of demonstrators in Tiananmen Square in Beijing memorialized Zhou Enlai and criticized Mao's closest associates, Zhou's opponents. In June the government announced that Mao would no longer receive foreign visitors. In July an earthquake devastated the city of Tangshan in Hebei Province. These events, added to the deaths of the three Communist leaders, contributed to a popular sense that the "mandate of heaven" had been withdrawn from the ruling party. At best the nation was in a state of serious political uncertainty.

Deng Xiaoping, the logical successor as premier, received a temporary setback after Zhou's death, when radicals launched a major counterassault against him. In April 1976 Deng was once more removed from all his public posts, and a relative political unknown, Hua Guofeng, a Political Bureau member, vice premier, and minister of public security, was named acting premier and party first vice chairman.

Even though Mao Zedong's role in political life had been sporadic and shallow in his later years, it was crucial. Despite Mao's alleged lack of mental acuity, his influence in the months before his death remained such that his orders to dismiss Deng and appoint Hua Guofeng were accepted immediately by the Political Bureau. The political system had polarized in the years before Mao's death into increasingly bitter and irreconcilable factions. While Mao was alive—and playing these factions off against each other—the contending forces were held in check. His death resolved only some of the problems inherent in the succession struggle.

The radical clique most closely associated with Mao and the Cultural Revolution became vulnerable after Mao died, as Deng had been after Zhou Enlai's demise. In October, less than a month after Mao's death, Jiang Qing and her three principal associates—denounced as the Gang of Four (see Glossary)—were arrested with the assistance of two senior Political Bureau members, Minister of National Defense Ye Jianying (1897–1986) and Wang Dongxing, commander of the CCP's elite bodyguard. Within days it was formally announced that Hua Guofeng had assumed the positions of party chairman, chairman of the party's Central Military Commission, and premier.

The Post-Mao Period, 1976–78

The jubilation following the incarceration of the Gang of Four and the popularity of the new ruling triumvirate (Hua Guofeng, Ye Jianying, and Li Xiannian, a temporary alliance of necessity) were succeeded by calls for the restoration to power of Deng Xiaoping and the elimination of leftist influence throughout the political system. By July 1977, at no small risk to undercutting Hua Guofeng's legitimacy as Mao's successor and seeming to contradict Mao's apparent will, the Central Committee exonerated Deng Xiaoping from responsibility for the Tiananmen Square incident. Deng admitted some shortcomings in the events of 1975, and finally, at a party Central Committee session, he resumed all the posts from which he had been removed in 1976.

The post-Mao political order was given its first vote of confidence at the Eleventh National Party Congress, held August 12–18, 1977. Hua was confirmed as party chairman, and Ye Jianying, Deng Xiaoping, Li Xiannian, and Wang Dongxing were elected vice chairmen. The congress proclaimed the formal end of the Cultural Revolution, blamed it entirely on the Gang of Four, and reiterated that "the fundamental task of the party in the new historical period is to build China into a modern, powerful socialist country by the end of the twentieth century." Many contradictions still were apparent, however, in regard to the Maoist legacy and the possibility of future cultural revolutions.

The new balance of power clearly was unsatisfactory to Deng, who sought genuine party reform and, soon after the National Party Congress, took the initiative to reorganize the bureaucracy and redirect policy. His longtime protégé Hu Yaobang replaced Hua supporter Wang Dongxing as head of the CCP Organization

Department. Educational reforms were instituted, and Cultural Revolution-era verdicts on literature, art, and intellectuals were overturned. The year 1978 proved a crucial one for the reformers. Differences among the two competing factions—that headed by Hua Guofeng (soon to be branded a leftist) and that led by Deng and the more moderate figures—became readily apparent by the time the Fifth National People's Congress was held in February and March 1978. Serious disputes arose over the apparently disproportionate development of the national economy, the Hua forces calling for still more large-scale projects that China could ill afford. In the face of substantive losses in leadership positions and policy decisions, the leftists sought to counterattack with calls for strict adherence to Mao Zedong Thought and the party line of class struggle. Rehabilitations of Deng's associates and others sympathetic to his reform plans were stepped up. Not only were many of those purged during the Cultural Revolution returned to power, but individuals who had fallen from favor as early as the mid-1950s were rehabilitated. It was a time of increased political activism by students, whose big-character posters attacking Deng's opponents—and even Mao himself—appeared with regularity.

China and the Four Modernizations, 1979–82

The culmination of Deng Xiaoping's re-ascent to power and the start in earnest of political, economic, social, and cultural reforms were achieved at the Third Plenum of the National Party Congress's Eleventh Central Committee in December 1978. The Third Plenum is considered a major turning point in modern Chinese political history. "Left" mistakes committed before and during the Cultural Revolution were "corrected," and the "two whatevers" policy ("support whatever policy decisions Chairman Mao made and follow whatever instructions Chairman Mao gave") was repudiated. The classic party line calling for protracted class struggle was officially exchanged for one promoting the Four Modernizations. In the future, the attainment of economic goals would be the measure of the success or failure of policies and individual leadership; in other words, economics, not politics, was in command. To effect such a broad policy redirection, Deng placed key allies on the Political Bureau (including Chen Yun as an additional vice chairman and Hu Yaobang as a member) while positioning Hu Yaobang as secretary general of the CCP and head of the party's Propaganda Department. Although assessments of the Cultural Revolution and Mao were deferred, a decision was announced on "historical questions left over from an earlier period." The 1976 Tiananmen Square incident, the 1959 removal of Peng Dehuai, and other now infamous political machinations were reversed in favor of the new leadership. New agricultural policies intended to loosen political restrictions on peasants and allow them to produce more on their own initiative were approved.

Rapid change occurred in the subsequent months and years. The year 1979 witnessed the formal exchange of diplomatic recognition between the People's Republic and the United States, a border war between China and Vietnam, the fledgling ''democracy movement'' (which had begun in earnest in November 1978), and the determination not to extend the thirty-year-old Treaty of Friendship, Alliance, and Mutual Assistance with the Soviet Union. All these events led to some criticism of Deng Xiaoping, who had to alter his strategy temporarily while directing his own political warfare against Hua Guofeng and the leftist elements in the party and government. As part of this campaign, a major document was presented at the September 1979 Fourth Plenum of the Eleventh Central Committee, giving a ''preliminary assessment'' of the entire thirty-year period of Communist rule. At the plenum, party Vice Chairman Ye Jianying pointed out the achievements of the CCP while admitting that the leadership had made serious political errors affecting the people. Furthermore, Ye declared the Cultural Revolution ''an appalling catastrophe'' and ''the most severe setback to [the] socialist cause since [1949].'' Although Mao was not specifically blamed, there was no doubt about his share of responsibility. The plenum also marked official acceptance of a new ideological line that called for ''seeking truth from facts'' and of other elements of Deng Xiaoping's thinking. A further setback for Hua was the approval of the resignations of other leftists from leading party and state posts. In the months following the plenum, a party rectification campaign ensued, replete with a purge of party members whose political credentials were largely achieved as a result of the Cultural Revolution. The campaign went beyond the civilian ranks of the CCP, extending to party members in the PLA as well.

Economic advances and political achievements had strengthened the position of the Deng reformists enough that by February 1980 they were able to call the Fifth Plenum of the Eleventh Central Committee. One major effect of the plenum was the resignation of the members of the ''Little Gang of Four'' (an allusion to the original Gang of Four, Mao's allies)—Hua's closest collaborators and the backbone of opposition to Deng. Wang Dongxing, Wu De, Ji Dengkui, and Chen Xilian were charged with ''grave [but unspecified] errors'' in the struggle against the Gang of Four and demoted from the Political Bureau to mere Central Committee membership. In turn, the Central Committee elevated Deng's protégés Hu Yaobang and Zhao Ziyang to the Standing Committee of the Political Bureau and the newly restored party Secretariat. Under the title of secretary general, Hu Yaobang took over day-to-day running of the party (see The First Wave of Reform, 1979–84, ch. 11). Especially poignant was the posthumous rehabilitation of the late president and one-time successor to Mao, Liu Shaoqi, at the Fifth Plenum. Finally, at the Fifth National People's Congress session in August and September that year, Deng's preeminence in government was consolidated when he gave up his vice premiership and Hua Guofeng resigned as premier in favor of Zhao Ziyang.

One of the more spectacular political events of modern Chinese history was the month-long trial of the Gang of Four and six of Lin Biao's closest associates. A 35-judge special court was convened in November 1980 and issued a 20,000-word indictment against the defendants. The indictment came more than four years after the arrest of Jiang Qing and her associates and more than nine years after the arrests of the Lin Biao group. Beyond the trial of ten political pariahs, it appeared that the intimate involvement of Mao Zedong, current party chairman Hua Guofeng, and the CCP itself were on trial. The prosecution wisely separated political errors from actual crimes. Among the latter were the usurpation of state power and party leadership; the persecution of some 750,000 people, 34,375 of whom died during the period 1966–76; and, in the case of the Lin Biao defendants, the plotting of the assassination of Mao. In January 1981 the court rendered guilty verdicts against the ten. Jiang Qing, despite her spirited self-vindication and defense of her late husband, received a death sentence with a two-year suspension; later, Jiang Qing's death sentence was commuted to life imprisonment. So enduring was Mao's legacy that Jiang Qing appeared to be protected by it from execution. The same sentence was given to Zhang Chunqiao, while Wang Hongwen was given life and Yao Wenyuan twenty years. Chen Boda and the other Lin Biao faction members were given sentences of between sixteen and eighteen years. The net effect of the trial was a further erosion of Mao's prestige and the system he created. In pre-trial meetings, the party Central Committee posthumously expelled CCP vice chairman Kang Sheng and Political Bureau member Xie Fuzhi from the party because of their participation in the "counterrevolutionary plots" of Lin Biao and Jiang Qing. The memorial speeches delivered at their funerals were also rescinded. There was enough adverse pre-trial testimony that Hua Guofeng reportedly offered to resign the chairmanship before the trial started.

In June 1981 the Sixth Plenum of the Eleventh Central Committee marked a major milestone in the passing of the Maoist era. The Central Committee accepted Hua's resignation from the chairmanship and granted him the face-saving position of vice chairman. In his place, CCP secretary general Hu Yaobang became chairman. Hua also gave up his position as chairman of the party's Central Military Commission in favor of Deng Xiaoping. The plenum adopted the 35,000-word "Resolution on Certain Questions in the History of Our Party Since the Founding of the People's Republic of China." The resolution reviewed the sixty years since the founding of the CCP, emphasizing party activities since 1949. A major part of the document condemned the ten-year Cultural Revolution and assessed Mao Zedong's role in it. "Chief responsibility for the grave 'Left' error of the 'cultural revolution,' an error comprehensive in magnitude and protracted in duration, does indeed lie with Comrade Mao Zedong. . . . [and] far from making a correct analysis of many problems, he confused right and wrong and the people with the enemy. . . . Herein lies his tragedy." At the same time, Mao was praised for seeking to correct personal and party shortcomings throughout his life, for leading the effort that brought the demise of Lin Biao, and for having criticized Jiang Qing and her cohort. Hua too was recognized for his contributions in defeating the Gang of Four but was branded a "whateverist." Hua also was criticized for his anti-Deng Xiaoping posture in the period 1976–77.

Several days after the closing of the plenum, on the occasion of the sixtieth anniversary of the founding of the CCP, new party chairman Hu Yaobang declared that "although Comrade Mao Zedong made grave mistakes in his later years, it is clear that if we consider his life work, his contributions to the Chinese revolution far outweigh his errors. . . . His immense contributions are immortal." These remarks may have been offered in an effort to repair the extensive damage done to the Maoist legacy and by extension to the party itself. Hu went on, however, to praise the contributions of Zhou Enlai, Liu Shaoqi, Zhu De, Peng Dehuai, and a score of other erstwhile enemies of the late chairman. Thus the new party hierarchy sought to assess, and thus close the books on, the Maoist era and move on to the era of the Four Modernizations. The culmination of Deng's drive to consolidate his power and ensure the continuity of his reformist policies among his successors was the calling of the Twelfth National Party Congress in September 1982 and the Fifth Session of the Fifth National

People's Congress in December 1982 (see The First Wave of Reform, 1979–84, ch. 11).

* * *

Chinese history is a vast field of intellectual inquiry. Advances in archaeology and documentary research constantly produce new results and numerous new publications. An excellent and concise survey of the entire course of Chinese history up to the 1970s is *China: Tradition and Transformation* by John K. Fairbank and Edwin O. Reischauer. For a more in-depth review of modern Chinese history (beginning of the Qing dynasty to the early 1980s), Immanuel C.Y. Hsü's *The Rise of Modern China* should be consulted. Hsü's book is particularly useful for its chapter-by-chapter bibliography. Maurice Meisner's *Mao's China and After: A History of the People's Republic* presents a comprehensive historical analysis of post-1949 China and provides a selected bibliography.

There are a number of excellent serial publications covering Chinese history topics. These include *China Quarterly, Chinese Studies in History,* and *Journal of Asian Studies.* The Association for Asian Studies' annual *Bibliography of Asian Studies* provides the most comprehensive list of monographs, collections of documents, and articles on Chinese history. (For further information and complete citations, see Bibliography.)

Chapter 2. Physical Environment and Population

A fierce white tiger graces this Han dynasty (206 B.C.–A.D. 220) decorative, circular facade tile.

REMARKABLY VARIED LANDSCAPES suggest the disparate climate and broad reach of China, the third largest country in the world in terms of area. China's climate ranges from subarctic to tropical. Its topography includes the world's highest peaks, tortuous but picturesque river valleys, and vast plains subject to life-threatening but soil-enriching flooding. These characteristics have dictated where the Chinese people live and how they make their livelihood.

The majority of China's people live in the eastern segment of the country, the traditional China Proper. Most are peasants living, as did their forebears, in the low-lying hills and central plains that stretch from the highlands eastward and southward to the sea. Agriculture predominates in this vast area, generally favored by a temperate or subtropical climate. The meticulously tilled fields are evidence in part of the government's continuing concern over farm output and the food supply.

Although migration to urban areas has been restricted since the late 1950s, as of the end of 1985 about 37 percent of the population was urban. An urban and industrial corridor formed a broad arc stretching from Harbin in the northeast through the Beijing area and south to China's largest city, the huge industrial metropolitan complex of Shanghai.

The uneven pattern of internal development, so strongly weighted toward the eastern part of the country, doubtless will change little even with developing interest in exploiting the mineral-rich and agriculturally productive portions of the vast northwest and southwest regions. The adverse terrain and climate of most of those regions have discouraged dense population. For the most part, only ethnic minority groups have settled there.

The "minority nationalities" are an important element of Chinese society. In 1987 there were 55 recognized minority groups, comprising nearly 7 percent of the total population. Because some of the groups were located in militarily sensitive border areas and in regions with strategic minerals, the government tried to maintain benevolent relations with the minorities. But the minorities played only a superficial role in the major affairs of the nation.

China's ethnically diverse population is the largest in the world, and the Chinese Communist Party and the government work strenuously to count, control, and care for their people. In 1982 China conducted its first population census since 1964. It was by far the most thorough and accurate census taken under Communist rule and confirmed that China was a nation of more than 1 billion people, or about one-fifth of the world's population. The census provided demographers with a wealth of accurate data on China's age-sex structure, fertility and mortality rates, and population density and distribution. Useful information also was gathered on minority ethnic groups, urban population, and marital status. For the first time since the People's Republic of China was founded, demographers had reliable information on the size and composition of the Chinese work force.

Beginning in the mid-1950s, the Chinese government introduced, with varying degrees of enthusiasm and success, a number of family planning, or population control, campaigns and programs. The most radical and controversial was the one-child policy publicly announced in 1979. Under this policy, which had different guidelines for national minorities, married couples were officially permitted only one child. Enforcement of the program, however, varied considerably from place to place, depending on the vigilance of local population control workers.

Health care has improved dramatically in China since 1949. Major diseases such as cholera, typhoid, and scarlet fever have been brought under control. Life expectancy has more than doubled, and infant mortality has dropped significantly. On the negative side, the incidence of cancer, cerebrovascular disease, and heart disease has increased to the extent that these have become the leading causes of death. Economic reforms initiated in the late 1970s fundamentally altered methods of providing health care; the collective medical care system was gradually replaced by a more individual-oriented approach.

More liberalized emigration policies enacted in the 1980s facilitated the legal departure of increasing numbers of Chinese who joined their overseas Chinese relatives and friends. The Four Modernizations program (see Glossary), which required access of Chinese students and scholars, particularly scientists, to foreign education and research institutions, brought about increased contact with the outside world, particularly the industrialized nations. Thus, as China moved toward the twenty-first century, the diverse resources and immense population that it had committed to a comprehensive process of modernization became ever more important in the interdependent world.

Physical Environment

China stretches some 5,000 kilometers across the East Asian landmass in an erratically changing configuration of broad plains,

Karst formations on the Li Jiang near Guilin
Courtesy
Douglass M. Dolan

Overlooking Pagoda of the Six Harmonies on the Qiantang Jiang, Hangzhou
Courtesy
Zhejiang Slide Studio

expansive deserts, and lofty mountain ranges, including vast areas of inhospitable terrain. The eastern half of the country, its seacoast fringed with offshore islands, is a region of fertile lowlands, foothills and mountains, and subtropical areas. The western half of China is a region of sunken basins, rolling plateaus, and towering massifs, including a portion of the highest tableland on earth. The vastness of the country and the barrenness of the western hinterland have important implications for defense strategy (see Doctrine, Strategy, and Tactics, ch. 14). In spite of many good harbors along the approximately 18,000-kilometer coastline, the nation has traditionally oriented itself not toward the sea but inland, developing as an imperial power whose center lay in the middle and lower reaches of the Huang He (Yellow River) on the northern plains.

Figures for the size of China differ slightly depending on where one draws a number of ill-defined boundaries. The official Chinese figure is 9.6 million square kilometers, making the country substantially smaller than the Soviet Union, slightly smaller than Canada, and somewhat larger than the United States. China's contour is reasonably comparable to that of the United States and lies largely at the same latitudes.

Boundaries

In 1987 China's borders, more than 20,000 kilometers of land frontier shared with nearly all the nations of mainland East Asia, were disputed at a number of points. In the western sector, China claimed portions of the 41,000-square-kilometer Pamir Mountains area, a region of soaring mountain peaks and glacial valleys where the borders of Afghanistan, Pakistan, the Soviet Union, and China meet in Central Asia. North and east of this region, some sections of the border remained undemarcated in 1987. The 6,542-kilometer frontier with the Soviet Union has been a source of continual friction. In 1954 China published maps showing substantial portions of Soviet Siberian territory as its own. In the northeast, border friction with the Soviet Union produced a tense situation in remote regions of Nei Monggol Autonomous Region (Inner Mongolia) and Heilongjiang Province along segments of the Ergun He (Argun River), Heilong Jiang (Amur River), and Wusuli Jiang (Ussuri River) (see fig. 3). Each side had massed troops and had exchanged charges of border provocation in this area. In a September 1986 speech in Vladivostok, Soviet leader Mikhail S. Gorbachev offered the Chinese a more conciliatory position on Sino-Soviet border rivers. In 1987 the two sides resumed border talks that had been broken off after the 1979 Soviet invasion of Afghanistan (see

Sino-Soviet Relations, ch. 12; The Soviet Union, ch. 14). Although the border issue remained unresolved as of late 1987, China and the Soviet Union agreed to consider the northeastern sector first.

A major dispute between China and India focuses on the northern edge of their shared border, where the Aksai Chin area of northeastern Jammu and Kashmir is under Chinese control but claimed by India. Eastward from Bhutan and north of the Brahmaputra River (Yarlung Zangbo Jiang) lies a large area controlled and administered by India but claimed by the Chinese in the aftermath of the 1959 Tibetan revolt. The area was demarcated by the British McMahon Line, drawn along the Himalayas in 1914 as the Sino-Indian border; India accepts and China rejects this boundary. In June 1980 China made its first move in twenty years to settle the border disputes with India, proposing that India cede the Aksai Chin area in Jammu and Kashmir to China in return for China's recognition of the McMahon Line; India did not accept the offer, however, preferring a sector-by-sector approach to the problem. In July 1986 China and India held their seventh round of border talks, but they made little headway toward resolving the dispute. Each side, but primarily India, continued to make allegations of incursions into its territory by the other.

China, Taiwan, and Vietnam all claim sovereignty over both the Xisha (Paracel) and the Nansha (Spratly) islands, but the major islands of the Xishas are occupied by China. The Philippines claims an area known as Kalayaan (Freedom Land), which excludes the Nansha in the west and some reefs in the south. Malaysia claims the islands and reefs in the southernmost area, and there also is a potential for dispute over the islands with Brunei.

The China-Burma border issue was settled October 1, 1960, by the signing of the Sino-Burmese Boundary Treaty. The first joint inspection of the border was completed successfully in June 1986. In 1987 the island province of Taiwan continued to be under the control of the Guomindang authorities (see Sino-United States Relations, ch. 12).

Terrain and Drainage

Terrain and vegetation vary greatly in China. Mountains, hills, and highlands cover about 66 percent of the nation's territory, impeding communication and leaving limited level land for agriculture. Most ranges, including all the major ones, trend east-west. In the southwest, the Himalayas and the Kunlun Mountains enclose the Qing Zang Plateau, which encompasses most of Xizang Autonomous Region (also known as Tibet) and part of Qinghai Province. It is the most extensive plateau in the world, where

Figure 3. China-Soviet Union Border Area

elevations average more than 4,000 meters above sea level and the loftiest summits rise to more than 7,200 meters.

From the Qing Zang Plateau, other less-elevated highlands, rugged east-west trending mountains, and plateaus interrupted by deep depressions fan out to the north and east. A continental scarp marks the eastern margin of this territory extending from the Greater Hinggan Range in northeastern China, through the Taihang Shan (a range of mountains overlooking the North China Plain) to the eastern edge of the Yunnan-Guizhou Plateau in the south (see fig. 4). Virtually all of the low-lying areas of China—the regions of dense population and intensive cultivation—are found east of this scarp line.

East-west ranges include some of Asia's greatest mountains. In addition to the Himalayas and the Kunlun Mountains, there are

Figure 3. (continued)

the Gangdise Shan (Kailas) and the Tian Shan ranges. The latter stands between two great basins, the massive Tarim Basin to the south and the Junggar Basin to the north. Rich deposits of coal, oil, and metallic ores lie in the Tian Shan area. The largest inland basin in China, the Tarim Basin measures 1,500 kilometers from east to west and 600 kilometers from north to south at its widest parts.

The Himalayas form a natural boundary on the southwest as the Altai Mountains do on the northwest. Lesser ranges branch out, some at sharp angles from the major ranges. The mountains give rise to all the principal rivers.

The spine of the Kunlun Mountains separates into several branches as it runs eastward from the Pamir Mountains. The northernmost branches, the Altun Shan and the Qilian Shan, rim the

Qing Zang Plateau in west-central China and overlook the Qaidam Basin, a sandy and swampy region containing many salt lakes. A southern branch of the Kunlun Mountains divides the watersheds of the Huang He and the Chang Jiang (Yangtze River). The Gansu Corridor, west of the great bend in the Huang He, was traditionally an important communications link with Central Asia.

North of the 3,300-kilometer-long Great Wall, between Gansu Province on the west and the Greater Hinggan Range on the east, lies the Nei Monggol Plateau, at an average elevation of 1,000 meters above sea level. The Yin Shan, a system of mountains with average elevations of 1,400 meters, extends east-west through the center of this vast desert or steppe peneplain. To the south is the largest loess plateau in the world, covering 600,000 square kilometers in Shaanxi Province, parts of Gansu and Shanxi provinces, and some of Ningxia-Hui Autonomous Region. Loess is a yellowish soil blown in from the Nei Monggol deserts. The loose, loamy material travels easily in the wind, and through the centuries it has veneered the plateau and choked the Huang He with silt.

Because the river level drops precipitously toward the North China Plain, where it continues a sluggish course across the delta, it transports a heavy load of sand and mud from the upper reaches, much of which is deposited on the flat plain. The flow is channeled mainly by constantly repaired manmade embankments; as a result the river flows on a raised ridge several meters—in some places more than ten meters— above the plain, and waterlogging, floods, and course changes have recurred over the centuries. Traditionally, rulers were judged by their concern for or indifference to preservation of the embankments. In the modern era, the new leadership has been deeply committed to dealing with the problem and has undertaken extensive flood control and conservation measures.

Flowing from its source in the Qing Zang highlands, the Huang He courses toward the sea through the North China Plain, the historic center of Chinese expansion and influence. Han (see Glossary) people have farmed the rich alluvial soils of the plain since ancient times, constructing the Grand Canal for north-south transport (see The Imperial Period, ch. 1). The plain itself is actually a continuation of the Dongbei (Manchurian) Plain to the northeast but is separated from it by the Bo Hai Gulf, an extension of the Huang Hai (Yellow Sea).

Like other densely populated areas of China, the plain is subject not only to floods but to earthquakes. For example, the mining and industrial center of Tangshan, about 165 kilometers east of Beijing, was leveled by an earthquake in July 1976 that reportedly also killed 242,000 people and injured 164,000.

The Qin Ling mountain range, a continuation of the Kunlun Mountains, divides the North China Plain from the Chang Jiang Delta and is the major physiographic boundary between the two great parts of China Proper (see Glossary). It is in a sense a cultural boundary as well, influencing the distribution of custom and language. South of the Qin Ling divide are the densely populated and highly developed areas of the lower and middle plains of the Chang Jiang and, on its upper reaches, the Sichuan Basin, an area encircled by a high barrier of mountain ranges.

The country's longest and most important waterway, the Chang Jiang is navigable over much of its length and has a vast hydroelectric potential. Rising on the Qing Zang Plateau, the Chang Jiang traverses 6,300 kilometers through the heart of the country, draining an area of 1.8 million square kilometers before emptying into the East China Sea. The roughly 300 million people who live along its middle and lower reaches cultivate a great rice- and wheat-producing area. The Sichuan Basin, favored by a mild, humid climate and a long growing season, produces a rich variety of crops; it is also a leading silk-producing area and an important industrial region with substantial mineral resources.

Second only to the Qin Ling as an internal boundary is the Nan Ling, the southernmost of the east-west mountain ranges. The Nan Ling overlooks the part of China where a tropical climate permits two crops of rice to be grown each year. Southeast of the mountains lies a coastal, hilly region of small deltas and narrow valley plains; the drainage area of the Zhu Jiang (Pearl River) and its associated network of rivers occupies much of the region to the south. West of the Nan Ling, the Yunnan-Guizhou Plateau rises in two steps, averaging 1,200 and 1,800 meters in elevation, respectively, toward the precipitous mountain regions of the eastern Qing Zang Plateau.

The Hai He, like the Zhu Jiang and other major waterways, flows from west to east. Its upper course consists of five rivers that converge near Tianjin, then flow seventy kilometers before emptying into the Bo Hai Gulf. Another major river, the Huai He, rises in Henan Province and flows through several lakes before joining the Chang Jiang near Yangzhou.

Inland drainage involving a number of upland basins in the north and northeast accounts for about 40 percent of the country's total drainage area. Many rivers and streams flow into lakes or diminish in the desert. Some are useful for irrigation.

China's extensive territorial waters are principally marginal seas of the western Pacific Ocean; these waters wash the shores of a long and much-indented coastline and approximately 5,000 islands.

Figure 4. Topography and Drainage

The Yellow, East China, and South China seas, too, are marginal seas of the Pacific Ocean. More than half the coastline (predominantly in the south) is rocky; most of the remainder is sandy. The Bay of Hangzhou roughly divides the two kinds of shoreline.

Climate

Monsoon winds, caused by differences in the heat-absorbing capacity of the continent and the ocean, dominate the climate. Alternating seasonal air-mass movements and accompanying winds are moist in summer and dry in winter. The advance and retreat of the monsoons account in large degree for the timing of the rainy season and the amount of rainfall throughout the country. Tremendous differences in latitude, longitude, and altitude give rise to sharp variations in precipitation and temperature within China. Although most of the country lies in the temperate belt, its climatic patterns are complex.

China's northernmost point lies along the Heilong Jiang in Heilongjiang Province in the cold-temperate zone; its southernmost point, Hainan Island, has a tropical climate (see table 4, Appendix A). Temperature differences in winter are great, but in summer the diversity is considerably less. For example, the northern portions of Heilongjiang Province experience an average January mean temperature of below 0°C, and the reading may drop to minus 30°C; the average July mean in the same area may exceed 20°C. By contrast, the central and southern parts of Guangdong Province experience an average January temperature of above 10°C, while the July mean is about 28°C.

Precipitation varies regionally even more than temperature. China south of the Qin Ling experiences abundant rainfall, most of it coming with the summer monsoons. To the north and west of the range, however, rainfall is uncertain. The farther north and west one moves, the scantier and more uncertain it becomes. The northwest has the lowest annual rainfall in the country and no precipitation at all in its desert areas.

Wildlife

China lies in two of the world's major zoogeographic regions, the Palearctic and the Oriental. The Qing Zang Plateau, Xinjiang and Nei Monggol autonomous regions, northeastern China, and all areas north of the Huang He are in the Palearctic region. Central, southern, and southwest China lie in the Oriental region. In the Palearctic zone are found such important mammals as the river fox, horse, camel, tapir, mouse hare, hamster, and jerboa. Among the species found in the Oriental region are the civet cat, Chinese pangolin, bamboo rat, tree shrew, and also gibbon and various other species of monkeys and apes. Some overlap exists between the two regions because of natural dispersal and migration, and deer or antelope, bears, wolves, pigs, and rodents are found in all of the diverse climatic and geological environments. The famous giant panda is found only in a limited area along the Chang Jiang.

Population

The Data Base

The People's Republic conducted censuses in 1953, 1964, and 1982. In 1987 the government announced that the fourth national census would take place in 1990 and that there would be one every ten years thereafter. The 1982 census, which reported a total population of 1,008,180,738, is generally accepted as significantly more reliable, accurate, and thorough than the previous two. Various international organizations eagerly assisted the Chinese in conducting the 1982 census, including the United Nations Fund for Population Activities which donated US$15.6 million for the preparation and execution of the census.

The nation began preparing for the 1982 census in late 1976. Chinese census workers were sent to the United States and Japan to study modern census-taking techniques and automation. Computers were installed in every provincial-level unit except Xizang and were connected to a central processing system in the Beijing headquarters of the State Statistical Bureau. Pretests and small-scale trial runs were conducted and checked for accuracy between 1980 and 1981 in twenty-four provincial-level units. Census stations were opened in rural production brigades (see Glossary) and urban neighborhoods. Beginning July 1, 1982, each household sent a representative to a census station to be enumerated. The census required about a month to complete and employed approximately 5 million census takers.

The 1982 census collected data in nineteen demographic categories relating to individuals and households. The thirteen areas concerning individuals were name, relationship to head of household, sex, age, nationality, registration status, educational level, profession, occupation, status of nonworking persons, marital status, number of children born and still living, and number of births in 1981. The six items pertaining to households were type (domestic or collective), serial number, number of persons, number of births in 1981, number of deaths in 1981, and number of registered persons absent for more than one year. Information was gathered in a number of important areas for which previous data were either

Landscape on the Grand Canal
Courtesy Xinhua News Agency

extremely inaccurate or simply nonexistent, including fertility, marital status, urban population, minority ethnic groups, sex composition, age distribution, and employment and unemployment (see table 5, Appendix A).

A fundamental anomaly in the 1982 statistics was noted by some Western analysts. They pointed out that although the birth and death rates recorded by the census and those recorded through the household registration system were different, the two systems arrived at similar population totals (see Differentiation, ch. 3). The discrepancies in the vital rates were the result of the under-reporting of both births and deaths to the authorities under the registration system; families would not report some births because of the one-child policy and would not report some deaths so as to hold on to the rations of the deceased. Nevertheless, the 1982 census was a watershed for both Chinese and world demographics. After an eighteen-year gap, population specialists were given a wealth of reliable, up-to-date figures on which to reconstruct past demographic patterns, measure current population conditions, and predict future population trends. For example, Chinese and foreign demographers used the 1982 census age-sex structure as the base population for forecasting and making assumptions about future fertility trends. The data on age-specific fertility and mortality rates provided the necessary base-line information for making population projections. The census data also were useful for estimating future manpower potential, consumer needs, and utility, energy, and health-service requirements. The sudden abundance of demographic data helped population specialists immeasurably in their efforts to estimate world population. Previously, there had been no accurate information on these 21 percent of the earth's inhabitants. Demographers who had been conducting research on global population without accurate data on the Chinese fifth of the world's population were particularly thankful for the 1982 census.

Mortality and Fertility

In 1949 crude death rates were probably higher than 30 per 1,000, and the average life expectancy was only 32 years. Beginning in the early 1950s, mortality steadily declined; it continued to decline through 1978 and remained relatively constant through 1987. One major fluctuation was reported in a computer reconstruction of China's population trends from 1953 to 1987 produced by the United States Bureau of the Census (see table 6, Appendix A; data in this table may vary from officially reported statistics). The computer model showed that the crude death rate increased dramatically during the famine years associated with the Great Leap Forward (1958–60, see Glossary), resulting in approximately 30 million deaths above the expected level.

According to Chinese government statistics, the crude birth rate followed five distinct patterns from 1949 to 1982. It remained stable from 1949 to 1954, varied widely from 1955 to 1965, experienced fluctuations between 1966 and 1969, dropped sharply in the late 1970s, and increased from 1980 to 1981. Between 1970 and 1980, the crude birth rate dropped from 36.9 per 1,000 to 17.6 per 1,000. The government attributed this dramatic decline in fertility to the *wan xi shao* (later marriages, longer intervals between births, and fewer children) birth control campaign. However, elements of socioeconomic change, such as increased employment of women in both urban and rural areas and reduced infant mortality (a greater percentage of surviving children would tend to reduce demand for additional children), may have played some role (see Labor Force, this ch.). To the dismay of authorities, the birth rate increased in both 1981 and 1982 to a level of 21 per 1,000, primarily as a result of a marked rise in marriages and first births. The rise was an indication of problems with the one-child policy of 1979 (see Population Control Programs, this ch.). Chinese sources, however, indicated that the birth rate decreased to 17.8 in 1985 and remained relatively constant thereafter.

In urban areas, the housing shortage may have been at least

partly responsible for the decreased birth rate. Also, the policy in force during most of the 1960s and the early 1970s of sending large numbers of high school graduates to the countryside deprived cities of a significant proportion of persons of childbearing age and undoubtedly had some effect on birth rates (see The Cultural Revolution Decade, 1966–76, ch. 1).

Primarily for economic reasons, rural birth rates tended to decline less than urban rates. The right to grow and sell agricultural products for personal profit and the lack of an old-age welfare system were incentives for rural people to produce many children, especially sons, for help in the fields and for support in old age. Because of these conditions, it is unclear to what degree propaganda and education improvements had been able to erode traditional values favoring large families.

Population Control Programs

Initially, China's post-1949 leaders were ideologically disposed to view a large population as an asset. But the liabilities of a large, rapidly growing population soon became apparent. For one year, starting in August 1956, vigorous propaganda support was given to the Ministry of Public Health's mass birth control efforts. These efforts, however, had little impact on fertility. After the interval of the Great Leap Forward, Chinese leaders again saw rapid population growth as an obstacle to development, and their interest in birth control revived.

In the early 1960s, propaganda, somewhat more muted than during the first campaign, emphasized the virtues of late marriage. Birth control offices were set up in the central government and some provincial-level governments in 1964. The second campaign was particularly successful in the cities, where the birth rate was cut in half during the 1963–66 period. The chaos of the Cultural Revolution brought the program to a halt, however.

In 1972 and 1973 the party mobilized its resources for a nationwide birth control campaign administered by a group in the State Council (see The State Council, ch. 10). Committees to oversee birth control activities were established at all administrative levels and in various collective enterprises. This extensive and seemingly effective network covered both the rural and the urban population. In urban areas public security headquarters included population control sections. In rural areas the country's "barefoot doctors" (see Glossary) distributed information and contraceptives to people's commune (see Glossary) members. By 1973 Mao Zedong was personally identified with the family planning movement, signifying a greater leadership commitment to controlled population growth than ever before. Yet until several years after Mao's death in 1976, the leadership was reluctant to put forth directly the rationale that population control was necessary for economic growth and improved living standards.

Population growth targets were set for both administrative units and individual families. In the mid-1970s the maximum recommended family size was two children in cities and three or four in the country. Since 1979 the government has advocated a one-child limit for both rural and urban areas and has generally set a maximum of two children in special circumstances. As of 1986 the policy for minority nationalities was two children per couple, three in special circumstances, and no limit for ethnic groups with very small populations. The overall goal of the one-child policy was to keep the total population within 1.2 billion through the year 2000, on the premise that the Four Modernizations (see Glossary) program would be of little value if population growth was not brought under control.

The one-child policy was a highly ambitious population control program. Like previous programs of the 1960s and 1970s, the one-child policy employed a combination of propaganda, social pressure, and in some cases coercion. The one-child policy was unique, however, in that it linked reproduction with economic cost or benefit.

Under the one-child program, a sophisticated system rewarded those who observed the policy and penalized those who did not. Couples with only one child were given a "one-child certificate" entitling them to such benefits as cash bonuses, longer maternity leave, better child care, and preferential housing assignments. In return, they were required to pledge that they would not have more children. In the countryside, there was great pressure to adhere to the one-child limit. Because the rural population accounted for approximately 60 percent of the total, the effectiveness of the one-child policy in rural areas was considered the key to the success or failure of the program as a whole.

In rural areas the day-to-day work of family planning was done by cadres at the team and brigade levels who were responsible for women's affairs and by health workers. The women's team leader made regular household visits to keep track of the status of each family under her jurisdiction and collected information on which women were using contraceptives, the methods used, and which had become pregnant. She then reported to the brigade women's leader, who documented the information and took it to a monthly meeting of the commune birth-planning committee. According to reports, ceilings or quotas had to be adhered to; to satisfy these cutoffs, unmarried young people were persuaded to postpone marriage, couples without children were advised to "wait their turn," women with unauthorized pregnancies were pressured to have abortions, and those who already had children were urged to use contraception or undergo sterilization. Couples with more than one child were exhorted to be sterilized.

The one-child policy enjoyed much greater success in urban than in rural areas. Even without state intervention, there were compelling reasons for urban couples to limit the family to a single child. Raising a child required a significant portion of family income, and in the cities a child did not become an economic asset until he or she entered the work force at age sixteen. Couples with only one child were given preferential treatment in housing allocation. In addition, because city dwellers who were employed in state enterprises received pensions after retirement, the sex of their first child was less important to them than it was to those in rural areas (see Urban Society, ch. 3).

Numerous reports surfaced of coercive measures used to achieve the desired results of the one-child policy. The alleged methods ranged from intense psychological pressure to the use of physical force, including some grisly accounts of forced abortions and infanticide. Chinese officials admitted that isolated, uncondoned abuses of the program occurred and that they condemned such acts, but they insisted that the family planning program was administered on a voluntary basis using persuasion and economic measures only. International reaction to the allegations were mixed. The UN Fund for Population Activities and the International Planned Parenthood Association were generally supportive of China's family planning program. The United States Agency for International Development, however, withdrew US$10 million from the Fund in March 1985 based on allegations that coercion had been used.

Observers suggested that an accurate assessment of the one-child program would not be possible until all women who came of childbearing age in the early 1980s passed their fertile years. As of 1987 the one-child program had achieved mixed results. In general, it was very successful in almost all urban areas but less successful in rural areas. The Chinese authorities must have been disturbed by the increase in the officially reported annual population growth rate (birth rate minus death rate): from 12 per 1,000, or 1.2 percent in 1980 to 14.1 per 1,000, or 1.4 percent in 1986. If the 1986 rate is maintained to the year 2000, the population will exceed 1.2 billion.

Rapid fertility reduction associated with the one-child policy has potentially negative results. For instance, in the future the elderly might not be able to rely on their children to care for them as they have in the past, leaving the state to assume the expense, which could be considerable. Based on United Nations statistics and data provided by the Chinese government, it was estimated in 1987 that by the year 2000 the population 60 years and older (the retirement age is 60 in urban areas) would number 127 million, or 10.1 percent of the total population; the projection for 2025 was 234 million elderly, or 16.4 percent. According to one Western analyst, projections based on the 1982 census show that if the one-child policy were maintained to the year 2000, 25 percent of China's population would be age 65 or older by the year 2040.

Density and Distribution

Overall population density in 1986 was about 109 people per square kilometer. Density was only about one-third that of Japan and less than that of many other countries in Asia and in Europe. The overall figure, however, concealed major regional variations and the high person-land ratio in densely populated areas. In the 11 provinces, special municipalities, and autonomous regions along the southeast coast, population density was 320.6 people per square kilometer (see fig. 5).

In 1986 about 94 percent of the population lived on approximately 36 percent of the land. Broadly speaking, the population was concentrated in China Proper, east of the mountains and south of the Great Wall. The most densely populated areas included the Chang Jiang Valley (of which the delta region was the most populous), Sichuan Basin, North China Plain, Zhu Jiang Delta, and the industrial area around the city of Shenyang in the northeast.

Population is most sparse in the mountainous, desert, and grassland regions of the northwest and southwest. In Nei Monggol Autonomous Region, portions are completely uninhabited, and only a few sections have populations more dense than ten people per square kilometer. The Nei Monggol, Xinjiang, and Xizang autonomous regions and Gansu and Qinghai provinces comprise 55 percent of the country's land area but in 1985 contained only 5.7 percent of its population (see table 7, Appendix A).

Migration

Internal

China has restricted internal movement in various ways. Official efforts to limit free migration between villages and cities began as early as 1952 with a series of measures designed to prevent individuals without special permission from moving to cities to take advantage of the generally higher living standards there.

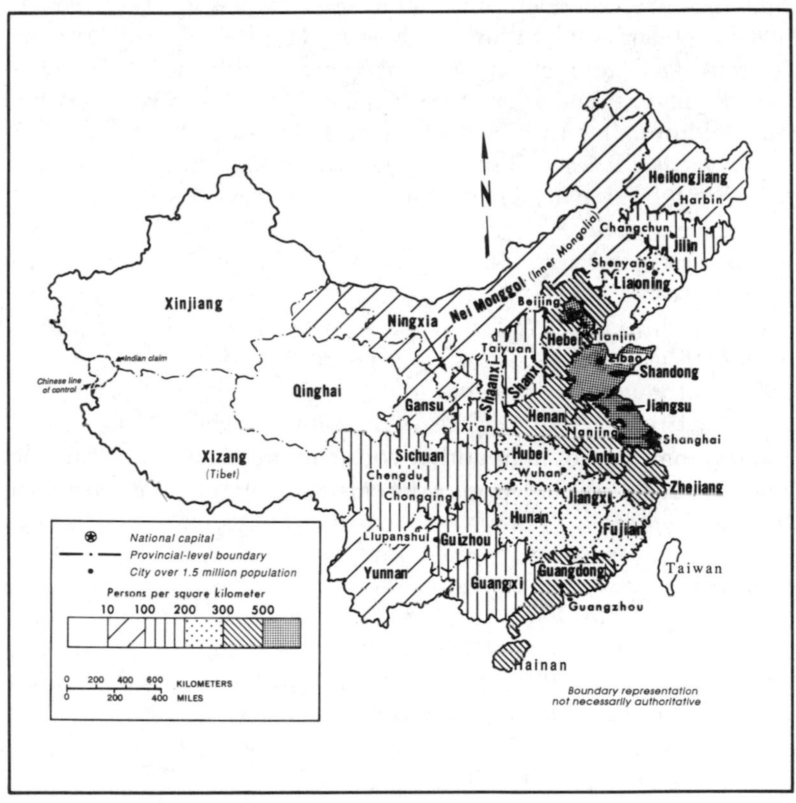

Source: Based on *Zhongguo 1982 Nian Renkou Pucha Ziliao* (1982 Population Census of China), Beijing, March 1985.

Figure 5. Population Density, 1982

The party decreased migration to cities during the 1960s and 1970s for economic and political reasons (see The Politics of Modernization, ch. 11). In the early stages of the Cultural Revolution, large numbers of urban youths were "sent down" to the countryside for political and ideological reasons. Many relocated youths were eventually permitted to return to the cities, and by the mid-1980s most had done so (see The Cultural Revolution Decade, 1966–76, ch. 1).

The success of the agricultural reforms under Deng Xiaoping in the late 1970s and early 1980s dramatically increased the food supply in China's cities, making it possible for more people to come in from rural areas and survive without food ration cards. Because of the increased food supply, the authorities temporarily relaxed the enforcement of migration restrictions. This relaxation, however, was short-lived, and in May 1984 new measures strengthened residence regulations and reinstated official control over internal migration. Additionally, in March 1986 a draft revision of the 1957 migration regulations was presented to the Standing Committee of the Sixth National People's Congress calling for stricter population control policies.

Nonetheless, migration from rural areas to urban centers continued. The problem of too-rapid urbanization was exacerbated by the agricultural responsibility system (see Glossary), which forced a reallocation of labor and left many agricultural workers unemployed.

The central government attempted to control movement through the household registration system and promote development of small cities and towns, but within this system many people were still able to migrate primarily for employment or educational purposes (see Differentiation, ch. 3). Leaving their place of official registration for days, months, or even years, unemployed agricultural workers found jobs in construction, housekeeping, or commune-run shops or restaurants. This temporary mobility was permitted by authorities because it simultaneously absorbed a large amount of surplus rural labor, improved the economies of rural areas, and satisfied urban requirements for service and other workers. The most significant aspect of the temporary migration, however, was that it was viewed as a possible initial step toward the development of small, rural-oriented urban centers that could bring employment and urban amenities to rural areas.

Although the temporary migration into the cities was seen as beneficial, controlling it was a serious concern of the central government. An April 1985 survey showed that the "floating" or nonresident population in eight selected areas of Beijing was 662,000, or 12.5 percent of the total population. The survey also showed that people entered or left Beijing 880,000 times a day. In an effort to control this activity, neighborhood committees and work units (*danwei*—see Glossary) were required to comply with municipal regulations issued in January 1986. These regulations stipulated that communities and work units keep records on visitors, that those staying in Beijing for up to three days must be registered, and that those planning to stay longer must obtain temporary residence permits from local police stations.

Although some cities were crowded, other areas of China were underpopulated. For example, China had little success populating the frontier regions. As early as the 1950s, the government began to organize and fund migration for land reclamation, industrialization, and construction in the interior and frontier regions. Land reclamation was carried out by state farms located largely in Xinjiang-Uygur Autonomous Region and Heilongjiang Province. Large numbers of migrants were sent to such outlying regions as Nei Monggol Autonomous Region and Qinghai Province to work in factories and mines and to Xinjiang-Uygur Autonomous Region to develop agriculture and industry. In the late 1950s, and especially in the 1960s, during the Cultural Revolution, many city youths were sent to the frontier areas. Much of the resettled population returned home, however, because of insufficient government support, harsh climate, and a general inability to adjust to life in the outlying regions. China's regional population distribution was consequently as unbalanced in 1986 as it had been in 1953. Nevertheless, efforts were still underway in 1987 to encourage migration to the frontier regions.

Urbanization

In 1987 China had a total of twenty-nine provincial-level administrative units directly under the central government in Beijing. In addition to the twenty-one provinces (*sheng*), there were five autonomous regions (*zizhiqu*) for minority nationalities, and three special municipalities (*shi*)—the three largest cities, Shanghai, Beijing, and Tianjin. (The establishment of Hainan Island as a provincial-level unit separate from Guangdong Province was scheduled to take place in 1988.) A 1979 change in provincial-level administrative boundaries in the northeast region restored Nei Monggol Autonomous Region to its original size (it had been reduced by a third in 1969) at the expense of Heilongjiang, Jilin, and Liaoning provinces. Urban areas were further subdivided into lower-level administrative units beginning with municipalities and extending down to the neighborhood level (see Local Administration, ch. 10).

The pace of urbanization in China from 1949 to 1982 was relatively slow because of both rapid growth of the rural population and tight restrictions on rural-urban migration for most of that period. According to the 1953 and 1982 censuses, the urban population as a percentage of total population increased from 13.3 to 20.6 percent during that period. From 1982 to 1986, however, the urban population increased dramatically to 37 percent of the total population. This large jump resulted from a combination of factors. One was the migration of large numbers of surplus agricultural workers, displaced by the agricultural responsibility system, from rural to urban areas (see Agricultural Policies, ch. 6). Another was a 1984 decision to broaden the criteria for classifying an area as a city or town. During 1984 the number of towns meeting the new urban criteria increased more than twofold, and the urban town population doubled. In the mid-1980s demographers expected the proportion of the population living in cities and towns to be around 50 percent by the turn of the century. This urban growth was expected to result primarily from the increase in the number of small- and medium-sized cities and towns rather than from an expansion of existing large cities.

China's statistics regarding urban population sometimes can be misleading because of the various criteria used to calculate urban population. In the 1953 census, *urban* essentially referred to settlements with populations of more than 2,500, in which more than 50 percent of the labor force were involved in nonagricultural pursuits. The 1964 census raised the cut-off to 3,000 and the requirement for nonagricultural labor to 70 percent. The 1982 census used the 3,000/70 percent minimum but introduced criteria of 2,500 to 3,000 and 85 percent as well. Also, in calculating urban population, the 1982 census made a radical change by including the agricultural population residing within the city boundaries. This explains the dramatic jump in urban population from the 138.7 million reported for year-end 1981 to the 206.6 million counted by the 1982 census. In 1984 the urban guidelines were further loosened, allowing for lower minimum population totals and nonagricultural percentages. The criteria varied among provincial-level units.

Although China's urban population—382 million, or 37 percent of the total population, in the mid-1980s—was relatively low by comparison with developed nations, the number of people living in urban areas in China was greater than the total population of any country in the world except India and the Soviet Union. The four Chinese cities with the largest populations in 1985 were Shanghai, with 7 million; Beijing, with 5.9 million; Tianjin, with 5.4 million; and Shenyang, with 4.2 million. The disproportionate distribution of population in large cities occurred as a result of the government's emphasis after 1949 on the development of large cities over smaller urban areas. In 1985 the 22 most populous cities in China had a total population of 47.5 million, or about 12 percent of China's total urban population. The number of cities with populations of at least 100,000 increased from 200 in 1976 to 342 in 1986 (see table 8, Appendix A).

In 1987 China was committed to a three-part strategy to control urban growth: strictly limiting the size of big cities (those of 500,000 or more people); developing medium-sized cities (200,000 to 500,000); and encouraging the growth of small cities (100,000 to 200,000). The government also encouraged the development of small market and commune centers that were not then officially designated as urban places, hoping that they eventually would be transformed into towns and small cities. The big and medium-sized cities were viewed as centers of heavy and light industry, and small cities and towns were looked on as possible locations for handicraft and workshop activities, using labor provided mainly from rural overflow.

Emigration and Immigration

Through most of China's history, strict controls prevented large numbers of people from leaving the country. In modern times, however, periodically some have been allowed to leave for various reasons. For example, in the early 1960s, about 100,000 people were allowed to enter Hong Kong. In the late 1970s, vigilance against illegal migration to Hong Kong was again relaxed somewhat. Perhaps as many as 200,000 reached Hong Kong in 1979, but in 1980 authorities on both sides resumed concerted efforts to reduce the flow.

In 1983 emigration restrictions were eased as a result in part of the economic open-door policy. In 1984 more than 11,500 business visas were issued to Chinese citizens, and in 1985 approximately 15,000 Chinese scholars and students were in the United States alone. Any student who had the economic resources, from whatever source, could apply for permission to study abroad. United States consular offices issued more than 12,500 immigrant visas in 1984, and there were 60,000 Chinese with approved visa petitions in the immigration queue.

Export of labor to foreign countries also increased. The Soviet Union, Iraq, and the Federal Republic of Germany requested 500,000 workers, and as of 1986 China had sent 50,000. The signing of the United States-China Consular Convention in 1983 demonstrated the commitment to more liberal emigration policies. The two sides agreed to permit travel for the purpose of family reunification and to facilitate travel for individuals who claim both Chinese and United States citizenship. Emigrating from China remained a complicated and lengthy process, however, mainly because many countries were unwilling or unable to accept the large numbers of people who wished to emigrate. Other difficulties included bureaucratic delays and in some cases a reluctance on the part of Chinese authorities to issue passports and exit permits to individuals making notable contributions to the modernization effort.

The only significant immigration to China has been by the overseas Chinese (see Glossary), who in the years since 1949 have been offered various enticements to return to their homeland. Several million may have done so since 1949. The largest influx came in 1978–79, when about 160,000 to 250,000 ethnic Chinese fled

Vietnam for southern China as relations between the two countries worsened. Many of these refugees were reportedly settled in state farms on Hainan Island in the South China Sea.

Minority Nationalities

Demographic Overview

Approximately 93 percent of China's population is considered Han. Sharp regional and cultural differences, including major variations in spoken Chinese, exist among the Han, who are a mingling of many peoples. All the Han nonetheless use a common written form of Chinese and share the social organization, values, and cultural characteristics universally recognized as Chinese (see Han Diversity and Unity, ch. 3).

Officially, China has fifty-six "nationality" groups, including the Han. The Chinese define a nationality as a group of people of common origin living in a common area, using a common language, and having a sense of group identity in economic and social organization and behavior. Altogether, China has fifteen major linguistic regions generally coinciding with the geographic distribution of the major minority nationalities (see fig. 6). Members of non-Han groups, referred to as the "minority nationalities," constitute only about 7 percent of the total population but number more than 70 million people and are distributed over 60 percent of the land.

Some minority nationalities can be found only in a single region; others may have settlements in two or more. In general, however, the minorities are concentrated in the provinces and autonomous regions of the northwest and the southwest. In Xizang, Xinjiang, and Nei Monggol autonomous regions, minorities occupy large frontier areas; many are traditionally nomadic and engage primarily in pastoral pursuits. Minority groups in Yunnan and Guizhou provinces and in the Guangxi-Zhuang Autonomous Region are more fragmented and inhabit smaller areas.

According to the 1982 census, approximately 95 percent of Xizang's civilian population of 1.9 million are Tibetan (Zang nationality). An internally cohesive group, the Tibetans have proven the most resistant of the minority groups to the government's integration efforts. Xinjiang, which is as vast and distant from Beijing as Xizang, is the minority area next in demographic and political significance. Despite a large-scale immigration of Han since the 1950s, in 1985 around 60 percent of Xinjiang's 13.4 million population belonged to minority nationalities. Of these, the most important were 6.1 million Uygurs and more than 900,000 Kazaks, both Turkic-speaking Central Asian peoples (see table 9, Appendix A).

Figure 6. Distribution of Major Minority Nationalities

Provinces with large concentrations of minorities include Yunnan, where the Yi and other minority groups comprised an estimated 32 percent of the population in 1985; Guizhou, home of more than half of the approximately 4 million Miao; and sparsely populated Qinghai, which except for the area around the provincial capital of Xining is inhabited primarily by Tibetans and other minority nationality members, amounting in 1986 to approximately 37 percent of the total provincial population. Additionally, in 1986 minority nationalities constituted approximately 16 percent of the population of Nei Monggol Autonomous Region. The Guangxi-Zhuang Autonomous Region contains almost all of the approximately 13.5 million members of what is China's largest minority nationality, the Zhuang; most of them, however, are highly assimilated.

Because many of the minority nationalities are located in politically sensitive frontier areas, they have acquired an importance greater than their numbers. Some groups have common ancestry with peoples in neighboring countries. For example, members of the Shan, Korean, Mongol, Uygur and Kazak, and Yao nationalities are found not only in China but also in Burma, Korea, the Mongolian People's Republic, the Soviet Union, and Thailand, respectively. If the central government failed to maintain good relations with these groups, China's border security could be jeopardized (see Threat Perception, ch. 14). Since 1949 Chinese officials have declared that the minorities are politically equal to the Han majority and in fact should be accorded preferential treatment because of their small numbers and poor economic circumstances. The government has tried to ensure that the minorities are well represented at national conferences and has relaxed certain policies that might have impeded their socioeconomic development.

The minority areas are economically as well as politically important. China's leaders have suggested that by the turn of the century the focus of economic development should shift to the northwest. The area is rich in natural resources, with uranium deposits and abundant oil reserves in Xinjiang-Uygur Autonomous Region. Much of China's forestland is located in the border regions of the northeast and southwest, and large numbers of livestock are raised in the arid and semiarid northwest. Also, the vast amount of virgin land in minority areas can be used for resettlement to relieve population pressures in the densely populated regions of the country.

In the early 1980s, the central government adopted various measures to provide financial and economic assistance to the minority areas. The government allotted subsidies totaling approximately ¥6,000 million (for value of the yuan, see Glossary) in 1984 to balance any deficits experienced in autonomous areas inhabited by minority nationalities. After 1980 the autonomous regions of Nei Monggol, Xinjiang, Xizang, Guangxi, and Ningxia and the provinces of Yunnan, Guizhou, and Qinghai were permitted to keep all revenues for themselves. The draft state budget written in April 1986 allocated a special grant of ¥800 million to the underdeveloped minority nationality areas over and above the regular state subsidies. The standard of living in the minority areas improved dramatically from the early to the mid-1980s. In Xizang Autonomous Region, annual per capita income increased from ¥216 in 1983 to ¥317 in 1984 (national per capita income was ¥663 in 1983 and ¥721 in 1984). The per capita net income of the minority areas in Yunnan Province increased from ¥118 in 1980 to ¥263 in 1984, for an increase of 81.3 percent. Overall, however, the minority areas remained relatively undeveloped in 1986.

Policy

Since 1949 government policy toward minorities has been based on the somewhat contradictory goals of national unity and the protection of minority equality and identity. The state constitution of 1954 declared the country to be a "unified, multinational state" and prohibited "discrimination against or oppression of any nationality and acts which undermine the unity of the nationalities." All nationalities were granted equal rights and duties. Policy toward the ethnic minorities in the 1950s was based on the assumption that they could and should be integrated into the Han polity by gradual assimilation, while permitted initially to retain their own cultural identity and to enjoy a modicum of self-rule. Accordingly, autonomous regions were established in which minority languages were recognized, special efforts were mandated to recruit a certain percentage of minority cadres, and minority culture and religion were ostensibly protected. The minority areas also benefited from substantial government investment.

Yet the attention to minority rights took place within the larger framework of strong central control. Minority nationalities, many with strong historical and recent separatist or anti-Han tendencies, were given no rights of self-determination. With the special exception of Xizang in the 1950s, Beijing administered minority regions as vigorously as Han areas, and Han cadres filled the most important leadership positions. Minority nationalities were integrated into the national political and economic institutions and structures. Party statements hammered home the idea of the unity of all the nationalities and downplayed any part of minority history that identified insufficiently with China Proper. Relations with the minorities were strained because of traditional Han attitudes of cultural superiority. Central authorities criticized this "Han chauvinism" but found its influence difficult to eradicate.

Pressure on the minority peoples to conform were stepped up in the late 1950s and subsequently during the Cultural Revolution. Ultraleftist ideology maintained that minority distinctness was an inherently reactionary barrier to socialist progress. Although in theory the commitment to minority rights remained, repressive assimilationist policies were pursued. Minority languages were looked down upon by the central authorities, and cultural and religious freedom was severely curtailed or abolished. Minority group members were forced to give up animal husbandry in order to grow crops that in some cases were unfamiliar. State subsidies were reduced, and some autonomous areas were abolished. These policies caused a great deal of resentment, resulting in a major rebellion in Xizang in 1959 and a smaller one in Xinjiang in 1962, the latter bringing about the flight of some 60,000 Kazak herders across the border to the Soviet Union. Scattered reports of violence in minority areas in the 1966–76 decade suggest that discontent was high at that time also.

After the arrest of the Gang of Four (see Glossary) in 1976, policies toward the ethnic minorities were moderated regarding language, religion and culture, and land-use patterns, with the admission that the assimilationist policies had caused considerable alienation. The new leadership pledged to implement a bona fide system of autonomy for the ethnic minorities and placed great emphasis on the need to recruit minority cadres.

Although the minorities accounted for only about 7 percent of China's population, the minority deputies to the National People's Congress made up 13.5 percent of all representatives to the congress in 1985, and 5 of the 22 vice chairmen of its Standing Committee (23 percent) in 1983 were minority nationals. A Mongol, Ulanhu, was elected vice president of China in June 1983. Nevertheless, political administration of the minority areas was the same as that in Han regions, and the minority nationalities were subject to the dictates of the Chinese Communist Party. Despite the avowed desire to integrate the minorities into the political mainstream, the party was not willing to share key decision-making powers with the ethnic minorities. As of the late 1970s, the minority nationality cadres accounted for only 3 to 5 percent of all cadres.

Under the leadership of Deng Xiaoping, the Chinese government in the mid-1980s was pursuing a liberal policy toward the national minorities. Full autonomy became a constitutional right, and policy stipulated that Han cadres working in the minority areas learn the local spoken and written languages. Significant concessions were made to Xizang, historically the most nationalistic of the minority areas. The number of Tibetan cadres as a percentage of all cadres in Xizang increased from 50 percent in 1979 to 62 percent in 1985. In Zhejiang Province the government formally decided to assign only cadres familiar with nationality policy and sympathetic to minorities to cities, prefectures, and counties with large numbers of minority people. In Xinjiang the leaders of the region's fourteen prefectural and city governments and seventy-seven of all eighty-six rural and urban leaders were of minority nationality.

Labor Force

A 10-percent sample tabulation of census questionnaires from the 1982 census provided badly needed statistical data on China's working population and allowed the first reliable estimates of the

Jinuo musicians, Yunnan Province
Courtesy China Pictorial
Va dancer, southwest China
Courtesy Xinhua News Agency

labor force's size and characteristics. The quality of the data was considered to be quite high, although a 40-million-person discrepancy existed between the 10-percent sample and the regular employment statistics. This discrepancy can be explained by the combination of inaccurate employment statistics and varying methods of calculation and scope of coverage. The estimated mid-1982 labor force was 546 million, or approximately 54 percent of the total population. Males accounted for slightly more than half of the estimated labor force, and the labor force participation rates for persons age fifteen years and older were among the highest in the world.

The 10-percent sample showed that approximately three-fourths of the labor force worked in the agricultural sector. According to the State Statistical Bureau, in the mid-1980s more than 120 million people worked in the nonagricultural sector. The sample revealed that men occupied the great majority of leadership positions. The average worker was a youthful thirty-three years old, and three out of every four workers were under forty-five years of age. The working population had a low education level. Less than 40 percent of the labor force had more than a primary school education, and 30 percent were illiterate or semiliterate.

In mid-1982 the overall unemployment rate was estimated to be about 5 percent. Of the approximately 25 million unemployed, 12 million were men and 13 million were women. The unemployment rate was highest in the northeast and lowest in the south. The unemployment rates were higher than those of East Asian, Southeast Asian, and Pacific island countries for which data were available but were lower than the rates found in North America and Europe. Virtually all of the unemployed persons in cities and towns were under twenty years of age.

Health Care

Since the founding of the People's Republic, the goal of health programs has been to provide care to every member of the population and to make maximum use of limited health-care personnel, equipment, and financial resources. The emphasis has been on preventive rather than on curative medicine on the premise that preventive medicine is "active" while curative medicine is "passive." The health-care system has dramatically improved the health of the people, as reflected by the remarkable increase in average life expectancy from about thirty-two years in 1950 to sixty-nine years in 1985.

After 1949 the Ministry of Public Health was responsible for all health-care activities and established and supervised all facets of health policy. Along with a system of national, provincial-level, and local facilities, the ministry regulated a network of industrial and state enterprise hospitals and other facilities covering the health needs of workers of those enterprises. In 1981 this additional network provided approximately 25 percent of the country's total health services. Health care was provided in both rural and urban areas through a three-tiered system. In rural areas the first tier was made up of barefoot doctors working out of village medical centers. They provided preventive and primary-care services, with an average of two doctors per 1,000 people. At the next level were the township health centers, which functioned primarily as out-patient clinics for about 10,000 to 30,000 people each. These centers had about ten to thirty beds each, and the most qualified members of the staff were assistant doctors. The two lower-level tiers made up the "rural collective health system" that provided most of the country's medical care. Only the most seriously ill patients were referred to the third and final tier, the county hospitals, which served 200,000 to 600,000 people each and were staffed by senior doctors who held degrees from 5-year medical schools. Health care in urban areas was provided by paramedical personnel assigned to factories and neighborhood health stations. If more professional care was necessary the patient was sent to a district hospital, and the most serious cases were handled by municipal hospitals. To ensure a higher level of care, a number of state enterprises and government agencies sent their employees directly to district or municipal hospitals, circumventing the paramedical, or barefoot doctor, stage.

An emphasis on public health and preventive treatment characterized health policy from the beginning of the 1950s. At that time the party began to mobilize the population to engage in mass "patriotic health campaigns" aimed at improving the low level of environmental sanitation and hygiene and attacking certain diseases. One of the best examples of this approach was the mass assaults on the "four pests"—rats, sparrows, flies, and mosquitoes—and on schistosoma-carrying snails. Particular efforts were devoted in the health campaigns to improving water quality through such measures as deep-well construction and human-waste treatment. Only in the larger cities had human waste been centrally disposed. In the countryside, where "night soil" has always been collected and applied to the fields as fertilizer, it was a major source of disease. Since the 1950s, rudimentary treatments such as storage in pits, composting, and mixture with chemicals have been implemented.

As a result of preventive efforts, such epidemic diseases as cholera, plague, typhoid, and scarlet fever have almost been eradicated. The mass mobilization approach proved particularly successful in the fight against syphilis, which was reportedly eliminated by the 1960s.

The incidence of other infectious and parasitic diseases was reduced and controlled. Relaxation of certain sanitation and antiepidemic programs since the 1960s, however, may have resulted in some increased incidence of disease. In the early 1980s, continuing deficiencies in human-waste treatment were indicated by the persistence of such diseases as hookworm and schistosomiasis. Tuberculosis, a major health hazard in 1949, remained a problem to some extent in the 1980s, as did hepatitis, malaria, and dysentery. In the late 1980s, the need for health education and improved sanitation was still apparent, but it was more difficult to carry out the health-care campaigns because of the breakdown of the brigade system. By the mid-1980s China recognized the acquired immune deficiency syndrome (AIDS) virus as a serious health threat but remained relatively unaffected by the deadly disease. As of mid-1987 there was confirmation of only two deaths of Chinese citizens from AIDS, and monitoring of foreigners had begun. Following a 1987 regional World Health Organization meeting, the Chinese government announced it would join the global fight against AIDS, which would involve quarantine inspection of people entering China from abroad, medical supervision of people vulnerable to AIDS, and establishment of AIDS laboratories in coastal cities. Additionally, it was announced that China was experimenting with the use of traditional medicine to treat AIDS.

In the mid-1980s the leading causes of death in China were similar to those in the industrialized world: cancer, cerebrovascular disease, and heart disease. Some of the more prevalent forms of fatal cancers included cancer of the stomach, esophagus, liver, lung, and colon-rectum. The frequency of these diseases was greater for men than for women, and lung cancer mortality was much greater in higher income areas. The degree of risk for the different kinds of cancers varied widely by region. For example, nasopharyngeal cancer was found primarily in south China, while the incidence of esophageal cancer was higher in the north.

To address concerns over health, the Chinese greatly increased the number and quality of health-care personnel, although in 1986 serious shortages still existed. In 1949 only 33,000 nurses and 363,000 physicians were practicing; by 1985 the numbers had risen dramatically to 637,000 nurses and 1.4 million physicians. Some 436,000 physicians' assistants were trained in Western medicine and had 2 years of medical education after junior high school. Official Chinese statistics also reported that the number of paramedics increased from about 485,400 in 1975 to more than 853,400 in 1982. The number of students in medical and pharmaceutical colleges in China rose from about 100,000 in 1975 to approximately 160,000 in 1982.

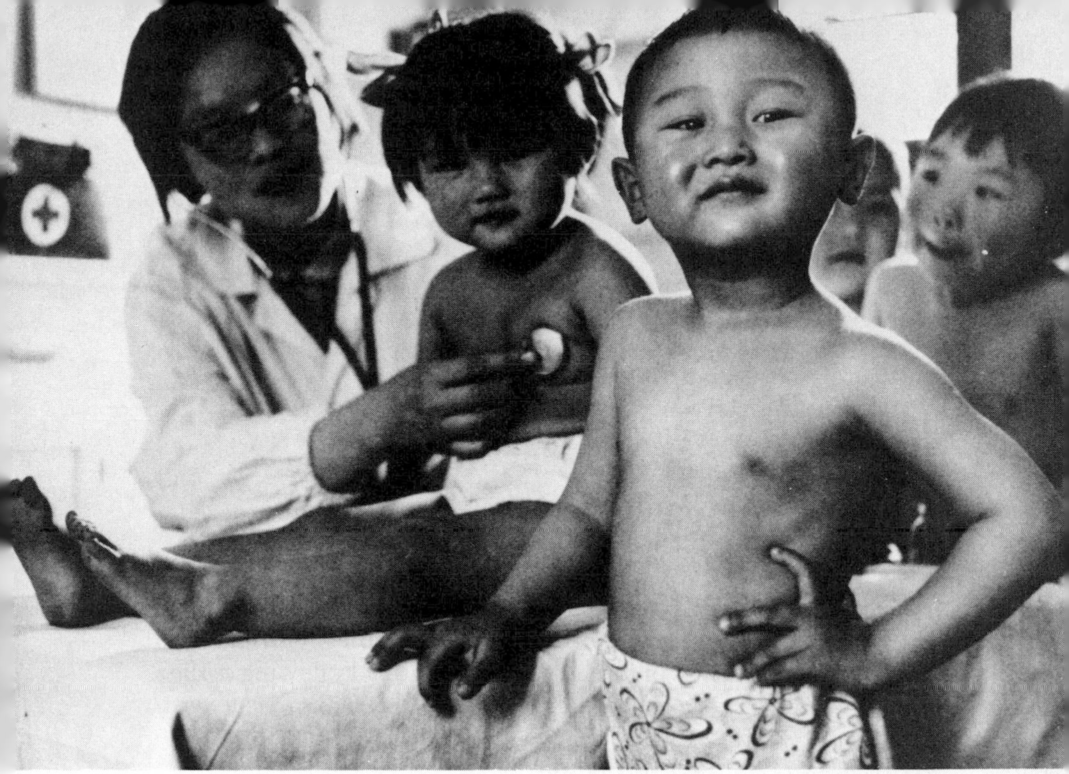

Health care for China's new generation
Courtesy
Xinhua News Agency

Boy with stuffed panda at the Beijing Zoo
Courtesy Stephanie Marcus

Efforts were made to improve and expand medical facilities. The number of hospital beds increased from 1.7 million in 1976 to 2.2 million in 1984, or to 2 beds per 1,000 compared with 4.5 beds per 1,000 in 1981 in the United States. The number of hospitals increased from 63,000 in 1976 to 67,000 in 1984, and the number of specialized hospitals and scientific research institutions doubled during the same period.

The availability and quality of health care varied widely from city to countryside. According to 1982 census data, in rural areas the crude death rate was 1.6 per 1,000 higher than in urban areas, and life expectancy was about 4 years lower. The number of senior physicians per 1,000 population was about 10 times greater in urban areas than in rural ones; state expenditure on medical care was more than ¥26 per capita in urban areas and less than ¥3 per capita in rural areas. There were also about twice as many hospital beds in urban areas as in rural areas. These are aggregate figures, however, and certain rural areas had much better medical care and nutritional levels than others.

In 1987 economic reforms were causing a fundamental transformation of the rural health-care system. The decollectivization of agriculture resulted in a decreased desire on the part of the rural populations to support the collective welfare system, of which health care was a part. In 1984 surveys showed that only 40 to 45 percent of the rural population was covered by an organized cooperative medical system, as compared with 80 to 90 percent in 1979.

This shift entailed a number of important consequences for rural health care. The lack of financial resources for the cooperatives resulted in a decrease in the number of barefoot doctors, which meant that health education and primary and home care suffered and that in some villages sanitation and water supplies were checked less frequently. Also, the failure of the cooperative health-care system limited the funds available for continuing education for barefoot doctors, thereby hindering their ability to provide adequate preventive and curative services. The costs of medical treatment increased, deterring some patients from obtaining necessary medical attention. If the patients could not pay for services received, then the financial responsibility fell on the hospitals and commune health centers, in some cases creating large debts.

Consequently, in the post-Mao era of modernization, the rural areas were forced to adapt to a changing health-care environment. Many barefoot doctors went into private practice, operating on a fee-for-service basis and charging for medication. But soon farmers demanded better medical services as their incomes increased, bypassing the barefoot doctors and going straight to the commune health centers or county hospitals. A number of barefoot doctors left the medical profession after discovering that they could earn a better living from farming, and their services were not replaced. The leaders of brigades, through which local health care was administered, also found farming to be more lucrative than their salaried positions, and many of them left their jobs. Many of the cooperative medical programs collapsed. Farmers in some brigades established voluntary health-insurance programs but had difficulty organizing and administering them.

Although the practice of traditional Chinese medicine was strongly promoted by the Chinese leadership and remained a major component of health care, Western medicine was gaining increasing acceptance in the 1970s and 1980s. For example, the number of physicians and pharmacists trained in Western medicine reportedly increased by 225,000 from 1976 to 1981, and the number of physicians' assistants trained in Western medicine increased by about 50,000. In 1981 there were reportedly 516,000 senior physicians trained in Western medicine and 290,000 senior physicians trained in traditional Chinese medicine. The goal of China's medical professionals is to synthesize the best elements of traditional and Western approaches.

In practice, however, this combination has not always worked smoothly. In many respects, physicians trained in traditional medicine and those trained in Western medicine constitute separate groups with different interests. For instance, physicians trained in Western medicine have been somewhat reluctant to accept "unscientific" traditional practices, and traditional practitioners have sought to preserve authority in their own sphere. Although Chinese medical schools that provided training in Western medicine also provided some instruction in traditional medicine, relatively few physicians were regarded as competent in both areas in the mid-1980s.

The extent to which traditional and Western treatment methods were combined and integrated in the major hospitals varied greatly. Some hospitals and medical schools of purely traditional medicine were established. In most urban hospitals, the pattern seemed to be to establish separate departments for traditional and Western treatment. In the county hospitals, however, traditional medicine received greater emphasis.

Traditional medicine depends on herbal treatments, acupuncture, acupressure, moxibustion (the burning of herbs over acupuncture points), and "cupping" of skin with heated bamboo. Such approaches are believed to be most effective in treating minor and chronic diseases, in part because of milder side effects. Traditional treatments may be used for more serious conditions as well, particularly for such acute abdominal conditions as appendicitis, pancreatitis, and gallstones; sometimes traditional treatments are used in combination with Western treatments. A traditional method of orthopedic treatment, involving less immobilization than Western methods, continued to be widely used in the 1980s.

Although health care in China developed in very positive ways by the mid-1980s, it exacerbated the problem of overpopulation. In 1987 China was faced with a population four times that of the United States and over three times that of the Soviet Union. Efforts to distribute the population over a larger portion of the country had failed: only the minority nationalities seemed able to thrive in the mountainous or desert-covered frontiers. Birth control programs implemented in the 1970s succeeded in reducing the birth rate, but estimates in the mid-1980s projected that China's population will surpass the 1.2 billion mark by the turn of the century, putting still greater pressure on the land and resources of the nation.

* * *

A thorough, scholarly study of China's geography is Zhao Songqiao's *Physical Geography of China,* which contains a number of detailed maps and charts, as well as interesting photographs and Landsat images. The China Handbook Editorial Committee's *China Handbook Series: Geography* provides a less technical overview of the physical environment and includes brief summaries of the topography, climate, and administrative divisions of China's provinces, autonomous regions, and special municipalities.

A good overview of China's population is provided in a series of articles found in *China's Economy Looks Toward the Year 2000, Volume 1: The Four Modernizations*, a collection of papers published by the United States Congress Joint Economic Committee. It opens with a general assessment of population policies and problems and continues with articles on the 1982 census results, family planning, the labor force, and material poverty. An article written by H. Yuan Tien, entitled "China: Demographic Billionaire," in *Population Bulletin* also provides a good demographic overview.

China's One-Child Family Policy, edited by Elisabeth Croll, Delia Davin, and Penny Kane, is an excellent analysis of the radical policy first announced in 1979. The work discusses the origins, problems, and prospects of the one-child policy. Tien's "Redirection of the Chinese Family" provides a concise overview of the one-child policy and its implications. (For further information and complete citations, see Bibliography.)

Chapter 3. The Social System

A Tang dynasty (A.D. 618–906) female dancer

CHINA, THE WORLD'S LARGEST SOCIETY, is united by a set of values and institutions that cut across extensive linguistic, environmental, and subcultural differences. Residents of the southern and northern regions of the country might not understand each other's speech, enjoy each other's favorite foods, or make a living from each other's land, and they might describe each other with derogatory stereotypes. Nonetheless, they would regard each other as fellow Chinese, members of the same society, and different from the Vietnamese or Koreans, with whom some Chinese might seem to have more in common.

Chinese society, since the second decade of the twentieth century, has been the object of a revolution intended to change it in fundamental ways. In its more radical phases, such as the Great Leap Forward (1958-60) and the Cultural Revolution (1966-76), the revolution aimed at nothing less than the complete transformation of everything from the practice of medicine, to higher education, to family life. In the 1980s China's leaders and intellectuals considered the revolution far from completed, and they intended further social change to make China a fully modernized country. It had become increasingly clear that although many aspects of Chinese social life had indeed undergone fundamental changes as a result of both political movements and economic development, the transformation was less than total. Much of the past either lived on in modified form or served to shape revolutionary initiatives and to limit the choices open to even the most radical of revolutionaries.

Ethnic Boundaries

China is, like all large states, multiethnic; but one ethnic group—the Han Chinese (see Glossary)—dominates the politics, government, and economy. This account focuses on the Han, and it considers the minority peoples only in relation to the Han ethnic group (see Minority Nationalities, ch. 2).

Over the centuries a great many peoples who were originally not Chinese have been assimilated into Chinese society. Entry into Han society has not demanded religious conversion or formal initiation. It has depended on command of the Chinese written language and evidence of adherence to Chinese values and customs. For the most part, what has distinguished those groups that have been assimilated from those that have not has been the suitability of their environment for Han agriculture. People living in areas where Chinese-style agriculture is feasible have either been displaced or assimilated. The consequence is that most of China's minorities inhabit extensive tracts of land unsuited for Han-style agriculture; they are not usually found as long-term inhabitants of Chinese cities or in close proximity to most Han villages. Those living on steppes, near desert oases, or in high mountains, and dependent on pastoral nomadism or shifting cultivation, have retained their ethnic distinctiveness outside Han society. The sharpest ethnic boundary has been between the Han and the steppe pastoralists, a boundary sharpened by centuries of conflict and cycles of conquest and subjugation. Reminders of these differences are the absence of dairy products from the otherwise extensive repertoire of Han cuisine and the distaste most Chinese feel for such typical steppe specialties as tea laced with butter.

Official policy recognizes the multiethnic nature of the Chinese state, within which all "nationalities" are formally equal. On the one hand, it is not state policy to force the assimilation of minority nationalities, and such nonpolitical expressions of ethnicity as native costumes and folk dances are encouraged. On the other hand, China's government is a highly centralized one that recognizes no legitimate limits to its authority, and minority peoples in far western Xinjiang-Uygur Autonomous Region, for example, are considered Chinese citizens just as much as Han farmers on the outskirts of Beijing.

Official attitudes toward minority peoples are inconsistent, if not contradictory. Since 1949 policies toward minorities have fluctuated between tolerance and coercive attempts to impose Han standards. Tolerant periods have been marked by subsidized material benefits intended to win loyalty, while coercive periods such as the Cultural Revolution have attempted to eradicate "superstition" and to overthrow insufficiently radical or insufficiently nationalistic local leaders.

What has not varied has been the assumption that it is the central government that decides what is best for minority peoples and that national citizenship takes precedence over ethnic identity. In fact, minority nationality is a legal status in China. The government reserves for itself the right to determine whether or not a group is a minority nationality, and the list has been revised several times since the 1950s. In the mid-1980s the state recognized 55 minority nationalities, some with as few as 1,100 members. Minority nationalities are guaranteed special representation in the National People's Congress and the Chinese People's Political Consultative Conference (see Glossary). Areas where minorities form the majority of the population may be designated "autonomous" counties, prefectures, or regions, subject to the authority of the central government in Beijing rather than to provincial or subprovincial administrations. It is expected that local administrations in such regions will be staffed at least in part by minority nationals and that application of national policies will take into account local circumstances and special needs. In the early 1980s, for example, minority peoples were exempted from the strict limitations on the number of children per family dictated to the Han population.

Most Han Chinese have no contact with members of minority groups. But in areas such as the Xizang (also known as Tibet) or Xinjiang autonomous regions, where large numbers of Han have settled since the assertion of Chinese central government authority over them in the 1950s, there is clearly some ethnic tension (see Minority Nationalities, ch. 2). The tension stems from Han dominance over such previously independent or semi-autonomous peoples as the Tibetans and Uygurs, from Cultural Revolution attacks on religious observances, and from Han disdain for and lack of sensitivity to minority cultures. In the autonomous areas the ethnic groups appear to lead largely separate lives, and most Han in those areas either work as urban-based administrators and professionals or serve in military installations or on state farms. Since the late 1970s, the central authorities have made efforts to conciliate major ethnic minorities by sponsoring the revival of religious festivals and by increasing the level of subsidies to the poorest minority regions. Because of these efforts, other moderate government policies, and the geographic distribution and relatively small size of minority groups in China, the country has not suffered widespread or severe ethnic conflict.

Han Diversity and Unity

The differences among regional and linguistic subgroups of Han Chinese are at least as great as those among many European nationalities. Han Chinese speak seven or eight mutually unintelligible dialects, each of which has many local subdialects. Cultural differences (cuisine, costume, and custom) are equally great. Modern Chinese history provides many examples of conflict, up to the level of small-scale regional wars, between linguistic and regional groups.

Such diversities, however, have not generated exclusive loyalties, and distinctions in religion or political affiliation have not reinforced regional differences. Rather, there has been a consistent tendency in Chinese thought and practice to downplay intra-Han distinctions, which are regarded as minor and superficial. What all Han share is more significant than the ways in which they differ.

In conceptual terms, the boundary between Han and non-Han is absolute and sharp, while boundaries between subsets of Han are subject to continual shifts, are dictated by local conditions, and do not produce the isolation inherent in relations between Han and minority groups.

Han ethnic unity is the result of two ancient and culturally central Chinese institutions, one of which is the written language. Chinese is written with ideographs (sometimes called characters) that represent meanings rather than sounds, and so written Chinese does not reflect the speech of its author. The disjunction between written and spoken Chinese means that a newspaper published in Beijing can be read in Shanghai or Guangzhou, although the residents of the three cities would not understand each other's speech. It also means that there can be no specifically Cantonese (Guangzhou dialect) or Hunanese literature because the local speech of a region cannot be directly or easily represented in writing. (It is possible to add local color to fiction, cite colloquialisms, or transcribe folk songs.) Therefore, local languages have not become a focus for regional self-consciousness or nationalism. Educated Chinese tend to regard the written ideographs as primary, and they regard the seven or eight spoken Han Chinese dialects as simply variant ways of pronouncing the same ideographs. This is linguistically inaccurate, but the attitude has significant political and social consequences. The uniform written language in 1987 continued to be a powerful force for Han unity.

The other major force contributing to Han ethnic unity has been the centralized imperial state. The ethnic group takes its name from the Han dynasty (206 B.C.–A.D. 220; see The Imperial Era, ch. 1). Although the imperial government never directly controlled the villages, it did have a strong influence on popular values and culture. The average peasant could not read and was not familiar with the details of state administration or national geography, but he was aware of belonging to a group of subcontinental scope. Being Han, even for illiterate peasants, has meant conscious identification with a glorious history and a state of immense proportions. Peasant folklore and folk religion assumed that the imperial state, with an emperor and an administrative bureaucracy, was the normal order of society. In the imperial period, the highest prestige went to scholar-officials, and every schoolboy had the possibility, at least theoretically, of passing the civil service examinations and becoming an official.

The prestige of the state and its popular identification with the highest values of Chinese civilization were not accidents; they were the final result of a centuries-long program of indoctrination and

Confucius observing the practice of rules of conduct among the members of society. Woodcut. Courtesy Library of Congress

education directed by the Confucian scholar-officials. Traditional Chinese society can be distinguished from other premodern civilizations to the extent that the state, rather than organized religious groups or ethnic segments of society, was able to appropriate the symbols of wisdom, morality, and the common good. The legacy for modern Chinese society has been a strong centralized government that has the right to impose its values on the population and against which there is no legitimate right of dissent or secession.

Traditional Society and Culture

The leaders who directed the efforts to change Chinese society after the establishment of the People's Republic of China in 1949 were raised in the old society and had been marked with its values. Although they were conscious revolutionaries, they could not wholly escape the culture into which they had been born. Nationalists as well as revolutionaries, they had no intention of transforming China into a replica of any foreign country. They had an ambivalent attitude toward their country's past and its traditional society, condemning some aspects and praising others. Furthermore, as practical administrators, China's post-1949 leaders devoted energy and attention to changing some aspects of traditional society, such as rural land tenure and the content of education, while leaving other aspects, such as family structure, largely untouched. Change in Chinese society, therefore, has been less than total and less consistent than has often been claimed by official spokesmen. To understand contemporary society, it is necessary to be familiar with past legacies, particularly in the realm of values and in areas of social life, such as family organization, where transformation has not been a high-priority political goal.

China's traditional values were contained in the orthodox version of Confucianism, which was taught in the academies and tested in the imperial civil service examinations. These values are distinctive for their this-worldly emphasis on society and public administration and for their wide diffusion throughout Chinese society. Confucianism, never a religion in any accepted sense, is primarily concerned with social order. Social harmony is to be achieved within the state, whose administrators consciously select the proper policies and act to educate both the rulers and the subject masses. Confucianism originated and developed as the ideology of professional administrators and continued to bear the impress of its origins (see The Ancient Dynasties; The Imperial Era, ch. 1).

Imperial-era Confucianists concentrated on this world and had an agnostic attitude toward the supernatural. They approved of ritual and ceremony, but primarily for their supposed educational and psychological effects on those participating. Confucianists tended to regard religious specialists (who historically were often rivals for authority or imperial favor) as either misguided or intent on squeezing money from the credulous masses. The major metaphysical element in Confucian thought was the belief in an impersonal ultimate natural order that included the social order. Confucianists asserted that they understood the inherent pattern for social and political organization and therefore had the authority to run society and the state.

The Confucianists claimed authority based on their knowledge, which came from direct mastery of a set of books. These books, the Confucian Classics, were thought to contain the distilled wisdom of the past and to apply to all human beings everywhere at all times (see Culture and the Arts, ch. 4). The mastery of the Classics was the highest form of education and the best possible qualification for holding public office. The way to achieve the ideal society was to teach the entire people as much of the content of the Classics as possible. It was assumed that everyone was educable and that everyone needed educating. The social order may have been natural, but it was not assumed to be instinctive. Confucianism put great stress on learning, study, and all aspects of socialization. Confucianists preferred internalized moral guidance to the external force of law, which they regarded as a punitive force applied to those unable to learn morality. Confucianists saw the ideal society as a hierarchy, in which everyone knew his or her proper place and duties. The existence of a ruler and of a state were taken for granted, but Confucianists held that rulers had to demonstrate their fitness to rule by their "merit." The essential point was that heredity was an insufficient qualification for legitimate authority. As practical administrators, Confucianists came to terms with hereditary kings and emperors but insisted on their right to educate rulers in the principles of Confucian thought. Traditional Chinese thought thus combined an ideally rigid and hierarchical social order with an appreciation for education, individual achievement, and mobility within the rigid structure.

Diffusion of Values

While ideally everyone would benefit from direct study of the Classics, this was not a realistic goal in a society composed largely of illiterate peasants. But Confucianists had a keen appreciation for the influence of social models and for the socializing and teaching functions of public rituals and ceremonies. The common people were thought to be influenced by the examples of their rulers and officials, as well as by public events. Vehicles of cultural transmission, such as folk songs, popular drama, and literature and the arts, were the objects of government and scholarly attention. Many scholars, even if they did not hold public office, put a great deal of effort into popularizing Confucian values by lecturing on morality, publicly praising local examples of proper conduct, and "reforming" local customs, such as bawdy harvest festivals. In this manner, over hundreds of years, the values of Confucianism were diffused across China and into scattered peasant villages and rural culture.

The Confucian Legacy

Traditional values have clearly shaped much of contemporary Chinese life. The belief in rule by an educated and functionally unspecialized elite, the value placed on learning and propagating an orthodox ideology that focuses on society and government, and the stress on hierarchy and the preeminent role of the state were all carried over from traditional society. Some of the more radical and extreme policies of the 1950s and 1960s, such as attacks on intellectuals and compulsory manual labor for bureaucrats, can only be understood as responses to deep-rooted traditional attitudes. The role of model workers and soldiers, as well as official concern for the content and form of popular literature and the arts, also reflects characteristically Chinese themes. In the mid-1980s a number of

Chinese writers and political leaders identified the lingering hold of "feudal" attitudes, even within the Chinese Communist Party (CCP), as a major obstacle to modernization. They identified such phenomena as authoritarianism, unthinking obedience to leaders, deprecation of expert knowledge, lack of appreciation for law, and the failure to apply laws to leaders as "feudal" legacies that were not addressed in the early years of China's revolution.

Traditional Social Structure

Throughout the centuries some 80 to 90 percent of the Chinese population have been farmers. The farmers supported a small number of specialized craftsmen and traders and also an even smaller number of land- and office-holding elite families who ran the society. Although the peasant farmers and their families resembled counterparts in other societies, the traditional Chinese elite, often referred to in English as the gentry, had no peers in other societies. The national elite, who comprised perhaps 1 percent of China's population, had a number of distinctive features. They were dispersed across the country and often lived in rural areas, where they were the dominant figures on the local scene. Although they held land, which they rented to tenant farmers, they neither possessed large estates like European nobles nor held hereditary titles. They achieved their highest and most prestigious titles by their performance on the central government's triennial civil service examinations. These titles had to be earned by each generation, and since the examinations had strict numerical quotas, competition was fierce. Government officials were selected from those who passed the examinations, which tested for mastery of the Confucian Classics. Elite families, like everyone else in China, practiced partible inheritance, dividing the estate equally among all sons. The combination of partible inheritance and the competition for success in the examinations meant that rates of mobility into and out of the elite were relatively high for a traditional agrarian society.

The imperial state was staffed by a small civil bureaucracy. Civil officials were directly appointed and paid by the emperor and had to have passed the civil service examinations. Officials, who were supposed to owe their primary loyalty to the emperor, did not serve in their home provinces and were generally assigned to different places for each tour of duty. Although the salary of central officials was low, the positions offered great opportunities for personal enrichment, which was one reason that families competed so fiercely to pass the examinations and then obtain an appointment. For most officials, officeholding was not a lifetime career. They served one or a few tours and then returned to their home districts and families,

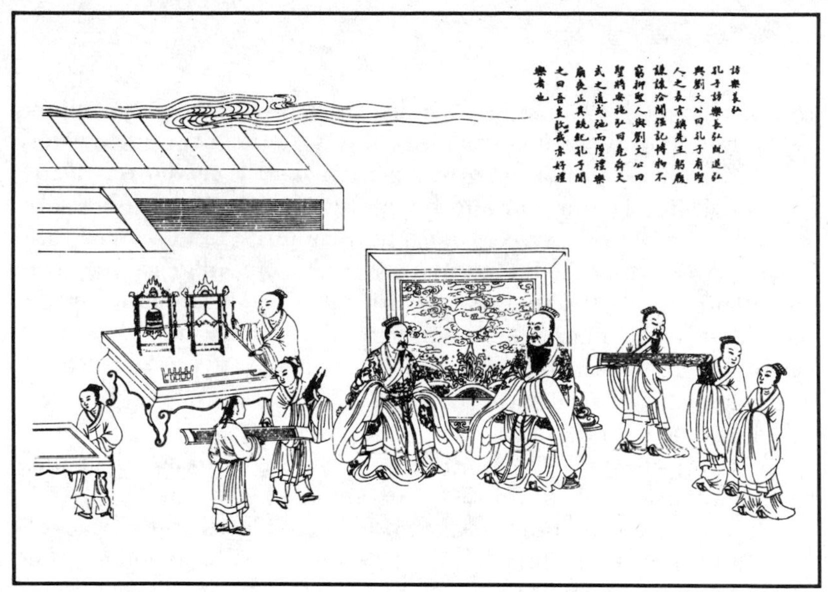

Musicians with a variety of instruments important to Confucian rituals
Courtesy Library of Congress

where their wealth, prestige, and network of official contacts made them dominant figures on the local scene.

The Examination System

In late imperial China the status of local-level elites was ratified by contact with the central government, which maintained a monopoly on society's most prestigious titles. The examination system and associated methods of recruitment to the central bureaucracy were major mechanisms by which the central government captured and held the loyalty of local-level elites. Their loyalty, in turn, ensured the integration of the Chinese state and countered tendencies toward regional autonomy and the breakup of the centralized system. The examination system distributed its prizes according to provincial and prefectural quotas, which meant that imperial officials were recruited from the whole country, in numbers roughly proportional to a province's population. Elites all over China, even in the disadvantaged peripheral regions, had a chance at succeeding in the examinations and achieving the rewards of officeholding.

The examination system also served to maintain cultural unity and consensus on basic values. The uniformity of the content of the examinations meant that the local elite and ambitious would-be elite all across China were being indoctrinated with the same values. Even though only a small fraction (about 5 percent) of those who attempted the examinations passed them and received titles, the study, self-indoctrination, and hope of eventual success on a subsequent examination served to sustain the interest of those who took them. Those who failed to pass (most of the candidates at any single examination) did not lose wealth or local social standing; as dedicated believers in Confucian orthodoxy, they served, without the benefit of state appointments, as teachers, patrons of the arts, and managers of local projects, such as irrigation works, schools, or charitable foundations.

In late traditional China, then, education was valued in part because of its possible payoff in the examination system. The overall result of the examination system and its associated study was cultural uniformity—identification of the educated with national rather than regional goals and values. This self-conscious national identity underlies the nationalism so important in China's politics in the twentieth century (see Republican China, ch. 1).

Social Stratification

Traditional thought accepted social stratification as natural and considered most social groups to be organized on hierarchical principles. In the ideal Confucian scheme of social stratification, scholars were at the highest level of society, followed by farmers, then by artisans, with merchants and soldiers in last place.

In society at large, the highest and most prestigious positions were those of political generalists, such as members of the emperor's council or provincial governors. Experts, such as tax specialists or physicians, ranked below the ruling political generalists. Although commerce has been a major element of Chinese life since the early imperial period, and wealthy merchants have been major figures in Chinese cities, Confucianists disparaged merchants. Commercial success never won respect, and wealth based on commerce was subject to official taxes, fees, and even confiscation. Upward mobility by merchants was achieved by cultivating good relations with powerful officials and educating their sons in the hope they might become officials. Although dynasties were founded by military conquest, Confucian ideology derogated military skill. Common soldiers occupied a low position in society and were recruited from its lowest ranks. Chinese civilization, however, includes a significant military tradition, and generals and strategists usually were held in high esteem.

Most of China's population was composed of peasant farmers, whose basic role in supporting the rulers and the rest of society was recognized as a positive one in Confucian ideology. In practical terms, farming was considered a hard and insecure life and one that was best left if an opportunity was available.

In Chinese communities the factors generating prestige were education, abstention from manual labor, wealth expended on the arts and education, a large family with many sons, and community service and acts of charity. Another asset was an extensive personal network that permitted one to grant favors and make introductions and recommendations. There was no sharp line dividing the elite from the masses, and social mobility was possible and common.

Stratification and Families

Before 1950 the basic units of social stratification and social mobility were families. Although wealthy families were often quite large, with as many as thirty people in three or four generations living together on a common budget, most families contained five or six people. In socioeconomic terms, late traditional China was composed of a large number of small enterprises, perhaps as many as 100 million farms and small businesses. Each was operated by a family, which acted not only as a household but also as a commercial enterprise. The family head also was the trustee of the estate and manager of the family business. Families could own property, such as land or shops, and pass it on to the next generation.

About 80 percent of the population were peasant farmers, and land was the fundamental form of property. Although many peasant families owned no land, large estates were rare by the eighteenth and nineteenth centuries. Peasant families might own all of the land they worked, or own some and rent some from a landowner, or rent all their land. Regardless of the form of tenure, the farm was managed as a unit, and the head of household was free to decide what to plant and how to use the labor of family members. Land could be bought and sold in small parcels, as well as mortgaged and rented in various forms of short-term and long-term contracts. The consequence was that in most villages peasant families occupied different steps on the ladder of stratification; they did not form a uniformly impoverished mass. At any time, peasant families were distinguished by the amount of land that they owned and worked compared with the percentage of their income they paid in rent. Over time, peasant families rose or fell in small steps as they bought land or were forced to sell it.

Most non-farm enterprises, commercial or craft, were similarly small businesses run by families. The basic units were owned by families, which took a long-term view of their prospects and attempted to shift resources and family personnel from occupation to occupation to adapt to economic circumstances. In all cases, the long-term goal of the head of the family was to ensure the survival and prosperity of the family and to pass the estate along to the next generation. The most common family strategy was to diversify the family's economic activities. Such strategies lay behind the large number of small-scale enterprises that characterized Chinese society before 1950. Farming and landowning were secure but not very profitable. Commerce and money-lending brought in greater returns but also carried greater risks. A successful farm family might invest in a shop or a food-processing business, while a successful restaurant owner might buy farmland, worked by a sharecropping peasant family, as a secure investment. All well-to-do families invested in the education of sons, with the hope of getting at least one son into a government job. The consequence was that it was difficult to draw a class line dividing landlords, merchants, and government workers or officials.

Social Mobility

Formal education provided the best and most respected avenue of upward mobility, and by the nineteenth century literacy rates in China were high for a traditional peasant society. Chances of receiving a good education were highest for the upper classes in and around coastal cities and lowest for the farmers of the interior. If schooling was not available, there were other avenues of mobility. Rural people could move to cities to seek their fortunes (and in some cases the cities were in Southeast Asia or the Americas). People could go into business, gamble on the market for perishable cash crops, try money-lending on a small scale or, as a long shot, join the army or a bandit group. Late traditional society offered alternate routes to worldly success and a number of ways to change one's position in society; but in all routes except education the chances of failure outweighed those of success.

In many cases, whether in business or banditry, success or failure depended to a great degree on luck. The combination of population pressure, the low rate of economic growth, natural disasters, and endemic war that afflicted the Chinese population in the first half of the twentieth century meant that many families lost their property, some starved, and almost all faced the probability of misfortune (see Republican China, ch. 1). From the perspective of individuals and individual families, it is likely that from 1850 to 1950 the chances of downward mobility increased and the ability to plan ahead with confidence decreased.

A tea stall in the Fragrant Hills outside Beijing
Courtesy Stephanie Marcus

Open-air shop, Yangzhou, Jiangsu Province
Courtesy Stephanie Marcus

Social Change

After the establishment of the People's Republic in 1949, the uncertainty and risks facing small-scale socioeconomic units were replaced by an increase in the scale of organization and bureaucratization, with a consequent increase in predictability and personal security. The tens of millions of small enterprises were replaced by a much smaller number of larger enterprises, which were organized in a bureaucratic and hierarchical manner. Collectivization of land and nationalization of most private businesses meant that families no longer had estates to pass along. Long-term interests for families resided primarily with the work unit (collective farm, office, or factory) to which they belonged.

Mobility in most cases consisted of gaining administrative promotions within such work units. Many of the alternate routes to social mobility were closed off, and formal education continued to be the primary avenue of upward mobility. In villages the army offered the only reasonable alternative to a lifetime spent in the fields, and demobilized soldiers staffed much of the local administrative structure in rural areas. For the first time in Chinese history, the peasant masses were brought into direct contact with the national government and the ruling party, and national-level politics came to have a direct impact on the lives of ordinary people. The formerly local, small-scale, and fragmented power structure was replaced by a national and well-integrated structure, operating by bureaucratic norms. The unpredictable consequences of market forces were replaced by administrative allocation and changing economic policies enforced by the government bureaucracy.

The principal transformation of society took place during the 1950s in a series of major campaigns carried out by the party. In the countryside, an initial land reform redistributed some land from those families with an excess to those with none. This was quickly followed by a series of reforms that increased the scale of organization, from seasonal mutual aid teams (groups of joint-support laborers from individual farming households), to permanent mutual aid teams, to voluntary agricultural cooperatives, to compulsory agricultural cooperatives, and finally to large people's communes (see Glossary). In each step, which came at roughly two-year intervals, the size of the unit was increased, and the role of inherited land or private ownership was decreased. By the early 1960s, an estimated 90 million family farms had been replaced by about 74,000 communes. During the same period, local governments took over commerce, and private traders, shops, and markets were replaced by supply and marketing cooperatives and the commercial

Free market, Guilin
Courtesy
Douglass M. Dolan

Street-side shoe repair shop
Courtesy Stephanie Marcus

bureaus of local government. In the cities, large industries were nationalized and craft enterprises were organized into large-scale cooperatives that became branches of local government. Many small shops and restaurants were closed down, and those that remained were under municipal management.

In both city and countryside, the 1950s saw a major expansion of the party and state bureaucracies, and many young people with relatively scarce secondary or college educations found secure white-collar jobs in the new organizations. The old society's set of formal associations—everything from lineages (clans), to irrigation cooperatives, to urban guilds and associations of persons from the same place of origin, all of which were private, small-scale, and usually devoted to a single purpose—were closed down. They were replaced by government bureaus or state-sponsored mass associations, and their parochial leaders were replaced by party members. The new institutions were run by party members and served as channels of information, communication, and political influence.

The basic pattern of contemporary society was established by 1960, and all changes since then, including the reforms of the early and mid-1980s, have represented only modifications and adjustments to the pattern. The pattern is cellular; most people belong to one large, all-embracing unit, such as a factory, government office, or village. The unit is run by a party branch, operates (or should operate) under common administrative rules and procedures, and reflects the current policies of the party. The consequence has been that most aspects of social differentiation, stratification, mobility, and tensions are now played out within an institutional framework. Most of the questions about any individual's life and prospects can be answered by specifying the unit—the social cell—with which that individual is associated.

Differentiation

Although much of the social structure of modern China can be interpreted as reflecting basic drives for security and equality, qualities in short supply before 1950, not all organizations and units are alike or equal. There are four major axes of social differentiation in modern China. To some extent they overlap and reinforce each other, but each rests on distinct and separate grounds.

The Work Place

Work units (*danwei*) belong to the state or to collectives. State-owned units, typically administrative offices, research institutes, and large factories, offer lifetime security, stable salaries, and benefits that include pensions and free health care. Collectives include the entire agricultural sector and many small-scale factories, repair shops, and village- or township-run factories, workshops, or service enterprises. Employees on the state payroll enjoy the best benefits modern China has to offer. The incomes of those in the collective sector are usually lower and depend on the performance of the enterprise. They generally lack health benefits or pensions, and the collective units usually do not provide housing or child-care facilities. In 1981 collective enterprises employed about 40 percent of the nonagricultural labor force, and most of the growth of employment since 1980 has come in this sector. Even though the growth since 1980 of individual businesses and small private enterprises, such as restaurants and repair services, has provided some individuals with substantial cash incomes, employment in the state sector remains most people's first choice. This reflects the public's recognition of that sector's superior material benefits as well as the traditional high prestige of government service.

"Security and equality" have been high priorities in modern China and have usually been offered within single work units. Because there is no nationwide insurance or social security system and because the income of work units varies, the actual level of benefits and the degree of equality (of incomes, housing, or opportunities for advancement) depend on the particular work unit with which individuals are affiliated. Work units are responsible for chronic invalids or old people without families, as well as for families confronted with the severe illness or injury of the breadwinner. Equality has always been sought within work units (so that all factory workers, for example, received the same basic wage, or members of a collective farm the same share of the harvest), and distinctions among units have not been publicly acknowledged. During the Cultural Revolution, however, great stress was placed on equality in an abstract or general sense and on its symbolic acting out. Administrators and intellectuals were compelled to do manual labor, and the uneducated and unskilled were held up as examples of revolutionary virtue.

In the mid-1980s many people on the lower fringes of administration were not on the state payroll, and it was at this broad, lower level that the distinction between government employees and non-government workers assumed the greatest importance. In the countryside, village heads were collective-sector workers, as were the teachers in village primary schools, while workers for township governments (and for all levels above them) and teachers in middle schools and universities were state employees. In the armed forces, the rank and file who served a three- to five-year enlistment at very low pay were considered citizens serving their military obligation rather than state employees. Officers, however, were state employees, and that distinction was far more significant than their rank. The distinction between state and collective-sector employment was one of the first things considered when people tried to find jobs for their children or a suitable marriage partner.

Communist Party Membership

Every unit in China, from the villages through the armed forces, is run by the party, which has a monopoly on political power (see Membership, ch. 10). Party members are in a sense the heirs of the traditional gentry. They are a power-holding elite, dispersed over the whole country, and serve as intermediaries between their own communities or units and the nation. They are recruited from the population at large on universalistic grounds of "merit," and they claim authority by their mastery of an ideology that focuses on government and public order. The ideology is contained in books, and party members are expected to be familiar with the basic texts, to continue studying them throughout their careers, and to apply them in concrete situations.

The differences between the traditional elite and the party are obvious. Party members are supposed to be revolutionaries, be devoted to changing society rather than restoring it, come from and represent the peasants and workers, and be willing to submit themselves totally and unreservedly to the party. On the whole, party members are distinctly less bookish and more military-oriented and outwardly egalitarian than traditional elites. Party members have been preferentially recruited from the poor peasantry of the interior, from the army, and from the ranks of industrial workers; intellectuals have usually found it difficult to enter the party. The party is represented in every village and every large or medium-sized enterprise in the country. The scope of its actions and concerns is much greater than that of its traditional predecessors.

Relatively speaking, there are more party members than there were traditional gentry. In 1986 the Chinese Communist Party had 44 million members in 2.6 million local party branches. This meant that about 8 percent of China's adult population belonged to the party. Not all party members hold state jobs: some hold village and township-level positions, and many armed forces enlisted personnel join the party during their service. (Indeed, a chance to join the party has been one of the major attractions of military service for peasant youth.)

Party members direct all enterprises and institutions and dominate public life and discussion. Anyone with ambitions to do more than his or her daily job or work in a narrow professional specialty must join the party. Membership is selective, and candidates must demonstrate their zeal, devotion to party principles, and willingness to make a total commitment to the party. Ideally, membership is a complete way of life, not a job, and selection for membership depends more on assessment of an individual's total personality and "moral" character than on specific qualifications or technical skills. While this could probably be said of all communist parties, Chinese Communist Party members certainly mirror China's traditional mandarins, who were political generalists rather than technical specialists. Party members are the intermediaries who link enterprises and communities with high-level structures, and they can belong to more than one organization, such as a factory and a municipal party body. Party membership is virtually a requirement for upward mobility or for opportunities to leave one's original work unit.

Urban-Rural Distinctions

In modern China, legal distinction is made between urban and rural dwellers, and movement from rural to urban status is difficult. Urban life is felt to be far preferable, and living standards and opportunities for such advantages as education are much better in the cities. This firm and absolute distinction, which had no precedent in traditional society, is the result of a set of administrative decisions and policies that have had major, if unintended, consequences for social organization. Modern Chinese society has been marked by an extraordinary degree of residential immobility, and internal migration and population movement have been limited by state control. For most of the period since 1958, there has been no legal way to move out of villages or from small cities to large cities. Although people have not inherited estates and private property, they have inherited rural or urban status, which has been a major determinant of living standards and life chances.

China's cities grew rapidly in the early and mid-1950s as rural people moved in to take advantage of the employment opportunities generated by economic growth and the expansion of heavy industry. The authorities became alarmed at this influx, both because of the cost of providing urban services (food supply, waste disposal) and because of the potential problems of unemployed or semi-employed migrants creating squatter settlements. Additionally, Chinese leaders held a certain anti-urban bias and tended to regard China's cities as unproductive. They accused city residents of living off the countryside and indulging in luxury consumption. Extolling large, smoking factories, they sought to engage the population in the manufacture of utilitarian commodities, like steel or trucks. The authorities demonstrated their bias against commerce and service trades by closing down many shops and markets. Since 1958 they have employed household registration and food rationing systems to control urban growth and general migration (see Migration, ch. 2).

In the 1980s the distinction between urban and rural status grew mainly out of the food distribution and rationing system. Rural registrants were assumed to be growing their own staple foods, and there was no provision for state allocation of grain to them. The state monopolized the trade in grain; it collected grain in the countryside as a tax or as compulsory purchase and used it to supply its functionaries and the urban population (see Internal Trade and Distribution, ch. 8). Urban status entitled one to purchase an allotment of grain, oil, and various other staple items. These were rationed, and a ration coupon as well as money was necessary to obtain grain legally. Ration coupons were good only in their own localities. The rationing system served several purposes. They included the fair distribution of scarce goods, prevention of private speculation in staple foods, and residence control. In addition, the police in cities kept household registration records and could make unannounced inspections, usually at night, looking for people who did not have legal permission to reside in a city. The controls have not been foolproof and have worked more effectively in times of shortages and strict political control.

In the 1980s the reasons for the administrative barriers around cities were fairly straightforward. Incomes and living standards in China's cities are two to three times higher than in the countryside. In addition, more urban dwellers have secure state jobs with their associated benefits. State investment has been concentrated in heavy industry, mostly urban, and agriculture and the rural sector have been left to their own devices, after meeting their tax obligations. The ironic consequence of a rural and peasant-based revolution has been a system that has acted, intentionally or not, to increase the social and economic gap between country and city.

Regional Distinctions

Regional distinctions in ways of life and standards of living were marked in traditional China and continue to have a strong influence on contemporary Chinese society. China's size, poorly developed transportation system, and state controls on migration mean that regional differences in income and in life chances remain large. Contemporary Chinese commentary, while certainly explicit on the role of class, has tended to ignore regional variation. This may reflect the characteristic emphasis on Chinese unity and uniformity, as well as the difficulty of fitting regional analysis into a Marxist framework. Nevertheless, both geographical position and a community's position in administrative and regional hierarchies act to limit income from sideline occupations, cash crops, village industries, and even such matters as marriage choices.

Incomes and educational standards in the 1980s were highest in the productive lower Chang Jiang (Yangtze River) Valley and central Guangdong Province regions and lowest in the semi-arid highlands of the northwest and the Yunnan-Guizhou Plateau, as they had been since the late nineteenth century. The lowest incomes and living standards were in the peripheral areas inhabited by minority nationalities. Within all regions, there were distinctions between urban cores, intermediate areas, and peripheries. Villages on the outskirts of major cities had more opportunities for production of cash crops such as vegetables, more opportunities in sideline occupations or subcontracting for urban factories, and easier access to urban services and amenities. Higher village incomes were reflected in better housing, higher school attendance, well-appointed village meeting halls, and a high level of farm and domestic mechanization. For settlements on the periphery, however, even if only a short distance from urban centers, transportation was difficult. Such settlements had changed little in appearance since the 1950s and devoted most of their land and work force to growing staple grains. Many children in these villages dropped out of school before completing primary education, as physical strength and endurance were more highly regarded than book learning.

There is clearly a degree of overlap in the four fields of social differentiation (work units, party membership, urban-rural distinctions, and regional distinctions). The top of the hierarchy is occupied by those who work in state organizations, belong to the party, live in a major city, and inhabit a prosperous region. Correspondingly, the least favored inhabitants are peasants whose villages are located in the remote parts of poor regions. What is most impressive about social differentiation in modern China is the extent to which key variables such as region and rural or urban status are ascribed, and not easily changed by individual effort. This is the negative side of the security and stability that attracted China's populace to the party and its programs.

Common Patterns

The cellular structure of contemporary Chinese society and the Chinese Communist Party's single-party rule mean that almost all social organizations share common characteristics (see Social

Change, this ch.). The same general description (an all-embracing social unit, whose members are assigned to it for life and which is organized on bureaucratic principles, subordinate to higher administrative levels, and managed by a branch of the party) applies to villages, schools, administrative offices, factories, or army units. All of these are work units.

Work Units

In some ways, Chinese work units (*danwei*) resemble the large-scale bureaucratic organizations that employ most people in economically developed societies. The unit is functionally specialized, producing a single product or service, and is internally organized into functional departments, with employees classified and rewarded according to their work skills. Professional managers run the organization, enforce internal regulations and work rules, and negotiate with other work units and administrative superiors.

Chinese work units, however, have many distinctive qualities. Workers usually belong to the same unit for their entire working life. The degree of commitment to the unit and the extent to which the unit affects many aspects of the individual worker's life have no parallel in other societies. Chinese work units are highly corporate, closed, permanent, and all-embracing groups. In most cases, people are either born into their units (villages count as units) or are assigned to them when they enter the work force.

Units supply their members with much more than a wage. Housing in the cities is usually controlled and assigned by work units. Consequently, one's neighbors are often one's workmates. If child-care facilities are available, they will most often be provided by the work unit. Recreation facilities will be provided by the work unit. Political study is carried out with one's workmates. In the cities many people meet prospective spouses either at work or through the introduction of fellow workers. For most people, social mobility takes the form of working their way up within the organization.

If goods are in short supply, they will be rationed through work units. This was the case with bicycles and sewing machines in the 1970s. The same can apply to babies. As part of China's planned birth policy, unit supervisors monitor the fertility of married women and may decide whose turn it is to have a baby (see Population Control Programs, ch. 2). At the other end of the life cycle, pensions and funeral expenses are provided by work units. Travel to another city usually requires the written permission of one's work unit before a ticket can be purchased or food coupons for one's destination issued. Every unit is managed by party members, who are responsible for personnel matters. Outside the farm sector, a written dossier is kept for every member of a unit. Units are often physically distinct, occupying walled compounds whose exits are monitored by gatekeepers. The unit is thus a total community, if not a total institution, and unit membership is the single most significant aspect of individual identity in contemporary China.

Since the 1950s the individual's political life too has been centered in the work unit. Political campaigns have meant endless meetings and rallies within the unit, and when individuals were to be criticized or condemned for political deviation or bad class origins, it was done within the work unit, by fellow workers. In the post-Mao Zedong era, many people were working side by side with others whom they had publicly condemned, humiliated, or physically beaten fifteen or twenty years before. Much of the quality of life within a unit derives from the long-term nature of membership and human relations and from the impossibility of leaving. Members seem most often to aim for affable but somewhat distant ties of "comradeship" with each other, reserving intimate friendships for a few whom they have known since childhood or schooldays.

The work-unit system, with its lifetime membership—sometimes referred to as the "iron rice bowl" (see Glossary)—and lack of job mobility, is unique to contemporary China. It was developed during the 1950s and early 1960s with little discussion or publicity. Its origins are obscure; it most likely arose through the efforts of party cadres whose background was rural and whose experience was largely in the army and in the disciplined and all-embracing life of party branches.

The special characteristics of the Chinese work unit—such as its control over the work and lives of its members and its strict subordination to administrative superiors who control the resources necessary to its operation—make the unit an insular, closed entity. Units are subject to various administrative hierarchies; reports go up and orders come down. The Chinese Communist Party, as a nationwide body, links all units and, in theory, monopolizes channels of communication and command (see Chinese Communist Party, ch. 10). Vertical, command relations seem to work quite effectively, and the degree of local compliance with the orders of superior bodies is impressive. Conversely, horizontal relations with other units are often weak and tenuous, presenting a problem especially for the economy.

Wages and Benefits

Much of any worker's total compensation (wages, benefits, and official and unofficial perquisites) is determined by membership in a particular work unit. There is considerable variation in the benefits associated with different work units. Although the wage structure is quite egalitarian when compared with those of other countries, wages are only part of the picture (see Income Distribution, ch. 5). Many of the limited goods available in China cannot be bought for money (see Retail Sales, ch. 8). Rather, they are available only to certain favored work units. Housing is an obvious example. Many collective enterprises may have no housing at all or offer only rudimentary dormitories for young, unmarried workers.

High-level administrative cadres and military officers may earn three or four times more than ordinary workers; in addition, the government often grants them superior housing, the unlimited use of official automobiles and drivers, access to the best medical care in the country, opportunities for travel and vacations, and the right to purchase rare consumer goods either at elite shops or through special channels. Although China is a socialist state, it is not exactly a welfare state. Pensions, medical benefits, and survivors' benefits are provided through work units and come out of the unit's budget. The amount and nature of benefits may vary from unit to unit. The state, through local government bodies, does provide some minimal welfare benefits, but only to those with no unit benefits or family members able to support them.

Retirees who have put in twenty-five or thirty years in a state-run factory or a central government office can expect a steady pension, most often at about 70 percent of their salary, and often continue to live in unit housing, especially if they have no grown children with whom they can live. In many cases, workers have been able to retire and have their children replace them. In other cases, some large state enterprises have started smaller sideline or subcontracting enterprises specifically to provide employment for the grown children of their workers. In contrast, peasants and those employed in collective enterprises generally receive no pensions and must depend on family members for support.

Informal Mechanisms of Exchange

In China formal exchanges of everything from goods and services to information are expected to go through official channels, under the supervision of bureaucrats. Administrative channels, however, are widely acknowledged to be inadequate and subject to inordinate delays. People respond by using and developing informal mechanisms of exchange and coordination. The most general term for such informal relations is *guanxi* (personal connections). Such ties are the affair of individuals rather than

Construction workers near the Beijing International Airport
Courtesy Rinn-Sup Shinn
Factory workers pose for picture, Beijing
Courtesy Rinn-Sup Shinn

institutions and depend on the mutually beneficial exchange of favors, services, introductions, and so on. In China such ties are created or cultivated through invitations to meals and presentation of gifts.

Personal relations are morally and legally ambiguous, existing in a gray and ill-defined zone. In some cases, personal connections involve corruption and favoritism, as when powerful cadres "enter through the back door" to win admission to college or university for their children or to place their relatives or clients in secure, state-sector jobs. In other cases, though, the use of such contacts is absolutely necessary for the survival of enterprises. Most Chinese factories, for example, employ full-time "purchasing agents," whose task is to procure essential supplies that are not available through the cumbersome state allocation system. As the economic reforms of the early 1980s have expanded the scope of market exchanges and the ability of enterprises to make their own decisions on what to produce, the role of brokers and agents of all sorts has expanded. In the countryside, village and township cadres often act as brokers, finding markets for the commodities produced by specialized farming households and tracking down scarce inputs, such as fertilizer or fuel or spare parts for agricultural machinery.

Although the form and operation of *guanxi* networks clearly has traditional roots, as well as parallels in overseas Chinese (see Glossary) societies and in Hong Kong and Taiwan, they are not simply inheritances or holdovers from the traditional past. Personal connections and informal exchanges are a basic part of modern Chinese society, are essential to its regular functioning, and are in many ways a response to the specific political and economic structures of that society. They thrive in the absence of formal, public, and overt means of exchange and may be considered a response to scarcity and to blocked official channels of communication. In modern China, those with the most extensive networks of personal connections are cadres and party members, who have both the opportunity to meet people outside their work units and the power to do favors.

Rural Society

Collectivization and Class Status

The first major action to alter village society was the land reform of the late 1940s and early 1950s, in which the party sent work teams to every village to carry out its land reform policy. This in itself was an unprecedented display of administrative and political power. The land reform had several related goals. The work teams were to redistribute some (though not all) land from the wealthier families or land-owning trusts to the poorest segments of the population and so to effect a more equitable distribution of the basic means of production; to overthrow the village elites, who might be expected to oppose the party and its programs; to recruit new village leaders from among those who demonstrated the most commitment to the party's goals; and to teach everyone to think in terms of class status rather than kinship group or patron-client ties. In pursuit of the last goal, the party work teams convened extensive series of meetings, and they classified all the village families either as landlords, rich peasants, middle peasants, or poor peasants. These labels, based on family landholdings and overall economic position roughly between 1945 and 1950, became a permanent and hereditary part of every family's identity and, as late as 1980, still affected, for example, such things as chances for admission to the armed forces, colleges, universities, and local administrative posts and even marriage prospects.

The collectivization of agriculture was essentially completed with the establishment of the people's communes in 1958. Communes were large, embracing scores of villages. They were intended to be multipurpose organizations, combining economic and local administrative functions (see Agricultural Policies, ch. 6). Under the commune system the household remained the basic unit of consumption, and some differences in standards of living remained, although they were not as marked as they had been before land reform. Under such a system, however, upward mobility required becoming a team or commune cadre or obtaining a scarce technical position such as a truck driver's.

Decollectivization

Under the collectivized system, grain production kept up with population growth (China's population nearly doubled from 1950 to 1980), and the rural population was guaranteed a secure but low level of subsistence (see Population, ch. 2). But the collectivized system seemed to offer few possibilities for rapid economic growth. There was some discontent with a system that relied so heavily on orders from above and made so little allowance for local conditions or local initiative. In the late 1970s, administrators in provincial-level units with extensive regions of low yields and consequent low standards of living began experimenting with new forms of tenure and production. In most cases, these took the form of breaking up the collective production team (see Glossary), contracting with individual households to work assigned portions of collective land, and expanding the variety of crops or livestock that could be produced. The experiments were deemed successful and popular, and they soon spread to all districts. By the winter of 1982–83, the people's communes were abolished; they were replaced by administrative townships and a number of specialized teams or businesses that often leased such collective assets as tractors and provided services for money.

The agricultural reforms of the early 1980s led to a confusingly large number of new production arrangements and contracts. Underlying the variability of administrative and contractual forms were several basic principles and trends. In the first place, land, the fundamental means of production, remained collective property. It was leased, allocated, or contracted to individual households, but the households did not own the land and could not transfer it to other households. The household became, in most cases, the basic economic unit and was responsible for its own production and losses. Most economic activity was arranged through contracts, which typically secured promises to provide a certain amount of a commodity or sum of money to the township government in return for the use of land, or workshops, or tractors.

The goal of the contracting system was to increase efficiency in the use of resources and to tap peasant initiative. The rigid requirement that all villages produce grain was replaced by recognition of the advantages of specialization and exchange, as well as a much greater role for markets. Some "specialized households" devoted themselves entirely to production of cash crops or provision of services and reaped large rewards. The overall picture was one of increasing specialization, differentiation, and exchange in the rural economy and in society in general. Rural incomes increased rapidly, in part because the state substantially increased the prices it paid for staple crops and in part because of economic growth stimulated by the expansion of markets and the rediscovery of comparative advantage.

The Role of the Household

Decollectivization increased the options available to individual households and made household heads increasingly responsible for the economic success of their households. In 1987, for example, it was legally possible to leave the village and move into a nearby town to work in a small factory, open a noodle stand, or set up a machine repair business. Farmers, however, still could not legally move into medium-sized or large cities. The Chinese press reported an increased appreciation in the countryside for education and an increased desire for agriculturally oriented newspapers and journals, as well as clearly written manuals on such profitable trades as rabbit-raising and beekeeping. As specialization and division of labor increased, along with increasingly visible differences in income and living standards, it became more difficult to encompass most of the rural population in a few large categories. During the early 1980s, the pace of economic and social change in rural China was rapid, and the people caught up in the change had difficulty making sense of the process.

Consequences of Rural Reform

The state retained both its powers and its role in the rural economy in the 1980s. Decollectivization, like the collectivization of the 1950s, was directed from the top down. Sometimes, apparently, it was imposed on communities that had been content with their collective methods. But in permitting households and communities greater leeway to decide what to produce and in allowing the growth of rural markets and small-scale industries, the state stepped back from the close supervision and mandatory quotas of the 1960s and 1970s.

Decollectivization obviated the supervisory functions of low-level cadres, who no longer needed to oversee work on the collective fields. Some cadres became full-time administrators in township offices, and others took advantage of the reforms by establishing specialized production households or by leasing collective property at favorable rates. Former cadres, with their networks of connections and familiarity with administrative procedures, were in a better position than ordinary farmers to take advantage of the opportunities offered by the growth of markets and commercial activity. Even those cadres not wholly devoted to increasing their own families' income found that to serve their fellow villagers as expected it was necessary to act as entrepreneurs. Village-level cadres in the mid-1980s were functioning less as overseers and more as extension agents and marketing consultants (see Post-Mao Policies, ch. 6).

By 1987 rural society was more open and diverse than in the 1960s and 1970s, and the rigid collective units of that period, which had reflected the state's overwhelming concern for security, had been replaced by networks and clusters of smaller units. The new, looser structure demonstrated the priority placed on efficiency and economic growth. Basic security, in the sense of an adequate supply of food and guarantees of support for the disabled, orphaned, or aged, was taken for granted. Less than half of China's population remembered the insecurity and risks of pre-1950 society, but the costs and inefficiencies of the collective system were fresh in their minds. Increased specialization and division of labor were trends not likely to be reversed. In the rural areas the significance of the work unit appeared to have diminished, although people still lived in villages, and the actions of low-level administrative cadres still affected ordinary farmers or petty traders in immediate ways.

The state and its officials still dominated the economy, controlled supplies of essential goods, taxed and regulated businesses and markets, and awarded contracts. The stratification system of the Maoist period had been based on a hierarchy of functionally unspecialized cadres directing the labors of a fairly uniform mass of peasants. It was replaced in the 1980s by a new elite of economically specialized households and entrepreneurs who had managed to come to terms with the administrative cadres who controlled access to many of the resources necessary for economic success. Local cadres still had the power to impose fees, taxes, and all manner of exactions. The norms of the new system were not clear, and the economic and social system continued to change in response to the rapid growth of rural commerce and industry and to national economic policies and reforms.

Regulations and Favors

Increased commercial activity produced a high degree of normative ambiguity, especially in areas like central Guangdong and Jiangsu provinces, where rural economic growth was fastest. Neither the proper role of local officials nor the rights and obligations of new entrepreneurs or traders were clear. The line between the normal use of personal contacts and hospitality and extraordinary and criminal favoritism and corruption was ambiguous. There were hints of the development of a system of patron-client ties, in which administrative cadres granted favors to ordinary farmers in return for support, esteem, and an occasional gift. The increased number of corruption cases reported in the Chinese press and the widespread assumption that the decollectivization and rural economic reforms had led to growing corruption probably reflected both the increased opportunities for deals and favors of all sorts and the ambiguous nature of many of the transactions and relationships. The party's repeated calls for improved "socialist spiritual civilization" and the attempts of the central authorities both to create a system of civil law and to foster respect for it can be interpreted as responses to the problem (see The First Wave of Reform, 1979–84, ch. 11; Return to Socialist Legality, ch. 13). On the local level, where cadres and entrepreneurs were engaged in constant negotiation on the rules of their game, the problem was presumably being addressed in a more straightforward fashion.

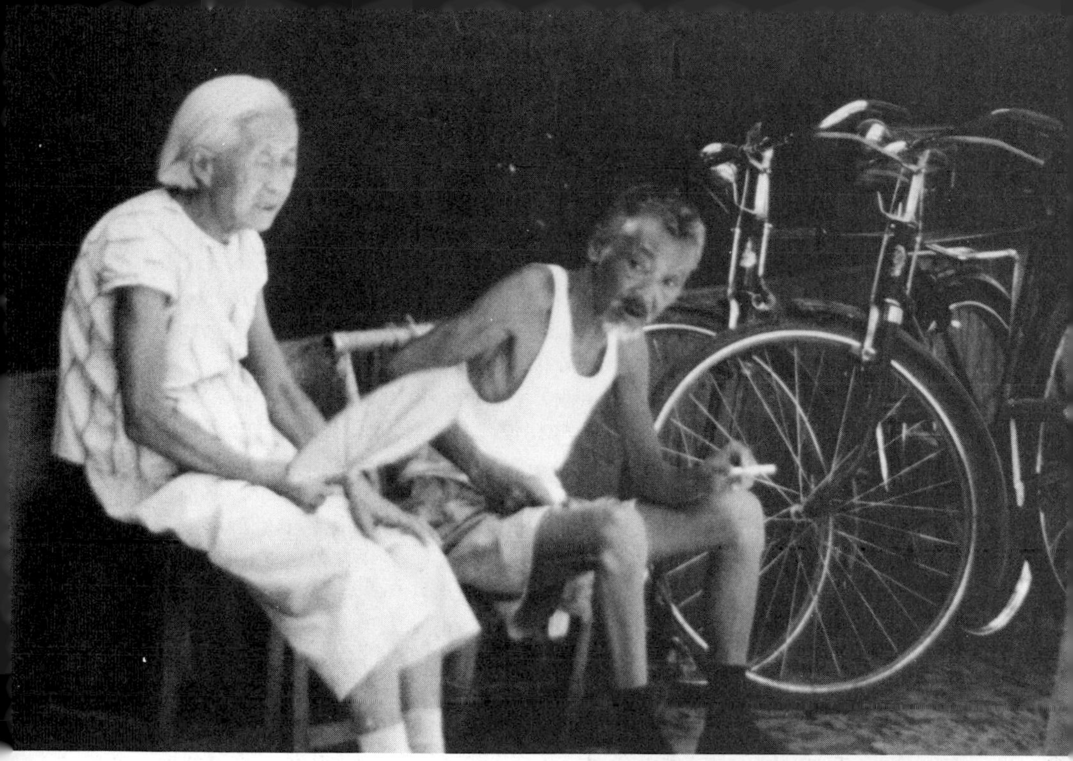

Grandparents
near Tiananmen Square
Courtesy Stephanie Marcus

An elderly attendant
surveys his kingdom,
Forbidden City, Beijing.
Courtesy Stephanie Marcus

Family and Household

In past Chinese society, the family provided every individual's support, livelihood, and long-term security. Today the state guarantees such security to those with no families to provide for them, and families and work units share long-term responsibility for the individual. The role of families has changed, but they remain important, especially in the countryside. Family members are bound, in law and custom, to support their aged or disabled members. The state, acting through work units, provides support and benefits only when families cannot. Households routinely pool income, and any individual's standard of living depends on the number of household wage earners and the number of dependents. In both cities and villages, the highest incomes usually are earned by households with several wage earners, such as unmarried adult sons or daughters.

In late traditional society, family size and structural complexity varied directly with class. Rural landlords and government officials had the largest families, poor peasants the smallest. The poorest segment of the population, landless laborers, could not afford to marry and start families. The need to provide for old age and the general association between the numbers of sons surviving to adulthood and long-term family success motivated individuals to create various nonstandard family forms. Couples who produced no sons, or no children at all, adopted or purchased infants outright. Families with daughters but no sons tried to find men willing to marry their daughters and move into their families, abandoning their original families and sometimes even their original surnames. Families with daughters but no property to attract a son-in-law were sometimes forced to sell their daughters as concubines or prostitutes. The variation in family size and complexity was the result of variation in class position and of the dual role of the household as both family and economic enterprise.

In contemporary society, rural families no longer own land or pass it down to the next generation. They may, however, own and transmit houses. Rural families pay medical expenses and school fees for their children. Under the people's commune system in force from 1958 to 1982, the income of a peasant family depended directly on the number of laborers it contributed to the collective fields. This, combined with concern over the level of support for the aged or disabled provided by the collective unit, encouraged peasants to have many sons. Under the agricultural reforms that began in the late 1970s, households took on an increased and more responsible economic role. The labor of family members is still the primary determinant of income. But rural economic growth and commercialization increasingly have rewarded managerial and technical skills and have made unskilled farm labor less desirable. As long as this economic trend continues in the countryside in the late 1980s, peasant families are likely to opt for fewer but better educated children.

The consequence of the general changes in China's economy and the greater separation of families and economic enterprises has been a greater standardization of family forms since 1950. In 1987 most families approximated the middle peasant (a peasant owning some land) norm of the past. Such a family consisted of five or six people and was based on marriage between an adult son and an adult woman who moved into her husband's family. The variant family forms—either the very large and complex or those based on minor, nonstandard forms of marriage—were much less common. The state had outlawed concubinage, child betrothal, and the sale of infants or females, all of which were formerly practiced, though not common. Increased life expectancy meant that a greater proportion of infants survived to adulthood and that more adults lived into their sixties or seventies. More rural families were able to achieve the traditional goal of a three-generation family in the 1980s. There were fewer orphans and young or middle-aged widows or widowers. Far fewer men were forced to retain lifelong single status. Divorce, although possible, was rare, and families were stable, on-going units.

A number of traditional attitudes toward the family have survived without being questioned. It is taken for granted that everyone should marry, and marriage remains part of the definition of normal adult status. Marriage is expected to be permanent. That marriage requires a woman to move into her husband's family and to become a daughter-in-law as well as a wife is still largely accepted. The norm of patrilineal descent and the assumption that it is sons who bear the primary responsibility for their aged parents remain. The party and government have devoted great effort to controlling the number of births and have attempted to limit the number of children per couple (see Population Control Programs, ch. 2). But the authorities have not attempted to control population growth by suggesting that some people should not marry at all.

In the past, kinship principles were extended beyond the domestic group and were used to form large-scale groups, such as lineages. Lineages were quite distinct from families; they were essentially corporate economic-political groups. They controlled land and, in some areas of China, dominated whole villages and sets of villages and held title to most of the farmland. Like most other late traditional associations, lineages were dominated by wealthy and educated elites. Ordinary peasants paid as much of their crop to their lineage group as they might have to a landlord. The Communists denounced these organizations as feudal systems by means of which landlords exploited others. The lineages were suppressed in the early 1950s and their land confiscated and redistributed in the land reform. Communal worship of distant lineage ancestors lost much of its justification with the dissolution of the lineage estate and was easily suppressed over the next several years. Domestic ancestor worship, in which members of a single family worshiped and memorialized their immediate ancestors, continued at least until 1966 and 1967, in the early stages of the Cultural Revolution, when Red Guards destroyed altars and ancestral tablets. In 1987 the party was still condemning ancestor worship as superstitious but had made little effort to end it.

Marriage

The Marriage Law of 1950 guaranteed everyone the freedom to choose his or her marriage partner. Nevertheless, especially in the countryside, there are few opportunities to meet potential mates. Rural China offers little privacy for courtship, and in villages there is little public tolerance for flirting or even extended conversation between unmarried men and women. Introductions and go-betweens continue to play a major role in the arrangement of marriages. In most cases each of the young people, and their parents, has an effective veto over any proposed match.

In the past, marriage was seen as the concern of families as well as of the two parties to the match. Families united by marriage were expected to be of equivalent status, or the groom's family to be of somewhat higher status. This aspect of marriage patterns has continued while the definitions of status have changed. Because inherited wealth has been eliminated as a significant factor, evaluation has shifted to estimates of earning power and future prosperity. The most desirable husbands have been administrative cadres, party members, and employees of large state enterprises. Conversely, men from poor villages have had difficulty finding wives. From the early 1950s to the late 1970s, when hereditary class labels were very significant, anyone with a ''counterrevolutionary'' background, that is, anyone previously identified with the landlord or even rich peasant class, was a bad prospect for marriage. Such pariahs often had no choice but to marry the offspring of other families with ''bad'' class backgrounds. At the other end of the social scale, there appears to be a high level of intermarriage among the children of high-level cadres.

Community Structure

Most rural Chinese live in one of some 900,000 villages, which have an average population of from 1,000 to 2,000 people. Villages have never been self-contained, self-sufficient units, and the social world of Chinese peasants has extended beyond their home villages. Almost all new wives come into a village from other settlements, and daughters marry out. All villagers have close kinship ties with families in other villages, and marriage go-betweens shuttle from village to village.

Before 1950 clusters of villages centered on small market towns that linked them to the wider economy and society. Most peasants were only a few hours' walk or less from a market town, which provided not only opportunities to buy and sell but also opportunities for entertainment, information, social life, and a host of specialized services. The villages around a market formed a social unit that, although less immediately visible than the villages, was equally significant.

From the early 1950s on, China's revolutionary government made great efforts to put the state and its ideology into direct contact with the villages and to sweep aside the intermediaries and brokers who had traditionally interpreted central policies and national values for villagers. The state and the party were generally successful, establishing unprecedented degrees of political and ideological integration of villages into the state and of village-level awareness of state policies and political goals.

The unintended consequence of the economic and political policies of the 1950s and 1960s was to increase the closed, corporate quality of China's villages and to narrow the social horizons of villagers. Land reform and the reorganization of villages as subunits of people's communes meant that villages became collective landholding units and had clear boundaries between their lands and those of adjacent villages. Central direction of labor on collective fields made the former practices of swapping labor between villages impossible. The household registration and rationing systems confined villagers to their home settlements and made it impossible for them to seek their fortune elsewhere. Cooperation with fellow villagers and good relations with village leaders became even more important than they had been in the past. The suppression of rural markets, which accompanied the drive for self-sufficiency in grain production and other economic activities, had severe social as well as economic consequences. Most peasants had neither reason nor opportunity for regular trips to town, and their opportunities for exchange and cooperation with residents of other villages were diminished. Villages became work units, with all that that implied.

Decollectivization in the early 1980s resulted in the revival of rural marketing, and a limited relaxation of controls on outmigration opened villages and diminished the social boundaries around them. The social world of peasants expanded, and the larger marketing community took on more significance as that of the village proper was diminished. Village membership, once the single most important determinant of an individual's circumstances, became only one of a number of significant factors, which also included occupation, personal connections, and managerial talent.

Urban Society

There is considerable confusion in both Chinese and foreign sources over definitions of urban places and hence considerable variation in estimates of China's urban population (see Migration, ch. 2). The problem of determining the size of the urban population reflects inconsistent and changing administrative categories; the distinction between rural and urban household registry and between categories of settlements; the practice of placing suburban or rural districts under the administration of municipal governments; and the differences in the status accorded to small towns. In sociological terms, *urban* refers to an area characterized by a relatively high degree of specialization in occupational roles, many special-purpose institutions, and uniform treatment of people in impersonal settings. In this sense, a Chinese market town is more urban than a village, and settlements become more urban as they grow in size and economic complexity. Large municipalities like Beijing and Shanghai have the highest degree of division of labor and the most specialized institutions.

Distinctive Features

Legal status as an urban dweller in China is prized (see Differentiation, this ch.). As a result of various state policies and practices, contemporary Chinese urban society has a distinctive character, and life in Chinese cities differs in many ways from that in cities in otherwise comparable developing societies. The most consequential policies have been the household registration system, the legal barriers to migration, the fostering of the all-embracing work unit, and the restriction of commerce and markets, including the housing market. In many ways, the weight of official control and supervision is felt more in the cities, whose administrators are concerned with controlling the population and do so through a dual administrative hierarchy. The two principles on which these control structures are based are locality and occupation. Household registers are maintained by the police, whose presence is much stronger in the cities than in the countryside (see Public Security Forces, ch. 13). Cities are subdivided into districts, wards, and finally into small units of some fifteen to thirty households, such as all those in one apartment building or on a small lane. For those employed in large organizations, the work unit either is coterminous with the residential unit or takes precedence over it; for those employed in small collective enterprises or neighborhood shops, the residential committee is their unit of registration and provides a range of services.

The control of housing by work units and local governments and the absence of a housing market have led to a high degree of residential stability (see The Work Place, this ch.). Most urban residents have spent decades in the same house or apartment. For this reason, urban neighborhoods are closely knit, which in turn contributes to the generally low level of crime in Chinese cities.

Since the early 1950s, the party leadership has consistently made rapid industrialization a primary goal and, to this end, has generally favored investment in heavy industry over consumption. For cities, these policies have meant an expansion of factories and industrial employment, along with a very low level of spending in such "nonproductive" areas as housing or urban transit systems (see Economic Policies, 1949–80, ch. 5). The emphasis on production and heavy industry and the discouragement of consumption and exchange, along with state takeovers of commerce and the service sector, led to cities having many factories but no peddlers, snack stalls, or entertainment districts. In the 1950s and early 1960s, major efforts were made to bring women into the paid labor force. This served the goals of increasing production and achieving sexual equality through equal participation in productive labor, a classic Marxist remedy for sexual inequality. By 1987 almost all young and middle-aged women in the cities worked outside the home.

Chinese cities, in contrast to those in many developing countries, contain a high proportion of workers in factories and offices and a low proportion of workers in the service sector. Workers enjoy a high level of job security but receive low wages. Between 1963 and 1977 most wages were frozen, and promotions and raises were very rare. Even with the restoration of material incentives in the late 1970s, two general wage raises in the 1980s, and increased opportunities for bonuses and promotions, wages remained low and increased primarily with seniority. As in most parts of the world, one reason that so many Chinese urban women are in the work force is that one income is not enough to support a family.

In the 1980s it was possible to purchase such consumer durables as television sets and bicycles on the market, but housing remained scarce and subject to allocation by work units or municipal housing bureaus. Although housing was poor and crowded, Chinese neighborhoods had improved greatly over the slum conditions that existed before 1950. Most people were gainfully employed at secure if low-paying jobs; the municipal government provided a minimal level of services and utilities (water and sanitation); the streets were fairly clean and orderly; and the crime rate was low (see Wages and Benefits, this ch.; Living Standards, ch. 5).

Housing

Chinese urban dwellers, as a category, receive subsidies on food, housing, and transportation services. In the 1980s such subsidies came to occupy an increasingly large share of the state budget. Even with subsidies, food purchases took the largest share of household budgets. Rents, in contrast, were very low, seldom taking more than 5 percent of household income even with water and electricity charges included. Little new housing was built between 1950 and 1980, and although more urban housing was erected between 1980 and 1985 than in the previous thirty years, housing remained in short supply. Entire families often lived in one room and shared cooking and toilet facilities with other families. Marriages were sometimes delayed until housing became available from the municipal office or the work unit. Young people were expected to live with their parents at least until marriage. This was consonant with traditional family patterns but was also reinforced by the shortage of housing. The pattern of long-term residential stability and great pressure on the stock of available housing meant that city neighborhoods were less stratified by occupation or income than those of many other countries. Not only were incomes more egalitarian to begin with, but more money could not buy a bigger or better equipped apartment. Managers and technical specialists lived under much the same conditions as manual workers, often in the same buildings. While many urban families enjoyed higher real incomes in the 1980s, they usually could not translate those incomes into better housing, as peasants could.

The combination of full adult employment with a minimal service sector put heavy burdens on urban households. By the 1980s both the public and the government recognized the burdens on urban households and the associated drain on the energies of workers, managers, and professionals. After 1985 more money was budgeted for housing and such municipal services as piped-in cooking gas. But state encouragement of the private or collective service sector

Workers' mid-rise housing, Beijing
Courtesy Robert L. Worden

Entrance to a private residence in north China
Courtesy Rinn-Sup Shinn

had greater effect. Unemployed urban youth were permitted and sometimes advised to set up small restaurants or service establishments. Peasants were permitted to come into cities to sell produce or local products. Municipal authorities seemed to ignore the movement of substantial numbers of rural people into the urban service sector as peddlers, carpenters, and other skilled workers or, occasionally, as domestic workers. In the mid-1980s the Chinese press reported an influx of teenage girls from the country seeking short-term work as housekeepers or nannies. Like other rural migrants, they usually used ties with relatives or fellow villagers resident in the city to find positions.

Families and Marriage

Urban families differ from their rural counterparts primarily in being composed largely of wage earners who look to their work units for the housing, old-age security, and opportunities for a better life that in the countryside are still the responsibility of the family. With the exception of those employed in the recently revived urban service sector (restaurants, tailoring, or repair shops) who sometimes operate family businesses, urban families do not combine family and enterprise in the manner of peasant families. Urban families usually have multiple wage earners, but children do not bring in extra income or wages as readily as in the countryside. Urban families are generally smaller than their rural counterparts, and, in a reversal of traditional patterns, it is the highest level managers and cadres who have the smallest families. Late marriages and one or two children are characteristic of urban managerial and professional groups. As in the past, elite family forms are being promoted as the model for everyone.

Three-generation families are not uncommon in cities, and a healthy grandparent is probably the ideal solution to the child-care and housework problems of most families. About as many young children are cared for by a grandparent as are enrolled in a work-unit nursery or kindergarten, institutions that are far from universal. Decisions on where a newly married couple is to live often depend on the availability of housing. Couples most often establish their own household, frequently move in with the husband's parents, or, much less often, may move in with the wife's parents. Both the state and the society expect children to look after their aged parents. In addition, a retired worker from a state enterprise will have a pension and often a relatively desirable apartment as well. Under these circumstances elderly people are assets to a family. Those urban families employing unregistered maids from the countryside are most likely those without healthy grandparents.

Families play less of a role in marriage choices in cities than in the countryside, at least in part because the family itself is not the unit promising long-term security and benefits to its members. By the late 1970s, perhaps half of all urban marriages were the result of introductions by workmates, relatives, or parents. The marriage age in cities has been later than that in the countryside, which reflects greater compliance with state rules and guidelines as well as social and economic factors common to many other countries. People in cities and those with secondary and postsecondary education or professional jobs tend to marry later than farmers. In China it is felt that marriage is appropriate only for those who have jobs and thus are in a position to be full members of society. Peasant youth, who have an automatic claim on a share of the collective fields and the family house, qualify, but college students or urban youths who are "waiting for assignment" to a lifetime job do not. In any case, work-unit approval is necessary for marriage.

Urban weddings are usually smaller and more subdued than their rural counterparts, which reflects the diminished role of the families in the process. More guests will be workmates or friends of the bride and groom than distant kin or associates of the parents. The wedding ceremony focuses on the bride and groom as a couple rather than on their status as members of families. Similarly, a brief honeymoon trip rather than a three-day celebration in which the entire village plays a part is an increasingly common practice. Long engagements are common in cities, sometimes because the couple is waiting for housing to become available.

Providing for the Next Generation

Although Chinese families continue to be marked by respect for parents and a substantial degree of filial subordination, parents have weighty obligations toward their children as well. Children are obliged to support parents in their old age, and parents are obliged to give their children as favorable a place in the world as they can. In the past this meant leaving them property and providing the best education or training possible. For most rural parents today the choice of a career for their children is not a major issue. Most children of peasants will be peasants like their parents, and the highest realistic ambition is a position as a low-level cadre or teacher or perhaps a technician. The primary determinant of a rural child's status and well-being remains his or her family, which is one reason for the intense concern with the marriage choices of sons and daughters and for the greater degree of parental involvement in those decisions.

Urban parents are less concerned with whom their children marry but are more concerned with their education and eventual careers. Urban parents can expect to leave their children very little in the way of property, but they do their best to prepare them for secure and desirable jobs in the state sector. The difficulty is that such jobs are limited, competition is intense, and the criteria for entry have changed radically several times since the early 1950s. Many of the dynamics of urban society revolve around the issue of job allocation and the attempts of parents in the better-off segments of society to transmit their favored position to their children. The allocation of scarce and desirable goods, in this case jobs, is a political issue and one that has been endemic since the late 1950s. These questions lie behind the changes in educational policy, the attempts in the 1960s and 1970s to settle urban youth in the countryside, the upheaval of the Cultural Revolution, and the post-1980 encouragement of small-scale private and collective commerce and service occupations in the cities. All are attempts to solve the problem, and each attempt has its own costs and drawbacks.

Opportunities and Competition

Cities, by definition, are places with a high degree of occupational specialization and division of labor. They are places offering their inhabitants a range of occupational choice and also, to the degree that some occupations are seen as better than others, competition for the better occupations. Cities also provide the training for specialized occupations, either in schools or on the job.

In China there is a cultural pattern stressing individual achievement and upward mobility. These are best attained through formal education and are bound up with the mutual expectations and obligations of parents and children. There is also a social structure in which a single, bureaucratic framework defines desirable positions, that is, managerial or professional jobs in the state sector or secure jobs in state factories. Banned migration, lifetime employment, egalitarian wage structures, and the insular nature of work units were intended by the state, at least in part, to curtail individual competition. Nevertheless, some jobs are still seen as preferable to others, and it is urbanites and their children who have the greatest opportunities to compete for scarce jobs. The question for most families is how individuals are selected and allocated to those positions. The lifetime tenure of most jobs and the firm control of job allocation by the party make these central issues for parents in the favored groups and for local authorities and party organizations.

Between the early 1950s and mid-1980s, policies on recruitment of personnel and their allocation to desirable jobs changed several times. As the costs and drawbacks of each method became apparent, pressure mounted to change the policy. In the early and mid-1950s, the problem was not acute. State offices were expanding rapidly, and there were more positions than people qualified to fill them. Peasants moved into cities and found employment in the expanding industrial sector. Most of those who staffed the new bureaucratic sectors were young and would not begin to retire until the 1980s and 1990s. Those who graduated from secondary schools or universities, however, or were discharged from the armed forces in the late 1950s and early 1960s found few jobs of the sort they were qualified for or had expected to hold.

Attempts to manage the competition for secure jobs were among the many causes of the radical, utopian policies of the period from 1962 to 1976. Among these, the administrative barriers erected between cities and countryside and the confinement of peasants and their children to their villages served to diminish competition and perhaps to lower unrealistic expectations. Wage freezes and the rationing of both staples and scarce consumer goods in cities attempted to diminish stratification and hence competition. The focusing of attention on the sufferings and egalitarian communal traditions of the past, which was so prominent in Maoist rhetoric and replaced the future orientation of the 1950s, in part diverted attention from frustrations with the present. Tensions were most acute within the education system, which served, as it does in most societies, to sort children and select those who would go on to managerial and professional jobs. It was for this reason that the Cultural Revolution focused so negatively on the education system. Because of the rising competition in the schools and for the jobs to which schooling could lead, it became increasingly evident that those who did best in school were the children of the "bourgeoisie" and urban professional groups rather than the children of workers and peasants (see Education Policy, ch. 4).

Cultural Revolution-era policies responded with public deprecation of schooling and expertise, including closing of all schools for a year or more and of universities for nearly a decade, exaltation of on-the-job training and of political motivation over expertise, and preferential treatment for workers and peasant youth. Educated urban youth, most of whom came from "bourgeois" families, were persuaded or coerced to settle in the countryside, often in remote frontier districts. Because there were no jobs in the cities, the party expected urban youth to apply their education in the countryside as primary school teachers, production team accountants, or barefoot doctors (see Glossary); many did manual labor. The policy was intensely unpopular, not only with urban parents and youth but also with peasants and was dropped soon after the fall of the Gang of Four (see Glossary) in late 1976. During the late 1970s and early 1980s, many of the youth who had been sent down to the countryside managed to make their way back to the cities, where they had neither jobs nor ration books. By the mid-1980s most of them had found jobs in the newly expanded service sector (see Internal Trade and Distribution, ch. 8).

In terms of creating jobs and mollifying urban parents, the 1980s policies on urban employment have been quite successful. The jobs in many cases are not the sort that educated young people or their parents would choose, but they are considerably better than a lifelong assignment to remote frontier areas.

The Maoist policies on education and job assignment were successful in preventing a great many urban "bourgeois" parents from passing their favored social status on to their children. This reform, however, came at great cost to the economy and to the prestige and authority of the party itself.

Examinations, Hereditary Transmission of Jobs, and Connections

Beginning in the late 1970s, China's leaders stressed expertise and education over motivation and ideology and consequently placed emphasis again on examinations. Competition in the schools was explicit, and examinations were frequent. A major step in the competition for desirable jobs was the passage from senior middle school to college and university, and success was determined by performance on a nationwide college and university entrance examination (see Education Policy, ch. 4). Examinations also were used to select applicants for jobs in factories, and even factory managers had to pass examinations to keep their positions. The content of these examinations has not been made public, but their use represents a logical response to the problem of unfair competition, favoritism, and corruption.

One extreme form of selection by favoritism in the 1980s was simple hereditary transmission, and this principle, which operated on a de facto basis in rural work units, seems to have been fairly widely used in China's industrial sector. From the 1960s to the 1980s, factories and mines in many cases permitted children to replace their parents in jobs, which simplified recruitment and was an effective way of encouraging aging workers to retire. The government forbade this practice in the 1980s, but in some instances state-run factories and mines, especially those located in rural or remote areas, used their resources to set up subsidiaries or sideline enterprises to provide employment for their workers' children. The leaders of these work units evidently felt responsible for providing employment to the children of unit members.

The party and its role in personnel matters, including job assignments, can be an obstacle to the consistent application of hiring standards. At the grass-roots level, the party branch's control of job assignments and promotions is one of the foundations of its power, and some local party cadres in the mid-1980s apparently viewed the expanded use of examinations and educational qualifications as a threat to their power. The party, acting through local employment commissions, controlled all job assignments. Party members occupied the most powerful and desirable positions; the way party members were evaluated and selected for positions remained obscure. Local party cadres were frequently suspected by the authorities of using their connections to secure jobs for their relatives or clients (see Informal Mechanisms of Exchange, this ch.).

Women

Traditional Chinese society was male-centered. Sons were preferred to daughters, and women were expected to be subordinate to fathers, husbands, and sons. A young woman had little voice in the decision on her marriage partner (neither did a young man). When married, it was she who left her natal family and community and went to live in a family and community of strangers where she was subordinate to her mother-in-law. Far fewer women were educated than men, and sketchy but consistent demographic evidence would seem to show that female infants and children had higher death rates and less chance of surviving to adulthood than males. In extreme cases, female infants were the victims of infanticide, and daughters were sold, as chattels, to brothels or to wealthy families. Bound feet, which were customary even for peasant women, symbolized the painful constraints of the female role.

Protests and concerted efforts to alter women's place in society began in China's coastal cities in the early years of the twentieth century. By the 1920s formal acceptance of female equality was common among urban intellectuals. Increasing numbers of girls attended schools, and young secondary school and college students approved of marriages based on free choice. Footbinding declined rapidly in the second decade of the century, the object of a nationwide campaign led by intellectuals who associated it with national backwardness.

Nevertheless, while party leaders condemned the oppression and subordination of women as one more aspect of the traditional society they were intent on changing, they did not accord feminist issues very high priority. In the villages, party members were interested in winning the loyalty and cooperation of poor and lower-middle-class male peasants, who could be expected to resist public criticism of their treatment of their wives and daughters. Many party members were poor and lower-middle-class peasants from the interior, and their attitudes toward women reflected their background. The party saw the liberation of women as depending, in a standard Marxist way, on their participation in the labor force outside the household.

The position of women in contemporary society has changed from the past, and public verbal assent to propositions about the equality of the sexes and of sons and daughters seems universal. Women attend schools and universities, serve in the People's Liberation Army, and join the party. Almost all urban women and the majority of rural women work outside the home. But women remain disadvantaged in many ways, economic and social, and there seems no prospect for substantive change.

The greatest change in women's status has been their movement into the paid labor force. The jobs they held in the 1980s, though, were generally lower paying and less desirable than those of men. Industries staffed largely by women, such as the textiles industry, paid lower wages than those staffed by men, such as the steel or mining industries. Women were disproportionately represented in collective enterprises, which paid lower wages and offered fewer benefits than state-owned industries. In the countryside, the work of males was consistently better rewarded than that of women, and most skilled and desirable jobs, such as driving trucks or repairing machines, were held by men. In addition, Chinese women suffered the familiar double burden of full-time wage work and most of the household chores as well.

As there come to be both more opportunities and more explicit competition for them in both city and countryside, there are some hints of women's being excluded from the competition. In the countryside, a disproportionate number of girls drop out of primary school because parents do not see the point of educating a daughter who will marry and leave the family and because they need her labor in the home. There are fewer female students in key rural and urban secondary schools and universities. As economic growth in rural areas generates new and potentially lucrative jobs, there is a tendency in at least some areas for women to be relegated to agricultural labor, which is poorly rewarded. There have been reports in the Chinese press of outright discrimination against women in hiring for urban jobs and of enterprises requiring female applicants to score higher than males on examinations for hiring.

On the whole, in the 1980s women were better off than their counterparts 50 or a 100 years before, and they had full legal equality with men. In practice, their opportunities and rewards were not entirely equal, and they tended to get less desirable jobs and to retain the burden of domestic chores in addition to full-time jobs.

Religion

Traditionally, China's Confucian elite disparaged religion and religious practitioners, and the state suppressed or controlled organized religious groups. The social status of Buddhist monks and Taoist priests was low, and ordinary people did not generally look up to them as models. In the past, religion was diffused throughout the society, a matter as much of practice as of belief, and had a weak institutional structure. Essentially the same pattern continues in contemporary society, except that the ruling elite is even less religious and there are even fewer religious practitioners.

The attitude of the party has been that religion is a relic of the past, evidence of prescientific thinking, and something that will fade away as people become educated and acquire a scientific view of the world. On the whole, religion has not been a major issue. Cadres and party members, in ways very similar to those of Confucian elites, tend to regard many religious practitioners as charlatans out to take advantage of credulous people, who need protection. In the 1950s many Buddhist monks were returned to secular life, and monasteries and temples lost their lands in the land reform. Foreign missionaries were expelled, often after being accused of spying, and Chinese Christians, who made up only a very small proportion of the population, were the objects of suspicion because of their foreign contacts. Chinese Christian organizations were established, one for Protestants and one for Roman Catholics, which stressed that their members were loyal to the state and party. Seminaries were established to train "patriotic" Chinese clergy, and the Chinese Catholic Church rejected the authority of the Vatican, ordaining its own priests and installing its own bishops. The issue in all cases, whether involving Christians, Buddhists, or members of underground Chinese sects, was not so much doctrine or theology as recognition of the primacy of loyalty to the state and party. Folk religion was dismissed as superstition. Temples were for the most part converted to other uses, and public celebration of communal festivals stopped, but the state did not put much energy into suppressing folk religion.

During the early stages of the Cultural Revolution, in 1966 and 1967, Red Guards destroyed temples, statues, and domestic ancestral tablets as part of their violent assault on the "four olds" (old ideas, culture, customs, and habits). Public observances of ritual essentially halted during the Cultural Revolution decade. After 1978, the year marking the return to power of the Deng Xiaoping reformers, the party and state were more tolerant of the public expression of religion as long as it remained within carefully defined limits (see Political Realignments at the Party Center, ch. 11). Some showcase temples were restored and opened as historical sites, and some Buddhist and even Taoist practitioners were permitted to wear their robes, train a few successors, and perform rituals in the reopened temples. These actions on the part of the state can be interpreted as a confident regime's recognition of China's traditional past, in the same way that the shrine at the home of Confucius in Shandong Province has been refurbished and opened to the public. Confucian and Buddhist doctrines are not seen as a threat, and the motive is primarily one of nationalistic identification with China's past civilization.

Similar tolerance and even mild encouragement is accorded to Chinese Christians, whose churches were reopened starting in the late 1970s. As of 1987 missionaries were not permitted in China, and some Chinese Catholic clergy were imprisoned for refusing to recognize the authority of China's "patriotic" Catholic Church and its bishops.

The most important result of state toleration of religion has been improved relations with China's Islamic and Tibetan Buddhist minority populations. State patronage of Islam and Buddhism also plays a part in China's foreign relations (see Relations with the Third World, ch. 12). Much of traditional ritual and religion survives or has been revived, especially in the countryside. In the mid-1980s the official press condemned such activities as wasteful and reminded rural party members that they should neither participate in nor lead such events, but it did not make the subject a major issue. Families could worship their ancestors or traditional gods in the privacy of their homes but had to make all ritual paraphernalia (incense sticks, ancestral tablets, and so forth) themselves, as it was no longer sold in shops. The scale of public celebrations was muted, and full-time professional clergy played no role. Folk religious festivals were revived in some localities, and there was occasional rebuilding of temples and ancestral halls. In rural areas, funerals were the ritual having the least change, although observances were carried out only by family members and kin, with no professional clergy in attendance. Such modest, mostly household-based folk religious activity was largely irrelevant to the concerns of the authorities, who ignored or tolerated it.

Trends and Tensions

By the mid-1980s the pace of social change in China was increasing, and, more than in any decade since the 1950s, fundamental changes in the structure of society seemed possible. The ultimate direction of social changes remained unclear, but social trends and tensions that could generate social change were evident. These trends were toward greater specialization and division of labor and toward new, more open and loosely structured forms of association (see Rural Society; Urban Society, this ch.). The uniform pattern of organization of work units in agriculture, industry, public administration, and the military was beginning to shift to an organization structured to reflect its purpose. Education and technical qualification were becoming more significant for attaining high status in villages, industries, the government, or the armed forces. Opportunities for desirable jobs remained limited, however, and competition for those jobs or for housing, urban residence, or college admission was keen.

The primary tension in Chinese society resulted from the value political leaders and ordinary citizens placed on both the social values of security and equality and the goals of economic growth and modernization. China remained a society in which all desired goods were in short supply, from arable land to secure nonmanual jobs, to a seat on a city bus. Crowding was normal and pervasive. Competition and open social strife were restrained by the public belief that scarce goods were being distributed as equitably as possible and that no individual or group was being deprived of livelihood or a fair share. In the mid-1980s Chinese authorities feared that social disorder might result from popular discontent over price increases or the conspicuous wealth of small segments of the population, such as free-market traders. The press frequently condemned the expressions of jealousy and envy that some people directed at those who were prospering by taking advantage of the opportunities the reformed economy offered. The rise in living standards in the 1980s may have contributed to rising expectations that could not be met without considerably more economic growth.

The tension between security and economic growth was reflected in the people's attitudes toward the work unit and the degree of control it exercised over their lives. There was no apparent reason why even a socialist, planned economy had to organize its work force into closed, insular, and sometimes nearly hereditary units. People generally liked the security and benefits provided by their units but disliked many other aspects of "unit life," such as the prohibition on changing jobs. Limited surveys in cities indicated that most people were assigned to work units arbitrarily, without regard to their wishes or skills, and felt little loyalty toward or identification with their work units. People adapted to unit life but reserved loyalties for their families at the one extreme and for the nation and "the people" at the other.

Rural reforms had essentially abolished the work unit in the countryside, along with its close control over people's activities. State and party control over the rural economy and society persisted, but individuals were accorded more autonomy, and most rural people seemed to welcome the end of production teams and production brigades (see Glossary). The success of these rural reforms made modification or even abolition of work units in the urban and state sectors a possibility.

By the mid-1980s the Chinese press and academic journals were discussing recruitment and movement of employees among work units. Although the discussion initially focused on scientists and technicians, whose talents were often wasted in units where they could not make full use of them, the questions raised were of general import. Such blocked mobility was recognized by China's leadership as an impediment to economic growth, and a "rational" flow of labor was listed as a goal for reform of the economy and the science and technology system (see The Reform Program, ch. 9). But few concrete steps had been taken to promote labor mobility, although government resolutions granted scientists and technicians the right to transfer to another unit, subject to the approval of their original work unit. The issue was politically sensitive, as it touched on the powers and perquisites of the party and of managers. Managers often refused permission to leave the unit, even to those scientists and engineers who had the formal right to apply for a transfer.

Similarly, foreign-funded joint ventures, on which China's government placed its hopes for technology transfer, found it impossible to hire the engineers and technicians they needed for high-technology work. There may have been personnel at other enterprises in the same city eager to work for the new firm, but there was no way to transfer them. In 1986 the State Council, in a move that had little immediate effect but considerable potential, decreed that henceforth state enterprises would hire people on contracts good for only a few years and that these contract employees would be free to seek other jobs when their contracts expired (see The State Council, ch. 10). The contract system did not apply, as of late 1986, to workers already employed in state enterprises, but it did indicate the direction in which at least some leaders wished to go.

The fundamental issues of scarcity, equity, and opportunity lay behind problems of balance and exchange among work units, among the larger systems of units such as those under one industry ministry, or between city and country (see Differentiation, this ch.; Urban Society, this ch.; Reform of the Economic System Beginning in 1979, ch. 5; Lateral Economic Cooperation, ch. 8). One of the major goals of the economic reform program in the mid-1980s was to break down barriers to the exchange of information, personnel, and goods and services that separated units, industrial systems, and geographic regions. National-level leaders decried the waste of scarce resources inherent in the attempts of industries or administrative divisions to be self-sufficient in as many areas as possible, in their duplication of research and production, and in their tendencies to hoard raw materials and skilled workers. Attempts to break down administrative barriers (such as bans on the sale of industrial products from other administrative divisions or the refusal of municipal authorities to permit factories subordinate to national ministries to collaborate with those subordinate to the municipality) were often frustrated by the efforts of those organizations that perceived themselves as advantageously placed to maintain the barriers and their unduly large share of the limited goods. Economic growth and development, which accelerated in the 1980s, was giving rise to an increasingly differentiated economic and occupational structure, within which some individuals and enterprises succeeded quite well.

Economic reforms in rural areas generated a great income spread among households, and some geographically favored areas, such as central Guangdong and southern Jiangsu provinces, experienced more rapid economic growth than the interior or mountainous areas. The official position was that while some households were getting rich first, no one was worse off and that the economy as a whole was growing. Press commentary, however, indicated a fairly high level of official concern over public perceptions of growing inequality. The problem confronting China's leaders was to promote economic growth while retaining public confidence in society's fundamental equity and fair allocation of burdens and rewards.

The major question was whether the basic pattern of Chinese society, a cellular structure of equivalent units coordinated by the ruling party, would continue with modifications, or whether its costs were such that it would be replaced by a different and less uniform system. In the late 1980s, either alternative seemed possible. The outcome would depend on both political forces and economic pressures. In either case, balancing individual security with opportunity would remain the fundamental task of those who direct Chinese society.

* * *

Among the best works on China's traditional society and culture are Derk Bodde's brief overview, *China's Traditional Culture: What and Whither?* and the American missionary Arthur H. Smith's *Village Life in China* and *Chinese Characteristics,* both written after many years in Shandong Province and north China at the end of the nineteenth century. Late traditional society is detailed in G. William Skinner's *The City in Late Imperial China.* Chinese society during World War II is presented in Graham Peck's *Two Kinds of Time.* Sociologist C. K. Yang's *A Chinese Village in Early Communist Transition* supplies a field study of a village just outside Guangzhou and an account of the initial stages of the transformation of rural society in 1949. Ida Pruitt's *A Daughter of the Han* is a well-done life history of a servant woman from Shandong Province. The changes of the 1950s are summarized in Franz Schurmann's authoritative *Ideology and Organization in Communist China.* Ezra F. Vogel's *Canton under Communism* and Lynn T. White's *Careers in Shanghai* cover the transformation of urban society. The Cultural Revolution is covered in William Hinton's *Hundred Day War* and Stanley Rosen's *Red Guard Factionalism and the Cultural Revolution in Guangzhou.* Susan Shirk's *Competitive Comrades* illuminates competition within urban schools and its consequences. *Son of the Revolution* by Liang Heng and Judith Shapiro and *To the Storm* by Yue Daiyu and Carolyn Wakeman provide autobiographical accounts of the Cultural Revolution and its aftermath.

Two primary texts on modern Chinese society, based on interviews in Hong Kong in the mid-1970s, are *Village and Family in Contemporary China* and *Urban Life in Contemporary China* written by sociologists Martin King Whyte and William L. Parish. Also based on interviews in Hong Kong are *Chen Village* by Anita Chan, Richard Madsen, and Jonathan Unger; Chan's *Children of Mao*; and Madsen's *Morality and Power in a Chinese Village.*

The most important English-language journal covering modern Chinese society is the *China Quarterly* published in London. Social trends and official policies are described in a range of English-language journals published in China; the primary ones are *Beijing Review* and *China Daily.* (For further information and complete citations, see Bibliography.)

Chapter 4. Education and Culture

A somber figure playing a sheng, *a reed-pipe instrument, is represented by a Tang dynasty (A.D. 618–907) clay tomb figure.*

SINCE THE REPUDIATION of the Cultural Revolution (1966–76), the development of the education system in China has been geared particularly to the advancement of economic modernization. Among the notable official efforts to improve the system were a 1984 decision to formulate major laws on education in the next several years and a 1985 plan to reform the education system. In unveiling the education reform plan in May 1985, the authorities called for nine years of compulsory education and the establishment of the State Education Commission (created the following month). Official commitment to improved education was nowhere more evident than in the substantial increase in funds for education in the Seventh Five-Year Plan (1986–90), which amounted to 72 percent more than funds allotted to education in the previous plan period (1981–85). In 1986 some 16.8 percent of the state budget was earmarked for education, compared with 10.4 percent in 1984.

Since 1949, education has been a focus of controversy in China. As a result of continual intraparty realignments, official policy alternated between ideological imperatives and practical efforts to further national development. But ideology and pragmatism often have been incompatible. The Great Leap Forward (1958–60) and the Socialist Education Movement (1962–65) sought to end deeply rooted academic elitism, to narrow social and cultural gaps between workers and peasants and between urban and rural populations, and to "rectify" the tendency of scholars and intellectuals to disdain manual labor. During the Cultural Revolution, universal education in the interest of fostering social equality was an overriding priority.

The post-Mao Zedong Chinese Communist Party leadership viewed education as the foundation of the Four Modernizations. In the early 1980s, science and technology education became an important focus of education policy. By 1986 training skilled personnel and expanding scientific and technical knowledge had been assigned the highest priority. Although the humanities were considered important, vocational and technical skills were considered paramount for meeting China's modernization goals. The reorientation of educational priorities paralleled Deng Xiaoping's strategy for economic development. Emphasis also was placed on the further training of the already-educated elite, who would carry on the modernization program in the coming decades. Renewed emphasis on modern science and technology, coupled with the recognition of the relative scientific superiority of the West, led to the adoption, beginning in 1976, of an outward-looking policy that encouraged learning and borrowing from abroad for advanced training in a wide range of scientific fields.

Beginning at the Third Plenum of the Eleventh National Party Congress Central Committee in December 1978, intellectuals were encouraged to pursue research in support of the Four Modernizations and, as long as they complied with the party's "four cardinal principles"—upholding socialism, the dictatorship of the proletariat, the leadership of the party, and Marxism-Leninism-Mao Zedong Thought—they were given relatively free rein. But when the party and the government determined that the strictures of the four cardinal principles had been stretched beyond tolerable limits, they did not hesitate to restrict intellectual expression.

Literature and the arts also experienced a great revival in the late 1970s and 1980s. Traditional forms flourished once again, and many new kinds of literature and cultural expression were introduced from abroad.

Education Policy

During the Cultural Revolution, higher education in particular suffered tremendous losses; the system was shut down, and a rising generation of college and graduate students, academicians and technicians, professionals and teachers, was lost. The result was a lack of trained talent to meet the needs of society, an irrationally structured higher education system unequal to the needs of the economic and technological boom, and an uneven development in secondary technical and vocational education. In the post-Mao period, China's education policy continued to evolve. The pragmatist leadership, under Deng Xiaoping, recognized that to meet the goals of modernization it was necessary to develop science, technology, and intellectual resources and to raise the population's education level. Demands on education—for new technology, information science, and advanced management expertise—were levied as a result of the reform of the economic structure and the emergence of new economic forms. In particular, China needed an educated labor force to feed and provision its 1-billion-plus population.

By 1980 achievement was once again accepted as the basis for admission and promotion in education. This fundamental change reflected the critical role of scientific and technical knowledge and professional skills in the Four Modernizations. Also, political activism was no longer regarded as an important measure of individual

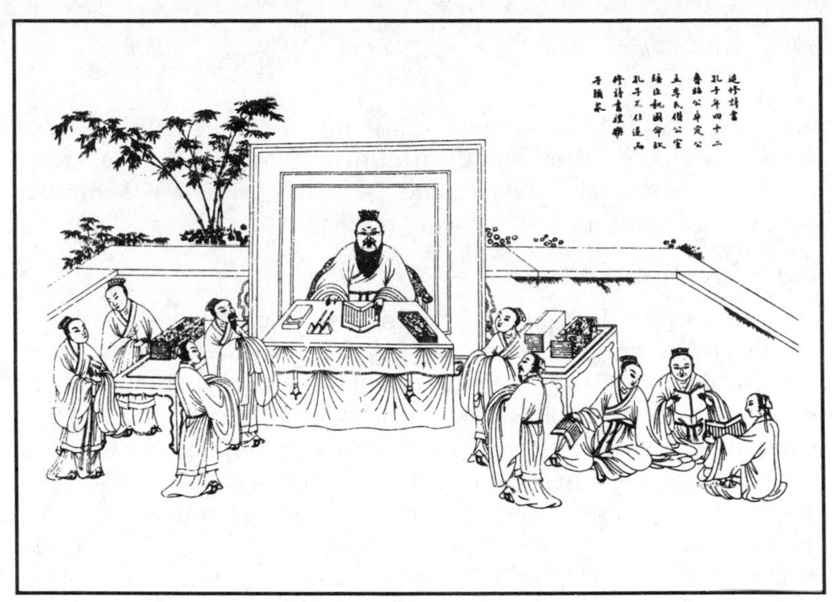

Teacher and students in a traditional academic setting. Woodcut.
Courtesy Library of Congress

performance, and even the development of commonly approved political attitudes and political background was secondary to achievement. Education policy promoted expanded enrollments, with the long-term objective of achieving universal primary and secondary education. This policy contrasted with the previous one, which touted increased enrollments for egalitarian reasons. In 1985 the commitment to modernization was reinforced by plans for nine-year compulsory education and for providing good quality higher education.

Deng Xiaoping's far-ranging educational reform policy, which involved all levels of the education system, aimed to narrow the gap between China and other developing countries. Modernizing China was tied to modernizing education. Devolution of educational management from the central to the local level was the means chosen to improve the education system. Centralized authority was not abandoned, however, as evidenced by the creation of the State Education Commission. Academically, the goals of reform were to enhance and universalize elementary and junior middle school education; to increase the number of schools and qualified teachers; and to develop vocational and technical education. A uniform standard for curricula, textbooks, examinations, and teacher qualifications (especially at the middle-school level) was established, and considerable autonomy and variations in and among the provinces, autonomous regions, and special municipalities were allowed. Further, the system of enrollment and job assignment in higher education was changed, and excessive government control over colleges and universities was reduced.

The Education System

To provide for its population, China has a vast and varied school system. There are preschools, kindergartens, schools for the deaf and for the blind, key schools (similar to college preparatory schools), primary schools, secondary schools (comprising junior and senior middle schools, secondary agricultural and vocational schools, regular secondary schools, secondary teachers' schools, secondary technical schools, and secondary professional schools), and various institutions of higher learning (consisting of regular colleges and universities, professional colleges, and short-term vocational universities). In terms of access to education, China's system represented a pyramid; because of the scarcity of resources allotted to higher education, student numbers decreased sharply at the higher levels. Although there were dramatic advances in primary education after 1949, achievements in secondary and higher education were not as great.

Although the government has authority over the education system, the Chinese Communist Party has played a role in managing education since 1949. The party established broad education policies and under Deng Xiaoping, tied improvements in the quality of education to its modernization plan. The party also monitored the government's implementation of its policies at the local level and within educational institutions through its party committees. Party members within educational institutions, who often have a leading management role, are responsible for steering their schools in the direction mandated by party policy.

New Directions

The May 1985 National Conference on Education recognized five fundamental areas for reform to be discussed in connection with implementing the party Central Committee's "Draft Decision on Reforming the Education System." The reforms were intended to produce "more able people"; to make the localities responsible for developing "basic education" and systematically implement a nine-year compulsory education program; to improve secondary education; to develop vocational and technical education; to reform the graduate-assignment system of institutions of higher education and to expand their management and decision-making powers; and to give administrators the necessary encouragement and authority to ensure smooth progress in educational reform.

The National Conference on Education paved the way for the abolition of the Ministry of Education and the establishment of the State Education Commission, both of which occurred in June 1985. Created to coordinate education policy, the commission assumed roles previously played by the State Planning Commission and the Ministry of Education. As a State Council commission, the new State Education Commission had greater status than the old Ministry of Education had had and was in charge of all education organizations except military ones (see The State Council, ch. 10). Although the State Education Commission assumed a central role in the administration of education, the reform decentralized much of the power previously wielded by the Ministry of Education and its constituent offices and bureaus, which had established curriculum and admissions policies in response to the State Planning Commission's requirements.

The State Education Commission, with its expanded administrative scope and power, was responsible for formulating guiding principles for education, establishing regulations, planning the progress of educational projects, coordinating the educational programs of different departments, and standardizing educational reforms. Simplification of administration and delegation of authority were made the bases for improving the education system. This devolution of management to the provinces, autonomous regions, and special municipalities meant local governments had more decision-making power and were able to develop basic education. State-owned enterprises, mass organizations, and individuals were encouraged to pool funds to accomplish education reform. Local authorities used state appropriations and a percentage of local reserve financial resources (basically township financial revenues) to finance educational projects.

Compulsory Education Law

The Law on Nine-Year Compulsory Education, which took effect July 1, 1986, established requirements and deadlines for attaining universal education tailored to local conditions and guaranteed school-age children the right to receive education. People's congresses at various local levels were, within certain guidelines and according to local conditions, to decide the steps, methods, and deadlines for implementing nine-year compulsory education in accordance with the guidelines formulated by the central authorities. The program sought to bring rural areas, which had four to six years of compulsory schooling, into line with their urban counterparts. Education departments were exhorted to train millions of skilled workers for all trades and professions and to offer guidelines, curricula, and methods to comply with the reform program and modernization needs.

Provincial-level authorities were to develop plans, enact decrees and rules, distribute funds to counties, and administer directly a few key secondary schools. County authorities were to distribute funds to each township government, which were to make up any deficiencies. County authorities were to supervise education and teaching and to manage their own senior middle schools, teachers' schools, teachers' in-service training schools, agricultural vocational schools, and exemplary primary and junior middle schools. The remaining schools were to be managed separately by the county and township authorities.

The compulsory education law divided China into three categories: cities and economically developed areas in coastal provinces and a small number of developed areas in the hinterland; towns and villages with medium development; and economically backward areas. By November 1985 the first category—the larger cities and approximately 20 percent of the counties (mainly in the more developed coastal and southeastern areas of China) had achieved universal 9-year education. By 1990 cities, economically developed areas in coastal provincial-level units, and a small number of developed interior areas (approximately 25 percent of China's population) and areas where junior middle schools were already popularized were targeted to have universal junior-middle-school education. Education planners envisioned that by the mid-1990s all workers and staff in coastal areas, inland cities, and moderately developed areas (with a combined population of 300 million to 400 million people) would have either compulsory 9-year or vocational education and that 5 percent of the people in these areas would have a college education—building a solid intellectual foundation for China. Further, the planners expected that secondary education and university entrants would also increase by the year 2000.

The second category targeted under the 9-year compulsory education law consisted of towns and villages with medium-level development (around 50 percent of China's population), where universal education was expected to reach the junior-middle-school level by 1995. Technical and higher education was projected to develop at the same rate.

The third category, economically backward (rural) areas (around 25 percent of China's population) were to popularize basic education without a timetable and at various levels according to local economic development, though the state would "do its best" to support educational development. The state also would assist education in minority nationality areas (see Minority Nationalities, ch. 2). In the past, rural areas, which lacked a standardized and universal primary education system, had produced generations of illiterates; only 60 percent of their primary school graduates had met established standards.

As a further example of the government's commitment to nine-year compulsory education, in January 1986 the State Council drafted a bill passed at the Fourteenth Session of the Standing Committee of the Sixth National People's Congress that made it illegal for any organization or individual to employ youths before they had completed their nine years of schooling. The bill also authorized free education and subsidies for students whose families had financial difficulties.

Key Schools

"Key schools," shut down during the Cultural Revolution, reappeared in the late 1970s and, in the early 1980s, became an integral part of the effort to revive the lapsed education system. Because educational resources were scarce, selected ("key") institutions—usually those with records of past educational accomplishment—were given priority in the assignment of teachers, equipment, and funds. They also were allowed to recruit the best students for special training to compete for admission to top schools at the next level. Key schools constituted only a small percentage of all regular senior middle schools and funneled the best students into the best secondary schools, largely on the basis of entrance scores. In 1980 the greatest resources were allocated to the key schools that would produce the greatest number of college entrants.

In early 1987 efforts had begun to develop the key school from a preparatory school into a vehicle for diffusing improved curricula, materials, and teaching practices to local schools. Moreover, the appropriateness of a key school's role in the nine-year basic education plan was questioned by some officials because key schools favored urban areas and the children of more affluent and better educated parents. In 1985 entrance examinations and the key-school system had already been abolished in Changchun, Shenyang, Shenzhen, Xiamen, and other cities, and education departments in Shanghai and Tianjin were moving to establish a student recommendation system and eliminate key schools. In 1986 the Shanghai Educational Bureau abolished the key junior-middle-school system to ensure "an overall level of education."

Primary Education

Primary Schools

The development of primary education in so vast a country as China was a formidable accomplishment. In contrast to the 20-percent enrollment rate before 1949, in 1985 about 96 percent of primary-school-age children were enrolled in approximately 832,300 primary schools (see table 10, Appendix A). This enrollment figure compared favorably with the record figures of the late 1960s and early 1970s, when enrollment standards were more egalitarian. In 1985 the World Bank estimated that enrollments in primary schools would decrease from 136 million in 1983 to 95 million in the late 1990s and that the decreased enrollment would reduce the number of teachers needed. Qualified teachers, however, would continue to be in demand.

Under the Law on Nine-Year Compulsory Education, primary schools were to be tuition-free and reasonably located for the convenience of children attending them; students would attend primary schools in their neighborhoods or villages. Parents paid a small fee per term for books and other expenses such as transportation, food, and heating. Previously, fees were not considered a deterrent to attendance, although some parents felt even these minor costs were more than they could afford. Under the education reform, students from poor families received stipends, and state enterprises, institutions, and other sectors of society were encouraged to establish their own schools. A major concern was that scarce resources be conserved without causing enrollment to fall and without weakening of the better schools. In particular, local governments were warned not to pursue middle-school education blindly while primary-school education was still developing, or to wrest money, teaching staff, and materials from primary schools.

Children usually entered primary school at seven years of age for six days a week. The two-semester school year consisted of 9.5 months, with a long vacation in July and August. Urban primary schools typically divided the school week into twenty-four to twenty-seven classes of forty-five minutes each, but in the rural areas the norm was half-day schooling, more flexible schedules, and itinerant teachers. Most primary schools had a five-year course, except in such cities as Beijing and Shanghai, which had reintroduced six-year primary schools and accepted children at six and one-half years rather than seven. The primary-school curriculum consisted of Chinese, mathematics, physical education, music, drawing, and elementary instruction in nature, history, and geography, combined with practical work experiences around the school compound.

Kindergarten children
Courtesy Xinhua News Agency

A general knowledge of politics and moral training, which stressed love of the motherland, love of the party, and love of the people (and previously love of Chairman Mao), was another part of the curriculum. A foreign language, often English, was introduced in about the third grade. Chinese and mathematics accounted for about 60 percent of the scheduled class time; natural science and social science accounted for about 8 percent. *Putonghua* (common spoken language, see Glossary) was taught in regular schools and pinyin romanization in lower grades and kindergarten. The State Education Commission required that all primary schools offer courses on communist ideology and morality. Beginning in the fourth grade, students usually had to perform productive labor two weeks per semester to relate classwork with production experience in workshops or on farms and subordinate it to academic study. Most schools had after-hour activities at least one day per week—often organized by the Young Pioneers—to involve students in recreation and community service.

By 1980 the percentage of students enrolled in primary schools was high, but the schools reported high dropout rates and regional enrollment gaps (most enrollees were concentrated in the cities). Only one in four counties had universal primary education. On the average, 10 percent of the students dropped out between each grade. During the 1979–83 period, the government acknowledged the "9–6–3" rule, that is, that nine of ten children began primary school, six completed it, and three graduated with good performance. This meant that only about 60 percent of primary students actually completed their five year program of study and graduated, and only about 30 percent were regarded as having primary-level competence. Statistics in the mid-1980s showed that more rural girls than boys dropped out of school.

Within the framework of the Law on Nine-Year Compulsory Education and the general trend toward vocational and technical skills, attempts were made to accommodate and correct the gap between urban and rural education. Urban and key schools almost invariably operated on a six day full-time schedule to prepare students for further education and high-level jobs. Rural schools generally operated on a flexible schedule geared to the needs of the agricultural seasons and sought to prepare students for adult life and manual labor in lower-skilled jobs. They also offered a more limited curriculum, often only Chinese, mathematics, and morals. To promote attendance and allow the class schedule and academic year to be completed, agricultural seasons were taken into account. School holidays were moved, school days shortened, and full-time, half-time, and spare-time classes offered in the slack agricultural seasons. Sometimes itinerant teachers were hired for mountain villages and served one village in the morning, another village in the afternoon.

Rural parents were generally well aware that their children had limited opportunities to further their education. Some parents saw little use in having their children attend even primary school, especially after the establishment of the agricultural responsibility system (see Glossary). Under that system, parents preferred that their children work to increase family income—and withdrew them from school—for both long and short periods of time (see Agricultural Policies, ch. 6).

Preschool Education

Preschool education, which began at age three and one-half, was another target of education reform in 1985. Preschool facilities were to be established in buildings made available by public enterprises, production teams, municipal authorities, local groups, and families. The government announced that it depended on individual organizations to sponsor their own preschool education and that preschool education was to become a part of the welfare services of various government organizations, institutes, and state- and collectively operated enterprises. Costs for preschool education varied according to services rendered. Officials also called for more preschool teachers with more appropriate training.

Special Education

The 1985 National Conference on Education also recognized the importance of special education, in the form of programs for gifted children and for slow learners. Gifted children were allowed to skip grades. Slow learners were encouraged to reach minimum standards, although those who did not maintain the pace seldom reached the next stage. For the most part, children with severe learning problems and those with handicaps and psychological needs were the responsibilities of their families. Extra provisions were made for blind and severely hearing-impaired children, although in 1984 special schools enrolled fewer than 2 percent of all eligible children in those categories. The China Welfare Fund, established in 1984, received state funding and had the right to solicit donations within China and from abroad, but special education remained a low government priority.

Secondary Education

Middle Schools

Secondary education in China has a complicated history. In the early 1960s, education planners followed a policy called "walking on two legs," which established both regular academic schools and separate technical schools for vocational training. The rapid expansion of secondary education during the Cultural Revolution created serious problems; because resources were spread too thinly, educational quality declined. Further, this expansion was limited to regular secondary schools; technical schools were closed during the Cultural Revolution because they were viewed as an attempt to provide inferior education to children of worker and peasant families. In the late 1970s, government and party representatives criticized what they termed the "unitary" approach of the 1960s, arguing that it ignored the need for two kinds of graduates: those with an academic education (college preparatory) and those with specialized technical education (vocational). Beginning in 1976 with the renewed emphasis on technical training, technical schools reopened, and their enrollments increased (as did those of key schools, also criticized during the Cultural Revolution). In the drive to spread vocational and technical education, regular secondary-school enrollments fell. By 1986 universal secondary education was part of the nine year compulsory education law that made primary education (six years) and junior-middle-school education (three years) mandatory. The desire to consolidate existing schools and to improve the quality of key middle schools was, however, under the education reform, more important than expanding enrollment.

Chinese secondary schools are called middle schools and are divided into junior and senior levels. In 1985 more than 104,000 middle schools (both regular and vocational) enrolled about 51 million students. Junior, or lower, middle schools offered a three year course of study, which students began at twelve years of age. Senior, or upper, middle schools offered a two or three year course, which students began at age fifteen.

The regular secondary-school year usually had two semesters, totaling nine months. In some rural areas, schools operated on a shift schedule to accommodate agricultural cycles. The academic curriculum consisted of Chinese, mathematics, physics, chemistry, geology, foreign language, history, geography, politics, physiology, music, fine arts, and physical education. Some middle schools also offered vocational subjects. There were thirty or thirty-one periods a week in addition to self-study and extracurricular activity. Thirty-eight percent of the curriculum at a junior middle school was in Chinese and mathematics, 16 percent in a foreign language. Fifty percent of the teaching at a senior middle school was in natural sciences and mathematics, 30 percent in Chinese and a foreign language.

Rural secondary education has undergone several transformations since 1980, when county-level administrative units closed some schools and took over certain poorer schools run by the people's communes (see Glossary). In 1982 the communes were eliminated. In 1985 educational reform legislation officially placed rural secondary schools under local administration. There was a high dropout rate among rural students in general and among secondary students in particular, largely because of parental attitudes. All students, however, especially males, were encouraged to attend secondary school if it would lead to entrance to a college or university (still regarded as prestigious) and escape from village life.

In China a senior-middle-school graduate is considered an educated person, although middle schools are viewed as a training ground for colleges and universities. And, while middle-school students are offered the prospect of higher education, they are also confronted with the fact that university admission is limited. Middle schools are evaluated in terms of their success in sending graduates on for higher education, although efforts persist to educate young people to take a place in society as valued and skilled members of the work force.

Vocational and Technical Schools

Both regular and vocational secondary schools sought to serve modernization needs. A number of technical and "skilled-worker" training schools reopened after the Cultural Revolution, and an effort was made to provide exposure to vocational subjects in general secondary schools (by offering courses in industry, services, business, and agriculture). By 1985 there were almost 3 million vocational and technical students.

Under the educational reform tenets, polytechnic colleges were to give priority to admitting secondary vocational and technical school graduates and providing on-the-job training for qualified workers. Education reformers continued to press for the conversion of about 50 percent of upper secondary education into vocational education, which traditionally had been weak in the rural areas. Regular senior middle schools were to be converted into vocational middle schools, and vocational training classes were to be established in some senior middle schools. Diversion of students from academic to technical education was intended to alleviate skill shortages and to reduce the competition for university enrollment. Although enrollment in technical schools of various kinds had not yet increased enough to compensate for decreasing enrollments in regular senior middle schools, the proportion of vocational and technical students to total senior-middle-school students increased from about 5 percent in 1978 to almost 36 percent in 1985, although development was uneven. Further, to encourage greater numbers of junior-middle-school graduates to enter technical schools, vocational and technical school graduates were given priority in job assignments, while other job seekers had to take technical tests.

In 1987 there were four kinds of secondary vocational and technical schools: technical schools that offered a four year, post-junior middle course and two- to three-year post-senior middle training in such fields as commerce, legal work, fine arts, and forestry; workers' training schools that accepted students whose senior-middle-school education consisted of two years of training in such trades as carpentry and welding; vocational technical schools that accepted either junior- or senior-middle-school students for one- to three-year courses in cooking, tailoring, photography, and other services; and agricultural middle schools that offered basic subjects and agricultural science.

These technical schools had several hundred different programs. Their narrow specializations had advantages in that they offered in-depth training, reducing the need for on-the-job training and thereby lowering learning time and costs. Moreover, students were more motivated to study if there were links between training and future jobs. Much of the training could be done at existing enterprises, where staff and equipment were available at little additional cost.

There were some disadvantages to this system, however. Under the Four Modernizations, technically trained generalists were needed more than highly specialized technicians. Also, highly specialized equipment and staff were underused, and there was an overall shortage of specialized facilities to conduct training. In addition, large expenses were incurred in providing the necessary facilities and staff, and the trend in some government technical agencies was toward more general technical and vocational education.

Further, the dropout rate continued to have a negative effect on the labor pool as upper-secondary-school technical students dropped out and as the percentage of lower-secondary-school graduates entering the labor market without job training increased. Occupational rigidity and the geographic immobility of the population, particularly in rural areas, further limited educational choices.

Although there were 668,000 new polytechnic school enrollments in 1985, the Seventh Five-Year Plan called for annual increases of 2 million mid-level skilled workers and 400,000 senior technicians, indicating that enrollment levels were still far from sufficient. To improve the situation, in July 1986 officials from the State Education Commission, State Planning Commission, and Ministry of Labor and Personnel convened a national conference on developing China's technical and vocational education. It was decided that technical and vocational education in rural areas should accommodate local conditions and be conducted on a short-term basis. Where conditions permitted, emphasis would be placed on organizing technical schools and short-term training classes. To alleviate the shortage of teachers, vocational and technical teachers' colleges were to be reformed and other colleges and universities were to be mobilized for assistance. The State Council decision to improve training for workers who had passed technical examinations (as opposed to unskilled workers) was intended to reinforce the development of vocational and technical schools.

Higher Education

Background

Higher education reflects the changes in political policies that have occurred in contemporary China. Since 1949 emphasis has continually been placed on political re-education, and in periods of political upheaval, such as the Great Leap Forward and the Cultural Revolution, ideology has been stressed over professional or technical competence. During the early stages of the Cultural Revolution, tens of thousands of college students joined Red Guard (see Glossary) organizations, effectively closing down the higher education system (see The Cultural Revolution Decade, 1966–76, ch. 1). In general, when universities reopened in the early 1970s, enrollments were reduced from pre-Cultural Revolution levels, and admission was restricted to individuals who had been recommended by their work unit (*danwei*—see Glossary) possessed good political credentials, and had distinguished themselves in manual labor. In the absence of stringent and reasonably objective entrance examinations, political connections became increasingly important in securing the recommendations and political dossiers necessary to qualify for university admission. As a result, the decline in educational quality was profound. Deng Xiaoping reportedly wrote Mao Zedong in 1975 that university graduates were "not even capable of reading a book" in their own fields when they left the university. University faculty and administrators, moreover, were demoralized by what they faced.

Efforts made in 1975 to improve educational quality were unsuccessful. By 1980 it appeared doubtful that the politically oriented admission criteria had accomplished even the purpose of increasing enrollment of worker and peasant children. Successful candidates for university entrance were usually children of cadres and officials who used personal connections that allowed them to "enter through the back door." Students from officials' families would accept the requisite minimum two year work assignment in the countryside, often in a suburban location that allowed them to remain close to their families. Village cadres, anxious to please the parent-official, gladly recommended these youths for university placement after the labor requirement had been met. The child of an official family was then on his or her way to a university without having academic ability, a record of political activism, or a distinguished work record.

After 1976 steps were taken to improve educational quality by establishing order and stability, and calling for an end to political contention on university campuses, and expanding university enrollments. This pressure to maintain quality and minimize expenditures led to efforts both to run existing institutions more efficiently and to develop other college and university programs. As a result, labor colleges for training agro-technicians and factory-run colleges for providing technical education for workers were established. In addition, eighty-eight institutions and key universities were provided with special funding, top students and faculty members, and other support, and they recruited the most academically qualified students without regard to family background or political activism.

Modernization Goals in the 1980s

The commitment to the Four Modernizations required great advances in science and technology. Under the modernization program, higher education was to be the cornerstone for training and research. Because modernization depended on a vastly increased and improved capability to train scientists and engineers for needed breakthroughs, the renewed concern for higher education and academic quality—and the central role that the sciences were expected to play in the Four Modernizations—highlighted the need for scientific research and training. This concern can be traced to the critical personnel shortages and qualitative deficiencies in the sciences resulting from the unproductive years of the Cultural Revolution, when higher education was shut down. In response to the need for scientific training, the Sixth Plenum of the Twelfth National Party Congress Central Committee, held in September 1986, adopted a resolution on the guiding principles for building a socialist society that strongly emphasized the importance of education and science.

Reformers realized, however, that the higher education system was far from meeting modernization goals and that additional changes were needed. The Provisional Regulations Concerning the Management of Institutions of Higher Learning, promulgated by the State Council in 1986, initiated vast changes in administration and adjusted educational opportunity, direction, and content. With the increased independence accorded under the education reform, universities and colleges were able to choose their own teaching plans and curricula; to accept projects from or cooperate with other socialist establishments for scientific research and technical development in setting up ''combines'' involving teaching, scientific research, and production; to suggest appointments and removals of vice presidents and other staff members; to take charge of the distribution of capital construction investment and funds allocated by the state; and to be responsible for the development of international exchanges by using their own funds.

The changes also allowed the universities to accept financial aid from work units and decide how this money was to be used without asking for more money from departments in charge of education. Further, higher education institutions and work units could sign contracts for the training of students.

Higher education institutions also were assigned a greater role in running interregional and interdepartmental schools. Within their state-approved budgets, universities secured more freedom to allocate funds as they saw fit and to use income from tuition and

Students from Tongji University, Shanghai, work with construction models under direction of Western adviser.
Courtesy Xinhua News Agency

technical and advisory services for their own development, including collective welfare and bonuses.

There also was a renewed interest in television, radio, and correspondence classes. Some of the courses, particularly in the college-run factories, were serious, full-time enterprises, with a two- to three-year curriculum.

Entrance Examinations and Admission Criteria

National examinations to select students for higher education (and positions of leadership) were an important part of China's culture, and, traditionally, entrance to a higher education institution was considered prestigious. Although the examination system for admission to colleges and universities has undergone many changes since the Cultural Revolution, it remains the basis for recruiting academically able students. When higher education institutions were reopened in the early 1970s, candidates for entrance examinations had to be senior-middle-school graduates or the equivalent, generally below twenty-six years of age. Work experience requirements were eliminated, but workers and staff members needed permission from their enterprises to take the examinations.

Each provincial-level unit was assigned a quota of students to be admitted to key universities, a second quota of students for regular universities within that administrative division, and a third quota of students from other provinces, autonomous regions, and special municipalities who would be admitted to institutions operated at the provincial level. Provincial-level administrative units selected students with outstanding records to take the examinations. Additionally, preselection examinations were organized by the provinces, autonomous regions, and special municipalities for potential students (from three to five times the number of places allotted). These candidates were actively encouraged to take the examination to ensure that a sufficient number of good applicants would be available. Cadres with at least two years of work experience were recruited for selected departments in a small number of universities on an experimental basis. Preferential admission treatment (in spite of lower test scores) was given to minority candidates, students from disadvantaged areas, and those who agreed in advance to work in less developed regions after graduation.

In December 1977, when uniform national examinations were reinstated, 5.7 million students took the examinations, although university placement was available for only the 278,000 applicants with the highest scores. In July 1984, about 1.6 million candidates (30,000 fewer than in 1983) took the entrance examinations for the 430,000 places in China's more than 900 colleges and universities. Of the 1.6 million examinees, more than 1 million took the test for placement in science and engineering colleges; 415,000 for places in liberal arts colleges; 88,000 for placement in foreign language institutions; and 15,000 for placement in sports universities and schools. More than 100,000 of the candidates were from national minority groups. A year later, there were approximately 1.8 million students taking the 3-day college entrance examination to compete for 560,000 places. Liberal arts candidates were tested on politics, Chinese, mathematics, foreign languages, history, and geography. Science and engineering candidates were tested on politics, Chinese, mathematics, chemistry, and biology. Entrance examinations also were given in 1985 for professional and technical schools, which sought to enroll 550,000 new students.

Other innovations in enrollment practices included allowing colleges and universities to admit students with good academic records but relatively low entrance-examination scores. Some colleges were allowed to try an experimental student recommendation system—fixed at 2 percent of the total enrollment for regular colleges and 5 percent for teachers' colleges—instead of the traditional entrance examination. A minimum national examination score was established for admission to specific departments at specially designated colleges and universities, and the minimum score for admission to other universities was set by provincial-level authorities. Key universities established separate classes for minorities. When several applicants attained the minimum test score, the school had the option of making a selection, a policy that gave university faculty and administrators a certain amount of discretion but still protected admission according to academic ability.

In addition to the written examination, university applicants had to pass a physical examination and a political screening. Less than 2 percent of the students who passed the written test were eliminated for reasons of poor health. The number disqualified for political reasons was unknown, but publicly the party maintained that the number was very small and that it sought to ensure that only the most able students actually entered colleges and universities.

By 1985 the number of institutions of higher learning had again increased—to slightly more than 1,000. The State Education Commission and the Ministry of Finance issued a joint declaration for nationwide unified enrollment of adult students—not the regular secondary-school graduates but the members of the work force who qualified for admission by taking a test. The State Education Commission established unified questions and time and evaluation criteria for the test and authorized provinces, autonomous regions, and special municipalities to administer the test, grade the papers in a uniform manner, and determine the minimum points required for admission. The various schools were to enroll students according to the results. Adult students needed to have the educational equivalent of senior-middle-school graduates, and those applying for release or partial release from work to study were to be under forty years of age. Staff members and workers were to apply to study job-related subjects with review by and approval of their respective work units. If employers paid for the college courses, the workers had to take entrance examinations. In 1985 colleges enrolled 33,000 employees from various enterprises and companies, approximately 6 percent of the total college enrollment.

In 1985 state quotas for university places were set, allowing both for students sponsored by institutions and for those paying their own expenses. This policy was a change from the previous system in which all students were enrolled according to guidelines established in Beijing. All students except those at teachers' colleges, those who had financial difficulties, and those who were to work under adverse conditions after graduation had to pay for their own tuition, accommodations, and miscellaneous expenses.

Changes in Enrollment and Assignment Policies

The student enrollment and graduate assignment system also

was changed to reflect more closely the personnel needs of modernization. By 1986 the state was responsible for drafting the enrollment plan, which took into account future personnel demands, the need to recruit students from outlying regions, and the needs of trades and professions with adverse working conditions. Moreover, a certain number of graduates to be trained for the People's Liberation Army were included in the state enrollment plan. In most cases, enrollment in higher education institutions at the employers' request was extended as a supplement to the state student enrollment plan. Employers were to pay a percentage of training fees, and students were to fulfill contractual obligations to the employers after graduation. The small number of students who attended colleges and universities at their own expense could be enrolled in addition to those in the state plan.

Accompanying the changes in enrollment practices were reforms, adopted in 1986, in the faculty appointment system, which ended the "iron rice bowl" (see Glossary) employment system and gave colleges and universities freedom to decide what departments, majors, and numbers of teachers they needed. Teachers in institutions of higher learning were hired on a renewable contract basis, usually for two to four years at a time. The teaching positions available were teaching assistant, lecturer, associate professor, and professor. The system was tested in eight major universities in Beijing and Shanghai before it was instituted nationwide at the end of 1985. University presidents headed groups in charge of appointing professors, lecturers, and teaching assistants according to their academic levels and teaching abilities, and a more rational wage system, geared to different job levels, was inaugurated. Universities and colleges with surplus professors and researchers were advised to grant them appropriate academic titles and encourage them to work for their current pay in schools of higher learning where they were needed. The new system was to be extended to schools of all kinds and other education departments within two years.

Under the 1985 reforms, all graduates were assigned jobs by the state; a central government placement agency told the schools where to send graduates. By 1985 Qinghua University and a few other universities were experimenting with a system that allowed graduates to accept job offers or to look for their own positions. For example, of 1,900 Qinghua University graduates in 1985, 1,200 went on to graduate school, 48 looked for their own jobs, and the remainder were assigned jobs by the school after consultation with the students. The college students and postgraduates scheduled to graduate in 1986 were assigned primarily to work in forestry, education, textiles, and the armaments industry. Graduates still were needed in civil engineering, computer science, finance, and English.

Scholarship and Loan System

In July 1986 the State Council announced that the stipend system for university and college students would be replaced with a new scholarship and loan system. The new system, to be tested in selected institutions during the 1986–87 academic year, was designed to help students who could not cover their own living expenses but who studied hard, obeyed state laws, and observed discipline codes. Students eligible for financial aid were to apply to the schools and the China Industrial and Commercial Bank for low-interest loans. Three categories of students eligible for aid were established: top students encouraged to attain all-around excellence; students specializing in education, agriculture, forestry, sports, and marine navigation; and students willing to work in poor, remote, and border regions or under harsh conditions, such as in mining and engineering. In addition, free tuition and board were to be offered at teachers' colleges, and the graduates were required to teach at least five years in primary and middle schools. After graduation, a student's loans were to be paid off by his or her employer in a lump sum, and the money was to be repaid to the employer by the student through five years of payroll deductions.

Study Abroad

In addition to loans, another means of raising educational quality, particularly in science, was to send students abroad to study. A large number of Chinese students studied in the Soviet Union before educational links and other cooperative programs with the Soviet Union were severed in the late 1950s. In the 1960s and 1970s, China continued to send a small number of students abroad, primarily to European universities. In October 1978 Chinese students began to arrive in the United States; their numbers accelerated after normalization of relations between the two countries in January 1979, a policy consistent with modernization needs. Although figures vary, more than 36,000 students, including 7,000 self-supporting students (those who paid their own way, received scholarships from host institutions, or received help from relatives and "foreign friends"), studied in 14 countries between 1978 and 1984. Of this total, 78 percent were technical personnel sent abroad for advanced study. As of mid-1986 there were 15,000 Chinese scholars and graduates in American universities, compared with the total of 19,000 scholars sent between 1979 and 1983.

Chinese students sent to the United States generally were not typical undergraduates or graduate students but were mid-career scientists, often thirty-five to forty-five years of age, seeking advanced training in their areas of specialization. Often they were individuals of exceptional ability who occupied responsible positions in Chinese universities and research institutions. Fewer than 15 percent of the earliest arrivals were degree candidates. Nearly all the visiting scholars were in scientific fields.

Educational Investment

Many of the problems that had hindered higher educational development in the past continued in 1987. Funding remained a major problem because science and technology study and research and study abroad were expensive. Because education was competing with other modernization programs, capital was critically short. Another concern was whether or not the Chinese economy was sufficiently advanced to make efficient use of the highly trained technical personnel it planned to educate. For example, some observers believed that it would be more realistic to train a literate work force of low-level technicians instead of research scientists. Moreover, it was feared that using an examination to recruit the most able students might advance people who were merely good at taking examinations. Educational reforms also made some people uncomfortable by criticizing the traditional practice of rote memorization and promoting innovative teaching and study methods.

The prestige associated with higher education caused a demand for it. But many qualified youths were unable to attend colleges and universities because China could not finance enough university places for them. To help meet the demand and to educate a highly trained, specialized work force, China established alternate forms of higher education—such as spare-time, part-time, and radio and television universities.

China cannot afford a heavy investment, either ideologically or financially, in the education of a few students. Since 1978 China's leaders have modified the policy of concentrating education resources at the university level, which, although designed to facilitate modernization, conflicted directly with the party's principles. The policies that produced an educated elite also siphoned off resources that might have been used to accomplish the compulsory nine year education more speedily and to equalize educational opportunities in the city and the countryside. The policy of key schools has been modified over the years. Nevertheless, China's leaders believe an educated elite is necessary to reach modernization goals.

Wang Tingxi,
a "national model teacher"
from Hunan Province
Courtesy
Xinhua News Agency

Young sportsmen
Courtesy
Xinhua News Agency

Teachers

Among the most pressing problems facing education reformers was the scarcity of qualified teachers, which has led to a serious stunting of educational development. In 1986 there were about 8 million primary- and middle-school teachers in China, but many lacked professional training. Estimates indicated that in order to meet the goals of the Seventh Five-Year Plan and realize compulsory 9-year education, the system needed 1 million new teachers for primary schools, 750,000 new teachers for junior middle schools, and 300,000 new teachers for senior middle schools. Estimates predict, however, that the demand for teachers will drop in the late 1990s because of an anticipated decrease in primary-school enrollments.

To cope with the shortage of qualified teachers, the State Education Commission decreed in 1985 that senior-middle-school teachers should be graduates with two years' training in professional institutes and that primary-school teachers should be graduates of secondary schools. To improve teacher quality, the commission established full-time and part-time (the latter preferred because it was less costly) in-service training programs. Primary-school and preschool in-service teacher training programs devoted 84 percent of the time to subject teaching, 6 percent to pedagogy and psychology, and 10 percent to teaching methods. In-service training for primary-school teachers was designed to raise them to a level of approximately two years' postsecondary study, with the goal of qualifying most primary-school teachers by 1990. Secondary-school in-service teacher training was based on a unified model, tailored to meet local conditions, and offered on a spare-time basis. Ninety-five percent of its curricula was devoted to subject teaching, 2 to 3 percent to pedagogy and psychology, and 2 to 3 percent to teaching methods. There was no similar large-scale in-service effort for technical and vocational teachers, most of whom worked for enterprises and local authorities.

By 1985 there were more than 1,000 teacher training schools—an indispensable tool in the effort to solve the acute shortage of qualified teachers. These schools, however, were unable to supply the number of teachers needed to attain modernization goals through 1990. Although a considerable number of students graduated as qualified teachers from institutions of higher learning, the relatively low social status and salary levels of teachers hampered recruitment, and not all of the graduates of teachers' colleges became teachers. To attract more teachers, China tried to make teaching a more desirable and respected profession. To this end, the government designated September 10 as Teachers' Day, granted teachers pay raises, and made teachers' colleges tuition free. To further arrest the teacher shortage, in 1986 the central government sent teachers to underdeveloped regions to train local schoolteachers.

Because urban teachers continued to earn more than their rural counterparts and because academic standards in the countryside had dropped, it remained difficult to recruit teachers for rural areas. Teachers in rural areas also had production responsibilities for their plots of land, which took time from their teaching. Rural primary teachers needed to supplement their pay by farming because most were paid by the relatively poor local communities rather than by the state.

Adult Education

Role in Modernization

Because only 4 percent of the nation's middle-school graduates are admitted to universities, China has found it necessary to develop other ways of meeting the demand for education. Adult education has become increasingly important in helping China meet its modernization goals. Adult, or "nonformal," education is an alternative form of higher education that encompasses radio, television, and correspondence universities, spare-time and part-time universities, factory-run universities for staff and workers, and county-run universities for peasants, many operating primarily during students' off-work hours. These alternative forms of education are economical. They seek to educate both the "delayed generation"—those who lost educational opportunities during the Cultural Revolution—and to raise the cultural, scientific, and general education levels of workers on the job.

Alternative Forms

Schools have been established by government departments, businesses, trade unions, academic societies, democratic parties (see Glossary), and other organizations. In 1984 about 70 percent of China's factories and enterprises supported their own part-time classes, which often were referred to as workers' colleges. In Beijing alone, more than ninety adult-education schools with night schools enrolled tens of thousands of students. More than 20,000 of these students graduated annually from evening universities, workers' colleges, television universities, and correspondence schools—more than twice the number graduating from regular colleges and universities. The government spent ¥200 (for value of the yuan—see Glossary) to ¥500 per adult education student and at least ¥1,000 per regular university student. In 1984 approximately 1.3 million students enrolled in television, correspondence, and evening universities, about a 30-percent increase over 1983.

Spare-time education for workers and peasants and literacy classes for the entire adult population were other components of basic education. Spare-time education included a very broad range of educational activities at all levels. Most spare-time schools were sponsored by factories and run for their own workers; they provided fairly elementary education, as well as courses to upgrade technical skills. Most were on-the-job training and retraining courses, a normal part of any industrial system. These schools continually received publicity in the domestic media as a symbol of social justice, but it was unclear whether they received adequate resources to achieve this end.

China's educational television system began in 1960 but was suspended during the Cultural Revolution in 1966. In 1979 the Central Radio and Television University was established in Beijing with branches in twenty-eight provincial-level universities. Many Central Radio and Television University students are recent senior-middle-school graduates who scored just below the cut-off point for admission to conventional colleges and universities. Full-time (who take four courses) and part-time students (two courses) have at least two years' work experience, and they return to their jobs after graduation. Spare-time students (one course) study after work. Students whose work units grant them permission to study in a television university are paid their normal wages; expenses for most of their books and other educational materials are paid for by the state. A typical Central Radio and Television University student spends up to six hours a day over a three-year period watching lectures on videotapes produced by some of the best teachers in China. These lectures are augmented by face-to-face tutoring by local instructors and approximately four hours of homework each evening. The major problem with the system is that there are too few television sets.

In 1987 the Central Television and Radio University had its programs produced, transmitted, and financed by the Ministry of Radio, Cinema, and Television (see Telecommunications Services, ch. 8). The State Education Commission developed its curriculum and distributed its printed support materials. Curriculum included both basic, general-purpose courses in science and technology and more specialized courses. Programs in English-language instruction were particularly popular. The Central Television and Radio University offered more than 1,000 classes in Beijing and its suburbs and 14 majors in 2- to 3-year courses through 56 working centers.

Students who passed final examinations were given certificates entitling them to the same level of remuneration as graduates of regular, full-time colleges and universities. The state gave certain allowances to students awaiting jobs during their training period.

Literacy and Language Reform

The continuing campaigns to eradicate illiteracy also were a part of basic education. Chinese government statistics indicated that of a total population of nearly 1.1 billion in 1985, about 230 million people were illiterate or semiliterate. The difficulty of mastering written Chinese makes raising the literacy rate particularly difficult. In general, language reform was intended to make written and spoken Chinese easier to learn, which in turn would foster both literacy and linguistic unity and serve as a foundation for a simpler written language. In 1951 the party issued a directive that inaugurated a three-part plan for language reform. The plan sought to establish universal comprehension of a standardized common language, simplify written characters, and introduce, where possible, romanized forms based on the Latin alphabet. In 1956 *putonghua* was introduced as the language of instruction in schools and in the national broadcast media, and by 1977 it was in use throughout China, particularly in the government and party, and in education. Although in 1987 the government continued to endorse the goal of universalizing *putonghua*, hundreds of regional and local dialects continued to be spoken, complicating interregional communication.

A second language reform required the simplification of ideographs because ideographs with fewer strokes are easier to learn. In 1964 the Committee for Reforming the Chinese Written Language released an official list of 2,238 simplified characters most basic to the language. Simplification made literacy easier, although people taught only in simplified characters were cut off from the wealth of Chinese literature written in traditional characters. Any idea of replacing ideographic script with romanized script was soon abandoned, however, by government and education leaders.

A third area of change involved the proposal to use the pinyin romanization system more widely. Pinyin (first approved by the National People's Congress in 1958) was encouraged primarily to facilitate the spread of *putonghua* in regions where other dialects and languages are spoken. By the mid-1980s, however, the use of pinyin was not as widespread as the use of *putonghua*.

Retaining literacy was as much a problem as acquiring it, particularly among the rural population. Literacy rates declined between 1966 and 1976. Political disorder may have contributed to the decline, but the basic problem was that the many Chinese ideographs can be mastered only through rote learning and are often forgotten because of disuse.

Policy Toward Intellectuals

Background

The current status of Chinese intellectuals reflects traditions established in the imperial period. For most of this period, government officials were selected from among the literati on the basis of the Confucian civil service examination system (see Restoration of Empire, ch. 1; Traditional Society and Culture, ch. 3). Intellectuals were both participants in and critics of the government. As Confucian scholars, they were torn between their loyalty to the emperor and their obligation to "correct wrong thinking" when they perceived it. Then, as now, most intellectual and government leaders subscribed to the premise that ideological change was a prerequisite for political change. Historically, Chinese intellectuals rarely formed groups to oppose the established government. Rather, individual intellectuals or groups of intellectuals allied themselves with cliques within the government to lend support to the policies of that clique.

With the abolition of the civil service examination system in 1905 and the end of the last imperial dynasty in 1911, intellectuals no longer had a vehicle for direct participation in the government. Although the absence of a strong national government would have been expected to provide a favorable situation for maximum intellectual independence, other inhibiting factors—such as the concentration of intellectuals in foreign-controlled treaty ports, isolated from the mainstream of Chinese society, or in universities dependent on government or missionary financing—remained. Probably the greatest obstacle to the development of an intellectual community free of outside control was the rising tide of nationalism coupled with the fear of being accused of selling out to foreign interests. In 1927 the newly established Guomindang government in Nanjing attempted to establish an intellectual orthodoxy based on the ideas of Sun Yat-sen, but intellectuals continued to operate with a certain degree of freedom in universities and treaty ports (see Nationalism and Communism, ch. 1). Following the Japanese invasion and occupation of large parts of China in the 1930s, the Guomindang government tightened control over every aspect of life, causing a large number of dissident intellectuals to seek refuge in Communist-administered areas or in Hong Kong.

When the People's Republic of China was established in 1949, intellectuals came under strict government control. Educated overseas Chinese (see Glossary) were invited to return home, and those intellectuals who remained in China were urged to contribute their technical expertise to rebuilding the country. Intellectuals were expected to serve the party and the state. Independent thinking was stifled, and political dissent was not tolerated.

In mid-1956 the Chinese Communist Party felt secure enough to launch the Hundred Flowers Campaign (see Glossary), soliciting criticism under the classical "double hundred" slogan "Let a hundred flowers bloom, let the hundred schools of thought contend." "Let a hundred flowers bloom" applied to the development of the arts, and "let the hundred schools of thought contend" encouraged the development of science. The initiation of this campaign was followed by the publication in early 1957 of Mao Zedong's essay "On the Correct Handling of Contradictions among the People," in which he drew a distinction between "constructive criticisms among the people" and "hateful and destructive criticism between the enemy and ourselves." In August 1957, when it was clear to the leadership that widespread criticism of the party and party cadres had gotten out of hand, the Anti-Rightist Campaign was launched to suppress all divergent thought and firmly reestablish orthodox ideology. Writers who had answered the party's invitation to offer criticisms and alternative solutions to China's problems were abruptly silenced, and many were sent to reform camps or internal exile. By the early 1960s, however, a few intellectuals within the party were bold enough to again propose policy alternatives, within stringent limits.

When the Cultural Revolution began, in 1966, party functionaries assumed positions of leadership at most research institutes and universities, and many schools were closed or converted to "soldiers', workers', and peasants' universities." Intellectuals, denounced as the "stinking ninth category," either were purged or had their work heavily edited for political "purity," which severely hampered most serious research and scholarship.

Following the fall of Lin Biao, minister of national defense and Mao's heir apparent, in 1971, the atmosphere for intellectuals began to improve. Under the aegis of Zhou Enlai and later Deng Xiaoping, many intellectuals were restored to their former positions and warily resumed their pre-Cultural Revolution duties. In January 1975 Zhou Enlai set out his ambitious Four Modernizations (see Glossary) program and solicited the support of China's intellectuals in turning China into a modern industrialized nation by the end of the century (see The Cultural Revolution Decade, 1966–76; The Post-Mao Period, 1976–78, ch. 1).

Post-Mao Development

The Third Plenum of the Eleventh National Party Congress Central Committee in December 1978 officially made the Four Modernizations basic national policy and reemphasized the importance of intellectuals in achieving them. The policy of "seeking truth from facts" was stressed, and scholars and researchers were given freer rein to pursue scientific research. Most mainstream intellectuals were content to avoid political involvement and to take on the role of scholar-specialists within their spheres of competence, with the understanding that as long as they observed the four cardinal principles—upholding socialism, the dictatorship of the proletariat, the leadership of the party, and Marxism-Leninism-Mao Zedong Thought—they would be permitted to conduct their research with minimal bureaucratic interference. This was accomplished more easily in the natural sciences, which are generally recognized as apolitical, than in the social sciences, humanities, and the arts.

The first serious challenge to the more tolerant policy toward intellectuals came in 1980, as conservative ideologues in the military and the party stepped up their calls to combat "bourgeois liberalization," a loosely defined appellation for any writing or activity believed to stretch the limits of the four cardinal principles. By early 1981 opposition to "bourgeois liberalization" was focused on Bai Hua, a writer with the Political Department of what was then the Wuhan Military Region. Bai had long been a strong advocate for relaxation of cultural and social policy, but what especially alarmed the guardians of cultural orthodoxy was his screenplay "Bitter Love," which depicted the frustrated patriotism of an old painter who faces misunderstanding and ill-treatment when he returns to China from the United States. When the screenplay first appeared in a nationally circulated literary magazine in the fall of 1979, it caused little stir. The motion picture version, however, which was shown to selected officials, drew strong censure. A commentary in the April 18, 1981, issue of *Jiefangjun Bao* (Liberation Army Daily) accused Bai Hua of violating the four cardinal principles and described the screenplay as an example of "bourgeois liberalization." The commentary was reprinted in the next month's issue of *Jiefangjun Wenyi* (Liberation Army Literature and Art), along with other articles critical of "Bitter Love." Over the next few months the criticism was taken up by most civilian newspapers, and the acting minister of culture, Zhou Weizhi, singled out "Bitter Love" for attack in a speech delivered to the Twentieth Session of the Fifth National People's Congress Standing Committee in September. Finally, Bai Hua yielded to the ostracism and wrote a letter of self-criticism addressed to *Jiefangjun Bao* and *Wenyibao* (Literary Gazette), in which he apologized for a "lack of balance" in "Bitter Love" and for failing to recognize the power of the party and the people to overcome obstacles in Chinese society. Bai Hua was out of public view for the next year but remained active, writing four short stories in the period. In January 1983 he was invited by the Ministry of Culture to participate in a Shanghai conference on film scripts, and in May of that year the Beijing People's Art Theater presented his new historical play, "The King of Wu's Golden Spear and the King of Yue's Sword," thought by many to be a veiled criticism of Mao Zedong and perhaps even of Deng Xiaoping. Although the "Bitter Love" controversy caused considerable anxiety in the intellectual community, it is as noteworthy for what it did not do as for what it did do. Unlike previous campaigns in which writers and all of their works were condemned, criticism in this case focused on one work, "Bitter Love." Neither Bai Hua's other works nor his political difficulties in the 1950s and 1960s were part of the discussion. In fact, as if to emphasize the limited nature of the campaign, at its height in May 1981 Bai was given a national prize for poetry by the Chinese Writers' Association.

After a mild respite in 1982 and most of 1983, "antibourgeois liberalization" returned in full force in the short-lived campaign against "spiritual pollution" launched by a speech given by Deng Xiaoping at the Second Plenum of the Twelfth Central Committee in October 1983. In the speech, Deng inveighed against advocates of abstract theories of human nature, "bourgeois humanitarianism," "bourgeois liberalization," and socialist alienation, as well as the growing fascination in China with "decadent elements" from Western culture. Conservatives, led by Political Bureau member Hu Qiaomu and party Propaganda Department head Deng Liqun, used the campaign in an effort to oppose those aspects of society that they disliked. The campaign soon was out of control and extended to areas beyond the scope that Deng Xiaoping had intended, raising fears at home and abroad of another Cultural Revolution.

Because of the campaign against spiritual pollution, intellectuals (including scientists and managerial and technical personnel) and party and government cadres were hesitant to take any action that could expose them to criticism. Peasants, whose production had greatly increased under the responsibility system adopted in 1981, felt uncertain about the future course of central policy (see Post-Mao Policies, ch. 6). Because of this, many of them returned their specialized certificates and contracts to local authorities, sold their equipment, and lowered production targets. Many ordinary citizens, especially the young, resented the sudden interference in their private lives. Foreign businessmen and government leaders expressed serious reservations about the investment climate and China's policy of opening to the world.

Because of these adverse results, the central leadership reevaluated the campaign and limited it to theoretical, literary, and artistic circles and did not permit it to extend to science and technology, the economy, or rural areas. All ideological, theoretical, literary, and artistic issues were to be settled through discussion, criticism, and self-criticism, without resorting to labeling or attacks. By January 1984 the campaign against spiritual pollution had died out, and attention was once more turned to reducing leftist influence in government and society.

Following the campaign's failure, and perhaps because of it, the position and security of intellectuals improved significantly. In 1984 the party and government turned their attention to promoting urban economic reforms. A more positive approach to academic and cultural pursuits was reflected in periodic exhortations in the official press calling on the people to support and encourage the building of "socialist spiritual civilization," a term used to denote general intellectual activity, including ethics and morality, science, and culture.

Writers and other intellectuals were heartened by a speech delivered by Hu Qili, secretary of the party Secretariat, to the Fourth National Writers' Congress (December 29, 1984, to January 5, 1985). In the speech, Hu decried the political excesses that produced derogatory labels and decrees about what writers should and should not write and called literary freedom "a vital part of socialist literature." But as writers began to test the limits of the free expression called for by Hu Qili, they were reminded of their "social responsibilities," a thinly veiled warning for them to use self-censorship and to remain within the limits of free expression.

These limits, still poorly defined, were tested once again when Song Longxian, a young researcher at Nanjing University, using the pseudonym Ma Ding, published an article entitled "Ten Changes in Contemporary Chinese Economic Research" in the November 2, 1985, issue of the trade union paper *Gongren Ribao* (Workers' Daily). The article urged a pragmatic approach to economic theory and sharply attacked much previous economic research. A somewhat toned-downed version was republished in a subsequent issue of *Beijing Review*, a weekly magazine for foreign readers, and immediately became the center of a controversy continuing well into 1986. Ma Ding's supporters, however, far outnumbered his critics and included some important government officials. In May 1986 the editor of *Gongren Ribao*, writing in another economic journal, summed up the controversy. He termed the criticism of the article of far greater significance than the article itself and commended the "related departments" for handling the "Ma Ding incident very prudently" and "relatively satisfactorily," and he expressed the hope that "more people in our country, particularly leaders," would join in "providing powerful protection to the theoretical workers who are brave enough to explore."

In 1986 there were numerous calls for a new Hundred Flowers Campaign, and there were indications that these calls were being orchestrated from the top. At a May 1986 conference to commemorate the thirtieth anniversary of the original Hundred Flowers Campaign, Zhu Houze, new head of the party's Propaganda Department, sounded the keynote when he said, "Only through the comparison and contention of different viewpoints and ideas can people gradually arrive at a truthful understanding. . . ." Qin Jianxian, editor of *Shijie Jingji Daobao* (World Economic Journal), carried this theme further when he called for "unprecedented shocks to political, economic, and social life as well as to people's ideas, spiritual state, lifestyle, and thinking methods." In a July 1986 interview with *Beijing Review*, Wang Meng, the newly appointed minister of culture, held out great expectations for a new Hundred Flowers Campaign that he said "could arouse the enthusiasm of writers and artists and give them the leeway to display their individual artistic character." During the summer of 1986, expectations were raised for a resolution to come out of the Sixth Plenum of the Twelfth Central Committee in September, a resolution that General Secretary Hu Yaobang promised would have a "profound influence on the development of spiritual civilization." The actual document, however, was a watered-down compromise that fell far short of expectations. It became clear that intellectual policy is not a matter to be easily resolved in the short-term but requires lengthy debate.

Culture and the Arts

Traditional Literature

Classics

China has a wealth of classical literature, both poetry and prose, dating from the Eastern Zhou dynasty (770–221 B.C.) and including the Classics attributed to Confucius (see The Zhou Period, ch. 1; Traditional Society and Culture, ch. 3). Among the most important classics in Chinese literature is the *Yijing* (Book of Changes), a manual of divination based on eight trigrams attributed to the mythical emperor Fu Xi. (By Confucius' time these eight trigrams had been multiplied to sixty-four hexagrams.) The *Yijing* is still used by adherents of folk religion. The *Shijing* (Classic of Poetry) is made up of 305 poems divided into 160 folk songs; 74 minor festal songs, traditionally sung at court festivities; 31 major festal songs, sung at more solemn court ceremonies; and 40 hymns and eulogies, sung at sacrifices to gods and ancestral spirits of the royal house. The *Shujing* (Classic of Documents) is a collection of documents and speeches alleged to have been written by rulers and officials of the early Zhou period and before. It contains the best examples of early Chinese prose. The *Liji* (Record of Rites), a restoration of the original *Lijing* (Classic of Rites), lost in the third century B.C., describes ancient rites and court ceremonies. The *Chun Qiu* (Spring and Autumn) is a historical record of the principality of Lu, Confucius' native state, from 722 to 479 B.C. It is a log of concise entries probably compiled by Confucius himself. The *Lunyu* (Analects) is a book of pithy sayings attributed to Confucius and recorded by his disciples.

Early Prose

The proponents of the Hundred Schools of Thought in the Warring States period made important contributions to Chinese prose style (see The Hundred Schools of Thought, ch. 1). The writings of Mo Zi (Mo Di; 470–391 B.C.?), Mencius (Meng Zi; 372–289 B.C.), and Zhuang Zi (369–286 B.C.) contain well-reasoned, carefully developed discourses and show a marked improvement in organization and style over what went before. Mo Zi is known for extensively and effectively using methodological reasoning in his polemic prose. Mencius contributed elegant diction and, along with Zhuang Zi, is known for his extensive use of comparisons, anecdotes, and allegories. By the third century B.C., these writers had developed a simple, concise prose noted for its economy of words, which served as a model of literary form for over 2,000 years.

Early Poetry

Among the earliest and most influential poetic anthologies was the *Chuci* (Songs of Chu), made up primarily of poems ascribed to the semilegendary Qu Yuan (ca. 340–278 B.C.) and his follower Song Yu (fourth century B.C.). The songs in this collection are more lyrical and romantic and represent a different tradition from the earlier *Shijing*. During the Han dynasty (206 B.C.–A.D. 220), this form evolved into the *fu*, a poem usually in rhymed verse except for introductory and concluding passages that are in prose, often in the form of questions and answers. The era of disunity that followed the Han period saw the rise of romantic nature poetry heavily influenced by Taoism.

Classical poetry reached its zenith during the Tang dynasty (A.D. 618–907). The early Tang period was best known for its *lüshi* (regulated verse), an eight-line poem with five or seven words in each line; *zi* (verse following strict rules of prosody); and *jueju* (truncated verse), a four-line poem with five or seven words in each line. The two best-known poets of the period were Li Bai (701–762) and Du Fu (712–770). Li Bai was known for the romanticism of his poetry; Du Fu was seen as a Confucian moralist with a strict sense of duty toward society.

Later Tang poets developed greater realism and social criticism and refined the art of narration. One of the best known of the later Tang poets was Bai Juyi (772–846), whose poems were an inspired and critical comment on the society of his time.

Subsequent writers of classical poetry lived under the shadow of their great Tang predecessors, and although there were many fine poets in subsequent dynasties, none reached the level of this period. As the classical style of poetry became more stultified, a more flexible poetic medium, the *ci*, arrived on the scene. The *ci*, a poetic form based on the tunes of popular songs, some of Central Asian origin, was developed to its fullest by the poets of the Song dynasty (960–1279).

As the *ci* gradually became more literary and artificial after Song times, the *san qu*, a freer form, based on new popular songs, developed. The use of *san qu* songs in drama marked an important step in the development of vernacular literature.

Later Prose

The Tang period also saw a rejection of the ornate, artificial style of prose developed in the previous period and the emergence of a simple, direct, and forceful prose based on Han and pre-Han writing. The primary proponent of this neoclassical style of prose, which heavily influenced prose writing for the next 800 years, was Han Yu (768–824), a master essayist and strong advocate of a return to Confucian orthodoxy.

Vernacular fiction became popular after the fourteenth century, although it was never esteemed in court circles. Covering a broader range of subject matter and longer and less highly structured than literary fiction, vernacular fiction includes a number of masterpieces. The greatest is the eighteenth-century domestic novel *Hong Lou Meng* (Dream of the Red Chamber). A semiautobiographical work by a scion of a declining gentry family, *Hong Lou Meng* has been acknowledged by students of Chinese fiction to be the masterwork of its type.

Modern Prose

In the New Culture Movement (1917–23; see Glossary), literary writing style was largely replaced by the vernacular in all areas of literature (see Nationalism and Communism, ch. 1). This was brought about mainly by Lu Xun (1881–1936), China's first major stylist in vernacular prose (other than the novel), and the literary reformers Hu Shi (1891–1962) and Chen Duxiu (1880–1942).

The late 1920s and 1930s were years of creativity in Chinese fiction, and literary journals and societies espousing various artistic theories proliferated. Among the major writers of the period were Guo Moruo (1892–1978), a poet, historian, essayist, and critic; Mao Dun (1896–1981), the first of the novelists to emerge from the League of Left-Wing Writers and one whose work reflected the revolutionary struggle and disillusionment of the late 1920s; and Ba Jin (b. 1904), a novelist whose work was influenced by Ivan Turgenev and other Russian writers. In the 1930s Ba Jin produced a trilogy that depicted the struggle of modern youth against the age-old dominance of the Confucian family system. Comparison often is made between *Jia* (Family), one of the novels in the trilogy, and *Hong Lou Meng*. Another writer of the period was the gifted satirist and novelist Lao She (1899–1966). Many of these writers became important as administrators of artistic and literary policy after 1949. Most of those still alive during the Cultural Revolution were either purged or forced to submit to public humiliation (see The Cultural Revolution Decade, 1966–76, ch. 1).

The League of Left-Wing Writers was founded in 1930 and included Lu Xun in its leadership. By 1932 it had adopted the Soviet doctrine of socialist realism, that is, the insistence that art must concentrate on contemporary events in a realistic way, exposing the ills of nonsocialist society and promoting the glorious future under communism. After 1949 socialist realism, based on Mao's famous 1942 "Yan'an Talks on Literature and Art," became the uniform style of Chinese authors whose works were published. Conflict, however, soon developed between the government and the writers. The ability to satirize and expose the evils in contemporary society that had made writers useful to the Chinese Communist Party before its accession to power was no longer welcomed. Even more unwelcome to the party was the persistence among writers of what was deplored as "petty bourgeois idealism," "humanitarianism," and an insistence on freedom to choose subject matter.

At the time of the Great Leap Forward, the government increased its insistence on the use of socialist realism and combined with it so-called revolutionary realism and revolutionary romanticism (see The Great Leap Forward, 1958–60, ch. 1). Authors were permitted to write about contemporary China, as well as other times during China's modern period—as long as it was accomplished with the desired socialist revolutionary realism. Nonetheless, the political restrictions discouraged many writers. Although authors were encouraged to write, production of literature fell off to the point that in 1962 only forty-two novels were published.

During the Cultural Revolution, the repression and intimidation led by Mao's fourth wife, Jiang Qing, succeeded in drying up all cultural activity except a few "model" operas and heroic stories. Although it has since been learned that some writers continued to produce in secret, during that period no significant literary work was published.

Literature in the Post-Mao Period

The arrest of Jiang Qing and the other members of the Gang of Four (see Glossary) in 1976, and especially the reforms initiated at the Third Plenum of the Eleventh Central Committee in December 1978, led more and more older writers and some younger writers to take up their pens again. Much of the literature discussed the serious abuses of power that had taken place at both the national and the local levels during the Cultural Revolution. The writers decried the waste of time and talent during that decade and bemoaned abuses that had held China back. At the same time, the writers expressed eagerness to make a contribution to building Chinese society.

This literature, often called "the literature of the wounded," contained some disquieting views of the party and the political system. Intensely patriotic, these authors wrote cynically of the political leadership that gave rise to the extreme chaos and disorder of the Cultural Revolution. Some of them extended the blame to the entire generation of leaders and to the political system itself. The political authorities were faced with a serious problem: how could they encourage writers to criticize and discredit the abuses of the Cultural Revolution without allowing that criticism to go beyond what they considered tolerable limits?

During this period, a large number of novels and short stories were published; literary magazines from before the Cultural Revolution were revived, and new ones were added to satisfy the seemingly insatiable appetite of the reading public. There was a special interest in foreign works. Linguists were commissioned to translate recently published foreign literature, often without carefully considering its interest for the Chinese reader. Literary magazines specializing in translations of foreign short stories became very popular, especially among the young.

It is not surprising that such dramatic change brought objections from some leaders in government and literary and art circles, who feared it was happening too fast. The first reaction came in 1980 with calls to combat "bourgeois liberalization," a campaign that was repeated in 1981. These two difficult periods were followed by the campaign against spiritual pollution in late 1983, but by 1986 writers were again enjoying greater creative freedom (see Policy Toward Intellectuals, this ch.).

Traditional Arts

Drama

Traditional drama, often called "Chinese opera," grew out of the *zaju* (variety plays) of the Yuan dynasty (1279–1368) and continues to exist in 368 different forms, the best known of which is Beijing Opera, which assumed its present form in the mid-nineteenth century and was extremely popular in the Qing dynasty (1644–1911) court. In Beijing Opera, traditional Chinese string and percussion instruments provide a strong rhythmic accompaniment to the acting. The acting is based on allusion: gestures, footwork, and other body movements express such actions as riding a horse, rowing a boat, or opening a door. Spoken dialogue is divided into recitative and Beijing colloquial speech, the former employed by serious characters and the latter by young females and clowns. Character roles are strictly defined. The traditional repertoire of Beijing Opera includes more than 1,000 works, mostly taken from historical novels about political and military struggles.

In the early years of the People's Republic, the development of Beijing Opera was encouraged; many new operas on historical and modern themes were written, and earlier operas continued to be performed. As a popular art form, opera has usually been the first of the arts to reflect changes in Chinese policy. In the mid-1950s, for example, it was the first to benefit under the Hundred Flowers Campaign. Similarly, the attack in November 1965 on Beijing Deputy Mayor Wu Han and his historical play, "Hai Rui's Dismissal from Office," signaled the beginning of the Cultural Revolution. During the Cultural Revolution, most opera troupes were disbanded, performers and scriptwriters were persecuted, and all operas except the eight "model operas" approved by Jiang Qing and her associates were banned. After the fall of the Gang of Four in 1976, Beijing Opera enjoyed a revival and continued to be a

Beijing Opera characters. The figure at right is Baogong, a high official known for his upright and unbending character.
Courtesy Xinhua News Agency

very popular form of entertainment both in theaters and on television.

In traditional Chinese theater, no plays were performed in the vernacular or without singing. But at the turn of the twentieth century, Chinese students returning from abroad began to experiment with Western plays. Following the May Fourth Movement of 1919, a number of Western plays were staged in China, and Chinese playwrights began to imitate this form. The most notable of the new-style playwrights was Cao Yu (b. 1910). His major works—"Thunderstorm," "Sunrise," "Wilderness," and "Peking Man"—written between 1934 and 1940, have been widely read and performed in China.

In the 1930s, theatrical productions performed by traveling Red Army cultural troupes in Communist-controlled areas were consciously used to promote party goals and political philosophy. By the 1940s theater was well-established in the Communist-controlled areas.

In the early years of the People's Republic, Western-style theater was presented mainly in the form of "socialist realism." During the Cultural Revolution, however, Western-style plays were condemned as "dead drama" and "poisonous weeds" and were not performed.

Following the Cultural Revolution, Western-style theater experienced a revival. Many new works appeared, and revised and banned plays from China and abroad were reinstated in the national repertoire. Many of the new plays strained at the limits of creative freedom and were alternately commended and condemned, depending on the political atmosphere. One of the most outspoken of the new breed of playwrights was Sha Yexin. His controversial play "The Imposter," which dealt harshly with the favoritism and perquisites accorded party members, was first produced in 1979. In early 1980 the play was roundly criticized by Secretary General Hu Yaobang—the first public intervention in the arts since the Cultural Revolution. In the campaign against bourgeois liberalism in 1981 and the antispiritual pollution campaign in 1983, Sha and his works were again criticized. Through it all Sha continued to write for the stage and to defend himself and his works in the press. In late 1985 Sha Yexin was accepted into the Chinese Communist Party and appointed head of the Shanghai People's Art Theater, where he continued to produce controversial plays.

Music

Chinese music appears to date back to the dawn of Chinese civilization, and documents and artifacts provide evidence of a well-developed musical culture as early as the Zhou dynasty (1027–221 B.C.). The Imperial Music Bureau, first established in the Qin dynasty (221–207 B.C.), was greatly expanded under the Han emperor Wu Di (140–87 B.C.) and charged with supervising court music and military music and determining what folk music would be officially recognized. In subsequent dynasties, the development of Chinese music was strongly influenced by foreign music, especially that of Central Asia.

Chinese vocal music has traditionally been sung in a thin, nonresonant voice or in falsetto and is usually solo rather than choral. All traditional Chinese music is melodic rather than harmonic. Instrumental music is played on solo instruments or in small ensembles of plucked and bowed stringed instruments, flutes, and various cymbals, gongs, and drums. The scale has five notes.

The New Culture Movement of the 1910s and 1920s evoked a great deal of lasting interest in Western music as a number of Chinese musicians who had studied abroad returned to perform Western classical music and to compose works of their own based on the Western musical notation system. Symphony orchestras were formed in most major cities and performed to a wide audience in the concert halls and on radio. Popular music—greatly influenced by Western music, especially that of the United States—also gained a wide audience in the 1940s. After the 1942 Yan'an Forum on Literature and Art, a large-scale campaign was launched in the Communist-controlled areas to adapt folk music to create revolutionary songs to educate the largely illiterate rural population on party goals.

After the establishment of the People's Republic, revolutionary songs continued to be performed, and much of the remainder of popular music consisted of popular songs from the Soviet Union with the lyrics translated into Chinese. Symphony orchestras flourished throughout the country, performing Western classical music and compositions by Chinese composers. Conservatories and other institutions of musical instruction were developed and expanded in the major cities. A number of orchestras from Eastern Europe performed in China, and Chinese musicians and musical groups participated in a wide variety of international festivals.

During the height of the Cultural Revolution, musical composition and performance were greatly restricted. After the Cultural Revolution, musical institutions were reinstated and musical composition and performance revived. In 1980 the Chinese Musicians' Association was formally elected to the International Musicological Society. Chinese musical groups toured foreign countries, and foreign musical organizations performed in China. In the mid-1980s popular ballads and Western folk and classical music still drew the greatest audiences, but other kinds of music, including previously banned Western jazz and rock and roll, were being performed and were receiving increasing acceptance, especially among young people.

Painting and Calligraphy

In imperial times, painting and calligraphy were the most highly appreciated arts in court circles and were produced almost exclusively by amateurs—aristocrats and scholar-officials—who alone had the leisure to perfect the technique and sensibility necessary for great brushwork. Calligraphy was thought to be the highest and purest form of painting. The implements were the brush pen, made of animal hair, and black inks made from pine soot and animal glue. In ancient times, writing, as well as painting, was done on silk. But after the invention of paper in the first century A.D., silk was gradually replaced by the new and cheaper material. Original writings by famous calligraphers have been greatly valued throughout China's history and are mounted on scrolls and hung on walls in the same way that paintings are.

Painting in the traditional style involves essentially the same techniques as calligraphy and is done with a brush dipped in black or colored ink; oils are not used. As with calligraphy, the most popular materials on which paintings are made are paper and silk. The finished work is then mounted on scrolls, which can be hung or rolled up. Traditional painting also is done in albums and on walls, lacquerwork, and other media.

Beginning in the Tang dynasty (A.D. 618–907), the primary subject matter of painting was the landscape, known as *shan-shui* (mountain-water) painting. In these landscapes, usually monochromatic and sparse, the purpose was not to reproduce exactly the appearance of nature but rather to grasp an emotion or atmosphere so as to catch the "rhythm" of nature. In Song dynasty (960–1279) times, landscapes of more subtle expression appeared; immeasurable distances were conveyed through the use of blurred outlines, mountain contours disappearing into the mist, and impressionistic treatment of natural phenomena. Emphasis was placed on the spiritual qualities of the painting and on the ability of the artist to reveal the inner harmony of man and nature, as perceived according to Taoist and Buddhist concepts (see The Hundred Schools of Thought, ch. 1).

Beginning in the thirteenth century, there developed a tradition of painting simple subjects—a branch with fruit, a few flowers, or one or two horses. Narrative painting, with a wider color range and a much busier composition than the Song painting, was immensely popular at the time of the Ming dynasty (1368–1644).

During the Ming period, the first books illustrated with colored woodcuts appeared. As the techniques of color printing were perfected, illustrated manuals on the art of painting began to be published. *Jieziyuan Huazhuan* (Manual of the Mustard Seed Garden), a five-volume work first published in 1679, has been in use as a technical textbook for artists and students ever since.

Beginning with the New Culture Movement, Chinese artists started to adopt Western techniques. It also was during this time that oil painting was introduced to China.

In the early years of the People's Republic, artists were encouraged to employ socialist realism. Some Soviet socialist realism was imported without modification, and painters were assigned subjects and expected to mass-produce paintings. This regimen was considerably relaxed in 1953, and after the Hundred Flowers Campaign of 1956–57, traditional Chinese painting experienced a significant revival. Along with these developments in professional art circles, there was a proliferation of peasant art depicting everyday life in the rural areas on wall murals and in open-air painting exhibitions.

During the Cultural Revolution, art schools were closed, and publication of art journals and major art exhibitions ceased. Nevertheless, amateur art continued to flourish throughout this period.

Following the Cultural Revolution, art schools and professional organizations were reinstated. Exchanges were set up with groups of foreign artists, and Chinese artists began to experiment with new subjects and techniques.

Contemporary Performing Arts

Motion Pictures

Motion pictures were introduced to China in 1896, but the film industry was not started until 1917. During the 1920s film technicians from the United States trained Chinese technicians in Shanghai, an early filmmaking center, and American influence continued to be felt there for the next two decades. In the 1930s and 1940s, several socially and politically important films were produced.

The film industry continued to develop after 1949. In the 17 years between the founding of the People's Republic and the Cultural Revolution, 603 feature films and 8,342 reels of documentaries and newsreels were produced. The first wide-screen film was produced in 1960. Animated films using a variety of folk arts, such as papercuts, shadow plays, puppetry, and traditional paintings, also were very popular for entertaining and educating children.

During the Cultural Revolution, the film industry was severely restricted. Most previous films were banned, and only a few new ones were produced. In the years immediately following the Cultural Revolution, the film industry again flourished as a medium of popular entertainment. Domestically produced films played to large audiences, and tickets for foreign film festivals sold quickly.

In the 1980s the film industry fell on hard times, faced with the dual problems of competition from other forms of entertainment and concern on the part of the authorities that many of the popular thriller and martial arts films were socially unacceptable. In January 1986 the film industry was transferred from the Ministry of Culture to the newly formed Ministry of Radio, Cinema, and Television to bring it under "stricter control and management" and to "strengthen supervision over production."

Radio and Television

Radio and television expanded rapidly in the 1980s as important means of mass communication and popular entertainment (see Telecommunications, ch. 8; The Media, ch. 10). By 1985 radio reached 75 percent of the population through 167 radio stations, 215 million radios, and a vast wired loudspeaker system. Television, growing at an even more rapid rate, reached two-thirds of the population through more than 104 stations (up from 52 in 1984 and 44 in 1983); an estimated 85 percent of the urban population had access to television. As radio and television stations grew, the content of the programming changed drastically from the political lectures and statistical lists of the previous period. Typical radio listening included soap operas based on popular novels and a variety of Chinese and foreign music. Most television shows were entertainment, including feature films, sports, drama, music, dance, and children's programming. In 1985 a survey of a typical week of television programming made by the Shanghai publication *Wuxiandian Yu Dianshi* (Journal of Radio and Television) revealed that more than half of the programming could be termed entertainment; education made up 24 percent of the remainder of the programming and news 15 percent. A wide cross section of international news was presented each evening. Most news broadcasts were borrowed from foreign news organizations, and a Chinese summary was dubbed over. China Central Television also contracted with several foreign broadcasters for entertainment programs. Between 1982 and 1985, six United States television companies signed agreements to provide American programs to China.

One of China's many folk arts is juggling.
Courtesy Douglass M. Dolan

Folk and Variety Arts

Folk and variety arts have a long history in China. One of the oldest forms of folk art is puppetry. Puppeteers use various kinds of puppets, including marionettes, rod puppets, cloth puppets, and wire puppets in performances incorporating folk songs and dances and some dialogues. The subject matter is derived mainly from children's stories and fables. The shadow play is a form of puppetry that is performed by moving figures made of animal skins or cardboard held behind a screen lit by lamplight. The subject matter and singing style in shadow plays are closely related to local opera. Another popular folk art is the *quyi*, which consists of various kinds of storytelling and comic monologues and dialogues, often to the accompaniment of clappers, drums, or stringed instruments.

Variety arts, including tightrope walking, acrobatics, animal acts, and sleight of hand date back at least as far as the Han dynasty (206 B.C.–A.D. 220) and were very popular in the imperial court. Later, many of these feats were incorporated into the traditional theater, and they continued to be performed by itinerant troupes. As these troupes traveled around the countryside, they developed and enriched their repertoire. Since 1949 these art forms have gained new respectability. Troupes have been established in the provinces, autonomous regions, and special municipalities, and theaters specifically dedicated to the variety arts have been built in major cities. Some troupes have become world famous, playing to packed houses at home and on foreign tours.

Publishing

Background

Publishing in China dates from the invention of woodblock printing around the eighth century A.D. and was greatly expanded with the invention of movable clay type in the eleventh century. From the tenth to the twelfth century, Kaifeng, Meishan, Hangzhou, and Jianyang were major printing centers. In the nineteenth century, China acquired movable lead type and photogravure printing plates and entered the age of modern book and magazine printing. The largest of the early publishing houses were the Commercial Press (Shangwu Yinshuguan), established in 1897, and the China Publishing House (Zhonghua Shuju), established in 1912, both of which were still operating in 1987. Following the May Fourth Movement of 1919, publishers, especially those associated with various groups of intellectuals, proliferated. During the Chinese civil war, New China Booksellers (Xinhua Shudian) published a large amount of Marxist literature and educational materials in the Communist-controlled areas. On the eve of the establishment of the People's Republic in 1949, there were over 700 New China Booksellers offices.

Between 1949 and 1952, the New China Booksellers offices scattered throughout the country were nationalized and given responsibility for publishing, printing, and distribution. Also, several small private publishers were brought under joint state-private ownership, and by 1956 all private publishers had been nationalized. After a brief flourishing during the Hundred Flowers Campaign of 1956–57, the publishing industry came under strong political pressure in the Anti-Rightist Campaign of 1957 (see The Transition to Socialism, 1953–57, ch. 1). The industry had not fully recovered from this campaign when it was plunged into the Cultural Revolution, a period in which publishing was severely curtailed and limited mainly to political tracts supporting various campaigns. Following the Cultural Revolution, publishing again flourished in unprecedented ways. In 1982 the China National Publishing Administration, the umbrella organization of Chinese publishers, was placed under the Ministry of Culture, but actual management of the industry was directed through four systems of administration: direct state administration; administration by committees or organizations of the State Council or the party Central Committee;

armed forces administration; and administration by provinces, autonomous regions, or special municipalities.

In 1984 statistics showed that 17 of the country's 418 publishing establishments were in Shanghai, whereas Beijing was home to 160 publishers. In 1985 plans were announced to foster the growth of the publishing industry in Chongqing, Xi'an, Wuhan, and Shenyang to take some of the workload from Beijing and Shanghai.

Different publishers were assigned to specific kinds of publications. For example, the People's Publishing House was responsible for publishing works on politics, philosophy, and the social sciences; the People's Literature Publishing House produced ancient and modern Chinese and foreign literature and literary history and theory; the China Publishing House had the principal responsibility for collating and publishing Chinese classical literary, historical, and philosophical works, and the Commercial Press was the principal publisher of Chinese-to-foreign-language reference works and translations of foreign works in the social sciences. Other publishers dealt with works in specialized fields of science.

In addition to the routine method of distributing books to bookstores in major cities, other methods of distribution were devised to meet the special needs of readers in urban and rural areas throughout the country. Mobile bookshops made regular visits to factories, mines, rural villages, and People's Liberation Army units, and service was provided in those locations through which individuals could request books. Arrangements were made with the libraries of educational institutions and enterprises to supply them with the books that they required, and books specifically applicable to certain industries were systematically recommended and provided to the departments concerned. Also, book fairs and exhibits frequently were provided at meetings and in public parks on holidays and other special occasions.

Newspapers

In 1987 China had two news agencies, the Xinhua (New China) News Agency and the China News Service (Zhongguo Xinwenshe) (see The Media, ch. 10). Xinhua was the major source of news and photographs for central and local newspapers. The official newspapers *Renmin Ribao* (People's Daily) and *Guangming Ribao* (Enlightenment Daily), and the People's Liberation Army's *Jiefangjun Bao* (Liberation Army Daily) continued to have the largest circulation. In addition to these major party and army organs, most professional and scientific organizations published newspapers or journals containing specialized information in fields as varied as astronomy and entomology. Local morning and evening newspapers concentrating on news and feature stories about local people and events were extremely popular, selling out each day shortly after they arrived at the newsstands. In June 1981 the English-language *China Daily* began publication. This newspaper, which was provided for foreigners living or traveling in China but which also was read by a large number of Chinese literate in English, offered international news and sports from the major foreign wire services as well as interesting domestic news and feature articles. *Cankao Xiaoxi* (Reference News), an official news organ that carried foreign news items in Chinese translation, was available to cadres and their families. In 1980 it enjoyed a circulation of 11 million, but, with the subsequent proliferation of other news sources, its circulation dropped to 4 million in 1985, causing the subscription policy to be changed to make it available to all Chinese. Another source of foreign reporting was *Cankao Ziliao* (Reference Information), a more restricted Chinese reprint of foreign reportage available only to middle- and upper-level cadres. Both of these publications often included foreign reports critical of China.

Libraries and Archives

Very early in Chinese civilization, scholars had extensive private libraries, and all of the imperial dynasties constructed libraries and archives to house literary treasures and official records. The first modern libraries, however, did not appear in China until the late nineteenth century; even then, library service grew slowly and sporadically. In 1949 there were only fifty-five public libraries at the county level and above, most concentrated in major coastal commercial centers.

Following the founding of the People's Republic, government and education leaders strove to develop library services and make them available throughout the country. The National Book Coordination Act of 1957 authorized the establishment of two national library centers, one in Beijing and the other in Shanghai, and nine regional library networks. Even so, libraries still were scarce, and those facilities that were available were cramped and offered only rudimentary services. Seeing the lack of libraries as a major impediment to modernization efforts, government leaders in the early 1980s took special interest in the development of library services. The special concentration of funds and talent began to produce significant results. By 1986 China had over 200,000 libraries, including a national library and various public, educational, scientific, and military libraries. More than forty Chinese institutions of higher learning also had established library-science or

Anhui Provincial Library
Courtesy Alfonz Lengyel

information-science departments. There were more than 2,300 public libraries at the county level and above, containing nearly 256 million volumes, and below the county level some 53,000 cultural centers included a small library or reading room.

The country's main library, the National Library of China, in central Beijing, housed a rich collection of books, periodicals, newspapers, maps, prints, photographs, manuscripts, microforms, tape recordings, and inscriptions on bronze, stone, bones, and tortoiseshells. In 1987 a new National Library building, one of the world's largest library structures, was completed in the western suburbs. The Shanghai Municipal Library, one of the largest public libraries in the country, contained over 7 million volumes, nearly 1 million of which were in foreign languages. The Beijing University Library took over the collections of the Yanjing University Library in 1950 and by the mid-1980s—with more than 3 million volumes, one-fourth of them in foreign languages—was one of the best university libraries in the country.

On the basis of the General Rules for Archives published in 1983, historical archives were being expanded at the provincial and county levels. Two of the most important archives were the Number One Historical Archives of China, located in Beijing containing the archives of the Ming and Qing dynasties, and the Number Two Historical Archives of China, located in Nanjing containing the archives of the Guomindang period. A number of foreign scholars have been granted access to these archives. In 1987 public and research libraries still faced serious space, management, and service problems. Even with the special efforts being made to solve these problems, it was clear that they would not be quickly resolved.

In the late 1980s, China was experiencing an active educational and cultural life. Students were staying in school longer, educational standards were being raised, and facilities were being improved. Intellectuals were encouraged to develop their expertise, especially in the scientific and technical spheres, and a wide variety of traditional and foreign literary and art forms were allowed to flourish. This situation was likely to continue as long as it served the interest of economic modernization and posed no threat to the political establishment.

* * *

Several general works provide a good overview of China's education and culture. However, because the most important educational reforms did not evolve or become effective until 1985-86, and were still changing in 1987, these books generally did not address many of the latest educational reforms. Some of the most valuable books available include *China Issues and Prospects in Education, Annex 1, 1985* by the World Bank, which provides an overview of the system, detailed statistics, and projections; John Cleverly's *The Schooling of China*, which has excellent chapters on the anatomy of the educational system and its problems and prospects; and Ruth Hayhoe's *Contemporary Chinese Education*, which has valuable chapters on primary, secondary, and teacher education. Other informative works are the chapter on "Education" by Stanley Rosen in a book he co-edited with John Burns, entitled *Policy Conflicts in Post-Mao China*, and a brief article by Eli Seifman in the March 1986 issue of *Asian Thought and Society*.

Carol Lee Hamrin and Timothy Cheek's *China's Establishment Intellectuals*, Merle Goldman's *China's Intellectuals*, and Michael S. Duke's *Blooming and Contending* are indispensable sources of information on Chinese intellectual policy past and present. Liu Wu-chi's *An Introduction to Chinese Literature* gives an excellent summary of traditional literature and drama, and C.T. Hsia's *A History of Modern Chinese Fiction* gives insight into modern Chinese literature before the Cultural Revolution. *Encyclopedia of China Today*, edited by Fredric M. Kaplan, Julian M. Sobin, and Stephen Andors, contains valuable information about linguistic reform and gives a good overview of the arts in the post-Cultural Revolution period.

The *Zhongguo Chuban Nianjian* (China Publishing Yearbook), put out by the Commercial Press since 1980, provides rare data on that industry. Chi Wang's "An Overview of Libraries in the People's Republic of China" in the September 1984 issue of *China Exchange News* is an excellent source on Chinese libraries in the 1980s.

Other useful articles providing information on the changes and directions of China's education and cultural policy can be found in various issues of *Beijing Review*, *China News Analysis*, *China Exchange News*, *China Reconstructs*, and the Foreign Broadcast Information Service *Daily Report: China*, and the Joint Publications Research Service *China Report: Political, Sociological, and Military Affairs*. *People's Republic of China Yearbook* also provides useful information and statistics. (For further information and complete citations, see Bibliography.)

Chapter 5. Economic Context

A Sui dynasty (A.D. 581–617) architectural house model made of clay shows the complexity of that period's construction.

IN THE LATE 1980s the Chinese economy was a system in transition, moving cautiously away from central planning and gradually adopting some of the institutions and mechanisms of a market economy. The process of economic reform began in earnest in 1979, after Chinese leaders concluded that the Soviet-style system that had been in place since the 1950s was making little progress in improving the standard of living of the Chinese people and also was failing to close the economic gap between China and the industrialized nations.

The first major success of the economic reform program was the introduction of the responsibility system of production in agriculture, a policy that allowed farm families to work a piece of land under contract and to keep whatever profits they earned. By 1984 the responsibility system had dramatically increased food production, and the government had eliminated the people's communes—the hallmark of Chinese socialism for over twenty years. In most other sectors of the economy the role of government was reduced, managers were given more decision-making power, enterprises were encouraged to produce for profit, the role of the private sector increased, and experimentation with new forms of ownership began in the state sector. Constraints on foreign trade were relaxed, and joint ventures with foreign firms were officially encouraged as sources of modern technology and scarce foreign exchange. With rising incomes, greater incentives, and rapid growth in the service and light industrial sectors, the People's Republic of China began to exhibit some of the traits of a consumer society.

Movement toward a market system, however, was complex and difficult, and in 1987 the transition was far from complete. Relaxing restrictions on economic activity quickly alleviated some of China's most pressing economic difficulties, but it also gave rise to a new set of problems. Inflation—the greatest fear of Chinese consumers—became a problem for the first time since the early 1950s, and along with new opportunities to seek profit came growing inequality in income distribution and new temptations for crime, corruption, and Western cultural styles, regarded by many older Chinese people as decadent and "spiritually polluting." The state still owned and controlled the largest nonagricultural enterprises, and the major industries were still primarily guided by the central plan.

Thus, the Chinese economy in the late 1980s was very much a mixed system. It could not be accurately described as either a centrally planned economy or a market economy. The leadership was committed to further expansion of the reform program as a requisite for satisfactory economic growth, but at the same time it was compelled to keep a tight grip on key aspects of the economy—particularly inflation and grain production—to prevent the emergence of overwhelming political discontent. Under these circumstances, forces in the economic system worked against each other, producing what the Chinese leadership called internal "contradictions." On the one hand, the economy was no longer tightly controlled by the state plan because of the large and growing market sector. On the other hand, the market could not operate efficiently because many commodities were still under government control and most prices were still set or restricted by government agencies. Under the leadership of Deng Xiaoping, the entire nation was "riding the tiger"—making great progress but not entirely in control—and therefore unable to stop the process without risk.

Despite the burst of progress in the 1980s, the Chinese economy still shared many basic characteristics with the economies of other developing countries. The gross national product per capita in 1986 was ¥849 (for value of the yuan—see Glossary), or about US$228 (at the 1986 exchange rate), reflecting the low average level of labor productivity. As in many countries that did not begin sustained industrialization efforts until the middle of the twentieth century, the majority of the Chinese labor force—over 60 percent—was still employed in agriculture, which produced around 30 percent of the value of national output. Agricultural work still was performed primarily by hand. Modern equipment was in general use in industry but was largely typified by outdated designs and low levels of efficiency.

In other respects China's economy was quite different from those of most developing nations. The most important difference was that the Chinese economy—although in the midst of far-reaching changes—was organized as a socialist system, directed by a central planning structure. The predominance of state and collective ownership, firm central control over the financial system, redistribution of resources among regions, rationing of grain, and subsidized provision of housing resulted in a pattern of income distribution that was much narrower than those in almost all other developing countries. There was relatively little true capitalism in the form of private ownership of productive assets. Agricultural land was farmed under lease by farm households but was formally owned by villages, towns, and townships—the collective units that had replaced the rural commune system.

In the mid-1980s most Chinese were still very poor by American standards, but several important measures indicated that the quality of their lives was considerably better than implied by the level of gross national product (GNP) per capita. According to World Bank data, in 1984 energy consumption per person was 485 kilograms of oil equivalent, higher than that for any other country ranked as a low-income country and greater than the average for lower middle-income countries. In 1983 the daily calorie supply per capita was 2,620—11 percent above the basic requirement and nearly as high as the average for countries classified as upper middle-income countries. Significantly, infant mortality in 1985 was 39 per 1,000, well below the average for upper middle-income countries, and life expectancy at birth was 69 years, higher than the average for upper middle-income countries.

Despite the major economic gains made by China since 1949 and the dramatic advances of the 1980s, serious imbalances and deficiencies have persisted. Contributing to these deficiencies were the political turmoil that disrupted the economy during the Cultural Revolution decade (1966–76), insufficient flexibility in the planning process, and serious inaccuracies in price structures. Power shortages, inadequate transportation and communication networks, shortages of technicians and other highly trained personnel, insufficient foreign exchange for procurement of advanced technology from other countries, and inadequate legal and administrative provisions for both foreign and domestic trade further hindered modernization.

An important by-product of the reform program since the late 1970s has been an enormous increase in the amount of information available on the economy. The government collected and published basic national economic data in the 1950s, but the centralized statistics-keeping system broke down at the end of the 1950s, and very little statistical information was available during the 1960s and early 1970s. It was not until 1979 that the State Statistical Bureau ended the statistical "blackout" with the publication of an economic statistical communiqué. In subsequent years the State Statistical Bureau published larger and more frequent compendia, including annual almanacs of the economy and annual statistical yearbooks, which became progressively more sophisticated and informative. In addition, most provincial-level units and cities, as well as the major industries and economic sectors, such as coal mining and agriculture, began to produce their own specialized statistical yearbooks. In the early 1980s, numerous new periodicals, many of which specialized in economic data and analysis, started publication. Although Chinese statistical definitions and practices still differed from those in the West in many respects and the accuracy of some figures was called into doubt even by Chinese economists, foreign analysts in 1987 had access to a rich and growing body of data that would support extensive analysis of the Chinese economy.

General Nature of the Economy

Throughout most of the nineteenth and twentieth centuries, as during much of earlier Chinese history, the economy was barely able to meet the basic needs of the country's huge population—the largest in the world (see Population, ch. 2). In normal years the economy produced just about the amount of food required to meet the minimum nutritional requirements of the populace. In times of drought, flood, warfare, or civil disorder, there was not enough food, and before 1949 such conditions often led to starvation on a vast scale. Under the government of the People's Republic, food shortages were countered by redistributing supplies within China and by importing grain from abroad, which successfully averted famine except in the catastrophic years of 1959, 1960, and 1961.

Despite formidable constraints and disruptions, the Chinese economy was never stagnant. Production grew substantially between 1800 and 1949 and increased fairly rapidly after 1949. Before the 1980s, however, production gains were largely matched by population growth, so that productive capacity was unable to outdistance essential consumption needs significantly, particularly in agriculture. Grain output in 1979 was about twice as large as in 1952, but so was the population. As a result, little surplus was produced even in good years. Further, few resources could be spared for investment in capital goods, such as machinery, factories, mines, railroads, and other productive assets. The relatively small size of the capital stock caused productivity per worker to remain low, which in turn perpetuated the economy's inability to generate a substantial surplus (see fig. 7).

China's socialist system, with state ownership of most industry and central control over planning and the financial system, has enabled the government to mobilize whatever surplus was available and greatly increase the proportion of the national economic output devoted to investment. Western analysts estimated that investment accounted for about 25 percent of GNP in the 30 years after 1949, a rate surpassed by few other countries. Because of the comparatively low level of GNP, however, even this high rate of investment secured only a small amount of resources relative to the size of the country and the population. In 1978, for instance, only 16 percent of the GNP of the United States went into gross

A traditional country peddler. Woodcut.
Courtesy Woodcuts of Wartime China

investment, but this amounted to US$345.6 billion, whereas the approximately 25 percent of China's GNP that was invested came to about the equivalent of US$111 billion and had to serve a population 4.5 times the size of that in the United States. The limited resources available for investment prevented China from rapidly producing or importing advanced equipment. Technological development proceeded gradually, and outdated equipment continued to be used as long as possible. Consequently, many different levels of technology were in use simultaneously (see Historical Development of Science and Technology Policy, ch. 9). Most industries included some plants that were comparable to modern Western facilities, often based on imported equipment and designs. Equipment produced by Chinese factories was generally some years behind standard Western designs. Agriculture received a smaller share of state investment than industry and remained at a much lower average level of technology and productivity. Despite a significant increase in the availability of tractors, trucks, electric pumps, and mechanical threshers, most agricultural activities were still performed by people or animals (see Agricultural Policies, ch. 6).

Although the central administration coordinated the economy and redistributed resources among regions when necessary, in practice most economic activity was very decentralized, and there was

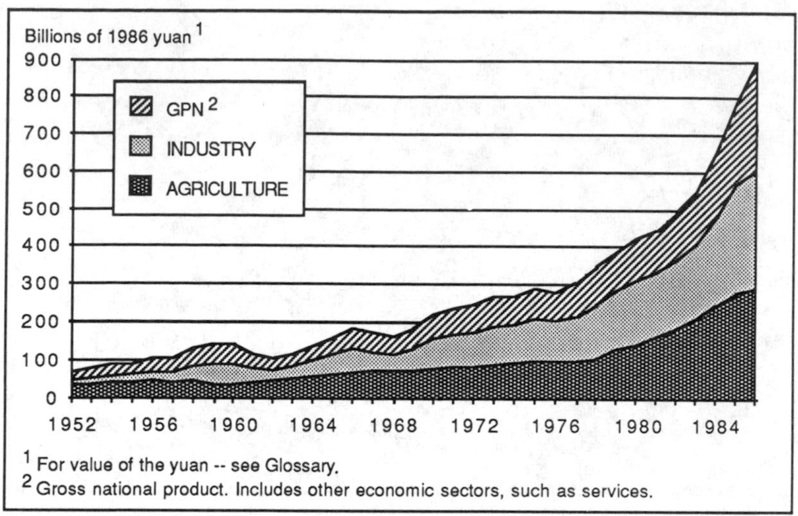

Source: Based on information from China, State Statistical Bureau, *Statistical Yearbook of China, 1986,* Hong Kong, 1986.

Figure 7. Gross National Product and Major Economic Sectors, 1952–86

relatively little flow of goods and services between areas (see Internal Trade and Distribution, ch. 8). About 75 percent of the grain grown in China, for instance, was consumed by the families that produced it. One of the most important sources of growth in the economy was the improved ability to exploit the comparative advantages of each locality by expanding transportation capacity. The communications and transportation sectors were growing and improving but still could not carry the volume of traffic required by a modern economy because of the scarcity of investment funds and advanced technology (see Transportation; Telecommunications, ch. 8).

Because of limited interaction among regions, the great variety of geographic zones in China, and the broad spectrum of technologies in use, areas differed widely in economic activities, organizational forms, and prosperity (see Physical Environment, ch. 2). Within any given city, enterprises ranged from tiny, collectively owned handicraft units, barely earning subsistence-level incomes for their members, to modern state-owned factories, whose workers received steady wages plus free medical care, bonuses, and an assortment of other benefits. The agricultural sector was diverse, accommodating well-equipped, "specialized households" that supplied scarce products and services to local markets; wealthy suburban villages specializing in the production of vegetables, pork, poultry, and eggs to sell in free markets in the nearby cities; fishing villages on the seacoast; herding groups on the grasslands of Nei Monggol Autonomous Region (Inner Mongolia); and poor, struggling grain-producing villages in the arid mountains of Shaanxi and Gansu provinces. The economy had progressed in major ways since 1949, but after four decades experts in China and abroad agreed that it had a great distance yet to go.

Economic Policies, 1949–80

When the Chinese Communist Party came to power in 1949, its leaders' fundamental long-range goals were to transform China into a modern, powerful, socialist nation. In economic terms these objectives meant industrialization, improvement of living standards, narrowing of income differences, and production of modern military equipment. As the years passed, the leadership continued to subscribe to these goals. But the economic policies formulated to achieve them were dramatically altered on several occasions in response to major changes in the economy, internal politics, and international political and economic developments.

An important distinction emerged between leaders who felt that the socialist goals of income equalization and heightened political consciousness should take priority over material progress and those who believed that industrialization and general economic modernization were prerequisites for the attainment of a successful socialist order. Among the prominent leaders who considered politics the prime consideration were Mao Zedong, Lin Biao, and the members of the Gang of Four (see Glossary). Leaders who more often stressed practical economic considerations included Liu Shaoqi, Zhou Enlai, and Deng Xiaoping. For the most part, important policy shifts reflected the alternating emphasis on political and economic goals and were accompanied by major changes in the positions of individuals in the political power structure. An important characteristic in the development of economic policies and the underlying economic model was that each new policy period, while differing significantly from its predecessor, nonetheless retained most of the existing economic organization. Thus the form of the economic model and the policies that expressed it at any given point in Chinese history reflected both the current policy emphasis and a structural foundation built up during the earlier periods.

Recovery from War, 1949–52

In 1949 China's economy was suffering from the debilitating effects of decades of warfare. Many mines and factories had been damaged or destroyed. At the end of the war with Japan in 1945, Soviet troops had dismantled about half the machinery in the major industrial areas of the northeast and shipped it to the Soviet Union. Transportation, communication, and power systems had been destroyed or had deteriorated because of lack of maintenance. Agriculture was disrupted, and food production was some 30 percent below its pre-war peak level. Further, economic ills were compounded by one of the most virulent inflations in world history.

The chief goal of the government for the 1949–52 period was simply to restore the economy to normal working order. The administration moved quickly to repair transportation and communication links and revive the flow of economic activity. The banking system was nationalized and centralized under the People's Bank of China. To bring inflation under control by 1951, the government unified the monetary system, tightened credit, restricted government budgets at all levels and put them under central control, and guaranteed the value of the currency. Commerce was stimulated and partially regulated by the establishment of state trading companies (commercial departments), which competed with private traders in purchasing goods from producers and selling them to consumers or enterprises. Transformation of ownership in industry proceeded slowly. About a third of the country's enterprises had been under state control while the Guomindang government was in power (1927–49), as was much of the modernized transportation sector. The Chinese Communist Party immediately made these units state-owned enterprises upon taking power in 1949. The remaining privately owned enterprises were gradually brought under government control, but 17 percent of industrial units were still completely outside the state system in 1952.

In agriculture a major change in landownership was carried out. Under a nationwide land reform program, titles to about 45 percent of the arable land were redistributed from landlords and more prosperous farmers to the 60 to 70 percent of farm families that previously owned little or no land. Once land reform was completed in an area, farmers were encouraged to cooperate in some phases of production through the formation of small "mutual aid teams" of six or seven households each. Thirty-nine percent of all farm households belonged to mutual aid teams in 1952. By 1952 price stability had been established, commerce had been restored, and industry and agriculture had regained their previous peak levels of production. The period of recovery had achieved its goals (see Rural Society, ch. 3; Agricultural Policies, ch. 6).

The First Five-Year Plan, 1953–57

Having restored a viable economic base, the leadership under Mao Zedong, Zhou Enlai, and other revolutionary veterans was prepared to embark on an intensive program of industrial growth and socialization. For this purpose the administration adopted the Soviet economic model, based on state ownership in the modern sector, large collective units in agriculture, and centralized economic planning. The Soviet approach to economic development was manifested in the First Five-Year Plan (1953–57) (see The Transition to Socialism, ch. 1; Organization, ch. 7). As in the Soviet economy, the main objective was a high rate of economic growth, with primary emphasis on industrial development at the expense of agriculture and particular concentration on heavy industry and capital-intensive technology. Soviet planners helped their Chinese counterparts formulate the plan. Large numbers of Soviet engineers, technicians, and scientists assisted in developing and installing new heavy industrial facilities, including many entire plants and pieces of equipment purchased from the Soviet Union. Government control over industry was increased during this period by applying financial pressures and inducements to convince owners of private, modern firms to sell them to the state or convert them into joint public-private enterprises under state control. By 1956 approximately 67.5 percent of all modern industrial enterprises were state owned, and 32.5 percent were under joint public-private ownership. No privately owned firms remained. During the same period, the handicraft industries were organized into cooperatives, which accounted for 91.7 percent of all handicraft workers by 1956.

Agriculture also underwent extensive organizational changes. To facilitate the mobilization of agricultural resources, improve the efficiency of farming, and increase government access to agricultural products, the authorities encouraged farmers to organize increasingly large and socialized collective units. From the loosely structured, tiny mutual aid teams, villages were to advance first to lower-stage, agricultural producers' cooperatives, in which families still received some income on the basis of the amount of land they contributed, and eventually to advanced cooperatives, or collectives. In the advanced producers' cooperatives, income shares were based only on the amount of labor contributed. In addition, each family was allowed to retain a small private plot on which to grow vegetables, fruit, and livestock for its own use. The collectivization process began slowly but accelerated in 1955 and 1956. In 1957 about 93.5 percent of all farm households had joined advanced producers' cooperatives.

In terms of economic growth the First Five-Year Plan was quite successful, especially in those areas emphasized by the Soviet-style development strategy. A solid foundation was created in heavy industry. Key industries, including iron and steel manufacturing, coal mining, cement production, electricity generation, and machine building were greatly expanded and were put on a firm, modern technological footing. Thousands of industrial and mining enterprises were constructed, including 156 major facilities. Industrial production increased at an average annual rate of 19 percent between 1952 and 1957, and national income grew at a rate of 9 percent a year.

Despite the lack of state investment in agriculture, agricultural output increased substantially, averaging increases of about 4 percent a year. This growth resulted primarily from gains in efficiency brought about by the reorganization and cooperation achieved through collectivization. As the First Five-Year Plan wore on, however, Chinese leaders became increasingly concerned over the relatively sluggish performance of agriculture and the inability of state trading companies to increase significantly the amount of grain procured from rural units for urban consumption.

The Great Leap Forward, 1958–60

Before the end of the First Five-Year Plan, the growing imbalance between industrial and agricultural growth, dissatisfaction with inefficiency, and lack of flexibility in the decision-making process convinced the nation's leaders—particularly Mao Zedong—that the highly centralized, industry-based Soviet model was not appropriate for China. In 1957 the government adopted measures to shift a great deal of the authority for economic decision making to the provincial-level, county, and local administrations. In 1958 the Second Five-Year Plan (1958–62), which was intended to continue the policies of the first plan, was abandoned. In its place the leadership adopted an approach that relied on spontaneous heroic efforts by the entire population to produce a dramatic "great leap" in production for all sectors of the economy at once (see The Great Leap Forward, 1958–60, ch. 1; Rural Society, ch. 3; The 1950s, ch. 6). Further reorganization of agriculture was regarded as the key to the endeavor to leap suddenly to a higher stage of productivity. A fundamental problem was the lack of sufficient capital to invest heavily in both industry and agriculture at the same time. To overcome this problem, the leadership decided to attempt to create capital in the agricultural sector by building vast irrigation and water control works employing huge teams of farmers whose labor was not being fully utilized. Surplus rural labor also was to be employed to support the industrial sector by setting up thousands of small-scale, low-technology, "backyard" industrial projects in farm units, which would produce machinery required for agricultural development and components for urban industries. Mobilization of surplus rural labor and further improvements in agricultural efficiency were to be accomplished by a "leap" to the final stage of agricultural collectivization—the formation of people's communes.

People's communes were created by combining some 20 or 30 advanced producers' cooperatives of 20,000 to 30,000 members on average, although membership varied from as few as 6,000 to over 40,000 in some cases. When first instituted, the communes were envisaged as combining in one body the functions of the lowest level of local government and the highest level of organization in agricultural production. Communes consisted of three organizational levels: the central commune administration; the production brigade (roughly equivalent to the advanced producers' cooperatives, or a traditional rural village); and the production team, which generally consisted of around thirty families. At the inception of the Great Leap Forward, the communes were intended to acquire all ownership rights over the productive assets of their subordinate units and to take over most of the planning and decision making for farm activities. Ideally, communes were to improve efficiency by moving farm families into dormitories, feeding them in communal mess halls, and moving whole teams of laborers from task to task. In practice, this ideal, extremely centralized form of commune was not instituted in most areas.

Ninety-eight percent of the farm population was organized into communes between April and September of 1958. Very soon it became evident that in most cases the communes were too unwieldy to carry out successfully all the managerial and administrative functions that were assigned to them. In 1959 and 1960, most production decisions reverted to the brigade and team levels, and eventually most governmental responsibilities were returned to county and township administrations. Nonetheless, the commune system was retained and continued to be the basic form of organization in the agricultural sector until the early 1980s.

During the Great Leap Forward, the industrial sector also was expected to discover and use slack labor and productive capacity to increase output beyond the levels previously considered feasible. Political zeal was to be the motive force, and to "put politics in command" enterprising party branches took over the direction of many factories. In addition, central planning was relegated to a minor role in favor of spontaneous, politically inspired production decisions from individual units.

The result of the Great Leap Forward was a severe economic crisis. In 1958 industrial output did in fact "leap" by 55 percent, and the agricultural sector gathered in a good harvest. In 1959, 1960, and 1961, however, adverse weather conditions, improperly constructed water control projects, and other misallocations of resources that had occurred during the overly centralized communization movement resulted in disastrous declines in agricultural output. In 1959 and 1960, the gross value of agricultural output fell by 14 percent and 13 percent, respectively, and in 1961 it dropped a further 2 percent to reach the lowest point since 1952. Widespread famine occurred, especially in rural areas, according to 1982 census figures, and the death rate climbed from 1.2 percent in 1958 to 1.5 percent in 1959, 2.5 percent in 1960, and then dropped back to 1.4 percent in 1961. From 1958 to 1961, over 14 million people apparently died of starvation, and the number of reported births was about 23 million fewer than under normal conditions. The government prevented an even worse disaster by canceling nearly all orders for foreign technical imports and using the country's foreign exchange reserves to import over 5 million tons of grain a year beginning in 1960. Mines and factories continued to expand output through 1960, partly by overworking personnel and machines but largely because many new plants constructed during the First Five-Year Plan went into full production in these years. Thereafter, however, the excessive strain on equipment and workers, the effects of the agricultural crisis, the lack of economic coordination, and, in the 1960s, the withdrawal of Soviet assistance caused industrial output to plummet by 38 percent in 1961 and by a further 16 percent in 1962.

Readjustment and Recovery: "Agriculture First," 1961–65

Faced with economic collapse in the early 1960s, the government sharply revised the immediate goals of the economy and devised a new set of economic policies to replace those of the Great Leap Forward. Top priority was given to restoring agricultural output and expanding it at a rate that would meet the needs of the growing population. Planning and economic coordination were to be revived—although in a less centralized form than before the Great Leap Forward—so as to restore order and efficient allocation of resources to the economy. The rate of investment was to be reduced and investment priorities reversed, with agriculture receiving first consideration, light industry second, and heavy industry third.

In a further departure from the emphasis on heavy industrial development that persisted during the Great Leap Forward, the government undertook to mobilize the nation's resources to bring about technological advancement in agriculture. Organizational changes in agriculture mainly involved decentralization of production decision making and income distribution within the commune structure. The role of the central commune administration was greatly reduced, although it remained the link between local government and agricultural producers and was important in carrying out activities that were too large in scale for the production brigades. Production teams were designated the basic accounting units and were responsible for making nearly all decisions concerning production and the distribution of income to their members. Private plots, which had disappeared on some communes during the Great Leap Forward, were officially restored to farm families (see Importance of Agriculture Recognized; Planning and Organization, ch. 6).

Economic support for agriculture took several forms. Agricultural taxes were reduced, and the prices paid for agricultural products were raised relative to the prices of industrial supplies for agriculture. There were substantial increases in supplies of chemical fertilizer and various kinds of agricultural machinery, notably small electric pumps for irrigation. Most of the modern supplies were concentrated in areas that were known to produce "high and stable yields" in order to ensure the best possible results.

In industry, a few key enterprises were returned to central state control, but control over most enterprises remained in the hands of provincial-level and local governments. This decentralization had taken place in 1957 and 1958 and was reaffirmed and strengthened in the 1961–65 period. Planning rather than politics once again guided production decisions, and material rewards rather than revolutionary enthusiasm became the leading incentive for production. Major imports of advanced foreign machinery, which had come to an abrupt halt with the withdrawal of Soviet assistance starting in 1960, were initiated with Japan and West European countries.

During the 1961–65 readjustment and recovery period, economic stability was restored, and by 1966 production in both agriculture and industry surpassed the peak levels of the Great Leap Forward period. Between 1961 and 1966, agricultural output grew at an average rate of 9.6 percent a year. Industrial output was increased in the same years at an average annual rate of 10.6 percent, largely by reviving plants that had operated below capacity after the economic collapse in 1961. Another important source of growth in this period was the spread of rural, small-scale industries, particularly coal mines, hydroelectric plants, chemical fertilizer plants, and agricultural machinery plants. The economic model that emerged in this period combined elements of the highly centralized, industrially oriented, Soviet-style system of the First Five-Year Plan with aspects of the decentralization of ownership and decision making that characterized the Great Leap Forward and with the strong emphasis on agricultural development and balanced growth of the "agriculture first" policy. Important changes in economic policy occurred in later years, but the basic system of ownership, decision-making structure, and development strategy that was forged in the early 1960s was not significantly altered until the reform period of the 1980s.

Events During the Cultural Revolution Decade, 1966–76

The Cultural Revolution was set in motion by Mao Zedong in 1966 and called to a halt in 1968, but the atmosphere of radical leftism persisted until Mao's death and the fall of the Gang of Four in 1976 (see The Cultural Revolution Decade, 1966–76, ch. 1). During this period, there were several distinct phases of economic policy.

High Tide of the Cultural Revolution, 1966–68

The Cultural Revolution, unlike the Great Leap Forward, was primarily a political upheaval and did not produce major changes in official economic policies or the basic economic model. Nonetheless, its influence was felt throughout urban society, and it profoundly affected the modern sector of the economy. Agricultural production stagnated, but in general the rural areas experienced less turmoil than the cities. Production was reduced in the modern nonagricultural sectors in several ways. The most direct cause of production halts was the political activity of students and workers in the mines and factories. A second cause was the extensive disruption of transportation resulting from the requisitioning of trains and trucks to carry Red Guards (see Glossary) around the country. Output at many factories suffered from shortages of raw materials and other supplies. A third disruptive influence was that the direction of factories was placed in the hands of revolutionary committees, consisting of representatives from the party, the workers, and the People's Liberation Army, whose members often had little knowledge of either management or the enterprise they were supposed to run. In addition, virtually all engineers, managers, scientists, technicians, and other professional personnel were "criticized," demoted, "sent down" to the countryside to "participate in labor," or even jailed, all of which resulted in their skills and knowledge being lost to the enterprise. The effect was a 14-percent decline in industrial production in 1967. A degree of order was restored by the army in late 1967 and 1968, and the industrial sector returned to a fairly high rate of growth in 1969.

Other aspects of the Cultural Revolution had more far-reaching effects on the economy. Imports of foreign equipment, required for technological advancement, were curtailed by rampant xenophobia. Probably the most serious and long-lasting effect on the economy was the dire shortage of highly educated personnel caused by the closing of the universities. China's ability to develop new technology and absorb imported technology would be limited for years by the hiatus in higher education (see Higher Education, ch. 4).

Resumption of Systematic Growth, 1970–74

As political stability was gradually restored, a renewed drive for coordinated, balanced development was set in motion under the leadership of Premier Zhou Enlai. To revive efficiency in industry, Chinese Communist Party committees were returned to positions of leadership over the revolutionary committees, and a campaign was carried out to return skilled and highly educated personnel to the jobs from which they had been displaced during the Cultural Revolution. Universities began to reopen, and foreign contacts were expanded. Once again the economy suffered from imbalances in the capacities of different industrial sectors and an urgent need for increased supplies of modern inputs for agriculture. In response to these problems, there was a significant increase in investment, including the signing of contracts with foreign firms for the construction of major facilities for chemical fertilizer production, steel finishing, and oil extraction and refining. The most notable of these contracts was for thirteen of the world's largest and most modern chemical fertilizer plants (see Chemicals, ch. 7). During this period, industrial output grew at an average rate of 8 percent a year.

Agricultural production declined somewhat in 1972 because of poor weather but increased at an average annual rate of 3.8 percent for the period as a whole. The party and state leadership undertook a general reevaluation of development needs, and Zhou Enlai presented the conclusions in a report to the Fourth National People's Congress in January 1975. In it he called for the Four Modernizations (see Glossary). Zhou emphasized the mechanization of agriculture and a comprehensive two-stage program for the modernization of the entire economy by the end of the century.

The Gang of Four, 1974–76

During the early and mid-1970s, the radical group later known as the Gang of Four attempted to dominate the power center through their network of supporters and, most important, through their control of the media. More moderate leaders, however, were developing and promulgating a pragmatic program for rapid modernization of the economy that contradicted the set of policies expressed in the media. Initiatives by Zhou Enlai and Deng Xiaoping were vehemently attacked in the press and in political campaigns as "poisonous weeds." Using official news organs, the Gang of Four advocated the primacy of nonmaterial, political incentives, radical reduction of income differences, elimination of private farm plots, and a shift of the basic accounting unit up to the brigade level in agriculture. They opposed the strengthening of central planning and denounced the use of foreign technology.

In the face of such contradictory policy pronouncements and uncertain political currents, administrators and economic decision makers at all levels were virtually paralyzed. Economic activity slowed, and the incipient modernization program almost ground to a halt. Uncertainty and instability were exacerbated by the death of Zhou Enlai in January 1976 and the subsequent second purge of Deng Xiaoping in April. The effects of the power struggle and policy disputes were compounded by the destruction resulting from the Tangshan earthquake in July 1976. Output for the year in both industry and agriculture showed no growth over 1975. The interlude of uncertainty finally ended when the Gang of Four was arrested in October—one month after Mao's death.

The Post-Mao Interlude, 1976–78

After the fall of the Gang of Four, the leadership under Hua Guofeng—and by July 1977 the rehabilitated Deng Xiaoping—reaffirmed the modernization program espoused by Zhou Enlai in 1975. They also set forth a battery of new policies for the purpose of accomplishing the Four Modernizations. The new policies strengthened the authority of managers and economic decision makers at the expense of party officials, stressed material incentives for workers, and called for expansion of the research and education systems (see The Post-Mao Period, 1976–78, ch. 1). Foreign trade was to be increased, and exchanges of students and "foreign experts" with developed countries were to be encouraged. This new policy initiative was capped at the Fifth National People's Congress in February and March 1978, when Hua Guofeng presented the draft of an ambitious ten-year plan for the 1976–85 period. The plan called for high rates of growth in both industry and agriculture and included 120 construction projects that would require massive and expensive imports of foreign technology.

Between 1976 and 1978, the economy quickly recovered from the stagnation of the Cultural Revolution. Agricultural production was sluggish in 1977 because of a third consecutive year of adverse weather conditions but rebounded with a record harvest in 1978. Industrial output jumped 14 percent in 1977 and increased by 13 percent in 1978.

Reform of the Economic System, Beginning in 1979

At the milestone Third Plenum of the National Party Congress Eleventh Central Committee in December 1978, the party leaders decided to undertake a program of gradual but fundamental reform of the economic system. They concluded that the Maoist version of the centrally planned economy had failed to produce efficient economic growth and had caused China to fall far behind not only the industrialized nations of the West but also the new industrial powers of Asia: Japan, the Republic of Korea, Singapore, Taiwan, and Hong Kong. In the late 1970s, while Japan and Hong Kong rivaled European countries in modern technology, China's citizens had to make do with barely sufficient food supplies, rationed clothing, inadequate housing, and a service sector that was inadequate and inefficient. All of these shortcomings embarrassed China internationally.

The purpose of the reform program was not to abandon communism but to make it work better by substantially increasing the role of market mechanisms in the system and by reducing—not eliminating—government planning and direct control. The process of reform was incremental. New measures were first introduced experimentally in a few localities and then were popularized and disseminated nationally if they proved successful. By 1987 the program had achieved remarkable results in increasing supplies of food and other consumer goods and had created a new climate of dynamism and opportunity in the economy. At the same time, however, the reforms also had created new problems and tensions, leading to intense questioning and political struggles over the program's future.

The Period of Readjustment, 1979–81

The first few years of the reform program were designated the "period of readjustment," during which key imbalances in the economy were to be corrected and a foundation was to be laid for a well-planned modernization drive. The schedule of Hua Guofeng's ten-year plan was discarded, although many of its elements were retained. The major goals of the readjustment process were to expand exports rapidly; overcome key deficiencies in transportation, communications, coal, iron, steel, building materials, and electric power; and redress the imbalance between light and heavy industry by increasing the growth rate of light industry and reducing investment in heavy industry. Agricultural production was stimulated in 1979 by an increase of over 22 percent in the procurement prices paid for farm products.

The central policies of the reform program were introduced experimentally during the readjustment period. The most successful reform policy, the contract responsibility system of production in agriculture, was suggested by the government in 1979 as a way for poor rural units in mountainous or arid areas to increase their incomes. The responsibility system allowed individual farm families to work a piece of land for profit in return for delivering a set amount of produce to the collective at a given price. This arrangement created strong incentives for farmers to reduce production costs and increase productivity. Soon after its introduction the responsibility system was adopted by numerous farm units in all sorts of areas.

Agricultural production was also stimulated by official encouragement to establish free farmers' markets in urban areas, as well as in the countryside, and by allowing some families to operate as "specialized households," devoting their efforts to producing a scarce commodity or service on a profit-making basis (see Post-Mao Policies, ch. 6).

In industry, the main policy innovations increased the autonomy of enterprise managers, reduced emphasis on planned quotas, allowed enterprises to produce goods outside the plan for sale on the market, and permitted enterprises to experiment with the use of bonuses to reward higher productivity. The government also tested a fundamental change in financial procedures with a limited number of state-owned units: rather than remitting all of their profits to the state, as was normally done, these enterprises were allowed to pay a tax on their profits and retain the balance for reinvestment and distribution to workers as bonuses.

The government also actively encouraged the establishment of collectively owned and operated industrial and service enterprises as a means of soaking up some of the unemployment among young people and at the same time helping to increase supplies of light industrial products. Individual enterprise—true capitalism—also was allowed, after having virtually disappeared during the Cultural Revolution, and independent cobblers, tailors, tinkers, and vendors once again became common sights in the cities. Foreign-trade procedures were greatly eased, allowing individual enterprises and administrative departments outside the Ministry of Foreign Trade (which became the Ministry of Foreign Economic Relations and Trade in 1984) to engage in direct negotiations with foreign firms. A wide range of cooperation, trading, and credit

Shanghai's Baoshan iron and steel works
Courtesy Xinhua News Agency

arrangements with foreign firms were legalized so that China could enter the mainstream of international trade (see Foreign Trade, ch. 8).

Reform and Opening, Beginning in 1982

The period of readjustment produced promising results, increasing incomes substantially; raising the availability of food, housing, and other consumer goods; and generating strong rates of growth in all sectors except heavy industry, which was intentionally restrained. On the strength of these initial successes, the reform program was broadened, and the leadership under Deng Xiaoping frequently remarked that China's basic policy was "reform and opening," that is, reform of the economic system and opening to foreign trade.

In agriculture the contract responsibility system was adopted as the organizational norm for the entire country, and the commune structure was largely dismantled. By the end of 1984, approximately 98 percent of all farm households were under the responsibility system, and all but a handful of communes had been dissolved. The communes' administrative responsibilities were turned over to township and town governments, and their economic roles were assigned to townships and villages. The role of free markets for farm produce was further expanded and, with increased marketing possibilities and rising productivity, farm incomes rose rapidly (see Post-Mao Policies, ch. 6).

In industry the complexity and interrelation of production activities prevented a single, simple policy from bringing about the kind of dramatic improvement that the responsibility system achieved in agriculture. Nonetheless, a cluster of policies based on greater flexibility, autonomy, and market involvement significantly improved the opportunities available to most enterprises, generated high rates of growth, and increased efficiency. Enterprise managers gradually gained greater control over their units, including the right to hire and fire, although the process required endless struggles with bureaucrats and party cadres. The practice of remitting taxes on profits and retaining the balance became universal by 1985, increasing the incentive for enterprises to maximize profits and substantially adding to their autonomy. A change of potentially equal importance was a shift in the source of investment funds from government budget allocations, which carried no interest and did not have to be repaid, to interest-bearing bank loans. As of 1987 the interest rate charged on such loans was still too low to serve as a check on unproductive investments, but the mechanism was in place.

The role of foreign trade under the economic reforms increased far beyond its importance in any previous period. Before the reform period, the combined value of imports and exports had seldom exceeded 10 percent of national income. In 1980 it was 15 percent, in 1984 it was 21 percent, and in 1986 it reached 35 percent. Unlike earlier periods, when China was committed to trying to achieve self-sufficiency, under Deng Xiaoping foreign trade was regarded as an important source of investment funds and modern technology. As a result, restrictions on trade were loosened further in the mid-1980s, and foreign investment was legalized. The most common foreign investments were joint ventures between foreign firms and Chinese units. Sole ownership by foreign investors also became legal, but the feasibility of such undertakings remained questionable.

The most conspicuous symbols of the new status of foreign trade were the four coastal special economic zones (see Glossary), which were created in 1979 as enclaves where foreign investment could receive special treatment. Three of the four zones—the cities of Shenzhen, Zhuhai, and Shantou—were located in Guangdong Province, close to Hong Kong. The fourth, Xiamen, in Fujian Province, was directly across the strait from Taiwan. More significant for China's economic development was the designation in April 1984 of economic development zones in the fourteen largest

Roadside stand on the route to the Ming tombs near Beijing
Courtesy Stephanie Marcus
North China fruit seller
Courtesy Ann Matles

coastal cities—including Dalian, Tianjin, Shanghai, and Guangzhou—all of which were major commercial and industrial centers. These zones were to create productive exchanges between foreign firms with advanced technology and major Chinese economic networks.

Domestic commerce also was stimulated by the reform policies, which explicitly endeavored to enliven the economy by shifting the primary burden of the allocation of goods and services from the government plan to the market. Private entrepreneurship and free-market activities were legalized and encouraged in the 1980s, although the central authorities continuously had to fight the efforts of local government agencies to impose excessive taxes on independent merchants. By 1987 the state-owned system of commercial agencies and retail outlets coexisted with a rapidly growing private and collectively owned system that competed with it vigorously, providing a wider range of consumption choices for Chinese citizens than at any previous time.

Although the reform program achieved impressive successes, it also gave rise to several serious problems. One problem was the challenge to party authority presented by the principles of free-market activity and professional managerial autonomy. Another difficulty was a wave of crime, corruption, and—in the minds of many older people—moral deterioration caused by the looser economic and political climate. The most fundamental tensions were those created by the widening income disparities between the people who were "getting rich" and those who were not and by the pervasive threat of inflation. These concerns played a role in the political struggle that culminated in party general secretary Hu Yaobang's forced resignation in 1987 (see Resistance and the Campaign Against Bourgeois Liberalization, ch. 11). Following Hu's resignation, the leadership engaged in an intense debate over the future course of the reforms and how to balance the need for efficiency and market incentives with the need for government guidance and control. The commitment to further reform was affirmed, but its pace, and the emphasis to be placed on macroeconomic and microeconomic levers, remained objects of caution.

Structure and Operation of the Economy

Roles of the Government and the Party

Under China's socialist political and economic system, the government was explicitly responsible for planning and managing the national economy. The State Constitution of 1982 specifies that the state is to guide the country's economic development and that the State Council is to direct its subordinate bodies in drawing up and carrying out the national economic plan and the state budget (see Constitutional Framework, ch. 10). A major portion of the governmental apparatus was devoted to managing the economy; all but a few of the more than 100 ministries, commissions, administrations, bureaus, academies, and corporations under the State Council were concerned with economic matters (see The State Council, ch. 10).

Each significant economic sector was supervised and controlled by one or more of these organizations, which included the People's Bank of China, State Planning Commission, State Economic Commission, State Machine-Building Industry Commission, and the ministries of agriculture, animal husbandry, and fishery; coal industry; commerce; communications; finance; light industry; metallurgical industry; petroleum industry; railways; textile industry; and water resources and electric power. Several aspects of the economy were administered by specialized departments under the State Council, including the State Statistical Bureau, General Administration of Civil Aviation of China, and China Travel and Tourism Bureau. Each of the economic organizations under the State Council directed the units under its jurisdiction through subordinate offices at the provincial and local levels.

Economic policies and decisions adopted by the National People's Congress and the State Council were passed on to the economic organizations under the State Council, which incorporated them into the plans for the various sectors of the economy. Economic plans and policies were implemented by a variety of direct and indirect control mechanisms. Direct control was exercised by designating specific physical output quotas and supply allocations for some goods and services. Indirect instruments—also called "economic levers"—operated by affecting market incentives. These included levying taxes, setting prices for products and supplies, allocating investment funds, monitoring and controlling financial transactions by the banking system, and controlling the allocation of scarce key resources, such as skilled labor, electric power, transportation, steel, and chemical fertilizer. A major objective of the reform program was to reduce the use of direct controls and to increase the role of indirect economic levers. Major state-owned enterprises still received detailed plans specifying physical quantities of key inputs and products from their ministries. Even these units, however, were increasingly affected by prices and allocations that were determined through market interaction and only indirectly influenced by the central plan.

By 1987 the majority of state-owned industrial enterprises, which were managed at the provincial level or below, were partially regulated by a combination of specific allocations and indirect controls, but they also produced goods outside the plan for sale in the market. Important, scarce resources—for example, engineers or finished steel—might be assigned to this kind of unit in exact numbers. Less critical assignments of personnel and materials would be authorized in a general way by the plan, but with procurement arrangements left up to the enterprise management. Enterprises had increasing discretion over the quantities of inputs purchased, the sources of inputs, the variety of products manufactured, and the production process.

Collectively owned units and the agricultural sector were regulated primarily by indirect instruments. Each collective unit was "responsible for its own profit and loss," and the prices of its inputs and products provided the major production incentives.

Consumer spending was subject to a limited degree of direct government influence but was primarily determined by the basic market forces of income levels and commodity prices. Before the reform period, key goods were rationed when they were in short supply, but by the mid-1980s availability had increased to the point that rationing was discontinued for everything except grain, which could also be purchased in the free markets.

Foreign trade was supervised by the Ministry of Foreign Economic Relations and Trade, General Administration of Customs, and Bank of China, the foreign exchange arm of the Chinese banking system, which controlled access to the scarce foreign currency required for imports. Because of the reduced restrictions on foreign trade, however, there were broad opportunities for individual work units to engage in exchanges with foreign firms without much interference from official agencies (see Organization of Foreign Trade, ch. 8).

The role of the government in the economy was buttressed by the pervasive influence of the Chinese Communist Party. The structure of the party organization paralleled that of the government but also extended below the lowest level of government into individual work units. Important economic decision makers at all levels, from the members of the State Council down to the managers of factories, either were party members themselves or worked closely with colleagues who were party members. The party served as a powerful supplementary network for transmitting and implementing the economic goals and policies of the government.

Although the government dominated the economy, the extent of its control was limited by the sheer volume of economic activity. Furthermore, the concept of government supervision of the economy had changed—at least in the minds of the advocates of reform—from one of direct but stifling state control to one of indirect guidance of a more dynamic economy (see The First Wave of Reform, 1979–84, ch. 11).

The Two Major Sectors: Agriculture and Industry

The two most important sectors of the economy were agriculture and industry, which together employed 80 percent of the labor force and in 1985 produced 72 percent of GNP. The two sectors differed in nearly all respects. Technology, labor productivity, and incomes advanced much more rapidly in industry than in agriculture. Agricultural output was vulnerable to the effects of weather, while industry was more directly influenced by political upheavals. The organization of industry was based on state and collective ownership, planning, and wage labor, while that of agriculture was built around household farming, self-reliance, and market incentives. The disparities between the two sectors combined to form an economic-cultural-social gap between the rural and urban areas—the major division in Chinese society.

Agriculture

In the late 1980s, China remained a predominantly agricultural country. As of 1985 about 63 percent of the population lived in rural areas, and nearly 63 percent of the national labor force was engaged in agriculture (see Migration; Labor Force, ch. 2). Modern technology had spread slowly in the vast farm areas, and the availability of modern supplies was less than adequate, causing growth in agricultural output to lag behind production increases in the rest of the economy. The proportion of GNP produced by agriculture declined from over 43 percent in the early 1950s to about 29 percent in 1985. The low agricultural growth rate as compared with other sectors of the economy reflected the fact that the average farmer had far less machinery and electric power and fewer other modern production aids to work with than the average worker in industry. Under the responsibility system (see Glossary), farm households and collective organizations purchased large amounts of new machinery, particularly small tractors and trucks. The horsepower of agricultural machinery per farmer increased by almost 30 percent between 1979 and 1985 but still came to less than 1 horsepower per person.

Before the early 1980s, most of the agricultural sector was organized according to the three-tier commune system (see Rural Society, ch. 3; Agricultural Policies, ch. 6). There were over 50,000 people's communes, most containing around 30,000 members. Each commune was made up of about sixteen production brigades, and each production brigade was composed of around seven production teams. The production teams were the basic agricultural collective units. They corresponded to small villages and typically included about 30 households and 100 to 250 members. The communes, brigades, and teams owned all major rural productive assets and provided nearly all administrative, social, and commercial services in the countryside. The largest part of farm family incomes consisted of shares of net team income, distributed to members according to the amount of work each had contributed to the collective effort. Farm families also worked small private plots and were free to sell or consume their products.

By the end of 1984, approximately 98 percent of the old production teams had adopted the contract responsibility system, and all but 249 communes had been dissolved, their governmental functions passed on to 91,000 township and town governments. Production team organizations were replaced by 940,000 village committees. Under the responsibility system, farm families no longer devoted most of their efforts to collective production but instead generally signed contracts with the village or town to cultivate a given crop on a particular piece of land. After harvest a certain amount of the crop had to be sold to the unit at a predetermined price, and any output beyond that amount was the property of the family, either to be sold in the market or to be consumed. Beyond the amount contracted for delivery to the collective, farmers were allowed to determine for themselves what and how to produce.

Market activity played a central role in the rural economy of the 1980s. Farmers sold a growing share of their produce in rural or urban free markets and purchased many of the inputs that had formerly been supplied by the team or brigade. A prominent new institution that thrived in the market environment was the "specialized household." Specialized households operated in the classic pattern of the entrepreneur, buying or renting equipment to produce a good or service that was in short supply locally. Some of the most common specialties were trucking, chicken raising, pig raising, and technical agricultural services, such as irrigation and pest control. Many of the specialized households became quite wealthy relative to the average farmer.

The new economic climate and the relaxation of restrictions on the movements of rural residents gave rise to numerous opportunities for profit-making ventures in the countryside. Towns, villages, and groups of households referred to as "rural economic unions" established small factories, processing operations, construction teams, catering services, and other kinds of nonagricultural concerns. Many of these organizations had links with urban

Chinese and American technicians conduct a drilling operation at the Antibao coal mine, Shanxi Province
Courtesy Xinhua News Agency

enterprises that found the services of these rural units to be less expensive and more efficient than those of their formal urban counterparts.

The growth of these nonagricultural enterprises in the countryside created a large number of new jobs, making it possible for many workers who were no longer needed in agriculture to "leave the land but stay in the country," significantly changing the structure of the rural economy and increasing rural incomes. In 1986 nonagricultural enterprises in the countryside employed 21 percent of the rural labor force and for the first time produced over half the value of rural output.

Although the chief characteristic of the new rural system was household farming for profit, collective organizations still played a major role. Agricultural land still was owned by township or town governments, which determined the crops farmers contracted to grow and the financial terms of the contracts. Many township, town, and village governments also engaged in major entrepreneurial undertakings, establishing factories, processing mills, brick works, and other large-scale enterprises. Finally, the maintenance and operation of public works, such as irrigation systems, power plants, schools, and clinics, generally still was regarded as the responsibility of the collective administrations.

Four percent of the nation's farmland was cultivated by state farms, which employed 4.9 million people in 1985. State farms were owned and operated by the government much in the same way as an industrial enterprise. Management was the responsibility of a director, and workers were paid set wages, although some elements of the responsibility system were introduced in the mid-1980s. State farms were scattered throughout China, but the largest numbers were located in frontier or remote areas, including Xinjiang-Uygur Autonomous Region in the northwest, Nei Monggol Autonomous Region, the three northeastern provinces of Heilongjiang, Jilin, and Liaoning and the southeastern provinces of Guangdong, Fujian, and Jiangxi.

Industry

The industrial sector employed only about 17 percent of the labor force in 1985 but, as a result of much higher labor productivity than the agricultural sector, accounted for over 46 percent of national income. Industrial units were very diverse in size and technological sophistication, ranging from tiny handicraft manufacturing enterprises to giant modern complexes producing such goods as steel, chemical fertilizer, and synthetic fibers. The majority of the country's large industrial units were clustered in the major industrial centers in the northeast, the Beijing-Tianjin-Tangshan area, the Chang Jiang (Yangtze River) Valley, and Shanghai. Small and medium-size units were found throughout the country, and a number of first-rank plants were located far from the leading cities (see Geographical Distribution of Industry, ch. 7). Ownership of industrial enterprises fell into three general categories: state ownership, urban collective ownership, and rural collective ownership. Industry was dominated by the state-owned sector, which included the largest, most technically advanced, and most important enterprises.

In 1985 state-owned enterprises produced 70 percent of national industrial output by value, held 75 percent of fixed industrial assets, and employed 46 percent of the industrial labor force (including rural industrial enterprises). Although all of these units were owned by "the state" in the abstract sense, operational control and effective ownership of specific enterprises were divided among the different levels of government. A few of the largest enterprises were under the direct authority of their respective ministries in the central government. Most major enterprises were owned by the province, autonomous region, or special municipality where they were located or were subject to shared control by the central ministry and the provincial-level government. Small and medium-size units usually were owned by city, prefecture, county, or town governments. Control of some enterprises was shared with higher administrative levels.

Workers in state-owned enterprises were paid regular wages according to an established pay scale, as well as bonuses that were supposed to be related to personal or enterprise performance or both. In addition, they received a number of important benefits, including free health care, subsidized housing, and subsidies for such work-related expenses as special clothing and commuting costs. The average income of industrial workers was considerably higher than that of most farmers and was much more stable.

Urban, collectively owned enterprises (owned by the workers) for the most part were small units equipped with relatively little machinery. Many of these units were engaged in handicraft production or other labor-intensive activities, such as manufacturing furniture or assembling simple electrical items. In the late 1970s and early 1980s, the government promoted them as a means of using surplus labor to increase supplies of consumer and export goods. By 1985 urban collective industrial enterprises employed over 17 million people, 20 percent of the total industrial labor force. These enterprises held only 13 percent of all industrial fixed assets but produced 19 percent of total industrial output value.

Rural, collectively owned industrial enterprises—commonly referred to as "township enterprises"—were the most rapidly growing portion of the industrial sector in the mid-1980s. The government regarded them as a means of expanding industrialization (without further taxing the overcrowded major urban centers), alleviating rural unemployment, and increasing supplies of industrial products in rural areas. Most of the township enterprises were operated by township and town governments, but a large number of very small units were operated by private cooperative organizations called "rural economic unions." In 1985 township enterprises employed 30 million workers, over a third of the total industrial labor force. The value of their fixed assets, however, was only 12 percent of the national total, and their output value came to less than 10 percent of the national total. Nonetheless, in 1985 their income grew by 44 percent over the 1984 levels. The most common products of township industries were building materials, agricultural machinery, textiles, and processed foods.

Other Important Sectors

Transportation, the postal system, and telecommunications employed over 12 million people in 1985. Long-distance transportation was carried primarily by railroads, inland waterways, and highways. The government-run railroad network was the backbone of the freight system, and rail lines extended to nearly all parts of China. In most areas, however, the rail system had too few feeder lines and was inadequately integrated. Much of the rail system had been improved in the 1980s; many heavily used stretches were converted to double track or upgraded, and several key new lines were constructed to relieve congested areas. Most locomotives in use in the early 1980s were picturesque but outdated steam engines. By 1987, however, several railroad districts had converted entirely to more modern and efficient diesel or electric locomotives, and domestic production of modern engines was supplemented by imported models. Within their limitations the railroads functioned fairly efficiently and made intensive use of the rail network. In 1986 the railroads carried 874.5 billion ton-kilometers of freight, 45 percent of the national freight total and a 7.8 percent increase over 1985. They also carried nearly 1.1 billion passengers, 20 percent of the national total. Despite reasonably good performance, the ability of the economy to move goods between cities and regions was severely limited by deficiencies in the system, and improvement of the railroads continued to be a high priority for state investment (see Railroads, ch. 8).

Inland navigation grew more quickly than the rail system and in 1986 carried 827.8 billion ton-kilometers of freight, nearly as much as the railroads. The principal inland waterway was the Chang Jiang and its tributaries, which constituted the major artery linking the industrial and agricultural areas of central China and the southwest to the great port and industrial center of Shanghai. Improvements to the water routes enabled larger and faster modern vessels to use them, extended their navigable length, and reduced the amount of time they were closed each year. In addition to modern vessels, the lakes, rivers, and canals were plied by thousands of motorized and nonmotorized traditional craft of all sizes (see Inland Waterways, ch. 8).

Local road networks were extensive, but many were narrow and unpaved, and all were overcrowded with trucks, jeeps, buses, carts pulled by tractors and animals, bicycles, pedestrians, and grain laid out to dry by local farmers. Owing to rapid increases in the volume of private and work-unit trucking, highway freight traffic was the fastest growing major portion of the transportation system aside from ocean shipping. In 1986 highway freight traffic totaled 259.6 billion ton-kilometers, an increase of 47 percent over 1985, and 80 percent of the volume was carried by vehicles that were not managed by state highway departments. In 1986 buses served 4.3 billion passengers for relatively short trips (see Highways and Roads, ch. 8).

Civil aviation provided important links both to isolated areas of the country and to foreign nations. It carried, however, only a small fraction of total freight and passenger traffic (see Civil Aviation, ch. 8).

The service sector expanded quickly during the reform period, making up for major deficiencies that had developed in the preceding quarter century. In the 1950s and 1960s, services were regarded as nonproductive and were therefore neglected. During the Cultural Revolution, they were relentlessly attacked as "remnants of capitalism." By the late 1970s, the service trades, such as food service, barbering, laundering, tailoring, and repair work, were seriously understaffed and were far from able to meet the needs of the population. Furthermore, they were all concentrated in large, inefficient state-owned units. The service occupations requiring advanced training, such as health care, education, and legal services, were decimated by the breakdown of the education system during the Cultural Revolution decade.

Revival of the service sector was a well-publicized goal of the reform program. Legalization of private and collective enterprise quickly led to the appearance of tinkers, cobblers, tailors, barbers, and small food-service stands, particularly in the free markets.

Between 1978 and 1985, the number of people engaged in the service trades, retail sales, and catering grew from only 6.1 million to over 25 million, of whom 21 million were in collective or individual enterprises. In 1986 the government further stimulated the growth of the sector by leasing to private individuals or groups a large number of small, state-owned, service establishments, including restaurants, repair shops, and barber shops, that had consistently been operating at a loss under state management.

Other service sectors that employed significant quantities of labor included health care, education and culture, and government administration. These sectors were important to the national economy and employed over 25 million people.

China produced nearly all of its own medicines and medical equipment, but most hospitals were poorly equipped by Western standards. A more serious shortage was the relatively small number of doctors and other highly trained medical personnel. In 1985 some 4.3 million people worked in health-care institutions. Of these, 1.4 million were doctors—including 336,000 doctors of traditional (rather than Western) medicine, 637,000 were nurses, and 1.4 million were midwives, laboratory technicians, pharmacists, and other technical personnel. The number of doctors of Western medicine grew by over 35 percent between 1978 and 1985, and renewed contact with the West opened training opportunities in Europe, the United States, and Japan.

Only a little over 10 percent of all Chinese received free medical care. Free care was provided to government workers, military personnel, teachers, college students, and workers in state-owned enterprises. A portion of the medical expenses incurred by their dependent family members was covered by the work units. Most rural towns and villages operated voluntary cooperative medical systems (see Health Care, ch. 2).

Educational and cultural institutions employed 12.7 million people in 1985. This total included 871,000 teachers and staff in institutions of higher education, an increase of 68 percent over the number in 1978, reflecting the intensive reconstruction of the education system in the 1980s. There were nearly 8 million people working in government administration in 1985.

Planning

Until the 1980s the economy was directed and coordinated by means of economic plans that were formulated at all levels of administration. The reform program significantly reduced the role of central planning by encouraging off-plan production by state-owned units and by promoting the growth of collective and

Urban market
Courtesy Xinhua News Agency

individual enterprises that did not fall under the planning system. The government also endeavored to replace direct plan control with indirect guidance of the economy through economic levers, such as taxes and investment support. Despite these changes, overall direction of the economy was still carried out by the central plan, as was allocation of key goods, such as steel and energy.

When China's planning apparatus was first established in the early 1950s, it was patterned after the highly centralized Soviet system. That system basically depended on a central planning bureaucracy that calculated and balanced quantities of major goods demanded and supplied. This approach was substantially modified during the Great Leap Forward (1958–60; see Glossary), when economic management was extensively decentralized. During the 1960s and 1970s, the degree of centralization in the planning system fluctuated with the political currents, waxing in times of pragmatic growth and waning under the influence of the Cultural Revolution and the Gang of Four.

At the national level, planning began in the highest bodies of the central government. National economic goals and priorities were determined by the party's Central Committee, the State Council, and the National People's Congress. These decisions were then communicated to the ministries, commissions, and other agencies under the State Council to be put into effect through national economic plans.

The State Planning Commission worked with the State Economic Commission, State Statistical Bureau, the former State Capital Construction Commission, People's Bank of China, the economic ministries, and other organs subordinate to the State Council to formulate national plans of varying duration and import. Long-range plans as protracted as ten and twelve years also were announced at various times. These essentially were statements of future goals and the intended general direction of the economy, and they had little direct effect on economic activity. As of late 1987 the most recent such long-range plan was the draft plan for 1976-85, presented by Hua Guofeng in February 1978.

The primary form of medium-range plan was the five-year plan, another feature adopted from the Soviet system. The purpose of the five-year plan was to guide and integrate the annual plans to achieve balanced growth and progress toward national goals. In practice, this role was only fulfilled by the First Five-Year Plan (1953-57), which served effectively as a blueprint for industrialization. The second (1958-62), third (1966-70), fourth (1971-75), and fifth (1976-80) five-year plans were all interrupted by political upheavals and had little influence. The Sixth Five-Year Plan (1981-85) was drawn up during the planning period and was more a reflection of the results of the reform program than a guide for reform. The Seventh Five-Year Plan (1986-90) was intended to direct the course of the reforms through the second half of the 1980s, but by mid-1987 its future was already clouded by political struggle.

A second form of medium-range planning appeared in the readjustment and recovery periods of 1949-52, 1963-65, and 1979-81, each of which followed a period of chaos—the civil war, the Great Leap Forward, and the Gang of Four, respectively. In these instances, normal long- and medium-range planning was suspended while basic imbalances in the economy were targeted and corrected. In each case, objectives were more limited and clearly defined than in the five-year plans and were fairly successfully achieved.

The activities of economic units were controlled by annual plans. Formulation of the plans began in the autumn preceding the year being planned, so that agricultural output for the current year could be taken into account. The foundation of an annual plan was a "material balance table." At the national level, the first step in the preparation of a material balance table was to estimate—for each province, autonomous region, special municipality, and enterprise under direct central control—the demand and supply for each centrally controlled good. Transfers of goods between provincial-level units were planned so as to bring quantities supplied and demanded into balance. As a last resort, a serious overall deficit in a good could be made up by imports.

The initial targets were sent to the provincial-level administrations and the centrally controlled enterprises. The provincial-level counterparts of the state economic commissions and ministries broke the targets down for allocation among their subordinate counties, districts, cities, and enterprises under direct provincial-level control. Counties further distributed their assigned quantities among their subordinate towns, townships, and county-owned enterprises, and cities divided their targets into objectives for the enterprises under their jurisdiction. Finally, towns assigned goals to the state-owned enterprises they controlled. Agricultural targets were distributed by townships among their villages and ultimately were reduced to the quantities that villages contracted for with individual farm households.

At each level, individual units received their target input allocations and output quantities. Managers, engineers, and accountants compared the targets with their own projections, and if they concluded that the planned output quotas exceeded their capabilities, they consulted with representatives of the administrative body superior to them. Each administrative level adjusted its targets on the basis of discussions with subordinate units and sent the revised figures back up the planning ladder. The commissions and ministries evaluated the revised sums, repeated the material balance table procedure, and used the results as the final plan, which the State Council then officially approved.

Annual plans formulated at the provincial level provided the quantities for centrally controlled goods and established targets for goods that were not included in the national plan but were important to the province, autonomous region, or special municipality. These figures went through the same process of disaggregation, review, discussion, and reaggregation as the centrally planned targets and eventually became part of the provincial-level unit's annual plan. Many goods that were not included at the provincial level were similarly added to county and city plans.

The final stage of the planning process occurred in the individual producing units. Having received their output quotas and the figures for their allocations of capital, labor, and other supplies, enterprises generally organized their production schedules into ten-day, one-month, three-month, and six-month plans.

The Chinese planning system has encountered the same problems of inflexibility and inadequate responsiveness that have emerged in other centrally planned economies. The basic difficulty has been that it is impossible for planners to foresee all the needs of the economy and to specify adequately the characteristics of planned inputs and products. Beginning in 1979 and 1980, the first reforms were introduced on an experimental basis. Nearly all of these policies increased the autonomy and decision-making power of the various economic units and reduced the direct role of central planning. By the mid-1980s planning still was the government's main mechanism for guiding the economy and correcting imbalances, but its ability to predict and control the behavior of the economy had been greatly reduced.

The Budget

The nature of the state budget also was significantly altered by the reform program. Before 1979 the state budget was the financial component of the national economic plan. It was made up of the budgets of both the central government and the local governments and included the revenues and expenditures of all state-owned enterprises. All profits from state enterprises were remitted to the state budget, and investment funds were allocated from the state budget. Under the reform, there was increased separation of enterprises from direct state control. Enterprises now paid proportional taxes on their incomes rather than remitting their entire profits to the state. Investment funds were, in principle, no longer to be allocated directly to state enterprises from the state budget but were to be obtained from the banking system in the form of interest-bearing loans.

In 1985 total state revenues of ¥186.6 billion included ¥51.4 billion in income taxes from state-owned enterprises and only ¥4.4 billion in enterprise incomes. The largest category of revenues was industrial and commercial taxes, which amounted to ¥110.1 billion. Agricultural taxes were ¥4.2 billion, continuing the previous policy of levying only negligible taxes on the farm sector. Revenues also included borrowing equal to ¥9 billion, a practice followed annually since 1978. As of 1983 roughly 30 percent of total revenues were collected by the central government and 70 percent by local governments, while each accounted for about 50 percent of expenditures.

In 1985 the largest category of budget expenditure was appropriations for capital construction, which received 31.3 percent of the total allotment. Culture, education, science, and public health constituted the next largest category, with 17 percent of expenditures. National defense, which averaged 19 percent of budgetary expenditures in the 1960s and 1970s, received only 10.3 percent of the total in 1985. Administrative expenses were 7.7 percent of the budget and new technology in enterprises 5.5 percent. In 1984 the state paid out ¥37 billion in price subsidies, an amount equal to 24 percent of total expenditures in that year. The bulk of the subsidies—¥32 billion—was for consumer goods.

An important function of the state budget was to transfer resources from prosperous regions to poor regions. The budgets that were finally approved by the Ministry of Finance for the provinces, autonomous regions, and special municipalities allowed surplus funds from affluent areas to be transferred to cover planned expenditures in the deficit areas, while bringing the budget for the entire country into balance. The resulting pattern of revenue sharing between provincial-level administrations and the central government was one in which the advanced industrialized regions paid a much higher rate of net taxation than most areas, and the least-developed regions were heavily subsidized. For example, in 1985 Shanghai remitted ¥8.4 billion in profits and taxes, equal to 4.5 percent of national budget revenues, although it had only 1.1 percent of the national population.

The Banking System

The history of the Chinese banking system has been somewhat checkered. Nationalization and consolidation of the country's banks received the highest priority in the earliest years of the People's Republic, and banking was the first sector to be completely socialized. In the period of recovery after the Chinese civil war (1949–52), the People's Bank of China moved very effectively to halt raging inflation and bring the nation's finances under central control. Over the course of time, the banking organization was modified repeatedly to suit changing conditions and new policies.

The banking system was centralized early on under the Ministry of Finance, which exercised firm control over all financial services, credit, and the money supply. During the 1980s the banking system was expanded and diversified to meet the needs of the reform program, and the scale of banking activity rose sharply. New budgetary procedures required state enterprises to remit to the state only a tax on income and to seek investment funds in the form of bank loans. Between 1979 and 1985, the volume of deposits nearly tripled and the value of bank loans rose by 260 percent. By 1987 the banking system included the People's Bank of China, Agricultural Bank, Bank of China (which handled foreign exchange matters), China Investment Bank, China Industrial and Commercial Bank, People's Construction Bank, Communications Bank, People's Insurance Company of China, rural credit cooperatives, and urban credit cooperatives.

The People's Bank of China was the central bank and the foundation of the banking system. Although the bank overlapped in function with the Ministry of Finance and lost many of its responsibilities during the Cultural Revolution, in the 1970s it was restored to its leading position. As the central bank, the People's Bank of China had sole responsibility for issuing currency and controlling the money supply. It also served as the government treasury, the main source of credit for economic units, the clearing center for financial transactions, the holder of enterprise deposits, the national savings bank, and a ubiquitous monitor of economic activities.

Another financial institution, the Bank of China, handled all dealings in foreign exchange. It was responsible for allocating the country's foreign exchange reserves, arranging foreign loans, setting exchange rates for China's currency, issuing letters of credit, and generally carrying out all financial transactions with foreign firms and individuals. The Bank of China had offices in Beijing and other cities engaged in foreign trade and maintained overseas offices in major international financial centers, including Hong Kong, London, New York, Singapore, and Luxembourg.

The Agricultural Bank was created in the 1950s to facilitate financial operations in the rural areas. The Agricultural Bank provided financial support to agricultural units. It issued loans, handled state appropriations for agriculture, directed the operations of the rural credit cooperatives, and carried out overall supervision of rural financial affairs. The Agricultural Bank was headquartered in Beijing and had a network of branches throughout the country. It flourished in the late 1950s and mid-1960s but languished thereafter until the late 1970s, when the functions and autonomy of the Agricultural Bank were increased substantially to help promote higher agricultural production. In the 1980s it was restructured again and given greater authority in order to support the growth and diversification of agriculture under the responsibility system.

The People's Construction Bank managed state appropriations and loans for capital construction. It checked the activities of loan recipients to ensure that the funds were used for their designated construction purpose. Money was disbursed in stages as a project progressed. The reform policy shifted the main source of investment funding from the government budget to bank loans and increased the responsibility and activities of the People's Construction Bank.

Rural credit cooperatives were small, collectively owned savings and lending organizations that were the main source of small-scale financial services at the local level in the countryside. They handled deposits and short-term loans for individual farm families, villages, and cooperative organizations. Subject to the direction of the Agricultural Bank, they followed uniform state banking policies but acted as independent units for accounting purposes. In 1985 rural credit cooperatives held total deposits of ¥72.5 billion.

Urban credit cooperatives were a relatively new addition to the banking system in the mid-1980s, when they first began widespread operations. As commercial opportunities grew in the reform period, the thousands of individual and collective enterprises that sprang up in urban areas created a need for small-scale financial services that the formal banks were not prepared to meet. Bank officials therefore encouraged the expansion of urban credit cooperatives as a valuable addition to the banking system. In 1986 there were more than 1,100 urban credit cooperatives, which held a total of ¥3.7 billion in deposits and made loans worth ¥1.9 billion.

In the mid-1980s the banking system still lacked some of the services and characteristics that were considered basic in most countries. Interbank relations were very limited, and interbank borrowing and lending were virtually unknown. Checking accounts were used by very few individuals, and bank credit cards did not exist. In 1986 initial steps were taken in some of these areas. Interbank borrowing and lending networks were created among twenty-seven cities along the Chang Jiang and among fourteen cities in north China. Interregional financial networks were created to link banks in eleven leading cities all over China, including Shenyang, Guangzhou, Wuhan, Chongqing, and Xi'an and also to link the branches of the Agricultural Bank. The first Chinese credit card, the Great Wall Card, was introduced in June 1986 to be used for foreign exchange transactions. Another financial innovation in 1986 was the opening of China's first stock exchanges since 1949. Small stock exchanges began operations somewhat tentatively in Shenyang, Liaoning Province, in August 1986 and in Shanghai in September 1986.

Throughout the history of the People's Republic, the banking system has exerted close control over financial transactions and the money supply. All government departments, publicly and collectively owned economic units, and social, political, military, and educational organizations were required to hold their financial balances as bank deposits. They were also instructed to keep on hand only enough cash to meet daily expenses; all major financial transactions were to be conducted through banks. Payment for goods and services exchanged by economic units was accomplished by debiting the account of the purchasing unit and crediting that of the selling unit by the appropriate amount. This practice effectively helped to minimize the need for currency.

Since 1949 China's leaders have urged the Chinese people to build up personal savings accounts to reduce the demand for consumer goods and increase the amount of capital available for investment. Small branch offices of savings banks were conveniently located throughout the urban areas. In the countryside savings were deposited with the rural credit cooperatives, which could be found in most towns and villages. In 1986 savings deposits for the entire country totaled over ¥223.7 billion.

Prices

Determination of Prices

Until the reform period of the late 1970s and 1980s, the prices of most commodities were set by government agencies and changed infrequently. Because prices did not change when production costs or demand for a commodity altered, they often failed to reflect the true values of goods, causing many kinds of goods to be misallocated and producing a price system that the Chinese government itself referred to as "irrational."

The best way to generate the accurate prices required for economic efficiency is through the process of supply and demand, and government policy in the 1980s increasingly advocated the use of prices that were "mutually agreed upon by buyer and seller," that is, determined through the market. The prices of products in the farm produce free markets were determined by supply and demand, and in the summer of 1985 the state store prices of all food items except grain also were allowed to float in response to market conditions. Prices of most goods produced by private and collectively owned enterprises in both rural and urban areas generally were free to float, as were the prices of many items that state-owned enterprises produced outside the plan. Prices of most major goods produced by state-owned enterprises, however, along with the grain purchased from farmers by state commercial departments for retail sales in the cities, still were set or restricted by government agencies and still were not sufficiently accurate.

In 1987 the price structure in China was chaotic. Some prices were determined in the market through the forces of supply and demand, others were set by government agencies, and still others were produced by procedures that were not clearly defined. In many cases, there was more than one price for the same commodity, depending on how it was exchanged, the kind of unit that produced it, or who the buyer was. While the government was not pleased with this situation, it was committed to continued price reform. It was reluctant, however, to release the remaining fixed prices

Selling fish under the floating-price policy, Jiangsu Province
Courtesy Xinhua News Agency

because of potential political and economic disruption. Sudden unpredictable price changes would leave consumers unable to continue buying some goods; some previously profitable enterprises under the old price structure would begin to take losses, and others would abruptly become very wealthy.

The Role of Prices

As a result of the economic reform program and the increased importance of market exchange and profitability, in the 1980s prices played a central role in determining the production and distribution of goods in most sectors of the economy. Previously, in the strict centrally planned system, enterprises had been assigned output quotas and inputs in physical terms. Now, under the reform program, the incentive to show a positive profit caused even state-owned enterprises to choose inputs and products on the basis of prices whenever possible. State-owned enterprises could not alter the amounts or prices of goods they were required to produce by the plan, but they could try to increase their profits by purchasing inputs as inexpensively as possible, and their off-plan production decisions were based primarily on price considerations. Prices were the main economic determinant of production decisions in agriculture and in private and collectively owned industrial enterprises despite the fact that regulations, local government fees or harassment, or arrangements based on personal connections often prevented enterprises from carrying out those decisions.

Consumer goods were allocated to households by the price mechanism, except for rationed grain. Families decided what commodities to buy on the basis of the prices of the goods in relation to household income.

Problems in Price Policy

The grain market was a typical example of a situation in which the government was confronted with major problems whether it allowed the irrational price structure to persist or carried out price reform. State commercial agencies paid farmers a higher price for grain than the state received from the urban residents to whom they sold it. In 1985 state commercial agencies paid farmers an average price of ¥416.4 per ton of grain and then sold it in the cities at an average price of ¥383.3 a ton, for a loss of ¥33.1 per ton. Ninety million tons were sold under this arrangement, causing the government to lose nearly ¥3 billion. If the state reduced the procurement price, farmers would reduce their grain production. Because grain was the staple Chinese diet, this result was unacceptable. If the state increased the urban retail price to equal the procurement price, the cost of the main food item for Chinese families would rise 9 percent, generating enormous resentment. But even this alternative would probably not entirely resolve the problem, as the average free-market price of grain—¥510.5 a ton in 1987—indicated that its true value was well above the state procurement price.

There was no clear solution to the price policy dilemma. The approach of the government was to encourage the growth of non-planned economic activity and thereby expand the proportion of prices determined by market forces. These market prices could then serve as a guide for more accurate pricing of planned items. It was likely that the Chinese economy would continue to operate with a dual price system for some years to come.

Inflation

One of the most striking manifestations of economic instability in China in the 1930s and 1940s was runaway inflation. Inflation peaked during the Chinese civil war of the late 1940s, when wholesale prices in Shanghai increased 7.5 million times in the space of 3 years. In the early 1950s, stopping inflation was a major government objective, accomplished through currency reform, unification and nationalization of the banks, and tight control over prices and the money supply. These measures were continued until 1979, and China achieved a remarkable record of price stability. Between 1952 and 1978, retail prices for consumer goods grew at an average rate of only 0.6 percent a year.

During the reform period, higher levels of inflation appeared when government controls were reduced. The first serious jump in the cost of living for urban residents occurred in 1980, when consumer prices rose by 7.5 percent. In 1985 the increase was 11.9 percent, and in 1986 it was 7.6 percent. There were several basic reasons for this burst of inflation after thirty years of steady prices. First, the years before the reform saw a generally high rate of investment and concentration on the manufacture of producer goods. The resultant shortage of consumer commodities caused a gradual accumulation of excess demand: personal savings were relatively large, and, in the late 1970s and early 1980s, there was a booming market for such expensive consumer durables as watches and television sets. Second, the real value of many items changed as some resources became more scarce and as technology altered both manufacturing processes and products. The real cost of producing agricultural products rose with the increased use of modern inputs. Manufactured consumer goods that were more technologically advanced and more expensive than those previously on the market—such as washing machines and color television sets—became available.

During the early 1980s, both consumer incomes and the amount of money in circulation increased fairly rapidly and, at times, unexpectedly. Consumer incomes grew because of the reform program's emphasis on material incentives and because of the overall expansion in productivity and income-earning possibilities. The higher profits earned and retained by enterprises were passed on to workers, in many cases, in the form of wage hikes, bonuses, and higher subsidies. At the same time, the expanded and diversified role of the banking system caused the amounts of loans and deposits to increase at times beyond officially sanctioned levels, injecting unplanned new quantities of currency into the economy.

Living Standards

Progress since 1949

Before 1949 the Chinese economy was characterized by widespread poverty, extreme income inequalities, and endemic insecurity of livelihood. By means of centralized economic planning, the People's Republic was able to redistribute national income so as to provide the entire population with at least the minimal necessities of life (except during the "three bad years" of 1959, 1960, and 1961) and to consistently allocate a relatively high proportion of national income to productive investment. Equally important to the quality of life were the results of mass public-health and sanitation campaigns, which rid the country of most of the conditions that had bred epidemics and lingering disease in the past. The most concrete evidence of improved living standards was that average national life expectancy more than doubled, rising from around thirty-two years in 1949 to sixty-nine years in 1985 (see Mortality and Fertility; Health Care, ch. 2).

In 1987 the standard of living in China was much lower than in the industrialized countries, but nearly all Chinese people had adequate food, clothing, and housing. In addition, there was a positive trend toward rapid improvements in living conditions in the 1980s as a result of the economic reforms, though improvements in the standard of living beyond the basic level came slowly. Until the end of the 1970s, the fruits of economic growth were largely negated by population increases, which prevented significant advances in the per capita availability of food, clothing, and housing beyond levels achieved in the 1950s (see Population, ch. 2). The second major change in the standard of living came about as a result of the rapid expansion of productivity and commerce generated by the reform measures of the 1980s. After thirty years of austerity and marginal sufficiency, Chinese consumers suddenly were able to buy more than enough to eat from a growing variety of food items. Stylish clothing, modern furniture, and a wide array of electrical appliances also became part of the normal expectations of ordinary Chinese families.

Food

While food production rose substantially after 1949, population increases were nearly as great until the 1980s. Production of grain, the source of about 75 percent of the calories in the Chinese diet, grew at an average rate of 2.7 percent a year between 1952 and 1979, while population growth averaged almost 2 percent a year. Total grain output per capita grew from 288 kilograms a year in 1952 to 319 kilograms in 1978, an increase of only 11 percent in 26 years. In 1984, however, a remarkably good harvest produced 396 kilograms of grain per capita, an increase of 24 percent in only 6 years. In 1985 grain output fell below the peak level of 1984, to 365 kilograms per person, and recovered only partially in 1986 to 369 kilograms per capita (see table B; Crops, ch. 6).

Other important food items that remained in short supply before the economic reforms included edible oil, sugar, and aquatic products. Production of oil-bearing crops increased at an average rate of about 2 percent a year from 1952 to 1979, and annual consumption of edible oil was less than 2 kilograms per person in 1979. Between 1978 and 1985, output grew at over 16 percent a year, and annual consumption increased to 5.1 kilograms per person. Sugar production grew at an average annual rate of 4.5 percent after 1952, but in 1979 consumption per person still was only 3.5 kilograms per year. From 1979 to 1985, sugar production grew by 10 percent a year, and the total amount of sugar available per person rose to 5.6 kilograms in 1985. Output of aquatic products rose at an average rate of only 2 percent a year between 1957 and 1978 and declined slightly in 1979; between 1979 and 1985, however, output grew at an average rate of 8.5 percent a year, and individual annual consumption rose from 3.2 kilograms to 4.9 kilograms.

Pork, eggs, and vegetables were increasingly available before the 1980s (see Animal Husbandry, ch. 6). Annual consumption of pork—the most commonly eaten meat in China—grew from 5.9 kilograms per person in 1952 to 7.5 kilograms per person in the mid-1970s. In 1979 a sharp increase in procurement prices for pork brought about a surge in supply—to 9.6 kilograms per person. Beginning in 1980, availability increased steadily, reaching

14 kilograms of pork per capita in 1985, an increase of 9 percent each year from 1978. Consumption of fresh eggs followed a similar pattern, climbing from an average of just over one kilogram per person in 1952 to almost two kilograms in 1978. The economic reforms elicited rapid increases in the supply of eggs, as they had with pork, and by 1985 consumption had more than doubled, to 5 kilograms of eggs per person a year, for an increase of over 14 percent a year.

Vegetables were the major supplement to grain in the Chinese diet and were very important nutritionally. In 1957 annual vegetable consumption per capita in Chinese cities averaged 109 kilograms and by 1981 had grown to 152 kilograms. Household survey data indicated that in 1985 vegetable consumption had leveled off, at 148 kilograms per person per year in urban areas and 131 kilograms in the countryside, as people used their higher incomes to increase their purchases of more expensive foods, such as meat, fish, and edible oil.

As of the late 1970s, famine and malnutrition were no longer major problems in China, but the average diet lacked variety and provided little more than basic nutritional requirements. Protein, in particular, was barely adequate for health maintenance. By the mid-1980s the availability of food had improved dramatically. Bustling street markets offered a good variety of fruits and vegetables throughout the year, and per capita consumption of high-protein foods—meat, poultry, eggs, and fish—increased by 63 percent over the 1979 level, to nearly 27 kilograms a year in 1985.

Clothing

Before the reform period, clothing purchases were restricted by rationing. Cotton cloth consumption was limited to between four and six meters a year per person in the 1970s. In the 1980s one of the most visible signs of the economic "revolution" was the appearance in Chinese cities of large quantities of relatively modern, varied, colorful, Western-style clothes, a sharp contrast to the monotone image of blue and gray suits that typified Chinese dress in earlier years. Cloth consumption increased from eight meters per person in 1978 to almost twelve meters in 1985, and rationing was ended in the early 1980s. Production of synthetic fibers more than tripled during this period; in 1985 synthetics constituted 40 percent of the cloth purchased (see Textiles, ch. 7). Consumers also tripled their purchases of woolen fabrics in these years and bought growing numbers of garments made of silk, leather, or down. In 1987 Chinese department stores and street markets carried clothing

Table B. Economic Indicators, Selected Years, 1952–86

	Unit	1952	1957	1965	1970	1975	1980	1983	1984	1985	1986
GNP [1]	billions of 1985 United States dollars [2]	33	50	65	96	126	169	210	239	268	288
Population	millions	575	647	725	830	924	987	1,025	1,035	1,045	1,060
Per capita GNP	1985 United States dollars [3]	57	77	89	116	136	171	205	231	257	272
Grain	millions of tons	164	195	195	240	285	321	387	407	379	391
Cotton	-do-	1.3	1.6	2.1	2.3	2.4	2.7	4.6	6.3	4.1	3.5
Crude steel	-do-	1.3	5.3	12.2	17.8	23.9	37.1	40.0	43.5	46.8	51.9
Crude oil	-do-	0.4	1.5	11.3	30.7	77.1	105.9	106.1	114.6	124.9	130.7
Coal	-do-	66	131	232	354	482	620	715	789	872	883
Agricultural production index	n.a.	100	120	123	142	169	188	248	283	302	313
Industrial production index	n.a.	100	245	478	855	1,271	1,911	2,222	2,524	2,966	3,239
Exports	billions of 1985 United States dollars [2]	0.8	1.6	2.2	2.3	7.3	18.3	22.2	26.1	27.4	30.9
Imports	-do-	1.1	1.5	2.0	2.3	7.5	19.5	21.4	27.4	42.3	42.9

n.a.—not applicable.

[1] Gross national product.

[2] Converted from 1985 yuan at the average 1985 exchange rate of US$100 = ¥293.67.

[3] GNP expressed in constant United States dollars does not fully reflect China's national economic performance because of differences in income definitions, inaccurate prices, and exchange rate changes unrelated to economic forces.

Sources: Based on information from China, State Statistical Bureau, *Statistical Yearbook of China, 1986*, Hong Kong, 1986; and *China Daily*, various issues, 1987.

in a large variety of styles, colors, quality, and prices. Many people displayed their new affluence with relatively expensive and stylish clothes, while those with more modest tastes or meager incomes still could adequately outfit themselves at very low cost.

Consumer Goods

As with food supplies and clothing, the availability of housewares went through several stages. Simple, inexpensive household items, like thermoses, cooking pans, and clocks were stocked in department stores and other retail outlets all over China from the 1950s on. Relatively expensive consumer durables became available more gradually. In the 1960s production and sales of bicycles, sewing machines, wristwatches, and transistor radios grew to the point that these items became common household possessions, followed in the late 1970s by television sets and cameras (see Other Consumer Goods, ch. 7). In the 1980s supplies of furniture and electrical appliances increased along with family incomes. Household survey data indicated that by 1985 most urban families owned two bicycles, at least one sofa, a writing desk, a wardrobe, a sewing machine, an electric fan, a radio, and a television. Virtually all urban adults owned wristwatches, half of all families had washing machines, 10 percent had refrigerators, and over 18 percent owned color televisions. Rural households on average owned about half the number of consumer durables owned by urban dwellers. Most farm families had 1 bicycle, about half had a radio, 43 percent owned a sewing machine, 12 percent had a television set, and about half the rural adults owned wristwatches.

Housing

Housing construction in towns and cities lagged behind urban population growth. A 1978 survey of housing conditions in 192 cities found that their combined population had increased by 83 percent between 1949 and 1978, but housing floor space had only grown by 46.7 percent. In 1978 there were only 3.6 square meters of living space per inhabitant in these cities, a reduction of 0.9 square meter since 1949. To remedy this problem, construction of modern urban housing became a top priority in the late 1970s, and by the mid-1980s new high-rise apartment blocks and the tall cranes used in their construction were ubiquitous features of large cities. Some apartments in the new buildings had their own lavatories, kitchens, and balconies, but others shared communal facilities. Nearly all were of much higher quality than older houses, many of which were built of mud bricks and lacked plumbing.

By 1981 living space in urban housing had increased to 5.3 square meters per person, and by 1985 the figure was 6.7 square meters (see Housing Construction, ch. 7). Despite this progress, scarcity of housing continued to be a major problem in the cities, and many young married couples had to live with parents or make do with a single room (see Housing, ch. 3).

Housing conditions in rural areas varied widely. During the 1960s and 1970s, thousands of production brigades built sturdy, sanitary houses and apartments and in many cases entire new villages. With the introduction of the responsibility system and the more than doubling of rural incomes in the early 1980s, another wave of housing construction took place as farm families moved quickly to invest in their major personal assets—their homes—which for the most part were privately owned. Many farm family houses lacked running water, but virtually all had electricity and were considerably more spacious than urban dwellings. In 1980 farm homes averaged 9.4 square meters of living space per person, and by 1985 the figure had risen to 14.7 square meters. Despite extensive construction of new housing, in poorer regions some farm families still lived in traditional dwellings, such as mud-brick and thatch houses or, in some regions, cave houses. Many of the nomadic herders in Nei Monggol, Xinjiang, and Xizang (Tibet) autonomous regions still lived in tents or felt yurts. In the Chang Jiang Valley and in south China, some fishing and boat transportation communities continued to live on their vessels (see Minority Nationalities, ch. 2).

Income Distribution

Income differences in China since the 1950s have been much smaller than in most other countries. There was never any attempt, however, at complete equalization, and a wide range of income levels remained. Income differences grew even wider in the 1980s as the economic reform policies opened up new income opportunities. More than two-thirds of all urban workers were employed in state-owned units, which used an eight-grade wage system. The pay for each grade differed from one industry to another, but generally workers in the most senior grades earned about three times as much as beginning workers, senior managers could earn half again as much as senior workers, and engineers could earn twice as much as senior workers. In 1985 the average annual income of people employed in state-owned units was ¥1,213. An important component of workers' pay was made up of bonuses and subsidies. In 1985 bonuses contributed 13 percent of the incomes of workers in state-owned units; subsidies for transportation, food, and clothing added another 15 percent. One of the most important subsidies—one that did not appear in the income figures—

was for housing, nearly all of which was owned and allocated by the work unit and rented to unit members at prices well below real value. In 1985 urban consumers spent just over 1 percent of their incomes on housing (see Wages and Benefits; Urban Society, ch. 3).

The 27 percent of the urban labor force that was employed in collectively owned enterprises earned less on average than workers in state-owned units. The income of workers in collectively owned enterprises consisted of a share of the profit earned by the enterprise. Most such enterprises were small, had little capital, and did not earn large profits. Many were engaged in traditional services, handicrafts, or small-scale, part-time assembly work. In 1985 workers in urban collective units earned an average annual income of ¥968. In the more open commercial environment of the 1980s, a small but significant number of people earned incomes much larger than those in regular state-owned and collectively owned units. Employees of enterprises run by overseas Chinese (see Glossary), for instance, earned an average of ¥2,437 in 1985, over twice the average income of workers in state-owned units.

The small but dynamic domestic private sector also produced some lucrative opportunities. Private, part-time schools, which appeared in large numbers in the mid-1980s, offered moonlighting work to university professors, who could double or triple their modest incomes if they were from prestigious institutions and taught desirable subjects, such as English, Japanese, or electronics. Small-scale entrepreneurs could earn considerably more in the free markets than the average income. Business people who served as a liaison between foreign firms and the domestic economy could earn incomes many times higher than those of the best-paid employees of state-owned units. A handful of millionaire businessmen could be found in the biggest cities. These people had owned firms before 1949, cooperated with the government in the 1950s in return for stock in their firms, and then lost their incomes in the political turmoil of the Cultural Revolution. In the late 1970s and early 1980s, when these businessmen were politically rehabilitated, their incomes were returned with the accrued interest, and some suddenly found themselves quite wealthy. Although the number of people earning incomes far beyond the normal wage scale was tiny relative to the population, they were important symbols of the rewards of economic reform and received a great deal of media attention. In 1985 most of these people worked in enterprises classified as "units of other ownership" (private rather than state- or collectively owned enterprises). These enterprises employed only 440,000 people out of the total urban labor force of 128 million in 1985 and paid

Shuangyushu department store in Beijing; the sign advertises fabrics, apparel, shoes, and hats.
Courtesy Rinn-Sup Shinn

average annual salaries of ¥1,373, only slightly higher than the overall urban national average.

In China, as in other countries, an important determinant of the affluence of a household was the dependency ratio—the number of nonworkers supported by each worker. In 1985 the average cost of living for one person in urban areas was ¥732 a year, and the average state enterprise worker, even with food allowance and other benefits added to the basic wage, had difficulty supporting one other person. Two average wage earners, however, could easily support one dependent. Families with several workers and few or no dependents had substantial surplus earnings, which they saved or used to buy nonessential goods. An important positive influence on the per capita consumption levels of urban families was a decline in the number of dependents per urban worker, from 2.4 in 1964 to 0.7 in 1985. In farm families the dependency ratio fell from 1.5 in 1978 to 0.7 in 1985. Farm incomes rose rapidly in the 1980s under the stimulus of the responsibility system but on average remained considerably lower than urban incomes. Household surveys found that in 1985 average net per capita income for rural residents was ¥398, less than half the average per capita urban income, which was ¥821. The value of goods farmers produced and consumed themselves accounted for 31 percent of rural income in 1985. The largest component of income in kind was food, 58 percent of which was self-produced.

Farm family members on average consumed much less of most major kinds of goods than urban residents. For instance, a household survey found in 1985 that the average urban dweller consumed 148 kilograms of vegetables, 20 kilograms of meat, 2.6 kilograms of sugar, and 8 kilograms of liquor. At the same time, a survey of rural households found that the average rural resident consumed 131 kilograms of vegetables, 11 kilograms of meat, 1.5 kilograms of sugar, and 4 kilograms of liquor. Differences of a similar nature existed for consumer durables.

Another indication of the gap between urban and rural income levels was the difference in personal savings accounts, which in 1985 averaged ¥277 per capita for urban residents but only ¥85 per capita for the rural population. There was great variation in rural income levels among different provincial-level units, counties, towns, villages, and individual families. While the average net per capita income for rural residents in 1985 was ¥398, provincial-level averages ranged from a high of ¥805 for farm families living in Shanghai to a low of ¥255 for the rural population of Gansu Province.

The fundamental influence on rural prosperity was geography (see Physical Environment, ch. 2). Soil type and quality, rainfall, temperature range, drainage, and availability of water determined the kinds and quantities of crops that could be grown. Equally important geographic factors were access to transportation routes and proximity to urban areas (see Internal Trade and Distribution, ch. 8).

The highest agricultural incomes were earned by suburban units that were able to sell produce and sideline products in the nearby cities. Under the responsibility system, household incomes depended on the number of workers in each household and the household's success in holding down production costs and in supplying goods and services to local markets. Most of the rural families with the highest incomes—the "10,000-yuan households"—were "specialized households" that concentrated family efforts on supplying a particular service or good. Many of these families owned their own equipment, such as trucks or specialized buildings, and operated essentially as private concerns.

An increasingly important influence on rural incomes in the mid-1980s was the expansion of nonagricultural rural enterprises, often referred to as "township enterprises." These were factories, construction teams, and processing operations, most of which were owned by collectives, primarily villages, towns, and townships. Some were owned by voluntary groups of families. Township enterprises were considered by the government to be the main source of employment for rural workers who were leaving agriculture because of rising productivity under the responsibility system. By the end of 1986, township enterprises employed 21 percent of the rural labor force. The movement of rural labor into township enterprises helped to increase average rural incomes because of the higher productivity in nonagricultural jobs. In 1986 industrial workers in rural areas produced an average annual value of ¥4,300 per person, compared with about ¥1,000 per farmer in the same year.

The change in farm production from primarily collective to primarily household operations is reflected in household survey data on the sources of rural incomes. Before the 1980s farmers received income in the form of shares of the profits earned by their production teams plus supplementary income from household sideline activities. In 1978 two-thirds of the net income of farm families came from the collective, and only 27 percent was derived from household production. With the shift to the responsibility system these ratios were reversed. By 1982 the collective provided only 21 percent of farm income, while household production provided 69 percent. In 1985 the collective share of farm income had fallen to just over 8 percent, and the family production share had risen to 81 percent.

Perhaps the most serious gaps in living standards between rural and urban areas were in education and health care. Primary schools existed in most rural localities, and 80 percent of the country's primary-school teachers worked in rural schools. Secondary schools were less widely distributed; only 57 percent of the total number of secondary-school teachers served in rural schools. Most rural schools were less well equipped and their staffs less adequately trained than their urban counterparts. Health care had been greatly improved in rural areas in the 1960s and 1970s through sanitation campaigns and the introduction of large numbers of barefoot doctors (see Glossary), midwives, and health workers. Most modern hospitals, fully trained doctors, and modern medical equipment, however, were located in urban areas and were not easily accessible to rural families. In 1985 two-thirds of all hospital beds and medical staff personnel were located in urban hospitals. The economic reforms affected rural education and health care positively in places where farm communities used their higher incomes to improve schools and hospitals and negatively in localities where the reduced role of the collective resulted in deterioration of collective services (see Health Care, ch. 2; Primary Education, ch. 4; Secondary Education, ch. 4).

Potential for Achieving National Goals

By 1987, under the stimulus of the reform program, the Chinese economy had made major strides toward achieving modernization and improved living standards. The potential for further improvements in efficiency and productivity was greatly increased by the revival of the education system, the opening of the economy to broader trade and cooperation with other countries, the expanded use of the market to enliven commerce and production, and the increased decision-making power of individual economic units (see Modernization Goals in the 1980s, ch. 4; Trade Policy in the 1980s, ch. 8).

The country's most important resource was its labor force, the largest in the world. The rapid expansion and improvement of the education system that began in the late 1970s was creating larger numbers of workers who were skilled and well educated, as well as the first substantial numbers of advanced-degree holders to staff the nation's universities and research institutes. In addition, the decentralization of management encouraged the participation in planning and decision making of growing numbers of local and enterprise-level managers, planners, administrators, and scientists. It also trained future economic leaders for higher administrative responsibilities.

In terms of material resources, China was adequately endowed to meet the needs of modernization in all but a few materials. Under the new policy of encouraging cooperation and joint ventures with foreign firms, advanced technology was more widely used to exploit China's large deposits of iron ore and other important minerals, along with the country's vast coal and petroleum reserves and its enormous hydroelectric potential—the largest in the world. Much of the investment in expanding the transportation network in the 1980s was aimed at improving access to previously remote mineral and energy resources for both domestic needs and foreign trade.

The most stringent resource constraint was the limited amount of arable land, which actually declined in the 1980s as cropland was appropriated for new rural housing and urban expansion. Between 1978 and 1985, the total area sown to crops declined by over 4 percent. The loss of farmland, however, was more than compensated for by improved productivity of the land that remained under cultivation. Farmers expanded the irrigated area, increased fertilizer application, acquired improved crop varieties, and made better use of comparative advantage in determining which crops to grow, resulting in an average rate of growth in the value of crop production of better than 5 percent a year over the same 7-year

A supermarket run by the Sanlian Company in the Zhuhai special economic zone, Guangdong Province
Courtesy Xinhua News Agency

period. Although agricultural growth rates had begun to fall off in the mid-1980s, the incentives of the responsibility system and greater access to international technical advances suggested that the farm sector could continue to meet the needs of the growing economy in the foreseeable future.

The industrial sector, while much less advanced than those of the developed countries, was nonetheless a solid base for modernization. Industrial enterprises were dispersed throughout the country and included units capable of producing all major kinds of machinery, equipment, chemicals, building materials, and light industrial goods. Chinese enterprises could make most of the products required for modernization, and the growing pool of industrial technicians and managers was increasingly capable of effectively integrating advanced foreign technology into Chinese production processes. Key industries were being technologically strengthened by the purchase of advanced foreign equipment and the adoption of modern management techniques. Despite promising potential, formidable obstacles still impeded the drive for modernization. Physical restraints included a renewed increase in birth rates and population growth rates as the number of women of childbearing age began to rise in 1986 and 1987. Some crucial resources—especially educated personnel and modern equipment—

still were in very short supply because of the sheer size of the economy. In the realm of policy, the administration faced the daunting problem of trying to integrate market measures—for efficiency—with government planning and control, the source of stability. In 1987 both kinds of mechanisms exerted extensive influence, with the result that market efficiency was hindered by government intervention and government plans were undermined by off-plan activities. Finally, the most serious concern of government leaders was the possibility of future political upheavals. While nearly all Chinese people enjoyed better living conditions as a result of the progress achieved by the reform program, the new policies also had given rise to new social problems and political tensions. Increasing crime and corruption, greater emphasis on the profit motive, widening income disparities, and inflation aroused resistance in many conservative quarters and resulted in the political struggle that caused Hu Yaobang to be forced from his position as Chinese Communist Party general secretary in early 1987. By mid-1987 it was not yet clear what the outcome of the struggle would be or how it would affect the future course of economic reform.

* * *

Among the most useful works on economic development in China before 1949 are Mark Elvin's *The Pattern of the Chinese Past* and Dwight H. Perkins' *Agricultural Development in China, 1368–1968*. These books examine the fundamental relationships between technology, population, society, and economic growth in China. A good, brief integration of much of the scholarship on the Chinese economy in the modern period may be found in Ramon H. Myers' *The Chinese Economy Past and Present*. *China's Modern Economy in Historical Perspective*, edited by Perkins, is a valuable collection of articles by leading scholars dealing with various aspects of China's modern economic development. A concise description of the Chinese economy in the eighty years before 1949 is presented in two brief works by Albert Feuerwerker, *The Chinese Economy, ca. 1870–1911* and *Economic Trends in the Republic of China, 1912–1949*. The most authoritative and detailed sources of information on the economy of the People's Republic are the annual statistical yearbooks compiled by the State Statistical Bureau. As of 1987 the most recent was *Statistical Yearbook of China, 1986*, which contains updated information on most major aspects of the Chinese economy since 1949, as well as a set of explanatory notes that define the terms and measures used. Another useful annual Chinese publication is the *Almanac of China's Economy*. Recent general treatments of the Chinese economy by Western scholars include a good overview, *China's Political Economy* by Carl Riskin, and a mathematically oriented work, *The Chinese Economy* by Gregory C. Chow. Some of the earlier classic works on the post-1949 economy are *China's Economic Revolution* by Alexander Eckstein, *China's Economy* by Christopher Howe, *China's Economic System* by Audrey Donnithorne, *The Economy of the Chinese Mainland* by Ta-Chung Liu and Kung-Chia Yeh, and *The Chinese Economy under Communism* by Nai-Ruenn Chen and Walter Galenson. *China's Development Experience in Comparative Perspective*, edited by Robert F. Dernberger, is a collection of studies by noted economists dealing with China's modern economic development. A good description of the Maoist economic model is presented in John G. Gurley's *China's Economy and the Maoist Strategy*. The United States Congress Joint Economic Committee has published a series of useful volumes on the Chinese economy: *An Economic Profile of Mainland China* (1967); *People's Republic of China: An Economic Assessment* (1972); *China: A Reassessment of the Economy* (1975); *Chinese Economy Post-Mao* (1978); *China under the Four Modernizations* (1982); and *China's Economy Looks Toward the Year 2000* (1986). There are many useful works dealing with specific aspects of the Chinese economy. Economic planning is analyzed by Perkins in *Market Control and Planning in Communist China* and more recently by Nicholas R. Lardy in *Economic Growth and Distribution in China*. The banking system is described in *Money and Monetary Policy in Communist China* by Katherine H. Hsiao and in *China's Financial System* by William A. Byrd. *The Political Economy of Reform in Post-Mao China*, edited by Elizabeth J. Perry and Christine Wong, is a collection of insightful analyses of the reform process. Prominent among the many works on Chinese agriculture are *Food for One Billion: China's Agriculture since 1949* by Robert C. Hsu, *Agriculture in China's Modern Economic Development* by Lardy, and *The Chinese Agricultural Economy*, edited by Randolph Barker, Radha Sinha, and Beth Rose. Current economic information appears in several official English-language periodicals from China, including *Beijing Review*, *China Daily*, and *China Reconstructs*. Major periodicals published outside China that monitor the Chinese economy include *Asian Wall Street Journal*, *China Quarterly*, *Economist*, and *Far Eastern Economic Review*. (For further information and complete citations, see Bibliography.)

Chapter 6. Agriculture

The original of this Han dynasty (206 B.C.–A.D. 220) pottery sheep was discovered in Henan Province.

CHINA HAS THE WORLD'S LARGEST agricultural economy and one of the most varied. The nation stands first among all others in the production of rice, cotton, tobacco, and hogs and is a major producer of wheat, corn, millet, tea, jute, and hemp. This wide range of crops is possible because of the country's varied climate and agricultural zones. China participates on a large scale in international agricultural markets, both as an exporter and as an importer.

For over 4,000 years, China has been a nation of farmers. By the time the People's Republic of China was established in 1949, virtually all arable land was under cultivation; irrigation and drainage systems constructed centuries earlier and intensive farming practices already produced relatively high yields. But little prime virgin land was available to support population growth and economic development. However, after a decline in production as a result of the Great Leap Forward (1958–60), agricultural reforms implemented in the 1980s increased yields and promised even greater future production from existing cultivated land.

A successful agricultural sector is critical to China's development. First, it must feed more than 1 billion people, about 21 percent of the world's population, using only 7 percent of the world's arable land. Second, it must provide raw materials for the industrial sector. Third, agricultural exports must earn the foreign exchange needed to purchase key industrial items from other countries.

Since 1949 China's political leaders have tried a variety of large-scale social experiments to boost agricultural production. First, a massive land reform program eliminated landlords and gave land to those who farmed it. Next, farm families were progressively organized into cooperatives, collectives, and finally people's communes. After more than twenty-five years of experience with communes, officials abolished these institutions, which had become too bureaucratic and rigid to respond to the flexible requirements of agricultural production. Also, farm production incentives languished in the commune system. In 1978 China's leaders began a program of far-reaching agricultural reforms. Townships and villages were organized, and new incentives were incorporated into contractual relationships tying farmers to economic cooperatives and businesses.

Since the revolution in 1949, China has devoted most of its investments and administrative energy to the industrial sector.

Generally, the agricultural sector received special attention only when the leaders perceived that the sector was beginning to restrain China's overall economic development. Agricultural output basically kept pace with the growth of population but did not expand fast enough to raise living standards. Per capita consumption of grains, fibers, edible oil, sugar, fruits, vegetables, fish, meat, eggs, and dairy products remained low. The value of goods generated by the agricultural sector has grown, but not as fast as output generated by other sectors in the economy. In 1949 about half of the country's output came from the agricultural sector. This ratio dropped to 41 percent by 1955, declined to 31 percent by 1965, and fell another few percentage points in 1975 to 25 percent. But agricultural reforms initiated in the early 1980s brought a rise in agriculture to 33 percent of GNP in 1985. At the same time, more than 60 percent of the national labor force was employed in agriculture.

China in the late 1980s was thus poised to confront growing demands for agricultural production with a combination of time-tested farming methods and modern agro-technology. The size and diversity of the country—in geography and in population—however, presented a unique challenge to China's policy makers and implementors.

Resources Endowment

Arable land in China is scarce; little more than 10 percent of the total land area, most of it in the eastern third of the country, can be cultivated. This compares with more than 20 percent for the continental United States, which is slightly smaller than China. Further agricultural expansion would be relatively difficult because almost no land that could be profitably cultivated remains unused and because, despite intensive cultivation, yields from some marginal lands are low. Some possibility for expansion exists in thinly populated parts of the country, especially in the northeast, but the growing season there is short and the process of land reclamation prolonged and costly.

China Proper (see Glossary) is divided by the Qin Ling range into highly dissimilar north and south agricultural areas (see fig. 8). In semitropical south China, rainfall is relatively abundant and the growing season long. Rice is the predominant grain crop. The paddies can generally be irrigated with water from rivers or other sources. Although much of the soil is acid red clay, the heavy use of fertilizer (at one time organic but by the mid-1980s also including a large proportion of chemical nutrients) supports high yields. Frequently two or even three crops a year are cultivated on the

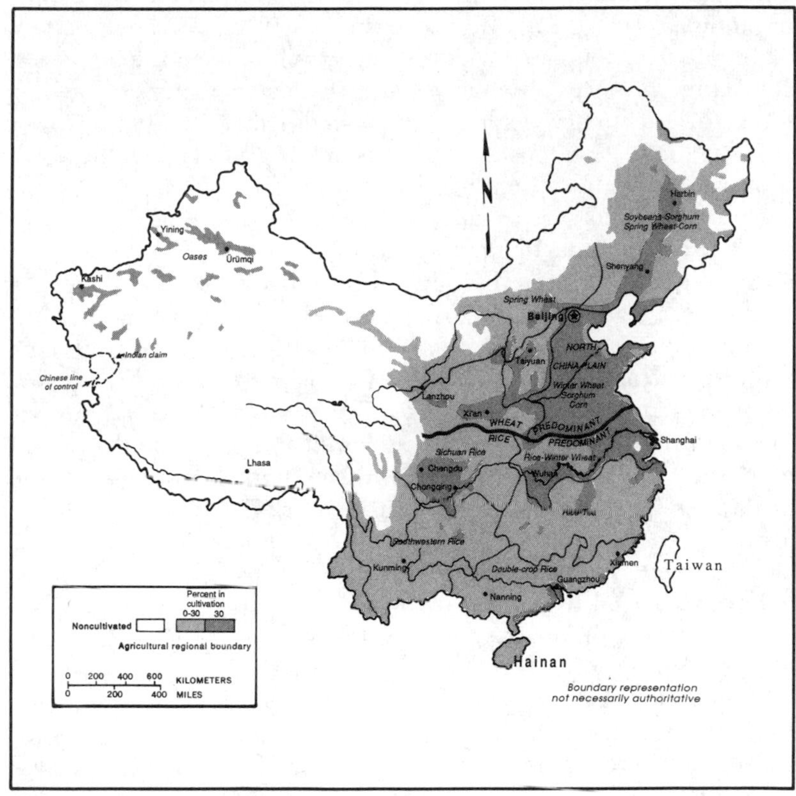

Figure 8. Agricultural Regions, 1987

same land. Food crops other than rice are also grown, most frequently in hilly areas or during the winter. These include potatoes and winter wheat. The highest grain yields in the country in the mid-1980s were generally found in the Sichuan Basin, the lower Chang Jiang (Yangtze River) Valley, and Guangdong and Fujian provinces, where multiple cropping of rice and other crops was the typical pattern. Cotton, tea, and industrial crops were also produced there.

Wheat has traditionally been the main crop in north China, a considerably drier region than south China. The winter wheat crop accounts for nearly 90 percent of China's total production. Spring wheat is grown mainly in the eastern portion of Nei Monggol Autonomous Region (Inner Mongolia) and the northeastern provinces. Other important grain crops include corn, sorghum, and millet. These are usually dryland crops. Since the late 1960s, irrigation has been greatly expanded, but water remains an important limiting factor. Compared with the south, soils in the north are generally better; however, because of the shorter growing season and colder, drier climate, yields per cultivated hectare tend to be lower and irrigation less extensive. Labor is not as abundant in the north as in the south, but cropping patterns tend to require less labor, and mechanization (especially of plowing) is more advanced.

The North China Plain, the most important growing area in north China, extends across several provinces. Winter wheat and corn are the leading grain crops; cotton is also grown, and Shandong Province produces peanuts. The North China Plain, although fertile, was traditionally subject to frequent floods and droughts, but water conservation measures ameliorated the problem (see Physical Environment, ch. 2). Winter wheat is grown in the mountainous areas west of this plain, but the climate is more severe and the danger of natural disasters even greater. The fertile soils of the northeastern plains have been used to plant corn, spring wheat, and even rice. High-quality soybeans are grown in the northeast and are exported to many Pacific Rim countries. Although Nei Monggol Autonomous Region produces some spring wheat and other grain, it is best known as a pastoral area.

Much of China's vast and generally inhospitable northwest and southwest regions is unsuitable for cultivation. Xinjiang-Uygur Autonomous Region in the northwest, like Nei Monggol Autonomous Region, is also best known as a pastoral area. In Xizang Autonomous Region (Tibet) in the southwest, most of the cultivated area has been irrigated, and special strains of wheat, rice, and barley suitable for the climate of that high-altitude region have been developed.

China's rural labor force in 1985 consisted of about 370 million people. The quality of the labor force had improved in the previous three decades, primarily because of the introduction of rural schools, which stressed elementary education (see Primary Education, ch. 4). Nevertheless, a large portion of the rural population was illiterate or semiliterate in 1987, and very few high school and college graduates lived in villages and towns. Lack of education continued to retard the spread of advanced technology in rural areas. The scarcity of cultivable land and the abundance of manpower led to the development of labor-intensive production in most parts of the country. And, although China's agriculture was less labor intensive than that in some neighboring countries, it was characterized by meticulous tending of the land and other techniques employed in East Asia for centuries.

In the 1980s the rural labor force also was employed in rural capital construction projects and small-scale industries. During the winter months, large numbers of rural people worked on construction and maintenance of irrigation or land-leveling projects. Where rural industrial plants existed, they usually employed a small proportion of the rural labor force, and many peasants also engaged in sideline activities, such as handicrafts. The government tightly limited migration from rural to urban areas (see Migration, ch. 2).

By the 1980s China had improved its agricultural resources, but important obstacles remained. The country's agricultural capital stock had been built up in large part by land modification. Through the centuries fields were leveled and consolidated, and substantial investments were made in building and modernizing irrigation facilities. Since the 1950s the production of mechanical agricultural equipment had been a major industry. But in the 1980s many observers still noted a shortage of transportation facilities to take crops to market and bring seed, fuel, and fertilizer to users (see Transportation, ch. 8). In addition to capital, China had available a supply of skilled labor and a stock of technical information on seed varieties and fertilizer use despite the damage done by the Cultural Revolution (1966–76; see Glossary).

Agricultural Policies

Agricultural policy has gone through three broad phases: the 1950s, when agriculture was collectivized, ending with the Great Leap Forward (1958–60; see Glossary); the period from 1961 to the death of Mao Zedong in 1976, when more agricultural progress came to depend on the supply of capital and modern inputs; and the period under the post-Mao leadership, which has been characterized by greater reliance on markets, prices, and incentives to boost production and to diversify output. (Inputs in this chapter refer to components of production such as land, labor, seed, fertilizer, machinery, tools, and irrigation water.)

The 1950s

During the 1950s the government of the new People's Republic made a concerted effort to redistribute land more equitably. Although many peasants owned part or all of the small holdings they farmed before 1949, tenancy was common, especially in south China. The Chinese Communist Party (CCP) implemented land reforms in areas under its control even before 1949, and subsequently landlords and wealthy peasants became targets of party attack. Their elimination as a class was a major aim of the land reform movement begun under the Agrarian Reform Law of

June 28, 1950 (see The Transition to Socialism, 1953–57, ch. 1). Collectivization of agriculture, which was accomplished in several stages, began about 1952.

The first stage of land reform was characterized by mutual aid teams. The mutual aid system was kept simple at first, involving only the temporary sharing of labor and some capital; individual households remained the basic unit of ownership and production. In 1954 mutual aid teams were organized with increasing rapidity into agricultural producers' cooperatives, which differed from mutual aid teams in that tools, draft animals, and labor were shared on a permanent basis. Cooperative members retained ownership of their land but secured a share in the cooperative by staking their plots along with those of other members in the common land pool. By 1956 the transformation of mutual aid teams into agricultural cooperatives was nearly complete. By the end of that year, moreover, the great majority of cooperatives had moved to a still higher stage of collectivization, having become advanced producers' cooperatives. These cooperatives contrasted with those of the earlier stage in that members no longer earned income based on shares of land owned. Instead, collective farm profits were distributed to members primarily on the basis of labor contributions. The average cooperative was made up of 170 families and more than 700 people. Although small private plots were permitted, most of the land was owned collectively by the cooperative. Another development in this period was the establishment of state farms in which land became the property of the state (see Planning and Organization, this ch.).

This degree of collectivization was achieved with much less turmoil than had occurred during collectivization in the Soviet Union. As in the Soviet Union, however, investment in the agricultural sector was kept low relative to industrial investment because planners chose to achieve more rapid growth of basic industries. But collectivization did not prevent the growth of agricultural production; grain production, for example, increased by 3.5 percent a year under the First Five-Year Plan (1953–57). Growth was achieved mainly through the intensified use of traditional agricultural techniques, together with some technical improvements.

Once collectivization was achieved and agricultural output per capita began to increase, the leadership embarked on the extremely ambitious programs of the Great Leap Forward of 1958–60 (see table 11, Appendix A). In agriculture this meant unrealistically high production goals and an even higher degree of collectivization than had already been achieved. The existing collectives were organized very rapidly into people's communes (see Glossary),

The Ming and Qing emperors prayed for a successful harvest at the Temple of Heaven in Beijing.
Courtesy Ronald E. Dolan

much larger units with an average of 5,400 households and a total of 20,000 to 30,000 members on average. The production targets were not accompanied by a sufficient amount of capital and modern inputs such as fertilizer; rather, they were to be reached in large measure by heroic efforts on the part of the peasants.

Substantial effort was expended during the Great Leap Forward on large-scale but often poorly planned capital construction projects, such as irrigation works. Because of the intense pressure for results, the rapidity of the change, and the inexperience and resistance of many cadres and peasants, the Great Leap Forward soon ran into difficulties. The peasants became exhausted from the unremitting pressure to produce. The inflation of production statistics, on the theory that accuracy mattered less than political effect, resulted in extravagant claims. Disruption of agricultural activity and transportation produced food shortages. In addition, the weather in 1959-61 was unfavorable, and agricultural production declined sharply (see fig. 9). By the early 1960s, therefore, agriculture was severely depressed, and China was forced to import grain (during the 1950s it had been a net exporter) to supply urban areas. Otherwise, an excessive amount of grain would have been extracted from rural areas (see Economic Policies, 1949-80, ch. 5).

Importance of Agriculture Recognized

Faced with this depression, the country's leaders initiated policies to strengthen the agricultural sector. The government increased incentives for individual and collective production, decentralized certain management functions, and expanded the role of private plots and markets. The people's commune system was reorganized so that production teams with 20 to 30 households and 90 to 140 people owned most of the assets, accounted for profits or losses, made economic decisions, and distributed income. Most important, the leadership embarked on policies designed to put "agriculture first" in planning, at least in principle. This meant more modern inputs for the countryside. Chemical fertilizer production and imports increased. Modern high-yielding seed varieties began to be developed. Irrigation facilities—many of which had been washed out during disastrous floods in 1959–61—were repaired and expanded, and the government began to provide more mechanical pumps and other irrigation equipment.

These improvements were not haphazard; most were focused on more advanced and productive areas. The intent was to build areas of modernized agriculture with high and stable yields that would form the basis for more stable agricultural production. In general, the places designated as "high- and stable-yield areas" were those with adequate irrigation and drainage, so that the payoff for greater use of fertilizer and new seeds would be higher.

Recovery

By the mid-1970s China's economy had recovered from the failures of the Great Leap Forward. In 1979 per capita grain output first surpassed previous peak levels achieved in 1957. In addition, small enterprises in the mid-1960s began to produce substantial quantities of chemical fertilizer. Government researchers developed fertilizer-responsive seeds. Focusing these inputs on the high- and stable-yield areas meant that parts of China that were already advanced tended to be favored over backward or less-developed regions, thus widening a gap that already had potentially serious implications (see Differentiation, ch. 3).

At the same time, the government urged poorer areas to rely mainly on their own efforts. This was symbolized, especially during the Cultural Revolution, by the campaign to "learn from Dazhai." Dazhai was a village in Shaanxi Province that overcame poverty and poor production conditions to become relatively wealthy. The authorities claimed that this was accomplished through self-reliance and struggle. Dazhai became a model of political organization and its leaders national emulation models as well.

These policies—"agriculture first," emphasis on the supply of modern inputs, and the Dazhai and other models—formed the framework for agricultural development from the early 1960s until the post-Mao era. The Cultural Revolution caused some disruption in the agricultural sector, such as political struggle sessions and changes in local leadership, but not nearly as much as in the industrial sector (see Trends in Industrial Production, ch. 7).

Post-Mao Policies

When the party leadership began to evaluate progress in the agricultural sector in the light of its campaign to move the nation toward the ambitious targets of the Four Modernizations (see Glossary), it noted disappointing failures along with some impressive gains. Furthermore, even though per capita grain production increased from the depressed levels of the early 1960s, output stagnated in the 1975–77 period, so that in 1978 per capita production was still not above average levels of the 1950s. Production of other major crops grew even more slowly. The leadership decided in 1978 to thoroughly revamp the rural economic system.

Top government and party leaders decided to dismantle the people's commune system and restructure it into a new rural system—the township-collective-household system—consisting of five parts: local government, party, state and collective economic entities, and households. Whereas the commune system integrated politics, administration, and economics into one unit, the new system was designed to have separate institutions handle specific functions. Townships, the basic unit of government in pre-commune days, were reconstructed to handle government and administrative functions. Party committees were to concentrate on party affairs. Economic collectives were organized to manage economic affairs. Households were encouraged to sign contracts with economic collectives.

The reform of the commune system fundamentally changed the way farmers were motivated to work. Nonmaterial incentive policies, such as intergroup competitions for red flags, were downplayed. Egalitarian distribution of grain rations declined, and the work payment system in effect on and off since the 1950s was scrapped (see Economic Policies, 1949–80, ch. 5). Rural cadres adopted an entirely new scheme to motivate farmers, called *baogan* (household production responsibility) system. Under *baogan*, economic cooperatives assigned specific plots of land to a family to cultivate for up to fifteen years. For each piece of land, the economic cooperative specified the quantity of output that had to be delivered to procurement stations. The contract also outlined household obligations, such as contributions to capital accumulation and welfare funds; the number of days to be contributed to maintenance

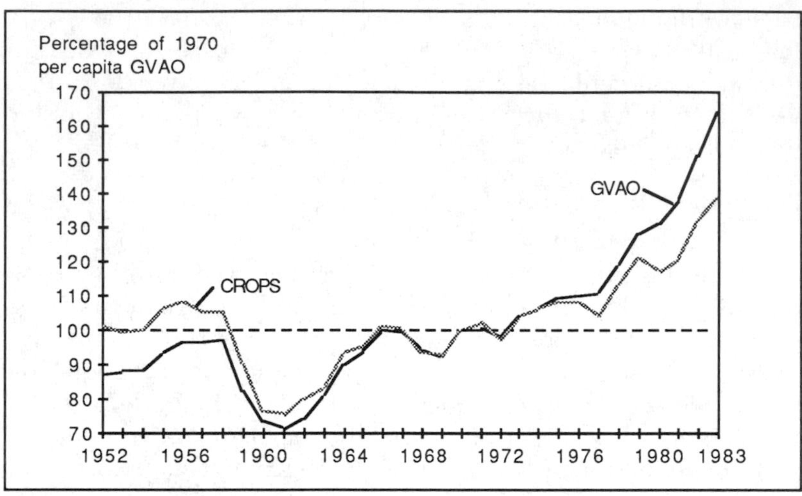

Source: Based on information in U.S. Department of Agriculture, Economic Research Service, *China: Review of Agriculture in 1981 and Outlook for 1982*, Washington, August 1982; 1983 estimated.

Figure 9. Per Capita Gross Value of Agricultural Output (GVAO) and Crop Production, 1952–83.

of water control systems; and debt repayment schedules. Output raised in excess of state and collective obligations was the reward to the household. Families could consume the surplus or sell it in rural markets as they wished. *Baogan* permitted families to raise income through hard work, good management, wise use of technology, and reduction of production costs.

While the overall level of investment within the agricultural sector did not change much during the reform period, substantial changes took place in investment patterns. National leaders called for greater investment in agriculture, but actual state expenditures declined in the first part of the 1980s. Whereas communes had invested considerable sums in agriculture, the rate of investment from the newly formed economic cooperatives was far below the rate before the reform. The revitalization and extension of the rural banking system (the Agricultural Bank and rural credit cooperatives) and favorable lending policies did provide a small but steady source of investment funds for the sector. The major change, however, was that after 1978 farm families were allowed to invest funds, and their investment in small tractors, rural industry, and housing was substantial. In 1983 rural households invested ¥21 billion (for the value of the yuan—see Glossary) in housing compared with ¥11 billion from state sources.

Mao Zedong's policy of self-reliance was relaxed, and his dictum "grow grain everywhere" was abandoned. Farm households began to produce crops and animals best suited for their natural conditions. Excellent cotton growing land in Shandong Province that had grown grain during the Cultural Revolution returned to growing cotton. Areas sown with grain crops declined, and areas sown with cotton, oilseeds, and other cash crops expanded. Reform policies also reduced major administrative barriers that had limited labor and capital from moving beyond commune boundaries. Households with insufficient labor or little inclination to farm were able to transfer land contracts to families that were interested in cultivation and animal husbandry. Rural workers were permitted to shift from crop cultivation to commercial, service, construction, and industrial activities in rural townships. Capital in rural areas was permitted to move across administrative boundaries, and individuals invested not only in their own farm production but also in business ventures outside their own villages.

The rural marketing system changed substantially in the post-Mao period. The system of mandatory sales of farm produce to local state purchasing stations ended, as did state rationing of food grains, cooking oil, and cotton cloth to consumers. Households with marketable surpluses had several options: goods could be consumed on the farm, sold in local markets, or sold to state stations according to signed purchase contracts. Rural markets disbanded during the Cultural Revolution were reopened, and the number of markets rose from 33,000 in 1978 to 61,000 in 1985. Total trade in these markets increased from ¥12.5 billion in 1978 to ¥63.2 billion in 1985. Consumers purchased food and daily necessities in stores run by the state, cooperatives, and private entrepreneurs and in local free markets. Coincident with these reforms, the state raised procurement prices to improve incentives and increase production by farmers. From 1966 to 1982, wheat and rice procurement prices rose by 66 percent, while oilseed prices increased 85 percent. To avoid urban discontent over high prices, the state absorbed the increasing additional costs, and retail prices for these goods remained constant.

The new policies quickly began to produce results. The gross value of agricultural output nearly doubled from 1978 to 1985. Production of grain, oilseeds, cotton, and livestock increased rapidly in this period (see Production, this ch.). Per capita net income of peasant households rose dramatically from ¥134 in 1978 to ¥397 in 1985, but income inequality increased. The demise of collective institutions, however, brought decreases in health, education, and welfare services. Less attention was paid to maintaining the environment, and some water, soil, and forest resources were wasted. Despite this, mid-1980s observers opined that prospects were good for an overall rise in rural prosperity.

Reforms in the late 1970s and early 1980s also swept away policies and administrative rules restricting business activity. Old commune production and brigade enterprises were reorganized, and a host of new firms were founded by economic cooperatives and citizens. Business activity included manufacturing, mining, transportation, catering, construction, and services. By the mid-1980s the value generated by these enterprises surpassed the value of output from raising crops and livestock.

Planning and Organization

The state's role in the mid-1980s was chiefly to plan production and manage resources. Among state institutions at the national level, the Ministry of Agriculture, Animal Husbandry, and Fishery was primarily responsible for coordinating agricultural programs. Other central bodies of importance in agricultural policy matters included the State Economic Commission; the State Planning Commission; the ministries of commerce, forestry, and the chemical industry; the State Statistical Bureau; and the Agricultural Bank; and various academies and institutions that conducted research on agricultural science, agricultural economics, and related subjects.

Between state institutions at the national level and the townships and villages at the base of the administrative hierarchy were various provincial-level, prefectural, and county-level government organs that also administered programs, including some agricultural research and extension activities. Some 2,000 county-level units coordinated programs and enforced policies with the economic cooperatives and households in their jurisdictions. County-level units sometimes operated their own chemical fertilizer plants or other factories producing basic agricultural items, and they helped direct the allocation of the materials produced to peasant farmers.

Some agricultural production occurred on state farms where workers received regular wages, like factory workers. State farms were mostly found on the fringes of the main agricultural areas, especially on newly reclaimed land and particularly in the northeast, where they nevertheless accounted for only about 4 percent of total cultivated land.

Most of the economic activity in rural areas took place within the context of collectively and privately owned enterprises.

Economic cooperatives, enterprises, and households were guided by their own self-sufficiency requirements, pursuit of profits, and compliance with annual economic plans. Forces of self-sufficiency continued to play an important role in decision making, especially as farm households allocated resources to ensure their own food grain rations. The pursuit of profit traditionally had been a driving force in rural areas, and although this energy had largely been curbed in the past, in the 1980s farmers were encouraged to seek profits.

The state drafted annual economic plans that were passed down through administrative channels to assist local cadres. Operators of farms and other enterprises reviewed the plan targets, which guided them to make proper economic decisions. The state has used both direct and indirect methods to affect decisions. In past decades cadres decided what would be produced, what production techniques were to be employed, and how output was to be distributed on the basis of annual plans. Indirect controls, such as prices and interest rates, became more important after 1980. Different combinations of the forces of self-sufficiency, profits, and state plans affected decision making for a given product in a given year. For example, in 1985 cotton farmers were told via state plans how much area to plant in cotton, whereas farmers received no state plans to sow fields with melons; rather, they planted melons in the hope of increasing profits.

The state continued to control the economic behavior of farm households, economic cooperatives, and enterprises through powerful political and administrative mechanisms in the late 1980s. The first of these mechanisms was the more than 83,000 township governments, which were responsible for civil and military affairs, public security (police), family planning, and statistics. Village committees numbered more than 940,000 and were subordinate to townships. Although they were not formal government institutions, they maintained public order, managed welfare services, and oversaw water conservancy projects. Probably the most powerful entities on the local level were Chinese Communist Party committees in townships and the subordinate party branches in villages. More than 20 million rural party members staffed posts and headed committees that supervised all aspects of rural life. They coordinated relations between party, government, and economic entities, and they ensured that party policies were followed. They nominated candidates to administrative posts and approved applications for military service, jobs, and opportunities for higher education (see Rural Society, ch. 3; The Cadre System, ch. 10).

The second mechanism—control of marketing functions—gave the state powerful tools to influence agricultural decisions. As in other centrally planned economies, the state was responsible for organizing and directing a major part of the flow of resources between sectors. It could achieve this using a variety of means, including prices and markets as well as direct controls. It needed to balance the needs of various sectors for input such as fuel, cement, timber, and machinery (as well as the needs of consumers in both rural and urban areas) in trying to meet its goals (see Structure and Operation of the Economy; Living Standards, ch. 5).

The government procured grain and other agricultural products from the peasants to supply urban areas and food-deficient regions with subsistence and to provide raw materials for textile and other light industries. Part of the required amount was obtained simply as a direct tax. The proportion obtained from taxes declined over time, however, and the tax in 1984 was less than 3 percent of the value of total production. The remainder was obtained through purchases by state procurement agencies.

In the period from 1957 to 1978, the state raised prices for agricultural produce while lowering the prices of basic items such as fertilizer and fuel used in agricultural production. This was necessary to promote the use of more fertilizer and fuel to obtain greater production and to provide incentives for the production and sale of agricultural commodities.

As a third mechanism, the state exercised considerable leverage in rural affairs through its control over credit and agricultural production supplies. The state owned and controlled some 27,000 agricultural banks that served rural areas and provided production loans. Agricultural banks also supervised the activities of more than 42,000 credit cooperatives that provided banking services for cooperatives and rural households and provided production and consumer loans to customers. The state controlled banking activities through administrative regulations, loan policy, and interest rates. The state regulated delivery of fertilizer, machinery, and fuel through its marketing channels. In addition, government control of water and electricity supplies provided the state with an important lever to induce farmers to comply with political policies and economic plans (see table 12, Appendix A).

Finally, local governments possessed considerable influence in local affairs because they delivered social welfare services. Economic cooperatives and peasant households were not likely to engage in activities that could lead to diminishing supplies of social services. Rural families desired and increasingly felt entitled to medical, education, welfare, and cultural benefits. Villages competed to have these facilities located within their boundaries, not only to have more convenient access to their services but also to take advantage of the employment opportunities they afforded.

Operational Methods and Inputs

China's farmers have long used techniques such as fertilization and irrigation to increase the productivity of their scarce land. Over time, many farming techniques have been modernized: chemical fertilizers have supplemented organic fertilizers, and mechanical pumps have come into use in irrigation. Government planners in the 1980s emphasized increased use of fertilizer, improved irrigation, mechanization of agriculture, and extension of improved seed varieties as leading features of the agricultural modernization program.

Cropping Patterns

All of these elements of modern agriculture are used in the context of the traditional intensive cropping patterns. To maximize year-round use of the land, two or more crops are planted each year where possible. Rice, wheat, cotton, vegetable, and other crop seedlings are sometimes raised in special seedbeds and then transplanted to fields. Transplanting shortens the time required for a crop to mature, which allows farmers the opportunity to squeeze in an additional crop each growing season. Another method to make optimum use of scarce land is to plant seedlings in a mature stand of another crop. For example, when planting winter wheat in October, farmers in the north leave spaces among the rows so that cotton seedlings can be planted or transplanted in April and May. Without intercropping, farmers could raise only one crop a year. Mechanization supports this intensive cropping pattern. Despite a huge rural labor force, labor shortages occur each season when farmers are required to harvest one crop and plant another in its place, all within the space of a few weeks. In the 1980s farmers invested in harvesting and planting machinery to overcome the shortage of labor. Seed breeders also supported intensive cropping patterns by selecting and breeding varieties that had shorter growing seasons.

Fertilizer

Intensive use of the arable soil made the use of fertilizer imperative to replace nutrients and to help improve yields. Organic fertilizers have long supplied the bulk of soil nutrients and have helped to maintain the structure of the soil. Over the centuries, use of organic fertilizers also increased with the growth in population and with the increased size of livestock herds. Peasants have traditionally used a large proportion of their labor in collecting organic materials for fertilizers. Use has been especially heavy in south China, where more intensive cropping has required more fertilizer and where the sources of fertilizer have been more abundant. Chemical fertilizers, however, have been used more widely since the 1960s. Use of chemical fertilizers in 1985 was more than 150 kilograms per hectare, measured in nutrient weight. The country's considerable future requirements will have to be met by chemical fertilizer because of the natural limits on rapid increases in production of organic fertilizers.

Production and imports of chemical fertilizers increased rapidly under the "agriculture first" programs of the early 1960s. The domestic industry was expanded, partly with the help of imported fertilizer factories, and production reached 1.7 million tons by 1965. Imports in 1965 were more than 600,000 tons. In the mid-1960s the government also began to emphasize the production of nitrogen fertilizer in small plants, usually operated by counties, that yielded about 10,000 tons per year. Their products were used locally, which helped conserve transportation resources. In 1972 the government contracted to import thirteen large-scale urea plants, each capable of producing more than 1 million tons of standard nitrogen fertilizer a year. By 1980 these were in operation, and total chemical fertilizer production in 1985 was 13.4 million tons, of which 12.3 million tons were nitrogen fertilizer. Imports added another 7.6 million tons.

In the 1980s chemical fertilizer use per hectare was less than the Japanese and Korean averages but more than the Indonesian and Indian averages. Future production and imports were likely to emphasize phosphate and potassium content in order to balance the nutrients obtained from organic fertilizers and from existing factories. Institutional reforms in the early 1980s encouraged households to cut costs and maximize earnings, which probably led to more efficient use of chemical fertilizer as farmers applied fertilizer to those crops giving the highest rates of return.

Mechanization

Post-Mao reforms dramatically affected farm mechanization. Most commune tractor stations were disbanded, and farm households were allowed to purchase equipment. The percentage of privately owned tractors increased from near zero in 1975 to more than 80 percent in 1985. The area plowed and planted by machine decreased in this period, but peasant use of tractors and trucks to transport goods soared dramatically. As much as 60 percent of tractor use was devoted to local hauling. Firms manufacturing farm

"Ploughing Corn." Woodcut.
Courtesy Woodcuts of Wartime China

machinery adjusted to the shift in rural organization by producing more small tractors, appropriate tractor-drawn equipment, better quality hand tools, and food and feed processing equipment. A rural electric power system—dams, generators, and transmission lines—had been under construction since 1949, and in 1987 most villages had access to electricity. In the period of the Four Modernizations, rural electric power consumption rose by 179 percent, from 18.3 billion kilowatt-hours in 1975 to 51.2 billion kilowatt-hours in 1985.

Despite the large stock and high production rate of tractors, most farm tasks in the mid-1980s were performed manually. Rice continued to be transplanted by hand, as local engineers had yet to develop and produce rice transplanters in substantial quantities. Only 36 percent of the land was plowed by machines, only 8 percent sown by machines, and only 3 percent of the crop area was harvested by machines. Draft animals continued to be important sources of power, and the number of animals increased sharply in the post-Mao period. Success in mechanization enabled surplus rural laborers to leave the fields to find jobs in rural industry and commerce. In the 1980s most observers believed that China would continue for some time to use mechanization to solve labor shortages at times of peak labor demand and to concentrate mechanization in areas of large-scale farming, as in the North China Plain and the northeast.

Water Conservancy

Irrigation was important in China's traditional agriculture, and some facilities existed as long as 2,000 years ago. The extension of water conservancy facilities by labor-intensive means was an important part of the agricultural development programs of the 1950s. During the Great Leap Forward, a number of water conservancy projects were undertaken, but with insufficient planning and capital. During the turmoil and bad weather of 1959–61, many water conservancy works were washed out by floods or otherwise destroyed, considerably reducing the irrigated acreage. Facilities were rebuilt in the early 1960s. By the 1980s irrigation facilities covered nearly half the cultivated land; systems installed since the late 1960s extended over a considerable part of north China, especially on the North China Plain.

In the era of post-Mao reform, irrigation and drainage systems expanded to increase the stock of stable and high-yielding land. The inventory of mechanical pumps also greatly increased; powered irrigation equipment reached almost 80 million horsepower in 1985. In this period the government began to charge fees for the water the farmers used, and farmers therefore limited the amount of water applied to their crops on a benefit cost basis. The reorganization of rural institutions weakened administrative measures necessary to make large-scale waterworks function. Lowered investment, poor maintenance, and outright damage to facilities lessened the effectiveness of the system. Adding additional acreage was likely to be increasingly costly because areas not under irrigation were remote from easily tapped water sources. In the mid-1980s government officials recognized the problems and undertook to correct them.

North China is chronically short of water and subject to frequent droughts (see Climate, ch. 2). A considerable proportion of its irrigation water comes from wells. Officials in the Ministry of Water Resources and Electric Power (and its predecessors) have periodically proposed diverting water from the Chang Jiang to irrigate the North China Plain. The enormous expense of constructing such a project has precluded its realization. Farmers have also been encouraged to use sprinkler systems, a more efficient use of scarce water resources than flood-type irrigation systems.

Pest Control

In 1987 the main method of weed and insect control continued to be labor-intensive cultivation. Fields were carefully tended, and a variety of biological controls, such as breeding natural enemies of crop pests, were used. Production and use of chemical herbicides and pesticides increased rapidly from the mid-1950s to the mid-1970s, but output fell subsequently by more than half (to about 200,000 tons) because the products were relatively ineffective, expensive, and highly toxic. Chemical pesticide use, therefore, was low compared with use in other countries.

Seed Varieties

Improved seed varieties have contributed significantly to improving crop yields. Highly fertilizer-responsive varieties came into use beginning in the mid-1960s. These were comparable to those developed outside China but were adapted to the shorter growing season imposed by multiple cropping. Their extensive use has complemented the large increases in fertilizer use and the increase in irrigated area. In the mid-1970s farmers began to plant hybrid rice, claiming yield increases of more than 20 percent. Hybrid rice is not used elsewhere because of the amount of labor it requires, but more than 6 million hectares of it were planted in the mid-1980s, accounting for 20 percent of total rice area. The China National Seed Company was established in 1978 to popularize improved seed varieties; it exported Chinese vegetable seeds and imported improved grain, cotton, forage, and oil seeds. About 5 percent of China's arable land was being used to raise seed in the mid-1980s, and the company operated more than 2,000 seed companies at provincial, prefectural, and county levels.

Agricultural Science

Agricultural science suffered from changes in policy and emphasis after the 1950s. The Cultural Revolution disrupted agricultural science training and research programs, but since the mid-1970s training and research programs have been restored. Government officials emphasized practical, production-oriented scientific work. The rural extension system popularized new techniques and new inputs, such as sprinkler irrigation systems. In 1987 eighty-four agricultural colleges and research institutes pursued research in seven broad fields: agriculture, forestry, aquatic production, land reclamation, mechanization, water conservation, and meteorology. In addition, almost 500 agricultural schools had a total staff of 29,000 teachers and 71,000 students. In the 1980s thousands of researchers and students were sent abroad (see Educational Investment, ch. 4). Research was being strengthened by the construction of sixteen regionally distributed agricultural experiment stations. New agricultural journals and societies were established to promote the dissemination of research results within the country. The Chinese sought technical information abroad as well through the import of technology and machinery and the international exchange of delegations.

Production

Five economic activities generated the bulk of agricultural output: crops, livestock, forestry, fishery, and sideline production (rural industry). Crop raising was the dominant activity, generating as much as 80 percent of the total value of output in the mid-1950s. The policy of stressing crop output was relaxed in the early 1980s, and by 1985 this figure fell to about 50 percent. The proportion of output generated by the livestock, forestry, and fishery sectors increased slowly after the 1950s. The sector that expanded the most rapidly was sideline production, whose share increased from 4 percent in 1955 to 30 percent in 1985.

The results of China's agricultural policies in terms of output have been mixed. Food consumption was maintained at subsistence level despite the catastrophic drop in production following the Great Leap Forward but failed to increase much above that level until the 1980s. Investment in irrigation and water control projects blunted the effects of severe weather on output, but in many parts of the country production continued to be negatively affected by the weather. Production rates varied considerably throughout the country, creating income inequalities. Despite rapid gains in rural areas in the 1980s, a substantial gap remained between rural and urban living standards (see Differentiation, ch. 3).

Crops

In the mid-1980s China's farmers annually planted crops on about 145 million hectares of land. Eighty percent of the land was sown with grain, 5 percent with oilseed crops, 5 percent with fruits, 3 percent with vegetables, 2 percent with fiber crops, and 0.5 percent with sugar crops and tobacco. Other crops made up the remaining 4 percent. In the 1960s and 1970s, when policies emphasized grain output, the area sown with grain exceeded 85 percent. After the reforms were launched in the early 1980s, the area sown with grain fell below 80 percent and the area sown with other crops expanded correspondingly.

Grain is China's most important agricultural product. It is the source of most of the calories and protein in the average diet and accounts for a sizable proportion of the value of agricultural production. China's statisticians define grain to include wheat, rice, corn, sorghum, millet, potatoes (at one-fifth their fresh weight), soybeans, barley, oats, buckwheat, field peas, and beans. Grain output paralleled the increase in population from 1949 through 1975 but

A bumper harvest at a granary in rural Jiangsu Province
Courtesy Xinhua News Agency
Harvesting rice, on the road from Wuxi to Suzhou
Courtesy Stephanie Marcus

rose rapidly in the decade between 1975 and 1985 (see table 13, Appendix A).

In 1987 China was the world's largest producer of rice, and the crop made up a little less than half of the country's total grain output. In a given year total rice output came from four different crops. The early rice crop grows primarily in provinces along the Chang Jiang and in provinces in the south; it is planted in February to April and harvested in June and July and contributes about 34 percent to total rice output. Intermediate and single-crop late rice grows in the southwest and along the Chang Jiang; it is planted in March to June and harvested in October and November and also contributed about 34 percent to total rice output in the 1980s. Double-crop late rice, planted after the early crop is reaped, is harvested in October to November and adds about 25 percent to total rice production. Rice grown in the north is planted from April to June and harvested from September to October; it contributes about 7 percent to total production.

All rice cultivation is highly labor intensive. Rice is generally grown as a wetland crop in fields flooded to supply water during the growing season. Transplanting seedlings requires many hours of labor, as does harvesting. Mechanization of rice cultivation is only minimally advanced. Rice cultivation also demands more of other inputs, such as fertilizer, than most other crops.

Rice is highly prized by consumers as a food grain, especially in south China, and per capita consumption has risen through the years. Also, as incomes have risen, consumers have preferred to eat more rice and less potatoes, corn, sorghum, and millet. Large production increases in the early 1980s and poor local transportation systems combined to induce farmers to feed large quantities of lower quality rice to livestock.

In 1987 China ranked third in the world as a producer of wheat. Winter wheat, which in the same year accounted for about 88 percent of total national output, is grown primarily in the Chang Jiang Valley and on the North China Plain. The crop is sown each fall from September through November and is harvested in May and June the subsequent year. Spring wheat is planted each spring in the north and northeast and is harvested in late summer. Spring wheat contributes about 12 percent of total wheat output.

Wheat is the staple food grain in north China and is eaten in the form of steamed bread and noodles. Per capita consumption has risen, and the demand for wheat flour has increased as incomes have risen. Wheat has been by far the most important imported grain.

Corn is grown in most parts of the country but is most common in areas that also produce wheat. Corn production has increased substantially over time and in some years has been second only to production of rice. Consumers have traditionally considered corn less desirable for human use than rice or wheat. Nevertheless, it frequently yields more per unit of land than other varieties of grain, making it useful for maintaining subsistence. As incomes rose in the early 1980s, consumer demand for corn as a food grain decreased, and increasing quantities of corn were allocated for animal feed.

Millet and sorghum are raised in the northern provinces, primarily in areas affected by drought. Millet is used primarily as a food grain. Sorghum is not a preferred food grain and in the 1980s was used for livestock feed and *maotai*, a potent alcoholic beverage.

Both Irish and sweet potatoes are grown in China. In the 1980s about 20 percent of output came from Irish potatoes grown mostly in the northern part of the country. The remaining 80 percent of output came primarily from sweet potatoes grown in central and south China (cassava output was also included in total potato production). Potatoes are generally considered to be a somewhat lower-quality food grain. Per capita consumption has declined through time. Potatoes are also used in the production of vodka and as a livestock feed.

Other grains, such as field peas, beans, and pulses, are grown throughout China. These grains are good sources of plant protein and add variety to the diet. Barley is a major grain produced in the lower Chang Jiang Basin. It is used for direct human consumption, livestock feed, and increasingly is in great demand as a feedstock to produce beer.

Soybeans, a leguminous crop, are also included in China's grain statistics. The northeast has traditionally been the most important producing area, but substantial amounts of soybeans are also produced on the North China Plain. Production of soybeans declined after the Great Leap Forward, and output did not regain the 10-million-ton level of the late 1950s until 1985. Population growth has greatly outstripped soybean output, and per capita consumption has fallen. Soybeans are a useful source of protein and fat, an important consideration given the limited amount of meat available and the grain- and vegetable-based diet. Oilseed cakes, by-products of soybean oil extraction, are used as animal feed and fertilizer.

Cotton is China's most important fiber crop. The crop is grown on the North China Plain and in the middle and lower reaches of the Chang Jiang Valley. In the 1970s domestic output did not meet demand, and significant quantities of raw cotton were imported. Production expanded dramatically in the early 1980s to reach a record 6 million tons in 1984. Although production declined to 4.2 million tons in 1985, China was still by far the largest cotton producer in the world. In the 1980s raw cotton imports ceased, and China became a major exporter of cotton.

Significant quantities of jute and hemp are also produced in China. Production of these crops expanded from 257,000 tons in 1955 to 3.4 million tons in 1985. Major producing provinces include Heilongjiang and Henan and also provinces along the Chang Jiang.

China is an important producer of oilseeds, including peanuts, rapeseed, sesame seed, sunflower seed, and safflower seed. Oilseed output in 1955 was 4.8 million tons. Output, however, did not expand between 1955 and 1975, which meant per capita oilseed availability decreased substantially because of population growth. Production from 1975 to 1985 more than tripled, to 15.5 million tons, but China continues to have one of the world's lowest levels of per capita consumption of oilseeds.

Sugarcane accounted for about 83 percent of total output of sugar crops in 1985. Major producing provinces include Guangdong, Fujian, and Yunnan provinces and Guangxi-Zhuang Autonomous Region. Production has grown steadily through the years from about 8 million tons in 1955 to over 51 million tons in 1985.

Sugar beet production accounted for the remaining 17 percent of total output in 1985. Major producing provinces and autonomous regions include Heilongjiang, Jilin, Nei Monggol, and Xinjiang. Sugar beet production rose from 1.6 million tons in 1955 to 8.9 million tons in 1985. Despite these impressive increases in output, per capita consumption was still very low, and large quantities were imported.

China is the world's largest producer of leaf tobacco. Farmers produce many kinds of tobacco, but flue-cured varieties often make up more than 80 percent of total output. Major producing areas include Henan, Shandong, Sichuan, Guizhou, and Yunnan provinces.

Tea and silk, produced mainly in the south, have traditionally been important commercial crops. The domestic market for these products has been substantial, and they continue to be important exports. Given China's different agricultural climatic regions, many varieties of vegetables are grown. Farmers raise vegetables in private plots for their own consumption. Near towns and cities, farmers grow vegetables for sale to meet the demand of urban consumers. Vegetables are an important source of vitamins and minerals in the diet.

Temperate, subtropical, and tropical fruits are cultivated in China. Output expanded from 2.6 million tons in 1955 to more than 11 million tons in 1985. Reforms in the early 1980s encouraged farmers to plant orchards, and the output of apples, pears, bananas, and citrus fruit was expected to expand in the late 1980s.

Animal Husbandry

In 1987 China had the largest inventory of hogs in the world. The number increased from about 88 million in 1955 to an estimated 331 million in 1985. Hogs are raised in large numbers in every part of China except in Muslim areas in the northwest. Most hogs are raised in pens by individual farm households, but in the mid-1980s the Chinese were constructing large mechanized feeding operations on the outskirts of major cities. Before the 1980s the state's major goal was to increase output with little regard to the ratio of meat to fat. In the 1980s consumers became more conscious of fat content, and breeders and raisers were shifting to the production of leaner hogs.

Draft animals are important sources of motive power in rural areas. Draft animal numbers increased steadily from about 56 million in 1955 to 67 million in 1985 despite rapid increases in the number of tractors and trucks in rural areas. Animals that provide draft power for crop cultivation and rural transportation include water buffalo, horses, mules, donkeys, oxen, and camels.

Sheep and goats are China's most important grazing animals. Most of these animals are bred in the semiarid steppes and deserts in the north, west, and northwest. The number of sheep and goats has expanded steadily from about 42 million in 1949 to approximately 156 million in 1985. Overgrazed, fragile rangelands have been seriously threatened by erosion, and in the late 1980s authorities were in the midst of a campaign to improve pastures and rangelands and limit erosion.

The dairy and poultry sectors of the livestock economy grew most rapidly in the 1980s. Dairy cows numbered just under 500,000 in 1978 but tripled to around 1.5 million in 1985. Consumers with rising incomes demanded more fresh and powdered milk for infants and elderly people. A large part of this increased demand was met by individual farmers who were permitted to purchase and own their animals. The government supported increased milk output by importing breeding animals and constructing large dairies and processing facilities. Most poultry was still grown in farmyard flocks, but reforms encouraged individuals and groups of households to invest in confined feeding operations. Egg output, especially, increased rapidly in the 1980s.

China's first modern feed mills were constructed in the 1970s, followed by many mills equipped with imported technology.

Production of mixed and compound feed grew rapidly, reaching more than 12 million tons in 1985. This development supported the growth of animal husbandry.

Forestry

Forests were cleared in China's main agricultural areas centuries ago. Most timber, therefore, comes from northeast China and the less densely populated parts of the northwest and southwest. The yield totaled around 60 million cubic meters in 1985. Bamboo poles and products are grown in the Chang Jiang Valley and in south China, and output reached 230 million poles in 1985. Rubber trees are cultivated in Guangdong Province; output rose steadily from 68,000 tons in 1975 to 190,000 tons in 1985. Other important forestry products include lacquer, tea oilseed, tung oil, pine resin, walnuts, chestnuts, plywood, and fiberboard.

The area covered by forests amounted to some 12 percent of total land area, which officials hoped to increase over the long term to 30 percent. Afforestation campaigns are carried out annually to re-establish forests, plant shelter belts, and set up soil stabilization areas. But because of continued overcutting of forests and low seedling survival rates in newly planted sections, China's forests are in a precarious situation. Better management and increased investment over a long period of time will be required to increase output of valuable forest products.

Fishery

Aquatic production increased slowly after the 1950s, reaching 6.2 million tons in 1985. Output is composed of both marine and freshwater fish, shellfish, and kelp. Marine products contributed 63 percent to total aquatic production. Fishermen collected more than 83 percent of marine output from the open seas. The remaining 17 percent of output came from sea farms along China's coasts.

The freshwater catch accounted for 37 percent of total aquatic output in the mid-1980s. Fish farming in ponds accounted for 80 percent of the total freshwater catch; only 20 percent was collected in natural rivers, lakes, and streams. Fish from all sources provides consumers with an important source of protein and added variety in their diet.

Sideline Production

In addition to improving the principal yield of agricultural units, the post-Mao economic reforms greatly stimulated sideline production in rural areas. Before 1984 sideline production generated by production brigades, production teams, and households included

Silkworms being fed mulberry leaves
Courtesy Nanjing Slide Studio
Clearing lotus pond, Hangzhou
Courtesy Douglass M. Dolan

hunting, fishing, collecting wild herbs, and producing family handicrafts, as well as various kinds of industry, commerce, transportation, and services. Sideline industrial output included fertilizer, farm machinery, textiles, bricks, electrical appliances, and various consumer goods. Sideline industrial activities also included processing cotton, grain, and oilseeds; mining coal, iron ore, and gold; and dredging gravel and sand. Among the services included in sideline output were barbering, entertainment, and catering. As part of the sideline economy, rural entities transported people and goods and operated retail stores; rural construction groups built dams, factory sites, roads, and houses. Of all kinds of sideline production, the state counted only the industrial output of enterprises operated by counties and communes in its total industrial output.

Output rose so rapidly that by 1985 the value of production generated in sidelines exceeded the value of principal crop and livestock production. To make the gross value of agricultural output more realistically represent agricultural production, statisticians in 1985 limited sideline production to hunting and fishing, collecting wild herbs, and producing family handicrafts. After 1985, therefore, there were at least three aggregate measures of economic performance: gross value of output; gross value of agricultural output (crops, livestock, forestry, aquatic, and sideline); and gross value of rural society, which included the gross value of agricultural output plus the value of rural industrial, transportation, construction, and other output (see Rural Industry, ch. 7).

Agricultural Trade

Since 1949 agricultural exports for most years have exceeded agricultural imports. China's officials have used this export surplus as an important source for financing the importation of high-priority industrial items. Agricultural exports have risen through the years but have not grown as fast as industrial exports. In 1970, for example, agricultural exports accounted for 45 percent of total exports, but in 1985 China's US$6.5 billion in agricultural exports was only 20 percent of the total exports.

In the 1970s agricultural imports accounted for about 30 percent of total imports. For example, of the US$7.1 billion worth of products imported in 1977, US$2.1 billion (30 percent) were agricultural products. In 1985 US$4.7 billion worth of agricultural products were imported, which was only 5 percent of the US$42.8 billion of total imports (see fig. 10; table 14, Appendix A). The ratio of agricultural imports to other imports was expected to rise in the late 1980s and 1990s.

Wheat has been imported nearly every year since the early 1950s. These imports averaged about 5 million tons in the 1960s and 1970s but rose to a peak of more than 13 million tons in 1982. Wheat imports fell as wheat output expanded rapidly, so that by 1985 imports fell to just under 5.5 million tons. Argentina, Australia, Canada, France, and the United States have been major sources of China's wheat imports.

China is one of the world's largest rice exporters, annually shipping out about 1 million tons. Rice exports go primarily to Asian and East European countries and to Cuba.

China is both an importer and an exporter of coarse grains. Up to 1984 sorghum, millet, and corn exports usually totaled only several hundred thousand tons but reached a peak of over 5 million tons in 1985 (see Crops, this ch.). In the mid-1980s corn was shipped primarily to Japan, North Korea, and the Soviet Union. Barley is imported as a livestock feed and as a feedstock to brew beer. Corn is imported for human consumption and for livestock feed. Quantities imported varied considerably depending on internal supply conditions and prices in international markets. Large quantities of corn were imported during the Great Leap Forward (when grain production fell dramatically), in the early 1970s, and at the end of the 1970s, when corn imports hit a peak of 3.6 million tons. Major coarse grain suppliers include Argentina, Australia, Canada, France, Thailand, and the United States.

Soybeans have been a major foreign exchange earner for most of this century. Static production and rising domestic demand for soybeans and soybean products meant a decline in exports until the early 1980s. For example, in 1981 Argentina and the United States shipped more than 500,000 tons of soybeans to China; these two countries and Brazil also exported soybean oil to China. Domestic production expanded in the early 1980s, however, and by 1985 soybean imports fell and exports exceeded 1 million tons. Also in the early 1980s, China began to ship soybean meal to Asian markets.

Before 1983 China was one of the world's largest importers of raw cotton. These imports averaged around 100,000 tons annually but climbed to a peak of nearly 900,000 tons in 1980. A dramatic increase in domestic cotton production filled domestic demand, and exports exceeded imports in 1983. In 1985 China shipped nearly 500,000 tons of raw cotton to Asian and European markets.

Sugar imports to China come primarily from Australia, Cuba, the Philippines, and Thailand. Quantities imported climbed steadily from 100,000 tons in 1955 to 500,000 tons in the mid-1970s and continued to rise dramatically to a peak of more than 2 million tons in 1985.

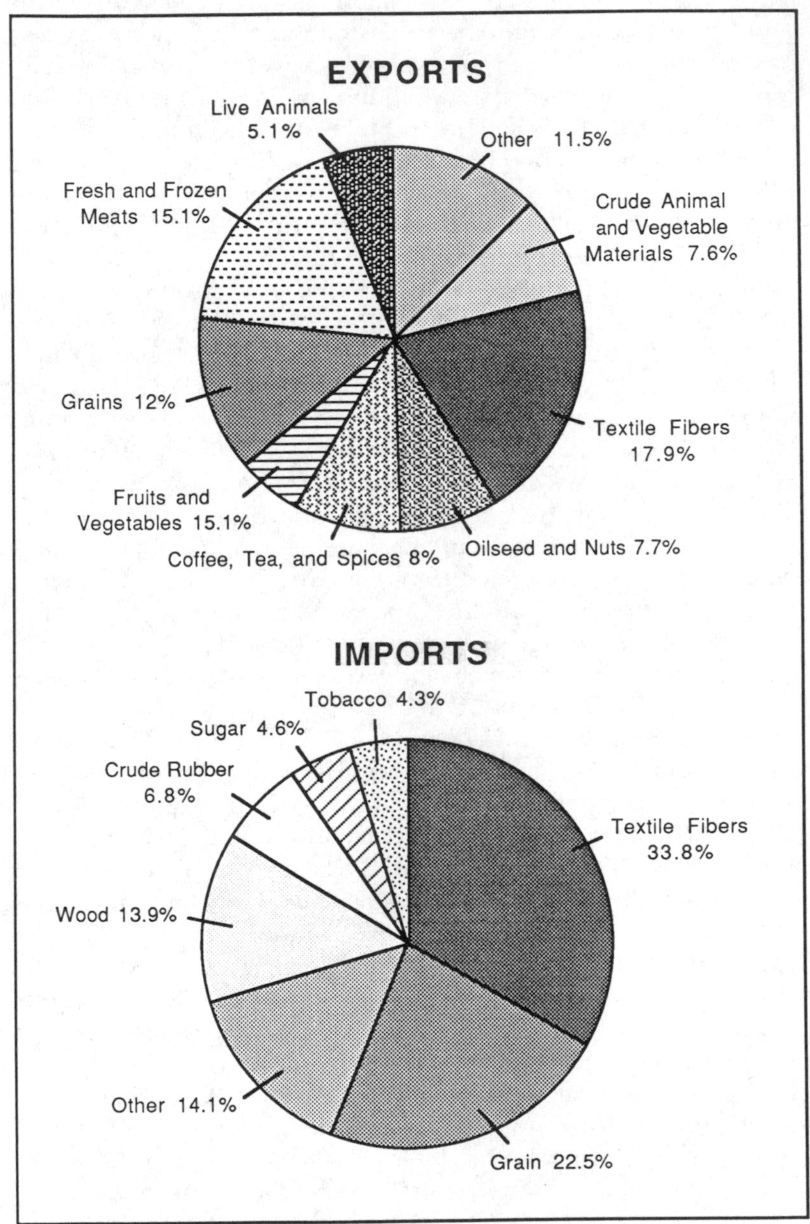

Figure 10. Composition of Agricultural Exports and Imports, 1985

In addition to the commodities just noted, China also exports a host of other products from its vast agricultural resources. Large quantities of live animals, meat, fish, vegetables, and fruits are shipped to Asian markets. Tea, spices, and essential oils are shipped to major international markets. China also exports animal products, such as hog bristles, fur, and other animal products.

Agricultural trade remains an important component of China's general agricultural modernization effort. China is likely to continue to import grain and other agricultural products for the foreseeable future. These imports would be used to maintain or improve living standards, especially in urban areas. In rural areas, imports help reduce the pressure for more procurement, freeing resources for increased consumption or investment in local agricultural programs.

In the long run, China may reduce the expenditure of foreign exchange needed to finance agricultural imports. These expenditures reduce the amount of other imports that can be used for modernization and investment in the nonagricultural sectors of the economy. Success in reducing agricultural imports will eventually depend on the development of domestic sources of supply, for which China hopes to rely in part on new production bases for marketable crops. Pressure for increased consumption is likely to continue. The increase in population and the need for more agricultural goods (including grain, industrial crops, and grain-consuming livestock) to support higher real incomes both in urban areas and in the new agricultural base areas will continue to be factors creating this pressure.

* * *

Useful general works on China's agricultural sector include Dwight H. Perkins' *Agricultural Development in China 1368–1968*; Randolph Barker, Radha Sinha, and Beth Rose's *The Chinese Agricultural Economy*; and Nicholas R. Lardy's *Agriculture in China's Modern Economic Development*. Since 1981 China's State Statistical Bureau has published data on the agricultural sector in annual statistical yearbooks. More detailed statistics, summary information, and policy statements are published by the Ministry of Agriculture, Animal Husbandry, and Fishery in its *Nongye Nianjian* (Agricultural Yearbook). The *China Daily*, printed in English and published in China, contains important data and policy statements. Thousands of Chinese-language books on agricultural topics, and newspapers such as *Zhongguo Nongbao* (China Agriculture), are available by purchase or subscription. *China Quarterly*, published in

London, occasionally contains articles on Chinese agriculture by foreign observers. The National Academy of Sciences Committee on Scholarly Communication with the People's Republic of China has published several interesting trip reports by United States agricultural delegations.

The United States government also publishes information and analysis concerning China. The Joint Economic Committee of the United States Congress periodically publishes a volume on China's economy; the 1986 edition is entitled *China's Economy Looks Toward the Year 2000*. Each year the United States Department of Agriculture publishes *China: Situation and Outlook Report*, which reviews China's agricultural production and trade for the past year and provides an outlook for the coming year. The department also publishes monthly forecasts of production and trade and prepares specialized reports on various topics. (For further information and complete citations, see Bibliography.)

Chapter 7. Industry

Perseverance characterizes this Western Han dynasty (206 B.C.–A.D. 9) female overseer excavated at an archaeological site in Yunnan Provice. The original was bronze with gold inlay.

CHINA'S INDUSTRIAL SECTOR has shown great progress since 1949, but in the late 1980s it remained undeveloped in many respects. Although the country manufactured nuclear weapons and delivery systems and could launch domestically produced satellites, many of its industries used technologies of the 1950s. Although China was one of the world's largest producers of fuel in the mid-1980s and had the world's largest hydroelectric power potential, frequent energy shortages caused lengthy factory shutdowns. Despite massive coal reserves in north China, transportation deficiencies necessitated coal imports to south China. Research institutes developed sophisticated industrial technologies, but bureaucratic and political obstacles impeded implementation.

To solve these and other problems, the Chinese leadership initiated sweeping economic reforms in the late 1970s. Although specific industrial reforms were not clearly defined, broad goals included loosening bureaucratic controls on enterprises and managers to promote a decentralization of authority. Other broad goals were to increase worker productivity by offering incentives; to give market forces greater influence on output mix, purchases, sales, and hiring; to make enterprises operate more efficiently and be responsible for profits and losses; and to restructure the price system to reflect supply and demand more accurately.

Another major goal of the reform program was development of light industry. Beginning with the First Five-Year Plan (1953–57), China adopted the Soviet model of economic development, stressing a heavy industrial base. However, this emphasis seriously strained China's resources and capital and led the leadership in the late 1970s to shift to development of light industry. Because light industry is labor intensive, this shift helped to alleviate unemployment. It also satisfied growing consumer demand, which had not been met because of overemphasis on heavy industry. Another reason for diversification into light industry was the desire to increase exports to obtain much-needed foreign currency.

By the mid-1980s industrial reforms had achieved substantial success in some areas. Industrial output was about twenty-five times that of 1952. A wide range of modern industries had been established, and the country was one of the world's leading producers of coal, textiles, and bicycles. There were major plants in almost every key industry, and a strong effort had been made to introduce manufacturing into undeveloped and rural areas. Light-industry output of consumer goods had increased dramatically. In some cases, enterprises reduced operating costs, managers were able to exercise greater autonomy, and technical innovations were implemented to increase efficiency.

Despite these bright spots in the 1980s, overall results were disappointing to Chinese economic planners. Major problems included failure to reform the price system, interference of local cadres in the managers' operation of enterprises, and perpetuation of the life tenure, "iron rice bowl" (see Glossary) system for workers. Rapid industrial growth made energy shortages one of the most critical problems facing the economy, limiting industrial enterprises and mines to 70 or 80 percent of capacity. According to China's energy planners, the country would have to quadruple electricity production to meet the gross value of industrial and agricultural output target for the year 2000. For a quick increase in output, the industry emphasized short-term development of thermal power plants. For the long term, China planned to rely on its vast hydroelectric power potential and nuclear power to meet electricity demand.

In the 1980s large-scale, centrally controlled plants dominated manufacturing. These large plants were supplemented with many small-scale town and township enterprises, which accounted for significant percentages of national output of coal, construction materials, and leather products.

Trends in Industrial Production

The shifts in economic policy typical of the People's Republic of China since 1949 have strongly affected industrial production (see Economic Policies, 1949–80, ch. 5). In the period of recovery from World War II and the Chinese civil war of 1945–49, industrial output more than doubled as plants were repaired and employment rose. The First Five-Year Plan concentrated on constructing plants and equipment for heavy industry, much of it with Soviet assistance. The machinery, iron and steel, and mining industries all built their foundations in this period. The increases in productive capacity resulted in a second doubling of output.

The Great Leap Forward (1958–60; see Glossary) saw production surge by 45 percent in 1958 as new plants went into operation, facilities operated beyond capacity, and great numbers of small local plants were established. But the overambitious plan to revamp China's economy soon encountered problems of misallocation and overextension of resources. The demands of the Great Leap Forward left the work force physically exhausted. As the overburdened economy began to collapse, growth fell to 22 percent in 1959 and

Glazed-ware finishing at Jingdezhen, a major porcelain-manufacturing center in Jiangxi Province
Courtesy Robert Tichane

4 percent in 1960. Output dropped precipitously in 1961 because of the earlier withdrawal of Soviet technicians, misallocation of resources, and a serious food shortage (see The 1950s, ch. 6). In 1962, with the restoration of planning and coordination, production began to recover. Industrial priorities were transferred from production of industrial goods to agricultural inputs and consumer goods. By 1965 most sectors of industry had regained their 1957 production levels.

In the early stages of the Cultural Revolution (1966–76; see Glossary), production declined when civil disturbances disrupted factories and transport in the big industrial cities. In 1967 output fell, and it remained below the 1966 level in 1968. After order was restored, production recovered in 1969 and grew by 18 percent in 1970. With resumption of growth and the beginning of the Fourth Five-Year Plan (1971–75), output grew by over 10 percent in 1971 and 1972 and by 13 percent in 1973. A wide-ranging program of investment in plants and equipment, including foreign imports, raised industrial capacity. Throughout the 1970s thousands of new, small-scale plants added significantly to levels of production, especially in coal, chemical fertilizer, cement, and electricity, although there were some setbacks. In the mid-1970s the influence of the Gang of Four (see Glossary) and disruption by the succession struggle again reduced industrial output. Political activities in factories and uncertainty of managers and planners caused growth to fall to 4.4 percent in 1974. Growth recovered to 10.3 percent in 1975 but fell to zero in 1976 in the uncertainty surrounding the deaths of Mao Zedong and Zhou Enlai, the second fall of Deng Xiaoping, and the destruction caused by the Tangshan earthquake (see The Post-Mao Period, 1976–78, ch. 1).

In 1977 and 1978, the Four Modernizations (see Glossary) effort began in earnest. Growth reached 14 percent in 1977, when political stability was restored and plants resumed full operation. The high growth rate in 1977 and 1978 caused a serious overheating of the economy, however. At the end of 1978, the leadership introduced a comprehensive economic reform. In 1979 the economy entered a period of readjustment, emphasizing a slower, more rational rate of growth. Policy stressed development of light industry and gave priority to the textile and consumer industries in supplying raw and unfinished materials, power, fuel, and finances. Capital investment in light industry increased from 5.4 percent in 1978 to about 8 percent in 1980. Between 1978 and 1981, the proportion of light industry in gross industrial output value increased by about 9 percent. The rate of capital construction decreased, and the government initiated a major drive to correct imbalances in the economy by gearing production to consumer needs and improving efficiency (see table 15, Appendix A).

In 1983 the government took measures to economize on fuel, energy, raw materials, and working capital. The policy experimentally granted enterprises more autonomy. It introduced new kinds of contracts, permitting limited competition among enterprises serving the same markets. The government began to allow market forces to determine production. At the Third Plenum of the Twelfth National Party Congress Central Committee in October 1984, the party officially reiterated its commitment to reform the urban economy, signaling a high priority for industrial modernization.

The Seventh Five-Year Plan (1986–90) called for greater responsiveness to consumer demand, increased efficiency, and a further assimilation of modern technology. The plan sought to accelerate development of the energy and raw-materials industries and control growth of manufacturing industries, making the two sectors develop more proportionately. Development of the transportation and communications sectors received high priority, and plans called for expanding the building industry. The leadership hoped to speed development of tertiary industry, such as restaurants and small shops, to meet consumer needs.

Organization

The government managed industry according to the kind and level of control, using various State Council organizations (see The State Council, ch. 10). In 1987 there were separate ministries concerned with industry, including those for aeronautics, astronautics, the chemical industry, the coal industry, the electronics industry, the metallurgical industry, the nuclear industry, the petroleum industry, the textile industry, light industry, railways, and water resources and electric power. There were two commissions concerned with industry—the National Defense Science, Technology, and Industry Commission and the State Machine-Building Industry Commission.

In 1986 the government recognized four kinds of economic enterprise ownership: "ownership by the whole people" (or state ownership), collective, individual, and other. Under state ownership, the productive assets of an enterprise were owned by the state, activities of the enterprise were determined by national economic plans, and profits or losses accrued to the state budget. Most of the largest modern enterprises were state owned and directly controlled by the central government. Many other enterprises also were state owned but were jointly supervised by the central government and authorities at the provincial, prefectural, or county levels. Profits from these enterprises were divided among the central and lower-level units (see Local Administration, ch. 10).

Under collective ownership, productive assets were owned by the workers themselves (in the case of an urban enterprise) or by the members of enterprises established by rural units. Profits and losses belonged to the members of the collective, and government authorities directed the enterprise loosely. Collectively owned enterprises were generally small and labor intensive, employing approximately 27 million people in cities and towns in 1983. Individual ownership belonged to the category of individual handicrafts in the 1950s; by the mid-1980s it also included individual enterprises with a maximum of thirty employees. The Chinese authorities left the "other" category undefined.

Geographical Distribution of Industry

Before 1949 industry was concentrated in the large coastal cities and in the northeast. Shanghai was the largest industrial center, followed by Anshan, Fushun, and Shenyang. Qingdao and Tianjin also were important industrial centers. Only a few cities in the interior had any modern industry; they included Wuhan, Chongqing, and Taiyuan (see fig. 11).

During the First Five-Year Plan, the government specifically emphasized development of the northeast and areas other than Shanghai, China's most important industrial base. Industrial sites were constructed in the north around the new steel mills at Baotou in Nei Monggol Autonomous Region (Inner Mongolia), and at Wuhan in Hubei Province. Industrial centers also arose in the southwest, mostly in Sichuan Province

In the 1950s industrial centers in east and northeast China accounted for approximately two-thirds of total industrial output. By 1983, however, industrial centers in the north, central-south, and southwest had increased their share of output to more than 40 percent. This increase was the result of a policy begun in the 1950s to gradually expand existing industrial bases to new areas, to build new bases in the north and central-south, and to establish a new base in the southwest.

From 1952 to 1983, central-south, southwest, and northwest China registered higher industrial growth than the east, northeast, and north regions. Total industrial output grew the fastest in the central-south region—from 13.7 percent of total output in 1952 to 18.6 percent in 1983 (see table 16, Appendix A). The government had stressed developing the interior regions since the 1950s, but by 1986 it had abandoned that strategy in order to develop areas with more established infrastructures. According to this plan, the south would continue growing, but the east and northeast would be the main benefactors.

Level of Technology

Despite marked improvement over the early years of the People's Republic, the technological level of Chinese industry generally remained quite low in the late 1980s. The Chinese made remarkable technological progress in some areas, such as nuclear weaponry, satellites, and computers; but overall the industrial sector lagged far behind that of the developed countries (see The Reform Program, ch. 9). Much of China's machinery and equipment dated from the 1950s and 1960s. The Soviet Union had provided technology assistance during the early and mid-1950s, but such aid ended in the late 1950s and early 1960s with the break in relations (see Sino-Soviet Relations, ch. 12).

One of the main reasons for lagging technology was the lack of coordination between research institutes and production enterprises. Between 1979 and 1984, the number of major scientific and technical research discoveries grew from 2,790 to 10,000, and the number of inventions approved by the state rose from 42 to 264. Most of the discoveries and inventions were never implemented. This

Figure 11. Major Industrial Facilities, 1987

was mainly because research institutes and production enterprises operated independently and had little or no exchange of information. Also, most enterprise managers were more concerned with meeting production quotas than with technological innovations.

There were no clear goals for research and development and no concept of the importance of research and development to industry. Instead, efforts were concentrated on research and development for purely scientific purposes. Therefore, China did not develop a broad base of industrial research and development. By the early 1980s only 8 percent of the total research and development work force was involved in industrial research compared with 72 percent in the United States and in the ensuing years the situation did not improve. Institutional obstacles and resource shortages also plagued research institutes.

In 1985 the Chinese Communist Party issued the "Resolution on the Reform of the Science and Technology Management System." The resolution sought to coordinate research and production more closely. Part of the overall strategy of the Four Modernizations was to redirect science and technology toward economic progress. Research institutes were to compete for contracts from various industries and operate on a fee-for-service basis. Emphasis went to cooperation among factories and universities and other institutes.

As of 1987 the status of this effort remained unclear. On the one hand, the metallurgical industry had applied more internal technological innovation than the electronics industry because the technologies in the former were more developed than in the latter. The metallurgical industry made a stronger effort to blend research and production in individual enterprises. Also, major metallurgical complexes had internal research facilities for new-product research. On the other hand, electronics was much more compartmentalized; by the late 1980s, there was no decisive breaking of the barriers between the technical and production elements.

China's assimilation of imported technology had mixed results in the mid-1980s. There had been some remarkable accomplishments, but they had taken a long time. For example, advanced West German cold-rolling technology had moved into the Anshan iron and steel complex in Liaoning Province. The electronics sector was not as successful because of shortages of raw materials, lack of a reliable power supply, low manpower skill, and a shortage of service and applications personnel. An exception was the Jiangnan semiconductor plant in Wuxi, Jiangsu Province, which received equipment from numerous Japanese and American companies. By 1987 it was highly productive. China's electronics industry, however, like most other industries, was far from implementing advanced technology, whatever its source.

Supplies of Industrial Resources

Capital

Since 1949 China has devoted a large percentage of investment to industry. By 1983 investment in industry was approximately 57 percent of investment in fixed assets. In 1984 about ¥44 billion (for value of the yuan—see Glossary), or roughly 30 percent of total state expenditures, was slated for capital construction. In 1981 the leadership attempted to limit uncontrolled, excessive investment in capital construction. The results were not especially positive—partly because of reinvestment by enterprises allowed to retain profits and partly because of foreign investment.

To supplement domestic sources of capital, China's leadership began allowing virtually all forms of foreign loans and credit by the end of 1979. By early 1980 the country had access to the equivalent of almost US$30 billion in foreign loans and credits extending through 1985. The Chinese also sought foreign capital by encouraging joint-venture projects between Chinese and foreign enterprises (see Foreign Trade, ch. 8). But in early 1986 foreign companies viewed China as a high-cost and high-risk investment area. In 1985 US$8.5 billion worth of foreign capital had been committed, compared with only US$500 million in the first quarter of 1986.

Labor

In the mid-1980s about 120 million people worked in the industrial sector (see Labor Force, ch. 2). In state-owned enterprises the annual output per worker (the Chinese measure of productivity) rose by 9.4 percent to ¥15,349. In 1987 there was a severe urban unemployment problem and consequently a virtually unlimited supply of unskilled and semiskilled labor. Skilled workers, engineers, scientists, technicians, and managerial personnel were in very short supply. During the Cultural Revolution, many specialists were forced to abandon their occupations, and most training and education programs ceased during the ten-year hiatus in higher education from 1966 to 1976 (see Education Policy, ch. 4). This led to a shortage of skilled personnel that seriously hampered the industrial sector's implementation of imported modern technology and independent development of new management and production forms. In 1980 a modern management training center was established in Dalian, Liaoning Province, with the help of foreign experts. In 1987 many Dalian graduates found it difficult to use their newly acquired skills because managerial autonomy was lacking, and many cadres had a vested interest in maintaining the status quo. It was unclear what effect students educated abroad were having on industry.

Raw Materials

China is well endowed with most of the important industrial ores, fuels, and other minerals. Only a few raw materials are not present in deposits large enough for domestic needs. Supplies of iron and coking coal, although of poor quality, are adequate. By the early to mid-1980s, China was a significant exporter of rare metals necessary for the aerospace and electronics industries. Nonetheless, China imported materials such as steel, pig iron, copper, and aluminum because of a large domestic demand and an inadequate transportation infrastructure (see Iron Ore; Other Minerals and Metals, this ch.).

Energy

Although China was the fourth largest world producer of fuel in 1985, energy shortages remained a major obstacle to industrial growth. Energy waste was considerable; to offset this, some energy prices were increased, and penalties for waste went into force.

Coal was the primary energy source, accounting in 1985 for more than 70 percent of total fuel consumption. Proven reserves were more than 700 billion tons, and estimated reserves were 3,000 billion tons. Onshore and offshore oil reserves in 1985 were around 5.3 billion tons, mostly untapped. China had the world's sixth largest electric power generating potential, but output still fell far short of demand. Total natural gas output for 1985 was 12.7 billion cubic meters; 15 billion cubic meters was set as the target for 1990. Natural gas and oil received equal weight in the Seventh Five-Year Plan (see Electric and Nuclear Power, this ch.).

Manufacturing

China's manufacturing sector developed according to the principle of "walking on two legs," a policy of self-reliance introduced in the 1950s. In the 1980s one leg consisted of the state-funded and state-controlled large and medium-sized plants with the most qualified personnel and the most advanced equipment. The other leg was small-scale plants using inferior equipment and large amounts of local labor. Together, the two sectors produced a wide range of industrial products. In most cases the larger plants accounted for the bulk of production, but the smaller enterprises were increasing their share and producing a significant percentage of cement, fertilizers, and farm machinery.

Iron and Steel

Before 1949 the iron and steel industry was small and dispersed; the Japanese had built the only modern steel facility just after World War I at Anshan, Liaoning Province. Although Japan eventually built nine blast furnaces in Anshan, total steel output by all plants never exceeded 1 million tons annually. Much of the Japanese equipment was either damaged in the Chinese civil war (1945-49) or removed by the Soviets at the end of World War II.

Since the establishment of the People's Republic, considerable investment has consistently gone to expand steel output. Steel production, however, has been very sensitive to changes in economic policies and political climate (see fig. 12). Steel output rose

Oil exploration in the Daqing oil field, Heilongjiang Province
Courtesy Xinhua News Agency

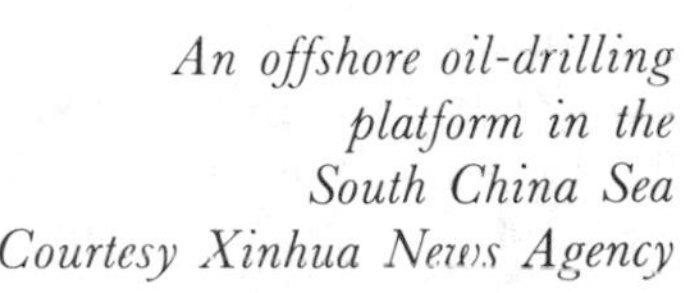

An offshore oil-drilling platform in the South China Sea
Courtesy Xinhua News Agency

steadily in the 1950s, when Soviet advisers helped establish the basis of the iron and steel industry, installing numerous Soviet-designed blast and open-hearth furnaces. The Great Leap Forward saw a significant increase in the number of primitive backyard furnaces producing poor-quality pig iron; numerous new, small, modern plants; overuse of large plants; and exaggerated production reports. In 1961 the industry broke down. Nearly all small plants were closed, and output fell to less than half the amount reported for 1960. From 1961 to 1965, output gradually recovered as equipment was repaired; basic oxygen furnaces were purchased from Austria and electric furnaces from Japan. Production fell in 1967 and 1968 during the Cultural Revolution but grew rapidly in the relative political stability from 1969 through the early 1970s. In the mid-1970s political upheaval retarded output, as did the catastrophic Tangshan earthquake of 1976. That event severely damaged the Tangshan steel plant and the Kailuan coal mines. The latter are major sources of coking coal. After 1976 output climbed steadily, reaching 34.5 million tons in 1979. Steel production for 1986 was 50 million tons.

Steel was viewed as the cornerstone or "key link" of both the Great Leap Forward and the Four Modernizations programs (see Economic Policies, 1949–80, ch. 5). But the post-Mao leadership was determined not to repeat the economically disastrous Great Leap Forward policies: in 1978 it called for a period of readjustment and a cutback in steel investment. It had set a goal, however, of producing 80 million tons of steel by 2000. Production targets were to be met by renovating and improving existing facilities, rather than building new ones. Improvements in existing plants reduced steel-industry energy consumption from 73.8 million tons of coal in 1978 to 69.1 million tons in 1983, and production increased by 26 percent. The Chinese realized they would need outside assistance to fully modernize their steel industry. They sought hardware, technology transfer, and managerial and planning assistance.

In 1987 China was the world's fifth largest producer of iron and steel but lagged far behind developed countries in production methods and quality. Most steel capacity was in open-hearth furnaces with basic oxygen furnaces, electric furnaces, and side-blown converters. Much of the iron and coking coal used in making steel was of low quality. Approximately 25 percent of the country's coal went for steel production in 1985. In 1985 capital construction, considered excessive by the Chinese, exacerbated existing shortages of rolled steel, and imports filled 25 percent of domestic demand.

The Ministry of Metallurgical Industry reported in 1985 that China had 13 plants capable of producing at least 1 million tons per year. Accounting for approximately 65 percent of total production, these mills were built mostly during the 1950s. The Anshan plant was the oldest and most productive of all, producing 7 million tons per year. The next largest was in Wuhan. It was constructed in the 1950s with Soviet aid. China began construction in 1978 on its first integrated steel complex, the Baoshan iron and steel works in Shanghai, but the completion date moved from 1982 to 1985 and finally to 1988.

Besides the larger plants, about 800 smaller mills were dispersed throughout the country in 1985. They ranged from specialty mills producing 500,000 tons per year to very small operations under local jurisdiction or other ministries. Many of the smaller mills were legacies of the Great Leap Forward, when local authorities had hurriedly established their own steel-making facilities. In the mid-1980s the government hoped to phase out these inefficient plants in favor of larger, more productive plants.

In the late 1980s, it was apparent that steel output would remain insufficient to meet the needs of the Four Modernizations. During the period covered by the Seventh Five-Year Plan, imports were expected to average 41 percent of domestic output. Thin rolled sheets, used to make such items as motor vehicles, washing machines, and refrigerators, were in extremely short supply. In 1984 China had to import about half its steel sheet and about 80 percent of its steel plate. Production of tubes and pipes also was inadequate, and approximately 50 percent of all tubes had to be imported. The country was most proficient in the production of steel bars, but it still had to import an estimated 1.8 million tons of rods and bars in 1984. In 1985 China imported a record 15 million tons of steel, more than two-thirds of it from Japan.

Machine Building

The machinery industry has been a leading priority since the founding of the People's Republic. The industry expanded from a few small assembly and repair facilities before 1949 to a large, widely distributed machine-building sector producing many kinds of modern equipment. However, as of 1987 the overall level of technology was still relatively backward. In the late 1970s and early 1980s, China intended to use large-scale imports to modernize the machinery industry but later decided that limiting imports to critical areas would be less costly. The former Ministry of Machine-Building Industry's plans called for about 60 percent of the industry's products in 1990 to reach the technological level of the

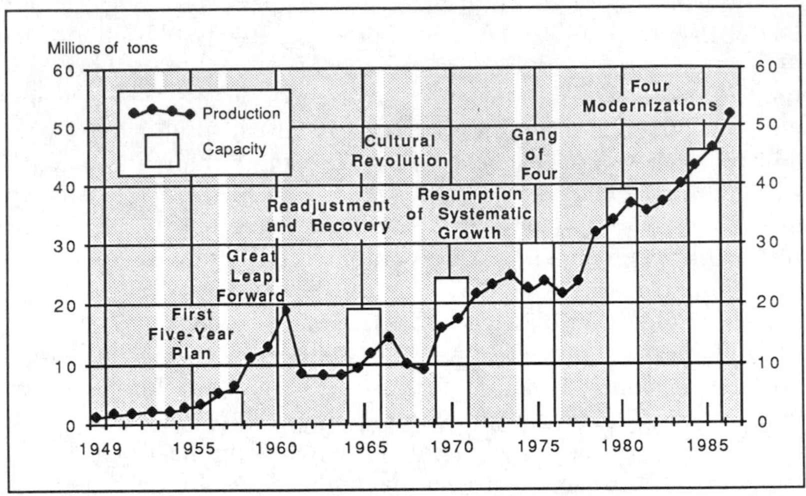

Figure 12. Steel Production and Capacity, 1948–86

industrialized countries during the 1970s and 1980s. Products built to international standards received priority in allocation of funds, materials, and energy.

In 1987 the machinery industry was distributed throughout the country. Nearly all counties and towns had one or more machine factories. Major machinery centers were Shanghai, Tianjin, Shenyang, Beijing, Harbin, Changchun, Taiyuan, Luoyang, Wuhan, Chongqing, Chengdu, Xi'an, and Lanzhou.

The machinery industry was selected by the State Council to lead the way in management reform. China's leaders realized that the quality of machinery would determine the success of modernization in all areas of the economy. The industry's extreme compartmentalization (a legacy of the Maoist obsession with self-reliance) showed a lack of communication among government offices or within regions. Skilled managers also were lacking.

Machine Tools

In 1986 about 120 major enterprises produced most of China's machine tools. Many of the large plants were in the east, north, and northeast, particularly in Beijing, Shanghai, Shenyang, Harbin, and Tianjin. In the early and mid-1980s, a number of agreements with foreign manufacturers aimed to help China upgrade its machine-tool industry. The Shanghai municipal government also asked assistance from the World Bank in preparing and financing a comprehensive modernization scheme for the Shanghai machine-tool industry.

Overall, the machine-tool industry was based on 1960s technology. Many of the tools had a service life of only five to seven years, compared with twelve to fifteen years in industrialized countries. The tools were generally unreliable and were poorly suited for precision work because of outdated design, low-quality purchased components, substandard manufacturing facilities, and a lack of production-management expertise.

Electric Power Equipment

By the early 1970s, major generator production centers in Harbin, Shanghai, Beijing, and Deyang (in Sichuan Province) had built both hydroelectric and thermal generators as large as 300 megawatts. There also were numerous small and medium-sized plants producing generators in the 3.2- to 80-megawatt range. As of 1986 China manufactured condenser-type turbo-generating units with capacities of 6,000 to 300,000 kilowatts; back-pressure extraction generating units with capacities of 12,000 to 50,000 kilowatts; geothermal facilities with capacities of 1,000 to 3,000 kilowatts; and hydroelectric power equipment consisting of generator equipment with an 18-million-kilowatt capacity. Deficiencies showed in power-generating equipment and transmission technology, and significant problems existed in direct-current transmission, particularly in converter technology. China continued to lack experience in design and production of high-volt-ampere transformers and circuit breakers.

Transportation Equipment

The automotive industry, which grew substantially after 1949, did not keep pace with the demands of modernization. In the early 1980s, demand was still low. A surge in demand resulted in the production of 400,000 vehicles and the importation of another 300,000 vehicles through early 1985. In the second half of 1985, stringent administrative measures curtailed most imports, and in early 1986 domestic production was reduced to 13 percent of that in early 1985. One cause for this was a large surplus created by high production and importation levels in 1984 and 1985. Although 1986 production levels were considered a short-term slowdown, the targets of the Seventh Five-Year Plan were quite low.

China's investment in the railroad industry during the Seventh Five-Year Plan was higher than that for any previous five-year plan, with an 80-percent increase over the Sixth Five-Year Plan (1981–85). The country allocated ¥10 billion to manufacture and purchase locomotives, and the remainder went to repair and rebuild obsolete equipment. During the Seventh Five-Year Plan, the Ministry of Railways set a production goal of 5,000 locomotives, including over 800 electric and over 2,000 diesel locomotives. The ministry also planned to manufacture 110,000 freight and 10,000 passenger cars. Despite these ambitious domestic production targets, China had to rely heavily on imported technology to modernize its railroad rolling stock.

From 1961 to 1987, China's maritime fleet grew faster than that of any other country in the world. During that time, the merchant fleet tonnage increased by an average 13.6 percent per year. From 1982 to 1987, Chinese shipyards produced 55 ships, including bulk cargo vessels, freighters, tankers, container ships, partial container ships, and passenger-cargo vessels, with a total deadweight tonnage of more than 700,000 million tons. At the end of 1985, about 17 percent of China's merchant fleet was built domestically.

In the late 1950s, China began developing its own aircraft, known as the Yun, or Y series. China built 135 civil aircraft between 1981 and 1985 and was scheduled to build hundreds more during the Seventh Five-Year Plan. Civil aircraft and aircraft engines were produced in large plants located primarily in Shanghai, Xi'an, Harbin, and Shenyang. Medium-sized factories produced the necessary test equipment, components, avionics, and accessories. China hoped for eventual self-reliance in all aircraft production, but it still imported aircraft in 1987.

Metallurgical Equipment

Much equipment in the metallurgical industry was based on Japanese designs of the 1930s and Soviet designs of the 1950s. Two-thirds of the major equipment at Anshan, one of the largest plants in China, was built during the 1930s and 1950s. In general, major metallurgical equipment was more technologically advanced than instruments and control systems. Measuring and monitoring instruments, essential to quality control, were in short supply.

Most of the iron- and steel-making equipment in general use was domestically produced. This included blast furnaces based on Chinese improvements to old Soviet designs, ore-beneficiation plants, open-hearth furnaces, electric furnaces, and a wide range of steel-finishing equipment. To achieve a higher technological level, various pieces of equipment were imported because China had not assimilated the technology necessary for domestic production. In most instances the industry imported only the main equipment, neglecting necessary control instruments and auxiliary technologies.

Electronics

In 1987 China's electronics industry was about ten to fifteen years behind those of the industrialized nations. Key problems were the inability to transfer technology from research to production and continued reliance on hand labor. Also, impatience to reach Western standards sometimes proved counterproductive. For example, instead of buying a complex item such as a microprocessor abroad, China chose to develop its own, at great expense.

In 1985 the electronics industry consisted of approximately 2,400 enterprises, 100 research institutions, 4 institutes of higher learning, and 20 secondary vocational schools. The industry employed some 1.4 million people, including 130,000 technical personnel. Besides the approximately 2,000 kinds of electronic components and large-scale integrated circuits produced by the industry, it made 400 varieties of electronic machinery, including electronic computers, television broadcast transmitters and receivers, and radar and communications equipment. In the 1980s China made great strides in the production of consumer electronic products, such as televisions, radios, and tape recorders.

Chemicals

China's chemical industry evolved from a negligible base in 1949, grew substantially in the 1950s and early 1960s, and received major emphasis in the late 1960s and 1970s. In 1984 chemical products served primarily agriculture and light industry. The three main areas of chemical manufacturing were chemical fertilizers, basic chemicals, and organically synthesized products. Chemical fertilizer was consistently regarded as the key to increased agricultural output. The output of many chemical products rose steadily, sometimes dramatically, from 1978 to 1986.

Except for a few items, such as soda ash and synthetic rubber, the great majority of chemical products, including fertilizer, came from small factories. Small-scale plants could be built more quickly and inexpensively than large, modern plants and were designed to use low-quality local resources, such as small deposits of coal or natural gas. They also minimized demands on the overworked transportation system.

Larger and more modern fertilizer plants were located in every special municipality, province, and autonomous region. In the early 1970s, China negotiated contracts with foreign firms for construction of thirteen large nitrogenous-fertilizer plants. By 1980 all thirteen plants had been completed, and ten were fully operational.

From 1980 to 1984, many inefficient fertilizer plants were shut down, and by 1984 additional plants were being built with the most advanced equipment available. To capitalize on China's rich mineral resources, the new plants were being constructed close to coal, phosphate, and potassium deposits.

Compared with advanced countries, China's chemical fertilizers lacked phosphate and potassium and contained too much nitrogen. To boost supplies of phosphate and potassium, China relied heavily on imports during the Sixth Five-Year Plan.

Basic chemical production grew rapidly after 1949. In 1985 production of sulfuric acid was approximately 6.7 million tons. Major production centers were in Nanjing and Lüda, and large plants were located at many chemical-fertilizer complexes. Soda-ash output in 1985 was 2 million tons; production was concentrated near major sources of salt, such as large coastal cities, Sichuan and Qinghai provinces, and Nei Monggol Autonomous Region. Production of caustic soda was scattered at large facilities in Lüda, Tianjin, Shanghai, Taiyuan, Shenyang, and Chongqing. In 1985 output of caustic soda was 2.4 million tons. Nitric acid and hydrochloric acid were produced in the northeast and in Shanghai and Tianjin.

The chemical industry's organic-synthesis branch manufactured plastics, synthetic rubber, synthetic fibers, dyes, pharmaceuticals, and paint. Plastics, synthetic rubber, and synthetic fibers such as nylon were particularly important in the modernization drive because they were used to produce such basic consumer goods as footwear and clothing. From 1979 to 1985, plastics production grew from 793,000 tons to 1.2 million tons and chemical fibers from 326,300 tons to 947,800 tons. The major centers for organic synthesis included Shanghai, Jilin, Beijing, Tianjin, Taiyuan, Jinxi, and Guangzhou. The industry received large amounts of foreign machinery in the 1970s.

Building Materials

Large-scale capital construction dramatically increased the demand for building materials. Like the chemical fertilizer industry, cement production featured simultaneous development of small-scale plants and large, modern facilities. Widespread construction of small-scale cement plants began in 1958. By the mid-1970s, these plants existed in 80 percent of China's counties; in 1984 they accounted for a major share of national cement output. These local plants varied widely in size and technology. In 1983 China produced approximately 108 million tons of cement, second in the world to the Soviet Union. In 1984 production increased 14 percent, to

A rotor-blade assembly being installed in an electric generator
Courtesy China Reconstructs

123 million tons and, except for Xizang (Tibet) and Ningxia-Hui autonomous regions, every province, autonomous region, and special municipality had plants capable of producing 500,000 tons of cement per year. In 1985 cement production increased to almost 146 million tons.

China's building-materials industry developed rapidly and reached an output value of ¥28.7 billion in 1984. It manufactured over 500 kinds of products and employed approximately 3.8 million people in 1984. These materials were used in the metallurgical, machinery, electronics, aviation, and national defense industries and in civil engineering projects. The main production centers for building materials were Beijing, Wuhan, and Harbin.

By the mid-1980s China was one of the world's primary producers of plate glass, a critical building material. Production in 1985 reached 49.4 million cases, and twenty urban glass factories each produced 500,000 cases annually. Three large glass plants, each having a production capacity of 1.2 million standard cases, were scheduled for completion in 1985 in Luoyang, Qinhuangdao, and Nanning.

Paper

In the early 1980s, China's serious shortage of productive forest combined with outdated technology to create a shortage of pulp and paper at a time of increasing demand. From 1981 to 1986, the annual growth rate of paper production was 7.3 percent. In 1986, however, only 20 percent of paper pulp was made of wood; the remainder derived from grass fiber.

China's more than 1,500 paper mills produced approximately 45.4 million tons and over 500 different kinds of machine-made paper in 1986. Approximately 1 million tons of pulp and paper were imported annually. In 1986 China focused on pollution control, increased product variety, reduced use of fiber and chemical ingredients, and more efficient use of energy as measures to improve production. China also sought foreign assistance to achieve these goals.

Textiles

China has a long and rich history in production of silk, bast fiber, and cotton textiles. The earliest silk producer, China began exporting to West Asia and Europe around 20 B.C. Ramie, a grass used to produce woven fabrics, fish lines, and fish nets, was first cultivated around 1000 B.C. and is found in the provinces of Hunan, Hubei, Sichuan, Guangdong, and Guizhou and the Guangxi-Zhuang Autonomous Region. Cotton spinning and weaving was the largest domestic industry in the late nineteenth and early twentieth centuries. After a respectable but inconsistent performance from 1949 to 1978, textile production increased significantly with the introduction of the responsibility system (see Glossary) for agriculture in 1979 (see Crops, ch. 6). By 1979 supplies of textiles had improved, the cloth-rationing system (in force since 1949) had ended, and the industry had begun to flourish.

From 1979 to 1984, the output value of the textile industry rose approximately 13 percent annually. In 1984 China had about 12,000 enterprises producing cotton and woolen goods, silk, linen, chemical fibers, prints and dyed goods, knitwear, and textile machinery. Textile production was 15.4 percent of the country's total industrial output value in 1984. Textile exports in 1984 (excluding silk goods) totaled US$4.2 billion, up 21.7 percent over 1983, and accounted for 18.7 percent of the nation's total export value. By 1986 textiles had replaced oil as the top foreign-exchange earner.

Traditionally, the coastal areas had the most modern textile equipment and facilities. Shanghai and Jiangsu Province were the nerve centers of the industry, accounting for 31.6 percent of the total gross-output value for textiles in 1983. Other major textile areas were Shandong, Liaoning, Hubei, Zhejiang, and Hebei provinces.

After 1949 cotton textile production was reorganized and expanded to meet consumer needs. Cotton cultivation increased

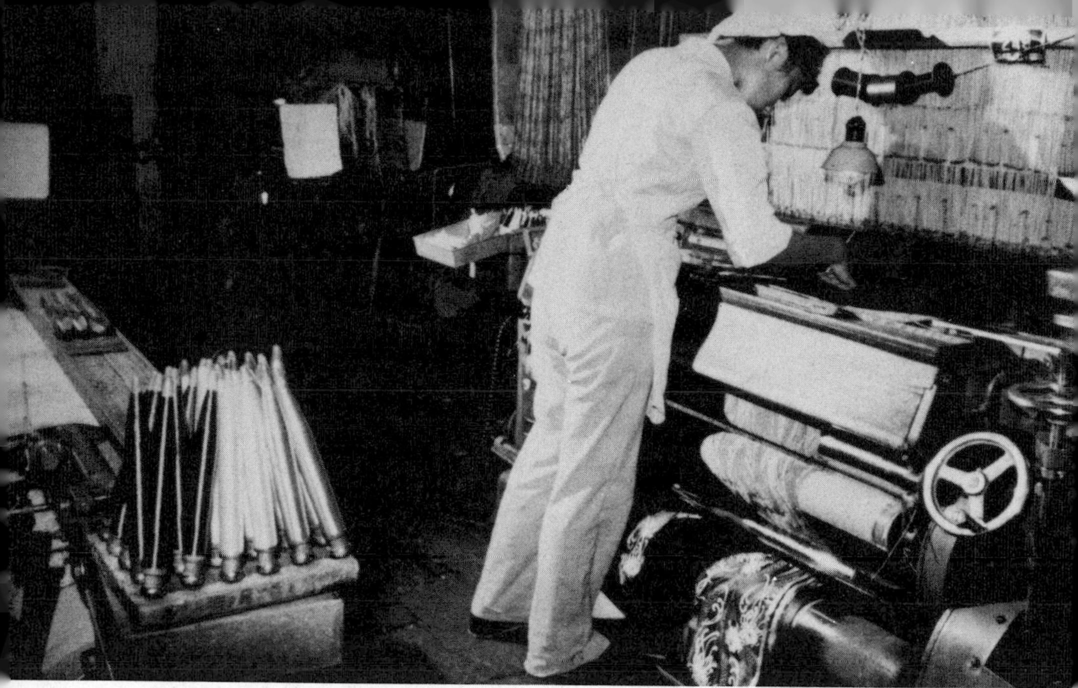

Silk textile weaver, Wuxi, Jiangsu Province
Courtesy Nanjing Slide Studio

in the areas around the established spinning centers in the port cities of Shanghai, Qingdao, Tianjin, and Guangzhou. New spinning and weaving facilities opened near the inland cotton-producing regions. In 1983 China produced 4.6 millions tons of cotton, more than double the 1978 total.

China still was the world's largest silk producer in 1985, manufacturing approximately 422,000 meters of silk textiles. Shanghai and Jiangsu and Zhejiang provinces were the main silk centers. In 1985 China also produced approximately 125,000 tons of knitting wool, 218 million meters of woolen piece goods, 3.5 million tons of yarn, and 541,000 tons of chemical fibers.

Food Processing

Food processing made significant advances in China after 1949. The most basic improvement was the nearly universal establishment of mechanized grain-milling facilities in rural production units. The processing of food into finished and packaged products also grew extensively.

Although a growing number of food products were packaged for export, China's food processing capacity was relatively low in the mid-1980s. An immense variety of baked goods and candies were produced for local consumption, and most Chinese continued to resist processed food. Rising standards of living, however, increased the demand for processed food because of its nutritional and hygienic advantages.

The beverage industry was very large and widespread. All regions had breweries and distilleries producing beer and a variety of domestic and Western alcoholic beverages. China successfully exported several varieties of beer and liquor, and domestic soft-drink production was widespread.

Other Consumer Goods

In the first thirty years of the People's Republic, many basic consumer goods were scarce because of the emphasis on heavy industry. The 1979 economic reform program resulted, however, in a consumer goods explosion. For example, television production increased from approximately 500,000 sets in 1978 to over 16 million sets by 1985. During the same period, bicycle output increased by a factor of about three and one-half, production of electric fans increased twelvefold, and the output of radios doubled. In the first half of 1985, compared with the same period in 1984, production of television sets, washing machines, electric fans, and refrigerators increased dramatically. Refrigerators, washing machines, and televisions included imported components. In 1985 economic planners decided to limit production of refrigerators because they estimated that supply would outstrip demand by 5.9 million units in 1990. The following year, authorities curbed production of televisions to emphasize quality over quantity.

Construction

Housing Construction

Modern housing has been in chronic shortage in contemporary China. Housing conditions in 1949 were primitive and crowded, and massive population growth since then has placed great strains on the nation's building industry. According to 1985 estimates, 46 million additional units of housing, or about 2.4 billion square meters of floor space, would be needed by the year 2000 to house every urban family. Adequate housing was defined as an average of eight square meters of living space per capita. As of 1985, however, the average per capita urban living space, for example, was only 6.7 square meters. Housing specialists suggested that the housing construction and allocation system be reformed and that the eight-square-meter target be achieved in two stages: six square meters by 1990 and the additional two square meters between 1990 and 2000. To help relieve the situation, urban enterprises were increasing investment in housing for workers. In 1985 housing built by state and collective enterprises in cities and towns totaled 130 million square meters of floor space. In the countryside, housing built by farmers was 700 million square meters.

Capital Construction

Since the 1950s, the capital construction industry has been plagued by excessive growth and compartmentalization. There were frequent cost overruns and construction delays, and resources were overtaxed. Project directors often failed to predict accurately the need for such elements as transportation, raw materials, and energy. A large number of small factories were built, providing surplus capacity at the national level but with deficient economies of scale at the plant level. Poor cooperation among ministries and provincial-level units resulted in unnecessary duplication. Because each area strove for self-sufficiency in all phases of construction, specialization suffered. Since the early years of the People's Republic, overinvestment in construction has been a persistent problem. Fiscal reforms in 1979 and 1980 exacerbated overinvestment by allowing local governments to keep a much greater percentage of the revenue from enterprises in their respective areas. Local governments could then use the retained earnings to invest in factories in their areas. These investments, falling outside the national economic plan, interfered with the central government's control of capital investment.

From 1979 to 1981 the economy underwent a "period of readjustment," during which the investment budget for capital construction was sharply reduced (see Reform of the Economic System, Beginning in 1979, ch. 5). This administrative solution to overinvestment proved ineffective, and later reforms concentrated on economic measures such as tax levies to discourage investment. The issuance of interest-bearing loans instead of grants was also intended to control construction growth. Despite reforms, capital construction continued at a heated pace in 1986. The majority of the new investment was unplanned, coming from loans or enterprises' internal capital.

During the Seventh Five-Year Plan, 925 medium- and large-scale projects were scheduled. The government planned to allocate ¥1.3 trillion for fixed assets, an increase of 70 percent over the Sixth Five-Year Plan. Forty percent of the funds were allocated for new projects and the remaining 60 percent for renovation or expansion of existing facilities. Some of the projects involved were power-generating stations, coal mines, railroads, ports, airports, and raw-material production centers.

Mining

Coal

In the first half of the twentieth century, coal mining was more developed than most industries. Such major mines as Fushun, Datong, and Kailuan produced substantial quantities of coal for railroads, shipping, and industry. Expansion of coal mining was a major goal of the First Five-Year Plan. The state invested heavily in modern mining equipment and in the development of large, mechanized mines. The "longwall" mining technique was adopted widely, and output reached 130 million tons in 1957.

During the 1960s and 1970s, investment in large mines and modern equipment lagged, and production fell behind the industry's growth. Much of the output growth during this period came from small local mines. A temporary but serious production setback followed the July 1976 Tangshan earthquake, which severely damaged China's most important coal center, the Kailuan mines. It took two years for production at Kailuan to return to the 1975 level.

In 1987 coal was the country's most important source of primary energy, meeting over 70 percent of total energy demand. The 1984 production level was 789 million tons. More than two-thirds of deposits were bituminous, and a large part of the remainder was anthracite. Approximately 80 percent of the known coal deposits were in the north and northwest, but most of the mines were located in Heilongjiang Province and east China because of their proximity to the regions of highest demand (see fig. 14).

Although China had one of the world's largest coal supplies, there still were shortages in areas of high demand, mainly because of an inadequate transportation infrastructure. The inability to transport domestic coal forced the Chinese to import Australian coal to south China in 1985. The industry also lacked modern equipment and technological expertise. Only 50 percent of tunneling, extracting, loading, and conveying activities were mechanized, compared with the 95-percent mechanization level found in European nations.

Iron Ore

China had iron-ore reserves totaling approximately 44 billion tons in 1980. In the mid-1980s, however, China relied on imports because of domestic transportation and production problems. Sizable iron-ore beds are distributed widely in about two-thirds of China's provinces and autonomous regions. The largest quantities are found in Liaoning Province, followed by Sichuan, Hebei,

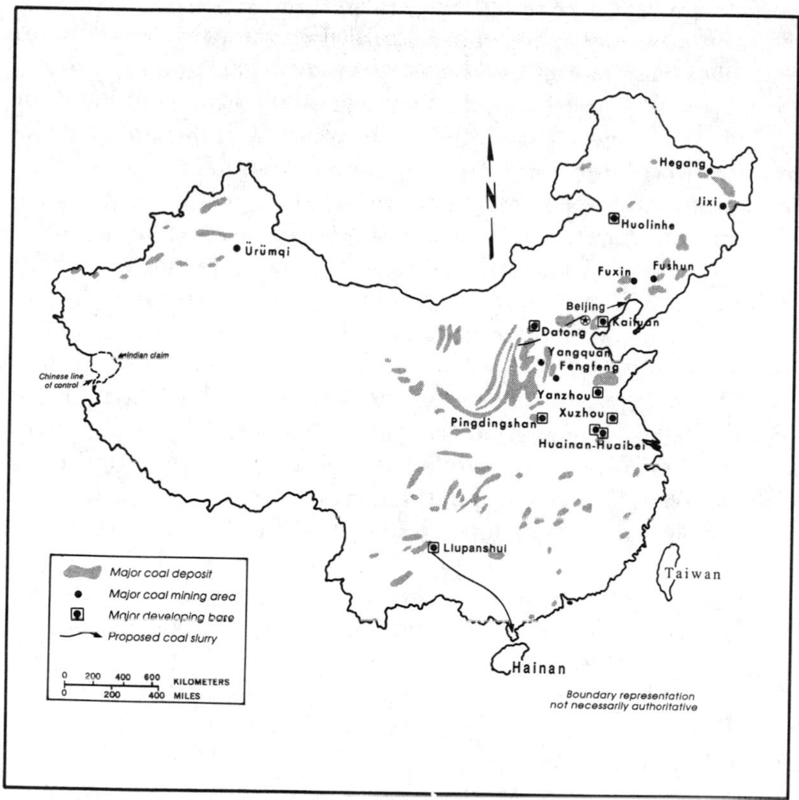

Figure 13. Coal Reserves and Major Mining Areas, 1987

Shanxi, Anhui, Hubei, Gansu, Shandong, and Yunnan provinces and Nei Monggol Autonomous Region.

In the mid-1980s mines lacked modern excavation, transportation, and ore-beneficiation equipment. Most of the ore mined had a low iron content and required substantial refining or beneficiation before use in blast furnaces. Most mines lacked modern plants for converting low-grade iron ore into concentrated pellets.

Other Minerals and Metals

After 1949 geological exploration discovered deposits of more than 130 useful minerals. China is among the world leaders in proven deposits of tungsten, antimony, rare earth metals, molybdenum, vanadium, titanium, pyrite, gypsum, barite, copper, tin, lead, zinc, aluminum, mercury, manganese, nickel, phosphorus, asbestos, fluorite, magnesite, and borax. Of these, China exported antimony, tin, and tungsten in significant quantities. In general, mineral extraction was inadequate for industrialization because of transportation bottlenecks and shortages of modern equipment for mining, smelting, and refining. A number of important mineral products were imported despite large domestic deposits, including aluminum, copper, and zinc.

Among the rare earth metals and ferroalloys, beryllium, tungsten, molybdenum, barium, manganese, mercury, niobium, zirconium, and titanium were present in large reserves and were extracted in adequate quantities. Deficiencies existed in chromium, platinum, and gold.

China produced sufficient quantities of most nonmetallic minerals to meet domestic needs. Barite, fluorite, salt, and talc were available in massive reserves and were exported in large quantities. Graphite, magnesite, phosphates, and pyrite were less abundant but generally satisfied domestic demand. Sulfur deposits were large, but quality was low and imports were necessary.

China is rich in uranium and has favorable geological conditions for the formation of uranium deposits. The ore is easy to mine and dress because of its relatively simple physical composition.

Energy

Oil and Natural Gas

Before 1949 China imported most of its oil. During the First Five-Year Plan it invested heavily in exploration and development of wells. In 1959 vast reserves were discovered in the Songhua Jiang (Sungari River)-Liaohe Basin in northeast China. The Daqing oil field in Heilongjiang Province became operational in 1960. Daqing was producing about 2.3 million tons of oil by 1963, and it continued to lead the industry through the 1970s. Further important discoveries, including the major oil fields of Shengli (in Shandong Province), and Dagang (in Tianjin special municipality) enabled China to meet domestic needs and eliminate nearly all imports by the mid-1960s (see fig. 15). In 1973, despite a steadily growing internal demand for petroleum products, output was large enough to export 1 million tons of crude oil to Japan. Exports increased to 6.6 million tons in 1974 and reached 13.5 millions tons in 1978. In 1985 exports of crude oil amounted to approximately 20 million tons, roughly 16 percent of total production. The majority of 1985 exports were to Japan, but the government also had released increasing quantities on the spot market and sent some to Singapore for refining. Although the government temporarily abandoned its drive to broaden its oil export base in 1986, 130.7 million tons of crude oil still were produced, an increase of 5.8 million tons over 1985.

Oil reserves are large and widely dispersed. In general, development is concentrated on deposits readily accessible from major industrial and population centers. Deposits in remote areas such as the Tarim, Junggar, and Qaidam basins remain largely unexplored. The quality of oil from the major deposits varies considerably. A few deposits, like the Shengli field, produce low-quality oil suitable mainly as fuel. Most of the oil produced in China from the big fields in the north and northeast is heavy, is low in sulfur, and has a very high paraffin content, making it difficult and expensive to extract and to refine.

Offshore exploration and drilling were first undertaken in the early 1970s and became more widespread and advanced as the decade progressed. Chinese and foreign oil experts believed that offshore deposits were extensive and could equal onshore reserves. Offshore operations relied heavily on foreign technology. In 1982 thirty-three foreign oil companies submitted bids for offshore drilling rights; twenty-seven eventually signed contracts. By the mid-1980s, when offshore exploration results were disappointing and only a handful of wells were actually producing oil, China began to emphasize onshore development. To continue offshore exploration, China established the China National Offshore Oil Corporation to assist foreign oil companies in exploring, developing, extracting, and marketing China's oil.

Offshore exploration and drilling were concentrated in areas in the South China Sea, Gulf of Tonkin, and Zhu Jiang (Pearl River) Delta in the south, and the Bo Hai Gulf in the north. Disputes between China and several neighboring countries complicated the future of oil development in several promising offshore locations (see Physical Environment, ch. 2).

Natural gas was a relatively minor source of energy. Output grew rapidly in the 1960s and 1970s. By 1985 production was approximately 12 billion cubic meters—about 3 percent of China's primary energy supply. The following year, output increased by 13 billion cubic meters. Sichuan Province possesses about half of China's natural gas reserves and annual production. Most of the remaining natural gas is produced at the Daqing and Shengli oil fields in the northeast. Other gas-producing areas include the coastal plain in Shanghai and in Jiangsu and Zhejiang provinces; the Huabei complex in Hebei Province; and the Liaohe oil field in Liaoning Province.

The exact size of China's natural gas reserves was unknown. Estimates ranged from 129 billion to 24.4 trillion cubic meters.

The Chinese hoped for a major discovery in the Zhongyuan Basin, a 5,180-square-kilometer area along the border of Henan and Shandong provinces. Major offshore reserves have been discovered. If successfully tapped, these could increase gas output by 50 percent. The largest unexploited natural gas potential is believed to be in Qinghai Province and Xinjiang-Uygur Autonomous Region.

A rudimentary petroleum-refining industry was established with Soviet aid in the 1950s. In the 1960s and 1970s, this base was modernized and expanded, partially with European and Japanese equipment. In 1986 Chinese refineries were capable of processing about 2.1 million barrels per day. By 1990 China plans to reach 2.5 million barrels per day.

In the 1970s China constructed oil pipelines and improved ports handling oil tankers. The first oil pipeline was laid from Daqing to the port of Qinhuangdao; 1,150 kilometers long, it became operational in 1974. The following year the pipeline was extended to Beijing; a second line connected Daqing to the port of Lüda and branched off to the Democratic People's Republic of Korea. A pipeline from Linyi in Shandong Province to Nanjing was completed in 1978, linking the oil fields of Shengli and Huabei to ports and refineries of the lower Chang Jiang region. In 1986 plans had been made to construct a 105-kilometer pipeline linking an offshore well with the Chinese mainland via Hainan Island.

Electric and Nuclear Power

From 1949 to the mid-1980s, China pursued an inconsistent policy on the development of electric power. Significant underinvestment in the readjustment period, starting in 1979, caused serious power shortages into the mid-1980s. Although China's hydroelectric power potential was the world's largest and the power capacity was the sixth largest, 1985 estimates showed that demand exceeded supply by about 40 billion kilowatt-hours per year. Because of power shortages, factories and mines routinely operated at 70- to 80-percent capacity, and in some cases factories only ran for 3 or 4 days a week. Whole sections of cities were frequently blacked out for hours.

China's leaders began to acknowledge the seriousness of the power shortage in 1979. The government took no positive steps until the mid-1980s, when it announced import of 10,000 megawatts of thermal power-plant capacity to serve the east's large population centers. It also launched a nationwide campaign to create an additional 5,000 megawatts of electric-power capacity. Under the Seventh Five-Year Plan, China planned to add 30,000 to 35,000 megawatts of capacity, a 55- to 80-percent increase over previous five-year plans.

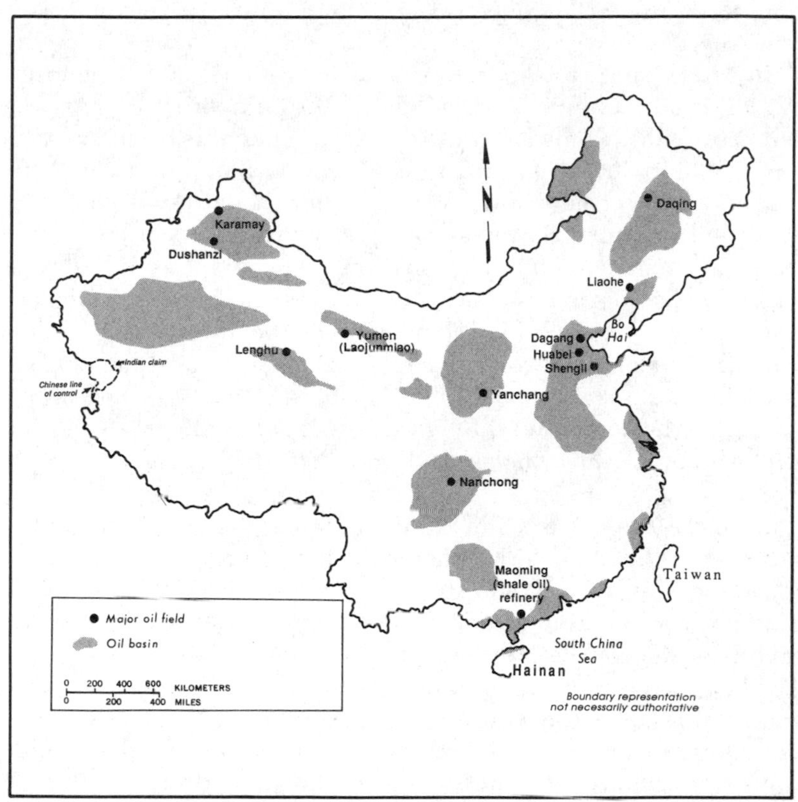

Figure 14. Major Oil Basins and Oil Fields, 1987

The leadership decided to build thermal power plants to meet the country's electricity needs, because such plants were relatively inexpensive and required construction lead times of only three to six years. In 1985 approximately 68 percent of generating capacity was derived from thermal power, mostly coal fired, and observers estimated that by 1990 its share would increase to 72 percent. The use of oil-fired plants peaked in the late 1970s, and by the mid-1980s most facilities had been converted back to coal. Only a few thermal plants were fueled by natural gas. Hydroelectric power accounted for only about 30 percent of generating capacity. Observers expected that during the Seventh Five-Year Plan, China would continue to emphasize the development of thermal power over hydroelectric power because of the need to expand the power supply quickly to keep pace with industrial growth. However, in the long term, hydroelectric power gradually was to be given priority over thermal power.

In 1986 China's total generating capacity was 76,000 megawatts: 52,000 from thermal plants and 24,000 from hydroelectric power sources. China planned to construct large generators having capacities of 100 to 300 megawatts to increase thermal power capacity. The new, larger generators would be much more efficient than generators having capacities of only fifty megawatts or less. With the larger generators, China would only have to increase coal consumption by 40 percent to achieve a 54-percent increase in generating capacity by 1990. Foreign observers believed that as China increased its grid network, it could construct power plants close to coal mines, then run power lines to the cities. This method would eliminate the costly and difficult transportation of coal to smaller urban plants, which had already created a significant pollution problem.

From 1949 to 1986, China built at least 25 large, 130 medium, and about 90,000 small-sized hydroelectric power stations. According to the Ministry of Water Resources and Electric Power, China's 1983 annual power output was 351.4 billion kilowatt-hours, of which 86 billion kilowatt-hours were generated by hydroelectric power. While construction of thermal plants was designed as a quick remedy for alleviating China's power shortages, the development of hydroelectric power resources was considered a long-term solution. The primary areas for the construction of hydroelectric power plants were the upper Huang He (Yellow River), the upper and middle stream tributaries and trunk of the Chang Jiang, and the Hongshui He in the upper region of the Zhu Jiang Basin. The construction of new hydroelectric power plants was expected to be a costly and lengthy process, undertaken with assistance from the United States, Canada, Kuwait, Austria, Norway, France, and Japan.

To augment its thermal and hydroelectric power capacity, China was developing a nuclear energy capability. China's nuclear industry began in the 1950s with Soviet assistance. Until the early 1970s, it had primarily military applications. In August 1972, however, reportedly by directive of Premier Zhou Enlai, China began developing a reactor for civilian energy needs. After Mao Zedong's death in 1976, support for the development of nuclear power increased significantly. Contracts were signed to import two French-built plants, but economic retrenchment and the Three Mile Island incident in the United States abruptly halted the nuclear program. Following three years of "investigation and demonstration," the leadership decided to proceed with nuclear power development. By 1990 China intended to commit between 60 and 70 percent of its nuclear industry to the civilian sector. By 2000 China planned to have a nuclear generating capacity of 10,000 megawatts, accounting for approximately 5 percent of the country's total generating capacity.

In 1986 a 300-megawatt domestically designed nuclear power plant was under construction at Qinshan, Zhejiang Province, with completion planned for 1989. Although most of the equipment in the plant was domestic, a number of key components were imported. The Seventh Five-Year Plan called for constructing two additional 600-megawatt reactors at Qinshan. Another plant, with two 900 megawatt reactors, was under construction at Daya Bay in Guangdong Province. The Daya Bay project was a joint venture with Hong Kong, with considerable foreign loans and expertise.

Rural Industry

From 1980 to 1986, the number of rural town and village enterprises rose from 1.4 million to more than 12.2 million. There were five kinds of town and township enterprises: township enterprises, village enterprises, cooperative enterprises, enterprises jointly run by several households, and household enterprises. In 1986 the assets of the enterprises at the township and village levels totaled ¥134 billion.

Their total output value for 1985 was ¥272.8 billion, 17 percent of the gross national output and 44 percent of the gross agricultural output. Rural enterprises absorbed a large portion of the surplus agricultural labor displaced by the agricultural responsibility system and the breakdown of the people's commune system (see Post-Mao Policies, ch. 6). This absorption helped the state greatly by eliminating state support of millions of displaced workers. In 1986 rural enterprises employed approximately 76 million people, or 20 percent of China's total work force.

The town and village enterprises made a significant contribution to overall economic growth. In 1985 an estimated 28 percent of coal, 53 percent of construction materials, 30 percent of paper, 20 percent of textile goods, 33 percent of garments, and 75 percent of leather products came from rural enterprises. The enterprises also made extensive progress in the export market, with 8,000 export-oriented factories, of which 870 were Chinese-foreign joint ventures. In 1985 town and village enterprises earned about ¥4 billion in foreign currency.

Despite the rapid growth and success of town and village enterprises, continued expansion faced obstacles in 1987. The government was trying to limit production because of economic and environmental concerns. Moreover, financial mismanagement, poor market analysis, rising energy and raw-material cost, substandard equipment, and constant interference from local government authorities hampered production and expansion. In certain areas, such as Zhejiang Province, efforts were made to solve some of the problems facing the rural enterprises. Local governments allowed the enterprises to keep 70 percent of profits, and of the remaining 30 percent remitted to the county government, 70 percent was invested in existing enterprises or used to establish new ones.

Defense Industry

China's defense industrial complex produced weapons and equipment based predominantly on Soviet designs of the 1950s and 1960s. Because of a lack of foreign exchange, a low short-term threat perception, and an emphasis on the other three of the Four Modernizations (agriculture, industry, and science and technology), China had decided to develop its defense industries gradually. It would rely primarily on domestic production, importing foreign technology only in areas of critical need.

The defense industries produced a wide range of military matériel. Large quantities of small arms and tanks were produced, and many were exported to Third World countries such as Iran. China had upgraded Soviet aircraft and was developing nuclear-powered ballistic-missile submarines, intercontinental ballistic missiles, and tanks equipped with infrared night-vision gear and laser range finders (see Military Modernization, ch. 14).

Because defense was assigned the lowest priority in the Four Modernizations in the 1970s, China's large defense sector has devoted an increasing amount of its resources to civilian production. For example, in the mid-1980s approximately one-third of the ordnance industry's output was allocated to civilian production, and the share was expected to rise to two-thirds by 1990. The defense sector produced a wide variety of products, ranging from furniture to telescopes, cameras to heavy machinery.

Despite the military's contribution to the industrial sector, in 1987 Chinese industry lagged far behind that of the industrialized nations. Much of industrial technology was seriously outdated. Severe energy shortages, transportation bottlenecks, and bureaucratic interference also hindered modernization. Although output was high in a number of industries, quality was often poor. However, China's industrial sector has made considerable progress since 1949. Output of most products has increased dramatically since the 1950s, and China now produces computers, satellites,

Oil tanks at Maoming, Guandong Province
Courtesy Xinhua News Agency

and other high-technology items. The reform program introduced in the late 1970s brought an era of more rational economic planning and laid the groundwork for more balanced and sustained industrial growth. As of 1987 China's leaders were aware of the need for greater industrial efficiency and productivity and were striving to achieve these goals.

* * *

Industrial growth before 1949 is outlined by John K. Chang in *Industrial Development in Pre-Communist China*. Thomas G. Rawski describes the development of the producer goods industries, both before and after the founding of the People's Republic, in *China's Transition to Industrialism*. A wealth of material on Chinese industry is found in the United States Congress Joint Economic Committee's *China's Economy Looks Toward the Year 2000*, which includes an overview article, as well as specific articles relating to the structure, management, ownership and control, and finance and planning of industry. It also describes and analyzes the energy sector in detail.

The second volume of *China: Socialist Economic Development* in the World Bank Country Study series, contains information on industrial organization, policy, strengths and weaknesses, and issues and challenges. Another World Bank Country Study, *China: Long-Term Development Issues and Options*, looks at some of the major development issues facing China to the year 2000. Two Rand studies, *Industrial Innovation in China with Special Reference to the Metallurgical Industry* and *Chinese Electronics Industry in Transition*, are excellent case studies, documenting China's attempt to modernize its outdated industrial sector. The annual *Statistical Yearbook of China* provides figures on a wide range of industrial categories. The semimonthly *China Business Review* provides well-researched articles on many topics related to industry, and the *Country Report: China, North Korea*, (formerly *Quarterly Economic Review of China, North Korea*) outlines economic events on a quarterly basis and provides annual summaries. (For further information and complete citations, see Bibliography.)

Chapter 8. Trade and Transportation

Rich in detail, this Tang dynasty (A.D. 618–907) pottery horse is typical of the lively art style of the period. The original on which this artist's rendition is based was polychromatic and stood about thirty-nine centimeters high.

TRADE AND TRANSPORTATION are the lifeblood of an economy. In the twenty-five years that followed the founding of the People's Republic of China in 1949, China's trade institutions and transportation and communications networks were built into a partially modern but somewhat inefficient system. The drive to modernize the economy that began in 1978 required a sharp acceleration in commodity flows and greatly improved efficiency in economic transactions. In the ensuing years economic reforms were adopted by the government to develop a "socialist planned commodity economy" that combined central planning with market mechanisms. These changes resulted in the decentralization and expansion of domestic and foreign trade institutions, a greatly enlarged role for free markets in the distribution of goods, and a prominent role for foreign trade and investment in economic development. Despite increased investment and development in the 1980s, the transportation and communications sectors were strained by the rapid expansion of production and the exchange of goods.

Transportation, postal services, communications, and trade, including services, employed about 6.3 percent of the national labor force in the mid-1980s—about 22 percent of the nonagricultural labor force. Chinese statistics estimate that these sectors produced about 7.4 percent of the gross national product in 1983.

Internal Trade and Distribution

Agriculture

Agricultural products were distributed in three major ways in China during the 1980s. They were either retained by the household (now the primary production unit) for distribution among its members, procured by the state, or sold in free rural or urban markets.

Approximately 63 percent of the population was located in rural areas, where the majority of the people worked in agriculture and rural industries. Under the responsibility system (see Glossary) for agriculture instituted in 1981, the household replaced the production team (see Glossary) as the basic production unit. Families contracted with the economic collective to farm a plot of land, delivered a set amount of grain or other produce and the agricultural tax to the state, and paid a fee to the collective. After meeting these obligations, the household was free to retain its surplus produce or sell it in free markets. Restrictions on private plots and household sideline production were lifted, and much of the production from these was also sold on free markets (see Post-Mao Policies; Planning and Organization, ch. 6).

Distribution of food and other agricultural goods to urban consumers, industry, and rural areas deficient in food was carried out primarily by the state and secondarily by producers or cooperatives. The state procured agricultural goods by means of taxes in kind and by purchases by state commercial departments (state trading companies) under the Ministry of Commerce. The agricultural tax was not large, falling from 12 percent of the total value of agricultural output in 1952 to 5 percent in 1979. In 1984 the number of agricultural and sideline products subject to state planning and purchasing quotas was reduced from twenty-nine to ten and included grains, edible oil, cured tobacco, jute, hemp, and pigs. In 1985 the system of state purchasing quotas for agricultural products was abolished. Instead, the state purchased grain and cotton under contract at a set price. Once contracted quotas were met, the grain and cotton were sold on the market at floating prices. If market prices fell below the listed state price, the state purchased all available market grain at the state price to protect the interests of producers. Vegetables, pigs, and aquatic products sold to urban, mining, and industrial areas were traded in local markets according to demand. Local commercial departments set the prices of these goods according to quality to protect the interests of urban consumers. All other agricultural goods were sold on the market to the state, to cooperatives, or to other producers. Restrictions on private business activities were greatly reduced, permitting peasants as well as cooperatives to transport agricultural goods to rural and urban markets and allowing a rapid expansion of free markets in the countryside and in cities. The number of wholesale produce markets increased by 450 percent between 1983 and 1986, reaching a total of 1,100 and easing pressure on the state produce distribution network, which had been strained by the burgeoning agricultural production engendered by rural reforms. In 1986 free markets, called "commodity fairs," numbered 61,000 nationwide.

Once food was procured and transported to urban areas, it was sold to consumers by state-owned stores and restaurants. In the mid-1980s food items were also available in free markets, where peasants sold their produce, and in privately owned restaurants. As noted previously, the prices of pigs, aquatic products, and vegetables were determined by local authorities according to quality and demand; prices of other products floated freely on the market. Except for grain, edible oil, and a few other rationed items,

Livestock are still an important form of power and transportation.
Courtesy Stephanie Marcus

Horse-drawn carts are still frequently seen in the countryside.
Courtesy Stephanie Marcus

food items were in good supply. Industrial goods used in agricultural production were sold to agricultural units in the 1980s. Local cooperatives or state supply and marketing bureaus sold most agricultural producer goods, including chemical fertilizers and insecticides, to households at set prices. The state also offered preferential prices for agricultural inputs to grain farmers to encourage grain production. Households were permitted to purchase agricultural machinery and vehicles to transport goods to market. In order to ensure that rural units could cover the costs of the increasing quantities of industrial inputs required for higher yields, the government periodically reduced the prices of the industrial goods sold to farmers, while raising the procurement prices for agricultural products. In the mid-1980s, however, the price gap between agricultural and industrial products was widening to the disadvantage of farmers.

Industry

After 1982, reforms moved China's economy to a mixed system based on mandatory planning, guidance planning (use of economic levers such as taxes, prices, and credit instead of administrative fiat), and the free market. In late 1984 further reforms of the urban industrial economy and commerce reduced the scope of mandatory planning, increased enterprise autonomy and the authority of professional managers, loosened price controls to rationalize prices, and cut subsidies to enterprises. These changes created a "socialist planned commodity economy," essentially a dual economy in which planned allocation and distribution are supplemented by market exchanges based on floating or free prices (see Prices, ch. 5).

As a result of these reforms, the distribution of goods used in industrial production was based on mandatory planning with fixed prices, guidance planning with floating prices, and the free market. Mandatory planning covered sixty industrial products, including coal, crude oil, rolled steel, nonferrous metals, timber, cement, electricity, basic industrial chemicals, chemical fertilizers, major machines and electrical equipment, chemical fibers, newsprint, cigarettes, and defense industry products. Once enterprises under mandatory planning had met the state's mandatory plans and supply contracts, they could sell surplus production to commercial departments or other enterprises. Prices of surplus industrial producer goods floated within limits set by the state. The state also had a planned distribution system for important materials such as coal, iron and steel, timber, and cement. Enterprise managers who chose to exceed planned production goals purchased additional

Bicycle repair shop in Beijing
Courtesy Rinn-Sup Shinn
Bicycle parking area in Beijing
Courtesy Rinn-Sup Shinn

materials on the market. Major cities established wholesale markets for industrial producer goods to supplement the state's allocation system.

Under guidance planning, enterprises try to meet the state's planned goals but make their own arrangements for production and sales based on the orientation of the state's plans, the availability of raw and unfinished materials and energy supplies, and the demands on the market. Prices of products under guidance planning either are unified prices or floating prices set by the state or prices negotiated between buyers and suppliers. Production and distribution of products not included in the state's plans are regulated by market conditions.

Lateral Economic Cooperation

China also undertook measures to develop ''lateral economic ties,'' that is, economic cooperation across regional and institutional boundaries. Until the late 1970s, China's planned economy had encouraged regional and organizational autarky, whereby enterprises controlled by a local authority found it almost impossible to do business with other enterprises not controlled by the same institution, a practice that resulted in economic waste and inefficiency. Lateral economic cooperation broke down some barriers in the sectors of personnel, resources, capital, technical expertise, and procurement and marketing of commodities. In order to promote increased and more efficient production and distribution of goods among regions and across institutional divisions, ties were encouraged among producers of raw and semifinished materials and processing enterprises, production enterprises and research units (including colleges and universities), civilian and military enterprises, various transportation entities, and industrial, agricultural, commercial, and foreign trade enterprises.

A multitiered network of transregional economic cooperation associations also was established. The Seventh Five-Year Plan (1986–90) divided China into three regions—eastern, central, and western, each with its own economic development plans. In addition to the three major regions, three echelons of economic cooperation zones were created. The first echelon—national-level economic development zones—cut across several provincial-level boundaries and linked major economic areas. Among these were the Shanghai Economic Zone, the Northeastern Economic Zone, the energy production bases centering on Shanxi Province, the Beijing-Tianjin-Tangshan Economic Zone, and the Southwestern Economic Zone. The second-echelon network linked provincial-level capitals with designated ports and cities along vital communication lines and included the Huaihai Economic Zone (consisting of fifteen coastal prefectures and cities in Jiangsu, Anhui, Henan, and Shandong provinces) and the Zhu Jiang Delta Economic Zone centered on the southern city of Guangzhou. The third tier of zones centered on provincial-level capitals and included the Nanjing Regional Economic Cooperation Association. Smaller-scale lateral economic ties below the provincial level, among prefectures, counties, and cities, also were formed.

Retail Sales

Retail sales in China changed dramatically in the late 1970s and early 1980s as economic reforms increased the supply of food items and consumer goods, allowed state retail stores the freedom to purchase goods on their own, and permitted individuals and collectives greater freedom to engage in retail, service, and catering trades in rural and urban areas. Retail sales increased 300 percent from 1977 to 1985, rising at an average yearly rate of 13.9 percent—10.5 percent when adjusted for inflation. In the 1980s retail sales to rural areas increased at an annual rate of 15.6 percent, outpacing the 9.7-percent increase in retail sales to urban areas and reflecting the more rapid rise in rural incomes. In 1977 sales to rural areas comprised 52 percent of total retail sales; in 1984 rural sales accounted for 59.2 percent of the total. Consumer goods comprised approximately 88 percent of retail sales in 1985, the remaining 12 percent consisting of farming materials and equipment.

The number of retail sales enterprises also expanded rapidly in the 1980s. In 1985 there were 10.7 million retail, catering, and service establishments, a rise of 850 percent over 1976. Most remarkable in the expansion of retail sales was the rapid rise of collective and individually owned retail establishments. Individuals engaged in businesses numbered 12.2 million in 1985, more than 40 times the 1976 figure. Furthermore, as state-owned businesses either were leased or turned over to collective ownership or were leased to individuals, the share of state-owned commerce in total retail sales dropped from 90.3 percent in 1976 to 40.5 percent in 1985.

In 1987 most urban retail and service establishments, including state, collective, and private businesses or vendors, were located either in major downtown commercial districts or in small neighborhood shopping areas. The neighborhood shopping areas were numerous and were situated so that at least one was within easy walking distance of almost every household. They were able to supply nearly all the daily needs of their customers. A typical neighborhood shopping area in Beijing would contain a one-story department store, bookstore, hardware store, bicycle repair shop, combined tea shop and bakery, restaurant, theater, laundry, bank, post office, barbershop, photography studio, and electrical appliance repair shop. The department stores had small pharmacies and carried a substantial range of housewares, appliances, bicycles, toys, sporting goods, fabrics, and clothing. Major shopping districts in big cities contained larger versions of the neighborhood stores as well as numerous specialty shops, selling such items as musical instruments, sporting goods, hats, stationery, handicrafts, cameras, and clocks.

Supplementing these retail establishments were free markets in which private and collective businesses provided services, hawked wares, or sold food and drinks. Peasants from surrounding rural areas marketed their surplus produce or sideline production in these markets. In the 1980s urban areas also saw a revival of "night markets," free markets that operated in the evening and offered extended service hours that more formal establishments could not match.

In rural areas, supply and marketing cooperatives operated general stores and small shopping complexes near village and township administrative headquarters. These businesses were supplemented by collective and individual businesses and by the free markets that appeared across the countryside in the 1980s as a result of rural reforms. Generally speaking, a smaller variety of consumer goods was available in the countryside than in the cities. But the lack was partially offset by the increased access of some peasants to urban areas where they could purchase consumer goods and market agricultural items.

A number of important consumer goods, including grain, cotton cloth, meat, eggs, edible oil, sugar, and bicycles, were rationed during the 1960s and 1970s. To purchase these items, workers had to use coupons they received from their work units. By the mid-1980s rationing of over seventy items had been eliminated; production of consumer goods had increased, and most items were in good supply. Grain, edible oil, and a few other items still required coupons. In 1985 pork rationing was reinstated in twenty-one cities as supplies ran low. Pork was available at higher prices in supermarkets and free markets.

Foreign Trade

History of Chinese Foreign Trade

Chinese foreign trade began as early as the Western Han dynasty (206 B.C.–A.D. 9), when the famous "silk route" through Central

Urban market in Qingdao, Shandong Province
Courtesy Xinhua News Agency

Asia was pioneered by Chinese envoys (see The Imperial Era, ch. 1). During later dynasties, Chinese ships traded throughout maritime Asia, reaching as far as the African coast, while caravans extended trade contacts in Central Asia and into the Middle East. Foreign trade was never a major economic activity, however, and Chinese emperors considered the country to be entirely self-sufficient. During parts of the Ming (1368–1644) and Qing (1644–1911) dynasties, trade was officially discouraged.

In the nineteenth century, European nations used military force to initiate sustained trade with China. From the time of the Opium War (1839–42) until the founding of the People's Republic in 1949, various Western countries and, starting in the 1890s, Japan compelled China to agree to a series of unequal treaties that enabled foreigners to establish essentially autonomous economic bases and operate with privileged status in China. Foreign privileges were abolished when the People's Republic came into being (see Emergence of Modern China, ch. 1).

Foreign trade did not account for a large part of the Chinese economy for the first thirty years of the People's Republic. As in most large, continental countries, the amount of commerce with other nations was small relative to domestic economic activity. During the 1950s and 1960s, the total value of foreign trade was only about 2 percent of the gross national product (GNP). In the 1970s trade grew rapidly but in 1979 still amounted to only about 6 percent of GNP.

The importance of foreign trade in this period, however, far exceeded its volume. Foreign imports alleviated temporary but critical shortages of food, cotton, and other agricultural products as well as long-term deficiencies in a number of essential items, including raw materials such as chrome and manufactured goods such as chemical fertilizer and finished steel products. The acquisition of foreign plants and equipment enabled China to utilize the more advanced technology of developed countries to speed its own technological growth and economic development.

During the 1950s China imported Soviet plants and equipment for the development program of the First Five-Year Plan (1953–57). At the same time, the Chinese government expanded exports of agricultural products to repay loans that financed the imports (see The First Five-Year Plan, ch. 5). Total trade peaked at the equivalent of US$4.3 billion in 1959, but a sudden decline in agricultural production in 1959–61 required China's leaders to suspend further imports of machinery to purchase foreign grain. Under a policy of "self-reliance," in 1962 total trade declined to US$2.7 billion. As the economy revived in the mid-1960s, plants and equipment again were ordered from foreign suppliers, and substantial growth in foreign trade was planned. But in the late 1960s, the chaos and antiforeign activities of the Cultural Revolution (1966–76; see Glossary) caused trade again to decline.

The pragmatic modernization drive led by party leaders Zhou Enlai and Deng Xiaoping and China's growing contacts with Western nations resulted in a sharp acceleration of trade in the early 1970s. Imports of modern plants and equipment were particularly emphasized, and after 1973 oil became an increasingly important export. Trade more than doubled between 1970 and 1975, reaching US$13.9 billion. Growth in this period was about 9 percent a year. As a proportion of GNP, trade grew from 1.7 percent in 1970 to 3.9 percent in 1975. In 1976 the atmosphere of uncertainty resulting from the death of Mao and pressure from the Gang of Four (see Glossary), whose members opposed reliance on foreign technology, brought another decline in trade.

Beginning in the late 1970s, China reversed the Maoist economic development strategy and, by the early 1980s, had committed itself to a policy of being more open to the outside world and widening foreign economic relations and trade. The opening up policy led to the reorganization and decentralization of foreign trade institutions, the adoption of a legal framework to facilitate foreign economic relations and trade, direct foreign investment, the creation of special economic zones (see Glossary) and "open cities," the rapid expansion of foreign trade, the importation of foreign technology and management methods, involvement in international financial markets, and participation in international foreign economic organizations. These changes not only benefited the Chinese economy but also integrated China into the world economy. In 1979 Chinese trade totaled US$27.7 billion—6 percent of China's GNP but only 0.7 percent of total world trade. In 1985 Chinese foreign trade rose to US$70.8 billion, representing 20 percent of China's GNP and 2 percent of total world trade and putting China sixteenth in world trade rankings.

Trade Policy in the 1980s

Under the policy of opening up to the outside world, exports, imports, and foreign capital were all assigned a role in promoting economic development. Exports earned foreign currency, which was used to fund domestic development projects and to purchase advanced foreign technology and management expertise. Imports of capital goods and industrial supplies and foreign loans and investment were used to improve the infrastructure in the priority areas of energy, transportation, and telecommunications and to modernize the machine-building and electronics industries. To earn more foreign currency and to conserve foreign exchange reserves, foreign capital was also used to expand production of export commodities, such as textiles, and of import substitutes, such as consumer goods.

China has adopted a variety of measures to promote its foreign economic relations, maximizing the role of imports, exports, and foreign capital in economic development. Foreign trade organizations were reorganized, and control of imports and exports was relaxed or strengthened depending on the balance of trade and the level of foreign exchange reserves. Heavy purchases of foreign plants and equipment resulted in import restraint from 1980 to 1983. Because of the expansion of exports in the mid-1980s, a large foreign reserve surplus, and the decentralized management of foreign trade, imports surged. Huge, uncontrolled purchases of consumer goods led to trade deficits in 1984 and 1985, resulting in the introduction of an import and export licensing system, stricter controls on foreign exchange expenditures, and the devaluation of the yuan in order to reduce the trade deficit and ensure that machinery, equipment, and semifinished goods, rather than consumer goods, were imported. In 1985 China had foreign exchange reserves of US$11.9 billion.

China joined a number of international economic organizations, becoming a member of the World Bank, the International Monetary

Fund, the Asian Development Bank, the General Agreement on Tariffs and Trade (GATT), and the Multi-Fiber Agreement. China became an observer of GATT in 1982 and formally applied to participate as a full member in July 1986. China also reversed its aversion to foreign capital, borrowing money from international lending organizations, foreign governments, and foreign commercial banks and consortia and permitting foreign banks to open branches in China. The Chinese government maintained a good credit rating internationally and did not pile up huge foreign debts like many other communist and developing countries. Between 1979 and 1985, China signed loans totaling US$20.3 billion, US$15.6 billion of which it already had used. Most loans went into infrastructure projects, such as energy and transportation, and funded raw materials imports. The Bank of China, the principal foreign exchange bank, established branches overseas and participated in international financial markets in Eurobonds and loan syndication.

Legal and institutional frameworks to facilitate foreign investment and trade also were created. Laws on taxation, joint ventures, foreign investments, and related areas were promulgated to encourage foreign investment. In 1979 China created four special economic zones in Shenzhen, Zhuhai, Shantou (in Guangdong Province), and Xiamen (in Fujian Province). The special economic zones essentially were export-processing zones designed to attract foreign investment, expand exports, and import technology and expertise. In 1984 fourteen coastal cities were designated "open cities." These too were intended to attract foreign funds and technology. But in 1985 the government decided to concentrate resources on only four of the cities: Dalian, Guangzhou, Shanghai, and Tianjin. Although the special economic zones and open cities had the power to grant investment incentives, problems with the red tape, bureaucratic interference, and lack of basic infrastructure resulted in less foreign investment and fewer high-technology projects than initially envisioned.

From 1979 to 1985, China received US$16.2 billion in foreign investment and used US$4.6 billion of that amount. By 1986 China had over 6,200 foreign-funded businesses, including 2,741 joint ventures, 3,381 cooperatively managed businesses, and 151 enterprises with sole foreign investment. Of the joint ventures, 70 percent were in production enterprises (manufacturing or processing) and 30 percent were service industries (primarily hotels or tourism). Hong Kong provided 80 percent of the joint-venture partners, the United States 7 percent, and Japan 6 percent.

A 22-million-ton berth at the Baoshan iron and steel works, Shanghai
Courtesy Xinhua News Agency

Organization of Foreign Trade

The increasingly complex foreign trade system underwent expansion and decentralization in the late 1970s and 1980s. In 1979 the Ministry of Foreign Trade's nine foreign trade corporations lost their monopoly on import and export transactions as the industrial ministries were permitted to establish their own foreign trade enterprises. The provincial branch corporations of the state foreign trade corporations were granted more autonomy, and some provinces, notably Fujian, Guangdong, and the special municipalities of Beijing, Tianjin, and Shanghai were permitted to set up independent, provincial-level import-export companies. Some selected provincial enterprises were granted autonomy in foreign trade decisions. In 1982 the State Council's Import-Export Control Commission, Foreign Investment and Control Commission, Ministry of Foreign Trade, and Ministry of Foreign Economic Relations were merged to form the Ministry of Foreign Economic Relations and Trade. In 1984 the foreign trade system underwent further decentralization. Foreign trade corporations under this and other ministries and under provincial-level units became independent of their parent organizations and were responsible for their own profits and losses. An agency system for foreign trade also was established, in which imports and exports were handled by specialized enterprises and corporations acting as agents on a commission basis.

Ministry of Foreign Economic Relations and Trade

The main functions of the Ministry of Foreign Economic Relations and Trade were to establish and supervise foreign trade policies; to work with the State Planning Commission in setting long-term foreign trade plans and annual quotas for imports and exports; to control imports and exports through licenses and quotas; to supervise the management of foreign trade corporations and enterprises; and to coordinate economic and trade relations with foreign governments and international economic organizations. The ministry also undertook international market research, led institutes of foreign economic relations and trade, and directed the General Administration of Customs.

Foreign Trade Corporations and Enterprises

In the late 1980s China had numerous specialized national corporations handling import and export transactions in such areas as arts and crafts, textiles, "native produce" and animal byproducts, foodstuffs of various kinds, chemicals, light industrial products, metals and minerals technology, industrial machinery and equipment, petrochemical and petroleum products, scientific instruments, aerospace technology and services, ships, and weapons (see table 2, Appendix B). Although nominally supervised by the Ministry of Foreign Economic Relations and Trade each of these corporations was responsible for its own profits and losses. Included among these enterprises, for example, was the Great Wall Industrial Corporation, which imported and exported transportation vehicles, satellites and other products associated with aerospace programs, mechanical equipment, electrical products, hardware and tools, medical apparatus, and chemicals. China Northern Industrial Corporation, subordinate to the Ministry of Ordnance Industry, used military production facilities to manufacture civilian products for export. The business activities of China Northern Industrial Corporation included the sale of heavy machinery, hardware and tools, and heavy-duty vehicles; light chemical industry products, such as plastic, paints, and coatings; and high-precision machinery and optical and optical-electronic equipment. Other corporations offered a variety of professional consulting services. One of these, the China International Economic Consultants Corporation, provided economic and legal expertise on investment and other economic activities.

Financial Transactions and Investment

Foreign exchange and reserves were controlled in the mid-1980s by the State Administration of Exchange Control under the People's Bank of China, the central bank. Foreign exchange allocations to banks, ministries, and enterprises were all approved by the State Administration of Exchange Control. The Bank of China, the foreign exchange arm of the People's Bank of China, lost its monopoly on all foreign exchange transactions in 1984 when the Agricultural Bank, People's Construction Bank, China Industrial and Commercial Bank, and China International Trust and Investment Corporation (CITIC) were permitted to deal in foreign currency. The Bank of China remained China's principal foreign exchange bank and provided loans for production and commercial transactions related to exports, set up branches overseas, maintained correspondent relations with foreign banks, and did research on international monetary trends. The Bank of China also was active in international financial markets through such activities as loan syndication and issuing of foreign bonds. CITIC, formed in 1979 to facilitate foreign investment in China, also borrowed and lent internationally and issued foreign bonds in addition to encouraging and participating in joint ventures, importing foreign technology and equipment, and making overseas investments. In 1986 CITIC was renamed CITIC Group and shifted its emphasis to power, metallurgical, and raw materials industries, which had trouble attracting investments. In late 1986 the CITIC Group had set up 47 joint ventures, invested in 114 domestic companies, and issued US$550 million in foreign bonds. The China Investment Bank was established in 1981 as a channel for medium- and long-term loans from international financial institutions such as the World Bank.

Other Organizations Involved in Trade

The State Council's State Planning Commission and State Economic Commission were involved in long-term planning for the development of foreign trade, and they developed national priorities for imports and exports. Several other organizations under the State Council were also involved in foreign trade matters: the Special Economic Zones Office, State Import and Export Commodities Inspection Administration, General Administration of Customs, and China Travel and Tourism Bureau. The China Council for the Promotion of International Trade (CCPIT) assisted the Ministry of Foreign Economic Relations and Trade in foreign trade relations. CCPIT handled trade delegations to and from China, organized foreign trade exhibitions in China and Chinese exhibitions in other countries, and published periodicals promoting Chinese trade. The People's Insurance Company of China expanded its operations in 1980 for the purpose of encouraging foreign trade. New categories of coverage offered to foreign firms included compensatory trade, satellite launching, nuclear power plant safety, offshore oil development insurance, insurance against contract failure, and insurance against political risk.

Composition of Foreign Trade

The dominant pattern of foreign trade after 1949 was to import industrial producer goods from developed countries and to pay for them with exports of food, crude materials, and light manufactures, especially textiles. The pattern was altered as circumstances demanded; in the period of economic collapse following the Great Leap Forward (1958–60; see Glossary), food imports increased from a negligible amount in 1959 to 39 percent of all imports in 1962. At the same time, imports of machinery and equipment dropped from 41 percent to 5 percent of the total. From this time on, food and live animals remained a significant, although declining, share of imports, amounting to 14.8 percent of the total in 1980 but dropping to 4.1 percent in 1985. The pattern also shifted over time as China's industrial sector expanded, gradually increasing the share of exports accounted for by manufactured goods. Manufactures provided only 30 percent of all exports in 1959, 37.9 percent in 1975, and grew to 44.9 percent in 1985.

Important changes occurred in several specific trade categories in the 1970s and 1980s (see table 17, Appendix A). Imports of textile fibers rose from 5.8 percent in 1975 to 10.7 percent in 1980 as the Chinese textile industry grew faster than domestic cotton supplies but then fell to 4 percent in 1985 as domestic cotton production increased. Imports of unfinished textile products also increased from 1.3 percent in 1975 to 5.3 percent in 1985 as a result of textile industry growth. Iron and steel accounted for approximately 20 percent of imports in the 1970s, fell to 11.6 percent in 1980, then rose to 14.9 percent in 1985. Imports of manufactured goods, machinery, and transportation equipment represented 62.6 percent of total import value in 1975, fell to 53.9 percent in 1980 as imports were cut back during the "period of readjustment" of the economy (1979–81), and rose again to 75.2 percent in 1985. On the export side, the share of foodstuffs fell to 12.5 percent in 1985. The fastest growing export item in the 1970s was petroleum, which was first exported in 1973. Petroleum rocketed to 12.1 percent of all exports in 1975, 22 percent in 1980, and 21.2 percent in 1985.

In the 1980s textile exports grew rapidly. Although exports of unfinished textiles remained about 14 percent of total exports, all categories of textile exports rose from 5 percent in 1975 to 18.7 percent in 1984. In 1986 textiles replaced petroleum as China's largest single export item.

Trading Partners

During the 1950s China's primary foreign trading partner was the Soviet Union. In 1959 trade with the Soviet Union accounted for nearly 48 percent of China's total. As relations between the two countries deteriorated in the early 1960s, the volume of trade fell, decreasing to only just over 7 percent of Chinese trade by 1966. During the 1970s trade with the Soviet Union averaged about 2 percent of China's total, while trade with all communist countries made up about 15 percent. In 1986, despite a trade pact with the Soviet Union, Chinese-Soviet trade, according to Chinese customs statistics, amounted to only 3.4 percent of China's total trade, while trade with all communist countries fell to 9 percent of the total (see table 18, Appendix A).

By the mid-1960s Japan had become China's leading trading partner, accounting for 15 percent of trade in 1966. Japan was China's most natural trading partner; it was closer to China than any other industrial country and had the best transportation links to it. The Japanese economy was highly advanced in those areas where China was weakest, especially heavy industry and modern technology, while China was well endowed with some of the important natural resources that Japan lacked, notably coal and oil. In the 1980s Japan accounted for over 20 percent of China's foreign trade and in 1986 provided 28.9 percent of China's imports and 15.2 percent of its exports. Starting in the late 1970s, China ran a trade deficit with Japan.

Beginning in the 1960s, Hong Kong was consistently the leading market for China's exports and its second largest partner in overall trade. In 1986 Hong Kong received 31.6 percent of Chinese goods sold abroad and supplied about 13 percent of China's imports. Hong Kong was a major market for Chinese foodstuffs and served as a transshipment port for Chinese goods reexported to other countries.

The United States banned trade with China until the early 1970s. Thereafter trade grew rapidly, and after the full normalization of diplomatic and commercial relations in 1979, the United States became the second largest importer to China and in 1986 was China's third largest partner in overall trade. Most American goods imported by China were either high-technology industrial products, such as aircraft, or agricultural products, primarily grain and cotton.

Western Europe has been important in Chinese foreign trade since the mid-1960s. The Federal Republic of Germany, in particular, was second only to Japan in supplying industrial goods to China during most of this period. China followed a policy of shopping widely for its industrial purchases, and it concluded deals of various sizes with nearly all of the West European nations. In 1986 Western Europe accounted for nearly 18 percent of China's foreign trade, with imports exceeding exports.

Third World countries have long served as a market for Chinese agricultural and light industrial products. In 1986 developing countries purchased about 15 percent of Chinese exports and supplied about 8 percent of China's imports.

Tourism

Between 1949 and 1974, the People's Republic was closed to all but selected foreign visitors. Beginning in the late 1970s, when the leadership decided to promote tourism vigorously as a means of earning foreign exchange, China quickly developed its own tourist industry. Major hotel construction programs greatly increased the number of hotels and guest houses, more historic and scenic spots were renovated and opened to tourists, and professional guides and other service personnel were trained. The expansion of domestic and international airline traffic and other tourist transportation facilities made travel more convenient. Over 250 cities and counties were opened to foreign visitors by the mid-1980s. Travelers needed only valid visas or residence permits to visit 100 locations; the remaining locales required travel permits from public security departments. In 1985 approximately 1.4 million foreigners visited China, and nearly US$1.3 billion was earned from tourism.

Transportation

Transportation is a major factor in China's national economy. For most of the period since 1949, however, transportation occupied a relatively low priority in China's national development. Inadequate transportation systems hindered the movement of coal from mine to user, the transportation of agricultural and light industrial products from rural to urban areas, and the delivery of imports and exports. As a result, the underdeveloped transportation system constrained the pace of economic development throughout the country. In the 1980s the updating of transportation systems was given priority, and improvements were made throughout the transportation sector (see fig. 15).

In 1986 China's transportation system consisted of long-distance

Figure 15. Railroads and Major Air and Sea Ports, 1987

hauling by railroads and inland waterways and medium-distance and rural transportation by trucks and buses on national and provincial-level highways. Waterborne transportation dominated freight traffic in east, central, and southwest China, along the Chang Jiang (Yangtze River) and its tributaries, and in Guangdong Province and Guangxi-Zhuang Autonomous Region, served by the Zhu Jiang (Pearl River) system. All provinces, autonomous regions, and special municipalities, with the exception of Xizang Autonomous Region (Tibet), were linked by railroads. Many double-track lines, electrified lines, special lines, and bridges were added to the system. Subways were operating in Beijing and Tianjin, and construction was being planned in other large cities. National highways linked provincial-level capitals with Beijing and major ports. Roads were built between large, medium, and small towns as well as between towns and railroad connections. The maritime fleet made hundreds of port calls in virtually all parts of the world, but the inadequate port and harbor facilities at home still caused major problems. Civil aviation underwent tremendous development during the 1980s. Domestic and international air service was greatly increased. In 1985 the transportation system handled 2.7 billion tons of goods. Of this, the railroads handled 1.3 billion tons; highways handled 762 million tons; inland waterways handled 434 million tons; ocean shipping handled 65 million tons; and civil airlines handled 195,000 tons. The 1985 volume of passenger traffic was 428 billion passenger-kilometers. Of this, railroad traffic accounted for 241.6 billion passenger-kilometers; road traffic, for 157.3 billion passenger-kilometers; waterway traffic, for 17.4 billion passenger-kilometers; and air traffic, for 11.7 billion passenger-kilometers.

Ownership and control of the different elements of the transportation system varied according to their roles and their importance in the national economy. The railroads were owned by the state and controlled by the Ministry of Railways. In 1986 a contract system for the management of railroad lines was introduced in China. Five-year contracts were signed between the ministry and individual railroad bureaus that were given responsibility for their profits and losses. The merchant fleet was operated by the China Ocean Shipping Company (COSCO), a state-owned enterprise. The national airline was run by the General Administration of Civil Aviation of China (CAAC). Regional airlines were run by provincial-level and municipal authorities. Highways and inland waterways were the responsibilities of the Ministry of Communications. Trucking and inland navigation were handled by government-operated transportation departments as well as by private enterprises.

Transportation was designated a top priority in the Seventh Five-Year Plan (1986–90). Under the plan, transportation-related projects accounted for 39 of 190 priority projects. Because most were long-term development projects, a large number were carried over from 1985, and only a few new ones were added. The plan called for an increase of approximately 30 percent in the volume of various kinds of cargo transportation by 1990 over 1985 levels. So each mode of transportation would have to increase its volume by approximately 5.4 percent annually during the 5-year period. The plan also called for updating passenger and freight transportation and improving railroad, waterways, and air transportation. To achieve these goals, the government planned to increase state and local investments as well as to use private funds.

The Seventh Five-Year Plan gave top priority to increasing the capacity of existing rail lines and, in particular, to improving the coal transportation lines between Shanxi Province and other provincial-level units and ports and to boosting total transportation capacity to 230 million tons by 1990. Other targets were the construction of 3,600 kilometers of new rail lines, the double-tracking of 3,300 kilometers of existing lines, and the electrification of 4,000 kilometers of existing lines.

Port construction also was listed as a priority project in the plan. The combined accommodation capacity of ports was to be increased by 200 million tons, as compared with 100 million tons under the Sixth Five-Year Plan (1981–85). Priority also was given to highway construction. China planned to build new highways and rebuild existing highways to a total length of 140,000 kilometers. At the end of the Seventh Five-Year Plan, the total length of highways was to be increased to 1 million kilometers from the existing 940,000 kilometers. Air passenger traffic was to be increased by an average of 14.5 percent annually over the 5-year period, and air transportation operations were to be decentralized. Existing airports were to be upgraded and new ones built.

Railroads

China's first railroad line was built in 1876. In the 73 years that followed, 22,000 kilometers of track were laid, but only half were operable in 1949. Between 1949 and 1985, more than 30,000 kilometers of lines were added to the existing network, mostly in the southwest or coastal areas where previous rail development had been concentrated. By 1984 China had 52,000 kilometers of operating track, 4,000 kilometers of which had been electrified. All provinces, autonomous regions, and special municipalities, with the exception of Xizang Autonomous Region, were linked by rail. Many double-track lines, electric lines, special lines, and railroad bridges were added to the system. Railroad technology also was upgraded to improve the performance of the existing rail network. There still were shortcomings, however. Most of the trunk lines were old, there was a general shortage of double-track lines, and Chinese officials admitted that antiquated management techniques still were being practiced. There were plans in the late 1980s to upgrade the rail system, particularly in east China, in the hope of improving performance.

China's railroads are heavily used. In 1986, the latest year for which statistics were available, railroads carried 1 billion passengers and 1.3 billion tons of cargo. The average freight traffic density was 15 million tons per route-kilometer, double that of the United

States and three times that of India. Turnaround time between freight car loadings averaged less than four days.

Between 1980 and 1985, China built about 3,270 kilometers of new track, converted 1,581 kilometers to double track, and electrified 2,500 kilometers of track. The total investment in this period amounted to over ¥21.4 billion (for value of the yuan—see Glossary). Railroads accounted for over two-thirds of the total ton-kilometers and over half the passenger-kilometers in China's transportation systems. China's longest electrified double-track railroad, running from Beijing to Datong, Shanxi Province, was opened for operation in 1984. One of the world's highest railroads, at 3,000 meters above sea level in Qinghai Province, also went into service in the same year, and improved doubletrack railroads, some of them electrified, offered a fast way to transport coal from Shanxi Province to the highly industrialized eastern part of the country and the port of Qinhuangdao for export.

Production and maintenance of modern locomotives also made an important contribution to increased rail capacity. Manufacturing output in the mid-1980s increased significantly when production of electric and diesel locomotives for the first time exceeded that of steam-powered ones. China hoped, in the long-run, to phase out its steam-powered locomotives. In the mid-1980s China had more than 280,000 freight cars and about 20,000 passenger cars. The country still was unable, however, to meet the transportation needs brought about by rapid economic expansion.

Subways

China's first subways opened to traffic in Beijing in 1970, and Tianjin in 1980, respectively, and subway systems were planned for construction in Harbin, Shanghai, and Guangzhou beginning in the 1980s. In its first phase, the Beijing subway system had 23.6 kilometers of track and 17 stations. In 1984 the second phase of construction added 16.1 kilometers of track and 12 stations, and in 1987 additional track and another station were added to close the loop on a now circular system. In 1987 there were plans to upgrade the signaling system and railcar equipment on seventeen kilometers of the first segment built. The subway carried more than 100 million passengers in 1985, or about 280,000 on an average day and 450,000 on a peak day. In 1987 this accounted for only 4 percent of Beijing's 9 million commuters. The Beijing subway authorities estimated that passenger traffic would increase 20 percent yearly. To accommodate the increase in riders, Beijing planned to construct an extension of a seven-kilometer subway line under Chang'an Boulevard, from Fuxing Gate in the east to Jianguo Gate

Train carrying petroleum products from Maoming, Guangdong Province Courtesy Xinhua News Agency

The Fuchengmen subway station in Beijing Courtesy Jiefangjun Bao

in the west. The Tianjin subway opened a five-kilometer line in 1980. The Shanghai subway was planned to have 14.4 kilometers of track in its first phase.

Highways and Roads

In 1986 China had approximately 962,800 kilometers of highways, 52,000 kilometers of which were completed between 1980 and 1985. During this period China also rebuilt 22,000 kilometers of highways in cities and rural areas. Nearly 110,000 kilometers of roads were designated part of a network of national highways, including roads linking provincial-level capitals with Beijing and China's major ports.

Provincial-level and local governments were responsible for their own transportation and road construction, some with foreign expertise and financing to hasten the process. Most financing and maintenance funds came from the provincial level, supplemented in the case of rural roads by local labor. In line with the increased emphasis on developing light industry and decentralizing agriculture, roads were built in large, medium-sized, and small towns and to railroad connections, making it possible for products to move rapidly between cities and across provincial-level boundaries. In 1986 approximately 780,000 kilometers of the roads, or 81 percent, were surfaced. The remaining 19 percent (fair-weather roads) were in poor condition, hardly passable on rainy days. Only 20 percent of the roads were paved with asphalt; about 80 percent had gravel surfaces. In addition, 60 percent of the major highways needed repair.

China's highways carried 660 million tons of freight and 410 million passengers in 1985. In 1984 the authorities began assigning medium-distance traffic (certain goods and sundries traveling less than 100 kilometers and passengers less than 200 kilometers) to highways to relieve the pressure on railroads. Almost 800 national highways were used for transporting cargo. Joint provincial-level transportation centers were designated to take care of cross-country cargo transportation between provinces, autonomous regions, and special municipalities. A total of about 15,000 scheduled rural buses carried 4.3 million passengers daily, and more than 2,300 national bus services handled a daily average of 450,000 passengers. The number of trucks and buses operated by individuals, collectives, and families reached 130,000 in 1984, about half the number of state-owned vehicles. In 1986 there were 290,000 private motor vehicles in China, 95 percent of which were trucks. Most trucks had a four- to five-ton capacity.

The automobile was becoming an increasingly important mode of transportation in China. The automotive industry gave priority to improving quality and developing new models rather than increasing production. Nevertheless, as a result of the introduction of modern technology through joint ventures with advanced industrialized countries, Chinese automobile production for 1985 surpassed 400,000 units.

Although cars and trucks were the primary means of highway transportation, in the mid-1980s carts pulled by horses, mules, donkeys, cows, oxen, and camels still were common in rural areas. Motor vehicles often were unable to reach efficient travel speeds near towns and cities in rural areas because of the large number of slow-moving tractors, bicycles, hand- and animal-drawn carts, and pedestrians. Strict adherence to relatively low speed limits in some areas also kept travel speeds at inefficient levels.

Bridges

In the late 1980s, China had more than 140,000 highway bridges. Their length totaled almost 4,000 kilometers. Among the best known were the Huang He (Yellow River) Bridge in Nei Monggol Autonomous Region (Inner Mongolia), the Liu Jiang Bridge in Guangxi-Zhuang Autonomous Region, the Ou Jiang Bridge in Zhejiang Province, the Quanzhou Bridge in Fujian Province, and four large bridges along the Guangzhou-Shenzhen highway. Five major bridges—including China's longest highway bridge, the 5,560-meter-long Huang He Bridge at Zhengzhou—were under construction during the mid-1980s, and a 10,282-meter-long railroad bridge across the Huang He on the Shandong-Henan border was completed in 1985.

Inland Waterways

Inland navigation is China's oldest form of transportation (see fig. 16). Despite the potential advantages of water transportation, it was often mismanaged or neglected in the past. Beginning in 1960 the network of navigable inland waterways decreased further because of the construction of dams and irrigation works and the increasing sedimentation. But by the early 1980s, as the railroads became increasingly congested, the authorities came to see water transportation as a much less expensive alternative to new road and railroad construction. The central government set out to overhaul the inefficient inland waterway system and called upon localities to play major roles in managing and financing most of the projects. By 1984 China's longest river, the Chang Jiang, with a total of 70,000 kilometers of waterways open to shipping on its main stream and 3,600 kilometers on its tributaries, became the nation's busiest shipping lane, carrying 72 percent of China's total waterborne traffic. An estimated 340,000 people and 170,000 boats were engaged in the water transportation business. More than 800 shipping enterprises and 60 shipping companies transported over 259 million tons of cargo on the Chang Jiang and its tributaries in 1984. Nationally, in 1985 the inland waterways carried some 434 million tons of cargo. In 1986 there were approximately 138,600 kilometers of inland waterways, 79 percent of which were navigable.

The Cihuai Canal in northern Anhui Province opened to navigation in 1984. This 134-kilometer canal linking the Ying He, a major tributary of the Huai He, with the Huai He's main course, had an annual capacity of 600,000 tons of cargo. The canal promoted the flow of goods between Anhui and neighboring provinces and helped to develop the Huai He Plain, one of China's major grain-producing areas.

Maritime Shipping

During the early 1960s, China's merchant marine had fewer than thirty ships. By the 1970s and 1980s, maritime shipping capabilities had greatly increased. In 1985 China established eleven shipping offices and jointly operated shipping companies in foreign countries. In 1986 China ranked ninth in world shipping with more than 600 ships and a total tonnage of 16 million, including modern roll-on and roll-off ships, container ships, large bulk carriers, refrigerator ships, oil tankers, and multipurpose ships. The fleet called at more than 400 ports in more than 100 countries.

The container ship fleet also was expanding rapidly. In 1984 China had only fifteen container ships. Seven more were added in 1985, and an additional twenty-two were on order. By the early 1980s, Chinese shipyards had begun to manufacture a large number of ships for their own maritime fleet. The China Shipping Inspection Bureau became a member of the Suez Canal Authority in 1984, empowering China to sign and issue seaworthiness certificates for ships on the Suez Canal and confirming the good reputation and maturity of its shipbuilding industry. In 1986 China had 523 shipyards of various sizes, 160 specialized factories, 540,000 employees, and more than 80 scientific research institutes. The main shipbuilding and repairing bases of Shanghai, Dalian, Tianjin, Guangzhou, and Wuhan had 14 berths for 10,000-ton-class ships and 13 docks.

The inadequacy of port and harbor facilities has been a longstanding problem for China but has become a more serious obstacle because of increased foreign trade. Beginning in the 1970s, the authorities gave priority to port construction. From 1972 to 1982, port traffic increased sixfold, largely because of the foreign trade

Figure 16. Principal Improved Inland Waterways, 1987

boom. The imbalance between supply and demand continued to grow. Poor management and limited port facilities created such backups that by 1985 an average of 400 to 500 ships were waiting to enter major Chinese ports on any given day. The July 1985 delay of more than 500 ships, for instance, caused huge losses. All of China's major ports are undergoing some construction. To speed economic development, the Seventh Five-Year Plan called for the construction by 1990 of 200 new berths—120 deep-water berths for ships above 10,000 tons and 80 medium-sized berths for ships below 10,000 tons—bringing the total number of berths to 1,200. Major port facilities were developed all along China's coast.

Civil Aviation

In 1987 China's civil aviation system was operated by the General

Administration of Civil Aviation of China (CAAC). By 1987 China had more than 229,000 kilometers of domestic air routes and more than 94,000 kilometers of international air routes. The more than 9 million passengers and 102,000 tons of freight traffic represented a 40 percent growth over the previous year. The air fleet consisted of about 175 aircraft and smaller turboprop transports. CAAC had 274 air routes, including 33 international flights to 28 cities in 23 countries, such as Tokyo, Osaka, Nagasaki, New York, San Francisco, Los Angeles, London, Paris, Frankfurt, East Berlin, Zurich, Moscow, Istanbul, Manila, Bangkok, Singapore, Sydney, and Hong Kong. Almost 200 domestic air routes connected such major cities as Beijing, Shanghai, Tianjin, Guangzhou, Hangzhou, Kunming, Chengdu, and Xi'an, as well as a number of smaller cities. The government had bilateral air service agreements with more than 40 countries and working relations with approximately 386 foreign airline companies. CAAC also provided air service for agriculture, forestry, communications, and scientific research.

The staff of CAAC was estimated at approximately 50,000 in the 1980s. The administration operated three training colleges to educate future airline personnel. In a bid to improve CAAC's services, more ticket offices were opened in major cities for domestic and international flights.

In the mid-1980s regional airlines began operations under the general aegis of CAAC. Wuhan Airlines, run by the Wuhan municipal authorities, started scheduled passenger flights to Hubei, Hunan, Guangdong, and Sichuan provinces in May 1986. Xizang also planned to set up its own airline to fly to Kathmandu and Hong Kong.

In the 1980s the central government increased its investment in airport construction, and some local governments also granted special funds for such projects. Lhasa Airport in Xizang, Jiamusi Airport in Heilongjiang Province, and Kashi and Yining airports in Xinjiang-Uygur Autonomous Region were expanded, and new airports were under construction in Xi'an, Luoyang, and Shenzhen. An investment of ¥500 million was planned for expanding runways and building new terminals and other airport facilities. In 1986 China had more than ninety civilian airports, of which eight could accommodate Boeing 747s and thirty-two could accommodate Boeing 737s and Tridents.

Postal Services

Postal service is administered by the Ministry of Posts and Telecommunications, which was established in 1949 and reestablished in 1973 after a two-year period during which the postal and telecommunications functions had been separated and the ministry downgraded to a subministerial level. Although postal service in China goes back some 2,500 years, modern postal services were not established until 1877 by the Qing government. Development was slow; by 1949 there was only 1 post office for every 370 square kilometers.

Since then the postal service has grown rapidly. In 1984 China had 53,000 post and telecommunications offices and 5 million kilometers of postal routes, including 240,000 kilometers of railroad postal routes, 624,000 kilometers of highway postal routes, and 230,000 kilometers of airmail routes. By 1985 post offices were handling 4.7 billion first-class letters and 25 billion newspapers and periodicals. In 1987, after a six-year hiatus, six-digit postal codes were ordered to be put into use.

Telecommunications

In 1987 China possessed a diversified telecommunications system that linked all parts of the country by telephone, telegraph, radio, and television. None of the telecommunications forms were as prevalent or as advanced as those in modern Western countries, but the system included some of the most sophisticated technology in the world and constituted a foundation for further development of a modern network.

Historical Development

When the People's Republic was founded in 1949, the telecommunications facilities in China were outdated, and many had been damaged or destroyed during the war years. In the 1950s existing facilities were repaired, and, with Soviet assistance, considerable progress was made toward establishing a long-distance telephone wire network connecting Beijing to provincial-level capitals. In addition, conference telephone service was initiated, radio communications were improved, and the production of telecommunications equipment was accelerated. Growth in telecommunications halted with the general economic collapse after the Great Leap Forward (1958–60) but revived in the 1960s after the telephone network was expanded and improved equipment was introduced, including imports of Western plants. An important component of the Fourth Five-Year Plan (1971–75) was a major development program for the telecommunications system. The program allotted top priority to scarce electronics and construction resources and dramatically improved all aspects of China's telecommunications capabilities. Microwave radio relay lines and buried cable lines were constructed to create a network of wideband carrier trunk lines, which covered the entire country. China was linked to the international telecommunications network by the installation of communications satellite ground stations and the construction of coaxial cables linking Guangdong Province with Hong Kong and Macao. Provincial-level units and municipalities rapidly expanded local telephone and wire broadcasting networks. Expansion and modernization of the telecommunications system continued throughout the late 1970s and early 1980s, giving particular emphasis to the production of radio and television sets and expanded broadcasting capabilities.

Telecommunications Services

In 1987 the Ministry of Posts and Telecommunications administered China's telecommunications systems and related research and production facilities. Besides postal services, some of which were handled by electronic means, the ministry was involved in a wide spectrum of telephone, wire, telegraph, and international communications (see Postal Services, this ch.). The Ministry of Radio and Television was established as a separate entity in 1982 to administer and upgrade the status of television and radio broadcasting. Subordinate to this ministry were the Central People's Broadcasting Station, Radio Beijing, and China Central Television. Additionally, the various broadcasting training, talent-search, research, publishing, and manufacturing organizations were brought under the control of the Ministry of Radio and Television. In 1986 responsibility for the movie industry was transferred from the Ministry of Culture to the new Ministry of Radio, Cinema, and Television (see Contemporary Performing Arts, ch. 4). The Chinese Communist Party's Propaganda Department coordinates the work of both telecommunications-related ministries.

As of 1987 the quality of telecommunications services in China had improved markedly over earlier years. A considerable influx of foreign technology and increased domestic production capabilities had a major impact in the post-Mao period.

The primary form of telecommunications in the 1980s was local and long-distance telephone service administered by six regional bureaus: Beijing (north region), Shanghai (east region), Xi'an (northwest region), Chengdu (southwest region), Wuhan (central-south region), and Shenyang (northeast region). These regional headquarters served as switching centers for provincial-level subsystems. By 1986 China had nearly 3 million telephone exchange lines, including 34,000 long-distance exchange lines with direct, automatic service to 24 cities. By late 1986 fiber optic communications technology was being employed to relieve the strain on

Chengdu Airport in Sichuan Province, a major air traffic center
Courtesy Sichuan People's Publishing House

existing telephone circuits. International service was routed through overseas exchanges located in Beijing and Shanghai. Guangdong Province had coaxial cable and microwave lines linking it to Hong Kong and Macao.

The large, continuously upgraded satellite ground stations, originally installed in 1972 to provide live coverage of the visits to China by U.S. president Richard M. Nixon and Japanese prime minister Kakuei Tanaka, still served as the base for China's international satellite communications network in the mid-1980s. By 1977 China had joined Intelsat and, using ground stations in Beijing and Shanghai, had linked up with satellites over the Indian and Pacific oceans.

In April 1984 China launched an experimental communications satellite for trial transmission of broadcasts, telegrams, telephone calls, and facsimile, probably to remote areas of the country. In February 1986 China launched its first fully operational telecommunications and broadcast satellite. The quality and communications capacity of the second satellite reportedly was much greater than the first. In mid-1987 both satellites were still functioning. With these satellites in place China's domestic satellite communication network went into operation, facilitating television and radio transmissions and providing direct-dial long-distance telephone, telegraph, and facsimile service. The network had ground stations in Beijing, Ürümqi, Hohhot, Lhasa, and Guangzhou, which also were linked to an Intelsat satellite over the Indian Ocean.

Telegraph development received lower priority than the telephone network largely because of the difficulties involved in transmitting the written Chinese language. Computer technology gradually alleviated these problems and facilitated further growth in this area. By 1983 China had nearly 10,000 telegraph cables and telex lines transmitting over 170 million messages annually. Most telegrams were transmitted by cables or by shortwave radio. Cut-microwave transmission also was used. Teletype transmission was used for messages at the international level, but some 40 percent of county and municipal telegrams still were transmitted by Morse code.

Apart from traditional telegraph and telephone services, China also had facsimile, low-speed data-transmission, and computer-controlled telecommunications services. These included on-line information retrieval terminals in Beijing, Changsha, and Baotou that enabled international telecommunications networks to retrieve news and scientific, technical, economic, and cultural information from international sources.

High-speed newspaper-page-facsimile equipment and Chinese-character-code translation equipment were used on a large scale. Sixty-four-channel program-controlled automatic message retransmission equipment and low-or medium-speed data transmission and exchange equipment also received extensive use. International telex service was available in coastal cities and special economic zones.

The Central People's Broadcasting Station controlled China's national radio network. Programming was administered by the provincial-level units. The station produced general news and cultural and educational programs. It also provided programs for minority groups in the Korean, Manchurian, Zang (Tibetan), Uygur, and Kazak languages, as well as programs directed toward Taiwan and overseas Chinese (see Glossary) listeners. Radio Beijing broadcast to the world in thirty-eight foreign languages, *putonghua* (see Glossary), and various dialects, including Amoy, Cantonese, and Hakka. It also provided English-language news programs aimed at foreign residents in Beijing. Medium-wave, shortwave, and FM stations reached 80 percent of the country—over 160 radio stations and 500 relay and transmission stations—with some 240 radio programs.

The nationwide network of wire lines and loudspeakers transmitted radio programs into virtually all rural communities and many urban areas. By 1984 there were over 2,600 wired broadcasting stations, extending radio transmissions to rural areas outside the range of regular broadcasting stations.

In 1987 China Central Television (CCTV), the state network, managed China's television programs. In 1985 consumers purchased 15 million new sets, including approximately 4 million color sets. Production fell far short of demand. Because Chinese viewers often gathered in large groups to watch publicly owned sets, authorities estimated that two-thirds of the nation had access to

A satellite dish and radio relay tower used in communications with remote areas of China
Courtesy China Transport

television. In 1987 there were about 70 million television sets, an average of 29 sets per 100 families. CCTV had four channels that supplied programs to the over ninety television stations throughout the country. Construction began on a major new CCTV studio in Beijing in 1985. CCTV produced its own programs, a large portion of which were educational, and the Television University in Beijing produced three educational programs weekly. The English-language lesson was the most popular program and had an estimated 5 to 6 million viewers. Other programs included daily news, entertainment, teleplays, and special programs. Foreign programs included films and cartoons. Chinese viewers were particularly interested in watching international news, sports, and drama (see Contemporary Performing Arts, ch. 4; The Media, ch. 10).

* * *

Descriptions of the evolving domestic and foreign trade systems are found in a variety of periodicals, including *China Daily*, *Far Eastern Economic Review*, *Asiaweek*, *China Trade Report*, *China Business Review*, and *Beijing Review*. Jean C. Oi's ''Peasant Grain Marketing and State Procurement: China's Grain Contracting System'' provides a good description of grain procurement and marketing. Useful articles on foreign trade are ''China's International Trade: Policy and Organizational Change and Their Place in the

'Economic Readjustment' " by Y.Y. Kueh and Christopher Howe and "Understanding Chinese Trade" by John Frankenstein. Valuable analyses of China's economic reforms and their impact on domestic and foreign trade appear in both volumes of the 1986 United States Congress Joint Economic Committee's *China's Economy Looks Toward the Year 2000* and in *China's Economy and Foreign Trade, 1981-85* by Nai-Ruenn Chen and Jeffrey Lee.

Transportation and telecommunications developments are described in the periodicals *China Transport* and *China Business Review*. (For further information and complete citations, see Bibliography.)

Chapter 9. Science and Technology

This glazed earthenware funerary object from the Eastern Han dynasty (A.D. 25–220) shows some of the intricacies of Chinese architecture of the era.

IN A SPEECH to the National Science Conference in March 1978, then-Vice Premier Deng Xiaoping declared: "The crux of the Four Modernizations is the mastery of modern science and technology. Without the high-speed development of science and technology, it is impossible to develop the national economy at a high speed." For more than a century China's leaders have called for rapid development of science and technology, and science policy has played a greater role in national politics in China than in many other countries. China's scientific and technical achievements are impressive in many fields. Although the World Bank classified it in the 1980s as a low-income, developing country, China has by its own efforts developed nuclear weapons, the ability to launch and recover satellites, a supercomputer, and high-yield hybrid rice. But the development of science and technology has been uneven, and significant achievements in some fields are matched by low levels in others.

The evolving structure of science and technology and frequent reversals of policy under the People's Republic have combined to give Chinese science a distinctive character. The variation in quality and achievements stems in part from a large and poorly educated rural populace and limited opportunities for secondary and college education—conditions common to all developing countries. The character of Chinese science also reflects concentration of resources in a few key fields and institutions, often with military applications. In more politically radical periods—such as the Great Leap Forward (1958–60) and the Cultural Revolution (1966–76)—efforts were made to expand the ranks of scientists and technicians by sharply reducing education and certification standards.

China's leaders have involved themselves in the formulation of science policy to a greater extent than have the leaders of most countries. Science policy also has played a significant part in the struggles between contending leaders, who have often acted as patrons to different sectors of the scientific establishment. Party leaders, not themselves scientifically trained, have taken science and scientists quite seriously, seeing them as keys to economic development and national strength. Party efforts to control science to "serve production" and generate economic and military payoffs, however, have met with repeated frustrations. The frustration in turn has contributed to frequent reversals of policy and has exacerbated the inherent tension between the scientific and political elites over the goals and control of the nation's science and technology. In any economic system there are likely to be tensions and divergences of interest between managers and scientists, but in China such tensions have been extreme and have led to repeated episodes of persecution of scientists and intellectuals. Science in China has been marked by uneven development, wide variation in quality of work, high level of involvement with politics, and high degree of policy discontinuity.

In the post-Mao era, the anti-intellectual policies of the Cultural Revolution have been reversed, and such top leaders as Deng Xiaoping have encouraged the development of science. But China's leaders in the 1980s remained, like their predecessors over the past 100 years, interested in science primarily as a means to national strength and economic growth. The policy makers' goal was the creation of a vigorous scientific and technical establishment that operates at the level of developed countries while contributing in a fairly direct way to agriculture, industry, and defense. The mid-1980s saw a major effort to reform the scientific and technical system through a range of institutional changes intended to promote the application of scientific knowledge to production. As in the past 100 years, policy makers and scientists grappled with such issues as the proportion of basic to applied research, the priorities of various fields of research, the limits of professional and academic freedom, and the best mechanisms for promoting industrial innovation and widespread assimilation of up-to-date technology.

Historical Development of Science and Technology Policy

Pre-1949 Patterns

Until the Ming dynasty (1368–1644), China was a world leader in technology and scientific discovery. Many Chinese inventions—paper and printing, gunpowder, porcelain, the magnetic compass, the sternpost rudder, and the lift lock for canals—made major contributions to economic growth in the Middle East and Europe. The outside world remained uninformed about Chinese work in agronomy, pharmacology, mathematics, and optics. Scientific and technological activity in China dwindled, however, after the fourteenth century. It became increasingly confined to little-known and marginal individuals who differed from Western scientists such as Galileo or Newton in two primary ways: they did not attempt to reduce the regularities of nature to mathematical form, and they did not constitute a community of scholars, criticizing each others' work and contributing to an ongoing program of research. Under the last two dynasties, the Ming (1368–1644) and the Qing

(1644–1911), China's ruling elite intensified its humanistic concentration on literature, the arts, and public administration and regarded science and technology as either trivial or narrowly utilitarian (see The Confucian Legacy, ch. 3).

Foreign Learning and Chinese Learning

Western mathematics and science were introduced to China in the seventeenth and eighteenth centuries by Jesuit missionaries but had little impact. In the nineteenth century, the trauma of repeated defeat at the hands of Western invaders (in 1840–41 and 1860) finally convinced some Chinese leaders of the need to master foreign military technology. As part of the Self-Strengthening Movement in the 1860s, a number of foreign-style arsenals, shipyards, and associated training schools were established (see The Self-Strengthening Movement, ch. 1). The initial effort to produce steamships and artillery led, step-by-step, to recognition of the need to master metallurgy, chemistry, mathematics, physics, and foreign languages. The last decades of the century saw the establishment, under the auspices either of the imperial government or of foreign missionaries, of secondary schools and colleges teaching science, as well as the movement of Chinese students to advanced studies in Japan, the United States, and Europe.

Individual Chinese students had no great difficulty mastering Western science, but the growth in their numbers and potential influence posed a challenge to the Confucian scholar-officials who dominated the imperial government and Chinese society. Such officials were reluctant to grant foreign-trained scientists and engineers a status equal to that of Confucian scholars, and they were suspicious of foreign ideas about politics and social organization, such as professional autonomy, freedom of speech and assembly, and experiments rather than written texts as validation of propositions. Nineteenth-century officials attempted to control the influx of foreign knowledge and values, distinguishing militarily useful technology, which was to be imported and assimilated, from foreign philosophy, religion, or political and social values, which were to be rejected. The slogan "Chinese learning for the essence, Western learning for utility" expressed this attitude. Although the terms were no longer used, the fundamental issue remained significant in the 1980s, as the Chinese Communist Party attempted to distinguish between beneficial foreign technology and harmful and "polluting" foreign ideas and practices. Throughout the twentieth century, China's political leaders have had a deeply ambivalent attitude toward science and technology, promoting it as necessary for national defense and national strength but fearing it as a carrier of threatening alien ideas and practices.

By 1900 China's science and technology establishment, minimal though it was, already manifested several features that would characterize it throughout the twentieth century. Although China's early scientific achievements were a source of national pride, they had no direct influence on the practice and teaching of science in China, which was based on foreign models and foreign training. As a group, China's scientists, with their foreign education, foreign-language competence, and exposure to foreign ideas of science as an autonomous, international, and professional activity, formed the most cosmopolitan element of the population. China's scientists, more than their foreign counterparts, were motivated by patriotism and the desire to help their country through their work, and many deliberately chose applied over basic scientific work. Chinese intellectuals were influenced by the Confucian teachings that intellectuals had special responsibilities toward their society and should play a role in public affairs. Much scientific work was done under government patronage, direction, and funding. The government, whether imperial or republican, was interested in science for what it could contribute to national development and military power, and it saw science as a means rather than as an end in itself. The first major publisher of translations of scientific works was the Jiangnan Arsenal, founded in Shanghai in 1866, which published nearly 200 basic and applied scientific texts originally written in English, French, or German.

In the first two decades of the twentieth century an increasing number of colleges and universities were founded, and growing numbers of Chinese students were educated abroad. The Science Society of China, whose membership included most of the country's leading scientists and engineers, was founded by Chinese students at Cornell University in 1914. In 1915 it began publication in China of a major journal, *Kexue* (Science), which was patterned on the journal of the American Association for the Advancement of Science. In 1922 the Society established a major biological research laboratory in Nanjing. The Society devoted itself to the popularization of science through an active and diverse publication program, the improvement of science education, and participation in international scientific meetings.

The establishment of the Guomindang government at Nanjing in 1927 was followed by the creation of several government research and training institutions (see Republican China, ch. 1). The Academia Sinica, founded in 1928, had a dozen research institutes, whose personnel did research and advised the government. The late 1920s and early 1930s saw the establishment of many research institutes, such as the Fan Memorial Biological Institute in Beijing and the Beijing Research Laboratory, which eventually formed departments in physics, biology, pharmacology, and other fields. Most of the research institutes were characterized both by very limited funds and personnel and by productive, high-quality scientific work. By the 1930s China possessed a number of foreign-trained scientists who did research of high quality, which they published in both Chinese and foreign scientific journals. These scientists worked in the major universities or in research institutes funded by the government or foreign organizations (such as missionary groups and the Rockefeller Foundation) and were concentrated in Beijing, Nanjing, and Shanghai.

Between 1937 and 1949, China's scientists and scientific work suffered the ravages of invasion, civil war, and runaway inflation. Funds to support research, never ample, almost totally disappeared, and most scientists were forced to devote most of their energies to teaching, administration, or a government job. In a change from the earlier pattern, many students opted not to return to China after foreign education, choosing instead to seek careers abroad.

Soviet Influence in the 1950s

After the establishment of the People's Republic in 1949, China reorganized its science establishment along Soviet lines—a system that remained in force until the late 1970s, when China's leaders called for major reforms. The Soviet model is characterized by a bureaucratic rather than a professional principle of organization, the separation of research from production, the establishment of a set of specialized research institutes, and a high priority on applied science and technology, which includes military technology.

The government's view of the purpose of scientific work was set forth in the September 1949 Common Program of the Chinese People's Political Consultative Conference (see Glossary), which stated, "Efforts should be made to develop the natural sciences in order to serve the construction of industry, agriculture, and the national defense." On November 1, 1949, the Chinese Academy of Sciences was founded, amalgamating research institutes under the former Academia Sinica and Beijing Research Academy (the former Beijing Research Laboratory). In March 1951 the government directed the academy to determine the requirements of the production sector of the economy and to adjust scientific research to meet those requirements. Scientists were to engage in research with significant and fairly immediate benefits to society and to work as members of collectives rather than as individuals seeking personal fame and recognition.

The Chinese Academy of Sciences was explicitly modeled on the Soviet Academy of Sciences, whose director, Sergei I. Vavilov, was consulted on the proper way to reorganize Chinese science. His book *Thirty Years of Soviet Science* was translated into Chinese to serve as a guide. Soviet influence also was realized through large-scale personnel exchanges. During the 1950s China sent about 38,000 people to the Soviet Union for training and study. Most of these (28,000) were technicians from key industries, but the total cohort included 7,500 students and 2,500 college and university teachers and postgraduate scientists. The Soviet Union dispatched some 11,000 scientific and technical aid personnel to China. An estimated 850 of these worked in the scientific research sector, about 1,000 in education and public health, and the rest in heavy industry. In 1954 China and the Soviet Union set up the Joint Commission for Cooperation in Science and Technology, which met annually until 1963 and arranged cooperation on over 100 major scientific projects, including those in nuclear science. When the Chinese Academy of Sciences completed a draft twelve-year plan for scientific development in 1956, it was referred to the Soviet Academy of Sciences for review. In October 1957 a high-level delegation of Chinese scientists accompanied Mao Zedong to Moscow to negotiate an agreement for Soviet cooperation on 100 of the 582 research projects outlined in the twelve-year plan.

The Soviet aid program of the 1950s was intended to develop China's economy and to organize it along Soviet lines. As part of its First Five-Year Plan (1953–57), China was the recipient of the most comprehensive technology transfer in modern industrial history. The Soviet Union provided aid for 156 major industrial projects concentrated in mining, power generation, and heavy industry. Following the Soviet model of economic development, these were large-scale, capital-intensive projects. By the late 1950s, China had made substantial progress in such fields as electric power, steel production, basic chemicals, and machine tools, as well as in production of military equipment such as artillery, tanks, and jet aircraft. The purpose of the program was to increase China's production of such basic commodities as coal and steel and to teach Chinese workers to operate imported or duplicated Soviet factories. These goals were met and, as a side effect, Soviet standards for materials, engineering practice, and factory management were adopted. In a move whose full costs would not become apparent for twenty-five years, Chinese industry also adopted the Soviet separation of research from production.

The adoption of the Soviet model meant that the organization of Chinese science was based on bureaucratic rather than professional principles. Under the bureaucratic model, leadership is in the hands of nonscientists, who assign research tasks in accordance with a centrally determined plan. The administrators, not the scientists, control recruitment and personnel mobility. The primary rewards are administratively controlled salary increases, bonuses, and prizes. Individual scientists, seen as skilled workers and as employees of their institutions, are expected to work as components of collective units. Information is controlled, is expected to flow only through authorized channels, and is often considered proprietary or secret. Scientific achievements are regarded as the result primarily of ''external'' factors such as the overall economic and political structure of the society, the sheer numbers of personnel, and adequate levels of funding. Under professional principles, which predominate in Western countries, scientists regard themselves as members of an international professional community that recruits and rewards its members according to its own standards of professional excellence. The primary reward is recognition by professional peers, and scientists participate in an elaborate network of communication, which includes published articles, grant proposals, conferences, and news of current and planned research carried by scientists who circulate from one research center to another.

"Reds" Versus "Experts" in the 1950s and 1960s

Tensions between scientists and China's communist rulers existed from the earliest days of the People's Republic and reached their height during the Cultural Revolution (see The Cultural Revolution Decade, 1966–76, ch. 1). In the early 1950s, Chinese scientists, like other intellectuals, were subjected to regular indoctrination intended to replace bourgeois attitudes with those more suitable to the new society. Many attributes of the professional organization of science, such as its assumption of autonomy in choice of research topics, its internationalism, and its orientation toward professional peer groups rather than administrative authorities, were condemned as bourgeois. Those scientists who used the brief period of free expression in the Hundred Flowers Campaign of 1956–57 (see Glossary)—to air complaints of excessive time taken from scientific work by political meetings and rallies or of the harmful effects of attempts by poorly educated party cadres to direct scientific work—were criticized for their ''antiparty'' stance, labeled as ''rightists,'' and sometimes dismissed from administrative or academic positions (see The Transition to Socialism, 1953–57, ch. 1).

The terminology of the period distinguished between "red" and "expert" (see Glossary). Although party leaders spoke of the need to combine "redness" with expertise, they more often acted as if political rectitude and professional skill were mutually exclusive qualities. The period of the Great Leap Forward saw efforts to reassign scientists to immediately useful projects, to involve the uneducated masses in such research work as plant breeding or pest control, and to expand rapidly the ranks of scientific and technical personnel by lowering professional standards. The economic depression and famine following the Great Leap Forward, and the need to compensate for the sudden withdrawal of Soviet advisers and technical personnel in 1960, brought a renewed but short-lived emphasis on expertise and professional standards in the early 1960s. The scientific establishment was attacked during the Cultural Revolution, causing major damage to China's science and technology. Most scientific research ceased. In extreme cases, individual scientists were singled out as "counterrevolutionaries" and made the objects of public criticism and persecution, and the research work of whole institutes was brought to a halt for years on end. The entire staffs of research institutes commonly were dispatched to the countryside for months or years to learn political virtue by laboring with the poor and lower-middle peasants. Work in the military research units devoted to nuclear weapons and missiles presumably continued, although the secrecy surrounding strategic weapons research makes it difficult to assess the impact of the Cultural Revolution in that sector.

In the most general sense, the Cultural Revolution represented the triumph of anti-intellectualism and the consistent, decade-long deprecation of scholarship, formal education, and all the qualities associated with professionalism in science. Intellectuals were assumed to be inherently counterrevolutionary, and it was asserted that their characteristic attitudes and practices were necessarily opposed to the interests of the masses. Universities were closed from the summer of 1966 through 1970, when they reopened for undergraduate training with very reduced enrollments and a heavy emphasis on political training and manual labor. Students were selected for political rectitude rather than academic talent. Primary and secondary schools were closed in 1966 and 1967, and when reopened were repeatedly disrupted by political struggle. All scientific journals ceased publication in 1966, and subscriptions to foreign journals lapsed or were canceled. For most of a decade China trained no new scientists or engineers and was cut off from foreign scientific developments.

During the decade between 1966 and 1976, China's leaders attempted to create a new structure for science and technology

China's HL-1 controlled-nuclear fusion experimental device
Courtesy Xinhua News Agency

characterized by mass participation, concentration on immediate practical problems in agriculture and industry, and eradication of distinctions between scientists and workers. Ideologues saw research as an inherently political activity and interpreted all aspects of scientific work, from choice of topic to methods of investigation, as evidence of an underlying political line. According to this view, research served the interests of one social class or another and required the guidance of the party to ensure that it served the interest of the masses.

The early 1970s were characterized by mass experimentation, in which large numbers of peasants were mobilized to collect data and encouraged to view themselves as doing scientific research. Typical projects included collecting information on new crop varieties, studying the effectiveness of locally produced insecticides, and making extensive geological surveys aimed at finding useful minerals or fossil fuels. Mao Zedong took a personal interest in earthquake prediction, which became a showcase of Cultural Revolution-style science. Geologists went to the countryside to collect folk wisdom on precursors of earthquakes, and networks of thousands of observers were established to monitor such signs as the level of water in wells or the unusual behavior of domestic animals. The emphasis in this activity, as in acupuncture anesthesia, was on immediate practical benefits, and little effort was made to integrate the phenomena observed into larger theoretical frameworks.

The effects of the extreme emphasis on short-term problems and the deprecation of theory were noted by Western scientists who visited China in the mid- and late 1970s. For example, work in research institutes affiliated with the petrochemical industry was described as excessively characterized by trial and error. In one case, large numbers of substances were tried as catalysts or modifiers of the wax crystals in crude oil, and little attention was given to the underlying chemical properties of the catalytic or modifying agents.

Rehabilitation and Rethinking, 1977–84

The Cultural Revolution's attacks on science and its deprecation of expertise were opposed by those within the government and party who were more concerned with economic development than with revolutionary purity. In the early 1970s, Premier Zhou Enlai and his associate Deng Xiaoping attempted to improve the working conditions of scientists and to promote research. At the January 1975 session of the Fourth National People's Congress, Zhou Enlai defined China's goal for the rest of the century as the Four Modernizations (see Glossary), that is, modernization of agriculture, industry, science and technology, and national defense. Although the policies proposed in the speech had little immediate effect, they were to become the basic guide for the post-Mao period. In 1975 Deng Xiaoping, then vice chairman of the Chinese Communist Party, vice premier of the government, and Zhou Enlai's political heir, acted as patron and spokesman for China's scientists (see Constitutional Framework, ch. 10). Under Deng's direction, three major policy documents—on science and technology, industry, and foreign trade—were drafted. Intended to promote economic growth, they called for rehabilitating scientists and experts, reimposing strict academic standards in education, and importing foreign technology. The proposals for reversing most of the Cultural Revolution policies toward scientists and intellectuals were denounced by the ideologues and followers of the Gang of Four (see Glossary) as "poisonous weeds." Zhou died in January 1976, and Deng was dismissed from all his posts in April. Deng's stress on the priority of scientific and technical development was condemned by the radicals as "taking the capitalist road." This dispute demonstrated the central place of science policy in modern Chinese politics and the link between science policies and the political fortunes of individual leaders.

Some of the immediate consequences of Mao's death and the subsequent overthrow of the Gang of Four in October 1976 were the reversals of science and education policies (see The Post-Mao Period, 1976–78, ch. 1). During 1977 the more vocal supporters of the Gang of Four were removed from positions of authority in research institutes and universities and replaced with professionally qualified scientists and intellectuals. Academic and research institutions that had been closed were reopened, and scientists were summoned back to their laboratories from manual labor in the countryside. Scientific journals resumed publication, often carrying reports of research completed before everything stopped in the summer of 1966. The media devoted much attention to the value of science and the admirable qualities of scientists. It denounced the repressive and anti-intellectual policies of the deposed Gang of Four, who were blamed for the failure of China's science and technology to match advanced international levels. The news media now characterized scientists and technicians as part of society's "productive forces" and as "workers" rather than as potential counterrevolutionaries or bourgeois experts divorced from the masses. Considerable publicity went to the admission or readmission of scientists to party membership.

The March 1978 National Science Conference in Beijing was a milestone in science policy. The conference, called by the party Central Committee, was attended by many of China's top leaders, as well as by 6,000 scientists and science administrators. Its main purpose was to announce publicly the government and party policy of encouragement and support of science and technology. Science and technology were assigned a key role in China's "New Long March" toward the creation of a modern socialist society by the year 2000. A major speech by Deng Xiaoping reiterated the concept of science as a productive force and scientists as workers, an ideological formulation intended to remove the grounds for the political victimization of scientists. Speeches by then-Premier Hua Guofeng and Vice Premier Fang Yi, the top government figure involved in science and technology, urged that scientists be given free rein in carrying out research as long as the work was in line with broad national priorities. Basic research was to be supported, although stress would continue to be placed on applied work, and China's scientists would be given wide access to foreign knowledge through greatly expanded international scientific and technical exchanges.

By 1978 substantial progress had been made toward restoring the science and technology establishment to its pre-Cultural Revolution state. Leaders with special responsibility for science and technology joined recently rehabilitated senior scientists in looking ahead and framing sweeping and very ambitious plans for further development. The draft Eight-Year Plan for the Development of Science and Technology, discussed at the 1978 National Science Conference, called for a rapid increase in the number of research workers, for catching up to advanced international levels by the mid-1980s, and for substantial work in such fields as lasers, manned space flight, and high-energy physics. For some scientists, and perhaps for their political sponsors as well, mastering technologies and developing Chinese capabilities in the most advanced areas of science were goals in themselves, regardless of the costs or of the likely benefits to the peasants and workers.

Both political leaders and media personnel seemed captivated by the vision of rapid economic growth and social transformation made possible by the wonders of science. Further, many leaders, not themselves scientifically trained, tended toward unrealistic expectations of the immediate benefits from research. This attitude, while different from the hostility to science exhibited during the Cultural Revolution, was based on a misunderstanding of the nature of scientific work and was therefore a poor foundation for science policy.

The plans for rapid advance in many scientific areas were associated with equally ambitious calls for economic growth and the large-scale import of complete factories. During 1979 it became

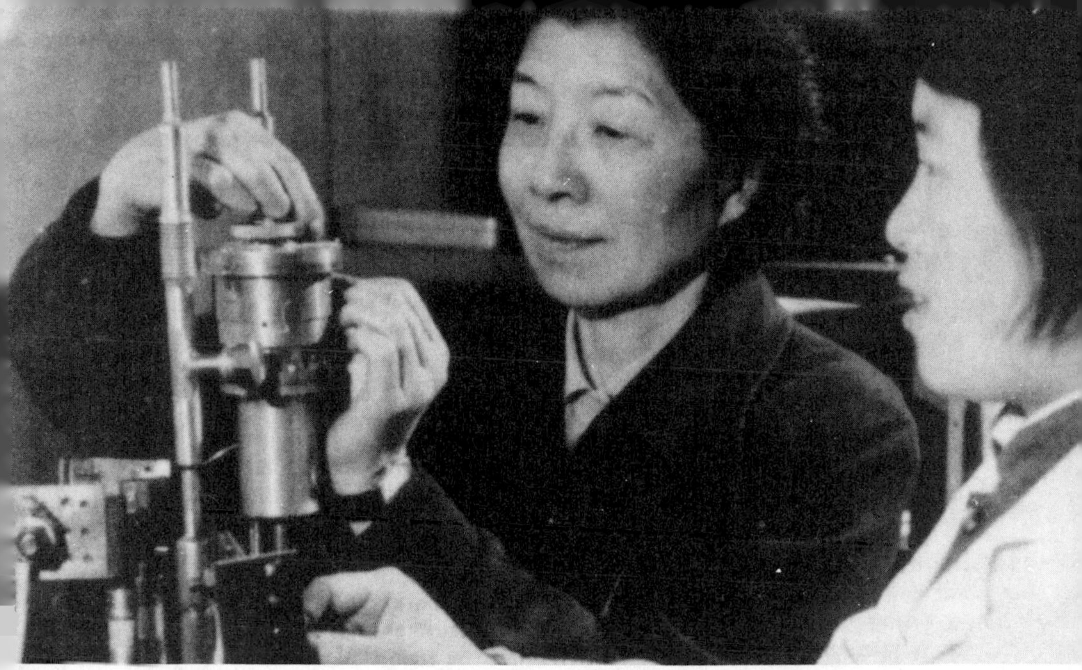

Physicists at the Chinese Academy of Sciences work on superconducting materials. Courtesy China Reconstructs

increasingly clear that China could not pay for all the imports or scientific projects wanted by all the ministries, regional authorities, and research institutes. It also became increasingly evident that those promoting the projects had overlooked financial constraints and severe shortages of scientific and technical manpower and that they lacked a comprehensive plan. In February 1981 a report of the State Science and Technology Commission reversed the overly ambitious 1978 eight-year scientific development plan and called for renewed emphasis on the application of science to practical problems and on training more scientists and engineers.

As scientists and administrators confronted the problems of applying and linking research with development, they became aware of the constraints of the existing system and of the extent to which the endemic difficulties in applying scientific knowledge were consequences of the Soviet-style structure for science and industry that China had uncritically adopted in the 1950s. Attention shifted to reforming the existing system and promoting greater efficiency and better use of scarce resources, such as trained manpower. Between 1981 and 1985, a number of new journals discussed China's scientific system and suggested improvements, while national and local administrators sponsored a wide range of experimental reforms and reorganizations of research bodies. The extensive discussion and experimentation culminated in a March 1985 decision of the party Central Committee calling for thorough reform of China's science system (see The Reform Program, this ch.).

Science and Technology in the 1980s

The Supply of Skilled Manpower

Research and development is a labor-intensive endeavor, in which the critical resource is the size and quality of the pool of trained manpower. China suffers both from an absolute shortage of scientists, engineers, and technicians and from maldistribution and misuse of those it has. Chinese statistics on the number and distribution of scientific personnel are neither complete nor consistent. According to the State Statistical Bureau, at the end of 1986 there were some 8.2 million personnel (out of 127.7 million workers) in the natural sciences working in state-owned enterprises, research institutes, and government offices. These numbers probably excluded military personnel and scientists in military research bodies, but they included support personnel in research institutes. "Scientific and technical personnel" comprised about 1.5 percent of all employed persons, but only about 350,000 of them were "research personnel." Their number had increased markedly from the 1970s as well-trained students began graduating from Chinese colleges and universities in substantial numbers and as postgraduates began returning from advanced training in foreign countries. Between 1979 and 1986, China sent over 35,000 students abroad, 23,000 of whom went to the United States.

More significant than sheer numbers of scientific personnel were their quality and distribution. The total numbers masked wide variations in educational background and quality, lumping together graduates of two-year institutions or those who had attended secondary or postsecondary schools during periods of low standards with those who had graduated from major institutions in the early 1960s or the 1980s, that is, before or after the period of the Cultural Revolution. The Cultural Revolution had removed an entire generation from access to university and professional training, creating a gap in the age distribution of the scientific work force. The scientific community included a small number of elderly senior scientists, often trained abroad before 1949, a relatively small group of middle-aged personnel, and a large number of junior scientists who had graduated from Chinese universities after 1980 or returned from study abroad. In the mid-1980s many of the middle-aged, middle-rank scientists had low educational and professional attainments, but generally they could be neither dismissed nor retired (because of China's practice of secure lifetime employment); nor could they be retrained, as colleges and universities allocated scarce places to younger people with much better qualifications. Scientists and engineers were concentrated in specialized research institutes, in heavy industry, and in the state's military research and military industrial facilities, which had the highest standards and the best-trained people. A very small proportion of scientists and engineers worked in light industry, consumer industry, small-scale collective enterprises, and small towns and rural areas.

Research Institutes

In the late 1980s, most Chinese researchers worked in specialized research institutes rather than in academic or industrial enterprises. The research institutes, of which there were about 10,000 in 1985, were, like their Soviet exemplars, directed and funded by various central and regional government bodies. Their research tasks were, in theory, assigned by higher administrative levels as part of an overall research plan; the research plan was, in theory, coordinated with an overall economic plan. Research institutes were the basic units for the conduct of research and the employment of scientists, who were assigned to institutes by government personnel bureaus. Scientists usually spent their entire working careers within the same institute. Research institutes functioned as ordinary Chinese work units, with the usual features of lifetime employment, unit control of rewards and scarce goods, and limited contact with other units not in the same chain of command (see Work Units, ch. 3). Each research institute attempted to provide its own staff housing, transportation, laboratory space, and instruments and to stockpile equipment and personnel. The limited channels for exchanges of information with other institutes often led to duplication or repetition of research.

National Organization and Administration

The research institutes belonged to larger systems or hierarchies, defined by the administrative bodies that directed and funded their subordinate institutes. Research institutes were grouped into five major subsystems, known in China as the "five main forces" (see fig. 17). The five subsystems were administratively distinct and had little contact or communication.

Chinese Academy of Sciences

In the late 1980s, the Chinese Academy of Sciences remained the most prestigious research agency in the natural sciences. It administered about 120 research institutes in various parts of China, with major concentrations in Beijing and Shanghai. In 1986 the academy employed 80,000 persons, over 40,000 of whom were scientific personnel. It also operated the elite Chinese University of Science and Technology, located in Hefei, Anhui Province, as well as its own printing plant and scientific instrument factory. Its institutes concentrated on basic research in many fields and did research (such as that on superconductor materials) that met international standards. The Chinese Academy of Sciences institutes employed China's best-qualified civilian scientists and had better laboratories, equipment, and libraries than institutes in the other four research systems. The academy's concentration on basic research was intended to be complemented by the work of the more numerous institutes affiliated with industrial ministries or local governments, which focused on applied research.

Although nominally subordinate to the State Science and Technology Commission, the Chinese Academy of Sciences in practice reported directly to the State Council (see The State Council, ch. 10). Before 1956 the academy was directly responsible for overall science planning, and in 1987 it retained a fairly high degree of institutional autonomy and influence on national science policy. The academy provided expert advice, when asked, to the State Council and its ministries, commissions, and agencies. Its specialized research institutes also did work for the military research and development program. Additionally, it had responsibility for multidisciplinary research, monitoring the level of technology in Chinese industries and suggesting areas where foreign technology should be purchased. During the 1980s the academy repeatedly was asked to pay more attention to the needs of production and the application of knowledge.

The membership of the Chinese Academy of Sciences included the nation's most senior and best-known scientists, some of whom had long-standing personal ties with senior political leaders. Such ties and the prestige of the academy helped it win favorable treatment in the state budgetary process and operate with relatively little outside interference. Its relatively privileged position generated resentment among those working in less well-funded institutes under the industrial ministries, whose workers—as well as some planners in the state administration—reportedly considered the academy both overfunded and overstaffed with theoreticians who contributed little to the national economy.

State Science and Technology Commission

The State Science and Technology Commission, a ministerial-level organ of the State Council, had responsibility for overseeing

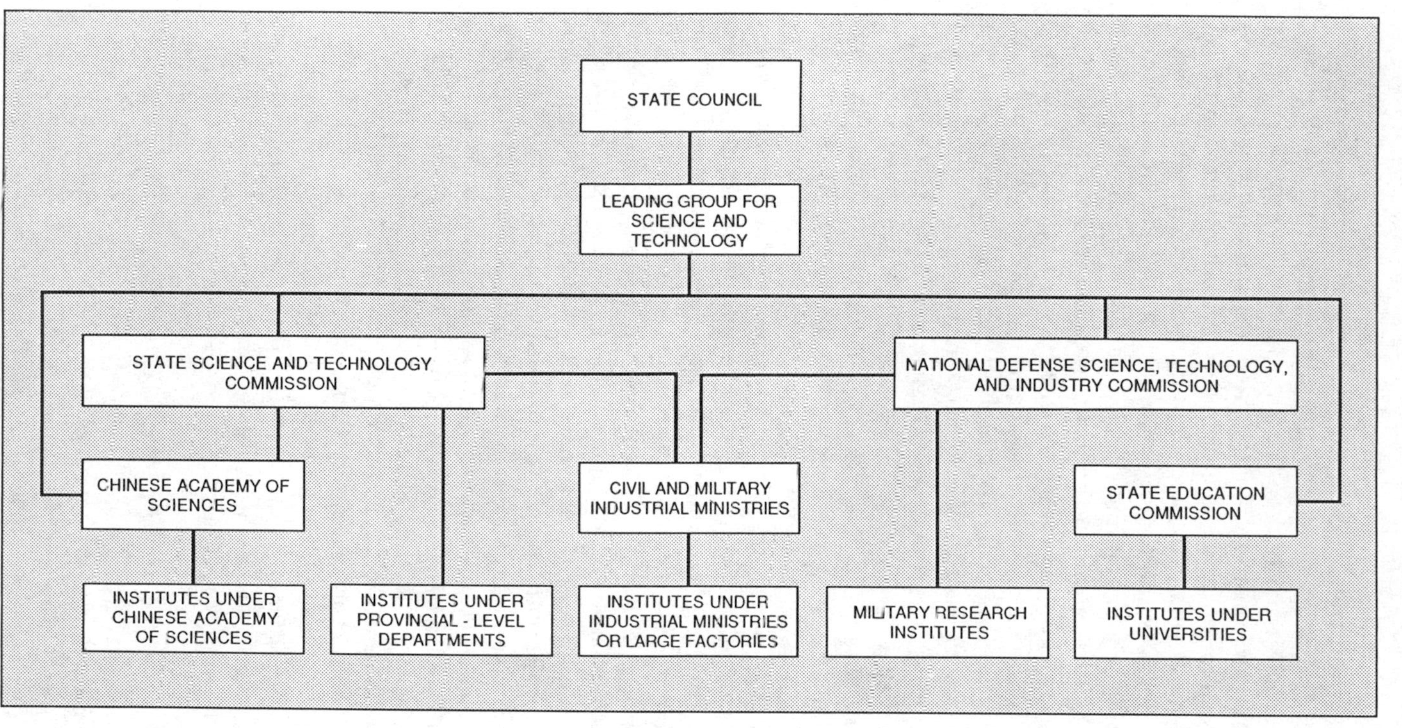

Figure 17. Organization of the Science and Technology Establishment

the work of civilian research institutes subordinate to the various industrial ministries, such as the Ministry of Electronics Industry and the Ministry of Coal Industry, or to provincial-level, prefectural, or municipal bureaus. More than 80 percent of China's 10,000 research institutes fell in this category, and their range of quality was considerable. Central planners and administrators considered the proliferation of low-quality research institutes a waste of scarce research funds, but as of mid-1987 they had not been able to overrule powerful ministries or local governments. Such institutes, which employed the majority of China's scientists and engineers, were expected to devote themselves to the application of science and to useful innovations and improvements to industrial processes and products. They had little direct contact with factories, and they reported their research results up the chain of command of their department or ministry, which was responsible for passing them on to factories. The scientists and engineers had little opportunity for interchanges with research institutes that were doing similar work but that were subordinate to a different ministry or commission.

The State Science and Technology Commission also has primary responsibility for coordinating science policy with the state's planning and budgeting operations, working in coordination with the State Planning Commission, the State Economic Commission, and the Ministry of Finance. The importance of science and science policy was indicated by the high state and party rank of the ministers and vice ministers placed in charge of the State Science and Technology Commission. Provincial-level units, responsible for budgeting, planning, and coordinating across administrative hierarchies, had their own science and technology commissions. The demarcation between the responsibilities of the Chinese Academy of Sciences and the State Science and Technology Commission in policy formulation and consultation was not entirely clear, and there was probably a certain degree of ambiguity and contention in their dealings with each other. The commission was apprised of the research being done at the academy institutes and approved the academy budget as a whole, but it could not direct the allocation of funds within the academy.

National Defense Science, Technology, and Industry Commission

Since the 1950s much of China's research and development effort has been channeled into military work. Military research facilities and factories are reported to have China's best-trained personnel, highest level of technology, and first priority for funding. Although the military sector has been shrouded in secrecy, its work has resulted in the largely independent development of nuclear and thermonuclear weapons, intercontinental ballistic missiles, nuclear submarines and submarine-launched ballistic missiles, and the successful launch and recovery of communications and reconnaissance satellites. Little information on the military research sector has been made public, and secrecy has been reinforced by isolation of many military research centers in the remote deserts and mountains of China's western regions. The overall level of China's military technology is not high by international standards, and the achievements in nuclear weapons and missiles have apparently resulted from projects featuring concentrated resources, effective coordination of distinct specialties and industries, and firm leadership directed at the achievement of a single, well-defined goal. The style recalls the 1940s Manhattan Project in the United States, and the accomplishments demonstrate the effectiveness of the Soviet-style "big push" mode of organizing research and development.

The military sector has developed in comparative isolation from the civilian economy, and until the 1980s its higher level of skills made little contribution to the national economy. Throughout the 1980s efforts have been made to break down some of the administrative barriers separating the military and civilian research and development systems. The military sector has been relatively privileged, and the spirit of self-reliance has been strong. Nevertheless, the rapid development of electronics and computer applications in the 1970s and 1980s rendered much of China's military industry obsolete. Consequently, pressure for more contact between the military research units and civilian institutes (which, with foreign contact and up-to-date foreign technology, may surpass the technical level of the military institutes) may be generated.

In 1987 the work of the military research institutes continued to be directed by the State Council's National Defense Science, Technology, and Industry Commission (NDSTIC). The NDSTIC was created in 1982 with the merger of the National Defense Science and Technology Commission, National Defense Industries Office, and Office of the Science, Technology, and Armament Commission of the party Central Military Commission. The NDSTIC functioned in a manner similar to the State Science and Technology Commission, concentrating on high-level planning and coordination across the vertical chains of command in which military research institutes and factories are organized.

Research in Colleges, Universities, and Enterprises

As a consequence of China's adopting the Soviet model for the organization of science and industry—featuring strict separation of research, production, and training—little research has been done in Chinese universities. The State Education Commission has provided only limited funding to support research, and through the 1980s the scale of research at most colleges and universities has been very modest. Since 1980 a few academic research institutes have been established in such areas as computer science. The World Bank has supported a major effort to increase research in Chinese universities and to make better use of the scarce skills of faculty members. On the whole, though, universities have continued to play only a minor role in scientific research.

Research institutes associated with or organized as constituent parts of productive enterprises have been quite rare and represent the smallest of the five systems of research institutes. Only the largest mines, oil fields, or factories, such as the Anshan iron and steel complex in Liaoning Province or the Yanshan petrochemical complex in Beijing, had their own research units, dedicated to solving immediate problems in production in the late 1980s. Enterprises concentrated on production, and their managers had little incentive to take the risks associated with innovation.

Planning Scientific Research

Since 1949 China has attempted, with mixed success, to organize research and development according to a centralized national plan. The various plans for scientific development that China has adopted since 1957 have been broad—listing topics and areas of priority without going into much detail or attempting to issue targets or dates to specific research institutes. From the 1950s through the mid-1980s, the "iron rice bowl" (see Glossary) of guaranteed employment and funding applied to research institutes and researchers as much as to any other enterprises or state-sector workers (see Economic Policies, 1949–80, ch. 5). No institute ever had its budget cut for failing to make a planned discovery, and no scientist was dismissed for failing to publish or to make progress in research.

Much of the initiative in research seems to have come from below, with institutes submitting proposals for projects and funding to the State Science and Technology Commission. The commission's plans were drawn up after conferences in which scientists and directors of institutes suggested work that seemed feasible and worthwhile. The Beijing headquarters of the commission had a staff of between 500 and 1,000, not all of whom had scientific or economic backgrounds. Some of their energies were devoted to communication and coordination with other elements of the central administration, such as the State Planning Commission and the State Economic Commission. The core of the responsibility and power

The Long March-3 satellite-carrier rocket ready for launch
Courtesy Xinhua News Agency

of the State Science and Technology Commission was in its allocation of funds for research and approval of projects. It possessed neither the manpower nor the expertise to monitor the work of the several thousand research institutes it oversaw, and of necessity it concentrated on major projects and relied on the advice of expert scientists and the regional scientific and technological commissions, which processed reports and applications for new projects. Much of its work consisted of "balancing" the competing requests for limited funds, and its decisions often were made on grounds other than scientific merit. Although China's leaders have addressed the rhetoric of centralized planning to scientific research, research activities have been more decentralized and more subject to pressures from powerful ministries and provincial-level governments.

Integration of Administrative Systems

In the late 1980s, two of the five research subsystems—the Chinese Academy of Sciences and the military system—were relatively privileged in receiving government financing and being supplied with scarce resources and historically had tended to form closed, self-sufficient domains. The system under the State Science and Technology Commission, which included the largest number of research institutes, was marked by wide variations in quality and a vertical, bureaucratic mode of organization that inhibited collaboration and exchange of information. Both the universities and the research institutes attached to large industrial complexes were short of funds and out of the mainstream of research. Overall, China's science and technology structure was marked by lopsided distribution of skilled manpower, pervasive fragmentation, compartmentalization, and duplication of research—an outcome of the 1950s decision to adopt a bureaucratic mode of organization for science and technology. Chinese policy makers were well aware of these problems and, over the years, had responded with two forms of organizational remedies: high-level coordinating bodies and mass scientific associations that cut across administrative boundaries.

Leading Group for Science and Technology

The growth of China's scientific system and the tendencies toward compartmentalization inherent in the Soviet mode of scientific and industrial organization, which it emulated, were matched by the creation of administrative bodies intended to coordinate the activities of vertically organized administrative hierarchies. Both the State Science and Technology Commission and the NDSTIC, which were formed by the amalgamation of earlier coordinating bodies founded as long ago as the mid-1950s, had this primary function. Efforts to fill the need for progressively more authoritative and comprehensive coordination culminated in the establishment of the State Council's Leading Group for Science and Technology in January 1983. The leading group, a special-purpose task force formed by the State Council to address problems that cut across administrative boundaries, was China's highest-level policy-making organ for science and technology. In 1987 its chairman was Premier Zhao Ziyang, and its membership included Fang Yi, state councillor and former head of the State Science and Technology Commission and the Chinese Academy of Sciences, and leading members of the State Science and Technology Commission, NDSTIC, State Planning Commission, State Economic Commission, State Education Commission, Chinese Academy of Sciences, and Ministry of Labor and Personnel. That the leading group was headed by the premier indicated both the significance China's leaders attached to science policy and the level of authority necessary to settle disputes and encourage cooperation.

China Association of Science and Technology

At the lower end of the administrative hierarchy, communication and cooperation were intended to be promoted by professional organizations, whose membership cut across administrative boundaries. The primary organization was the China Association of

Science and Technology, a nongovernment mass organization. Because it was funded by the government and, like all organizations in China, directed by party cadres, its autonomy had strict limits. The China Association of Science and Technology was an umbrella organization: as of 1986 it comprised 139 national scientific societies organized by discipline and 1.9 million individual members. It succeeded earlier scientific associations that had been founded in 1910–20. The China Association of Science and Technology served three major purposes. First, like professional associations in most countries, it brought individual scientists and administrators together with their professional peers from other work units at conferences, lectures, and joint projects, and it promoted communication across administrative boundaries. Second, the China Association of Science and Technology had a major role in the popularization of science and dissemination of scientific knowledge to the general public. This latter function was accomplished through the publication of popular-science journals and books aimed at an audience with a high-school education and through lecture series, refresher training for technicians and engineers, and consultation for farmers and rural and small-scale industries. Throughout the 1980s, the China Association of Science and Technology and its constituent associations served increasingly as consultants to government officials. Third, the China Association of Science and Technology played a major role in China's international scientific exchanges and hosted delegations of foreign scientists, sponsored international scientific conferences in China, participated in many joint research projects with foreign associations and scientific bodies, and represented China in many international science societies.

International Ties

Since emerging from the self-imposed isolation and self-reliance of the Cultural Revolution, China has expanded its international scientific exchanges to an unprecedented degree. The 1980s policy of opening up to the outside world, a basic element of Deng Xiaoping's prescription for modernization, was nowhere better exemplified than in science and technology policy (see China and the Four Modernizations, 1979–82, ch. 1). The goal was to help China's science and technology reach international standards as quickly as possible and to remedy the damage done by the Cultural Revolution. This was achieved by participating in international conferences, cooperating in projects with foreign scientists, and sending thousands of Chinese graduate students and senior researchers to foreign universities for training and joint research.

Scientific cooperation has come to play a significant part in China's foreign relations and diplomatic repertoire. Visits of Chinese leaders to foreign countries are often marked by the signing of an agreement for scientific cooperation. In mid-1987 China had diplomatic relations with 133 countries and formal, government-to-government agreements on scientific cooperation with 54 of them (see An Overview of China's Foreign Relations, ch. 12). When diplomatic relations were established between China and the United States in January 1979, the Joint Commission in Scientific and Technological Cooperation was founded. Since then, the two governments have signed twenty-eight agreements on scientific and technical cooperation in fields ranging from earthquake prediction to industrial management. China has mutually beneficial scientific exchange programs with both technically advanced nations and those having only a minimal scientific capability. Although China tended to receive aid from more scientifically advanced nations and to render aid to the less developed, the equality implied in scientific exchange made it a useful diplomatic form.

In 1987 China had scientific-exchange relations with 106 countries—usually in the form of agreements between the China Association of Science and Technology and a foreign equivalent. Incomplete statistics indicated that by 1986 Chinese scientists had completed over 500 joint projects with scientists in the United States and were working on 1,500 projects with counterparts in various West European countries, 300 with those in Eastern Europe, and at least 30 with Japanese researchers. In June 1986 the Chinese Academy of Sciences signed an agreement with the Soviet Academy of Sciences for scientific cooperation in unspecified fields. Many exchanges with the United States involved Chinese-American scientists and engineers, who collaborated with visiting Chinese researchers in the United States and visited China to lecture on their specialties and to advise scientific bodies.

By 1986 the China Association of Science and Technology or its constituent associations were full members of 96 international scientific societies and committees, and over 300 Chinese scientists held office in international scientific bodies. China also was an active participant in United Nations scientific activities in the 1980s. Luoyang, Henan Province, is the site of the United Nations Educational, Scientific and Cultural Organization's International Silt Research and Training Center, which specializes in problems of river silts. Apart from the 35,000 students China sent abroad for training between 1979 and 1986, approximately 41,000 Chinese scientists took part in various international exchanges. Between 1980 and 1986, China hosted 155 international academic conferences, which were attended by 10,000 foreign scholars and 30,000 Chinese participants. China also has employed substantial numbers of foreign experts, often retired scientists or engineers, as short-term consultants.

International exchanges represent one of the most successful aspects of the Chinese government's efforts to raise the level of science and demonstrate the strength of the centralized direction and funding possible under China's bureaucratic organization of science. The weaknesses of that mode of organization are evident in the less successful efforts to improve the internal functioning and productivity of the domestic science and technology establishment and have generated a major effort to reform that establishment.

The Reform Program

Shortcomings of the Science and Technology System

From the perspective of China's leaders, the entire science and technology system of the late 1980s, with its 8 million personnel and 10,000 research institutes, represented an expensive, underutilized and not very productive capital investment. Dissatisfaction with the system had become pervasive by the early 1980s, and both scientists and political leaders agreed on the necessity for fundamental reform. The primary complaint of the leadership was that, despite thirty years of policy statements, central plans, and political campaigns directed at the attitudes of scientists and engineers, science still was not serving the needs of the economy. Reformist political leaders and senior scientists identified a number of organizational problems that were inherent in the system adopted from the Soviet Union and that had been compounded by Chinese work-unit and lifetime job assignment practices (see Differentiation; Common Patterns, ch. 3).

In an October 1982 speech to the National Science Awards Conference, Premier Zhao Ziyang identified the following as primary problems: uneven development and lack of coordination among scientific fields; lack of communication between research and production units; duplication of research and facilities; rivalry among institutes, administrative bodies, and hierarchies; and maldistribution of personnel, with some units and fields overstaffed and others very short of skilled personnel. Zhao's speech drew upon and was followed by extensive discussions of management and organization by scientists and administrators. These discussions emphasized the prevalence of departmentalism, compartmentalism, and fragmentation of efforts. These problems, when combined with poor management, poorly educated managers, absence of incentives for good work or of penalties for poor performance, and absence of direct communication between research units and productive enterprises, resulted in the failure of the science and technology establishment to serve production and economic growth.

In the 1980s research institutes, like all Chinese work units, responded to an economic system in which supplies were uncertain by attempting to be as self-sufficient as possible. Exchanges of information, services, or personnel across the very strictly defined administrative boundaries were difficult, resulting in failure to share expensive imported equipment and in widespread duplication of facilities. The absence of information on work being done in other research institutes, even in the same city, frequently led to duplication and repetition of research.

Like all other workers in China, scientists were assigned to research institutes or universities by government labor bureaus. Such assignments frequently did not reflect specialized skills or training. Assignments were meant to be permanent, and it was very difficult for scientists or engineers to transfer to another work unit. In many cases, talents or specialized training were wasted. Institutes that may have had the funds to purchase advanced foreign equipment often had no way to hire a Chinese chemist or mathematician. Not only were China's scientists and engineers in short supply, many were underemployed or misemployed.

The Program

In March 1985, after extensive discussion, consultation, and experimentation, the party Central Committee called for sweeping reforms of science management. The reforms proposed in the "Decision on the Reform of the Science and Technology Management System" represented a major break with past practices, and they assumed corresponding reforms in the nation's industrial and economic systems. By changing the method of funding research institutes, encouraging the commercialization of technology and the development of a technology market, and rewarding individual scientists, the reforms of the mid-1980s were meant to encourage the application of science to the needs of industry. It was envisaged that most research institutes would support themselves through consulting and contract work and would cooperate with factories through partnerships, mergers, joint ventures, or other appropriate and mutually agreeable means. The ultimate goal was to encourage exchange and cooperation and to break down the compartmentalization characterizing China's research and development structure.

The principal means for accomplishing the reforms was changing the funding system to force research institutes to establish contact with productive enterprises and to do work directly supporting those enterprises. Direct allocation of funds to research institutes was to be phased out and replaced by a system under which institutes sold their services in the marketplace. The distinctions among institutes subordinate to the Chinese Academy of Sciences, the industrial ministries, provincial-level governments, colleges and universities, and even the NDSTIC were to be minimized, and all were to compete and collaborate in a single market-oriented system. Institutes doing basic research were to compete for grants from a National Natural Science Foundation (which was subsequently established). The reforms were not intended as a budget-cutting measure, and total state funding for science and technology was to be increased.

A technology market and the commercialization of technology in the late 1980s were to be developed to encourage the transfer of technology and the transformation of research results into products and services. Direct centralized administration and supervision of research were to decline, and institutes were to be headed by younger, technically qualified directors, who were to be given broad powers to select their own research topics and to seek out partners for cooperation and consultation. Scientific personnel were to receive better pay and benefits, recognition of their achievements, and the right to do supplementary consulting work and to transfer to units where their talents could be better utilized.

The Relation with Economic Reform

Implementing the reforms of the science and technology system, however, presupposed reforms of the economic, industrial, and local administrative systems (see Reform of the Economic System, Beginning in 1979, ch. 5). In general, science and technology reforms represented the application to that sector of the principles underlying the sweeping reforms of the economy proposed in the October 1984 "Decision of the Central Committee of the Chinese Communist Party on Reform of the Economic Structure." Both reform "decisions" emphasized greater autonomy for institutions, a greater role for the market, more competition, and rewards for the successful introduction of improved products and processes. In every case, the goal was increased productivity and economic benefit.

The central provisions of the 1980s reform related to funding, the technology market and cooperative ventures, and the rights and potential job mobility of individual researchers. The intent of the reformers was to change the basic conditions of the economic system, so that the self-interest that had pushed managers of factories and research institutes toward compartmentalization, duplication, and hoarding of resources would henceforth push them toward cooperation, division of labor, and orientation toward the needs of the market. Because these reforms represented a radical departure from the procedures developed since the 1950s, the leadership anticipated that their implementation would be slow, and it planned to phase them in over a number of years.

Perhaps because of the centrality of funding to the whole reform scheme and because the administrative machinery for handling budgets was already in place, many concrete provisions for funding research were adopted following the March 1985 Central Committee decision. In February 1986 the State Council promulgated provisional regulations under which science and technology projects listed in the annual state economic plan were to be completed as contract research, in which there would be nationwide open bidding on the contracts. Banks were to monitor expenditures under the contract. Institutes conducting basic research were to have their regular operating expenses guaranteed by the state, but all other income would come from competitive research grants. The government was to continue to fund completely the institutes working in public health and medicine, family planning, environmental science, technical information, meteorology, and agriculture. In 1986 the newly established National Natural Science Foundation, explicitly modeled on the United States National Science Foundation, disbursed its first competitive awards, totaling ¥95 million (for value of the yuan—see Glossary), to 3,432 research projects selected from 12,000 applications. The amount of money awarded to individual projects was not large, but the precedent of competition, disregard of administrative boundaries, and expert appraisal of individual or small-group proposals was established and widely publicized. And, early in 1987, the NDSTIC announced that henceforth weapons procurement and military research and development would be managed through contracts and competitive bidding.

Technology Markets and Joint Ventures

Commercializing technology requires markets, and China in the late 1980s had to develop market institutions to handle patents, the sale of technology, and consulting contracts. This was a major endeavor and one that promised to take many years. Deciding how to set prices for technology and how to write and enforce contracts for technical consulting proved difficult, largely because of the complexity of technology markets. Further, China lacked the legal and commercial frameworks to support such markets. Nevertheless, institutes and factories participated in "technology fairs" and established contractual relations in great numbers, with the total

The control center at the Baoshan iron and steel complex in Shanghai
Courtesy Xinhua News Agency

technology trade volume in 1986 reaching an estimated ¥2.3 billion. Research institutes and universities formed companies to sell technical services and develop products. Even the formerly self-contained Chinese Academy of Sciences set up companies to export specialty magnets and to develop optical products.

In the late 1980s, China's technology markets and efforts to commercialize scientific and technical knowledge were growing rapidly amid considerable confusion, ferment, and turmoil. Although progressing, the commercialization of technology was proving difficult to implement, and, perhaps for this reason, the State Council announced in February 1987 that most applied scientific research institutes were to be incorporated into large and medium-sized productive enterprises to coordinate research with the needs of production. The precise form the technology market would eventually take was not clear, but its development had wide support and was not likely to be halted or reversed.

Personnel and Job Mobility

From one perspective the most important element of China's science and technology system is its human capital—its trained scientists and engineers. By the 1980s it was widely recognized in the Chinese press that scientists, like all intellectuals, had been poorly treated, underpaid, and burdened with difficult living conditions that reduced their productivity. In many cases scientists' abilities were wasted because they were assigned to jobs outside their expertise or because their institute already had all the professionals in their field it needed and there was no way for them to change jobs (see Educational Investment, ch. 4). Many Chinese science policy writers were familiar with the conclusion of Western specialists that scientific progress and the effective application of science to practical problems are facilitated by personnel mobility. Accordingly, the March 1985 party Central Committee decision called for reform of the personnel system to promote a "rational flow" of scientific and technical personnel.

Throughout the late 1980s, however, job mobility and attempts to place scientists where their talents could have the greatest effect were the aspect of reform in which least was achieved. Transfer of scientists from one unit to another remained a major step, and a relatively infrequent one. According to the State Science and Technology Commission, 2 percent of scientists and engineers changed work units in 1983, and only 4 percent in 1985. Personnel still required the permission of their work unit heads to transfer, and that permission often was withheld. Many directors of institutes were accused of having a "feudal mentality," that is, regarding personnel as part of their unit's property.

The State Council reiterated in the mid-1980s that scientists and engineers had the right to do consulting work in their spare time. In practice, however, such spare-time consulting often created problems within the work unit as some institute directors attempted to confiscate payments for consulting or even to charge their personnel in the local courts with corruption and theft of state property. Although the press gave considerable publicity to scientists who had left the "iron rice bowl" of a Chinese Academy of Sciences institute to start their own business or to join a growing collective or rural factory, such resignations remained relatively rare. Possibly more common were practices whereby institutes detailed their personnel on temporary consulting contracts to productive enterprises.

The difficulties in transferring scientific personnel even when the Central Committee and the State Council made it official policy demonstrated the significance of China's unique work-unit system of employment and economic organization and the obstacles it presented to reform. Allowing personnel to decide for themselves to move out of the work units to which the state and the party assigned them would be a major break with the practices that have become institutionalized in China since 1949. Some observers believe that because of its potential challenge to the authority of the party, which controls personnel matters in all work units, job mobility for scientists, even though it would promote scientific productivity and the growth of the economy, may be too extreme a reform to be feasible (see Differentiation, ch. 3).

Technology Transfer

Policy

In the late 1980s, China's goals of modernization and rapid economic growth depended on the large-scale introduction of foreign technology. The task was to import technology to renovate and upgrade several thousand factories, mines, and power stations whose levels of productivity and energy efficiency were far below prevailing international standards. Since 1980 Chinese policy statements have stressed the need to improve existing facilities, to import technology rather than finished goods, and to renovate factories through selective purchase of key technology rather than through purchase of whole plants. This was an unprecedented problem, since China's previous experience with technology transfer, both in the massive Soviet technical-aid program of the 1950s and in the more modest purchases of fertilizer and petrochemical plants in the 1960s and early 1970s, featured large projects that brought in complete plants. In the 1980s much of the technology to be imported was production or process technology, representing better ways of producing items China already manufactured, such as truck transmissions or telephone cables. Such technology was usually the proprietary knowledge of foreign corporations, and China demonstrated an unprecedented willingness to cooperate with such firms. With the explicit aim of promoting technology imports, China made great efforts to attract foreign businesses and foreign capital and permitted joint ventures and even foreign-owned subsidiaries to operate in China.

China's economic planners gave priority in technology imports to electronics, telecommunications, electric-power generation and transmission, transportation equipment, and energy-saving devices. The degree of central control over technology imports fluctuated in the 1980s, reflecting changing foreign trade policies and foreign exchange balances, but the overall trend was toward devolution of decision making to those who use the technology or equipment. Bank loans and other means were made available to encourage end users to select appropriate technology.

Modes of Transfer

The transfer of proprietary technology from a foreign corporation is, among other things, a commercial transaction, and such transactions take many forms. Chinese authorities have selected joint-equity ventures as their preferred mode of technology transfer. In such ventures, both the foreign and the Chinese partner contribute capital, each provides what it has the advantage in (usually technology and access to world market for the foreign partner and labor and a factory for the Chinese partner), and management and profits are split. Many major foreign corporations with technology that China desires have been reluctant to risk their capital in such ventures. But enough have agreed to produce such items as jet airliners, computers, and machine tools that Chinese authorities can claim success for their policy.

Linking Technology and Economics

As they have accumulated experience in dealing with foreign corporations, Chinese economic administrators and enterprise managers have become better able to negotiate contracts that, while not full joint ventures, still permit the necessary training and consultation in the use of foreign technology. By the late 1980s, the transfer of foreign technology had become a normal commercial transaction. To an increasing extent, policy and practices for technology transfer were becoming part of general economic and foreign trade policies. China faced problems in assimilating technology in the factories that imported it and in deciding which foreign technologies to import. It was becoming clear to Chinese planners and foreign suppliers of technology that these problems reflected overall deficiencies in technical and management skills and that they were general economic and management problems. The solution to these problems was increasingly seen by Chinese administrators as lying in reforms of the economy and industrial management. The effort to import and assimilate foreign technology thus served to help unify technology policy and economic policy and to overcome the problems of the separation of science, technology, and the economy, which China's leaders had been trying to solve since the early 1950s.

* * *

Because of the continuity of the issues affecting China's science and technology, many of the studies carried out in the early 1960s are still useful. Among these are Leo A. Orleans' *Professional Manpower and Education in Communist China*, Wu Yuan-li and Robert B. Sheeks' *The Organization and Support of Scientific Research and Development in Mainland China*, and Cheng Chu-yuan's *Scientific and*

Engineering Manpower in Communist China, 1949–1963. Richard P. Suttmeier's 1974 *Research and Revolution: Science Policy and Societal Change in China* sets out most of the basic policy choices for science in China. Articles by Suttmeier and Denis Fred Simon cover most aspects of current science policy. *Science in Contemporary China*, edited by Orleans, assesses the state of science in China as of 1980. Rudi Volti's *Technology, Politics, and Society in China* and K.C. Yeh's *Industrial Innovation in China with Special Reference to the Metallurgical Industry* provide good overviews of China's science and technology system. Current news of policies and achievements in science and technology is available in such Chinese sources as *Beijing Review*, *China Daily*, and *China Exchange News*. Chinese reports and discussions of science and technology policy are translated and published in the Joint Publications Research Service's *China Report: Science and Technology*. (For further information and complete citations, see Bibliography.)

Chapter 10. Party and Government

Representation of a terra-cotta figure of a Qin dynasty (221–207 B.C.) general. The figure near the tomb of the first Qin emperor, Shi Huangdi, near present-day Xi'an, Shaanxi Province.

THE THIRD PLENUM of the Central Committee of the Eleventh National Party Congress, held in December 1978, marked a major turning point in China's development. The course was laid for the party to move the world's most populous nation toward the ambitious targets of the Four Modernizations. After a decade of turmoil brought about by the Cultural Revolution (1966–76), the new direction set at this meeting was toward economic development and away from class struggle. The plenum endorsed major changes in the political, economic, and social system. It also instituted sweeping personnel changes, culminating in the elevation of two key supporters of Deng Xiaoping and the reform program, Hu Yaobang and Zhao Ziyang, to the posts of general secretary of the party (September 1982) and premier of the State Council (September 1980), respectively. In January 1987 Hu Yaobang lost the position of general secretary when he failed to control violent student demonstrations. Zhao Ziyang became acting general secretary, in addition to serving as premier, pending confirmation by the Thirteenth National Party Congress, scheduled for October 1987.

Under the new and pragmatic leadership, the modernization program, slated to be well established by the year 2000, was to engage the energies and talents of the entire population in reaching the reform goals. But unlike in the past, acceptable class background was not to play a role in selecting and promoting participants for the national program. Intellectuals or those with advanced education were no longer negatively categorized. Class consciousness was being replaced by one that fostered initiative and encouraged each person to contribute according to his or her ability.

An initial challenge facing the reform leadership was to provide for a rational and efficient governing system to support economic development. In pursuit of that goal, the cult of personality surrounding Mao Zedong was unequivocally condemned and replaced by a strong emphasis on collective leadership. An example of this new emphasis was the party's restoration in February 1980 of its Secretariat, which had been suspended since 1966. The new party and state constitutions, both adopted in 1982, provided the institutional framework for the Four Modernizations program. These documents abolished the post of party chairman and restored the post of president of the People's Republic of China, thereby giving additional weight to government functions and providing a degree of balance to the authoritative party structure. Also, the government's role was broadened by the addition of standing committees and direct elections at subnational levels of the government's presiding body, the National People's Congress.

The political structure in 1987 seemed to represent consensus and continuity, but it continued to undergo the test of accommodation and a process of trial and error. The experimental approach was rooted in official recognition that the party and the government had to remain self-critical and responsive if they were to fulfill the expectations that the reform leaders had raised since 1978 of solving old problems and meeting new challenges. Some of the most sweeping changes concerned the party and government cadre system that was essential to the implementation and performance of the reform program. Manned by about 14 million cadres, the system was acknowledged officially to be overstaffed and sluggish. The drive to weed out tens of thousands of aged, inactive, and incompetent cadres was intensified. Even more revolutionary, the life tenure system for state and party cadres was abolished, and age limits for various offices were established. While removing superfluous personnel, the reform leaders stressed the importance of creating a "third echelon" of younger leadership to enter responsible positions and be trained for future authority. Between 1978 and 1987, some 470,000 younger officials reportedly were promoted to responsible positions.

The theoretical basis of the political system continued to be Marxism-Leninism-Mao Zedong Thought (which combined borrowings from Soviet ideology with Mao's theoretical writings), but with an unmistakable emphasis on the application of this doctrine to achieve desired results. The test of a reform was no longer how closely it reflected hallowed quotations or ideas—although reforms continued to be couched in proper doctrinal arguments—but whether or not it produced demonstrable benefits to the reform program. The banner slogan of the reform agenda was "socialism with Chinese characteristics." This slogan implied that considerable leeway would be allowed in doctrinal matters in order to achieve the overriding goal of rapid modernization. But reform leaders realized that successful implementation of the broad-ranging reform program required a stable, professional bureaucracy to direct the course of events. The course chosen included a more rational division of powers and functions for th party and government, and it provided a body of regulations and procedures to support the separation. Institutions were set up to maintain discipline and to audit bureaucratic records. In December 1986 the Standing Committee of the National People's Congress established the Ministry of Supervision to oversee the work of the government cadre. Of course, the primacy of the party over all other sociopolitical institutions was an unchanging fact of political life.

Another recognized requirement for a successful reform program was the decentralization of authority, including a greater voice and degree of accountability for local bodies in the formulation and implementation of programs and policies. In the 1980s government leaders instituted experimental programs at all levels to achieve this end. The party, wielding political power and having close access to reform leaders, appeared to act increasingly in an advisory role, guiding events in accordance with its own general policy and serving as an intermediary between government officials and front-line producers, for example, departmental administrators and enterprise managers. The role of the party was still being defined, but it appeared less focused on dictating the specific course of events.

Chinese Communist Party

Party Constitution

The party constitution adopted in September 1982 at the Twelfth National Party Congress clearly defines the powers and functions of the Chinese Communist Party (CCP), and it assigns the party a pivotal role in guiding national efforts toward a communist social system. Although the party constitution sets legal limits on CCP activities, the party's role in areas of political, ideological, and organizational leadership is authoritative and unquestioned.

The organizational principle that drives the Chinese political system is democratic centralism. Within the system, the democratic feature demands participation and expression of opinion on key policy issues from members at all levels of party organization. It depends on a constant process of consultation and investigation. At the same time, the centralist feature requires that subordinate organizational levels follow the dictates of superior levels. Once the debate has reached the highest level and decisions concerning policy have been made, all party members are obliged to support the Central Committee.

In the party constitution, and in other major policy statements, the CCP diminished the role of centralism by abolishing the post of party chairman, by prohibiting any future cult of personality, and by emphasizing the importance of collective leadership. Most of the aged revolutionary veterans who had worked for years under the highly centralized party organization dominated by Mao Zedong were made honorary advisers, elected to the Central Advisory Commission initiated at the Twelfth Congress. Although their prestige remained intact, these leaders were effectively removed from direct participation in the policy-making process. This development permitted their replacement by younger leaders more supportive of the Four Modernizations (see Glossary). In addition, the new party constitution emphasized the party's role in promoting socialist democracy, in developing and strengthening a socialist legal system, and in consolidating public resolve to carry out the modernization program.

The priorities expounded at the Twelfth National Party Congress were designed not only to improve the organizational cohesion and morale of the party and government but also to hasten prosperity and foster national power. The congress endorsed programs from the Eleventh National Party Congress that stressed stability and unity, balance between ideology and technical skill, collective rather than individual leadership, party discipline, training of successors at all levels of party organization, and a more relaxed climate for intraparty debate on major national and local issues. The economic policies of the Twelfth National Party Congress continued to be oriented toward growth, but the party's subsequent direction emphasized a more controlled growth program.

National Party Congresses

The National Party Congress is in theory the highest body of the CCP. (It should be distinguished from the National People's Congress, China's highest legislative body—see The National People's Congress, this ch.) After its ascent to power in 1949, the party held no congress until 1956. This was the eighth congress since the party's founding in 1921; (see table 1, Appendix B). The Ninth National Party Congress convened in April 1969, the tenth in August 1973, the eleventh in August 1977, and the twelfth in September 1982. The Thirteenth National Party Congress was scheduled for October 1987. The National Party Congress reviews reports on party activities since the last session, revises the party constitution, ratifies the party program for a specific period, and elects the Central Committee, which serves as the highest organ of the CCP when the National Party Congress is not in session. The congress has, however, neither the independence to generate legislative bills nor the effective power to check and balance the party and government bureaucracies. Although limited in its role—in effect it is a pro forma approval body—the National Party Congress performs a useful function as a forum for rising party cadres who represent all regions, ethnic groups, and functional groups. The delegates (there were 1,545 for the Twelfth National Party Congress) can observe firsthand the working of the party machine at the national level, gain a better perspective on the direction of political transformation planned by the leadership, and serve as communicators of party policies to the grass roots. Further, delegates can provide the top party leadership a sense of the response and progress made concerning key party programs in their home districts.

Central Committee and Political Bureau

Political power is formally vested in the much smaller CCP Central Committee and the other central organs answerable directly to this committee. The Central Committee is elected by the National Party Congress and is identified by the number of the National Party Congress that elected it. Central Committee meetings are known as plenums (or plenary sessions), and each plenum of a new Central Committee is numbered sequentially. Plenums are to be held at least annually. In addition, there are partial, informal, and enlarged meetings of Central Committee members where often key policies are formulated and then confirmed by a plenum. For example, the "Communiqué of the Third Plenum of the Eleventh Central Committee" (December 1978), which established the party's commitment to economic modernization, resulted from a month-long working meeting that preceded the Third Plenum.

The Central Committee's large size and infrequent meetings make it necessary for the Central Committee to direct its work through its smaller elite bodies—the Political Bureau and the even more select Political Bureau's Standing Committee—both of which the Central Committee elects. The Twelfth Central Committee consisted of 210 full members and 138 alternate members. The Political Bureau had twenty-three members and three alternate members. The Standing Committee—the innermost circle of power—had six members who were placed in the most important party and government posts. These six leaders were Hu Yaobang (who was demoted from party general secretary in January 1987), Ye Jianying (who died in October 1986, a year after resigning his Standing Committee post), Deng Xiaoping, Zhao Ziyang (who was named acting general secretary in January 1987), Li Xiannian, and Chen Yun.

The leadership was altered significantly at a special conference of delegates called the National Conference of Party Delegates, held September 18–23, 1985. The conference was convened on the authority of Article 12 of the 1982 party constitution, which provides for holding conferences of delegates between full congresses. These national conferences of delegates appear to be more authoritative than regular plenums. The conference was attended by 992 delegates, and it elected 56 new full members and 35 new alternate members to the Central Committee, while accepting the

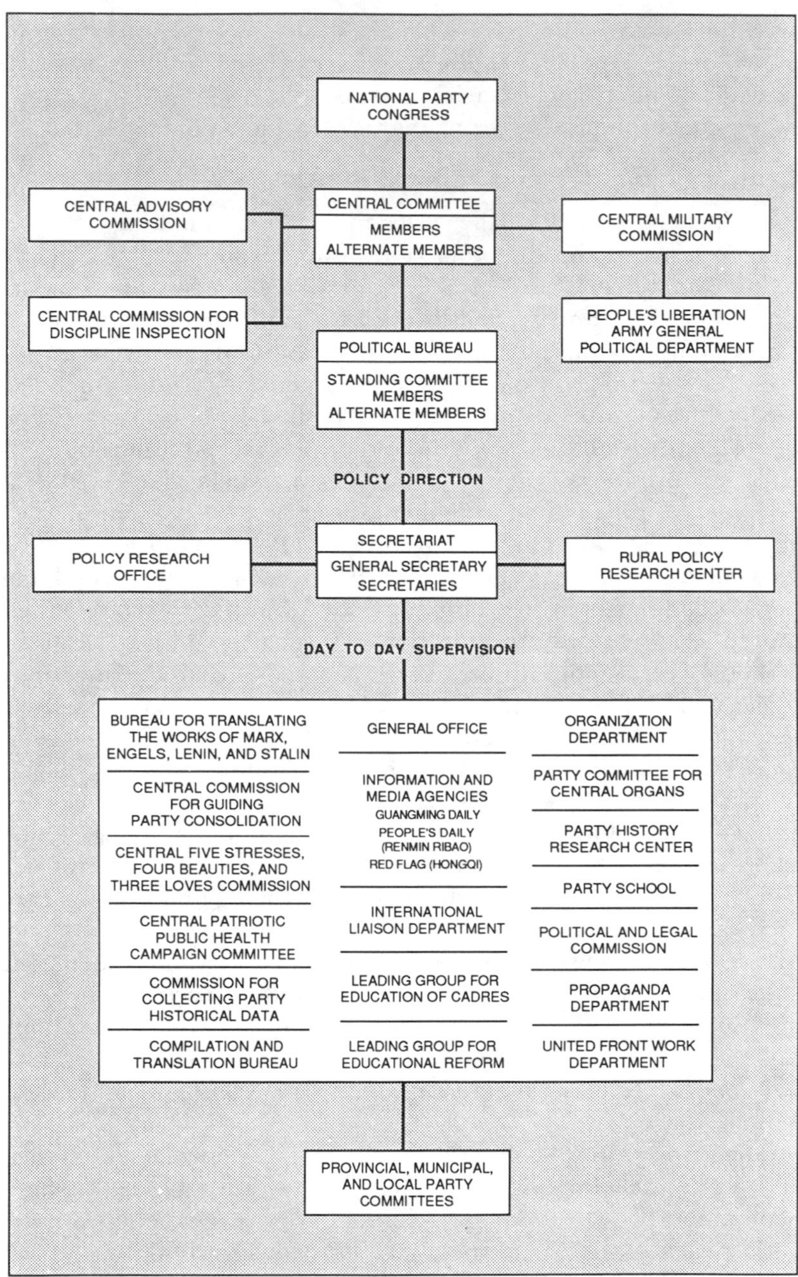

Figure 18. Organization of the Chinese Communist Party, 1987

resignations of 65 full and alternate members, including Ye Jianying and nine other senior Political Bureau members. The Fifth Plenum, which immediately followed the conference, elected six new members to the Political Bureau, dropped three from the party Secretariat, and added five new members to the latter body. The conference thus produced a sizable turnover in the senior party leadership and in a direction very favorable to Deng's reform program. Younger and better educated leaders who supported Deng's reforms replaced aging and long-inactive leaders. The other major accomplishment of the conference was its adoption of the "Proposal on the Seventh Five-Year Plan" (1986–90), the framework for developing the actual plan adopted at the Sixth National People's Congress in 1986 (see Reform of the Economic System, Beginning in 1979, ch. 5).

Secretariat

The day-to-day work of the CCP is carried out by the Secretariat and its various departments—all placed under the direction of the Political Bureau and its Standing Committee (see fig. 18). Headed by Hu Yaobang until January 1987, the Secretariat (suspended in 1966) was reestablished in February 1980 as the administrative center of the party apparatus, or, more aptly, as the party's inner cabinet. The Secretariat and its general secretary are elected by the CCP Central Committee. In early 1987 seven of the eleven members of the Secretariat held concurrent positions on the Political Bureau. This overlap in responsibilities permitted reform leaders to exercise greater control than in the past over policy implementation. In the same way, Secretariat members sitting on the Political Bureau have acquired a role in party policy making. The Secretariat evidently is used as a proving ground for successors to senior party leaders.

Central Military Commission

The CCP's Central Military Commission is also elected by the Central Committee and exercises authority over the military through the General Political Department of the People's Liberation Army (PLA). Since 1982 the party Central Military Commission has had a counterpart organization in the state Central Military Commission (see The National People's Congress, this ch.). In fact, the leadership of both bodies is identical. Nevertheless, because the party Central Military Commission reports directly to the powerful Central Committee, it is the authoritative body in matters of military policy (see Military Organization, ch. 14).

Other Party Organs

Another body, the Central Commission for Discipline Inspection, is chartered to monitor the implementation of party policy and to handle disciplinary matters regarding party organizations and members. The Central Advisory Commission was established by the 1982 Party Constitution to facilitate the transfer of power from the Long March (see Glossary) generation to younger and better educated successors. This body has consultative rather than decision-making powers. Its chairman is an ex-officio member of the Political Bureau's Standing Committee. Deng Xiaoping was made the first chairman of this body, both to lend it prestige and to encourage older leaders to retire.

Below the central level, party committees and congresses were formed in the twenty-one provinces, five autonomous regions, and three special municipalities directly under the central government. Taiwan was listed as a province but, of course, was not under China's administration. The party also was represented in various county subdivisions (which included the prefectures) and within the PLA from regional headquarters down to regimental level (see Military Organization, ch. 14). At the bottom of the party hierarchy were three kinds of basic organizations: general party branches, primary party committees, and party branches. These were set up in factories, shops, schools, offices, neighborhoods, PLA companies, and other places, depending on local circumstances and subject to approval by the appropriate party committees.

Party committees at the provincial level are elected by the provincial-level congresses that convene every five years and have as additional functions the election of a discipline inspection commission, advisory commissions, and delegates to the National Party Congress. The county-level party congress convenes every three years and elects a committee, standing committee, and secretary. Below the county and PLA regimental levels, the general branch committee meets twice a year and is elected for a two-year term. The party branch, or lowest level of party organization, meets four times a year and elects a branch committee for a two-year term. Every party member must be a member of a branch committee. Party branch committees and their members at the grass-roots level are the backbone of the party organization. This is also the level where admission and expulsion of party members takes place. Branch members exchange views on issues, become thoroughly informed concerning party goals and policies, and learn to accept party discipline.

Membership

In 1987 the CCP had 46 million members (4.3 percent of the national population). To qualify as party members, applicants must be at least eighteen years of age and must go through a one-year probationary period. Emphasis is placed on the applicant's technical and educational qualifications rather than on ideological criteria. Members are expected, however, to be both "red" and "expert" (see Glossary), and the need to make the party apparatus more responsive to the demands and wishes of the masses of the people is stressed.

A major corollary of the self-improvement and self-cleansing activities is an ongoing campaign to weed out corrupt and dishonest party officials from all levels of the party organizations. Ideally this is accomplished by persuasion, but if necessary by punishment. The party's seriousness concerning this campaign was underlined with its September 1986 expulsion of the governor and party deputy secretary of Jiangxi Province for "violations of law and discipline" and "unhealthy tendencies" that purportedly included corruption, moral degeneration, abuse of official power, intercession in favor of relatives and friends, leaking of secret information, and many other charges.

Significantly, the party also experimented with the direct election of its party committee members. In late 1984 Hu Yaobang prescribed election procedures for direct election under a limited franchise of the Shaanxi Province party secretary. This election process included involvement of a large number of cadres down to the county level, open nominations, and a series of runoff elections, reportedly with no interference from either the central party Secretariat or the provincial party committee. In addition, party election procedures required that the number of candidates be greater than the number of persons to be elected.

In 1987 efforts to upgrade organizational effectiveness, unity, and discipline were proceeding in accordance with a document adopted in September 1986 by the Sixth Plenum of the Twelfth Central Committee. The "Resolution of the Central Committee of the Communist Party of China on the Guiding Principles for Building a Socialist Society with an Advanced Culture and Ideology" shifted attention away from the controversial issue of "unhealthy tendencies" in the party to focus on the need for academic freedom, mass supervision of the party, and other aspects of political reform. The stated goal was to build a truly communist society, but one defined authoritatively as "socialism with Chinese characteristics." Party energies and discipline were to be directed at achieving this goal and removing all obstructions and obstructionists. Thus, while earlier the party had identified corruption as a prime target, this concern was replaced with attention to "indigenous feudal tendencies" that might hinder success in economic modernization (see The Third Wave of Reform, Beginning in 1986, ch. 11). The plenum endorsed the party's commitment to political reform and the extension of "socialist democracy and improving the socialist legal system, all for the purpose of facilitating socialist modernization."

Mass Organizations

In its efforts toward enlisting broad popular support and involvement, the CCP in 1987 continued to rely on mass organizations, "democratic parties" (see Glossary), and professional organizations. These organizations, affiliated directly and indirectly with the CCP, were without exception headed by and permeated with party cadres. As secondary or auxiliary vehicles for the party's "mass line," the organizations constituted a united front of support for the party line and policies and conveyed the impression desired by the party that the broad strata of the population endorsed and was unified behind the communist leadership. Moreover, mass organizations were used as a means to penetrate the society at large, encourage popular participation, mobilize the masses, and integrate them into party-directed political life.

Chinese People's Political Consultative Conference

The activities of the mass organizations in theory are represented by the Chinese People's Political Consultative Conference (CPPCC) but in actuality are directed by the United Front Work Department of the Central Committee. The CPPCC has national and local committees and is composed of a variety of groups and individuals: the Chinese Communist Party, the "eight democratic parties"; mass organizations, including the All-China Federation of Trade Unions, Communist Youth League, All-China Women's Federation, and All-China Federation of Industry and Commerce; minorities; compatriots from Hong Kong, Macao, and Taiwan; overseas Chinese (see Glossary); and outstanding scientists, educators, cultural figures, journalists, and medical professionals. In June 1983 the Sixth CPPCC held its first session, which was attended by 2,039 delegates, including representatives from the Chinese Communist Party (technically a member of the united front associated with the CPPCC). CPPCC national sessions usually are held in conjunction with the session of the National People's Congress. The CPPCC has as its basic functions providing political

China's party and state leaders in 1985: from left to right, Hu Yaobang, Deng Xiaoping, Li Xiannian, Zhao Ziyang, Deng Yingchao, and Peng Zhen
Courtesy Xinhua News Agency

consultancy on major state policies and encouraging a united front of patriotic intellectuals to contribute to modernization. The CPPCC is an important symbol of multiparty cooperation in China's modernization programs, and reform leaders have increasingly emphasized its role.

Democratic Parties

The eight "democratic parties" have existed since before 1950. They include the Revolutionary Committee of the Chinese Guomindang, founded in 1948 by dissident members of the mainstream Guomindang then under control of Generalissimo Chiang Kai-shek; China Democratic League, begun in 1941 by intellectuals in education and the arts; China Democratic National Construction Association, formed in 1945 by educators and national capitalists (industrialists and business people); China Association for Promoting Democracy, started in 1945 by intellectuals in cultural, education (primary and secondary schools), and publishing circles; Chinese Peasants' and Workers' Democratic Party, originated in 1930 by intellectuals in medicine, the arts, and education; China Zhi Gong Dang (Party for Public Interest), founded in 1925 to attract the support of overseas Chinese; Jiusan (September Third)

Society, founded in 1945 by a group of college professors and scientists to commemorate the victory of the "international war against fascism"; and Taiwan Democratic Self-Government League, created in 1947 by "patriotic supporters of democracy who originated in Taiwan and now reside on the mainland."

Trade Unions

The most prominent mass organizations were given key responsibility for supporting and implementing the reform program. CCP Secretariat member Hao Jianxiu, speaking to an executive meeting of the All-China Federation of Trade Unions, said that "as mass organizations of the working class, trade unions should stand at the forefront of the ongoing economic reform in China. They should blaze a new trail with distinct Chinese characteristics for conducting trade union activities." Specifically, Federation organizations were to aid members in acquiring modern scientific knowledge and technological skill. Within the membership and its affiliated organizations, intellectuals were to be protected and considered as members of the working class. Workers acquired the right to examine and discuss their factory director's principles, management plans, reform programs, budgets, and accounts. They also had the right to vote and to supervise and appraise leaders at all organizational levels. The workers' congress, held twice a year, was the organization empowered to exercise those rights. The regular organization that managed the daily affairs was the trade union body. These liberalizing changes were designed to improve workers' morale and thereby their productivity.

Communist Youth League

The Communist Youth League, the other primary communist organization, functioned as an all-purpose school for party members. Except for its top-ranking officials, the league's members, from fifteen to twenty-five years of age, were indoctrinated, trained, and prepared to serve as future party regulars. The league was organized on the party pattern. Its leader (in 1987 Song Defu) was identified as first secretary and member of the party's Central Committee. The Communist Youth League's eleventh congress, held in December 1982, was attended by about 2,000 delegates. The congress elected a central committee of 263 members and 51 alternate members. In 1987 the league included 52 million members attached to 2.3 million branches. They were required to carry out party policies, respect party discipline, and act as a "shock force and as a bridge linking the party with the broad masses of young people." Since 1984 the league's leadership has increased ties with youth organizations worldwide through friendly exchanges and cooperation. The Communist Youth League was responsible also for guiding the activities of the Young Pioneers (for children below the age of fifteen).

Women, Artists, Students, and Others

Among the other CPPCC groups, the All-China Women's Federation enlisted women in the party's effort to spread ideological awareness and to raise educational and technical levels. It also protected women's rights, promoted their welfare, and assisted them in family planning. The All-China Federation of Literary and Art Circles was guided by the principle "Let a hundred flowers bloom, let the hundred schools of thought contend," but with the stringent official qualification that all works must conform to the four cardinal principles (socialism, dictatorship of the proletariat, supporting the party leadership, and Marxism-Leninism-Mao Zedong Thought). The All-China Federation of Youth was designed as a patriotic united front, with the Communist Youth League as its "nucleus." An affiliated youth organization was the All-China Students' Federation for university and college students. The All-China Federation of Industry and Commerce took part in modernization efforts, offering consultant services in sciences and economics, training teachers and business managers, and running schools. The Chinese People's Association for Friendship with Foreign Countries was responsible for promoting friendly relations and mutual understanding on nongovernmental levels through foreign contacts and cultural exchanges. In 1985 the association had connections with more than 150 foreign countries. There were also several politically active groups among Chinese adherents of Buddhism, Islam, Taoism, and Christianity.

The Government

Constitutional Framework

The formal structure of government in 1987 was based on the State Constitution adopted on December 4, 1982, by the National People's Congress (NPC), China's highest legislative body. Three previous state constitutions—those of 1954, 1975, and 1978—had been superseded in turn. The 1982 document reflects Deng Xiaoping's determination to lay a lasting institutional foundation for domestic stability and modernization. The new State Constitution provides a legal basis for the broad changes in China's social and economic institutions and significantly revises government structure and procedures.

The 1982 State Constitution is a lengthy, hybrid document with 138 articles. Large sections were adapted directly from the 1978 constitution, but many of its changes derive from the 1954 constitution. Specifically, the new Constitution deemphasizes class struggle and places top priority on development and on incorporating the contributions and interests of nonparty groups that can play a central role in modernization. Accordingly, Article 1 of the State Constitution describes China as a "people's democratic dictatorship," meaning that the system is based on an alliance of the working classes—in communist terminology, the workers and peasants—and is led by the Communist Party, the vanguard of the working class. Elsewhere, the Constitution provides for a renewed and vital role for the groups that make up that basic alliance—the CPPCC, democratic parties, and mass organizations. The 1982 Constitution expunges almost all of the rhetoric associated with the Cultural Revolution (see Glossary) incorporated in the 1978 version. In fact, the Constitution omits all references to the Cultural Revolution and restates Mao Zedong's contributions in accordance with a major historical reassessment produced in June 1981 at the Sixth Plenum of the Eleventh Central Committee, the "Resolution on Some Historical Issues of the Party since the Founding of the People's Republic."

There also is emphasis throughout the 1982 State Constitution on socialist law as a regulator of political behavior. Thus, the rights and obligations of citizens are set out in detail far exceeding that provided in the 1978 constitution. Probably because of the excesses that filled the years of the Cultural Revolution, the 1982 Constitution gives even greater attention to clarifying citizens' "fundamental rights and duties" than the 1954 constitution did. The right to vote and to run for election begins at the age of eighteen except for those disenfranchised by law. The Constitution guarantees the freedom of religious worship as well as the "freedom not to believe in any religion" and affirms that "religious bodies and religious affairs are not subject to any foreign domination."

Article 35 of the 1982 State Constitution proclaims that "citizens of the People's Republic of China enjoy freedom of speech, of the press, of assembly, of association, of procession, and of demonstration." In the 1978 constitution, these rights were guaranteed, but so were the right to strike and the "four big rights," often called the "four bigs": to speak out freely, air views fully, hold great debates, and write big-character posters. In February 1980, following the Democracy Wall period (see Glossary), the four bigs were abolished in response to a party decision ratified by the National People's Congress. The right to strike was also dropped

Gate to Zhongnanhai, seat of the Chinese Communist Party and the State Council, Beijing
Courtesy Robert L. Worden

from the 1982 Constitution. The widespread expression of the four big rights during the student protests of late 1986 elicited the regime's strong censure because of their illegality. The official response cited Article 53 of the 1982 Constitution, which states that citizens must abide by the law and observe labor discipline and public order. Besides being illegal, practicing the four big rights offered the possibility of straying into criticism of the CCP, which was in fact what appeared in student wall posters. In a new era that strove for political stability and economic development, party leaders considered the four big rights politically destabilizing.

The new State Constitution is also more specific about the responsibilities and functions of offices and organs in the state structure. There are clear admonitions against familiar Chinese practices that the reformers have labeled abuses, such as concentrating power in the hands of a few leaders and permitting lifelong tenure in leadership positions. In addition, the 1982 Constitution provides an extensive legal framework for the liberalizing economic policies of the 1980s. It allows the collective economic sector not owned by the state a broader role and provides for limited private economic activity. Members of the expanded rural collectives have the right "to farm private plots, engage in household sideline production, and raise privately owned livestock." The primary emphasis is given to expanding the national economy, which is to be accomplished by balancing centralized economic planning with supplementary regulation by the market.

Another key difference between the 1978 and 1982 state constitutions is the latter's approach to outside help for the modernization program. Whereas the 1978 constitution stressed "self-reliance" in modernization efforts, the 1982 document provides the constitutional basis for the considerable body of laws passed by the NPC in subsequent years permitting and encouraging extensive foreign participation in all aspects of the economy. In addition, the 1982 document reflects the more flexible and less ideological orientation of foreign policy since 1978. Such phrases as "proletarian internationalism" and "social imperialism" have been dropped.

The National People's Congress

In the mid-1980s the NPC acquired heightened prominence. The NPC is defined in the 1982 Constitution as "the highest organ of state power" without being identified, as it was in the 1975 state constitution, as "under the leadership of the Communist Party of China." In addition, the Constitution states that "all power in the People's Republic of China belongs to the people." Although the preamble makes clear that the nation operates "under the leadership of the Communist Party of China and the guidance of Marxism-Leninism and Mao Zedong Thought," the trend has been to enhance the role of the NPC.

The major functions of the NPC are to amend the state constitution and enact laws; to supervise the enforcement of the state constitution and the law; to elect the president and the vice president of the republic; to decide on the choice of premier of the State Council upon nomination by the president; to elect the major officials of government; to elect the chairman and other members of the state Central Military Commission; to elect the president of the Supreme People's Court and the procurator-general of the Supreme People's Procuratorate; to examine and approve the national economic plan, the state budget, and the final state accounts; to decide on questions of war and peace; and to approve the establishment of special administrative regions and the "systems to be instituted there."

The NPC may also remove key government leaders, including the president and vice president and members of the State Council and state Central Military Commission. The 1982 State Constitution established the state Central Military Commission as the key governmental body charged with "directing the armed forces." While the party Central Military Commission provided the political direction for military policy making, the state Central Military Commission oversaw key military personnel appointments, managed PLA financial and material resources, developed regulations, and implemented statutes to provide a more rational and professional organizational basis for the PLA. The chairman of the state Central Military Commission—in a departure from earlier practices that put either the state president or the party chairman in command—was designated as the commander-in-chief of the armed forces.

The 3,000 members of the NPC meet once a year and serve 5-year terms. Delegates are elected by the people's congresses at the provincial level as well as by the PLA. Provincial delegations meet before each NPC session to discuss agenda items. There were 2,977 deputies at the First Session of the Sixth National People's Congress held from June 6 to 21, 1983. Because of the infrequent meetings, the NPC functions through a permanent body, the Standing Committee, whose members it elects (155 members in 1983). The Standing Committee's powers were enhanced in 1987 when it was given the ability to "enact and amend laws with the exception of those which should be enacted by the NPC," thus giving this body legislative powers. The Standing Committee presides over sessions of the NPC and determines the agenda, the routing of legislation, and nominations for offices. The NPC also has six permanent committees: one each for minorities, law, finance, foreign affairs, and overseas Chinese and one for education, science, culture, and health. Leaders of the NPC Standing Committee are invariably influential members of the CCP and leaders of major mass organizations. The Standing Committee has within it a smaller group that is led by the chairman of the Standing Committee (in 1987 Peng Zhen) and in 1987 included the vice chairmen and the secretary of the Standing Committee, comprising a total of twenty-one members.

In addition to the NPC's formal function, the Standing Committee is responsible, among other things, for conducting the election of NPC delegates; interpreting the State Constitution and laws; supervising the work of the executive, the state Central Military Commission, and judicial organs; deciding on the appointment and removal of State Council members on the recommendation of the premier; approving and removing senior judicial and diplomatic officials; ruling on the ratification and abrogation of treaties; and deciding on the proclamation of a state of war when the NPC is not in session.

Although in 1987 the NPC played a greater role than in earlier years, it did not determine the political course of the country. This remained the function of the CCP. Rather, the NPC played a consultative role. Another of its major functions was to serve as a symbol of the Communist regime's legitimacy and popular base. But with the emphasis in the mid-1980s on strengthening the democratic aspects of democratic centralism, the NPC may assume even more importance in decision making.

The State Council

In 1987 the top executive apparatus of the government was the State Council, the equivalent of the cabinet or council of ministers in many other countries (see fig. 19). Although formally responsible to the NPC and its Standing Committee in conducting a wide range of government functions both at the national and at the local levels, the State Council was responsive mainly to the CCP Secretariat, under the Political Bureau and its Standing Committee. This orientation was dictated by the fact that the senior members of the State Council were concurrently influential party leaders—a tie that has facilitated the party's centralized control over the state apparatus. It also tended to obscure distinctions between the party and the government, resulting in overcentralization of power in the hands of a few, and arbitrary behavior by, key leaders. Both excesses were condemned by reform leaders. Deng's intention was to introduce some checks and balances into the party and government sectors by clarifying their separate functions with administrative codes and regulations and by developing a legal base from which to enforce them.

The State Council met once a month and had a standing committee meeting twice a week that included the premier, vice premiers, a secretary, and state councillors. It was headed by the premier, Zhao Ziyang, who was re-elected to a five-year term in 1983. The membership of the State Council as of November 1986 included, in addition to the premier, five vice premiers (versus thirteen in 1980), the secretary, and eleven state councillors. As the chief administrative organ of government, its main functions were to formulate administrative measures, issue decisions and orders, and monitor their implementation; draft legislative bills for submission to the NPC or its Standing Committee; and prepare the economic plan and the state budget for deliberation and approval by the NPC. The State Council was the functional center of state power and clearinghouse for government initiatives at all levels. With the government's emphasis on economic modernization, the State Council clearly acquired additional importance and influence.

The State Council was supported by leading groups, which resembled institutionalized task forces and dealt with problems in the modernization program. For example, a leading group established in September 1986 was directed to investigate and suggest ways to eliminate the obstacles to foreign investment in China. In addition to the leading groups were offices that dealt with matters of ongoing concern. These included the Hong Kong and Macao Affairs Office and the Special Economic Zones Office. In 1987 the State Council structure also included thirty-two ministers in charge of ministries, nine ministers in charge of commissions, twenty-nine agencies for carrying out specialized functions, and eight major banking institutions (see table 3, Appendix B). (In 1980 there had been thirty-eight ministers presiding over ministries and eleven ministers in charge of commissions. The NPC Standing Committee established the new Ministry of Supervision in December 1986.) In a bureaucratic reorganization carried out mainly in 1982, thousands of elderly officials had been retired and replaced by younger and better educated officials. Reductions in leadership personnel in the bodies under the State Council were accompanied by reductions in the staff of these bodies from 49,000 to 32,000 members.

The Judiciary

The State Constitution of 1982 and the Organic Law of the People's Courts that went into effect on January 1, 1980, provide for a four-level court system. At the highest level is the Supreme People's Court, the premier appellate forum of the land, which supervises the administration of justice by all subordinate "local" and "special" people's courts. Local people's courts—the courts of the first instance—handle criminal and civil cases. These people's courts make up the remaining three levels of the court system and consist of "higher people's courts" at the level of the provinces, autonomous regions, and special municipalities; "intermediate people's courts" at the level of prefectures, autonomous prefectures, and municipalities; and "basic people's courts" at the level of autonomous counties, towns, and municipal districts (see Court Structure and Process, ch. 13).

In April 1986, at the Fourth Session of the Sixth National People's Congress, the General Principles of the Civil Code was approved as "one of China's basic laws." Consisting of more than 150 articles, the code is intended to regulate China's internal and external economic relations to establish a stable base conducive to trade and attractive to foreign investors. Many of its provisions define the legal status of economic entities and the property rights they exercise. The code clearly stipulates that private ownership of the means of production is protected by law and may not be seized or interfered with by any person or organization. It also

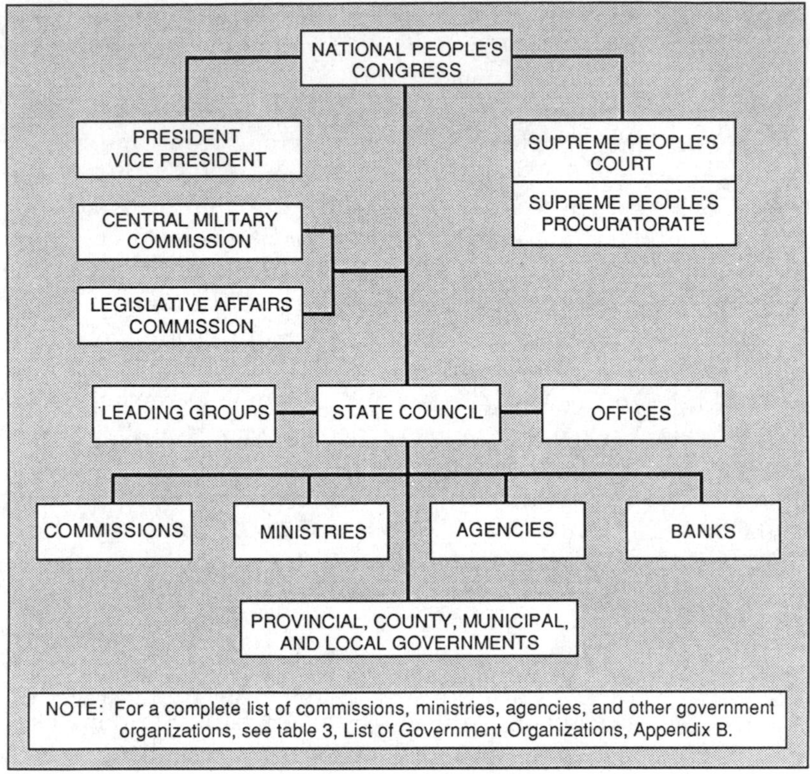

Figure 19. The Structure of the Government, 1987

recognizes partnerships and wholly foreign-owned or joint-venture enterprises (see Reform of the Economic System, Beginning in 1979, ch. 5).

Local Administration

Governmental institutions below the central level are regulated by the provisions of the State Constitution of 1982. These provisions are intended to streamline the local state institutions and make them more efficient and more responsive to grass-roots needs; to stimulate local initiative and creativity; to restore prestige to the local authorities that had been seriously diminished during the Cultural Revolution; and to aid local officials in their efforts to organize and mobilize the masses. As with other major reforms undertaken after 1978, the principal motivation for the provisions was to provide better support for the ongoing modernization program.

The state institutions below the national level were local people's congresses—the NPC's local counterparts—whose functions and powers were exercised by their standing committees at and above the county level when the congresses were not in session. The standing committee was composed of a chairman, vice chairmen, and members. The people's congresses also had permanent committees that became involved in governmental policy affecting their areas and their standing committees, and the people's congresses held meetings every other month to supervise provincial-level government activities. In May 1984 Peng Zhen described the relationship between the NPC Standing Committee and the standing committees at lower levels as "one of liaison, not of leadership." Further, he stressed that the institution of standing committees was aimed at transferring power to lower levels so as to tap the initiative of the localities for the modernization drive.

The administrative arm of these people's congresses was the local people's government. Its local organs were established at three levels: the provinces, autonomous regions, and special municipalities; autonomous prefectures, counties, autonomous counties (called *banners* in Nei Monggol Autonomous Region (Inner Mongolia)), cities, and municipal districts; and, at the base of the administrative hierarchy, administrative towns (*xiang*). The administrative towns replaced people's communes as the basic level of administration.

Reform programs have brought the devolution of considerable decision-making authority to the provincial and lower levels. Nevertheless, because of the continued predominance of the fundamental principle of democratic centralism, which is at the base of China's State Constitution, these lower levels are always vulnerable to changes in direction and decisions originated at the central level of government. In this respect, all local organs are essentially extensions of central government authorities and thus are responsible to the "unified leadership" of the central organs.

The people's congresses at the provincial, city, and county levels each elected the heads of their respective government organizations. These included governors and deputy governors, mayors and deputy mayors, and heads and deputy heads of counties, districts, and towns. The people's congresses also had the right to recall these officials and to demand explanations for official actions. Specifically, any motion raised by a delegate and supported by three others obligated the corresponding government authorities to respond. Congresses at each level examined and approved budgets and the plans for the economic and social development of their respective administrative areas. They also maintained public order, protected public property, and safeguarded the rights of citizens of all nationalities. (About 7 percent of the total population was composed of minority nationalities concentrated mainly in sensitive border areas.) All deputies were to maintain close and responsive contacts with their various constituents.

Before 1980 people's congresses at and above the county level did not have standing committees. These had been considered superfluous because the local congresses did not have a heavy workload and in any case could serve adequately as executive bodies for the local organs of power. The CCP's decision in 1978 to adopt the Four Modernizations as its official party line, however, produced a critical need for broad mass support and the means to mobilize that support for the varied activities of both party and state organs. In short, the new programs revealed the importance of responsive government. The CCP view was that the standing committees were better equipped than the local people's governments to address such functions as convening the people's congresses; keeping in touch with the grass roots and their deputies; supervising, inspecting, appointing, and removing local administrative and judicial personnel; and preparing for the election of local deputies to the next higher people's congresses. The use of standing committees was seen as a more effective and rational way to supervise the activities of the local people's governments than requiring that local administrative authorities check and balance themselves. The proclaimed purpose of the standing committee system was to make local governments more responsible and more responsive to constituents.

The establishment of the standing committees in effect also meant restoring the formal division of responsibilities between party and state authorities that had existed before 1966. The 1979 reform mandated that the party should not interfere with the administrative activities of local government organs and that its function should be confined to "political leadership" to ensure that the party's line was correctly followed and implemented. Provincial-level party secretaries, for instance, were no longer allowed to serve concurrently as provincial-level governors or deputy governors (chairmen or vice chairmen in autonomous regions, and mayors or deputy mayors in special municipalities), as they had been allowed to do during the Cultural Revolution. In this connection most officials who had held positions in the former provincial-level revolutionary committees were excluded from the new local people's governments. Some provincial-level officials who were purged during the Cultural Revolution were rehabilitated and returned to power.

The local people's congresses and their standing committees were given the authority to pass local legislation and regulations under the Organic Law of the People's Courts of 1980. This authority was granted only at the level of provinces, autonomous regions, and special municipalities. Its purpose was to allow local congresses to accommodate the special circumstances and actual needs of their jurisdictions. This measure was billed as a "major reform" instituted because "a unified constitution and a set of uniform laws for the whole country have proved increasingly inadequate" in coping with differing "local features or cultural and economic conditions." On July 17, 1979, *Renmin Ribao* (People's Daily) observed: "To better enforce the constitution and state laws, we must bring them more in line with the concrete realities in various areas and empower these areas to approve local laws and regulations so that they can decide certain major issues with local conditions in mind." The law explicitly stated, however, that the scope of legislation must be within the limits of the State Constitution and policies of the state, and that locally enacted bills must be submitted "for the record" to the Standing Committee of the NPC and to the State Council, which, according to the 1982 State Constitution, can annul them if they are found to "contravene the Constitution, the statutes, or the administrative rules and regulations."

In 1987 the party and the government continued to stress the importance of bringing about popular "supervision" over, for instance, the pivotal county-level administration. The importance of maintaining close ties with the masses, listening to their opinions, being concerned with their welfare, and serving their interests was emphasized. Such concern was ensured with the adoption of electoral procedures as part of the 1979 reform package that called for instituting direct elections of deputies to the local people's congresses at the county level. Under the old procedure, the electorate's only choice had been to vote for a slate of candidates equal in number to the number of deputies to be elected. Additional reforms provided for a more open process of nomination, a secret ballot with a choice of candidates, and the possibility of primary elections. The new election procedures were also extended to the election of government officials and of delegates to high-level people's congresses. (All of these reforms taken together offered the potential, in those areas where they were adopted, for significant change.) Experiments reportedly also were taking place in certain medium-sized cities, beginning in 1986, to increase participation by citizens in political activities and decision making. In December 1986 Beijing municipal authorities announced that the mid-1987 municipal elections would allow more than one candidate to run for election for each seat available. This announcement came as extensive student demonstrations in key urban centers were demanding broader democratic freedoms.

China's paramount leader Deng Xiaoping Courtesy Xinhua News Agency

CCP general secretary and member of the Standing Committee of the Political Bureau of the Chinese Communist Party, Zhao Ziyang Courtesy Xinhua News Agency

Official efforts to improve government performance at the grass-roots level continued in 1987. They had as a precedent a set of regulations, first enacted in 1952 and 1954, covering the activities of what are officially referred to as "basic-level mass autonomous organizations." Such organizations included the urban neighborhood committees, subdistrict offices, people's mediation committees, and public security committees. These regulations had been reissued in January 1980 by the NPC Standing Committee in an attempt to strengthen the grass-roots organizations. In addition, the 1982 State Constitution had proclaimed the establishment of residents' and villagers' committees to ensure public security and preserve social order; to provide public health services and mediate civil disputes; and, most important, to carry information to and from government organs. Another significant reform at the basic level was the establishment of the administrative town (xiang)

Li Peng, member of the Standing Committee of the Political Bureau of the Chinese Communist Party and future premier of the State Council
Courtesy Xinhua News Agency

President of the People's Republic of China, Yang Shangkun
Courtesy Xinhua News Agency

government to replace the commune. This reform freed the commune to function solely as an economic unit.

Another administrative reform directly related to economic modernization was the establishment in 1979 of the special economic zones, which included Shenzhen, Zhuhai, and Shantou, all in Guangdong Province, and Xiamen in Fujian Province. Supervising China's special economic zones were the Guangdong provincial committee in charge of the special economic zones, headquartered in Shenzhen, and the Xiamen Construction and Development Corporation. The Guangdong provincial committee controlled Zhuhai, Shenzhen, and Shantou and shared its authority over Shekou (a small port zone within Shenzhen) with the China Merchant Steam Navigation Company. The latter was a Hong Kong subsidiary of China's Ministry of Communications that had been empowered in 1979 to negotiate all foreign ventures in Shekou.

The special administrative region, another administrative unit, was developed to serve foreign policy goals. Article 31 of the State Constitution of 1982 empowers the NPC to enact laws to establish special administrative regions to accommodate local conditions. Hong Kong will come under this rule when Britain transfers its sovereignty over its former colony to China on July 1, 1997, as delineated in the Joint Declaration on the Question of Hong Kong, signed on September 26, 1984. Macao is slated to become a special administrative region on December 20, 1999, when Portugal is to transfer governmental authority over Macao to China, as stipulated in the Joint Declaration on the Question of Macao, initialed on March 26, 1987 (see Nationalism, ch. 12). In 1986 and 1987 the State Council's Hong Kong and Macao Affairs Office was drafting the Basic Law for the Hong Kong Special Administrative Region, which would define Hong Kong's system of government. The new law was due for completion in 1988.

The Cadre System

In 1987 the party and government cadre (*ganbu*) system, the rough equivalent of the civil service system in many other countries, was entering the final stages of a massive overhaul aimed at transforming the bureaucracy into an effective instrument of national policy. The term *cadre* refers to a public official holding a responsible or managerial position, usually full time, in party and government. A cadre may or may not be a member of the CCP, although a person in a sensitive position would almost certainly be a party member.

In an August 1980 speech, "On the Reform of the Party and State Leadership System," Deng Xiaoping declared that power was overcentralized and concentrated in the hands of individuals who acted arbitrarily, following patriarchal methods in carrying out their duties. Deng meant that the bureaucracy operated without the benefit of regularized and institutionalized procedures, and he recommended corrective measures such as abolishing the bureaucratic practice of life tenure for leading positions. In 1981 Deng proposed that a younger, better educated leadership corps be recruited from among cadres in their forties and fifties who had trained at colleges or technical secondary schools.

The theme of "streamlining and rejuvenating" the bureaucracy was taken up by Zhao Ziyang in early 1980 when he announced a major overhaul of the government. The number of vice premiers was reduced from 13 to 2, State Council agencies were cut by almost half, and the number of ministers and vice ministers was reduced from 505 to 167. The new appointees were younger and better

Wan Li was to become chairman of the Standing Committee of the National People's Congress in 1988
Courtesy Xinhua News Agency

educated than their predecessors. In January 1982 Deng called for a "revolution" in the bureaucracy, starting with its top levels. At that time, Deng envisioned reducing the size of the government bureaucracy by one-quarter over a two-year period. By retiring veteran cadres, the way could be opened for promoting younger, professionally competent cadres to positions of authority and thereby providing the effective leadership needed for China's modernization. In May 1982 the Central Committee reorganized and streamlined its internal structure by cutting staff in its 30 component departments by 17.3 percent. Subordinate bureaus were reduced by 11 percent. Almost half of the CCP Central Committee elected in September 1982 were new members, and 83 percent of the alternate members were newly elected.

Reorganization of the provincial-level party and government structures took place between late 1982 and May 1983. During this period, almost one-third of the provincial-level party first secretaries and all but three of the governors were replaced, most of them moving into advisory positions. Almost two-thirds of provincial-level leaders in 1986 were college or university educated. During 1983 and 1984, these reforms reached the prefectural, county, municipal, and town levels, reportedly resulting in a reduction in staff of 36 percent and an elevation in the percentage of college educated leaders to 44 percent.

Simultaneous with restructuring and rejuvenating the bureaucracy, a drive was begun to improve the party's working style and consolidate party organizations. The Second Plenum of the Twelfth Central Committee, held in October 1983, initiated such a program for the years 1984–86. Some 388,000 party members participated in the first stage of party rectification. These included high- and middle-ranking cadres in 159 leading organs in the central departments, provinces, autonomous regions, special municipalities, and PLA. This phase of the campaign lasted over a year and was accompanied by the recruitment of 340,000 technicians and 32,000 college and university graduates and postgraduates into the CCP. In addition, a campaign was launched to ferret out residual leftist influence from the Cultural Revolution period, factionalism, and corruption. Discipline inspection committees were reinstituted. Three kinds of party members were singled out as special targets: followers of the Gang of Four (see Glossary) or of Lin Biao, factionalists, and persons who "beat, smashed, and looted" during the Cultural Revolution. These members were to be expelled from the party. Lesser offenders requiring correction included party members with bureaucratic or patriarchal attitudes, those seeking personal power and position, and those inept or lazy in their work.

The principal objective of the reform leadership was to establish a system of steady, predictable rule through the creation of a professional bureaucracy. An important aspect of the program was personnel reform. Guidelines were issued that set age limits for key offices. A limit of sixty-five years of age was imposed for government ministers, sixty for vice ministers and department chiefs, and, for all other officials, sixty for men and fifty-five for women. The effect of this key reform was to bring to an end the lifetime tenure system that had been fundamental to China's bureaucracy since 1949. There was the additional stipulation that officeholders in the reconstructed bureaucracy be qualified both politically and professionally, that is, be both "red" and "expert." The reorganization and streamlining of provincial-level party and government bureaucracies followed the same procedures, including reducing the staff sizes and number of offices, lowering the average age, and raising the educational requirements for candidates for provincial-level leadership. These changes were considered essential to providing for a "third echelon" of leaders. This group could serve in positions of some authority, where they could be trained, observed, and evaluated as to their suitability for increased responsibility. Below the central level, the chosen age for leaders at the level of provinces, autonomous regions, and special municipalities was fifty-five; at the county level, between thirty and fifty years.

The second stage of party rectification, having the same goals as the first stage, began in the fall of 1984 and encompassed prefectural and county-level units. This stage involved some 13.5 million cadres, or about one-third of the party's membership. The third and final stage of the three-year party rectification campaign was launched in November 1985 and targeted party units "below the county level." This stage encompassed almost 20 million party members, about half the total membership of the party. These members belonged to the more than 1 million party branches throughout the rural areas. The campaign worked from the higher to the lower level organizations and proceeded methodically "in stages and groups." But while party pronouncements at previous stages of the rectification had complained about the perfunctory manner in which the campaigns were being managed, at this final stage the central authorities displayed notable leniency and caution. They feared that extensive restructuring and rebuilding of the local leadership had the potential to disrupt both production and social order. Even in cases of embezzlement, graft, and other "unhealthy practices," the party counseled circumspection and the employment of moderate measures. Subjecting local leaders to condemnation at mass meetings, a practice prevalent during the Cultural Revolution, was strictly forbidden.

In sum, the "revolution" being carried out in the bureaucratic structures of power was meant to reorient the system away from the style, procedures, and excesses of the Cultural Revolution and toward the most efficient and potentially successful methods for China's modernization. This reorientation required the massive retirement of veteran cadres and the recruitment of those knowledgeable in modern economics and technology to be trained in leadership positions. It was an enormous task and one that obviously met significant resistance from those who either did not understand the new requirements or saw them as a substantial threat to their position and livelihood. Nevertheless, in early 1987 the reform leadership appeared to be making very credible strides at fulfilling these goals.

The Media

Since 1978 the media had been one focus of the CCP's efforts to modernize key sectors of Chinese society, and it operated on the premise that more responsible and factual reporting would help to narrow the distance between the elite and the masses. The party hoped in this way to enlist mass support for its nation-building program. In 1987 the official media continued to play its assigned role as a vehicle through which to inform, educate, indoctrinate, control, and mobilize the masses.

Before 1978 the CCP used the mass media as a tool to "serve the interest of proletarian politics" or the party's "class struggle" and "mass line." Having these priorities, the party was concerned neither with openness nor accuracy. What the CCP considered information was more often than not the interpretation of events or data that would support the government's political, social, and economic programs. Timeliness of content was far less important than political or ideological utility. Before 1976 the party allowed no dissenting view to appear in print. The result was reporting and commentary that made information and propaganda all but synonymous.

With the ascendancy of the Deng Xiaoping reformers in 1978, the mass media began to display a different orientation and focus. It began to play a significant part in the CCP drive to popularize, first within the party, the notion of "practice being the only criterion of truth" and of "seeking truth from facts," rather than from petrified formulations. After March 1978 the party press no longer printed Mao's quotations in bold type. Moreover, it began to report more shortcomings and expose more criticism of the central authorities. In 1987 there still were considerable limits on criticism in the official media, however. Party general secretary Hu Yaobang, in a 1986 speech published in the party's daily organ *Renmin Ribao*, instructed editors that 80 percent of reporting should focus on achievements in modernization and only 20 percent on shortcomings.

China's extensive communication system includes both official and unofficial channels. Official means of communication include government directives and state documents, newspapers, periodicals, books, and other publications; radio and television; and drama, art, motion pictures, and exhibitions. Unofficial channels include handwritten wall newspapers, handbills, posters, street-corner skits, and theater (see Culture and the Arts, ch. 4). Of all these channels, the newspapers, periodicals, and electronic media continued in 1987 to play the most important part in communications.

Among the principal national newspapers in 1987, *Renmin Ribao* contained party and government directives, unsigned editorials, commentaries, and letters to the editor. The latter were often critical of local implementation of central policies. The PLA organ was *Jiefangjun Bao* (Liberation Army Daily). *Gongren Ribao* (Workers' Daily) dealt with labor matters, and *Guangming Ribao* (Enlightenment Daily) provided coverage of science, culture, and education. There were numerous other newspapers published both at the provincial-level and at the mass organization-level, but none of these had the prestige and authoritativeness associated with the party and army newspapers. Starting in 1978, party authorities permitted newspapers from south China provinces to circulate outside

China; in 1983 north China newspapers were given foreign circulation. There were also many specialty newspapers focusing on the economy, trade and finance, agriculture, the arts, youth affairs, and so on. By the end of 1984, post offices in China reportedly were distributing 734 different newspapers with a total circulation of 112.9 million, or a newspaper for every eighth person in China.

Hongqi (Red Flag), a journal published by the CCP Central Committee, provides guidance on questions of current political theory, explaining the direction of the party's Marxist analysis, setting forth the party line, and suggesting the proper methods for implementing it. A monthly until December 1979, *Hongqi* since has been published twice a month. The government also publishes its major reports and documents. For example, *Guowuyuan Gongbao* (State Council Bulletin), appearing three times a month, provides a summary of directives, prints notices, presents agreements signed with foreign countries, and registers central approval given to local government actions.

In addition to open official and unofficial documents, there is another large category of materials that is classified for internal use (*neibu*), as opposed to for public use (*gongkai*). These materials are published by party, government, academic, and professional organizations. Some publications have additional restrictions, such as for distribution only within the publishing unit. The most protected publication is entitled *Cankao Ziliao* (Reference Information) and is distributed to around 1,000 high officials daily. A similar internal use publication, but with a much wider readership, is the *Cankao Xiaoxi* (Reference News). This publication contains translations of selected foreign news articles, many of which are critical of China. These internally circulated materials generally are more reliable and detailed than those found in the open press.

The principal source of domestic news and the sole source of international news for the mass domestic newspapers and radio is the Xinhua (New China) News Agency. This government agency has departments dealing with domestic news, international news, domestic news for foreign news services, and foreign affairs. It maintains an extensive network of correspondents in ninety overseas bureaus. Xinhua also releases the *News Bulletin* in English, French, Spanish, Arabic, and Russian, totaling about 30,000 words per day, and provides special features to newspapers and magazines in more than 100 countries. Domestic branches of Xinhua can communicate with the head office over microwave communications. Internationally, a telecommunications network has been established linking Beijing with Paris, London, New York, Tokyo and Hong Kong. Further, Xinhua has rented an international communications satellite to file news to foreign countries and exchange news with foreign news agencies. It mails special features to newspapers and magazines in more than 100 countries. Another news agency, China News Service (Zhongguo Xinwenshe), provides news stories and photographs to Chinese newspapers and some radio and television stations in Hong Kong, Macao, and several foreign countries.

By 1984 electronic media included over 160 radio stations and 90 television stations (see Telecommunications, ch. 8). The Central People's Broadcasting Station, headquartered in Beijing and subordinate to the Ministry of Radio, Cinema, and Television, provided domestic service to every area of the country. Radio Beijing, China's overseas radio service, continued to expand its programming, initiating a news program in English for foreign residents in Beijing in January 1985. Television service was available in the major urban areas and was increasing its reach outside urban centers. China's television broadcasting was under the control of China Central Television (CCTV). In 1979 the network began an "open university" program. By 1984 China reported having "radio and television universities" in 326 cities and 1,168 counties throughout 28 provinces, autonomous regions, and special municipalities, making the use of television an important aspect of higher education in China (see Education Policy, ch. 4).

* * *

The dynamic nature and pace of political and social change in China have inspired a number of new works by China specialists. For discussion of the concepts basic to the cadre system, A. Doak Barnett's *Cadres, Bureaucracy, and Political Power in Communist China* is useful. Also useful is Franz Schurmann's *Ideology and Organization in Communist China*. Of specific relevance to this chapter is the State Constitution of 1982, which appears in *Beijing Review*, December 27, 1982, and the Party Constitution of 1982, which appears in *Beijing Review*, September 20, 1982. These two documents, as well as extensive summary material on other subjects, also appear in *People's Republic of China Year Book, 1985*. *China Quarterly* publishes in each issue a useful section entitled "Chronicle and Documentation" that contains factual information and analysis of key official meetings, events, foreign relations, and so on. In addition, two useful articles appearing in this publication are Melanie Manion's "The Cadre Management System Post-Mao: The Appointment, Promotion, Transfer and Removal of Party and State Leaders," and David S.G. Goodman's "The National CCP Conference of September 1985 and China's

Leadership Changes.'' Of particular use is James R. Townsend and Brantly Womack's *Politics in China*, which explains China's political and institutional framework and the governmental process. A similar and detailed work is Alan P.L. Liu's *How China Is Ruled*. Political and structural reforms are dealt with in the first volume of *China's Economy Looks Toward the Year 2000*, published by the United States Congress Joint Economic Committee. Another work that summarizes these subjects and includes a wide variety of selected documents covering key topics is *Policy Conflicts in Post-Mao China*, edited by John P. Burns and Stanley Rosen. (For further information and complete citations, see Bibliography.)

Chapter 11. The Political Process

An Eastern Han dynasty (A.D. 25–220) cavalryman awaits battle armed with a halberd. The bronze figure, about fifty-three centimeters high, was part of a group of mounted soldiers discovered in Gansu Province.

CHINA'S "SECOND REVOLUTION," a far-reaching program of reform designed by Deng Xiaoping, was initiated at the Third Plenum of the Eleventh Central Committee in December 1978. It marked a major turning point in China's modern political history, as it was intended to make China's institutions and political process supportive of the Four Modernizations, a national program of social and economic development. The first step was to recruit intellectuals and mobilize the population on a course of modernization. Ultimately, it was hoped, these efforts would produce what became identified as "socialism with Chinese characteristics."

To realize this lofty goal, several obstacles had to be overcome. The Cultural Revolution, under Mao Zedong's direction between 1966 and 1976, had divided Chinese society into competing factions. The deaths of Zhou Enlai and Mao Zedong in 1976 left the country without strong leadership and contributed further to social and political divisiveness. The need became obvious to replace Mao's premise of "class struggle as the key link"—which emphasized class conflict and disruptive mass campaigns—with a pragmatic style that stressed stability and a problem-solving approach to difficulties encountered in carrying out developmental programs. The overly centralized political system, patterned after the Soviet Union's Stalinist model, had to be revised to decentralize decision-making authority.

Probably the greatest impediment to the success of modernization was the unwieldy Chinese bureaucracy. Steeped in revolutionary tradition but advanced in age and largely untrained in modern administrative procedures, party and government cadres operated through personal connections and patriarchal attitudes. For the party and government to exercise effective control over modernization programs, these cadres would have to be replaced by younger and better trained administrators, a development that not surprisingly would provoke considerable resistance from within the bureaucracy. Finally, the means had to be found to engage urban workers, peasants, and intellectuals in China's modernization process by separating them from their traditional and often backward viewpoints and providing them with a more practical and scientific basis for their actions.

The substantial revisions to China's social, political, and ideological system, required for the success of the "second revolution," caused serious tensions within the political system. The introduction of major economic reforms also caused considerable strains. But the economic reform measures, first introduced in China's rural areas, provoked an enthusiastic response and a substantial following. With this success as a base, additional reform measures were prepared in October 1984 for introduction into China's more diverse and complicated urban sector. Concomitant with measures to promote rural and urban development, plans were made for substantial revision and reorganization of the political and administrative structure in China, particularly the party and government cadre system.

Because of the innovative nature of the political and economic reform programs, each wave of reform stimulated a constituency supporting its development. Beneficiaries of the new measures carried them out with enthusiasm, sometimes even taking them beyond their originally intended scope. At the same time, a substantial segment of the affected population found itself undercut and showed varying degrees of opposition to the reform initiatives. The reform measures, initially designed by China's top party leaders, took on a dimension of spontaneity as they were implemented. The dynamics of the reform process, generating degrees of support and opposition, played a substantial role in shaping the political process in China after 1978.

Operating within this context, China's top party leaders had a twofold task. First, they had to preserve a consensus among the senior party leadership (the Political Bureau) concerning the nature and content of reform measures and the pace at which they would be introduced. Second, that consensus had to survive the continual dislocations and permutations that accompanied the implementation process. Some reforms provoked instability by being zealously pursued; others bogged down in resistance. By 1987 it appeared that the resolution of these emerging issues and problems was accomplished mainly by internal bargaining among key leaders, who often represented major institutional interests, and by disciplinary measures. The latter case was exemplified by the forced resignation of party general secretary Hu Yaobang early in that year. In a more general sense, the major function of reform leadership was to maintain stability in the political system while preserving the momentum necessary for perpetuating the overall reform program. In short, as in other developing societies, China's leaders have had to manage the tensions inherent in a society undergoing rapid and thoroughgoing change.

Finally, Marxism-Leninism-Mao Zedong Thought—the official state ideology—needed continual substantive revision and changes in emphasis by China's political leadership. Under Mao Zedong's leadership, China's recognized ideal had been to create the true "socialist man." In the 1980s Deng Xiaoping set for his government the perhaps equally idealistic goal of leading the enormous population of this developing country, still imbued with "feudalistic" traditions, toward the achievement of a modern, developed state by the year 2000. It was a goal that seemed to require frequent revision if it were ever to be achieved.

Political Realignments at the Party Center

Chairman Hua Guofeng presided over the historic Third Plenum of the Eleventh Central Committee on December 18–22, 1978, his authority rooted in his generally acknowledged claim to be Mao Zedong's chosen successor. Viewed in historical context, Hua's role was that of a relatively minor figure temporarily bridging the gap between the radical leadership associated with Mao and the Cultural Revolution and the emergence of new political leaders who could consolidate national policy and assert credible authority (see The Post-Mao Period, 1976–78, ch. 1). Hua's political weakness was most graphically illustrated by the rehabilitation—for the second time—of Deng Xiaoping, in July 1977, and Deng's subsequent successful elevation of his protégés and initiation of a comprehensive reform program to realize the Four Modernizations.

This transitional period moved toward far-reaching reform and even a reassessment of Mao Zedong Thought. Economic development and material rewards to motivate producers replaced the Maoist emphasis on ideological goals and incentives. A stress on political stability supplanted the call to "continuing revolution." In Chinese academic circles, efforts were made to restore and raise academic standards, and party leaders stressed the importance of science and technology and the contribution of intellectuals in realizing modernization. The liberalization of expression in intellectual and cultural circles led to further questioning of the Cultural Revolution, Mao's role, and Mao Zedong Thought.

Between 1979 and 1981 it became necessary to "readjust" some of the reform programs and initiatives to effect a balance between reformist and conservative forces. The major issues dividing these forces were China's capacity to sustain rapid economic development and the political and cultural consequences of opening up to the world and allowing liberalization of expression and behavior. The retrenchment that followed was a readjustment and not an end to Deng Xiaoping's reform agenda.

Deng Xiaoping Consolidates Power

Deng's second rehabilitation marked another milestone in the career of one of the party's most remarkable leaders. Born in Sichuan Province in 1904, Deng was the son of a wealthy landlord. A bright student, he went to France on a work-study program in 1920. There Deng, like many other Chinese students, was radicalized and joined the nascent Chinese Communist Party. He had returned to China by 1926 and, after the party was forced underground in 1927, became involved in guerrilla activities (see Republican China, ch. 1). Eventually he joined the main body of the party and Red Army in Jiangxi Province. Deng participated in the Long March (see Glossary) and rose through the ranks of the Red Army to become a senior political commissar during the war against Japan (1937–45) and the Chinese civil war (1945–49). After the establishment of the People's Republic of China in 1949, he was assigned his home province of Sichuan, where he was made first secretary of the Southwest Regional Party Bureau. In 1952 Deng was transferred to Beijing and given several key positions, the highest of which was vice premier of the State Council—a remarkable development that he probably owed to Mao's favor.

In 1956 Deng was promoted over several more-senior party leaders to the Standing Committee of the Political Bureau and became secretary general of the party, that is, head of the party Secretariat. As secretary general, Deng became involved in the day-to-day implementation of party policies and had immediate access to the resources of the entire party bureaucracy. Consequently, Deng's power grew immensely. Because he perceived Mao's radical economic policies to have been harmful to China's development after 1958, Deng began to work more closely with State Chairman Liu Shaoqi. Deng's behavior irritated Mao, and his stress on results over ideological orthodoxy struck Mao as "revisionism" (see Glossary). During the Cultural Revolution, Deng was branded the "number-two capitalist roader in the party" (Liu Shaoqi was the "number-one capitalist roader," having allegedly abandoned socialism, see The Cultural Revolution Decade, 1966–76, ch. 1). In 1967 Deng was driven from power and sent to work in a tractor factory in Jiangxi Province.

After the excesses of the Cultural Revolution and the shock of an attempted military coup in 1971 by Lin Biao, Premier Zhou Enlai apparently recommended that Deng be brought back to aid in dealing with increasingly complex domestic and international issues. Mao agreed, and Deng returned in April 1973 as a vice premier. He rejoined the Political Bureau in December, becoming more active in national affairs as Zhou Enlai's health weakened. By early 1975 he was in charge of the work of the Central Committee as one of its vice chairmen. From this powerful vantage point,

Deng concentrated on moderating the effects of the more radical aspects of the policies introduced during the Cultural Revolution and on focusing national attention on economic development. He also continued to build his own political influence through restoring to high office many old cadres who had been purged during the Cultural Revolution. Mao again began to distrust Deng and, after Zhou's death, decided that Deng should once again be removed from his positions.

Deng has been described as aggressive, brash, impatient, and self-confident. He inspired respect among Chinese officials as a capable administrator and a brilliant intellect. He did not, however, inspire loyalty and devotion, and he admitted that his hard-driving personality often alienated others. In contrast to Mao, Deng offered no expansive socialist vision. Rather, Deng's message was a practical one: to make the Chinese people more prosperous and China a modern socialist state. Deng's pragmatic style arose primarily from his dedication to placing China among the world's great powers.

Deng consolidated his power and influence by removing his opponents from their power bases, elevating his protégés to key positions, revising the political institutional structure, retiring elderly party leaders who either were hesitant about his reform programs or too weak and incompetent to implement them, and raising up a replacement generation of leaders beholden to him and apparently enthusiastic about the reform program. As a first step toward achieving these goals, Deng set out to remove Hua Guofeng, apparently a firm believer in Mao's ideals, from the three pivotal positions of chairman of the party and of its powerful Central Military Commission and premier of the State Council. At that time, Deng was on the Political Bureau Standing Committee, vice chairman of the party Central Military Commission, and vice premier of the State Council.

At the Third Plenum, four new members were elected to the Political Bureau, all to varying degrees supporters of the reform program. Hu Yaobang, an energetic protégé of Deng Xiaoping, was elected, as was Wang Zhen, a Deng stalwart. Also elected were Deng Yingchao, widow of Zhou Enlai, and Chen Yun, architect of China's 1950s economic policy. Chen also became head of the newly established Central Commission for Discipline Inspection (see Other Party Organs, ch. 10). Following the plenum, Hu Yaobang was appointed secretary general of the party and head of its Propaganda Department. Further personnel changes beneficial to Deng occurred at the Fifth Plenum, held February 23–29, 1980. Hu Yaobang was elevated to the Standing Committee of the

Political Bureau, as was another Deng protégé, Zhao Ziyang. With these promotions, accompanied by the forced resignations of members associated with the Cultural Revolution, the Standing Committee was comprised of seven members, four of whom were strongly committed to party and economic reform.

Hua Guofeng's position was eroded further in mid-1980, when he was replaced as premier by Zhao Ziyang. A fast-rising provincial party official, Zhao spent his early career in Guangdong Province, where he gained expertise in managing agricultural affairs. Unlike Hua, whose political status had improved during the Cultural Revolution, Zhao Ziyang was purged in 1967 for supporting the policies of Mao's opponents. After his rehabilitation in 1972, Zhao worked briefly in Nei Monggol Autonomous Region (Inner Mongolia) and then returned to Guangdong Province. In 1975, a peak period in Deng's influence, Zhao was sent to troubled Sichuan Province as party first secretary. Under Zhao's leadership Sichuan Province returned to political and economic health. Zhao believed firmly in material incentives, and he promoted experiments in returning decision-making authority to the local work units, rather than centralizing it exclusively in provincial-level or central administrative bureaus.

Hua Guofeng's political isolation deepened when at the Central Committee's Sixth Plenum, in June 1981, he was replaced as party chairman by General Secretary Hu Yaobang. This key meeting reevaluated party history, including the Cultural Revolution, and charged Mao with major errors in his later years. Hua, having been identified with the "two whatevers" group ("support whatever policy decisions Chairman Mao made and follow whatever instructions Chairman Mao gave"), was marked for political oblivion. At this same meeting, Deng Xiaoping assumed Hua's former position as chairman of the party's Central Military Commission, advancing his goal of ridding the top military ranks of reform opponents. With these developments, Deng was poised for an even more thorough consolidation of the reform leadership at the upcoming Twelfth National Party Congress.

Institutionalizing Collective Leadership

Following the Third Plenum, one of Deng Xiaoping's major reform goals had been to produce an institutionalized and stable political system that could promote economic development. Economic reform was to be accompanied by political reform that would permit a greater range of personal and intellectual choices and include the opening up of debate on key issues of local and national concern.

A major part of this political reform had to do with implementing the concept of collective leadership. The cult of personality cultivated by Mao and those associated with him had made Chinese society subject to the whims of an aging and increasingly irrational revolutionary personality. To counter this style and project an image of political maturity and regularity, Deng declined to assume the party chairmanship. Even Hua Guofeng's demotion from senior leadership positions was done gradually and was cushioned by allowing Hua to retain his membership on the Central Committee. Overall, Deng's objective was to invert the practice of having power vested more in individuals than in institutions and to modify a decision-making process that operated by fiat, without regular procedures or an adequate information base.

A major step toward institutionalizing collective leadership was taken with the re-establishment of the party Secretariat in 1980 (see Secretariat, ch. 10). Its formation permitted the emplacement of promising younger leaders to manage and master day-to-day party affairs. Having supervisory authority over the various Central Committee departments, the Secretariat could provide the Political Bureau and its presiding Standing Committee with additional expertise in making decisions. By 1987 the Secretariat included eleven members, six of whom also served on the Political Bureau. The broad experience of its membership covered all major substantive areas, including party, government, and military affairs, agriculture, the national economy and planning, culture and propaganda, and industry and trade. In addition to drafting the major policy resolutions for Political Bureau deliberation and then supervising the implementation of party policy, the Secretariat used its expertise and organizational standing to exert pressure on the cumbersome Chinese bureaucracy to achieve the desired results.

The 1982 Party Constitution abolished the post of party chairman and expanded the base of political authority to include the Standing Committee of the Political Bureau, party general secretary, chairman of the party's Central Military Commission, first secretary of the Central Commission for Discipline Inspection, and chairman of the Central Advisory Commission. The premier also served on the Standing Committee, which thus included in its policy-making ranks representatives of the three major institutions—party, government, and military.

Another measure that promoted a more balanced distribution of power was the strengthening of senior governmental bodies. As premier, Zhao Ziyang presided over the State Council, a body crucial to the implementation of economic reform measures and, like the party Secretariat, supported by an abundance of research institutions to aid in decision making (see The State Council, ch. 10). By 1987 the State Council, the chief administrative organization of government and clearinghouse for government actions, was composed of twenty-two members, including Premier Zhao and five vice premiers who also served on the Political Bureau. Its Standing Committee of seventeen included senior members with long and recognized experience in all aspects of government. The State Council directed the work of the various government ministries, commissions, and agencies and verified that relevant party policies were being implemented.

The process of easing out unwanted leaders was institutionalized at the Twelfth National Party Congress in September 1982. Deng Xiaoping developed and headed the new central body, the party's Central Advisory Commission. Qualified members with at least forty years of party service were honored by being named to this body as consultants to the party and the government. This institutional innovation was intended to remove the superannuated veterans from real power positions while allowing them to remain at least at the fringes of power.

Besides providing for the graceful retirement of old revolutionary heroes and elderly leaders, at the Twelfth National Party Congress the reform leadership successfully consolidated its control of the party. Sixty percent of the members and alternate members on the newly elected Central Committee were newcomers and probable supporters of the reform program. Most of those elected had professional and technical qualifications, fulfilling another reform goal of infusing the bureaucracy with competent and talented officials.

A Successor Generation

An even more remarkable shift in the composition of party leadership occurred at the National Conference of Party Delegates in September 1985. Over 100 senior party leaders submitted their resignations, including 10 members of the Political Bureau and 64 members of the Central Committee. The officials reportedly gave their reason for retiring as a desire to make way for younger and better-educated leaders who were more equipped to lead China and guide the reform program. In fact, these retiring leaders were a mixed group, some of whom lacked the vigor and skills necessary to handle the complexities of reform, while others had reservations concerning the direction and pace of the reform program. Some even may have believed that it was best to turn over responsibilities to a younger leadership. In spite of this trend, Deng, who was himself eighty-two years old, and several other senior leaders

The Twelfth National Party Congress of the Chinese Communist Party, September 1982
Courtesy Xinhua News Agency

continued in office. Officially, he maintained that his requests to retire had all been turned down. In fact, the progress of the reform program was heavily dependent on Deng's continued central role.

Hu Yaobang's demotion in 1987 also raised questions about the quality of the selection process for top positions and even about the stability of the reforming Chinese political system. Hu had been viewed as Deng's successor as party leader, but he came under attack from within the Political Bureau for what was described as indirectly encouraging questioning of the communist system, for pushing the economic reforms beyond their intended limits, and for speaking out abruptly in international circles. Although Deng reportedly apprised Hu of his errors, Hu was said to have failed to change and thus was demoted in accordance with party disciplinary rules. Obvious attempts were made to ease the general shock of Hu's demotion, including allowing him to retain his seat on the Standing Committee of the Political Bureau and having him shown in the press in attendance at key meetings. It seemed likely that Hu would be demoted further, at the Thirteenth National Party Congress scheduled for October 1987. This would correspond to the treatment a few years before of Hua Guofeng and preserve the appearance that the party was handling leadership affairs rationally, in clear contrast to the era of Maoist purges.

The First Wave of Reform, 1979–84

In the process of introducing reforms, China's leaders for the most part have acted cautiously and introduced new programs incrementally. In the period of the Four Modernizations, they began a broad search of foreign sources for ideas to introduce and test in the Chinese environment. Their pragmatic approach entailed following the progress of newly introduced concepts closely in order to make any necessary mid-course corrections or deletions. Maintaining the momentum of the reform program required the leaders to interact constantly to meet the challenges, failures, and setbacks inherent in their experiment.

The major changes introduced by key reforms inevitably provoked tensions in the political system. Strains developed between those who would not benefit or could not adjust to the new conditions and those who saw the new opportunities afforded. The resulting pressures on the system required constant attention of and mediation by the top party leaders. The goals, contents, and progress of the reform program reportedly were reviewed and discussed regularly at the highest-level party meetings. Leaders on the Political Bureau Standing Committee strove for consensus on the contents of the reform program and its agenda and participated in an ongoing process of bargaining to reconcile different policy orientations and institutional interests. The competing interests that emerged throughout the country when a new wave of reform was introduced appeared to have spokesmen or advocates in the highest party circles. The issues that emerged were debated in authoritative party meetings with the aim of arriving at a consensus and preserving harmony on the reform agenda. If this became impossible, personnel changes tended to follow, as was the case when Hu Yaobang apparently broke the consensus, moving ahead of what the cautious and stability-minded leadership could accept as a safe and reasonable course.

In this way China, under Deng Xiaoping's leadership, appeared to follow the tenets of democratic centralism (see Glossary). Policies that originated at the authoritative party center were tested and evaluated in practice, and reports of their results, including problems and setbacks, were then channeled back to the system's center for debate. In the 1980s it became something of a leadership art to keep the reform program going, balance the tensions it provoked, and maintain the political system intact. Seen in this context, a key question became whether or not political leaders other than Deng Xiaoping would have the prestige and political skill needed to direct and preserve this delicate balance, especially after Deng passed from the scene.

The Opening Up Policy and Reform in the Countryside

The first reforms to affect China's economy were instituted between 1979 and 1984. The programs were systemic economic reforms aimed at revising China's foreign economic relations and refocusing the country's agricultural system. The desire to purchase foreign equipment and technology needed for China's modernization led to a policy of opening up to the outside world that would earn foreign exchange through tourism, exports, and arms sales (see Reform of the Economic System, Beginning in 1979, ch. 5). The opening up policy included sending large numbers of students abroad to acquire special training and needed skills. The effect was to make China more dependent on major sectors of the world economy and reverse the Maoist commitment to the ideal of self-reliance. Not everyone was satisfied with this radical departure. The conservative reformers were especially apprehensive about the corrupting cultural and ideological influences that they believed accompanied foreign exposure and imports.

In China's rural areas, the economic reform program decollectivized agriculture through a contract responsibility system (see Glossary) based on individual households (see Rural Society, ch. 3; Agricultural Policies, ch. 6). The people's communes (see Glossary) established under Mao were largely replaced with a system of family-based farming. The rural reforms successfully increased productivity, the amount of available arable land, and peasant per capita income. All of these were major reform achievements. Their success stimulated substantial support in the countryside for the expansion and deepening of the reform agenda.

While the opening up policy and rural reform produced significant benefits to the Chinese economy and won enthusiastic support for the Deng reformers, they also generated substantial problems and brought political opposition from conservative leaders. The Maoist ideal of self-reliance still had proponents among the leadership in the 1980s, and many were openly critical of the expanding foreign influences, especially in such areas as the special economic zones (see Glossary).

In rural areas, economic reform led to inequalities among economic regions and appeared in some instances to produce a new, potentially exploitative class of rich peasants. The official press contained accounts of peasants who carried the profit motive far beyond the intent of the reform program, engaging in smuggling, embezzlement, and blatant displays of newly acquired wealth. Thus, on the one hand, top leaders fully supporting the reform agenda could show major successes as they promoted further reform. On the other hand, those more concerned with ideological continuity and social stability could identify problems and areas of risk. The differing perceptions and responses of these reformist and conservative groups produced considerable tension in the political system.

Rectification and Reform

These results of the opening up policy and rural reform programs had important political repercussions at the national level. The question of borrowing from the West has been debated vigorously since the early nineteenth century. The concern has always been the impact of Western social, political, and cultural traditions, sometimes referred to derisively as the "flies and insects" that blow in along with culturally neutral scientific and technical information. This concern was especially prevalent among conservatives in the highest leadership circles and extended to the possibly corrosive effect of Western traditions on the party's Marxist-Leninist ideological foundation. To meet this challenge, in October 1983 the party launched a national program to improve "party style," organization, and ideology.

According to Chen Yun, a leading conservative and major figure in party rectification, the question of party style was crucial for the organization's very survival, especially because of the party's tarnished image and the perceived crisis of confidence and loss of prestige during the Cultural Revolution period. Improving party style required that organizational norms be restored, which entailed ridding the party of factionalism. It also demanded that measures be taken to counter corruption and the exercise of privilege. These frequently had taken the form of abuses by cadres who used personal relations and "back-door" benefits to further their own interests. Finally, improved party style required that political discipline be enforced in implementing party programs.

These goals were accomplished over the next three years, accompanied by thorough ideological education. The Second Plenum of the Twelfth Central Committee (October 11–12, 1983) affirmed that the policy of opening up to the outside world was entirely correct but condemned the "corrosive influence of decadent bourgeois ideology" that accompanied it and the "remnant feudal ideas" still pervasive within the party system, which required thorough rectification. In effect, linking the attempt to "clear away cultural contamination" with improving party style meant rejecting both the radical left, or those who still carried the taint of associations with the Cultural Revolution, and those on the right, who were considered by some party leaders to have become too involved in the trappings of Western ideas and practices.

At the same time that the party was attempting to discipline its own ranks, a drive was initiated within Chinese society to crack down on crime. Beginning in August 1983, the drive focused on the increase in serious crimes against social order: murder, robbery, burglary, rape, and arson. Explanations for the crime wave included the breakdown of law and order that had begun in the Cultural Revolution period and corrupting influences that had slipped in with the opening up policy (see Return to Socialist Legality, ch. 13).

A campaign against "spiritual pollution" was initiated by a speech given at the Second Plenum by Deng Xiaoping (see Policy Toward Intellectuals, ch. 4). The campaign targeted "decadent, moribund ideas of the bourgeoisie" that questioned the suitability of the socialist system or the legitimacy of the party's leading role. It also sought to establish a basis for ideological continuity between the emerging younger generation and the older, civil-war-era veterans. Conservative Political Bureau members attempted to use the campaign to rectify what they considered decadent behavior and corrosive liberal thought. Following this example, some lower-level party cadres began to exhibit behavior similar to that of the mass campaigns of the Cultural Revolution. Young men and women with long hair or Western-style clothing were subjected to ridicule and abuse. Peasants who had prospered were accused of selfishness; in response, some ceased to participate in rural reform. Intellectuals were again under suspicion, and party and government cadres adopted a "wait-and-see" attitude to avoid making political errors.

To avert potential instability and stagnation of the reform program, the authorities began to place limits on the spiritual pollution campaign: it was not to be pursued in the countryside, it was not to impede scientific research aimed at promoting modernization, and, most important, it was not to be implemented in the mass-campaign style of the Cultural Revolution.

By the spring of 1984 the full-scale media treatment of spiritual pollution had subsided, indicating that party leaders were able to confront the problems and build a consensus on how to contain the excesses and return to the reform program. In May, in a bow to the conservatives, Zhao Ziyang reported that although mistakes had been made in implementing the spiritual pollution campaign, the issue of spiritual pollution remained on the party agenda. The reform leadership thus eased the tensions within the system by acknowledging that reactions to the reform program would occur and by checking any obstructions, disruptions, or violence that emerged. This essentially conciliatory approach was necessary at least until opponents could be removed or reformed through a series of new appointments or through the continuing party rectification program.

The Second Wave of Reform, 1984–86

Reform of the urban industrial and commercial economy was formally initiated with the landmark "Decision of the Central Committee of the Chinese Communist Party on Reform of the Economic Structure" issued in October 1984. The radical changes contained in the urban program were revealed as it unfolded, and they heralded additional tensions. The urban program was accompanied by a less publicized but apparently spectacularly successful program for developing rural industry. These programs presented considerable challenges for the political system. The strain was intensified by the fact that the urban reform system was being implemented at a time when the party rectification program was extending below the central level, into all areas of society.

The Repercussions of Urban Reform

The party leadership benefited from the success of the rural reform program and the generally enthusiastic public response it generated. The leadership sought to use this success as a basis for tackling reform of the much more complicated and diverse urban sector. The overall goal of the highly experimental urban reform program has been to create a mixed economy in which the market plays a significant role and in which state planning is concerned more with regulating than with directing the economy. This approach, however, has led to tensions both in conceptualization and in the effects of reforms on people.

At the conceptual level, the reform's emphasis on leasing industrial and commercial enterprises to individuals and collectives raised the issue of diversification of ownership and challenged the orthodox concept of state ownership. The introduction of securities markets and stock exchanges raised the question of how many Western-style reforms China could absorb and still call itself a socialist country. The same question applied to the adoption of a controversial bankruptcy law. These emerging problems were bound to be troublesome to party leaders like Chen Yun, who adhered to more orthodox socialist concepts.

At the level of implementation, questions emerged concerning the speculation and exploitation that was believed to accompany the operation of stock exchanges. The introduction of bankruptcy provisions was viewed as contributing to unemployment and hardships for the workers. Also, the introduction of a labor contract system, while providing opportunities to motivated and competent workers, might well threaten the livelihood of the less skilled. Even the new value being placed on entrepreneurship challenged the

The Gate of Heavenly Peace (Tiananmen) in Beijing, entrance to the Forbidden City
Courtesy Robert L. Worden

previous way of life, in which the state made all decisions and provided the means of sustaining life.

Although these challenges were serious, the most important dimension of the reform program was its distribution of power and authority. This function can be viewed as the dominant political role of the urban reform program, affecting the structure and organization of the party itself.

The Decentralization of Power

To produce the desired "socialist planned commodity economy," China's reform leadership began to recognize the necessity of transferring more authority over economic decision making to urban factory managers. A "factory director responsibility system" was developed to encourage more local initiative, more efficient use of resources, and more skillful and judicious leadership by the front-line producers. The reform immediately met serious resistance from party secretaries attached to the factories, who until then had been responsible for factory management and especially for personnel decisions. In their view, the reform threatened party perquisites and usurped local party decision-making authority.

This major issue in industrial reform was introduced in the context of the party's ongoing efforts to redefine the proper party role, especially vis-à-vis the government. In the mid-1980s it appeared that party leaders would have to share power even further, this time with enterprise managers or economic reform managers. Mid-level party cadres, many of whom had become party members during the Cultural Revolution decade, were particularly prone to negative feelings, especially concerning the urban reform program. Their resistance and resentment found sympathy among national-level party and government conservatives like Peng Zhen, Deng Liqun, and others and provided a substantial base of support for these leaders when they presented their own, similar views in policy-making circles. At least the leaders at the top who advocated more gradual reform could point to this disgruntled mid-level party group as a reason for revising the pace and content of the reform agenda.

The Third Wave of Reform, Beginning in 1986

The reform program seems to have followed a logical sequence, building a base of support in the countryside, where issues and institutions were more clear-cut, and then moving on to the more diverse and politically complex urban areas. As the reform program began to confront major obstacles in this setting, the reform leaders, led by Deng Xiaoping, began to emphasize the need to extend reform to political structures in order to make political institutions and processes more supportive of the modernization program.

The need for further political reform was underlined by the continuing difficulty in implementing the factory-director responsibility system, a major goal of the reform program for 1986. Party cadres had already lost the privilege of life tenure and been subjected to the rigors and requirements of the party rectification programs. They would not easily forfeit operational control of economic enterprises.

Political Reform

The August 1980 address on reform made by Deng to the Political Bureau became the basis in 1987 for changes in the party and state leadership systems. In the 1980 speech, Deng had called for strengthening the people's congresses, separating party and government organizations, reforming the cadre system, and establishing an independent judiciary. By 1986 the leadership's apparently overriding interest in Deng's plan was to curtail excessive party interference in governmental and economic decision making, and it was therefore bound eventually to provoke apprehension and resistance. In early 1986, with responsibility for political reform resting in the party Secretariat, several reports were aired concerning party secretaries at lower levels who had refused to relinquish decision-making power to benefit local economic reform management. Many local unit secretaries had succeeded in reclaiming authority previously given up. While Deng and the central reform leaders emphasized that party interference in government affairs actually weakened party leadership, conservative leaders such as Peng Zhen continued to speak about party unity and spirit and about the more gradual means to political change. Gradual means included additional legislation and the proper functioning of democratic centralism.

In addition to the new emphasis on power sharing in economic management, pressures increased to realize the goals of "socialist democracy" by increasing participation in public affairs through direct elections from a field of candidates. In fact, it was a student protest over the local slate of officials for a people's congress election in Anhui Province that sparked the student demonstrations that spread throughout the country in late 1986. In extending the argument for increased freedoms and democratic practices, demonstrators began even to question the presiding role of the party in the political system. Demonstrations in at least seventeen cities, with participants in the tens of thousands, also threatened to disrupt the urban economy and the continuation of the economic reform program. The drive to decentralize power and to separate party from government authority created political strains already apparent from the fact that no authoritative statement on these key issues ensued from the Sixth Plenum of the Twelfth Central Committee held in September 1986. The student demonstrations that followed lent credibility to conservative ideologues in the Secretariat, such as Deng Liqun, who argued that continued political relaxation and reform would inevitably lead to social chaos.

Resistance and the Campaign Against Bourgeois Liberalization

In late 1986, during the critical period when the Chinese political system appeared threatened by student demonstrators burning copies of party official newspapers, General Secretary Hu Yaobang failed to act to restore order. Hu refused to denounce the demonstrators or their intellectual mentors or to retreat from the political reform agenda. Instead, Hu favored the introduction of more "democratization" or pluralism into the political system. He called for more movement on political reform than the system could bear. In effect, Hu had outstripped the consensus concerning the pace and content of the reform agenda. In response, Deng Xiaoping had to make the difficult decision to remove his protégé from the post of party general secretary, a step taken by unanimous decision at an extraordinary expanded Political Bureau meeting in January 1987. Hu was replaced by Zhao Ziyang, one of the chief architects of the economic reform program, who explained that democratic reforms in China required a "protracted" process for their implementation.

At the same time that Hu Yaobang was removed from office, a campaign was initiated against "bourgeois liberalization." Given heavy play in the official media, this campaign sought to discredit Western political concepts and emphasize the importance of adhering to the four cardinal principles (see Glossary). The campaign against bourgeois liberalization became the means for conservatives led by Political Bureau members Chen Yun, Peng Zhen, and Hu Qiaomu to express their opposition to some of the reforms, especially the pace of the reform agenda, and to the increased democratization advocated by Hu Yaobang. Having responded to major conservative concerns, Zhao then emphasized the limits that had been placed on the campaign against bourgeois liberalization. The ideological campaign was to be limited to the party, and it was neither to reach the rural areas nor to affect economic reform policies. In addition, experimentation in the arts and sciences was not to be discouraged by this campaign. The imposition of these limits was inspired no doubt in large part by the need to avoid disruptions such as those that had accompanied the spiritual pollution campaign in 1983 and 1984. Besides affirming his support for the ongoing campaign against bourgeois liberalization, within specified limits, Zhao stressed that the economic reform program—including opening up to the outside world—would continue.

In March 1987 Deng Xiaoping made it clear that political reform also was to continue and that a "tentative plan" for political reform would be included on the agenda of the Thirteenth National Party Congress in October 1987. Deng's revelation suggested that with Hu Yaobang removed, China's senior leadership had reached a consensus on the sensitive issue of political reform, which had been discussed by many of them in general and cautious terms for some time. Even conservative senior leaders such as Li Xiannian and Peng Zhen made statements supporting political reform. This development did not limit the likelihood of very intense debate before and during the next National Party Congress on the specific implementation of this most sensitive program. But it did suggest that, with Hu Yaobang's demotion, China's top leaders could discuss key details of the future role of the party in China's reformed political system at the upcoming congress.

The Politics of Modernization

In the years following the Third Plenum of the Eleventh Committee Central in 1978, certain key reforms set in motion a process of systemic change in society. Successful continuation of the reform program depended on the ability of China's senior leaders to respond to the constant challenges encountered in implementing these changes. Although a significant portion of the political system underwent major reform, a central question remaining in the late 1980s was whether or not the party could maintain stable central leadership. There was reason to question whether a consensus could be built within China's top leadership circles without the presence of a leader of the stature of Deng Xiaoping. With major bureaucratic interests to contend with and satisfy, and differing ideological orientations within the top leadership, strong central direction seemed to be the basic requirement for continuing reform.

The Components of Reform

The major components of 1980s political reform emphasized collective leadership, the re-establishment of the party Secretariat to implement party policy and to train a group of senior-level successors, the strengthening of the government apparatus to enable it to share more power and responsibility for the development of the reform program, and the removal of the military from a major and sustained role in politics. The introduction of direct elections and multiple candidates for people's congresses up to the county level broadened public participation in China's governmental and political processes. Also, the electoral process provided an expanded forum for assessing both the potential and the shortcomings of party reform policies. The intent to involve the public in the process of identifying and resolving problems that emerged in implementing the reform program also was extended to vocational groups. For example, workers' congresses were given increased leeway to examine, debate, and discuss the policies being carried out in factories and even to evaluate the performance of factory managers. Even though the governmental and vocational groups had no direct political power, their new public voice on reform elevated the political process at least one step above the secret, closed channels of the Maoist era. In institutionalizing the reform debate, the party also developed a more efficient means for shaping and channeling public debate.

Competing Bureaucratic Interests

The implementation of these components of political reform contributed to internal tensions and competition among the major bureaucracies—the party, government, and military. The party's status remained paramount within the system, but the delineation of its role became increasingly vague. Theoretically, the party was to act as the unifying force that would guide the society on the difficult path to modernization. In practice, especially at the middle levels of the structure, it appeared in the mid-1980s that implementation of the reform program was greatly diluting the power of party cadres. Many party members were retired to advisory capacities, increased emphasis was placed on separating the functions of the party and government, and much of the decision-making authority in the economic sphere was transferred to enterprise managers. All these factors eroded the party's once pervasive authority. Although the party continued to articulate the central policy for all levels of society, it offered fewer opportunities for members to achieve recognition and rewards after 1978, when concrete results became more important. All this brought widespread bureaucratic resistance to reform policies and their implementation.

Retirements, elevated entrance qualifications, and power sharing with enterprise managers also brought traumatic changes in government bureaucracy. Direct elections to people's congresses added a new element of uncertainty about the cadre selection process for government service. Wider public discussion of issues and more extensive press coverage subjected state cadres to additional demands and criticisms and sometimes to abuse. The new accountability offered opportunities for government cadres, but often they perceived it as a threat or a burden. It soon became another major source of the complaints conveyed to top leadership circles.

In the late 1980s, the People's Liberation Army continued as a major player in political circles and had representatives on the Political Bureau (see Civil-Military Relations, ch. 14). Its presence within senior party bodies significantly declined in the 1980s, however, as was apparent from the percentage of party Central Committee memberships held by military personnel. Military influence had reached a high point in 1969, when its representatives gained roughly half the seats on the party's Ninth Central Committee, but declined at the Tenth Central Committee (1973) and Eleventh Central Committee (1978). In 1982 full membership on the Twelfth Central Committee held by People's Liberation Army personnel dropped to around 20 percent. At the National Conference of Party Delegates held in September 1985, about half of those retired from the Central Committee were from the armed forces, and civilians replaced seven members of the Political Bureau who had military connections.

These trends reflected Deng Xiaoping's military reform goals of placing the People's Liberation Army under firm civilian leadership and transforming its ranks and organization into a modern, professional military establishment. Owing partly to its size and largely to its heavily Maoist revolutionary traditions, the military was essentially conservative and in 1987 continued to resist many of the reformers' policies. It seemed possible that Deng's successors might experience strong pressure from a revitalized People's Liberation Army to restore some of its lost political influence.

Deng Xiaoping's Seminal Role

Although post-Mao pronouncements by the Chinese Communist Party officially emphasized collective leadership, Deng Xiaoping clearly occupied center stage and acquired unique political stature in the party hierarchy (without even holding the titular number-one position). Following the consolidation of Deng's power at the Twelfth National Party Congress in 1982, the party issued *The Selected Works of Deng Xiaoping*. The book was intended to provide authoritative ideological backing for the reform program in progress and became required reading for party members. Another volume, entitled *Building Socialism with Chinese Characteristics*, issued in 1985, contained speeches and writings on economic policy, ideological questions, and foreign policy written by Deng after the Twelfth National Party Congress. A major purpose of the later work was to support the dramatic reforms introduced at the Third Plenum of that congress's Central Committee in October 1984. This book was re-released in March 1987 with additional speeches and remarks on intervening events, purportedly with the intention of providing extensive guidance for reform. Given the volume and frequency of publication, it became difficult for the reform leadership to avoid the appearance of creating a cult of personality around Deng.

Deng was an effective bridge between China's legendary revolutionary generation and the generation engaged in carrying out the Four Modernizations. At the same time, Deng's preeminence called attention to the succession issue. The resolution of problems emerging in the course of reform depended heavily on Deng's political backing and on his authoritative reform pronouncements. In large measure, Deng's published works would support later leaders by providing them an authoritative source with which to bolster their own reform measures. Like any body of writing, however, Deng's thoughts are open to interpretation and thus might as easily be used by an opposition group for its own ends.

Marxism-Leninism-Mao Zedong Thought Re-Thought

Continuous development of the means of production is a major goal of all Marxist governments. Under Mao, however, that goal was pursued in a manner that subordinated economic policy to the dictates of massive class struggle and, in the end, to political struggle carried up to the Political Bureau level. Mao, who admitted his own ignorance of economics, resented efforts to correct the problems caused by hasty agricultural collectivization and the Great Leap Forward (1958–60; see Glossary), and he initiated a political and ideological "struggle" against the 1950s reformers. This political campaign reached massive proportions during the Cultural Revolution, doing extensive damage to the economic, political, and social fabric of Chinese society.

In contrast, the post-Mao leadership so emphasized the issue of economic modernization that modernization began to shape the political process itself. Economic modernization became the basis of Deng Xiaoping's pragmatic reform policies. Despite disagreements over the content and pace of the reform program, Deng won solid support from other senior Chinese leaders who recognized the great danger of neglecting economic development and the well-being of the people.

The difference in political style between Mao and Deng was evident in their approach to opposition. When Mao perceived that party bureaucrats were blocking the full implementation of his radical programs, he set out in the early 1960s to purify the party. In contrast, faced with similar opposition in the 1980s, Deng sought points of agreement and built a coalition around an eclectic economic program.

The Role of Ideology

In the early 1950s, Mao borrowed Stalinist social and economic principles in promoting development. When these methods failed to produce immediate and spectacular results, Mao adopted a mass-campaign style of development derived from his experiences as a guerrilla leader. When applied to post-1949 problems, however, the style produced chaos. Mao's writings and speeches degenerated into rigid dogma that his followers insisted be followed to the letter. Deng, conversely, advocated a flexible and creative application of Marxist principles, even claiming that Marxism, as the product of an earlier age, did not provide all the means for addressing contemporary issues. Rather, he advocated taking a highly empirical approach known as "seeking truth from facts" in order to find the most effective means of dealing with problems. In Deng's approach, ideology itself was not the source of truth but merely an instrument for arriving at truth by experimentation, observation, and generalization.

To effect such a basic revision of Maoist ideology, Deng had to de-mystify Mao and reduce the towering image of the "Great Helmsman" to more human proportions. This was largely accomplished in June 1981, when the party's Sixth Plenum of the Eleventh Central Committee reassessed Mao's place in the history of the Chinese revolution. In the years after 1981, the leadership nevertheless continued to revere Mao's image as a revolutionary, nationalist, and modernizing symbol, especially when that image aided

The Chairman Mao Memorial Hall in Tiananmen Square with the Monument to the People's Heroes in the foreground, Beijing
Courtesy Robert L. Worden

Billboard-sized pictures and heroic statues of Mao Zedong once prevalent throughout China became less common in the 1980s. This one was prominently located at the front gates of the Beijing Iron and Steel College, Beijing, in 1986.
Courtesy Robert L. Worden

development of Deng's reform program (see China and the Four Modernizations, 1979–82, ch. 1).

Ideology and the Socialist Man

An important goal of Maoist ideology was the inculcation of certain prescribed values in party members and, by extension, in society as a whole. These included selfless dedication to the common good; an egalitarian concern with the uncomplicated expression of ideas in maxims or brief phrases understandable to all; and fervent commitment to ideal social behavior. In contrast, state ideology in the hands of Deng Xiaoping had a different purpose. The orientation was practical and less doctrinaire, aimed at fulfilling the goals of modernization. The official ideology was to be used to channel the individual's attempts to understand and practice modern concepts and methods. For example, in early 1987 the concept of village committees was introduced to give the massive rural population direct experience in self-management. It did not appear that these new bodies were meant to have substantive power but rather that they were intended to indoctrinate the population with modern approaches to social and political relations.

Paralleling this use of ideology as a cognitive tool was the party's policy of "emancipating the mind" and allowing debate to extend into subjects once considered "forbidden zones." China's scholars have argued publicly over issues such as the value of the commune system, the need for market concepts in a socialist economy, the historical impact of humanism, and even the current relevance of Marxism-Leninism. Student demonstrators in the mid-1980s went too far, however, by questioning the preeminent role of the party. At that point, the immediate official response was to subordinate creativity and experimentation to public recognition of the presiding role of the party and its ideology.

Ideology and Social Change

Since the Third Plenum of the Eleventh Central Committee in December 1978, party reformers have been committed to channeling the increased political awareness and energies of the population into a strengthened movement for change. The tensions that have emerged during each successive wave of reform have required intervention and policy decisions at senior party levels. These sometimes have taken the form of new initiatives. At other times, tensions have precipitated a conservative response. Overall, this political process has seemed to support a gradual but forward movement of the reform program.

Modernization, by its very nature, is a socially disruptive process.

In 1987, with many of the functions of the party apparatus still unclear even to party members and the question of Deng Xiaoping's successor still unsettled, the success of China's reform program was by no means assured.

* * *

Relatively few book-length studies of post-Mao politics are available. One of the more notable is John Gardner's *Chinese Politics and the Succession to Mao*, the major points of which are summarized and updated in his lengthy article "China under Deng." Key official documents for much of the post-Mao period can be found in *The People's Republic of China, 1979–1984*, edited by Harold Hinton. A valuable survey of the period is provided by A. Doak Barnett's "Ten Years after Mao."

Harry Harding's "Political Development in Post-Mao China," in Barnett and Ralph Clough's *Modernizing China: Post-Mao Reform and Development*, contains useful information on the post-1978 political scene. Articles by Harding, Carol Hamrin, and Christopher Clarke in the United States Congress Joint Economic Committee's *China's Economy Looks Toward the Year 2000* also are helpful in understanding the post-Mao era.

Andrew J. Nathan's *Chinese Democracy* skillfully analyzes the evolution of the Chinese conception of "democracy." Michel Oksenberg and Richard Bush, in "China's Political Evolution, 1972–1982," give extensive descriptions of the Chinese bureaucracy. Melanie Manion's "The Cadre Management System, Post-Mao: The Appointment, Promotion, Transfer, and Removal of Party and State Leaders" is a good examination of the cadre management system. David S. G. Goodman's "The National CCP Conference of September 1985 and China's Leadership Changes" presents extensive data on leadership developments in the mid-1980s.

Mao's China and After by Maurice Meisner and *Politics in China* by James R. Townsend and Brantly Womack provide general background on the post-1978 political history of China. Barnett's older *Cadres, Bureaucracy, and Political Power in Communist China* and Richard H. Solomon's *Mao's Revolution and the Chinese Political Culture* give excellent background on contemporary Chinese politics. Also, Franz Schurmann's seminal work, *Ideology and Organization in Communist China*, provides clear and extensive discussion on the basic elements of the Chinese political system.

Biographies of key Chinese leaders can be found in works by David Chang, Jerome Chen, Stuart Schram, and Dick Wilson. (For further information and complete citations, see Bibliography.)

Chapter 12. Foreign Relations

Waiting in eternity for battle, this terra-cotta archer was entombed with tens of thousands of similar figures toward the end of the Qin dynasty (221–207 B.C.) near Xi'an, Shaanxi Province.

IN THE 1980s CHINA pursued an independent foreign policy, formally disavowing too close a relationship with either the United States or the Soviet Union. The stated goals of this policy were safeguarding world peace, opposing all forms of hegemony, and achieving economic modernization at home. Chinese statements repeatedly emphasized the interrelation among these goals. In other words, China needed a peaceful international environment so that adequate resources could be devoted to its ambitious development plans for the rest of the twentieth century. The goal of economic modernization was a driving force behind China's increasingly active participation in world affairs, exemplified by its policy of opening up to the outside world, which greatly expanded Chinese economic relations with foreign countries. As part of what it called an "independent foreign policy of peace," Beijing had joined numerous international organizations, and it maintained diplomatic relations with more nations than at any time since the founding of the People's Republic of China in 1949. By mid-1987, China had diplomatic relations with 133 nations, and—in contrast with earlier periods—was willing to interact with governments of different social systems or ideologies on a basis of peaceful coexistence and mutual respect.

Although Chinese foreign policy since 1949 has had distinctive characteristics, the forces that shape Beijing's foreign policy and many of its overall goals have been similar to those of other nations. China has sought to protect its sovereignty and territorial integrity and to achieve independence of action, while interacting with both more powerful and less powerful countries. As with most other nations, Beijing's foreign relations have been conditioned by its historical experiences, nationalism and ideology, and the worldview of its leaders, as well as by the governmental structure and decision-making process. At times China's domestic policies have had wide-ranging ramifications for its foreign policy formulation.

Another characteristic Chinese foreign policy has had in common with that of many other countries is that the actual conduct of foreign relations sometimes has been at odds with official policy. Beijing's stress on ideology and principles in its official statements at times makes the contrast between statements and actions particularly noticeable. In addition, a nation's leaders must often make decisions in reaction to events and circumstances, rather than simply formulating a rational foreign policy based on their goals. The need to react to what has happened or what may happen adds an element of unpredictability to foreign policy decision making, as has been the case at several crucial junctures in Chinese foreign relations since 1949.

In addition to the aspects of foreign policy formulation and implementation that China has in common with other countries, China's foreign policy from 1949 to the late 1980s has had these characteristics: contrast between practicality and adherence to principles; fluctuation between militancy and peacefulness; tension between self-reliance and dependence on others; and contrast between China's actual and potential capabilities. These contradictory characteristics have created a confusing picture of Chinese foreign policy: is Chinese foreign policy basically pragmatic or primarily based on principles and ideology? Is China peace-loving or intent on fomenting world revolution? Is China's ultimate goal to be self-sufficient or economically interdependent with the rest of the world? And is China basically a poor, developing country that is at most a regional power or actually a nascent economic and military giant deserving of superpower status?

The response to these questions is that since 1949 Chinese foreign policy has reflected all of these contrasting features. Beijing has emphasized principles and ideology above everything else in foreign relations, especially during the 1950s and 1960s, but Chinese leaders have also shown a practical side that gave them the flexibility to change policies, sometimes drastically, when they deemed it in China's best interest. One of the most dramatic changes was the shift from an alliance with the Soviet Union against the United States and Japan in the 1950s to an explicitly anti-Soviet policy and rapprochement with Japan and the United States in the 1970s. Since 1949 Chinese foreign policy has fluctuated between periods of militancy, for example during the Cultural Revolution (1966–76), when China called for worldwide revolution, and periods when Beijing has been a chief proponent of peaceful coexistence among nations, such as during the mid-1950s and again during the 1980s. How self-reliant or dependent on others China should become in order to modernize has been a constant dilemma in Chinese policy since the nineteenth century. As this policy fluctuated, Chinese foreign relations have alternated between a tendency toward isolation and periods of openness to foreign assistance and influence. Finally, the contradiction between China's actual capabilities since 1949 and its perceived potential has been another salient and distinctive feature of its foreign relations. China's tremendous size, population, natural resources, military strength, and sense of history have placed it in the unusual position of being a poor, developing country that has often been treated as a major global power having a special relationship with the United States and the Soviet Union.

Evolution of Foreign Policy

Understanding the origins and forces shaping China's foreign policy provides a framework in which to view both the changes and the continuities in Chinese foreign policy from 1949 to the late 1980s. The origins of China's foreign policy can be found in its size and population, historical legacy, worldview, nationalism, and Marxism-Leninism-Mao Zedong Thought. These factors have combined with China's economic and military capabilities, governmental structure, and decision-making processes to make certain foreign policy goals prominent: security, sovereignty and independence, territorial integrity and reunification, and economic development.

Historical Legacy and Worldview

China's long and rich history as the world's oldest continuous civilization has affected Chinese foreign relations in various ways. For centuries the Chinese empire enjoyed basically unchallenged greatness and self-sufficiency (see The Imperial Era, ch. 1). China saw itself as the cultural center of the universe, a view reflected in the concept of the Middle Kingdom (Zhongguo, the Chinese word for China). For the most part, it viewed non-Chinese peoples as uncivilized barbarians. Although China was occasionally overrun and ruled by these "barbarians," as during the Yuan (1279–1368) and Qing (1644–1911) dynasties, the non-Chinese usually retained enough Chinese institutions to maintain a continuity of tradition. Because the Chinese emperor was considered the ruler of all mankind by virtue of his innate superiority, relations with other states or entities were tributary, rather than state-to-state relations between equals. Traditionally, there was no equivalent of a foreign ministry; foreign relations included such activities as tributary missions to the emperor made by countries seeking trade with China and Chinese military expeditions against neighboring barbarians to keep them outside China's borders. The first Europeans who sought trade with China, beginning in the sixteenth century, were received as tributary missions and had to conform to the formalities and rituals of the tribute system at the Chinese court. China's view of itself as the undisputed center of civilization—a phenomenon called sinocentrism—remained basically unchanged until the nineteenth century, when the Qing dynasty began to deteriorate under Western pressure.

A traditional concept related to China's view of itself as the Middle Kingdom that continues to have relevance is the idea of "using barbarians to control barbarians." In modern times, this practice has taken the form of using relations with one foreign power as a counterweight to relations with another. Two examples are China's policy of "leaning to one side" in the Sino-Soviet alliance of the 1950s for support against the United States and Beijing's rapprochement with the United States in the 1970s to counteract the Soviet threat China perceived at the time. China's strong desire for sovereignty and independence of action, however, seems to have made Chinese alliances or quasi-alliances short-lived.

Another effect of China's historical legacy is its tendency toward isolationism and an ambivalence about opening up to the outside world. In imperial times, China's foreign relations varied from dynasty to dynasty—from cosmopolitan periods like the Tang dynasty (A.D. 618–907) to isolationist periods such as the Ming dynasty (1368–1644), when few foreigners were allowed in the country. Overall, the sinocentric worldview and China's history of centuries of self-sufficiency favored isolation, which contributed to China's difficulty when confronted by expansionist Western powers in the nineteenth century. The debate over self-reliance and possible corruption by foreign influences or opening up to the outside world in order to modernize more quickly has continued for over a century and was still an issue in the late 1980s.

Nationalism

The importance of sovereignty and independence of action in Chinese foreign policy since 1949 has been closely related to Chinese nationalism. Just as Chinese national pride has been a natural outgrowth of China's long and rich historical tradition, the nationalism of Chinese leaders also has derived from the injustices China suffered in more recent history, in particular, China's domination by foreign powers from the nineteenth century until the end of World War II (see Emergence of Modern China, ch. 1). During this time, which China refers to as "the century of shame and humiliation," the formerly powerful imperial government devolved to what China calls "semicolonial" status, as it was forced to sign unequal treaties and grant foreigners special privileges of extraterritoriality. Foreign powers divided China into spheres of influence. Most debilitating and humiliating was the foreign military threat that overpowered China, culminating in Japan's invasion and occupation of parts of China in the late 1930s. The bitter recollection of China's suffering at the hands of foreign powers has continued to be a source of Chinese nationalistic sentiment since 1949.

The suspicion of foreign powers, opposition to any implication of inferior status, and desire to reassert sovereignty and independence have strongly influenced Chinese foreign policy. Examples of this attitude are Mao Zedong's statement in 1949 that "the Chinese people have stood up" and Deng Xiaoping's 1982 pronouncement that "no foreign country can expect China to be its vassal or expect it to swallow any bitter fruit detrimental to its interests."

A foreign policy goal closely related to nationalism has been the desire to achieve territorial integrity and to restore to Chinese sovereignty areas previously considered a part of China. Although China as of 1987 had not resolved border disputes with several of its neighbors, including India, the Soviet Union, and Vietnam (including islands in the South China Sea), Beijing had concluded boundary settlements with other nations, including Pakistan, Burma, Nepal, Afghanistan, the Democratic People's Republic of Korea (North Korea), and the Mongolian People's Republic (Mongolia). Negotiations on border issues, held intermittently with the Soviet Union since 1949 and with India since the early 1980s, continued to be held in 1987. The difficulty of resolving these issues seemed to reflect their relation to sensitive questions of national pride both in China and in neighboring countries and sometimes to questions of China's perceived national security interests (see Physical Environment, ch. 2). For example, Qing control over Outer Mongolia (present-day Mongolia) had lapsed long before 1949 and had been supplanted by Russian and then Soviet influence. Although it was most likely with reluctance and regret, China recognized Mongolia as a separate nation in 1949. By contrast, asserting sovereignty over another outlying area, Xizang (Tibet), was considered such an important strategic goal that military force was used to gain control there in 1950 and to reassert it in 1959.

Two other Chinese areas under the control of foreign powers are Hong Kong and Macao. According to Chinese statements, these "problems left over from history" were the result of imperialist aggression and the incompetence of Chinese rulers. Macao, the first European enclave on the Chinese coast, was occupied by Portugal in 1557 and ceded to Portugal under an 1887 treaty. Britain gained control of Hong Kong island and adjacent territory through three treaties with China in the nineteenth century. In the mid-1980s China concluded formal arrangements with Britain and Portugal for the return of these areas to Chinese sovereignty in 1997 (Hong Kong) and 1999 (Macao). Both agreements were made under a policy of "one country, two systems" (see Glossary), giving the areas a high degree of autonomy as "special administrative regions" of China. From the perspective of Chinese nationalism, negotiating the return of both Hong Kong and Macao to Chinese sovereignty before the end of the twentieth century was undoubtedly one of the major foreign policy accomplishments of Chinese leaders in the 1980s.

The most crucial of the issues of national reunification, however, remained unresolved in the late 1980s: the issue of Taiwan. Chiang Kai-shek and his forces fled to Taiwan after the founding of the People's Republic of China in 1949. The government they established there, the "Republic of China," continued to claim authority as the government of the Chinese nation almost four decades after the founding of the People's Republic. Although China's goal of reunifying Taiwan with the mainland remained unchanged, the previous, more militant Chinese policy of "liberating Taiwan" was replaced in the 1980s by the concept of reunification under the "one country, two systems" policy. The agreements on Hong Kong and Macao were considered by many observers as possible precedents for reunifying Taiwan with the mainland. Because of the legacy of mistrust between the leaders of the two sides and other complex factors, however, this difficult and long-standing problem did not appear close to resolution in the late 1980s.

The Influence of Ideology

An important influence on Chinese foreign policy that has especially affected China's interpretations of world events has been ideology, both Marxist-Leninist and Maoist. The ideological components of China's foreign policy, whose influence has varied over time, have included a belief that conflict and struggle are inevitable; a focus on opposing imperialism; the determination to advance communism throughout the world, especially through the Chinese model; and the Maoist concept of responding with flexibility while adhering to fundamental principles.

One of the most basic aspects of China's ideological worldview has been the assumption that conflict, though not necessarily military conflict, is omnipresent in the world. According to Marxist-Leninist analysis, all historical development is the result of a process of struggle, between classes within a nation, between nations themselves, or between broader forces such as socialism and imperialism. A basic tenet of Chinese leaders holds that the international situation is best understood in terms of the "principal contradictions" of the time. Once these contradictions are understood, they can be exploited in order to, as Mao said, "win over the many, oppose the few, and crush our enemies one by one." China has amplified the Leninist policy of uniting with some forces in order to oppose others more effectively in a united front (see Glossary).

Chinese leaders have urged the formation of various united fronts as they have perceived the contradictions in the world to change over time.

Perhaps because of the belief in struggle as necessary for progress, for most of its history after 1949 China considered world war inevitable. This changed in the 1980s, when Chinese leaders began to say that the forces for peace in the world had become greater than the forces for war. One reason for growing world stability was seen in ''multipolarization,'' that is, the growth of additional forces, such as the Third World and Europe, to counterbalance the tension between the United States and the Soviet Union. China's description of world events as a struggle between opposing forces, however, remained unchanged.

Opposition to imperialism—domination by foreign powers—is another major ideological component of Chinese foreign policy. The Leninist emphasis on the struggle against imperialism made sense to Chinese leaders, whose nationalism had evolved in part in reaction to China's exploitation by foreign powers during the nineteenth century. Although opposition to imperialism and hegemony has remained a constant, the specific target of the opposition has changed since 1949. In somewhat oversimplified terms, China focused on opposing United States imperialism in the 1950s; on opposing collusion between United States imperialism and Soviet revisionism in the 1960s; on combating Soviet social-imperialism or hegemony in the 1970s; and on opposing hegemony by either superpower in the 1980s.

The extent of China's determination to advance communism throughout the world is another component of its foreign policy that has fluctuated since 1949. In the early 1950s and during the 1960s, Chinese leaders called for worldwide armed struggle against colonialism and ''reactionary'' governments. China supplied revolutionary groups with rhetorical and, in some cases, material support. Central to support for leftist movements was the idea that they should take China as a model in their struggle for national liberation. Chinese leaders expressed the belief that China's experience was directly applicable to the circumstances in many other countries, but they also stressed the importance of each country's suiting its revolution to its own conditions—creating ambiguity about China's position on ''exporting'' revolution. For most of the time since 1949, China's dedication to encouraging revolution abroad has appeared to receive a lower priority than other foreign policy goals.

Militancy and support for worldwide revolution peaked during the Cultural Revolution, when China's outlook on liberation struggles seemed to take its cue from Lin Biao's famous 1965 essay "Long Live the Victory of People's War!" This essay predicted that the underdeveloped countries of the world would surround and overpower the industrial nations and create a new communist world order. As a result of alleged Chinese involvement in subversive activities in Indonesia and several African countries in the late 1960s, those nations broke off diplomatic relations with Beijing (see table 4, Appendix B).

By the 1980s China had lessened or discontinued its support for most of the revolutionary and liberation movements around the world, prominent exceptions being the Palestine Liberation Organization and resistance fighters in Cambodia and Afghanistan. Despite its shift toward cultivating state-to-state relations with established governments, many other countries continued to be suspicious of China's intentions. Especially in Asia, where Beijing previously supported many local communist parties, China's image as a radical power intent on fomenting world revolution continued to affect the conduct of its foreign relations into the late 1980s.

One of the major characteristics of Chinese foreign policy since 1949 has been its claim of consistently adhering to principles while particular interpretations and policies have changed dramatically. A statement by Mao Zedong seems to summarize this apparent contradiction: "We should be firm in principle; we should also have all flexibility permissible and necessary for carrying out our principles." Although claiming that, on the whole, China has never deviated from such underlying principles as independence and safeguarding peace, Chinese leaders have made major shifts in foreign policy based on their pragmatic assessment of goals and the international situation. Aiding this interpretation of the primacy of principles in Chinese foreign policy has been the emphasis on long-term goals. According to Chinese leaders, China has pursued a long-term strategy and is "definitely not swayed by expediency or anybody's instigation or provocation." In keeping with the view of Chinese foreign policy as constant and unvarying, Chinese pronouncements often describe their policy with words such as "always" and "never."

An example of how certain principles have provided a framework of continuity for Chinese foreign policy since 1949 is found in the Five Principles of Peaceful Coexistence (see Glossary) embodied in an agreement signed by China and India in 1954. The five principles played an important role in the mid-1950s, when China began to cultivate the friendship of newly independent nations of Asia and Africa. By the time of the Cultural Revolution, however, China was involved in acrimonious disputes with many of these same nations, and their relations could have been described as anything but "peacefully coexistent." The Five Principles of Peaceful Coexistence were reemphasized in the 1980s, were considered the basis for relations with all nations regardless of their social systems or ideology, and were made a part of the 1982 party constitution.

Decision Making and Implementation

Understanding the intricate workings of a government can be difficult, especially in a country such as China, where information related to leadership and decision making is often kept secret. Although it still was not possible to understand fully the structure of Chinese foreign-policy-related governmental and nongovernmental organizations or how they made or implemented decisions, more was known about them by the late 1980s than at any time previously.

After 1949 China's foreign relations became increasingly more complex as China established formal diplomatic relations with more nations, joined the United Nations (UN) and other international and regional political and economic organizations, developed ties between the Chinese Communist Party and foreign parties, and expanded trade and other economic relations with the rest of the world. These changes had affected foreign relations in significant ways by the late 1980s. The economic component of China's international relations increased dramatically from the late 1970s to the late 1980s; more ministries and organizations were involved in foreign relations than ever before; and the Chinese foreign policy community was more experienced and better informed about the outside world than it had been previously.

Despite the growing complexity of Chinese foreign relations, one fundamental aspect of foreign policy that has remained relatively constant since 1949 is that the decision-making power for the most important decisions has been concentrated in the hands of a few key individuals at the top of the leadership hierarchy. In the past, ultimate foreign policy authority rested with such figures as Mao Zedong and Zhou Enlai, while in the 1980s major decisions were understood to have depended on Deng Xiaoping. By the late 1980s, Deng had initiated steps to institutionalize decision making and make it less dependent on personal authority, but this transition was not yet complete.

In examining the workings of a nation's foreign policy, at least three dimensions can be discerned: the structure of the organizations involved, the nature of the decision-making process, and the ways in which policy is implemented. These three dimensions are interrelated, and the processes of formulating and carrying out policy are often more complex than the structure of organizations would indicate.

Government and Party Organizations

By the late 1980s, more organizations were involved in China's foreign relations than at any time previously. High-level party and government organizations such as the Central Committee, Political Bureau, party Secretariat, party and state Central Military Commissions, National People's Congress, and State Council and such leaders as the premier, president, and party general secretary all were involved in foreign relations to varying degrees by virtue of their concern with major policy issues, both foreign and domestic (see Chinese Communist Party; The Government, ch. 10). The party Secretariat and the State Council together carried the major responsibility for foreign policy decisions.

In the 1980s, as China's contacts with the outside world grew, party and government leaders at all levels increasingly were involved in foreign affairs. The president of the People's Republic fulfilled a ceremonial role as head of state and also was responsible for officially ratifying or abrogating treaties and agreements with foreign nations. In addition to meeting with foreign visitors, Chinese leaders, including the president, the premier, and officials at lower levels, traveled abroad regularly.

In the late 1980s, the Political Bureau, previously thought of as the major decision-making body, was no longer the primary party organization involved in foreign policy decision making. Instead, the State Council referred major decisions to the Secretariat for resolution and the Political Bureau for ratification. Under the party Secretariat, the International Liaison Department had primary responsibility for relations between the Chinese Communist Party and a growing number of foreign political parties. Other party organizations whose work was related to foreign relations were the United Front Work Department, responsible for relations with overseas Chinese (see Glossary), the Propaganda Department, and the Foreign Affairs Small Group.

Of the Chinese government institutions, the highest organ of state power, the National People's Congress, appeared to have only limited influence on foreign policy. In the 1980s the National People's Congress was becoming more active on the international scene by increasing its contacts with counterpart organizations in foreign countries. Through its Standing Committee and its Foreign Affairs Committee, the National People's Congress had a voice in foreign relations matters and occasionally prepared reports on foreign policy-related issues for other party and government bodies.

As the primary governmental organization under the National People's Congress, the State Council had a major role in foreign policy, particularly with regard to decisions on routine or specific matters, as opposed to greater questions of policy that might require party involvement. As in the past, the Ministry of Foreign Affairs was the most important institution involved in conducting day-to-day foreign relations, but by the 1980s many other ministries and organizations under the State Council had functions related to foreign affairs as well. These included the Ministry of Foreign Economic Relations and Trade, Ministry of Finance, Ministry of National Defense, Bank of China, People's Bank of China, and China Council for the Promotion of International Trade. In addition, over half of the ministries, overseeing such disparate areas as aeronautics, forestry, and public health, had a bureau or department concerned explicitly with foreign affairs. These offices presumably handled contacts between the ministry and its foreign counterparts.

Ministry of Foreign Affairs

Since 1949 the Ministry of Foreign Affairs has been one of China's most important ministries. Each area of foreign relations, divided either geographically or functionally, is overseen by a vice minister or assistant minister. For example, one vice minister's area of specialty was the Soviet Union and Eastern Europe, while another was responsible for the Americas and Australia. At the next level, the Ministry of Foreign Affairs was divided into departments, some geographical and some functional in responsibility. The regionally oriented departments included those concerned with Africa, the Americas and Oceania, Asia, the Middle East, the Soviet Union and Eastern Europe, Western Europe, Taiwan, and Hong Kong and Macao. The functional departments were responsible for administration, cadres, consular affairs, finance, information, international laws and treaties, international organizations and affairs, personnel, protocol, training and education, and translation. Below the department level were divisions, such as the United States Affairs Division under the Department of American and Oceanian Affairs.

A recurring problem for the foreign ministry and the diplomatic corps has been a shortage of qualified personnel. In the first years after the founding of the People's Republic, there were few prospective diplomats with international experience. Premier Zhou Enlai relied on a group of young people who had served under him in various negotiations to form the core of the newly established foreign ministry, and Zhou himself held the foreign ministry portfolio until 1958. In the second half of the 1960s, China's developing foreign affairs sector suffered a major setback during the Cultural Revolution, when higher education was disrupted, foreign-trained scholars and diplomats were attacked, all but one Chinese ambassador (to Egypt) were recalled to Beijing, and the Ministry of Foreign Affairs itself practically ceased functioning.

Since the early 1970s, the foreign affairs establishment has been rebuilt, and by the late 1980s, foreign affairs personnel were recruited from such specialized training programs as the ministry's Foreign Affairs College, College of International Relations, Beijing Foreign Languages Institute, and international studies departments at major universities. Foreign language study still was considered an important requirement, but it was increasingly supplemented by substantive training in foreign relations. Foreign affairs personnel benefited from expanded opportunities for education, travel, and exchange of information with the rest of the world. In addition, specialists from other ministries served in China's many embassies and consulates; for example, the Ministry of National Defense provided military attachés, the Ministry of Foreign Economic Relations and Trade provided commercial officers, and the Ministry of Culture and the State Education Commission provided personnel in charge of cultural affairs.

Ministry of Foreign Economic Relations and Trade

Since the late 1970s, economic and financial issues have become an increasingly important part of China's foreign relations. In order to streamline foreign economic relations, the Ministry of Foreign Economic Relations and Trade was established in 1982 through the merger of two commissions and two ministries (see Organization of Foreign Trade, ch. 8). By the late 1980s, this ministry was the second most prominent ministry involved in the routine conduct of foreign relations. The ministry had an extremely broad mandate that included foreign trade, foreign investment, foreign aid, and international economic cooperation. Through regular meetings with the Ministry of Foreign Affairs, the Ministry of Foreign Economic Relations and Trade participated in efforts to coordinate China's foreign economic policy with other aspects of its foreign policy. It was unclear how thoroughly this was accomplished.

Ministry of National Defense

In any nation, the interrelation of the political and military aspects of strategy and national security necessitates some degree of military involvement in foreign policy. The military's views on defense capability, deterrence, and perceptions of threat are essential components of a country's global strategy. As of the late 1980s, however, little information was available on foreign policy coordination between the military and foreign policy establishments. The most important military organizations with links to the foreign policy community were the Ministry of National Defense and the party and state Central Military Commissions. The Ministry of National Defense provides military attachés for Chinese embassies, and, as of 1987, its Foreign Affairs Bureau dealt with foreign attachés and military visitors. Working-level coordination with the Ministry of Foreign Affairs was maintained when, for example, high-level military leaders traveled abroad. In addition, the Ministry of National Defense's strategic research arm, the Beijing Institute for International Strategic Studies, carried out research on military and security issues with foreign policy implications.

In the late 1980s, the most important link between the military and foreign policy establishments appeared to be at the highest level, particularly through the party and state Central Military Commissions and through Deng Xiaoping, who was concurrently chairman of both commissions (see Central Military Commission, ch. 10; Military Organization, ch. 14). The views of the commissions' members on major foreign policy issues were almost certainly considered in informal discussions or in meetings of other high-level organizations they also belonged to, such as the Political Bureau, the Secretariat, or the State Council. It was significant, though, that compared with earlier periods fewer military leaders served on China's top policy-making bodies during the 1980s.

"People-to-People" Diplomacy

Since 1949 a significant forum for Chinese foreign relations has been cultural or "people-to-people" diplomacy. The relative isolation of the People's Republic during its first two decades increased the importance of cultural exchanges and informal ties with people of other countries through mass organizations and friendship societies. In some cases, activities at this level have signaled important diplomatic breakthroughs, as was the case with the American-Chinese ping-pong exchange in 1971. In addition to educational and cultural institutions, many other organizations, including the media, women's and youth organizations, and academic and professional societies, have been involved in foreign relations. Two institutes responsible for this aspect of Chinese diplomacy were associated with the Ministry of Foreign Affairs and staffed largely by former diplomats: the Chinese People's Association for

Friendship with Foreign Countries and the Chinese People's Institute of Foreign Affairs.

The Decision-Making Process

The most crucial foreign policy decisions in the mid-1980s were made by the highest-level leadership, with Deng Xiaoping as the final arbiter. A shift was underway, however, to strengthen the principles of collective and institutional decision making and, at the same time, to reduce party involvement in favor of increased state responsibility. In line with this trend, the State Council made foreign policy decisions regarding routine matters and referred only major decisions either to the party Secretariat or to informal deliberations involving Deng Xiaoping for resolution. When called upon to make decisions, the Secretariat relied largely on the advice of the State Council and members of China's foreign affairs community. The importance of the Political Bureau appeared to have lessened. Although individual members of the Political Bureau exerted influence on the shaping of foreign policy, the Political Bureau's role as an institution seemed to have become one of ratifying decisions, rather than formulating them. The division between party and government functions in foreign affairs as of the mid-1980s could therefore be summarized as party supremacy in overall policy making and supervision, with the government's State Council and ministries under it responsible for the daily conduct of foreign relations.

These high-level decision-making bodies comprised the apex of an elaborate network of party and government organizations and research institutes concerned with foreign policy. To support the formulation and implementation of policy, especially in a bureaucracy as complex and hierarchical as China's, there existed a network of small advisory and coordination groups. These groups functioned to channel research, provide expert advice, and act as a liaison between organizations. Perhaps the most important of these groups was the party Secretariat's Foreign Affairs Small Group. This group comprised key party and government officials, including the president, the premier, state councillors, the ministers of foreign affairs and foreign economic relations and trade, and various foreign affairs specialists, depending on the agenda of the meeting. The group possibly met weekly, or as required by circumstances. Liaison and advisory functions were provided by other groups, including the State Council's Foreign Affairs Coordination Point, the staff of the premier's and State Council's offices, and bilateral policy groups, such as one composed of ministers and vice ministers of the Ministry of Foreign Affairs and the Ministry

Chinese leader Deng Xiaoping meets American guest
Courtesy Liaowang

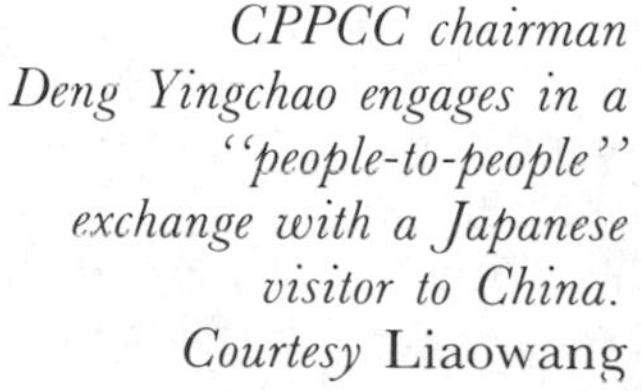

CPPCC chairman Deng Yingchao engages in a "people-to-people" exchange with a Japanese visitor to China.
Courtesy Liaowang

of Foreign Economic Relations and Trade, which met at least every few months.

In the late 1980s, the decision-making process for foreign policy matters followed a fairly hierarchical pattern. If a particular ministry was unable to make a decision because the purview of other ministries was involved, it would attempt to resolve the issue through informal discussion or through an interagency group. If that was not successful or if higher-level consideration was needed, the problem might be referred to the Foreign Affairs Coordination Point or to select members of the State Council for review. Certain major decisions would then be discussed by the Foreign Affairs Small Group before consideration by the party Secretariat itself. If the issue was extremely controversial or important, the final decision would be directed to the highest-level leadership, particularly Deng Xiaoping.

An Overview of China's Foreign Relations

Affected by the confluence of a myriad of factors, including its historical legacy, worldview, nationalism, ideology, the decision-making process in Beijing, and the international situation, China's foreign relations have had a rich and varied development in the years since 1949. Two aspects of Chinese foreign policy that have led to wide fluctuations over time are the degree of militancy or peacefulness Beijing has espoused and its ambivalence in choosing between self-reliance and openness to the outside world. Although dividing something as complex as foreign policy into time periods necessarily obscures certain details, Chinese foreign relations can be examined roughly by decades: the Sino-Soviet alliance of the 1950s, isolation and radicalism in the 1960s, increased international involvement in the 1970s, and the independent foreign policy of the 1980s. During each of these periods, China's relations with the rest of the world underwent significant changes.

Sino-Soviet Relations

After the founding of the People's Republic, the Chinese leadership was concerned above all with ensuring national security, consolidating power, and developing the economy. The foreign policy course China chose in order to translate these goals into reality was to form an international united front with the Soviet Union and other socialist nations against the United States and Japan. Although for a time Chinese leaders may have considered trying to balance Sino-Soviet relations with ties with Washington, by mid-1949 Mao Zedong declared that China had no choice but "leaning to one side"—meaning the Soviet side.

Soon after the establishment of the People's Republic, Mao traveled to Moscow to negotiate the 1950 Sino-Soviet Treaty of Friendship, Alliance, and Mutual Assistance. Under this agreement, China gave the Soviet Union certain rights, such as the continued use of a naval base at Lüda, Liaoning Province, in return for military support, weapons, and large amounts of economic and technological assistance, including technical advisers and machinery. China acceded, at least initially, to Soviet leadership of the world communist movement and took the Soviet Union as the model for development. China's participation in the Korean War (1950–53) seemed to strengthen Sino-Soviet relations, especially after the UN-sponsored trade embargo against China. The Sino-Soviet alliance appeared to unite Moscow and Beijing, and China became more closely associated with and dependent on a foreign power than ever before.

During the second half of the 1950s, strains in the Sino-Soviet alliance gradually began to emerge over questions of ideology, security, and economic development. Chinese leaders were disturbed by the Soviet Union's moves under Nikita Khrushchev toward de-Stalinization and peaceful coexistence with the West. Moscow's successful earth satellite launch in 1957 strengthened Mao's belief that the world balance was in the communists' favor—or, in his words, "the east wind prevails over the west wind"—leading him to call for a more militant policy toward the noncommunist world in contrast to the more conciliatory policy of the Soviet Union.

In addition to ideological disagreements, Beijing was dissatisfied with several aspects of the Sino-Soviet security relationship: the insufficient degree of support Moscow showed for China's recovery of Taiwan, a Soviet proposal in 1958 for a joint naval arrangement that would have put China in a subordinate position, Soviet neutrality during the 1959 tension on the Sino-Indian border, and Soviet reluctance to honor its agreement to provide nuclear weapons technology to China. And, in an attempt to break away from the Soviet model of economic development, China launched the radical policies of the Great Leap Forward (1958–60; see Glossary), leading Moscow to withdraw all Soviet advisers from China in 1960. In retrospect, the major ideological, military, and economic reasons behind the Sino-Soviet split were essentially the same: for the Chinese leadership, the strong desire to achieve self-reliance and independence of action outweighed the benefits Beijing received as Moscow's junior partner.

During the 1960s the Sino-Soviet ideological dispute deepened and spread to include territorial issues, culminating in 1969 in bloody armed clashes on their border. In 1963 the boundary dispute had come into the open when China explicitly raised the issue of territory lost through "unequal treaties" with tsarist Russia. After unsuccessful border consultations in 1964, Moscow began the process of a military buildup along the border with China and in Mongolia, which continued into the 1970s.

The Sino-Soviet dispute also was intensified by increasing competition between Beijing and Moscow for influence in the Third World and the international communist movement. China accused the Soviet Union of colluding with imperialism, for example by signing the Partial Nuclear Test Ban Treaty with the United States in 1963. Beijing's support for worldwide revolution became increasingly militant, although in most cases it lacked the resources to provide large amounts of economic or military aid. The Chinese Communist Party broke off ties with the Communist Party of the Soviet Union in 1966, and these had not been restored by mid-1987.

During the Cultural Revolution, China's growing radicalism and xenophobia had severe repercussions for Sino-Soviet relations. In 1967 Red Guards besieged the Soviet embassy in Beijing and harassed Soviet diplomats. Beijing viewed the Soviet invasion of Czechoslovakia in 1968 as an ominous development and accused the Soviet Union of "social imperialism." The Sino-Soviet dispute reached its nadir in 1969 when serious armed clashes broke out at Zhenbao (or Damanskiy) Island on the northeast border (see fig. 3). Both sides drew back from the brink of war, however, and tension was defused when Zhou Enlai met with Aleksey Kosygin, the Soviet premier, later in 1969.

In the 1970s Beijing shifted to a more moderate course and began a rapprochement with Washington as a counterweight to the perceived threat from Moscow. Sino-Soviet border talks were held intermittently, and Moscow issued conciliatory messages after Mao's death in 1976, all without substantive progress. Officially, Chinese statements called for a struggle against the hegemony of both superpowers, but especially against the Soviet Union, which Beijing called "the most dangerous source of war." In the late 1970s, the increased Soviet military buildup in East Asia and Soviet treaties with Vietnam and Afghanistan heightened China's awareness of the threat of Soviet encirclement. In 1979 Beijing notified Moscow it would formally abrogate the long-dormant Sino-Soviet Treaty of Friendship, Alliance, and Mutual Assistance but proposed bilateral talks. China suspended the talks after only one round, however, following the Soviet invasion of Afghanistan in 1979.

In the 1980s China's approach toward the Soviet Union shifted once more, albeit gradually, in line with China's adoption of an independent foreign policy and the opening up economic policy. Another factor behind the shift was the perception that, although the Soviet Union still posed the greatest threat to China's security, the threat was long-term rather than immediate. Sino-Soviet consultations on normalizing relations were resumed in 1982 and held twice yearly, despite the fact that the cause of their suspension, the Soviet presence in Afghanistan, remained unchanged. Beijing raised three primary preconditions for the normalization of relations, which it referred to as "three obstacles" that Moscow had to remove: the Soviet presence in of Afghanistan, Soviet support for Vietnam's invasion of Cambodia, and the presence of Soviet forces along the Sino-Soviet border and in Mongolia. For the first half of the 1980s, Moscow called these preconditions "third-country issues" not suitable for bilateral discussion, and neither side reported substantial progress in the talks.

Soviet leadership changes between 1982 and 1985 provided openings for renewed diplomacy, as high-level Chinese delegations attended the funerals of Soviet leaders Leonid Brezhnev, Yuriy Andropov, and Konstantin Chernenko. During this time, Sino-Soviet relations improved gradually in many areas: trade expanded, economic and technical exchanges were resumed (including the renovation of projects originally built with Soviet assistance in the 1950s), border points were opened, and delegations were exchanged regularly.

The Soviet position on Sino-Soviet relations showed greater flexibility in 1986 with General Secretary Mikhail S. Gorbachev's July speech at Vladivostok. Among Gorbachev's proposals for the Asia-Pacific region were several directed at China, including the announcement of partial troop withdrawals from Afghanistan and Mongolia, the renewal of a concession pertaining to the border dispute, and proposals for agreements on a border railroad, space cooperation, and joint hydropower development. Further, Gorbachev offered to hold discussions with China "at any time and at any level." Although these overtures did not lead to an immediate high-level breakthrough in Sino-Soviet relations, bilateral consultations appeared to gain momentum, and border talks were resumed in 1987. In the late 1980s, it seemed unlikely that China and the Soviet Union would resume a formal alliance, but Sino-Soviet relations had improved remarkably when compared with the previous two decades. Whether or not full normalization would include renewed relations between the Chinese and Soviet communist parties, as China had established with the East European communist parties, was uncertain as of mid-1987.

Sino-American Relations

China's relations with the other superpower, the United States, also have followed an uneven course. Chinese leaders expressed an interest in possible economic assistance from the United States during the 1940s, but by 1950 Sino-American relations could only be described as hostile. During its first two decades the People's Republic considered the United States "imperialist" and "the common enemy of people throughout the world."

The Korean War was a major factor responsible for setting relations between China and the United States in a state of enmity and mistrust, as it contributed to the United States policy of "containing" the Chinese threat through a trade embargo and travel restrictions, as well as through military alliances with other Asian nations. An important side effect of the Korean War was that Washington resumed military aid to Taiwan and throughout the 1950s became increasingly committed to Taiwan's defense, making the possibility of Chinese reunification more remote. After the United States-Taiwan Mutual Defense Treaty was signed in 1954, Taiwan became the most contentious issue between the United States and China, and remained so in the late 1980s, despite the abrogation of the treaty and the subsequent normalization of relations between Beijing and Washington in 1979.

In 1955 Premier Zhou Enlai made a conciliatory opening toward the United States in which he said the Chinese people did not want war with the American people. His statement led to a series of official ambassadorial-level talks in Geneva and Warsaw that continued fairly regularly for the next decade and a half. Although the talks failed to resolve fundamental conflicts between the two countries, they served as an important line of communication.

Sino-American relations remained at a stalemate during most of the 1960s. Political considerations in both countries made a shift toward closer relations difficult, especially as the United States became increasingly involved in the war in Vietnam, in which Washington and Beijing supported opposite sides. China's isolationist posture and militancy during the Cultural Revolution precluded effective diplomacy, and Sino-American relations reached a low point with seemingly little hope of improvement.

Several events in the late 1960s and early 1970s, however, led Beijing and Washington to reexamine their basic policies toward each other. After the Soviet Union's invasion of Czechoslovakia in 1968 and the Sino-Soviet border clashes in 1969, China saw its major threat as clearly coming from the Soviet Union rather than the United States and sought a closer relationship with Washington as a counterweight to Moscow. When President Richard M. Nixon assumed office in 1969, he explored rapprochement with China as part of his doctrine of reduced United States military involvement in Asia. Moves in this direction resulted in an American ping-pong team's trip to China and Henry A. Kissinger's secret visit, both in 1971, followed by Nixon's dramatic trip to China in 1972. The Shanghai Communiqué, a milestone document describing the new state of relations between the two countries, and signed by Nixon and Zhou Enlai, included a certain degree of ambiguity that allowed China and the United States to set aside differences, especially on the Taiwan issue, and begin the process of normalizing relations.

After the signing of the Shanghai Communiqué, however, movement toward United States-China normalization during the 1970s saw only limited progress. The United States and China set up liaison offices in each other's capitals in 1973, and bilateral trade grew unevenly throughout the decade. "People's diplomacy" played an important role, as most exchanges of delegations were sponsored by friendship associations. Chinese statements continued to express the view that both superpowers were theoretically adversaries of China, but they usually singled out the Soviet Union as the more "dangerous" of the two.

In the second half of the 1970s, China perceived an increasing Soviet threat and called more explicitly for an international united front against Soviet hegemony. In addition, rather than strictly adhering to the principle of self-reliance, China adopted an economic and technological modernization program that greatly increased commercial links with foreign countries. These trends toward strategic and economic cooperation with the West gave momentum to Sino-United States normalization, which had been at an impasse for most of the decade. Ties between China and the United States began to strengthen in 1978, culminating in the December announcement that diplomatic relations would be established as of January 1, 1979. In establishing relations, Washington reaffirmed its agreement that the People's Republic was the sole legal government of China and that Taiwan was an inalienable part of China. Deng Xiaoping's visit to the United States the following month was symbolic of the optimism felt in Beijing and Washington concerning their strategic alignment and their burgeoning commercial, technical, and cultural relations.

In the 1980s United States-China relations went through several twists and turns. By late 1981 China appeared to pull back somewhat from the United States as it asserted its independent foreign policy. Beijing began to express increasing impatience with the lack of resolution on the Taiwan issue. One of the main issues of contention was the Taiwan Relations Act, passed by the United States Congress in 1979, which provided for continuing unofficial relations between Washington and Taipei. In late 1981 China began to make serious demands that the United States set a firm timetable for terminating American arms sales to Taiwan, even threatening to retaliate with the possible downgrading of diplomatic relations. In early 1982 Washington announced it would not sell Taiwan more advanced aircraft than it had already provided, and in August, after several months of intense negotiations, China and the United States concluded a joint communiqué that afforded at least a partial resolution of the problem. Washington pledged to increase neither the quality nor the quantity of arms supplied to Taiwan, while Beijing affirmed that peaceful reunification was China's fundamental policy. Although the communiqué forestalled further deterioration in relations, Beijing and Washington differed in their interpretations of it. The Taiwan issue continued to be a "dark cloud" (to use the Chinese phrase) affecting United States-China relations to varying degrees into the late 1980s.

In addition to the question of Taiwan, other aspects of United States-China relations created controversy at times during the 1980s: Sino-American trade relations, the limits of American technology transfer to China, the nature and extent of United States-China security relations, and occasional friction caused by defections or lawsuits. Difficulties over trade relations have included Chinese displeasure with United States efforts to limit imports such as textiles and a degree of disappointment and frustration within the American business community over the difficulties of doing business in China. The issue of technology transfer came to the fore several times during the 1980s, most often with Chinese complaints about the level of technology allowed or the slow rate of transfer. China's dissatisfaction appeared to be somewhat abated by the United States 1983 decision to place China in the "friendly, nonaligned" category for technology transfer and the conclusion of a bilateral nuclear energy cooperation agreement in 1985.

Determining the nature and limits of security relations between China and the United States has been a central aspect of their relations in the 1980s. After a period of discord during the first years of the decade, Beijing and Washington renewed their interest in security-related ties, including military visits, discussions of international issues such as arms control, and limited arms and weapons technology sales.

Beginning in 1983, Chinese and United States defense ministers and other high-level military delegations exchanged visits, and in

1986 United States Navy ships made their first Chinese port call since 1949. The United States approved certain items, such as aviation electronics, for sale to China, restricting transfers to items that would contribute only to China's defensive capability. As of the late 1980s, it appeared that American assistance in modernizing China's arms would also be limited by China's financial constraints and the underlying principle of self-reliance.

Despite the issues that have divided them, relations between the United States and China continued to develop during the 1980s through a complex network of trade ties, technology-transfer arrangements, cultural exchanges, educational exchanges (including thousands of Chinese students studying in the United States), military links, joint commissions and other meetings, and exchanges of high-level leaders. By the second half of the 1980s, China had become the sixteenth largest trading partner of the United States, and the United States was China's third largest; in addition, over 140 American firms had invested in China. High-level exchanges, such as Premier Zhao Ziyang's visit to the United States and President Ronald Reagan's trip to China, both in 1984, and President Li Xiannian's 1985 tour of the United States demonstrated the importance both sides accorded their relations.

Relations with the Third World

Next in importance to its relations with the superpowers have been China's relations with the Third World. Chinese leaders have tended to view the developing nations of Asia, Africa, and Latin America as a major force in international affairs, and they have considered China an integral part of this major Third World force. As has been the case with China's foreign relations in general, policy toward the countries of the developing world has fluctuated over time. It has been affected by China's alternating involvement in and isolation from world affairs and by the militancy or peacefulness of Beijing's views. In addition, China's relations with the Third World have been affected by China's ambiguous position as a developing country that nevertheless has certain attributes more befitting a major power. China has been variously viewed by the Third World as a friend and ally, a competitor for markets and loans, a source of economic and military assistance, a regional power intent on dominating Asia, and a "candidate superpower" with such privileges as a permanent seat on the UN Security Council.

China's relations with the Third World have developed through several phases: the Bandung Line of the mid-1950s (named for a 1955 conference of Asian and African nations held in Bandung, Indonesia), support for liberation and world revolution in the 1960s, the pronouncement of the Theory of the Three Worlds and support for a "new international economic order" in the 1970s, and a renewed emphasis on the Five Principles of Peaceful Coexistence in the 1980s.

In the first years after the founding of the People's Republic, Chinese statements echoed the Soviet view that the world was divided into two camps, the forces of socialism and those of imperialism, with "no third road" possible. By 1953 China began reasserting its belief that the newly independent developing countries could play an important intermediary role in world affairs. In 1954 Zhou Enlai and Prime Minister Jawaharlal Nehru of India agreed on the Five Principles of Peaceful Coexistence as the underlying basis for conducting foreign relations. China's success in promoting these principles at the 1955 Bandung Conference helped China emerge from diplomatic isolation. By the end of the 1950s, however, China's foreign policy stance had become more militant. Statements promoting the Chinese revolution as a model and Beijing's actions in the Taiwan Strait (1958) and in border conflicts with India (1962) and Vietnam (1979), for example, alarmed many Third World nations.

During the 1960s China cultivated ties with Third World countries and insurgent groups in an attempt to encourage "wars of national liberation" and revolution and to forge an international united front against both superpowers. China offered economic, technical, and sometimes military assistance to other countries and liberation movements, which, although small in comparison with Soviet and United States aid, was significant considering China's own needs. Third World appreciation for Chinese assistance coexisted, however, with growing suspicions of China's militancy. Such suspicions were fed, for example, by Zhou Enlai's statement in the early 1960s that the potential for revolution in Africa was "excellent" and by the publication of Lin Biao's essay "Long Live the Victory of People's War!" in 1965. Discord between China and many Third World countries continued to grow. In some cases, as with Indonesia's charge of Chinese complicity in the 1965 coup attempt in Jakarta and claims by several African nations of Chinese subversion during the Cultural Revolution, bilateral disputes led to the breaking off of diplomatic relations. Although the Third World was not a primary focus of the Cultural Revolution, it was not immune to the chaos this period wrought upon Chinese foreign relations.

In the 1970s China began to redefine its foreign policy after the isolation and militancy of the late 1960s. China reestablished those of its diplomatic missions that had been recalled during the Cultural

Revolution and began the process of rapprochement with the United States. The People's Republic was admitted into the UN in 1971 and was recognized diplomatically by an increasing number of nations. China's major foreign policy statement during this time was Mao's Theory of the Three Worlds, which was presented publicly by Deng Xiaoping at the UN in 1974. According to this theory, the First World consisted of the two superpowers—the Soviet Union and the United States—both "imperialist aggressors" whose rivalry was the greatest cause of impending world war. The Third World was the main force in international affairs. Its growing opposition to superpower hegemony was exemplified by such world events as the Arab nations' control of oil prices, Egypt's expulsion of Soviet aid personnel in 1972, and the United States withdrawal from Vietnam. The Second World, comprising the developed countries of Europe plus Japan, could either oppress the Third World or join in opposing the superpowers. By the second half of the 1970s, China perceived an increased threat from the Soviet Union, and the theory was modified to emphasize that the Soviet Union was the more dangerous of the two superpowers.

The other primary component of China's Third World policy in the early 1970s was a call for radical change in the world power structure and particularly a call for a "new international economic order." Until the late 1970s, the Chinese principles of sovereignty, opposition to hegemony, and self-reliance coincided with the goals of the movement for a new international economic order. Chinese statements in support of the new order diminished as China began to implement the opening up policy, allow foreign investment, and seek technical assistance and foreign loans. China's critical opinion of international financial institutions appeared to change abruptly as Beijing prepared to join the International Monetary Fund and the World Bank in 1980. Chinese support for changes in the economic order stressed the role of collective self-reliance among the countries of the Third World, or "South-South cooperation," in the 1980s.

Also in the 1980s, China reasserted its Third World credentials and placed a renewed emphasis on its relations with Third World countries as part of its independent foreign policy. China stressed that it would develop friendly relations with other nations regardless of their social systems or ideologies and would conduct its relations on the basis of the Five Principles of Peaceful Coexistence. Beijing exchanged delegations with Third World countries regularly, and it made diplomatic use of cultural ties, for example, by promoting friendly links between Chinese Muslims and Islamic countries. Officially, China denied that it sought a leadership role in the Third World, although some foreign observers argued to the contrary. Beijing increasingly based its foreign economic relations with the Third World on equality and mutual benefit, expressed by a shift toward trade and joint ventures and away from grants and interest-free loans.

By the second half of the 1980s, China's relations with Third World nations covered the spectrum from friendly to inimical. Bilateral relations ranged from a formal alliance with North Korea, to a near-alliance with Pakistan, to hostile relations with Vietnam marked by sporadic border conflict. Many relationships have changed dramatically over time: for example, China previously had close relations with Vietnam; its ties with India were friendly during the 1950s but were strained thereafter by border tensions. Particularly in Southeast Asia, a legacy of suspicion concerning China's ultimate intentions affected Chinese relations with many countries.

As of 1987 only a few countries in the world lacked diplomatic ties with Beijing; among them were Honduras, Indonesia, Israel, Paraguay, Saudi Arabia, South Africa, the Republic of Korea, and Uruguay. Some of these had formal ties with Taiwan instead. China's growing interest in trade and technical exchanges, however, meant that in some cases substantial unofficial relations existed despite the absence of diplomatic recognition.

Relations with the Developed World

Since 1949 China's overriding concerns have been security and economic development. In working toward both of these goals, China has focused on its relations with the superpowers. Because most of the developed world, with the exception of Japan, is fairly distant from China and is aligned formally or informally with either the Soviet Union or the United States, China's relations with the developed world often have been subordinate to its relations with the superpowers. In the 1950s China considered most West European countries "lackeys" of United States imperialism, while it sided with Eastern Europe and the Soviet Union. As China's relations with the superpowers have changed, so have its ties with other developed nations. An example of this is that more than a dozen developed countries, including the Federal Republic of Germany, Spain, Japan, Australia, and New Zealand, all established diplomatic relations with China after the Sino-American rapprochement in the early 1970s.

The developed nations have been important to China for several reasons: as sources of diplomatic recognition, as alternative sources of trade and technology to reduce reliance on one or the other superpower, and as part of China's security calculations. In the

1980s China stressed the role of developed nations in ensuring peace in an increasingly multipolar world. Australia and Canada were important trading partners for China, but Beijing's most important relations with the developed world were with Japan and Europe.

Japan

Japan is by far the most important to China of the nonsuperpower developed nations. Among the reasons for this are geographical proximity and historical and cultural ties, China's perception of Japan as a possible resurgent threat, Japan's close relations with the United States since the end of World War II, and Japan's role as the third-ranking industrialized power in the world. Japan's invasion and occupation of parts of China in the 1930s was a major component of the devastation China underwent during the "century of shame and humiliation." After 1949 Chinese relations with Japan changed several times, from hostility and an absence of contact to cordiality and extremely close cooperation in many fields. One recurring Chinese concern in Sino-Japanese relations has been the potential remilitarization of Japan.

At the time of the founding of the People's Republic, Japan was defeated and Japanese military power dismantled, but China continued to view Japan as a potential threat because of the United States presence there. The Sino-Soviet Treaty of Friendship, Alliance, and Mutual Assistance included the provision that each side would protect the other from an attack by "Japan or any state allied with it," and China undoubtedly viewed with alarm Japan's role as the principal United States base during the Korean War. At the same time, however, China in the 1950s began a policy of attempting to influence Japan through trade, "people's diplomacy," contacts with Japanese opposition political parties, and through applying pressure on Tokyo to sever ties with Taipei. Relations deteriorated in the late 1950s when Chinese pressure tactics escalated. After the Sino-Soviet break, economic necessity caused China to reconsider and revitalize trade ties with Japan.

Sino-Japanese ties declined again during the Cultural Revolution, and the decline was further exacerbated by Japan's growing strength and independence from the United States in the late 1960s. China was especially concerned that Japan might remilitarize to compensate for the reduced United States military presence in Asia brought about under President Nixon. After the beginning of Sino-American rapprochement in 1971, however, China's policy toward Japan immediately became more flexible. By 1972 Japan and China had established diplomatic relations and agreed to conclude a separate peace treaty. The negotiations for the peace treaty were protracted and, by the time it was concluded in 1978, China's preoccupation with the Soviet threat led to the inclusion of an "antihegemony" statement. In fewer than three decades, China had signed an explicitly anti-Japanese treaty with the Soviet Union and a treaty having an anti-Soviet component with Japan.

From the 1970s into the 1980s, economic relations were the centerpiece of relations between China and Japan. Japan has been China's top trading partner since the 1960s. Despite concern in the late 1980s over a trade imbalance, the volume of Sino-Japanese trade showed no sign of declining. Relations suffered a setback in 1979 and 1980, when China canceled or modified overly ambitious plans made in the late 1970s to import large quantities of Japanese technology, the best-known example involving the Baoshan iron and steel complex in Shanghai. Lower expectations on both sides seemed to have created a more realistic economic and technological partnership by the late 1980s.

Chinese relations with Japan during the 1980s were generally close and cordial. Tension erupted periodically, however, over trade and technology issues, Chinese concern over potential Japanese military resurgence, and controversy regarding Japan's relations with Taiwan, especially Beijing's concern that Tokyo was pursuing a "two Chinas" policy. China joined other Asian nations in criticizing Japanese history textbooks that deemphasized past Japanese aggression, claiming that the distortion was evidence of the rise of militarism in Japan. By the late 1980s, despite occasional outbreaks of tension, the two governments held regular consultations, high-level leaders frequently exchanged visits, Chinese and Japanese military leaders had begun contacts, and many Chinese and Japanese students and tourists traveled back and forth.

Europe

Although it had been the European powers that precipitated the opening of China to the West in the nineteenth century, by 1949 the European presence was limited to Hong Kong and Macao. Europe exerted a strong intellectual influence on modern Chinese leaders (Marxism and Leninism of course originated in Europe), and some leaders, including Zhou Enlai and Deng Xiaoping, studied in Europe early in their careers. Nevertheless, China's geographic distance from Europe, its preoccupation with the superpowers, and the division of Europe after World War II have meant that China's relations with European nations usually have been subordinate to its relations with the Soviet Union and the United States.

East European nations were the first countries to establish diplomatic relations with China in 1949, following the Soviet Union's lead. In the early 1950s, through the Sino-Soviet alliance, China became an observer in the Council for Mutual Economic Assistance (Comecon), and Chinese relations with Eastern Europe included trade and receipt of limited amounts of economic and technical aid. The Sino-Soviet dispute was manifested in China's relations with certain East European countries, especially China's support for Albania's break with the Soviet Union in the late 1950s. After the Sino-Soviet split in the 1960s, the only East European nations maintaining significant ties with China until the late 1970s were Albania, Romania, and Yugoslavia. By the late 1980s, however, as Beijing's relations with Moscow improved and relations with governments and parties on the basis of "mutual respect and peaceful coexistence" were renewed, China's ties with the other nations of Eastern Europe also had improved noticeably, to include communist party ties.

China's ties with Western Europe were minimal for the first two decades of the People's Republic. Several West European nations, mostly in Scandinavia, established diplomatic relations with China in the early 1950s, and Britain and the Netherlands established ties with China at the chargé d'affaires level in 1954. In the late 1950s, Britain became the first Western nation to relax the trade embargo against China imposed during the Korean War. The establishment of diplomatic relations between China and France in 1964 also provided an opening for trade and other limited Chinese contacts with Western Europe until the 1970s.

China's relations with Western Europe grew rapidly in the 1970s, as more nations recognized China and diplomatic relations were established with the European Economic Community in 1975. In the second half of the 1970s, China's emphasis on an international united front against Soviet hegemony led to increased Chinese support for West European unity and for the role of the North Atlantic Treaty Organization. Ties with Western Europe also were featured prominently in Beijing's independent foreign policy of the 1980s. Furthermore, China's opening up to foreign trade, investment, and technology beginning in the late 1970s greatly improved Sino-European ties. One of the few major problems in China's relations with Western Europe in the post-Mao era was the downgrading of diplomatic ties with the Netherlands from 1981 to 1984 over the latter's sale of submarines to Taiwan.

China's Role in International Organizations

Participation in international organizations is perceived as an important measure of a nation's prestige as well as a forum through which a nation can influence others and gain access to aid programs and sources of technology and information. The People's Republic was precluded from participating actively in most mainstream international organizations for the first two decades of its existence because of its subordinate position in the Sino-Soviet alliance in the 1950s and the opposition of the United States after China's involvement in the Korean War. China repeatedly failed to gain admission to the UN. In 1971 Beijing finally gained China's seat when relations with the United States changed for the better. Taipei's representatives were expelled from the UN and replaced by Beijing's.

After becoming a member of the UN, China also joined most UN-affiliated agencies, including, by the 1980s, the World Bank and the International Monetary Fund. China's willingness, under the policy of opening up to the outside world beginning in the late 1970s, to receive economic and technical assistance from such agencies as the UN Development Program was a significant departure from its previous stress on self-reliance. In 1986 China renewed its application to regain its seat as one of the founding members of the General Agreement on Tariffs and Trade.

By the late 1980s, China had become a member of several hundred international and regional organizations, both those of major significance to world affairs, including the International Atomic Energy Agency, the World Intellectual Property Organization, and the International Olympic Committee, and associations or societies focused on such narrow subjects as acrobatics or the study of seaweed. Besides providing China a forum from which to express its views on various issues, membership in the 1970s and 1980s in increasing numbers of international groups gave Chinese foreign-affairs personnel wider knowledge and valuable international experience.

It is notable that by the late 1980s Beijing had *not* sought formal membership in several important international organizations representative of Third World interests: the Group of 77, the Nonaligned Movement, and the Organization of Petroleum Exporting Countries. Despite the emphasis China placed on Third World relations, China's independent foreign policy and special position as a somewhat atypical Third World nation made it seem unlikely in the late 1980s that China would seek more than observer status in these groups.

By the second half of the 1980s, China's participation in international organizations reflected the two primary goals of its independent foreign policy: furthering domestic economic development through cooperation with the outside world and promoting peace and stability by cultivating ties with other nations on an equal basis. As expressed by Zhao Ziyang in a 1986 report to the National People's Congress, "China is a developing socialist country with a population of over 1 billion. We are well aware of our obligations and responsibilities in the world. We will therefore continue to work hard on both fronts, domestic and international, to push forward the socialist modernization of our country and to make greater contributions to world peace and human progress."

* * *

In the 1970s and 1980s, Chinese foreign policy was the subject of numerous books and articles reflecting diverse perspectives and disciplinary approaches. Excellent coverage includes A. Doak Barnett's *China and the Major Powers in East Asia*, King C. Chen's *China and the Three Worlds* (which includes many relevant documents), Wang Gungwu's *China and the World since 1949*, Melvin Gurtov and Byong-Moo Hwang's *China under Threat*, Michael B. Yahuda's *China's Role in World Affairs*, and Robert C. North's *The Foreign Relations of China*. Richard H. Solomon's chapter in *The China Factor* covers China's relations with many countries in addition to its primary focus on United States-China relations. *China and the World*, edited by Samuel S. Kim, provides a comprehensive view of many facets of Chinese foreign relations. Barnett's *The Making of Foreign Policy in China* is a pathbreaking study of a subject previously little understood outside China.

The following periodicals often contain informative or analytical articles on Chinese foreign policy and relations with specific countries or regions: *Asian Survey*, *Asia Pacific Community*, *Asiaweek*, *China Quarterly*, *Current History*, *Far Eastern Economic Review*, *Foreign Affairs*, *Issues & Studies*, *Journal of Northeast Asian Studies*, *Pacific Affairs*, *Problems of Communism*, *Washington Quarterly*, and *World Today*. (For further information and complete citations, see Bibliography.)

Chapter 13. Criminal Justice and Public Security

This crossbowman is one of tens of thousands of warriors buried to guard Shi Huangdi, founder of the Qin dynasty (221–207 B.C.), in his afterlife. The figure's weapon did not survive the two millennia underground.

SWEEPING REFORMS IN CHINA'S legal system were announced at the Second Session of the Fifth National People's Congress held in June and July 1979. New laws on courts, procuratorates, crime, and trials were promulgated. The changes, effective as of January 1, 1980, reflected the leadership's conviction that if economic modernization was to succeed, the people—who had suffered through the humiliations, capricious arrests, and massive civil disorders of the Cultural Revolution (1966–76)—had to be assured that they no longer would be abused or incarcerated on the basis of hearsay or arbitrary political pronouncements.

From the perspective of the leaders of the Chinese Communist Party, moreover, codified laws and a strengthened legal system were seen as important means of preventing a possible return of radical policies and a repetition of the era when the Gang of Four ruled by fiat and inconsistent party regulations. Aside from establishing a legal code that would be more difficult for corrupt officials to manipulate, the new laws made the courts responsible for applying all but minor sanctions and made the police answerable to the courts. Procuratorates, which had fallen into disuse during the Cultural Revolution, were reinstituted to prosecute criminal cases, review court decisions, and investigate the legality of actions taken by the police and other government organizations. A greater role for the courts and independent investigations were expected to make it more difficult to introduce politically colored testimony into the courtrooms.

Hard labor still was the most common form of punishment in China in the 1980s. The penal system stressed reform rather than retribution, and it was expected that productive labor would reduce the penal institutions' cost to society. Even death sentences could be stayed by two-year reprieve. If a prisoner was judged to have reformed during that period, his or her sentence could be commuted to life or a fixed term at labor.

Neighborhood committees in the 1980s continued to be heavily involved in law enforcement and mediation of disputes at the local level. Among the enforcement procedures these committees used to influence both thought and behavior were criticism and collective responsibility.

In the period between 1980 and 1987, important progress was made in replacing the rule of men with the rule of law. Laws originally passed in 1979 and earlier were amended and augmented, and law institutes and university law departments that had been closed during the Cultural Revolution were opened to train lawyers and court personnel. It was only a beginning, but important steps had been taken in developing a viable legal system and making the government and the courts answerable to an objective standard.

The Legal System

Imperial China

Contemporary social control is rooted in the Confucian past. The teachings of Confucius have had an enduring effect on Chinese life and have provided the basis for the social order through much of the country's history. Confucians believed in the fundamental goodness of man and advocated rule by moral persuasion in accordance with the concept of *li* (propriety), a set of generally accepted social values or norms of behavior. *Li* was enforced by society rather than by courts. Education was considered the key ingredient for maintaining order, and codes of law were intended only to supplement *li*, not to replace it (see The Hundred Schools of Thought, ch. 1; Traditional Society and Culture, ch. 3).

Confucians held that codified law was inadequate to provide meaningful guidance for the entire panorama of human activity, but they were not against using laws to control the most unruly elements in the society. The first criminal code was promulgated sometime between 455 and 395 B.C. There were also civil statutes, mostly concerned with land transactions.

Legalism, a competing school of thought during the Warring States period (475–221 B.C.), maintained that man was by nature evil and had to be controlled by strict rules of law and uniform justice. Legalist philosophy had its greatest impact during the first imperial dynasty, the Qin (221–207 B.C.; see The Imperial Era, ch. 1).

The Han dynasty (206 B.C.–A.D. 220) retained the basic legal system established under the Qin but modified some of the harsher aspects in line with the Confucian philosophy of social control based on ethical and moral persuasion. Most legal professionals were not lawyers but generalists trained in philosophy and literature. The local, classically trained, Confucian gentry played a crucial role as arbiters and handled all but the most serious local disputes.

This basic legal philosophy remained in effect for most of the imperial era. The criminal code was not comprehensive and often not written down, which left magistrates great flexibility during trials. The accused had no rights and relied on the mercy of the court; defendants were tortured to obtain confessions and often served long jail terms while awaiting trial. A court appearance, at minimum, resulted in loss of face, and the people were reluctant and afraid to use the courts. Rulers did little to make the courts more appealing, for if they stressed rule by law, they weakened their own moral influence.

In the final years of the Qing dynasty (1644–1911), reform advocates in the government implemented certain aspects of the modernized Japanese legal system, itself originally based on German judicial precedents (see The Hundred Days' Reform and the Aftermath, ch. 1). These efforts were short-lived and largely ineffective.

The Republican Period

Following the overthrow of the Qing dynasty in 1911, China came under the control of rival warlords and had no government strong enough to establish a legal code to replace the Qing code. Finally, in 1927, Chiang Kai-shek's Guomindang forces were able to suppress the warlords and gain control of most of the country (see Republican China, ch. 1). Established in Nanjing, the Guomindang government attempted to develop Western-style legal and penal systems. Few of the Guomindang codes, however, were implemented nationwide. Although government leaders were striving for a Western-inspired system of codified law, the traditional Chinese preference for collective social sanctions over impersonal legalism hindered constitutional and legal development. The spirit of the new laws never penetrated to the grass-roots level or provided hoped-for stability. Ideally, individuals were to be equal before the law, but this premise proved to be more rhetorical than substantive. In the end, most of the new laws were discarded as the Guomindang became preoccupied with fighting the Chinese Communists and the invading Japanese.

Developments after 1949

Ideological Basis

According to Chinese communist ideology, the party controlled the state and created and used the law to regulate the masses, realize socialism, and suppress counterrevolutionaries. Since it was the party's view that the law and legal institutions existed to support party and state power, law often took the form of general principles and shifting policies rather than detailed and constant rules. The Communists wrote laws in simple enough language that every individual could understand and abide by them. Technical language and strict legal procedures for the police and the courts were dispensed with so as to encourage greater popular appreciation of the legal system.

Moreover, Mao Zedong maintained that revolution was continuous, and he opposed any legal system that would constrain it. Whereas Western law stressed stability, Mao sought constant change, emphasized the contradictions in society, and called for relentless class struggle. In this milieu, the courts were instruments for achieving political ends, and criminal law was used by the party to conduct class struggle. The emphasis was shifting constantly, and new "enemies" were often identified. Mao believed it unwise to codify a criminal law that later might restrain the party.

The Maoists wanted the administration of justice to be as decentralized as possible in order to be consistent with the "mass line" (see Glossary). Neighborhood committees and work units, supervised by local officials, used peer pressure to handle most legal problems in consonance with current central policies. The police and courts were left to handle only the most serious cases. In both traditional and contemporary China, political and legal theory tended to support such methods. Mao was unconcerned that a person contesting the result of a group decision had nowhere to go for redress.

After 1949 the party also greatly altered the character of the legal profession. A number of law schools were closed, and most of the teachers were retired. Legal work was carried on by a handful of Western-trained specialists and a large number of legal cadres hastily trained in China. From the beginning these two groups disagreed over legal policy, and the development of the legal system reflected their continuous debate over both form and substance.

The Western-trained specialists were Guomindang-era lawyers who chose to cooperate with the Communists. Because they were considered politically unreliable, the party initially ignored most of their arguments for a modern legal system. As the 1950s progressed, however, this group was instrumental in China's adoption of a legal system based on the system of the Soviet Union. In general, the specialists wanted codified law, enforced by a strict Soviet-style legal bureaucracy. Without such procedures, they felt, there would be too much arbitrariness, and eventually the legal system would become ineffective. Many of these specialists passed from the scene when the Soviet model was abandoned in the late 1950s, but some became party members and gained influential positions.

In the first thirty years of the People's Republic, the new legal cadres—chosen more for their ideological convictions than legal expertise—conducted the day-to-day legal work. These cadres favored the Maoist system of social and political control and regarded themselves as supervisors of the masses who subscribed to a common set of communist values. The new cadres saw this common ideology as providing better overall direction than strict legal controls could. They believed that China was too large to be governed by any single set of fixed rules or a legal bureaucracy. They preferred to administer justice by simplified directives tailored to the needs of local communities so that the people (and the new cadres) could participate fully in their implementation. As part of this plan, the cadres organized "study groups" to familiarize every citizen with current directives and circulars.

Most cultures agree that the purpose of criminal law is to control deviancy—the Chinese traditionally have sought to do so through peer groups rather than through the courts. This practice continued after 1949. Ideally, peers helped the deviant through criticism or *shuofu* (persuading by talking). The stress was on education and rehabilitation (see Glossary), a policy linked to the Confucian and Maoist tenet that, with patience and persuasion, a person can be reformed.

Early Years of the People's Republic, 1949–53

In 1949 the Communists abolished all Guomindang laws and judicial organs and established the Common Program, a statement of national purposes adopted by a September 1949 session of the Chinese People's Political Consultative Conference (see Glossary), as a provisional constitution. Under the Common Program, 148 mainly experimental or provisional laws and regulations were adopted to establish the new socialist rule. The most important and far-reaching of these laws dealt with marriage, land reform, counterrevolutionaries, and corruption. A three-level, single-appeal court system was established, and the Supreme People's Procuratorate and local people's procuratorates were instituted. The procuratorates were established to ensure that government organs at all levels, persons in government service, and all citizens strictly observed the Common Program and the policies, directives, laws, and decrees of the people's government. They also were to investigate and prosecute counterrevolutionary and other criminal cases; to contest illegal or improper judgments rendered by judicial organs at every level; and to investigate illegal measures taken by places of detention and labor-reform organs anywhere in the country. They were to dispose of cases submitted by citizens who were dissatisfied with the decision of "no prosecution" made by the procuratorial organs of lower levels and to intervene in important civil cases and administrative legal actions affecting the national interest.

The period 1949–52 was one of national integration, which came in the wake of decades of disunity, turmoil, and war, and included efforts to bring the diverse elements of a disrupted society into line with the new political direction of the state. The land reform movement of 1949–51 was accompanied, in 1950, by the movement to suppress counterrevolutionaries. In 1952 the *san fan* ("three anti") movement opposed corruption, waste, and bureaucratism, while the *wu fan* ("five anti") movement rallied against bribery, tax evasion, theft of state assets, cheating on government contracts, and theft of state economic secrets. During this period, few cases were brought to court (see The People's Republic of China, ch. 1). Instead, administrative agencies, especially the police, conducted mass trials during which large crowds of onlookers shouted accusations. Hundreds of thousands were executed as a result of those "trials" and many more were sent to prison or to labor camps. In the relatively few cases that were tried in formal courts, it was difficult to discern what laws were used as a basis for the judgment.

In 1952 the authorities launched a nationwide judicial reform movement "to rectify and purify the people's judicial organs at every level politically, organizationally, and ideologically, and to strengthen the party's leadership of judicial work." Guomindang-era judges were purged from the courts, and those who remained, having been tacitly cleared of charges of "flagrant counterrevolution" and sworn to uphold the mass line in judicial work, continued to press for a more regularized Soviet-style legal system. These judges were confident that the mass movements shortly would end and that the communist-run government eventually would see that it needed a more formal judicial structure. Indeed, at the instigation of the legal specialists, in 1953 the state began to promulgate separate criminal laws.

The Legal System under the 1954 State Constitution

The state constitution promulgated in September 1954 attempted to set down in legal form the central tasks of the country in the transition period of the mid-1950s and to regulate China's strides toward socialism. The state constitution provided the framework of a legal system much like that in effect in the Soviet Union from 1921 to 1928. Much of the Soviet legal code was translated into Chinese, and Soviet legal experts helped rewrite it to suit Chinese conditions.

The 1954 state constitution gave the Standing Committee of the National People's Congress the power to appoint and dismiss judicial personnel and to enact legal codes. The state constitution protected individuals from arrest and detention unless approved by the people's procuratorates, and it granted citizens freedom of speech, correspondence, demonstration, and religious belief. Citizens could vote and could run for election. They also acquired the right to an education, work, rest, material assistance in old age, and the ability to lodge complaints with state agencies. Each citizen was granted the right to a public trial and to offer a defense aided by a "people's lawyer." Citizens were granted equality before the law, and women were guaranteed equal legal rights. Under the 1954 state constitution, local procuratorates that had been responsible both to the procuratorate at the next higher level and to the government at the corresponding level were responsible only to the procuratorate at the next higher level. Technically, the judiciary became independent, and the Supreme People's Court became the highest judicial organ of the state.

Additionally, a law codification commission was set up to draft the first criminal code of the People's Republic and to describe criminal liability in detail. A set of rules for the proper conduct for police and judicial personnel was established, and it became the "political task" of the courts to determine what was or was not an offense. A criminal law, a code of criminal procedure, and a civil code were drafted, but none of these were enacted until twenty-five years later.

To cope with the anticipated need for more lawyers, law schools expanded and revamped their curricula. A large quantity of legal books and journals reappeared for use by law students. Although all lawyers were supposed to be conversant in the current ideology, many developed into "legal specialists" with more concern for the law then for ideology. Although this viewpoint would be condemned in 1957 when the Soviet-style legal system was rejected, in 1954 it appeared that China had taken a first step toward an orderly administration of justice.

Between 1954 and 1957, much effort was expended to make the legal system work, but the underlying conflict between the specialists and the cadres, who were more concerned about ideology than the legal system, remained. By 1956 the situation had polarized. The specialists argued that the period of intense class struggle was over and that all people should now be considered equal before the law and the state constitution. The cadres, on the other hand, contended that class struggle would never end and that separate standards should be applied to class enemies. They saw the specialists as obstructing the revolution—trying to subvert the new state and restore the rights of old class enemies.

In 1956 Mao personally launched a mass movement under the classical slogan "Let a hundred flowers bloom, let the hundred schools of thought contend'' (see The Transition to Socialism, 1953-57, ch. 1; Policy Toward Intellectuals, ch. 4). His essay ''On the Correct Handling of Contradictions among the People,'' published in early 1957, encouraged people to vent their criticisms as long as they were ''constructive'' (''among the people'') rather than ''hateful and destructive'' (''between the enemy and ourselves''). Mao was anxious to defuse the potential for a backlash against communist rule such as had occurred in Hungary and Poland.

The legal specialists were among the most vociferous critics of party and government policies. They complained that there were too few laws and that the National People's Congress was slow in enacting laws already drafted. They felt that legal institutions were maturing too slowly and that the poorly qualified cadres were obstructing the work of these institutions to suit their own political ends. The legal experts also spoke out against those, especially party members, who thought themselves above the law.

By August 1957 the criticisms of party and state policies were too broad and penetrating to be ignored. Mao and his supporters labeled the critics ''rightists'' and launched a campaign against them. Among the first victims of the Anti-Rightist Campaign were the specialists and their legal system. Mao objected to this system for several reasons—among them, his views that the Soviet model was too Westernized for China and that the judicial system was too constraining.

The specialists' proposals for a judiciary free from party and political interference were denounced and ridiculed. Mao did not want a judiciary that stood as an impartial arbiter between the party and anyone else. The principle of presumption of innocence was spurned, as was the notion that the law always should act ''in the interest of the state and the people'' rather than the party.

Many specialists were transferred to nonjudicial jobs and replaced by party cadres. All codification commissions stopped work, and no new laws were drafted. The number of law schools dropped sharply as most universities shifted their curriculum to more politically acceptable subjects. Later, during the Cultural Revolution (1966-76; see Glossary), almost all the remaining law schools were closed.

With the Anti-Rightist Campaign of mid-1957 and the Great Leap Forward (1958-60; see Glossary), a new mass line emerged. The Anti-Rightist Campaign halted the trend toward legal professionalism, which was seen as a threat to party control. The party leadership resolutely declared its power absolute in legal matters. The Great Leap Forward sought to rekindle revolutionary spirit among the people. The mass line, as it affected public order, advocated turning an increasing amount of control and judicial authority over to the masses. This meant greater involvement and authority for the neighborhood committees and grass-roots mass organizations.

The Anti-Rightist Campaign put an end to efforts that would have brought about some degree of judicial autonomy and safeguards for the accused, and the country moved toward police domination. By 1958 the police were empowered to impose sanctions as they saw fit. The party gave low priority to the courts, and, as many judicial functions were turned over to local administrative officials, few qualified people chose to stay with the still-operating courts. The number of public trials decreased, and by the early 1960s the court system had become mostly inactive. One unexpected by-product of the shift from formal legal organs to local administrative control was that criminal sentences became milder. Persons found guilty of grand theft, rape, or manslaughter were sentenced to only three to five years' imprisonment, and the death penalty rarely was imposed.

During the Great Leap Forward, the number of arrests, prosecutions, and convictions increased as the police dispensed justice "on the spot" for even minor offenses. Still, the excesses of the Great Leap Forward were milder than those of the 1949–52 period, when many of those arrested were summarily executed. Persons found guilty during the Great Leap Forward were regarded as educable. After 1960, during a brief period of ascendancy of the political moderates, there was some emphasis on rebuilding the judicial sector, but the Cultural Revolution nullified most of the progress that had been made under the 1954 state constitution.

The Legal System under the 1975 State Constitution

The state constitution adopted in January 1975 overwhelmingly drew its inspiration from Mao Zedong Thought. It stressed party leadership and reduced the power of the National People's Congress. The streamlined document (30 articles compared with 106 in 1954) reduced even further the constitutional restraints on the Maoists. The sole article in the new state constitution that pertained to judicial authority eliminated the procuratorate and transferred its functions and powers to the police. The marked increase in police power suited the radical leaders in the party hierarchy who wanted public security forces to have the power to arrest without having to go through other judicial organs.

The National People's Congress theoretically was still empowered to enact laws, select and reject state officials, and direct the judiciary. The party, however, was the ultimate arbiter, and the Supreme

People's Court was no longer designated the highest judicial body in the land but was only mentioned in passing as one of the courts exercising judicial authority.

Equality before the law, a provision of the 1954 state constitution, was eliminated. Moreover, people no longer had the right to engage in scientific research or literary or artistic creation nor the freedom to change residences. Some new rights were added, including the freedom to propagate atheism and to practice religion. Citizens also gained the "four big rights": the right to speak out freely, air views fully, hold great debates, and write big-character posters (see Glossary). These "new" forms of socialist revolution along with the right to strike were examples of radical political activism popularized during the Cultural Revolution that were revoked in 1979 (see The Government, ch. 10).

"Socialist legality" under the 1975 state constitution was characterized by instant, arbitrary arrest. Impromptu trials were conducted either by a police officer on the spot, by a revolutionary committee (the local government body established during the Cultural Revolution decade), or by a mob. Spur-of-the-moment circulars and party regulations continued to take the place of a code of criminal law or judicial procedure. For example, during demonstrations in Beijing's Tiananmen Square in early 1976, three demonstrators were seized by police and accused of being counterrevolutionaries in support of Deng Xiaoping. The three were "tried" by the "masses" during a two-hour "struggle meeting," a session where thousands of onlookers shouted their accusations. After this "trial," during which the accused were forbidden to offer a defense (even if they had wished to), the three were sentenced to an unspecified number of years in a labor camp. In contrast to the milder sentences of the 1957 period, sentencing under the state constitution of 1975 was severe. Death sentences were handed down frequently for "creating mass panic," burglary, rape, and looting.

Following the death of Mao in September 1976 and the arrest of the Gang of Four (see Glossary) less than a month later, the government took its first steps to set aside the 1975 state constitution and restore the pre-Cultural Revolution legal system. In January 1977 Premier Hua Guofeng directed legal experts to begin rebuilding judicial institutions in the spirit of the 1954 state constitution. The Chinese press began to carry stories about the virtues of the 1954 document and the Gang of Four's abuse of it. Later in the year, Hua announced that China had eight important tasks to fulfill, among them the reconstruction of formal legal institutions.

During the fall of 1977, the People's Liberation Army (PLA)

A policeman directs rush-hour traffic in Beijing. The slogan reads "Pay attention to Safety."
Courtesy Robert L. Worden

and militia began turning over the responsibility for public security to the civilian sector. Judicial and public security workers held meetings to seek ways "to strengthen the building of the legal forces . . . and socialist legal systems." A theoretical study group from the Supreme People's Court affirmed that the courts and the public security organs were solely responsible for maintaining public order, and they called on the people to accept the views of superior authorities.

The government set out to reorganize completely all judicial procedures and establish codes of criminal law and judicial procedure as quickly as possible. Law schools were reopened, professors were rehired to staff them, and legal books and journals reappeared. By the end of 1977, the legal system and the courts reportedly were stronger than at any time since the 1954–56 period.

Return to Socialist Legality

Developments under the 1978 State Constitution

A new constitution intended to provide a structural basis for the return to socialist legality was adopted at the Fifth National People's Congress in March 1978. Legal reform was deemed essential not only to prevent a return to power of the radicals but also to provide the legal structure for the economic development of the country envisioned by the party leadership.

The 1978 state constitution reaffirmed the principle—deleted in the 1975 state constitution—of the equality of all citizens before the law. It guaranteed the right to a public trial, except in cases involving national security, sex offenses, or minors, and reaffirmed a citizen's right to offer a defense—also omitted in 1975.

The National People's Congress called for new criminal, procedural, civil, and economic codes as quickly as possible, using the new state constitution as a guide. The delegates quoted Mao as having said in 1962 that "we not only need a criminal code but also a civil code," and they invoked Mao's authority against those who viewed regularizing the legal system as counterrevolutionary.

In November 1978 the Law Institute of the Chinese Academy of Social Sciences, working in conjunction with the Legal Affairs Commission of the National People's Congress proposed strengthening the socialist legal system, which, it explained, was based on democracy, socialist principles, and the worker-peasant alliance. The institute added that the system should be formulated, enforced, and used by the people for economic development and against groups such as the Gang of Four. The 1978 state constitution gave the National People's Congress sole authority to interpret, promulgate, and change laws. It also reestablished the people's procuratorates and made them responsible both to the procuratorate at the next higher level and to the people's government at the same level, as they had been before 1954.

In mid-1979 China promulgated a series of new statutes that included the country's first criminal law, the first criminal procedure law, and updated laws on courts and procuratorates. Extensive preparations preceded the announcements. Beginning in early 1979, for example, the media hosted debates on subjects such as judicial independence, presumption of innocence, and equality of all citizens before the law. A national conference of procuratorates in January 1979 stressed the need for thorough investigations in all cases and respect for evidence. The participants in the conference warned that extorted confessions would no longer be accepted and that the police could not make arrests without procuratorate approval. If circumstances did not permit prior approval, the approval had to be obtained after the fact or the detainee had to be released.

Judicial work conferences were held throughout China to make recommendations to the National People's Congress concerning an independent judiciary. According to the recommendations, Chinese courts in the future would base their judgments on the law, while continuing to "work under unified leadership of the local party committees." In short, party policy no longer would be the equivalent of the law, but judicial independence in China could still be modified by party guidance.

Peng Zhen, director of the Legal Affairs Commission and active in the reform efforts of the early 1960s, announced the new laws in June 1979 and had them published shortly thereafter. According to Peng's announcement, the laws were based on 1954 and 1963 drafts and provided a foundation for the socialist legal system and, ultimately, social democracy. He affirmed that the judiciary would be independent and subject only to the law; that all individuals, no matter how senior, would be equal before the law; and that party members and cadres would have to forego special treatment and set an example for the people. In November 1979 Peng was appointed secretary general of the Standing Committee of the Fifth National People's Congress, a position from which he could control the reconstruction of the legal system.

Among the laws approved by the Second Session of the Fifth National People's Congress to take effect January 1, 1980, was the Organic Law of the Local People's Congresses and the Local People's Governments. The revolutionary committees, which had assumed judicial authority in the 1967-76 period, were eliminated; their authority was assumed by local people's governments, and judicial responsibility was returned to the appropriate courts.

The Electoral Law for the National People's Congress and Local People's Congresses, also to take effect January 1, 1980, provided for the direct election of some procurators and judges. The Organic Law of the People's Courts was designed to create a more orderly environment and to assure the people that the chaotic years of the Cultural Revolution, with no courts and no legal guarantees, were over. The law, a revised version of 1954 drafts, guaranteed the accused equality before the law regardless of race, nationality, sex, social background, or religious beliefs and gave people the right to a lawyer. In certain cases, the lawyer would be court-appointed. The law called for independence of the judiciary from political interference. Courts were free to establish judicial committees to assist them in difficult cases, and there were provisions for citizens to be elected as assessors to participate with judges in adjudicating cases. The local language was to be the medium for conducting court proceedings and writing court decisions. Cases involving the death penalty were to be reviewed by the Supreme People's Court, and all defendants were entitled to appeal to the next higher court.

The Organic Law of the People's Procuratorates, an amended version of a 1954 law, made procurators responsible for supervising law enforcement by the police, courts, and administrative agencies. The procuratorate was linked to China's past in that it functioned like the censorial system of imperial China. It served as the eyes and ears of the government, just as the censorial system was the watchdog for the emperor.

The procurators were elected by local people's congresses and approved by the next higher procuratorial level to handle only criminal cases. The independence of the procuratorates was constitutionally guaranteed. Still, their responsibilities were difficult, especially in any case involving a high party official. According to the new law, procuratorates at all levels had to establish procuratorial committees, practice democratic centralism (see Glossary), and make decisions through discussion. Ideally, a procuratorate at a lower level would be led, rather than dictated to, by one at the next higher level. Each procuratorate was responsible to the standing committee of the people's congress at the corresponding level.

The 1980 Criminal Law was intended to protect state property as well as the personal and property rights of citizens against unlawful infringement by any person or institution. It safeguarded the fundamental rights stipulated in the 1978 state constitution and prescribed penalties for counterrevolutionary activities (crimes against the state) and other criminal offenses. Prevention of crime and rehabilitation through education (taking into account actual conditions in China in 1979) were stressed. Illegal incarcerations, fabrications, prosecutions, and intimidation were forbidden, but the provisions of the law did not apply retroactively.

The Criminal Law contained a provision prohibiting the criminal prosecution of a person who had "reactionary," that is, antiparty, ideas but who had committed no "reactionary" actions. As Peng Zhen pointed out in late 1979, because "most contradictions were among the people," involving constructive criticism not antagonistic to the party or state, punishment was inappropriate (see Policy Toward Intellectuals, ch. 4). As in some other areas of the law, the actual judicial disposition appeared at times to be at variance with this particular principle.

The law defined criminal acts and distinguished between actual crimes and accidents. It also established a statute of limitations both to demonstrate the "humanitarian spirit" of the penal code and to permit law enforcement officials to concentrate on crimes for which evidence was still available. The law retained the important legal principle of analogy, according to which acts not specifically defined might be considered crimes. Criminal charges could not be brought unless there was evidence that a crime had been committed; the sole basis for prosecution was verifiable evidence. The law also defined basic understandable rules of evidence. The death penalty could be imposed for flagrant counterrevolutionary acts and for homicide, arson, criminal intent in causing explosions, and other offenses of this nature. The 1983 revision of the law considerably increased the number of offenses punishable by the death penalty.

The Law on Criminal Procedure was promulgated to reform judicial procedures in enforcing the Criminal Law. It was designed to educate citizens, establish judicial jurisdictions, and streamline judicial appeal and review. The law described the relationship between public security organs (investigations and provisional apprehensions), the procuratorates (arrest approvals, possible procuratorial investigations, prosecutions, and supervision of the police and penal institutions), and the courts (trials and sentencing). It also guaranteed the accused the right to make a defense at a public trial with an advocate present.

The public security organs, procuratorates, and courts had to base their judgments on verified evidence using the law as a measure. There were strict time limits on court and police actions to prevent overly lengthy detention.

Legal Reforms in the 1982 State Constitution

In late 1982 the National People's Congress adopted a new state constitution, which was still in effect in mid-1987 (see Constitutional Framework, ch. 10). The 1982 State Constitution incorporates many provisions of the laws passed since 1978 and distinguishes between the functions of the state and of the party, mandating that "no organization or individual may enjoy the privilege of being above the Constitution and the law" (Article 5). This article has been interpreted by Chinese observers to include party leaders. The State Constitution also delineates the fundamental rights and duties of citizens, including protection from defamation of character, illegal arrest or detention, and unlawful search.

The National People's Congress and the local people's congresses continued to enact legislation to meet the juridical and other needs of their jurisdictions. The draft Law on Civil Procedure, in force from October 1982, provides guidelines for hearing civil cases. These cases constitute the majority of lawsuits in China, and in the 1980s the number was growing rapidly. In some of the lower courts almost all cases were civil.

A major problem in implementing new criminal and civil laws was a critical lack of trained legal personnel. In August 1980 the Standing Committee of the National People's Congress had sought to remedy this shortage by passing the Provisional Act on Lawyers of the People's Republic of China, which took effect on January 1, 1982. Before the law went into effect, there were only 1,300 legal advisory offices and 4,800 lawyers in China. By mid-1983 the number had increased to 2,300 legal advisory offices staffed by more than 12,000 lawyers (approximately 8,600 full time and 3,500 part time). To meet the growing demand for lawyers, law institutes and university law departments that had been closed during the Cultural Revolution were reopened, and additional ones were established. By mid-1985 approximately 3,000 lawyers per year were graduating from the 5 legal institutes and 31 university law departments located throughout the country.

The law also established legal advisory offices at every level of government and established the duties, rights, and qualifications of lawyers. Any Chinese citizen with the right to vote who has passed a professional competency test after formal training or after two to three years of experience in legal work can qualify as a lawyer. Lawyers are expected to act as legal advisers to government and nongovernment organizations and as both public and private litigants in civil suits, to defend the accused in criminal cases on request of the defendant or upon assignment of the court, and to offer legal advice at a nominal charge to anyone requesting it. The 1982 law guarantees that in carrying out these duties lawyers will be permitted to meet and to correspond with their clients without interference from any organization or individual. The law seems to have had a positive effect. Although there was a serious shortage of lawyers and great disparity in professional competence among those practicing, China in the mid-1980s was making progress in developing a corps of lawyers to meet its legal needs.

Court Structure and Process

Between the Anti-Rightist Campaign of 1957 and the legal reforms of 1979, the courts—viewed by the leftists as troublesome and unreliable—played only a small role in the judicial system. Most of their functions were handled by other party or government organs. In 1979, however, the National People's Congress began the process of restoring the judicial system. The world was able to see an early example of this reinstituted system in action in the showcase trial of the Gang of Four and six other members of the "Lin-Jiang clique" from November 1980 to January 1981 (see China and the Four Modernizations, 1979–82, ch. 1). The trial, which was publicized to show that China had restored a legal system that made all citizens equal before the law, actually appeared to many foreign observers to be more a political than a legal exercise.

Nevertheless, it was intended to show that China was committed to restoring a judicial system.

The Ministry of Justice, abolished in 1959, was reestablished under the 1979 legal reforms to administer the newly restored judicial system. With the support of local judicial departments and bureaus, the ministry was charged with supervising personnel management, training, and funding for the courts and associated organizations and was given responsibility for overseeing legal research and exchanges with foreign judicial bodies.

The 1980 Organic Law of the People's Courts (revised in 1983) and the 1982 State Constitution established four levels of courts in the general administrative structure. Judges are elected or appointed by people's congresses at the corresponding levels to serve a maximum of two five-year terms. Most trials are administered by a collegial bench made up of one to three judges and three to five assessors. Assessors, according to the State Constitution, are elected by local residents or people's congresses from among citizens over twenty-three years of age with political rights or are appointed by the court for their expertise. Trials are conducted in an inquisitorial manner, in which both judges and assessors play an active part in the questioning of all witnesses. (This contrasts with the Western adversarial system, in which the judge is meant to be an impartial referee between two contending attorneys.) After the judge and assessors rule on a case, they pass sentence. An aggrieved party can appeal to the next higher court.

The Organic Law of the People's Courts requires that adjudication committees be established for courts at every level. The committees usually are made up of the president, vice presidents, chief judges, and associate chief judges of the court, who are appointed and removed by the standing committees of the people's congresses at the corresponding level. The adjudication committees are charged with reviewing major cases to find errors in determination of facts or application of law and to determine if a chief judge should withdraw from a case. If a case is submitted to the adjudication committee, the court is bound by its decision. The Supreme People's Court stands at the apex of the judicial structure (see fig. 20). Located in Beijing, it has jurisdiction over all lower and special courts, for which it serves as the ultimate appellate court. It is directly responsible to the National People's Congress Standing Committee, which elects the court president (see The Judiciary, ch. 10).

China also has special military, railroad transport, water transport, and forestry courts. These courts hear cases of counterrevolutionary activity, plundering, bribery, sabotage, or indifference to

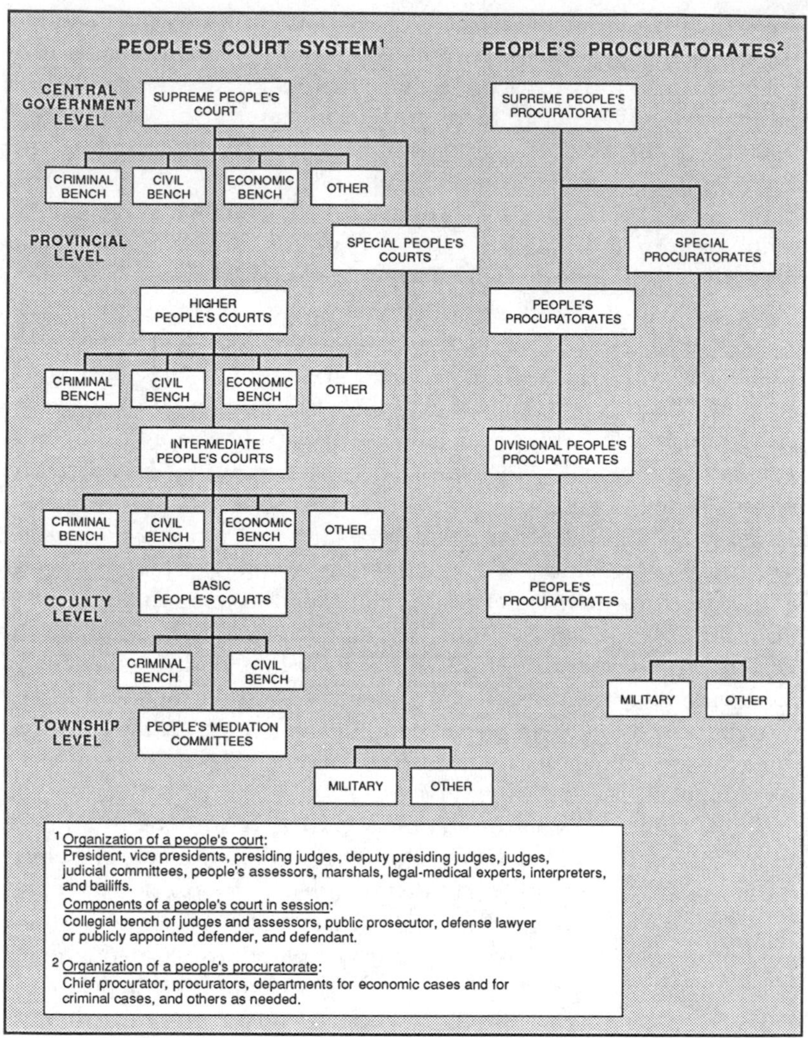

Figure 20. Organization of the People's Courts and People's Procuratorates, 1987

duty that result in severe damage to military facilities, work units, or government property or threaten the safety of soldiers or workers.

Military courts make up the largest group of special courts and try all treason and espionage cases. Although they are independent of civilian courts and directly subordinate to the Ministry of National Defense, military court decisions are reviewed by the

Supreme People's Court. Special military courts were first established in 1954 to protect the special interests of all commanders, political commissars, and soldiers, but they ceased to function during the Cultural Revolution. Military courts and procuratorates were reinstituted in October 1978, and open military trials resumed in December of that year.

Law Enforcement

An extensive public security system and a variety of enforcement procedures maintained order in China in 1987. Along with the courts and procuratorates, the country's judicial and public security agencies included the Ministry of Public Security and the Ministry of State Security, with their descending hierarchy of departments, bureaus, subbureaus, and stations.

Historical Background

Pre-Qin to 1949

However much the public security system may have been influenced by communist ideology and practice, it remained rooted directly in the traditional Chinese concept of governmental control through imposed collective responsibility. Even in the preimperial era, a system was proposed to organize the people into "groups of families which would be mutually responsible for each other's good behavior and share each other's punishments." The Qin (221-207 B.C.) and Han (206 B.C.-A.D. 220) dynasties made use of the concept, and the Song dynasty (960-1279) institutionalized it on a nationwide basis in the *bao jia* (tithing) system. It entailed the organization of family households into groups of ten, each unit being organized successively into a larger unit up to the county level of administration. Each family sent a representative to the monthly meeting of its unit, and each unit elected a leader to represent it at the next higher level. Since the head of each unit was responsible to the next higher level for the conduct of all members of his unit, the system served as an extension of the central government. Eventually, each group of families also was required to furnish men to serve in the militia. *Bao jia*, which alternately flourished or languished under later rulers and usually existed more in theory than in practice, was reinstituted during the Qing dynasty (1644-1911).

During the Qing period, the people's aversion to legalistic procedures and the rulers' preferences for socially and collectively imposed sanctions continued. Technically, the magistrate was to hear even minor criminal cases; but local elders and village leaders were allowed to handle most disputes, freeing the magistrate for more important work and saving the government expense. The people preferred to handle matters in this way, outside the intimidating court system.

Other practices for maintaining public order in China during the imperial era included the formation of mutual aid groups of farm households, which over time came to assume police functions. In a manner similar to twentieth-century means of ideological control, the Qing bureaucracy organized mass lectures that stressed the Confucian principle of obedience. Still another traditional form of policing was the appointment of censors to investigate corruption and misconduct up to the highest levels of government. Doing that job too well cost many censors their lives.

In 1932 Chiang Kai-shek's Guomindang government reinstituted the *bao jia* system. In the Guomindang's revised *bao jia* system, in addition to the chief, there were two officers of importance within each 100-family unit. The population officer maintained the records and reported all births, deaths, marriages, moves, and unlawful activities to the district office. The *bao jia* troop commander headed a self-defense unit and was responsible for maintaining law and order. In rural China, however, the local village was generally a self-contained world, and the peasants remained aloof from distant and higher-ranking centers of authority.

The Japanese were introduced to the *bao jia* system on Taiwan when they assumed control of the island after the Sino-Japanese War (1894–95), and they found the system highly suitable for administering occupied areas. They instituted modified versions of it in north China after 1937. The Japanese imposed severe restrictions on the population, and the system aided in taking the census, restricting movement, and conducting spot checks. Each household had to affix a wooden tablet on the front door with the names of all inhabitants inscribed. Anyone missing or not on the list during an inspection by Japanese troops was assumed to be an insurgent. Since there were not as many Japanese troops in south China as in the north, the local leaders assisted the Japanese in administering the areas. They also disseminated propaganda at neighborhood meetings and established self-defense and youth corps.

Developments Since 1949

The Communists were themselves products of Chinese society, and when they came to power in 1949 they liberally borrowed from these historical examples. They extensively organized the population and maintained the principles of mutual surveillance and mutual responsibility. They also retained the concept of self-defense forces. Communist control, however, exceeded that of *bao jia* or any other traditional system and extended into virtually every household. Under communist rule, the family was not considered an effective control mechanism. To achieve near-total control, a large number of administrative agencies and social organizations were established or adapted. Police forces resembling the Soviet police in organization, power, and activities were organized with the aid of Soviet advisers.

From 1949 to 1953, the newly established government of the People's Republic made use of the PLA, militia units made up of demobilized soldiers and other civilians, the police, and loyal citizens to put down resistance and establish order. Remnants of the Guomindang armed forces remained in pockets on the mainland, and communist efforts to enforce tax laws and agricultural rules provoked disturbances and riots. Extending responsibility for public order to include the police, military, and citizenry proved to be a highly effective arrangement, and the concept was written into the Common Program that preceded the 1954 state constitution.

The PLA and the militia continued to share responsibility for internal security and public order under the 1954 state constitution. The PLA's involvement in internal affairs was most extensive during the more turbulent period of the Cultural Revolution (see The Cultural Revolution Decade, 1966–76, ch. 1). Mao Zedong, perceiving that the public security cadres were protecting precisely the party leaders he wished to purge, directed youthful Red Guards to crush the police, courts, and procuratorates as well. The minister of public security, Luo Ruiqing (who concurrently served as the chief of staff of the PLA), was purged, soon followed by heads of the courts and procuratorates.

Initially, the military tried to remain uninvolved. But on Mao's orders, the PLA, which had once been told to support (actually to acquiesce to) the Red Guards, moved in to quell the chaos that Mao had inspired. The PLA gradually took over public security functions by establishing military control committees to replace the government bureaucracy. Revolutionary committees were set up as provincial-level and local administrative organs, usually with a PLA cadre in charge, and order gradually returned. By the summer of 1968 the Red Guards were being disbanded, and mass trials were used to punish and intimidate rioters.

With nineteen of China's twenty-nine provincial-level people's revolutionary committees headed by PLA commanders, the military again was in charge of administration and security throughout the country, but it badly needed help from experienced police officers. A policy of leniency toward most former officials evolved, and some public security cadres returned to work. The PLA also recruited inexperienced people to form auxiliary police units. These units were mass organizations with a variety of names reflecting their factional orientation. Perhaps the best known unit was the "Attack with Reason, Defend with Force Corps" named for the militant slogan of Mao's wife, Jiang Qing. Public security forces were composed largely of nonprofessionals and lacked the disciplined informant networks and personnel dossiers previously used to maintain order.

Beginning in 1968, the authorities called upon the PLA to help remove millions of urban dwellers from the overcrowded cities and relocate them to the countryside and to transport cashiered officials to special cadre schools for indoctrination and labor. The migration to the country mostly involved students and other youths for whom there were not enough jobs or places in the school system within the cities. Yet despite the discontent these campaigns caused, reported crime declined after 1970. Increased concern over the threat from the Soviet Union in the wake of armed clashes on the Sino-Soviet border in 1969 forced the PLA gradually to return to barracks, and control of the country reverted to the civilian leadership (see Civil-Military Relations, ch. 14).

The Beijing-based Central Security Regiment, also known as the 8341 Unit, was an important PLA law enforcement element. It was responsible over the years for the personal security of Mao Zedong and other party and state leaders. More than a bodyguard force, it also operated a nationwide intelligence network to uncover plots against Mao or any incipient threat to the leadership. The unit reportedly was deeply involved in undercover activities, discovering electronic listening devices in Mao's office and performing surveillance of his rivals. The 8341 Unit participated in the late 1976 arrest of the Gang of Four, but it reportedly was deactivated soon after that event.

The militia also participated in maintaining public order in the 1970s. Their involvement was especially evident in the 1973–76 period. In 1973 the Gang of Four, concerned over the transformation of the PLA into a more professional, less political, military force, took control of the urban militia from the PLA and placed it under local party committees loyal to them. For the next three years, the urban militia was used extensively to enforce radical political and social policies. It was the urban militia, along with the public security forces, that broke up the demonstrations in Tiananmen Square honoring the memory of Zhou Enlai in April 1976—the event that served as the pretext for the second purge of Deng Xiaoping (see The Cultural Revolution Decade, 1966–76, ch. 1). In rural areas the militia was more under the control of the PLA.

Public Security Forces

The Public Security System

In 1987 the Ministry of Public Security was the principal police authority. The ministry had functional departments for areas such as intelligence; police operations; prisons; and political, economic, and communications security. Subordinate to the ministry were provincial-level public security departments; public security bureaus and subbureaus at the county level (the bureaus located in the prefectures and large cities, the subbureaus in counties and municipal districts); and public security stations at the township level (see fig. 21). While public security considerations had a strong influence at all levels of administration, the police appeared to wield progressively greater influence at the lower levels of government.

The organization of local public security stations could be inferred from the tasks with which the police were charged. Generally, each station had sections for population control, pretrial investigations, welfare, traffic control, a detention center, and other activities.

In the 1980s the public security station—the police element in closest contact with the people—was supervised by the public security subbureau as well as by local governments and procuratorates. The procuratorate could assume direct responsibility for handling any case it chose, and it supervised investigations in those cases it allowed the public security station to conduct. A great deal of coordination occurred among the public security organs, the procuratorates, and the courts, so that a trial was unlikely to produce a surprise outcome.

The public security station generally had considerably broader responsibilities than a police station in the West, involving itself in every aspect of the district people's lives. In a rural area it had a chief, a deputy chief, a small administrative staff, and a small police force. In an urban area it had a greater number of administrative staff members and seven to eighteen patrolmen. Its criminal law activities included investigation, apprehension, interrogation, and temporary detention. The station's household section maintained a registry of all persons living in the area. Births, deaths, marriages, and divorces were recorded and confirmed through random household checks. The station regulated all hotels and required visitors who remained beyond a certain number of days to register. All theaters, cinemas, radio equipment, and printing presses also

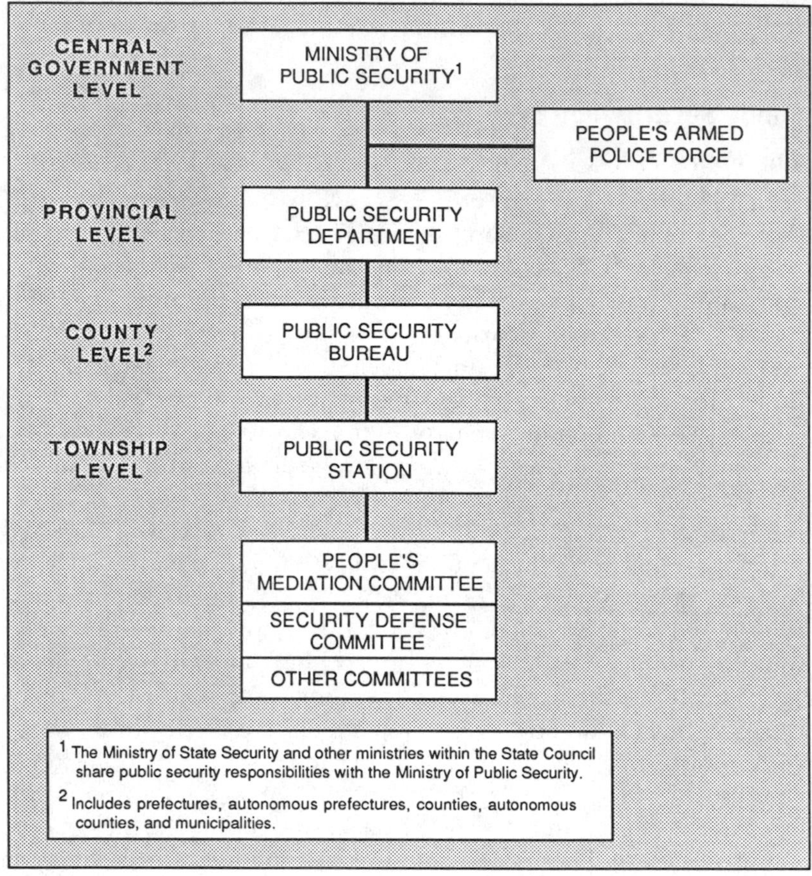

Figure 21. Organization of the Public Security System, 1987

were registered with the local public security station, permitting it to regulate gatherings and censor information effectively. It also regulated the possession, transportation, and use of all explosives, guns, ammunition, and poisons.

Another important police function was controlling change of residence. Without such controls, large numbers of rural residents undoubtedly would move to the overcrowded cities in search of better living standards, work, or education (see Migration, ch. 2; Urban Society, ch. 3). In April 1984 the State Council issued the Tentative Regulations Governing People's Republic of China Resident Identity. The regulations, to be implemented over a period of years, required all residents over sixteen years of age, except active-duty members of the PLA and the People's Armed Police Force and inmates serving sentences, to be issued resident identity cards by the Ministry of Public Security. The picture cards indicated the name, sex, nationality, date of birth, and address of the bearer. Cards for persons sixteen to twenty-five years of age were valid for ten years; those for persons between twenty-five and forty-five were valid for twenty years; and persons over forty-five were issued permanent cards. As of early 1987, only 70 million people had been issued identity cards, well below the national goal. Also, even those with resident identity cards preferred to use other forms of identification.

In the 1980s secret police operations employed agents, informers, and "roving spies." Police surveillance apparently was restricted to probation and parole. Plainclothes agents were posted at bus and railroad stations and other public places. Police informers denounced "bad elements" and assisted in surveillance of suspected political criminals. Roving spies were a special category of informant in the factories and work units and were ever watchful for dissidence or sabotage. Youths aspiring to be Communist Youth League members, or league members aspiring to be party members, sometimes cooperated as informants and agents for the police.

Public security officials also made extensive use of the authority granted them to impose administrative sanctions by two sets of documents. These were the 1957 Regulations on Reeducation Through Labor, which were reissued in 1979 with amendments, and the 1957 Regulations Governing Offenses Against Public Order, which were rescinded and replaced in 1986 by regulations of the same name. Offenders under the Regulations on Reeducation Through Labor might include "vagabonds, people who have no proper occupation, and people who repeatedly breach public order." The police could apprehend such individuals and sentence them to reeducation through labor with the approval of local labor-training administration committees. The 1957 regulations placed no limit on the length of sentences, but beginning in the early 1960s three or four years was the norm. The 1979 amended regulations, however, limited the length of reeducation through labor to three years with possible extension for extraordinary cases. The Regulations Governing Offenses Against Public Order empowered the police to admonish, fine, or detain people for up to fifteen days. Goods illegally in the possession of an offender were to be confiscated, and payment was imposed for damages or hospital fees in the event injury had been caused.

The criminal laws in force after January 1, 1980, restricted police powers regarding arrests, investigations, and searches. A public security official or a citizen could apprehend a suspect under emergency conditions, but a court or procuratorate was required to approve the arrest. The accused had to be questioned within twenty-four hours and his or her family or work unit notified of the detention "except in circumstances where notification would hinder the investigation or there was no way to notify them." Any premeditated arrest required a court or procuratorate warrant. The time that an accused could be held pending investigation was limited to three to seven days, and incarceration without due process was illegal.

Two officials were needed to conduct a criminal investigation. They were required to show identification and, apparently, to inform the accused of the crime allegedly committed before he or she was questioned. The suspect could refuse to answer only those questions irrelevant to the case. Torture was illegal.

The 1980 laws also provided that in conjunction with an arrest the police could conduct an emergency search; otherwise, a warrant was required. They had the right to search the person, property, and residence of an accused and the person of any injured party. They could intercept mail belonging to the accused and order an autopsy whenever cause of death was unclear.

In July 1980 the government approved new regulations governing police use of weapons and force. Police personnel could use their batons only in self-defense or when necessary to subdue or prevent the escape of violent criminals or rioters. Lethal weapons, such as pistols, could be used if necessary to stop violent riots, to lessen the overall loss of life, or to subdue surrounded but still resisting criminals. The regulations even governed use of sirens, police lights, and whistles.

The relationship between the police officers assigned to neighborhood patrols and the people was close. Police officers lived in a neighborhood on a long-term assignment and were expected to know all the residents personally. Their task was not only to prevent and punish crime but to promote desirable behavior by counseling and acting as role models. This positive side of the police officer's duties was a constant responsibility, but the bond between the public security units and the people was strengthened annually by means of "cherish-the-people" months, during which the police officer made a special effort to be of help, especially to the aged and the infirm.

Police were drawn from every segment of the population without restriction as to sex or ethnic origin. Selection was based on political loyalty, intelligence, and health, as it was for the PLA. Most recruits had Communist Youth League backgrounds or were former

PLA personnel. There was at least one police school in every provincial-level unit, and others were operated by municipalities. Usually those police designated for leadership positions attended the police schools, and patrolmen were trained at the unit and on the job. Legal training was emphasized as a method of improving the quality of the police forces. In 1985 three institutions of higher learning for police personnel—the University of Public Security, the University of Police Officers, and the Institute of Criminal Police—offered more than twenty special courses. Students were recruited from senior-middle-school graduates under twenty-two years of age, with a waiver to twenty-five years of age for those having a minimum of two years' experience in public security work.

The People's Armed Police Force

The People's Armed Police Force (PAPF), after a trial period in selected jurisdictions, was officially established at the national level in 1983. In line with the general policy of reducing the size of the armed forces and transferring responsibilities to the civilian sector, the newly established force was formed from internal security units reassigned from the PLA to the Ministry of Public Security and from border defense (customs) and fire-fighting units (see Military Modernization, ch. 14). In 1985 the PAPF consisted of approximately 600,000 volunteers and conscripts. With a general headquarters at the national level and subordinate division-level provincial or specialized units, regimental-level detachments, and battalion-level brigades, it retained its military organization.

PAPF units assigned to internal security were responsible for guarding party and state organizations and foreign embassies and consulates, as well as for responding to emergencies and maintaining law and order. Border defense units performed standard customs duties, such as inspecting vehicles and ships entering and leaving the country, and maintained surveillance against smugglers and drug traffickers. PAPF firefighting units were responsible for fire-prevention education as well as for fighting fires. PAPF units at every level worked in close cooperation with the armed forces and other public security organizations.

State Security

In June 1983 the National People's Congress, perceiving a growing threat of subversion and sabotage, established the Ministry of State Security under the State Council. This new ministry was charged with ensuring "the security of the state through effective measures against enemy agents, spies, and counterrevolutionary activities designed to sabotage or overthrow China's socialist system.'' At its inception, the ministry pledged to abide by the state constitution and the law and called upon the citizenry for their cooperation, reminding them of their constitutional obligations to ''keep state secrets'' and ''safeguard the security'' of the country. The Ministry of State Security reportedly acted in close coordination with the Ministry of Public Security, but as of mid-1987 little had been revealed about the actual workings of this counterintelligence organization.

Grass-Roots Organizations

Aspects of Chinese society also have contributed to shaping the contemporary structure for maintaining public order (see Urban Society, ch. 3). Urban and rural dwellers rarely change their residences. Amid the sprawling cities, neighborhoods remain close-knit communities. For the 80 percent of the population that lives in the countryside, home and place of work are the same. With little physical mobility, most villagers stay put for generations and know each other intimately. In such close-knit environments, where everyone is likely to know everyone else and notice most of what happens, mutual surveillance and peer pressure can be extremely effective (see Rural Society, ch. 3).

The structure of the public security system remained extensive in the 1980s, and the authority of its forces exceeded that of most police forces in the West. Nevertheless, public security agencies required and received the assistance of a wide-ranging network of grass-roots organizations to mobilize residents' responses to the government's call for observance of laws, lead the people in maintaining social order and public security, and settle disputes among residents.

In urban areas an average of 11 patrolmen were responsible for controlling an area containing 15,000 or more residents. A patrolman could not know all the people and their particular problems; he needed help. The local people's governments and congresses shared responsibility for public order but had no special personnel for the task. The armed forces were available, but they had other primary concerns and would be called out only in the most extreme circumstances.

To provide security beyond what could be provided by the police and to extend government control, a system of neighborhood or street committees had been established on a nationwide basis in 1954. The committees were charged with the responsibility of assisting the government in maintaining order. They usually controlled from 10,000 to 20,000 people and consisted of 3 to 7 full-time cadres. In the late 1970s, the size and functions of neighborhood committees

Inspecting the People's Armed Police Force
Courtesy Jiefangjun Huabao

were expanded. The neighborhood committees were specifically responsible for maintaining public order and were accountable to the local people's congress.

Residents' committees and residents' "small groups," also established in 1954, were subordinate to neighborhood committees. These were the genuine grass-roots organizations, staffed by unpaid local residents elected by their neighbors. They directly involved the people in controlling their neighborhoods, and they reduced the demands on formal state institutions by maintaining surveillance for the public security forces and mediating most civil disputes and minor criminal cases for the judiciary. A residents' committee supervised from 100 to 600 families with a staff of 7 to 17 members, one from each subordinate residents' small group. A residents' small group controlled fifteen to forty households. The public security organization in the countryside was also pervasive. From the 1950s to the early 1980s, it was structured along military lines. The people's commune (see Glossary) was the lowest level of government organization, with its administrative committee on a legal par with the local people's government in the urban areas. People's communes were subdivided into production brigades (see Glossary) and production teams (see Glossary). Each team elected a people's public security committee, which sent a representative to the committee at the brigade level. Physical control was mostly the responsibility of the militia units organized at the team, brigade, and commune levels. In the winter of 1982–83 communes were replaced by township governments, and grass-roots committees were patterned after urban committees (see Rural Society, ch. 3). These rural grass-roots committees were given legal status by the Draft Organic Regulations for Villagers' Committees approved by the National People's Congress in April 1987.

Residents' committees and small groups were staffed originally by housewives and retired persons but involved others as their functions expanded. Their pervasive presence made them a primary means for disseminating propaganda, and their grass-roots nature allowed for effective use of peer pressure in mediating disputes and controlling troublemakers. Perhaps 4 or 5 percent of the adult population exercised some authority in what Western experts have described as "participatory democracy in an extended form." The functional subunits, the residents' committees and residents' small groups, were particularly important in controlling the people.

People's mediation committees, guided and supervised jointly by the basic people's court and the public security station, performed an important function within the residents' committees. They settled minor disputes and disagreements using conciliation and peer pressure. Mediation committees were established originally in communist areas during the Chinese civil war (1945–49) as a natural outgrowth of traditional preferences for local mediation of disputes. Upon taking over the major cities of China in 1949, the Communists were confronted with a tremendous backlog of judicial cases. Mediation committees provided a means of resolving disputes while actively propagandizing and involving the people in the new government. Beginning in 1954 mediation committees were set up in neighborhoods, stores, schools, enterprises, factories, and workshops in the cities and in the production brigades and teams in the countryside.

In the 1980s the five- to eleven-member people's mediation committees were elected by popular vote to two-year terms with the option of being reelected. Members served without pay and could be removed at any time by the electors for dereliction of duty. They were responsible for settling disputes, strengthening popular unity, promoting production and order, and conducting propaganda activities. Parties in dispute came voluntarily to the mediation committee; people seemed to feel they should try mediation before proceeding to a lawsuit. Mediators' duties ranged from acting as go-betweens for parties who refused to talk to one another to defining issues, deciding questions of fact, and issuing tentative or advisory decisions. Mediation committees also exerted strong political, economic, social, and moral pressures upon one or both parties to gain "voluntary" compliance with the decisions. In addition to mediation committees, other officials, police officers, party members, and work supervisors were expected to serve as mediators. Members of the residents' committees and small groups who were not members of the mediation committees were also involved in the mediation process.

The Penal System

The Criminal Law that took effect on January 1, 1980, removed criminal punishment from the discretion of officials, whose arbitrary decisions were based on perceptions of the current party line, and established it on a legal basis. The specific provisions of that law listed eight categories of offenses.

The Statute on Punishment for Counterrevolutionary Activity approved under the Common Program in 1951 listed a wide range of counterrevolutionary offenses, punishable in most cases by the death penalty or life imprisonment. In subsequent years, especially during the Cultural Revolution, any activity that the party or government at any level considered a challenge to its authority could be termed counterrevolutionary. The 1980 law narrowed the scope of counterrevolutionary activity considerably and defined it as "any act jeopardizing the People's Republic of China, aimed at overthrowing the political power of the dictatorship of the proletariat and the socialist state." Under this category it included such specific offenses as espionage, insurrection, conspiracy to overthrow the government, instigating a member of the armed forces to turn traitor, or carrying out sabotage directed against the government.

Other offenses, in the order listed in the 1980 law, were transgressions of public security, defined as any acts which endanger people or public property; illegal possession of arms and ammunition; offenses against the socialist economic order, including smuggling and speculation; offenses against both the personal rights and the democratic rights of citizens, which range from homicide, rape, and kidnapping to libel; and offenses of encroachment on property, including robbery, theft, embezzlement, and fraud. There were also offenses against the public order, including obstruction of official business; mob disturbances; manufacture, sale, or transport of illegal drugs or pornography; vandalizing or illegally exporting cultural relics; offenses against marriage and the family, which include interference with the freedom of marriage and abandoning or maltreating children or aged or infirm relatives; and malfeasance, which specifically relates to state functionaries and includes such offenses as accepting bribes, divulging state secrets, dereliction of duty, and maltreatment of persons under detention or surveillance.

Under the 1980 law, these offenses were punishable when criminal liability could be ascribed. Criminal liability was attributed to intentional offenses and those acts of negligence specifically provided for by the law. There were principal and supplementary penalties. Principal penalties were public surveillance, detention, fixed-term imprisonment, life imprisonment, and death. Supplementary penalties were fines, deprivation of political rights, and confiscation of property. Supplementary penalties could be imposed exclusive of principal penalties. Foreigners could be deported with or without other penalties.

China retained the death penalty in the 1980s for certain serious crimes. The 1980 law required that death sentences be approved by the Supreme People's Court. This requirement was temporarily modified in 1981 to allow the higher people's courts of provinces, autonomous regions, and special municipalities to approve death sentences for murder, robbery, rape, bomb-throwing, arson, and sabotage. In 1983 this modification was made permanent. The death sentence was not imposed on anyone under eighteen years of age at the time of the crime nor "on a woman found to be pregnant during the trial." Criminals sentenced to death could be granted a stay of execution for two years, during which they might demonstrate their repentance and reform. In this case the sentence could be reduced. Mao was credited with having originated this idea, which some observers found cruel although it obviated many executions.

The overwhelming majority of prisoners were sentenced to hard labor. There were two categories of hard labor: the criminal penalty—"reform through labor"—imposed by the court and the administrative penalty—"reeducation through labor"—imposed outside the court system. The former could be any fixed number of years, while the latter lasted three or four years. In fact, those with either kind of sentence ended up at the same camps, which were usually state farms or mines but occasionally were factory prisons in the city.

The November 1979 supplementary regulations on "reeducation through labor" created labor training administration committees consisting of members of the local government, public security bureau, and labor department. The police, government, or a work unit could recommend that an individual be assigned to such reeducation, and, if the labor training administration committee agreed, hard labor was imposed without further due process. The police reportedly made heavy use of the procedure, especially with urban youths, and probably used it to move unemployed, youthful, potential troublemakers out of the cities.

In the early 1980s, the people's procuratorates supervised the prisons, ensuring compliance with the law. Prisoners worked eight hours a day, six days a week, and had their food and clothing provided by the prison. They studied politics, law, state policies, and current events two hours daily, half of that in group discussion. They were forbidden to read anything not provided by the prison, to speak dialects not understood by the guards, or to keep cash, gold, jewelry, or other goods useful in an escape. Mail was censored, and generally only one visitor was allowed each month.

Prisoners were told that their sentences could be reduced if they showed signs of repentance and rendered meritorious service. Any number of reductions could be earned totaling up to one-half the original sentence, but at least ten years of a life sentence had to be served. Probation or parole involved surveillance by the public security bureau or a grass-roots organization to which the convict periodically reported.

Crime by youthful offenders has been a matter of grave concern to the post-Mao leadership. In common with most societies, nearly all those charged with violent crime have been under thirty-five years of age. Criminal law makes special provisions for juvenile offenders. Offenders between fourteen and sixteen years of age are to be held criminally liable only if they commit homicide, robbery, arson, or "other offenses which gravely jeopardize public order," and offenders between fourteen and eighteen years of age "shall be given a lighter or mitigated penalty." In most cases juvenile offenders charged with minor infractions are dealt with by neighborhood committees or other administrative means. In serious cases juvenile offenders usually are sent to one of the numerous reformatories reopened in most cities under the Ministry of Education beginning in 1978.

In 1987 the crime rate remained low by international standards, and Chinese cities were among the safest in the world. The court system had been reestablished, and standard criminal, procedural, civil, and economic codes had been developed. Law schools, closed since the late 1950s, had been reopened, and new ones had been established to meet the growing need for lawyers and judges. Law enforcement organizations had been reorganized, civilianized, and made answerable to the courts and the procuratorates. But it would be unrealistic to assume that the old system of rule by party fiat could be changed in a short period of time. Opposition to the changes was pervasive at every level of the party and the government. Even its strongest supporters insisted that the legal system must be developed in accordance with the four cardinal principles—upholding socialism, the dictatorship of the proletariat, the leadership of the Chinese Communist Party, and Marxism-Leninism-Mao Zedong Thought. Given these limitations, it was clear that although much progress had been made in replacing the Mao era's arbitrary rule with a solid legal system, much still remained to be done.

* * *

Readers interested in further information on law in traditional China should consult *Law and Society in Traditional China* by Ch'ü T'ung-tsu and *Law in Imperial China* by Derk Bodde and Clarence Morris. Readers interested in studying traditional legal practices still in use in China should consult Phillip M. Chen's *Law and Justice* and Fu-shun Lin's *Chinese Law Past and Present*.

Justice in Communist China by Shao-chuan Leng and *The Criminal Process in the People's Republic of China, 1949–1963* by Jerome Alan Cohen are good sources on legal developments in the early years of the People's Republic, and Shao-chuan Leng and Hungdah Chiu's *Criminal Justice in Post-Mao China* is an indispensable source for Chinese legal developments in the 1980s. Other extremely useful articles providing information on the criminal justice and penal systems can be found in various issues of *Beijing Review*, *China News Analysis*, *Faxue Yanjiu* (Studies in Law), and Foreign Broadcast Information Service, *Daily Report:China*. (For further information and complete citations, see Bibliography.)

Chapter 14. National Defense

Two foot soldiers, one carrying a long bow, the other with a sword and shield. The artist's version is based on part of a decorative clay tile found in a tomb of the Southern and Northern Dynasties period (A.D. 420–588) at Dengxian, Henan Province.

CHINA HAS A LONG and glorious military tradition, dating back to the earliest days of recorded history. The martial exploits of kings and emperors, loyal generals and peasant rebels, and strategists and theorists are well known in Chinese high culture and folk tradition. Throughout the centuries, two tendencies have influenced the role of the military in national life, one in peacetime and the other in times of upheaval. In times of peace and stability, military forces were firmly subordinated to civilian control. The military was strong enough to overcome domestic rebellions and foreign invasion, yet it did not threaten civilian control of the political system. In times of disorder, however, new military leaders and organizations arose to challenge the old system, resulting in the militarization of political life. When one of these leaders became strong enough, he established a new political order ruling all China. After consolidating power, the new ruler or his successors subordinated the military to civilian control once again. In the past 150 years, a third factor entered the Chinese military tradition—the introduction of modern military technology and organization to strengthen military capabilities against domestic and foreign enemies. Since the beginning of the twentieth century, all three tendencies have been discernable in the role of the military in national life. These factors have been particularly apparent in the role of the People's Liberation Army in the rise to power of the Chinese Communist Party, in the military's role in the politics of the People's Republic of China, and in the efforts of Chinese leaders to modernize the armed forces.

After decades of development from a peasant guerrilla force to a conventional military organization capable of achieving long-sought national liberation, the People's Liberation Army pursued further technical competence and improved organization, with Soviet assistance, in the 1950s. Political involvement in the Great Leap Forward (1958–60) and the Cultural Revolution (1966–76) delayed these efforts until the late 1970s, when the People's Liberation Army embarked on a military modernization program, which had three major focuses. First, military modernization required both the strengthening of party control over the military and the continued disengagement of the armed forces from politics. These steps were necessary to ensure that a politically reliable yet professionally competent military would concentrate on the task of military reform. Second, defense modernization attempted to achieve improved combat effectiveness through organizational, doctrinal, training, educational, and personnel reforms (including recruitment, promotion, and demobilization). These reforms emphasized the development of combat capabilities in waging combined arms warfare. Third, military modernization was aimed at the transformation of the defense establishment into a system capable of independently sustaining modern military forces. This transformation necessitated the reorganization and closer integration of civilian and military science and industry and also the selective use of foreign technology.

Since the 1960s China had considered the Soviet Union the principal threat to its security; lesser threats were posed by long-standing border disputes with Vietnam and India. Beijing's territorial claims and economic interests made the South China Sea an area of strategic importance to China. Although China sought peaceful reunification of Taiwan with the mainland, it did not rule out the use of force against the island if serious internal disturbances, a declaration of independence, or a threatening alliance occurred.

The scope of foreign military cooperation has evolved gradually. In the 1950s China dealt only with communist nations and insurgencies. In the 1960s it began to provide military assistance to Third World nations to counteract Soviet and United States influence. Beginning in the late 1970s, China shifted its arms transfer policy away from military assistance in favor of commercial arms sales and began developing military ties with Western Europe and the United States. Chinese military contacts with foreign countries expanded rapidly with the introduction of the military modernization program and the policy of opening up to the outside world.

In the late 1980s, People's Liberation Army forces consisted of the various arms of the ground forces, and the Air Force, Navy, and Strategic Missile Force (also known as the Second Artillery Corps). The ground forces were divided into group armies and regional forces. Ground force equipment was largely of Soviet design and obsolescent, although some weaponry had been upgraded with foreign technology. The Air Force had serious technological deficiencies despite incremental improvements of aircraft. The Navy was developing a blue-water capability and sea-based strategic forces. China possessed a small but relatively credible nuclear deterrent force with an incipient second-strike capability. Paramilitary forces consisted of the militia, reserve service system, Production and Construction Corps, and People's Armed Police Force.

Historical Development, 1927–79

From the Founding of the People's Liberation Army to the Korean War

The People's Liberation Army (PLA) was built on several millennia of tradition and a century of Western military innovations. It traces its origins to the August 1, 1927, Nanchang Uprising in which Guomindang troops led by Chinese Communist Party leaders Zhu De and Zhou Enlai rebelled following the dissolution of the first Guomindang-Chinese Communist Party united front earlier that year. The survivors of that and other abortive communist insurrections, including the Autumn Harvest Uprising led by Mao Zedong, fled to the Jinggang Mountains along the border of Hunan and Jiangxi provinces. Joining forces under the leadership of Mao and Zhu, this collection of communists, bandits, Guomindang deserters, and impoverished peasants became the First Workers' and Peasants' Army, or Red Army—the military arm of the Chinese Communist Party. Using the guerrilla tactics that would later make Mao Zedong internationally famous as a military strategist, the Red Army survived several encirclement and suppression campaigns by superior Guomindang forces. But party internal politics forced the Red Army temporarily to abandon guerrilla warfare and resulted in the epic Long March of 1934–35 (see Nationalism and Communism, ch. 1). The Red Army's exploits during the Long March became legendary and remain a potent symbol of the spirit and prowess of the Red Army and its successor, the PLA. During that period, Mao's political power and his strategy of guerrilla warfare gained ascendancy in the party and the Red Army.

In 1937 the Red Army joined in a second united front with the Guomindang against the invading Japanese army (see Anti-Japanese War, ch. 1). Although nominally cooperating with the Guomindang, the Chinese Communist Party used the Red Army to expand its influence while leading the anti-Japanese resistance in north China. By the end of the war, the Red Army numbered approximately 1 million and was backed by a militia of 2 million. Although the Red Army fought several conventional battles against the Japanese (and Guomindang troops), guerrilla operations were the primary mode of warfare.

Mao's military thought grew out of the Red Army's experiences in the late 1930s and early 1940s and formed the basis for the "people's war" concept, which became the doctrine of the Red Army and the PLA. In developing his thought, Mao drew on the works of the Chinese military strategist Sun Zi (fourth century B.C.) and

Soviet and other theorists, as well as on the lore of peasant uprisings, such as the stories found in the classical novel *Shuihu Zhuan* (Water Margin) and the stories of the Taiping Rebellion (see Emergence of Modern China, ch. 1). Synthesizing these influences with lessons learned from the Red Army's successes and failures, Mao created a comprehensive politico-military doctrine for waging revolutionary warfare. People's war incorporated political, economic, and psychological measures with protracted military struggle against a superior foe. As a military doctrine, people's war emphasized the mobilization of the populace to support regular and guerrilla forces; the primacy of men over weapons, in which superior motivation compensated for inferior technology; and the three progressive phases of protracted warfare—strategic defensive, strategic stalemate, and strategic offensive. During the first stage, enemy forces were "lured in deep" into one's own territory to overextend, disperse, and isolate them. The Red Army established base areas from which to harass the enemy, but these bases and other territory could be abandoned to preserve Red Army forces. In the second phase, superior numbers and morale were applied to wear down the enemy in a war of attrition in which guerrilla operations predominated. During the final phase, Red Army forces made the transition to regular warfare as the enemy was reduced to parity and eventually defeated.

In the civil war following Japan's defeat in World War II, the Red Army, newly renamed the People's Liberation Army, again used the principles of people's war in following a policy of strategic withdrawal, waging a war of attrition, and abandoning cities and communication lines to the well-armed, numerically superior Guomindang forces (see Return to Civil War, ch. 1). In 1947 the PLA launched a counteroffensive during a brief strategic stalemate. By the next summer, the PLA had entered the strategic offensive stage, using conventional warfare as the Guomindang forces went on the defensive and then collapsed rapidly on the mainland in 1949. By 1950 the PLA had seized Hainan Island and Xizang (Tibet).

When the PLA became a national armed force in 1949, it was an unwieldy, 5-million-strong peasant army. In 1950 the PLA included 10,000 troops in the Air Force (founded in 1949) and 60,000 in the Navy (founded in 1950). China also claimed a militia of 5.5 million. At that time, demobilization of ill-trained or politically unreliable troops began, resulting in the reduction of military strength to 2.8 million in 1953.

China's new leaders recognized the need to transform the PLA, essentially an infantry army with limited mobility, logistics, ordnance, and communications, into a modern military force. The signing of the Sino-Soviet Treaty of Friendship, Alliance, and Mutual Assistance in February 1950 provided the framework for defense modernization in the 1950s. However, the Korean War was the real watershed in armed forces modernization. The Chinese People's Volunteers (as the military forces in Korea were called) achieved initial success in throwing back United Nations (UN) troops and, despite the PLA's first encounter with modern firepower, managed to fight UN forces to a stalemate. Nevertheless, China's Korean War experience demonstrated PLA deficiencies and stimulated Soviet assistance in equipping and reorganizing the military. The use of "human wave tactics" (unsupported, concentrated infantry attacks) against modern firepower caused serious manpower and matériel losses. Chinese air power also suffered heavy losses to superior UN forces. Finally, shortcomings in transportation and supply indicated the need to improve logistics capabilities.

Military Modernization in the 1950s and 1960s

Large-scale Soviet aid in modernizing the PLA, which began in the fall of 1951, took the form of weapons and equipment, assistance in building China's defense industry, and the loan of advisers, primarily technical ones. Mostly during the Korean War years, the Soviet Union supplied infantry weapons, artillery, armor, trucks, fighter aircraft, bombers, submarines, destroyers, and gunboats. Soviet advisers assisted primarily in developing a defense industry set up along Soviet organizational lines. Aircraft and ordnance factories and shipbuilding facilities were constructed and by the late 1950s were producing a wide variety of Soviet-design military equipment. Because the Soviet Union would not provide China with its most modern equipment, most of the weapons were outdated and lacked an offensive capability. Both Chinese dissatisfaction with this defensive aid and the Soviet refusal to supply China with nuclear bomb blueprints contributed to the withdrawal of Soviet advisers in 1960 (see Perception of Threat, this ch.; Sino-Soviet Relations, ch. 12).

In the early 1950s, China's leaders decided to reorganize the military along Soviet lines. In 1954 they established the National Defense Council, Ministry of National Defense, and thirteen military regions. The PLA was reconstituted according to Soviet tables of organization and equipment. It adopted the combined-arms concept of armor- and artillery-heavy mobile forces, which required the adoption of some Soviet strategy and tactics. PLA modernization according to the Soviet model also entailed creation of a professional officer corps, complete with Soviet-style uniforms, ranks, and insignia; conscription; a reserve system; and new rules of discipline. The introduction of modern weaponry necessitated raising the education level of soldiers and intensifying formal military training. Political education and the role of political commissars lost their importance as the modernization effort progressed.

The military's new emphasis on Soviet-style professionalism produced tensions between the party and the military. The party feared that it would lose political control over the military, that the PLA would become alienated from a society concentrating on economic construction, and that relations between officers and soldiers would deteriorate. The party reemphasized Mao's thesis of the supremacy of men over weapons and subjected the PLA to several political campaigns. The military, for its part, resented party attempts to strengthen political education, build a mass militia system under local party control, and conduct economic production activities to the detriment of military training. These tensions culminated in September 1959, when Mao Zedong replaced Minister of National Defense Peng Dehuai, the chief advocate of military modernization, with Lin Biao, who deemphasized military professionalism in favor of revolutionary purity (see The Great Leap Forward, 1958–60, ch. 1).

The ascension of Lin Biao and the complete withdrawal of Soviet assistance and advisers in 1960 marked a new stage in military development. The Soviet withdrawal disrupted the defense industry and weapons production, particularly crippling the aircraft industry. Although the military purchased some foreign technology in the 1960s, it was forced to stress self-reliance in weapons production. Lin Biao moved to restore PLA morale and discipline and to mold the PLA into a politically reliable fighting force. Lin reorganized the PLA high command, replaced the mass militia with a smaller militia under PLA control, and reformulated the Maoist doctrine of the supremacy of men over matériel. Lin stated that "men and matériel form a unity, with men as the leading factor," giving ideological justification to the reemphasis on military training. Political training, however, continued to occupy 30 to 40 percent of a soldier's time. At the same time, Lin instituted stricter party control, restored party organization at the company level, and intensified political education. In 1964 the prestige of the PLA as an exemplary, revolutionary organization was confirmed by the "Learn from the PLA" campaign. This campaign, which purported to disseminate the military's political-work experience throughout society, resulted in the introduction of military personnel into party and government organizations, a trend that increased after the Cultural Revolution began.

China's National Defense Science and Technology University in Beijing
Courtesy Jiefangjun Huabao

In the late 1950s and early 1960s, the PLA fought one internal and one external campaign: in Xizang against Tibetan rebels, and on the Sino-Indian border against India. In the first campaign, PLA forces overwhelmed poorly equipped Tibetan insurgents who rebelled in 1958–59 against the imposition of Chinese rule. The Sino-Indian border war broke out in October 1962 amid the deterioration of Sino-Indian relations and mutual accusations of intrusions into disputed territory. In this brief (one month) but decisive conflict, the PLA attacked Indian positions in the North-East Frontier Agency (later called Arunachal Pradesh), penetrating to the Himalayan foothills, and in Ladakh, particularly in the Aksai Chin region. After routing the Indian Army, the PLA withdrew behind the original "line of actual control" after China announced a unilateral cease-fire. Both campaigns were limited conflicts using conventional tactics.

The People's Liberation Army in the Cultural Revolution

The PLA played a complex political role during the Cultural Revolution (see The Cultural Revolution Decade, 1966–76, ch. 1). From 1966 to 1968, military training, conscription and demobilization, and political education virtually ceased as the PLA was ordered first to help promote the Cultural Revolution and then to reestablish order and authority. Although the Cultural Revolution initially developed separately in the PLA and in the party apparatus, the PLA, under the leadership of its radical leftist leader, Lin Biao, soon became deeply involved in civilian affairs. In early 1967 the military high command was purged, and regional military forces were instructed to maintain order, establish military control, and support the revolutionary left. Because many regional-force commanders supported conservative party and government officials rather than radical mass organizations, many provincial-level military leaders were purged or transferred, and Beijing ordered several main-force units to take over the duties of the regional-force units. In the summer of 1967, regional military organizations came under leftist attack, Red Guard factions obtained weapons, and violence escalated. By September the central authorities had called off the attack on the PLA, but factional rivalries between regional- and main-force units persisted. Violence among rival mass organizations, often backed by different PLA units, continued in the first half of 1968 and delayed the formation of revolutionary committees, which were to replace traditional government and party organizations. In July 1968 Mao abolished the Red Guards and ordered the PLA to impose revolutionary committees wherever such bodies previously had not been established.

Worries over military factionalism caused the leadership to curtail the Cultural Revolution and to initiate a policy of rotating military commanders and units. The Soviet invasion of Czechoslovakia, the enunciation of the Brezhnev Doctrine, the Soviet military buildup in its Far Eastern theater, and Sino-Soviet border clashes in the spring of 1969 brought about a renewed emphasis on some of the PLA's traditional military roles. In 1969 Lin Biao launched an extensive "war preparations" campaign; military training was resumed, and military procurement, which had suffered in the first years of the Cultural Revolution, rose dramatically. Military preparedness was further advanced along China's frontiers and particularly the Sino-Soviet border when the thirteen military regions were reorganized into eleven in 1970.

The PLA emerged from the more violent phase of the Cultural Revolution deeply involved in civilian politics and administration. It had committed 2 million troops to political activities and reportedly suffered hundreds of thousands of casualties. Regional military forces were almost completely absorbed in political work. PLA units did not withdraw fully from these duties until 1974. Following the sudden death of Lin Biao in 1971, the military began to disengage from politics, and civilian control over the PLA was reasserted. Lin's supporters in the PLA were purged, leaving some high-level positions in the PLA unfilled for several years. PLA officers who had dominated provincial-level and local party and government bodies resigned from those posts in 1973 and 1974. Military region commanders were reshuffled, and some purged military leaders were rehabilitated. Military representation in the national-level political organizations, following an all-time high at the Ninth National Party Congress in 1969, declined sharply at the Tenth National Party Congress in 1973 (see The Cultural Revolution Decade, 1966-76, ch. 1).

Along with the reassertion of civilian control over the military and the return to military duties came a shift of resources away from the defense sector. Defense procurement dropped by 20 percent in 1971 and shifted from aircraft production and intercontinental ballistic missile development to the modernization of the ground forces and medium-range ballistic missile and intermediate-range ballistic missile development.

Military Modernization in the 1970s

In January 1974 the PLA saw action in the South China Sea following a long-simmering dispute with the Republic of Vietnam (South Vietnam) over the Xisha (Paracel) Islands (see Vietnam, this ch.). South Vietnamese and PLA naval forces skirmished over 3 islands occupied by South Vietnamese troops, and the PLA successfully seized control of the islands in a joint amphibious operation involving 500 troops and air support.

By the mid-1970s concerns among Chinese leaders about military weakness, especially vis-à-vis the Soviet Union, resulted in a decision to modernize the PLA. Two initial steps were taken to promote military modernization. First, in 1975 vacant key positions in the military structure and the party Central Military Commission were filled. (The state Central Military Commission was not founded until 1982; see the National People's Congress, ch. 10). Nonetheless, to ensure party control of the PLA, civilians were appointed to key positions. Deng Xiaoping was appointed chief of general staff, while Gang of Four member Zhang Chunqiao was appointed director of the General Political Department. Second, in the summer following Premier Zhou Enlai's January 1975 proclamation of the Four Modernizations (see Glossary) as national policy, the party Central Military Commission convened an enlarged meeting to chart the development of military modernization. The military modernization program, codified in Central Directive No. 18 of 1975, instructed the military to withdraw from politics and to concentrate on military training and other defense matters. Factional struggles between party moderates and radicals in 1975 and 1976, however, led to the dismissal of Deng from all his posts and the delay of military modernization until after the death of Mao Zedong. Within a month of Mao's death, military leaders headed by Minister of National Defense Ye Jianying cooperated with party chairman Hua Guofeng to arrest the Gang of Four, thus ending a decade of radical politics.

The Chinese leadership resumed the military modernization program in early 1977. Three crucial events in the late 1970s shaped the course of this program: the second rehabilitation of Deng Xiaoping, the major civilian proponent of military modernization; the re-ordering of priorities in the Four Modernizations, relegating national defense modernization from third to fourth place (following agriculture, industry, and science and technology); and the Sino-Vietnamese border war of 1979. In July 1977, with the backing of moderate military leaders, Deng Xiaoping reassumed his position as PLA chief of general staff as well as his other party and state posts. At the same time, Deng became a vice chairman of the party Central Military Commission. In February 1980 Deng resigned his PLA position in favor of professional military commander Yang Dezhi; Deng improved his party Central Military Commission position, becoming chairman of it at the Sixth Plenum of the Eleventh Central Committee in June 1981. With enormous prestige in both the military and the civilian sectors, Deng vigorously promoted military modernization, the further disengagement of the military from politics, and the shift in national priorities to economic development at the expense of defense.

In 1977–78 military and civilian leaders debated whether the military or the civilian economy should receive priority in allocating resources for the Four Modernizations. The military hoped for additional resources to promote its own modernization, while civilian leaders stressed the overall, balanced development of the economy, including civilian industry and science and technology. By arguing that a rapid military buildup would hinder the economy and harm the defense industrial base, civilian leaders convinced the PLA to accept the relegation of national defense to last place in the Four Modernizations. The defense budget accordingly was reduced. Nonetheless, the Chinese military and civilian leadership remained firmly committed to military modernization.

The 1979 Sino-Vietnamese border war, although only sixteen days long, revealed specific shortcomings in military capabilities and thus provided an additional impetus to the military modernization effort. The border war, the PLA's largest military operation since the Korean War, was essentially a limited, offensive, ground-force campaign. China claimed victory, but the war had mixed results militarily and politically. Although the numerically superior Chinese forces penetrated about fifty kilometers into Vietnam, the PLA sustained heavy casualties. PLA performance suffered from poor mobility, weak logistics, and outdated weaponry. Inadequate communications, an unclear chain of command, and the lack of military ranks also created confusion and adversely affected PLA combat effectiveness.

Military Modernization

The military modernization begun in the late 1970s had three major focuses. First, under the political leadership of Deng Xiaoping, the military became disengaged from civilian politics and, for the most part, resumed the political quiescence that characterized its pre-Cultural Revolution role. Deng reestablished civilian control over the military by appointing his supporters to key military leadership positions, by reducing the scope of the PLA's domestic nonmilitary role, and by revitalizing the party political structure and ideological control system within the PLA.

Second, modernization required the reform of military organization, doctrine, education and training, and personnel policies to improve combat effectiveness in combined-arms warfare. Among the organizational reforms that were undertaken were the creation of the state Central Military Commission, the streamlining and reduction of superfluous PLA forces, civilianization of many PLA units, reorganization of military regions, formation of group armies, and enactment of the new Military Service Law in 1984. Doctrine, strategy, and tactics were revised under the rubric of "people's war under modern conditions," which envisaged a forward defense at selected locations near China's borders, to prevent attack on Chinese cities and industrial sites, and emphasized operations using combined-arms tactics. Reforms in education and training emphasized improving the military skills and raising the education levels of officers and troops and conducting combined-arms operations. New personnel policies required upgrading the quality of PLA recruits and officer candidates, improving conditions of service, changing promotion practices to stress professional competence, and providing new uniforms and insignia.

The third focus of military modernization was the transformation of the defense establishment into a system capable of independently maintaining a modern military force. As military expenditures remained relatively constant, reforms concentrated on reorganizing the defense research-and-development and industrial base to integrate civilian and military science and industry more closely. Foreign technology was used selectively to upgrade weapons. Defense industry reforms also resulted in China's entry into the international arms market and the increased production of civilian goods by defense industries. The scope of PLA economic activities was reduced, but the military continued to participate in

People's Liberation Army chemical-biological-radiological warfare training
Courtesy Jiefangjun Huabao
A unit of the People's Liberation Army armored force
Courtesy Xinhua News Agency

infrastructure development projects and initiated a program to provide demobilized soldiers with skills useful in the civilian economy.

Civil-Military Relations

Lines between civilian and military leadership and institutions in China are indistinct. All high-ranking military leaders have high-level party positions, and many high-ranking party officials have some military experience. When military leaders participate in national policy making, therefore, it is not clear whether their positions reflect PLA corporate interests or the interests of groups that cut across institutional lines. In general, in times where there was national leadership consensus on national policy, such as in the 1950s, the PLA was politically quiescent. Once the PLA was drawn into civilian politics during the Cultural Revolution, the military became divided along the lines of civilian factions. As long as the national leadership remained divided on a number of policy issues, the PLA, fearing factional struggles and political instability, was reluctant to leave the political scene. When Deng Xiaoping was rehabilitated in 1977, however, the stage was set for the withdrawal of the military from politics and a partial return to the PLA's previous political passivity.

Political Role of the People's Liberation Army

Deng Xiaoping's efforts in the 1980s to reduce the political role of the military stemmed from his desire to reassert civilian control over the military and to promote military modernization. To accomplish his objectives, Deng revitalized the civilian party apparatus and leadership and built a consensus on the direction of national policy. He also established personal control over the military through personnel changes, and he reduced the scope of the PLA's domestic political, economic, and social roles. Finally, he strengthened party control over the military through institutional reforms and political and ideological education. The revitalization of the party and the establishment of a consensus on national policy assured top military leaders of political stability and a vigorous party capable of handling national and regional affairs without extensive military participation (see China and the Four Modernizations, 1979–82, ch. 1).

Deng's personal political control was established over the military through his assumption of the position of chairman of the party Central Military Commission in June 1981 and through his appointment of his supporters to key positions in the party Central Military Commission, Ministry of National Defense, and the PLA's General Staff Department, General Political Department, and

General Logistics Department. Occasional replacement of military region and military district commanders also strengthened Deng's hand. Military leaders who objected to Deng's policies were replaced with more amenable personnel.

The creation of the state Central Military Commission in 1982 aimed to further strengthen civilian control over the military by stressing the PLA's role as defender of the state and by establishing another layer of supervision parallel to party supervision. The civilianization of several PLA corps and internal security units reduced the size of the PLA and the scope of its involvement in civilian affairs. The placement of defense industries under civilian control and the transfer or opening up of military facilities, such as airports and ports, to civilian authorities also limited the PLA's influence in economic and political matters. Propaganda using the PLA as a model for society also diminished, and emphasis was placed on the PLA's military rather than political role.

Party Control

In addition to making personnel changes, Deng revitalized party control over the PLA and diffused the military's political power by designating provincial-level, municipal, district, and county party committee secretaries to serve concurrently as the first political commissars of their equivalent-level units in the regional PLA. The percentage of PLA personnel permitted to join the party was limited by restricting party membership to military academy graduates. Political and ideological training stressed the military rather than the social, ideological, or economic role of the PLA. Special effort was made to discredit the PLA's role in the Cultural Revolution; the PLA's support for the left was described as incorrect because it caused factionalism within the military. While emphasizing the necessity and appropriateness of reforms to modernize the military, political education also sought to guarantee military support for Deng's reform agenda. Beginning in 1983 a rectification campaign (part of the party-wide rectification campaign aimed primarily at leftists) reinforced this kind of political and ideological training (see The First Wave of Reform, 1979–84, ch. 11).

Beginning in the late 1970s, Deng Xiaoping succeeded in decreasing military participation in national-level political bodies. Military representation on the Political Bureau fell from 52 percent in 1978 to 30 percent in 1982, and military membership in the party Central Committee declined from 30 percent in 1978 to 22 percent in 1982. Most professional military officers shared common views with the Deng leadership over military modernization and the fundamental direction of national policy, and they willingly limited their concerns to military matters. Nonetheless, some elements in the PLA continued to voice their opinions on nondefense matters and criticized the Deng reform program. Dissent centered on prestigious military leaders, notably Ye Jianying, who feared that ideological de-Maoification, cultural liberalization, and certain agricultural and industrial reforms deviated from Marxist values and ideals. The Deng leadership contained these criticisms with the help of the personnel changes, political education, and the rectification campaign just mentioned. In this way it was able to keep military dissent within bounds that did not adversely affect civil-military relations.

Popular Attitudes Toward the People's Liberation Army

Starting in the late 1970s, popular attitudes toward the PLA also underwent considerable changes. In the 1950s and 1960s, the military's prestige was very high because of its wartime exploits, because it was held up as a role model for society, and because of its participation in civilian construction projects. But the power gained by the PLA during the Cultural Revolution reawakened civilian resentment of military privileges and abuses of power. By the early 1980s, with the circumscription of the PLA's domestic role and the implementation of agricultural reforms offering greater opportunities for rural youth, the PLA's reputation as a prestigious, elite, Marxist-model organization and a promising channel for social mobility was severely tarnished. Society's perception of the military appeared to be returning to the traditional viewpoint that "one doesn't make nails out of good iron; one doesn't make soldiers out of good men." To restore this damaged image in the late 1980s, the media extolled the PLA's martial virtues and the great strides made in military modernization in recent years.

Military Organization

By 1987 changes in military organization indicated the importance Chinese leaders attached to structural reform in building military forces capable of waging modern, combined-arms warfare. These reforms included the creation of the state Central Military Commission parallel to the party Central Military Commission, reduction in force, reorganization of military regions, formation of group armies, enactment of the new Military Service Law, and reorganization of defense industries.

State and Party Central Military Commissions

At the apex of Chinese military organization stood two bodies—the state and party Central Military Commissions (see fig. 22).

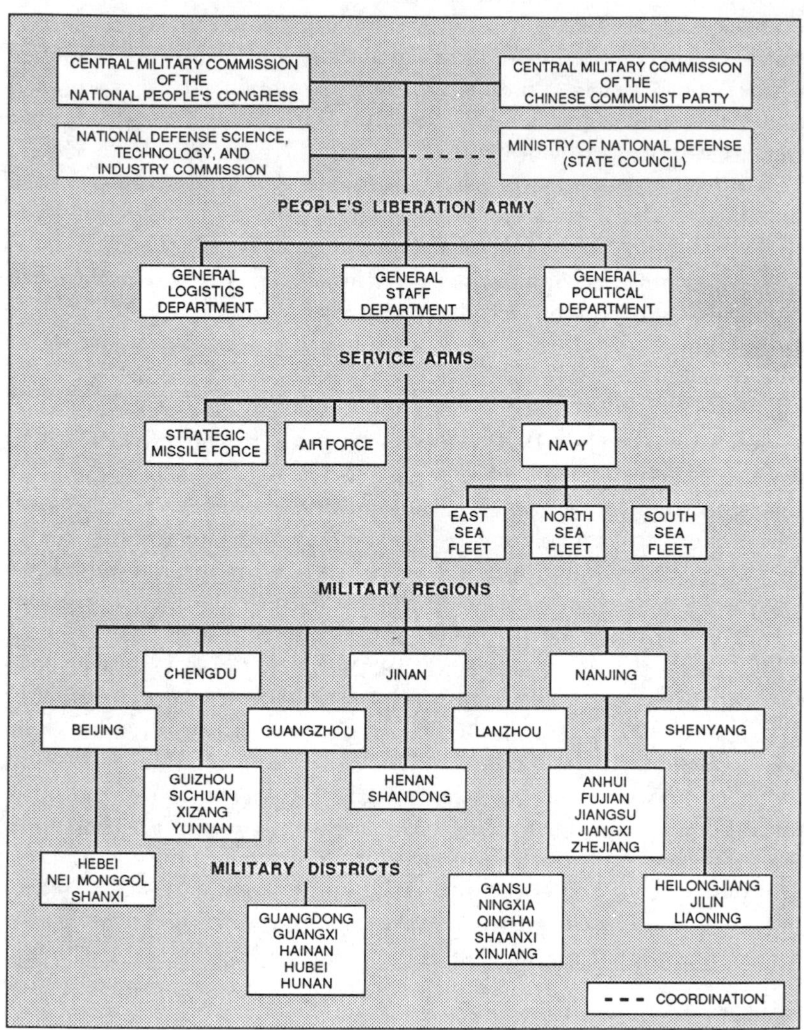

Figure 22. Organization of Military Establishment, 1987

The 1982 state Constitution created the state Central Military Commission as the state organ subordinate to the National People's Congress responsible for "directing the country's armed forces" (see Central Military Commission, ch. 10). The state Central Military Commission was the state's decision-making body in military affairs and directed and commanded the armed forces. The state Central Military Commission consisted of the chairman, who was commander in chief of the armed forces, an executive vice chairman, two vice chairmen, and four other members.

The party Central Military Commission, elected by the party Central Committee, exercised de facto, authoritative policy-making and operational control over the military. In addition to the chairman, the party Central Military Commission in 1987 included a permanent vice chairman who was concurrently secretary general, two vice chairmen, and four deputy secretaries general. The leadership of the state and party Central Military Commissions was identical, but the membership of the party Central Military Commission below the top leadership was thought to include regional commanders and service chiefs. Because the PLA has been under party control since its inception, the leadership of the party over the military did not change with the establishment of the state Central Military Commission. Although parallel leadership blurred the distinction between the two groups, the party Central Military Commission retained its traditional, preeminent position in charge of military affairs.

Ministry of National Defense and National Defense Science, Technology, and Industry Commission

Beneath the two Central Military Commissions were the Ministry of National Defense and the National Defense Science, Technology, and Industry Commission (NDSTIC), which separately took orders from the two Central Military Commissions but had no operational control over the PLA. The Ministry of National Defense was responsible for military modernization and provided administrative support for the PLA. It was responsible for planning, manpower, budget, foreign liaison, and training materials, but it possessed no policy-making or implementation authority. The NDSTIC—formed in August 1982 by merging the National Defense Science and Technology Commission, National Defense Industries Office, and Office of the Science, Technology, and Armaments Commission of the party Central Military Commission—was responsible for military research and development, weapons procurement, and coordination of the defense and civilian economic sectors (see Defense Industry and the Economic Role of the People's Liberation Army, this ch.).

Operational Control

In 1987 operational control of the PLA ran from the two Central Military Commissions to the PLA's three general departments: General Staff Department, General Political Department, and General Logistics Department. Below the department level ran parallel chains of command for operational, political, and logistical matters, each with its own separate communications facilities. Military policy originated in the party Political Bureau or the party Central Military Commission, became an operational order at the General Staff Department level, flowed through the military regions, and arrived at a main-force unit. Orders to regional forces also passed through the military district (provincial) level.

General Staff Department

The General Staff Department carried out staff and operational functions for the PLA and had major responsibility for implementing military modernization plans. Headed by the chief of general staff, the department served as the headquarters for the ground forces and contained headquarters for the three other armed services: Air Force, Navy, and Strategic Missile Force. The General Staff Department included functionally organized subdepartments for artillery, armored units, engineering, operations, training, intelligence, mobilization, surveying, communications, quartermaster services, and politics. Navy Headquarters controlled the North Sea Fleet, East Sea Fleet, and South Sea Fleet. Air Force Headquarters generally exercised control through the commanders of the seven military regions. Nuclear forces were directly subordinate to the General Staff Department. Conventional main, regional, and militia units were controlled administratively by the military region commanders, but the General Staff Department in Beijing could assume direct operational control of any main-force unit at will. Thus, broadly speaking, the General Staff Department exercised operational control of the main forces, and the military region commanders controlled the regional forces and, indirectly, the militia.

General Political Department

The General Political Department was responsible for ideological indoctrination, political loyalty, morale, personnel records, cultural activities, discipline, and military justice, and it provided the party structure for the PLA. It also published *Jiefangjun Bao* (Liberation Army Daily), the PLA's influential newspaper. The General Political Department director was at the head of a system of political commissars assigned to each echelon in the PLA. One of the primary tasks of the political commissar was the supervision of the party organization through party committees at the battalion level and above or through party branches in companies. Virtually all high-ranking officers in the military were party members. Until the early 1980s, when party membership in the PLA was restricted, an effort was made to have a party or Communist Youth League member in every unit down to the smallest maneuver element. Political commissars were equal in rank and authority to the commander of their echelon in peacetime but theoretically deferred to the commander during war. Commissars assumed many time-consuming chores, such as personnel problems, relations with civilians, and troop entertainment.

General Logistics Department

The General Logistics Department, headed by a director, was responsible for production, supply, transportation, housing, pay, and medical services. Historically, much of this support came from the civilian populace, and before the establishment of the General Logistics Department it was organized most often by commissars. PLA logistical resources in 1980 were far fewer than those of Western or Soviet forces; in the event of war the Chinese military would be heavily dependent upon the militia and civilians. In 1985 the General Logistics Department was reorganized, its staff cut by 50 percent, and some of its facilities turned over to the civilian sector.

Streamlining and Reduction in Force

Efforts began in the 1980s to streamline the PLA and organize it into a modern fighting force. The first step in reducing the 4.5-million-member PLA in the early 1980s was to relieve the PLA of some of its nonmilitary duties. The Railway Engineering Corps and the Capital Construction Engineering Corps were civilianized, and in 1983 the PLA internal security and border patrol units were transferred to the People's Armed Police Force.

In 1985 China reorganized its 11 military regions into 7 and began a 2-year program to reduce the force by 1 million. Eight military regions were merged into four—Chengdu, Jinan, Lanzhou, and Nanjing—and three key regions—Beijing, Guangzhou, and Shenyang—remained intact (see fig. 23). The PLA accomplished its 1-million-troop cut by streamlining the headquarters staffs of the three general departments, the military regions, and the military districts; reducing the size of the Air Force and the Navy; retiring older, undereducated, or incompetent officers; and transferring county- and city-level people's armed forces departments, which controlled the militia, to local civil authorities.

The PLA also reorganized its field armies (main-force armies) into group armies to increase its capability to wage combined-arms warfare. Breaking with the previously triangular organization of military units, the group armies combined formerly independent arms or services into a comprehensive combat unit. Group armies consisted of infantry and mechanized infantry divisions, tank divisions or brigades, and a number of artillery, antichemical, air defense, engineer, signal, reconnaissance, electronic countermeasure, and logistics troops. In the late 1980s, some group armies also had helicopter, air support, or naval units.

In 1987 PLA strength was about 3 million. Ground forces numbered about 2.1 million—the world's largest standing army; the Navy about 350,000—including those assigned to Naval Aviation, Coastal Defense Forces, and Marine Corps; the Air Force about 390,000; and the Strategic Missile Force about 100,000. The PLA was supported by an estimated 4.3 million basic (armed and trained) militia and 6 million ordinary (poorly armed and trained) militia. According to the 1984 Military Service Law, the militia, which was being combined with a newly developed reserve system, and the People's Armed Police Force also formed part of the Chinese armed forces (see Paramilitary Forces, this ch.). In 1986 reserve forces were included officially in the organizational system.

Doctrine, Strategy, and Tactics

From the early 1950s until the mid-1970s, people's war remained China's military doctrine. The PLA's force structure, however, which came to include nuclear weapons as well as artillery, combat aircraft, and tanks, did not reflect the concept of people's war. In the late 1970s, Chinese military leaders began to modify PLA doctrine, strategy, and tactics under the rubric of "people's war under modern conditions." This updated version of people's war lacked a systematic definition, but it permitted Chinese military leaders to pay tribute to Mao's military and revolutionary legacy while adapting military strategy and tactics to the needs of modern conventional and nuclear warfare. Elaborating on Mao's concept of active defense—tactically offensive action with a defensive strategy—Chinese strategy was designed to defeat a Soviet invasion before it could penetrate deeply into China. Chinese strategists envisaged a forward defense, that is, near the border, to prevent attack on Chinese cities and industrial facilities, particularly in north and northeast China. Such a defense-in-depth would require more positional warfare, much closer to the border, in the initial stages of a conflict. This strategy downplayed the people's war strategy of "luring in deep" in a protracted war, and it took into account the adaptations in strategy and tactics necessitated by technological advances in weaponry. The PLA emphasized military operations using modernized, combined arms tactics for the dual purpose of making the most effective use of current force structure and

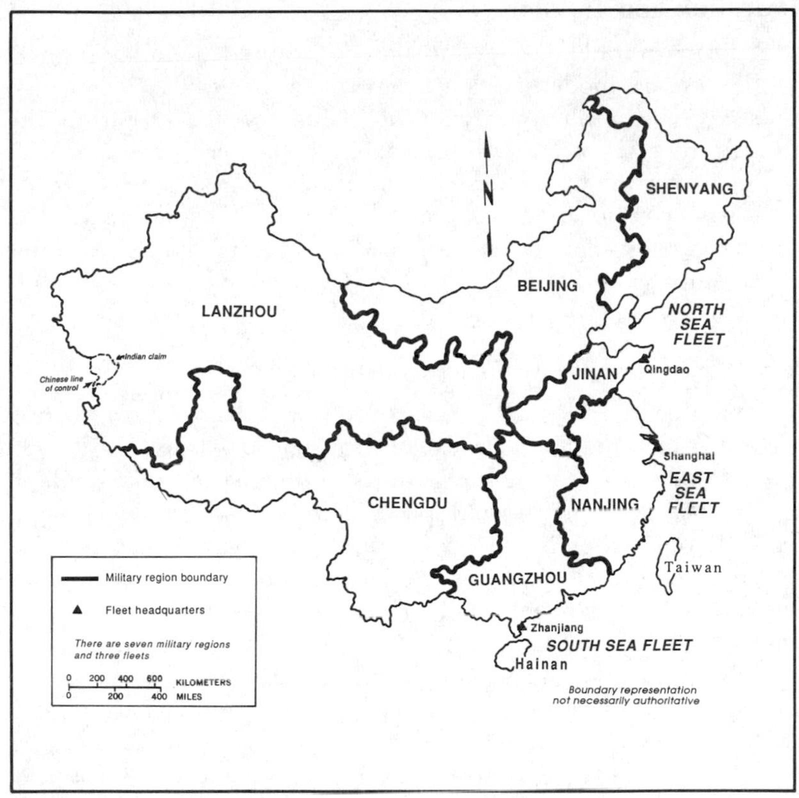

Source: Based on U.S. Central Intelligence Agency, China: Military Regions, 1986.

Figure 23. Military Regions and Fleet Commands, 1986

of preparing the armed forces for more advanced weaponry in the future.

The doctrine of "people's war under modern conditions" also incorporated the use of strategic and tactical nuclear weapons. China's own nuclear forces, which developed a second-strike capability in the early 1980s, provided Beijing with a credible, if minimum, deterrent against Soviet or United States nuclear attack. China repeatedly has vowed never to use nuclear weapons first, but it has promised retaliation against a nuclear attack. Chinese strategists also evinced an interest in tactical nuclear weapons, and the PLA has simulated battlefield use of such weapons in offensive and defensive exercises.

Education and Training

Reforms in training and education constituted an important part of the military modernization program in the 1980s. Senior officials recognized that improving the military skills and raising the education levels of both officers and troops were necessary prerequisites for the utilization of more advanced weaponry and the conduct of combined-arms operations. The PLA leadership focused education reforms on the military academy system and altered training to emphasize the officer corps, mechanized warfare, and combined arms operations.

Revitalization of the Military Academy System

Beginning in 1978, the PLA began to revive the military academy system, which the Cultural Revolution had devastated. By 1984 the system had over 100 institutions and consisted of 2 kinds of schools: command schools and specialized technical training centers. The PLA increased funding for military education, incorporated the study of foreign military experiences into the curriculum, and expanded contacts with foreign military academies. The rejuvenation of the military academies highlighted the emphasis placed on officer training. The PLA stipulated that most new officers should be military academy graduates, set minimum education levels for all officers, and established special classes to help officers meet those standards. Education and military-academy training thus became criteria for promotion, in addition to seniority, performance, and experience.

In 1986 the PLA introduced three measures that further strengthened the military academy system. First, at the top level the PLA's Military Academy, Political Academy, and Logistics Academy merged to form the National Defense University, China's senior military training and research institution. Second, a new, three-level training system for command officers was announced, whereby command officers would receive regular training at junior, middle, and higher military command academies. Third, noncommissioned officer (NCO) training entered the military academy system with the establishment of a naval academy for petty officers and an air force NCO academy and the creation of NCO classes in over forty ground force academies.

Training Reforms

Before the military modernization program began, PLA training was highly politicized and emphasized single-unit infantry troop training. Training reforms started with the depoliticization of training, whereby troops spent 80 percent of their time on military activities and 20 percent on political training. The scope of training then changed to concentrate on training officers capable of directing combined-arms warfare. Improved military education in the rejuvenated military academies provided some of this officer training. In addition, large-scale combined-arms exercises, which served to raise officer capabilities in commanding and coordinating combined-arms operations under combat conditions, occurred on a regular basis. These exercises stressed defense against attacking tanks, paratroopers, and aircraft and on occasion involved the simulated use of tactical nuclear weapons. The PLA also began using simulation equipment in training and in 1985 held its first completely simulated combat exercise. In 1986 the PLA training system underwent further reforms that complemented changes in military organization. A combined-arms tactical training center was created for training the newly formed group armies (former field armies) on a rotational basis. The training center coordinated group army exercises and utilized laser devices and simulation equipment in its training. The PLA also established a systematic training program for new recruits, replacing the old system in which inductees received basic training in their units. Under the new system, before new recruits were assigned to PLA units, they completed four months of training by a training regiment attached to a group army. The training regiments also trained squad leaders.

Personnel

Defense modernization brought changes to military personnel policies and practices. Personnel reforms emphasized upgrading the quality of recruits, improving conditions of service, altering promotion practices to stress professional competence over seniority or political loyalty, and providing new uniforms and insignia. The 1984 Military Service Law codified some of the changes in personnel policies and set the stage for further changes, such as the restoration of ranks.

Recruitment

The Military Service Law provided the legal basis for conscription, and it combined compulsory and voluntary service. All citizens between eighteen and twenty-two, regardless of sex, nationality, profession, family background, religion, or level of education, were obliged to perform military service. Almost 10 million men reached conscription age each year, but the PLA chose less than 10 percent of those eligible. A very small number of women were inducted annually. In the 1980s the PLA attempted to upgrade the quality of its inductees by changing recruiting practices. The PLA previously drew its recruits from rural youth of politically acceptable families. But the Military Service Law, the introduction of rural reforms offering greater economic opportunities for rural youth, and the PLA's requirements for higher educational levels caused recruitment to draw more recruits from better educated urban youth. Officers were drawn from military academy graduates; enlisted men and women who completed officer training in officially designated institutions and passed officer fitness tests; graduates of universities and special technical secondary schools; and civilian cadres and technical personnel recruited by nonmilitary units in the PLA. As a result of the new conscription and officer recruitment practices, the level of education in the PLA was much higher than that of the general population.

In 1987 approximately 100,000 women served in the PLA and represented one-tenth of the officer corps and one-quarter of the specialized technicians. Women served primarily in scientific research, communications, medical, and cultural units. Members of China's ethnic minorities also served in the PLA, but their percentage within the military was probably considerably lower than their proportion in the general population, partly because of their lower level of education and partly because of government and party suspicion of their loyalties.

Conditions of Service

The Military Service Law stipulated changes in conditions of service. Compulsory terms of service were three years for the ground forces and four for the Air Force and Navy. Soldiers could elect another term of one or two years in the ground forces and one year in the Navy and Air Force. After completing five years of compulsory service, a soldier could switch to voluntary service and could serve an eight- to twelve-year term until the age of thirty-five. The conscription law also made provisions for limited preferential treatment of service personnel and their families. However, military service was regarded by some as a hardship because of low pay, poor food, lowered marriage prospects, and difficulties in finding jobs after demobilization. To alleviate the unattractive aspects of military service and to help local economic development, the PLA instituted a program of dual-use training, whereby soldiers learned skills useful in civilian life in addition to military training (see Defense Industry and the Economic Role of the People's Liberation Army, this ch.).

Promotion

In the late 1970s, the PLA began altering its promotion practices to reflect the new emphasis on professional competence. Previously, there had been no retirement system in effect, and junior and field-grade officers had remained at their posts for many years with little opportunity for advancement. When promotion occurred, it was based on seniority, political rectitude, or a patron-client relationship. Officers advanced up a single chain of command, remaining in the same branch or service for life. In 1978 the PLA reinstituted the retirement system established by the 1955 Military Service Law and promulgated officer service regulations, which set retirement ages for military officers. Thus the PLA began a two-pronged effort to retire older officers and to promote younger, better educated, professionally competent officers. Older officers, including many over seventy years of age, were offered generous retirement packages as inducements to retire. The PLA also formulated new promotion standards that set minimum education levels for officers and emphasized education in military academies as a criterion for promotion. Officers below the age of forty had to acquire a secondary-school education by 1990 or face demotion. Furthermore, past promotion practices were to be discarded in favor of greater emphasis on formal training, higher education levels, and selection of more officers from technical and noncombat units. With the reduction in force begun in 1985, professional competence, education, and age became criteria for demobilization as well as promotion. By 1987 the PLA's promotion practices were based more on merit than they had been a decade earlier; nevertheless, political rectitude and *guanxi* (personal connections) continued to play an important role in promotion, and no centralized personnel system had been established.

Ranks, Uniforms, and Insignia

The 1984 Military Service Law also stipulated that military ranks would be reintroduced to the PLA. Military leaders justified the restoration of ranks as improving organization, discipline, and morale and facilitating coordinated operations among different arms and services, thus serving to modernize and regularize the military. The PLA's experience in the 1979 Sino-Vietnamese border war, in which the absence of ranks led to confusion on the battlefield, was another factor leading to the restoration of ranks. However, the rank system was not immediately implemented because "preparatory work" still needed to be done. Implementation was delayed by disputes in higher echelons in the PLA over who would receive what rank and by the long process of reducing the size of the military. In mid-1987 the PLA still had not restored its system of ranks. The ranks for officers reportedly were to be based on the 1955 rank system, which included one supreme marshal and ten marshals at the very top. Ground force and Air Force ranks were to be senior general, general, lieutenant general, major general, senior colonel, colonel, lieutenant colonel, major, senior captain, captain, first lieutenant, and second lieutenant. Naval officer ranks were to be senior admiral, admiral, vice admiral, rear admiral, senior captain, captain, commander, lieutenant commander, senior lieutenant, junior lieutenant, and ensign.

Although the restoration of ranks was delayed, in 1985 PLA personnel were issued new uniforms and service insignia. Officers at and above regimental level wore woolen and blended woolen uniforms; officers at battalion level and below and soldiers wore cotton uniforms. All personnel wore visored military caps, new collar insignia, and shoulder boards. The cap emblem was round with a design of five stars and the ideographs *bayi* (August 1st, the anniversary of the 1927 Nanchang Uprising) surrounded by wheat ears and cog wheels. Uniform colors were olive green for the ground forces; dark blue in winter, and a white jacket and dark blue trousers in summer for the Navy; and an olive green jacket and dark blue trousers for the Air Force. Officer jackets had epaulets and golden buttons with the five-star and August 1st design. Collar badges were red for the ground forces, black for the Navy, and blue for the Air Force. Personnel of the intraservice Strategic Missile Force wore distinctive patches but otherwise retained the uniform of their parent service. The new uniforms replaced the baggy, green fatigue uniforms that had made it hard to distinguish between officers and soldiers. The change in uniforms served the needs of military modernization by raising morale, strengthening discipline, and facilitating command and organization.

Defense Industry and the Economic Role of the People's Liberation Army

The transformation of China's defense establishment into a system capable of independently sustaining modern armed forces was one of the major goals of the military modernization program. In the late 1970s and 1980s, defense spending remained relatively constant despite the shift in resources in favor of overall economic development. Reforms focused on reorganizing the defense research-and-development and industrial base, more closely integrating civilian and military science and industry, and selectively utilizing foreign technology. China sold arms for hard currency to provide additional funds for defense industries. The PLA continued to play its role in economic development by participating in selective construction projects, providing dual-use training, and producing most of its food needs.

Military Expenditures

In the 1980s Chinese statistics indicated that defense spending represented a decreasing percentage of government expenditures, falling from 16 percent in 1980 to 8.3 percent of the state budget in 1987. However, United States Department of Defense studies suggested that the published budget figures understated defense spending by about one-half. With the growth of the Chinese economy under the modernization program, defense spending also represented a smaller percentage of the gross national product (GNP) than previously. United States Central Intelligence Agency analysts estimated that defense expenditures in 1978 absorbed 8 to 10 percent of GNP; in 1986 United States Department of Defense analysts estimated that China's military expenses fell within the range of 6 to 8 percent of GNP. Comparison of indices of defense procurement spending and industrial production from 1971 to 1983 revealed that the former increased by 15 percent, whereas the latter rose by 170 percent. These studies indicated that Chinese leaders have indeed subordinated military modernization to economic development.

United States Department of Defense officials in 1986 estimated Chinese defense spending by resources and force categories for the 1967 to 1983 period. Roughly 50 percent of defense expenditures were for weapons, equipment, and new facilities; 35 percent for operating costs; and 15 percent for research, development, and testing and evaluation. By service, these costs broke down to 25 percent for the ground forces; 15 percent for the Navy; 15 percent for strategic air defenses; 5 percent for ballistic missile forces; 5 percent for tactical air forces; and about 35 percent for command, logistics, personnel, intelligence, medical care, administration, research, development, testing and evaluation, and other support. Beginning in the late 1970s, China devoted more resources to its Strategic Missile Force, indicating an effort to increase its strategic security while modernizing the economy, and to national command and support activities, reflecting an emphasis on modernization of the defense structure.

Military Research and Development and the National Defense Science, Technology, and Industry Commission

The NDSTIC was the coordinating body for military research and development and industrial production. The NDSTIC reported to the party Central Military Commission's National Defense Industries Committee and the State Council's Leading Group for Science and Technology. The NDSTIC supervised weapons research and development, coordinated military production of defense industries, and controlled funding for weapons procurement. The establishment of the NDSTIC was a reform measure designed to break down the barriers between civilian and military research and development and industry. Military science and industry previously had been secretive, segregated, and privileged sectors, having material, financial, and personnel resources superior to those available to the civilian sector. The creation of the NDSTIC was one measure by which Chinese leaders hoped to facilitate the transfer of technology between the military and civilian sectors. The NDSTIC, in particular through its trading arm, China Xinshidai Corporation, coordinated procurement of foreign technology for military purposes.

Defense Industry

Beginning in 1978, Chinese leaders set out to transform the defense industries, which had a huge excess capacity and were criticized for having a "golden rice bowl" (rich but always begging for more). To utilize this excess capacity better and to break down the barriers between military and civilian industry, the machine-building ministries were reorganized, and civilians were appointed to manage them. The civilianized, renamed ministries and their responsibilities consisted of the Ministry of Nuclear Industry—nuclear weapons; Ministry of Aeronautics—aircraft; Ministry of Electronics Industry—electronics; Ministry of Ordnance Industry—munitions and armaments; Ministry of Astronautics—ballistic missiles and space systems; and China State Shipbuilding Corporation—naval construction. In 1986 the Ministry of Machine Building, which produced civilian heavy machinery and industrial equipment, and the Ministry of Ordnance Industry were consolidated into the new State Machine-Building Industry Commission as a way to strengthen the unified management of the national machine-building and weapons enterprises. In 1987 little information was available about this new commission or its relationship to the NDSTIC or to the State Economic Commission, whose Defense Bureau coordinated the civilian production of the defense industry. Further changes in defense industry structure occurred in 1986 and 1987, when inland defense enterprises were either relocated closer to transportation links or cities, closed down, or transferred to local civilian control and production.

Weapons Production

In 1987 China adopted a new contractual system for weapons research, development, and production. It was not clear from available information how this contract system would affect the role of the NDSTIC as the coordinating body for defense science and industry. Previously, the NDSTIC controlled procurement funding, reviewed proposals for weapons requirements funneled through the General Staff Department's Equipment Subdepartment, and coordinated with defense industries to produce the needed equipment. Under the new system, the state divided defense research and development funds into three categories: military equipment research, basic and applied sciences research, and unidentified technological services. The first type of appropriation went to military arms and services, which signed contracts with research institutes or enterprises to develop and manufacture the required weapons. The contract system involved the PLA, which had been removed to a large extent from such activities, in the development and manufacture of the weapons it would use. The second category of funds was devoted to basic research and applied science to help modernize the defense industry. The third category went to technological services necessary for research programs. This reform was another measure designed to integrate military and civilian industry by placing the military production of defense industries within the framework of the planned-commodity economy. The new system further sought to provide the military with better equipment at a minimum cost, to force the defense industry to upgrade weapons designs and improve production, to improve the management of weapons research and development through state application of economic levers, to promote cooperation between research institutes and factories, and to increase the decision-making powers of the enterprises.

Procurement of weapons and equipment represented 45 percent of the defense budget during the 1967 to 1983 period. This figure included 25 percent for aircraft, 15 percent for ground forces weapons, and about 10 percent each for naval and missile systems. China's military-industrial complex, the third largest in the world, produced a wide variety of weapons, including light arms and ammunition, armor, artillery, combat aircraft, fast-attack craft, frigates, destroyers, conventional and nuclear submarines, electronic equipment, tactical missiles, and ballistic missiles. With the notable exception of China's indigenously produced nuclear submarines, nuclear missiles, and satellites, most Chinese weaponry was based on Soviet designs of the 1950s and 1960s. Much of this equipment was obsolete or obsolescent, and beginning in the late

1970s China made great efforts to upgrade the equipment by changing indigenous designs or by incorporating Western technology. The greatest weaknesses were in conventional arms, precision-guided munitions, electronic warfare, and command, control, communications, and intelligence. China attempted to address these weaknesses by focusing military research on electronics—essential to progress in the previously mentioned areas—and by selectively importing key systems or technologies.

The Role of Foreign Military Technology

Following the withdrawal of Soviet aid and advisers in 1960, which crippled the defense industry and weapons production for several years, China stressed self-reliance in developing its own weaponry. The acquisition of foreign military technology became a contentious issue at times, particularly in the 1970s, when Maoists stressed complete self-reliance and more moderate leaders wished to import some foreign technology. The signing of an agreement to coproduce Rolls Royce Spey engines in 1975 signaled the resolution of that debate in favor of selective importation. Beginning in 1977, Chinese military delegations traveled abroad, particularly to Western Europe and, in the 1980s, to the United States, to visit Western defense manufacturers and to inspect the state of the art in military equipment. Chinese representatives showed great interest in a wide variety of weapons systems, but they made few purchases of complete weapons systems, concentrating instead on acquisition of selective components, equipment, or technologies and on concluding coproduction agreements.

China's selective approach to acquiring foreign military technology stemmed from the limited funds available for military modernization and the desire of Chinese leaders to avoid dependence on any one supplier. The selective approach also reflected the knowledge that assimilation of foreign technology could present problems because of the low level of Chinese military technology and lack of qualified personnel. Finally, the leadership realized that China's past emphasis on modifying foreign weapons and on reverse engineering had greatly limited China's weapons development capacity. To overcome weapons deficiency in the short run and achieve indigenous military research, development, and production in the long run, China's leaders combined the selective import of weapons and technology with improved technical training of defense personnel and development of the civilian economy.

China primarily was interested in obtaining defensive weapons from abroad to correct the PLA's most critical weaknesses. These weapons and equipment included antitank and antiaircraft missiles, armor-piercing ammunition, helicopters, trucks, jeeps, automobiles, and tank fire-control systems, engines, and turrets for the ground forces; antiship missiles, air defense systems, antisubmarine warfare systems, and electronic countermeasures systems for the Navy; and avionics, including fire control and navigation systems, for the Air Force. Observers opined that the entire military needed improved command, control, communications, and intelligence equipment and computers for command and logistics.

Arms Sales

China's entrance into the international arms market in the 1980s was closely related to reforms in the defense industry and the leadership's desire to acquire the foreign technology needed to modernize PLA weaponry. Before 1980 China provided arms to friendly Third World countries at concessionary prices (see Relations with the Third World, ch. 12). Because China transferred arms based on ideological and foreign policy considerations, terms were generous. Around 1980 China decided to sell weapons for profit to absorb excess capacity in the defense industry, make defense enterprises more economically viable, and earn the foreign currency required to purchase foreign military technology. China continued to sell military hardware at generous terms to some of its traditional friends and weapons customers, such as Pakistan, the Democratic People's Republic of Korea (North Korea), Egypt, Sudan, and Somalia. Hard-currency sales to Middle Eastern countries, however, particularly Iran and Iraq, accounted for the rapid increase in Chinese weapons sales in the 1980s. United States Arms Control and Disarmament Agency studies indicated that from 1979 to 1983 Chinese arms sales ranked eighth in the world, for a total of about US$3.5 billion, of which an estimated US$2.1 billion went to Middle Eastern countries. In 1979 arms sales accounted for 0.9 percent of total exports; in 1983 arms sales rose to 6.3 percent of total exports. By 1987 China had jumped to fifth place, ranking behind the United States, the Soviet Union, Britain, and France.

In the 1980s the defense industry and the PLA established a number of trading corporations to sell Chinese military hardware and to acquire foreign technology. The most prominent of these corporations were the China Xinshidai Corporation, affiliated with the NDSTIC; China Northern Industrial Corporation (commonly known as NORINCO), affiliated with the State Machine-Building Industry Commission; China National Aero-Technology Import and Export Corporation (CATIC), affiliated with the Ministry of Aeronautics; Great Wall Industrial Corporation and China Precision Machinery Import and Export Corporation, both affiliated with the

Ministry of Astronautics; China Electronics Import and Export Corporation, affiliated with the Ministry of Electronics Industry; China Shipbuilding Trading Corporation, affiliated with the China State Shipbuilding Corporation; and China Xinxing Corporation, affiliated with the PLA General Logistics Department. In 1984 these corporations began promoting Chinese weapons, actively seeking technology transfer and coproduction agreements with Western defense companies at international defense exhibitions in 1984.

Civilian Production

In late 1978 China initiated a policy of integrating civilian and military industry more closely in order to promote overall civilian economic development. This policy entailed civilianizing the machine-building ministries to make the defense industry more responsive to civilian control and needs; increasing defense industry production of civilian goods, particularly consumer goods; and transferring technology from the more advanced defense sector to the civilian sector of the economy. Production of civilian goods totaled 6.9 percent of total defense industry output in 1975. In 1980 it rose to 18 percent, and by 1985 it had jumped to 41.8 percent of total output. Chinese officials predicted that by 1990 about 80 percent of defense industry output would be civilian goods. The large excess capacity of the defense industry, resulting from declining orders from the PLA, made possible the rapid growth in civilian output. The defense industry manufactured a wide variety of goods for civilian use, including motor vehicles, optical equipment, television sets, electrical appliances, pharmaceuticals, and medical instruments and prostheses. Many of these products were consumer goods in high demand. For example, in 1985 the Ministry of Ordnance Industry manufactured 500,000 motorcycles, representing two-thirds of total motorcycle output, as well as 250,000 cameras, 450,000 bicycles, and 100,000 refrigerators.

Following the formulation of regulations and mechanisms for such transfers, defense industries began transferring technology to civilian industries on a large scale in the mid-1980s. Technology transfers provided defense enterprises with additional, lucrative sources of income and furnished civilian enterprises with a wide range of useful, advanced technology to modernize production. For example, the Ministry of Astronautics disseminated aerospace technology to light industry and to the petroleum, chemical engineering, machine-building, textile, communications, medical, and electronics industries.

Economic Roles of the People's Liberation Army

The PLA played a role in economic development practically from its inception. Beginning in the late 1930s and early 1940s, when the party was headquartered in Yan'an, the Red Army raised its own food. After 1949 the PLA became involved in economic reconstruction tasks—building railroads and factories, reclaiming wasteland, digging irrigation canals, establishing state farms, and participating in disaster relief operations. The PLA accepted its role as a force in economic construction and devoted segments of its structure, such as the Engineering Corps, Railway Engineering Corps, Capital Construction Engineering Corps, Signal Corps, and Production and Construction Corps, to building up the national infrastructure. However, PLA regional- and main-force units played a much smaller role in aiding the civilian economy.

This pattern continued into the 1980s. The PLA remained self-sufficient in food, participated in selective infrastructure development projects, and aided in disaster relief. From 1981 to 1985, the PLA contributed 110 million workdays to 44,500 construction projects, including the diversion of river water from the Luan He to Tianjin, construction of the Shengli oilfield in Shandong Province and the Huolinhe open-cut coal mine in Shaanxi Province, expansion of Zhanjiang port in Guangdong Province, and afforestation work involving the planting of 290 million trees.

The PLA contributed to economic development in two additional ways. First, in November 1984 the government decided to transfer some military facilities to civilian control or joint military-civilian use. These facilities included airfields, ports, docks, railroads, depots and warehouses, and recreational areas. The devolution of these facilities to civilian control helped to alleviate problems that plagued the civilian economy. Second, beginning in the late 1970s, the PLA operated a large-scale program of dual-use training, whereby PLA personnel learned skills useful to the growing economy. Under this program, officers and soldiers received military training and training in specialized skills, such as livestock breeding, cultivation, processing, construction, machine maintenance, repair of domestic appliances, motor vehicle repair, and driving. In 1986 the PLA trained more than 650,000 soldiers in 25,000 training courses at over 6,000 training centers. In early 1987 surveys indicated that over 70 percent of demobilized PLA personnel left the armed forces with skills they could use as civilians.

Perception of Threat

In the late 1980s, China viewed the Soviet Union as its principal military opponent. Simmering border disputes with Vietnam and India were perceived as lesser threats to security. China's burgeoning opening up policy, its claims to the Xisha (Paracel) and Nansha (Spratly) Islands, and the presence of offshore oil deposits made the South China Sea an area in which Beijing saw potential threats to its interests. Finally, although it did not regard Taiwan as a military threat, China nevertheless refused to rule out the use of force as a means of achieving reunification with Taiwan.

The Soviet Union

Despite common ideological roots, considerable Soviet assistance in the past, and warming relations since 1982, China in 1987 regarded the Soviet Union's military strength and foreign policy as the major threat to its security. Tensions in relations between the two countries had begun to escalate in the mid-1950s (see Sino-Soviet Relations, ch. 12). The 1968 Soviet invasion of Czechoslovakia and the buildup of Soviet forces in the Soviet Far East raised Chinese suspicions of Soviet intentions. Sharp border clashes between Soviet and Chinese troops occurred in 1969, roughly a decade after relations between the two countries had begun to deteriorate and some four years after a buildup of Soviet forces along China's northern border had begun. Particularly heated border clashes occurred in the northeast along the Sino-Soviet border formed by the Heilong Jiang (Amur River) and the Wusuli Jiang (Ussuri River), on which China claimed the right to navigate (see fig. 3). Border provocations occasionally recurred in later years—for example, in May 1978 when Soviet troops in boats and a helicopter intruded into Chinese territory—but major armed clashes were averted.

In the late 1970s, China decried what it perceived as a Soviet attempt to encircle it as the military buildup continued in the Soviet Far East and the Soviet Union signed friendship treaties with Vietnam and Afghanistan. In April 1979 Beijing notified Moscow that the thirty-year Treaty of Friendship, Alliance, and Mutual Assistance—under which the Soviets aided the PLA in its 1950s modernization—would not be renewed. Negotiations on improving Sino-Soviet relations were begun in 1979, but China ended them when the Soviet Union invaded Afghanistan late that year. In 1982 China and the Soviet Union resumed negotiations on normalizing relations. Although agreements on trade, science and technology, and culture were signed, political ties remained frozen because of Chinese insistence that the Soviet Union remove the three obstacles to improved Sino-Soviet relations. Although Chinese leaders publicly professed not to be concerned, the Soviet base at

Cam Ranh Bay in Vietnam, Soviet provision of MiG-23 fighters to North Korea, and Soviet acquisition of overflight and port calling rights from North Korea intensified Chinese apprehension about the Soviet threat. Soviet Communist Party General Secretary Mikhail S. Gorbachev's 1986 offer to withdraw some troops from Afghanistan and the Mongolian People's Republic (Mongolia) were seen by Beijing as a cosmetic gesture that did not lessen the threat to China.

In the mid-1980s the Soviet Union deployed about one-quarter to one-third of its military forces in its Far Eastern theater. In 1987 Soviet nuclear forces included approximately 171 SS-20 intermediate-range ballistic missiles, which China found particularly threatening, and 85 nuclear-capable long-range Backfire bombers. Approximately 470,000 Soviet ground force troops in 53 divisions were stationed in the Sino-Soviet border region, including Mongolia. Although 65 percent of these ground force divisions were only at 20 percent of full combat strength, they were provided with improved equipment, including T-72 tanks, and were reinforced by 2,200 aircraft, including new generation aircraft such as the MiG-23/27 Flogger fighter. Chinese forces on the Sino-Soviet border were numerically superior—1.5 million troops in 68 divisions—but technologically inferior. Although the PLA units in the Shenyang and Beijing military regions were equipped with some of the PLA's most advanced weaponry, few Chinese divisions were mechanized. The Soviet Union held tactical and strategic nuclear superiority and exceeded China in terms of mobility, firepower, air power, and antiaircraft capability. Chinese leaders reportedly did not consider a Soviet attack to be imminent or even likely in the short term. They believed that if the Soviets did attack, it would be a limited strike against Chinese territory in north or northeast China, rather than a full-scale invasion (see Doctrine, Strategy, and Tactics, this ch.).

Vietnam

China's relations with Vietnam began to deteriorate seriously in the mid-1970s (see An Overview of China's Foreign Relations, ch. 12). After Vietnam joined the Soviet-dominated Council for Mutual Economic Cooperation (Comecon) and signed the Treaty of Friendship and Cooperation with the Soviet Union in 1978, China branded Vietnam the "Cuba of the East" and called the treaty a military alliance. Incidents along the Sino-Vietnamese border increased in frequency and violence. In December 1978 Vietnam invaded Cambodia, quickly ousted the pro-Beijing Pol Pot regime, and overran the country. In February 1979 China attacked along virtually the entire Sino-Vietnamese border in a brief, limited campaign that involved ground forces only. In March Beijing declared its "lesson" finished and withdrew all its troops (see Historical Development, 1927-79, this ch.).

After the war, both China and Vietnam reorganized their border defenses. The border war strengthened Soviet-Vietnamese relations. The Soviet military role in Vietnam increased during the 1980s as the Soviets provided arms to Vietnam; moreover, Soviet ships enjoyed access to the harbors at Danang and Cam Ranh Bay, and Soviet reconnaissance aircraft operated out of Vietnamese airfields. Low-level conflict continued along the Sino-Vietnamese border as each side conducted artillery shelling and probed to gain high spots in the mountainous border terrain. Border incidents increased in intensity during the rainy season, when Beijing attempted to ease Vietnamese pressure against Cambodian resistance fighters. In 1986 China deployed twenty-five to twenty-eight divisions and Vietnam thirty-two divisions along their common border. Nevertheless, most observers doubted that China would risk another war with Vietnam in the near future.

India

Beijing considered recurring Sino-Indian border clashes a potential threat to its security. Negotiations since the 1962 Sino-Indian border war failed to resolve the conflicting border claims, and each side improved its military and logistics capabilities in the disputed regions. Since the war, China has continued its occupation of the Aksai Chin area, through which it built a strategic highway linking Xizang and Xinjiang autonomous regions. China had a vital military interest in maintaining control over this region, whereas India's primary interest lay in Arunachal Pradesh, its state in the northeast bordering Xizang Autonomous Region. In 1987, although India enjoyed air superiority, rough parity on the ground existed between the two military forces, which had a combined total of nearly 400,000 troops near the border. The Indian Army deployed eleven divisions in the region, backed up by paramilitary forces, whereas the PLA had fifteen divisions available for operations on the border. After a 1986 border clash and India's conversion of Arunachal Pradesh from union territory to state, tensions between China and India escalated. Both sides moved to reinforce their capabilities in the area, but neither ruled out further negotiations of their dispute. Most observers believe that the mountainous terrain, high-altitude climate, and concomitant logistic difficulties made it unlikely that a protracted or large-scale conflict would erupt on the Sino-Indian border.

South China Sea

The South China Sea area was strategically important to Beijing because of the discovery of offshore oil in China's 200-nautical-mile exclusive economic zone, increased foreign trade in the South China Sea, and China's territorial claims there. The Xisha and Nansha islands also were claimed, and some occupied, by Vietnam, Taiwan, the Philippines, and Malaysia. Beijing's claims to these island groups predated all others except those by the Guomindang authorities. In 1974 the PLA Navy ousted South Vietnamese forces from the Xisha and occupied some of the islands, which were valuable as Chinese fishing bases and guano sites. Although Chinese occupation of the Xisha effectively expanded its exclusive economic zone, the discovery of offshore oil deposits near Hainan Island intensified China's interest in both island groups. With the expansion of Chinese foreign trade, Beijing's interest grew in maintaining a naval presence in the Xisha Islands, which sit astride the strategic Hong Kong-Singapore shipping route. Chinese fishermen also used the Nansha Islands, but most of these were occupied by Vietnam, Taiwan, and the Philippines. In the 1980s the PLA Navy built up the South Sea Fleet, strengthened its naval facilities and deployments in the Xisha Islands, and conducted naval exercises in the South China Sea. To strengthen its military position in the Xisha Islands and protect itself against the Soviet base at Cam Ranh Bay, Beijing also reinforced its claim to the Nansha Islands.

Taiwan

Taiwan does not pose a military threat to China, despite Taipei's vow to "recover the mainland." Tensions in the Taiwan Strait decreased beginning in the late 1970s, when China called for peaceful reunification with Taiwan and reduction of PLA forces in Fujian Province opposite Taiwan. Nevertheless, Beijing refused to rule out the use of force against Taiwan in the event that Taiwan had serious internal disturbances or declared independence. In the late 1980s, a Chinese attack against Taiwan was considered unlikely by most observers. The Navy lacked the amphibious forces necessary to mount a full-scale invasion. The Navy had the capability to mount a blockade of Taiwan, but this measure also was considered unlikely.

Foreign Military Cooperation

In the 1950s China limited its military cooperation almost entirely to communist nations and to insurgent movements in Southeast

Asia. The Soviet Union provided China with substantial assistance, and with advice in modernizing the PLA and developing China's defense industry (see Military Modernization in the 1950s and 1960s, this ch.). China provided North Korea with arms and assistance, and the PLA and the Korean People's Army developed close ties because of their association in the Korean War. In 1961 China and North Korea signed a mutual defense agreement, and Chinese-North Korean military cooperation continued in the late 1980s. China also provided weapons and military and economic assistance to Vietnam, which ended in 1978 when relations between the two countries soured. In the 1950s and 1960s, China provided weapons to communist insurgent groups in Laos, Cambodia, Burma, Thailand, Malaysia, Indonesia, and the Philippines.

In the 1960s and 1970s, China began developing military ties with Third World nations in Asia and Africa, while maintaining or promoting cooperation with North Korea, the Democratic Republic of Vietnam (North Vietnam), and Albania. Chinese military cooperation with North Korea and North Vietnam stemmed from security considerations. Chinese military assistance to Third World countries arose from attempts to extend Chinese influence and counteract Soviet and United States influence. China became increasingly anti-Soviet in the 1970s. In the 1980s China developed close military ties and provided considerable military assistance to Pakistan, Bangladesh, and Sri Lanka in South Asia; Egypt in the Middle East; and Tanzania, Sudan, Somalia, Zaire, and Zambia in Africa.

In the late 1970s, the scope and tenor of foreign military cooperation changed with the shift to commercial arms sales, attempts to gain some influence in Eastern Europe, and improvement in relations with the United States and Western Europe. Chinese military assistance to communist insurgents, especially in Southeast Asia, tapered off. Nevertheless, China continued to provide weapons both to the Khmer Rouge and to noncommunist Cambodian resistance groups, and it developed close relations with and sold weapons to Thailand. Traditionally friendly states in South Asia continued to have close military ties with China and to purchase Chinese military hardware under generous terms. Chinese-Albanian relations deteriorated in the 1970s, and Beijing terminated all assistance in 1978. But at the same time, China began to exchange military delegations with two other East European countries—Yugoslavia and Romania. Chinese military relations with these two countries were limited and, especially in the case of Romania (a Warsaw Pact member), served to irritate the Soviet Union.

The Chinese Navy's Huangfeng class fast-attack craft
Courtesy Conmilit

A major change in foreign military cooperation occurred when China began developing military contacts with West European nations and the United States in the late 1970s and the 1980s. This change reflected China's desire to counter Soviet influence, especially in Europe, as well as to develop relations with modern armed forces. China needed advanced hardware and technology and organizational, training, personnel, logistics, and doctrinal concepts for modernizing the PLA. Chinese military ties with West European countries were strongest with Britain, France, and Italy. Chinese military relations with the United States developed rapidly in the 1980s and included exchanges of high-level military officials and working-level delegations in training, logistics, and education. The United States sold some weapons to China for defensive purposes, but China was unlikely to purchase large amounts of American arms because of financial and political constraints (see Sino-American Relations, ch. 12).

Beginning in 1979, when China introduced its policy of opening up to the outside world, military exchanges with foreign countries grew substantially (see Historical Legacy and Worldview, ch. 12). The PLA hosted 500 military delegations from 1979 to 1987 and sent thousands of military officials abroad for visits, study, and lectures. China received port calls from thirty-three foreign warships, including United States, British, French, and Australian ships, and it sent two naval ships to visit Pakistan, Bangladesh, and Sri Lanka in 1985. PLA departments, academies, and research institutes opened their doors to foreign military visitors. In 1987 China had ties with eighty-five foreign armies, posted Chinese military attachés in sixty countries, and hosted forty military attachés in Beijing.

Force Structure

Ground Forces

The PLA ground forces consisted of conventionally armed main and regional units and in 1987 made up over 70 percent of the PLA. It provided a good conventional defense but had only limited offensive potential and was poorly equipped for nuclear, biological, or chemical warfare. Main forces included about 35 group armies, comprising 118 infantry divisions, 13 armored divisions, and 33 artillery and antiaircraft artillery divisions, plus 71 independent regiments and 21 independent battalions of mostly support troops. Regional forces consisted of 73 divisions of border defense and garrison troops plus 140 independent regiments.

Under the old system, a field army consisted of three partially motorized infantry divisions and two regiments of artillery and antiaircraft artillery. Each field army division had over 12,000 personnel in three infantry regiments, one artillery regiment, one armored regiment, and one antiaircraft artillery battalion. Organization was flexible, the higher echelons being free to tailor forces for combat around any number of infantry divisions. At least theoretically, each division had its own armor and artillery—actual equipment levels were not revealed and probably varied—and the assets at army level and within the independent units could be apportioned as needed.

The new, main-force group armies typically included 46,300 troops in up to four divisions, believed to include infantry, armor, artillery, air defense, airborne, and air support elements. Although the new group armies were supposed to reflect a move to combined-arms operations, because of a lack of mechanization they continued to consist of infantry supported by armor, artillery, and other units. The 13 armored divisions each had 3 regiments and 240 main battle tanks but lacked adequate mechanized infantry support. There was little evidence of the use of armored personnel carriers during the Sino-Vietnamese border conflict in 1979, and tanks were used as mobile artillery and as support for dismounted infantry. Artillery forces emphasized towed guns, howitzers, and truck-mounted multiple rocket launchers. In the 1980s some self-propelled artillery entered service, but the PLA also produced rocket launchers as a cheaper but not totally effective alternative to self-propelled guns. There was a variety of construction equipment, mobile bridging, trucks, and prime movers. A new multiple rocket launcher for scattering antitank mines appeared in 1979, but mine-laying and mine-clearing equipment remained scarce.

Regional forces consisted of full-time PLA troops organized as independent divisions for garrison missions. Garrison divisions were static, artillery-heavy units deployed along the coastline and borders in areas of likely attack. Regional forces were armed less heavily than their main-force counterparts, and they were involved in training the militia. They were the PLA units commonly used to restore order during the Cultural Revolution.

In 1987 the PLA ground forces, which relied upon obsolescent but serviceable equipment, were most anxious to improve defenses against armored vehicles and aircraft. Most equipment was produced from Soviet designs of the 1950s, but weapons were being incrementally upgraded, some with Western technology. One example of upgraded, Soviet-design equipment was the Type 69 main battle tank, an improved version of the Type 59 main battle tank, itself based on the Soviet T-54. The Type 69 main battle tank had improved armor, a gun stabilizer, a fire control system including a laser range finder, infrared searchlights, and a 105mm smooth-bore gun. In 1987 the existence of a new, Type 80 main battle tank was revealed in the Western press. The tank had a new chassis, a 105mm gun, and a fire control system. Production of the Type 80 tank had not yet begun. The PLA was believed to have atomic demolition munitions, and there were unconfirmed reports that it also had tactical nuclear weapons. In any case, nuclear bombs and missiles in the Chinese inventory could be used in a theater role. The PLA had a scarcity of antitank guided missiles, tactical surface-to-air missiles, and electronics to improve communications, fire control, and sensors. China began production of the Soviet Sagger antitank missile in 1979 but lacked a more powerful, longer range, semiautomatic antitank guided missile. The PLA required a mobile surface-to-air missile and an infantry shoulder-fired missile for use against helicopters and certain other aircraft (see Appendix C).

Air Force

The primary mission of the PLA Air Force was the defense of the mainland, and most aircraft were assigned to this role. A smaller number of ground attack and bomber units were assigned to interdiction and possibly close air support, and some bomber units could be used for nuclear delivery. The force had only limited military airlift and reconnaissance capabilities.

The Soviet Union helped to establish the Air Force in 1949 and began to provide aircraft in late 1951. Production technology came two years later. By 1956 China was assembling F-4s (copies of MiG-15s) and eight years later was producing both the F-5 (MiG-17) and the F-6 (MiG-19) under license. Meanwhile, Soviet instructors were training the new pilots in Soviet tactics. The withdrawal of Soviet aid in 1960 crippled China's aircraft industry. The industry declined markedly through 1963, further hindered by the high priority accorded to the competing missile and nuclear weapons program. The aircraft industry began to recover in about 1965, however, when China began providing F-4s and F-5s to North Vietnam.

Chinese pilots saw considerable action in the Korean War and, to a lesser extent, during the Taiwan Strait crisis of 1958. During the China-Vietnam border conflict of 1979, the Chinese avoided air battles, probably at least partly because they lacked the confidence to challenge Vietnam's air force, which though far smaller was better armed and trained.

The Air Force underwent reorganization and streamlining as part of the reduction in force begun in 1985. Before the 1985 reorganization, the Air Force reportedly had four branches: air defense, ground attack, bombing, and independent air regiments. In peacetime the Air Force Directorate, under the supervision of the PLA General Staff Department, controlled the Air Force through air army headquarters located with, or in communication with, each of the seven military region headquarters. In war, control of the Air Force probably reverted to the regional commanders. In 1987 it was not clear how the reorganization and the incorporation of air support elements into the group armies affected air force organization.

The largest Air Force organizational unit was the division, which consisted of 17,000 personnel in three regiments. A typical air defense regiment had three squadrons of three flights; each flight had three or four aircraft. The Air Force also had 220,000 air defense personnel who controlled about 100 surface-to-air missile sites and over 16,000 antiaircraft guns. In addition, it had a large number of early-warning, ground-control-intercept, and air-base radars manned by specialized troops organized into at least twenty-two independent regiments.

In the 1980s the Air Force made serious efforts to raise the education level and improve the training of its pilots. Superannuated pilots were retired or assigned to other duties. All new pilots were

An Air Force pilot with his F-7/Fishbed jet fighter
Courtesy Xinhua News Agency

at least middle-school graduates. The time it took to train a qualified pilot capable of performing combat missions reportedly was reduced from four or five years to two years. Training emphasized raising technical and tactical skills in individual pilots and participation in combined-arms operations. Flight safety also increased.

In 1987 the Air Force had serious technological deficiencies—especially when compared with its principal threat, the Soviet Union—and had many needs that it could not satisfy. It needed more advanced aircraft, better avionics, electronic countermeasures equipment, more powerful aircraft weaponry, a low-altitude surface-to-air missile, and better controlled antiaircraft artillery guns. Some progress was made in aircraft design with the incorporation of Western avionics into the F-7 (a copy of the MiG-21) and F-8 (an indigenous model derived from various Soviet designs), the development of refueling capabilities for the B-6D bomber and the A-5 attack fighter, increased aircraft all-weather capabilities, and the production of the HQ-2J high-altitude surface-to-air missile and the C-601 air-to-ship missile.

Navy

Although naval personnel comprised only 12 percent of PLA strength, the PLA Navy ranked in 1987 as the third largest navy in the world. In 1987 the Navy consisted of the naval headquarters in Beijing; three fleet commands—the North Sea Fleet, based at Qingdao, Shandong Province; the East Sea Fleet, based at Shanghai; and the South Sea Fleet, based at Zhanjiang, Guangdong Province—and about 2,000 ships. The 350,000-person Navy included Naval Air Force units of 34,000 men, the Coastal Defense Forces of 38,000, and the Marine Corps of 56,500. Naval Headquarters, which controlled the three fleet commands, was subordinate to the PLA General Staff Department.

China's 1,500-kilometer coastline was protected by more than 100 diesel-powered Romeo- and Whiskey-class submarines, which could remain at sea only a limited time. Inside this protective ring and within range of shore-based aircraft were destroyers and frigates mounting Styx antiship missiles, depth-charge projectors, and guns up to 130mm. Any invader penetrating the destroyer and frigate protection would be swarmed by almost 900 fast-attack craft. Stormy weather could limit the range of these small boats, however, and curtail air support. Behind the inner ring were Coastal Defense Force personnel operating naval shore batteries of Styx missiles and guns, backed by ground force units deployed in depth.

In 1949 Mao asserted that "to oppose imperialist aggression, we must build a powerful navy." The Naval Academy was set up at Dalian in March 1950, mostly with Soviet instructors. The Navy was established in September 1950 by consolidating regional naval forces under General Staff Department command. It then consisted of a motley collection of ships and boats acquired from the Guomindang forces. The Naval Air Force was added two years later. By 1954 an estimated 2,500 Soviet naval advisers were in China—possibly one adviser to every thirty Chinese naval personnel—and the Soviet Union began providing modern ships. With Soviet assistance, the navy reorganized in 1954 and 1955 into the North Sea Fleet, East Sea Fleet, and South Sea Fleet, and a corps of admirals and other naval officers was established from the ranks of the ground forces. In shipbuilding the Soviets first assisted the Chinese, then the Chinese copied Soviet designs without assistance, and finally the Chinese produced vessels of their own design. Eventually Soviet assistance progressed to the point that a joint Sino-Soviet Pacific Ocean fleet was under discussion.

Through the upheavals of the late 1950s and 1960s the Navy remained relatively undisturbed. Under the leadership of Minister of National Defense Lin Biao, large investments were made in naval construction during the frugal years immediately after the Great Leap Forward. During the Cultural Revolution, a number of top naval commissars and commanders were purged, and naval forces were used to suppress a revolt in Wuhan in July 1967, but the service largely avoided the turmoil. Although it paid lip service to Mao and assigned political commissars aboard ships, the Navy continued to train, build, and maintain the fleets.

In the 1970s, when approximately 20 percent of the defense budget was allocated to naval forces, the Navy grew dramatically. The conventional submarine force increased from 35 to 100 boats, the number of missile-carrying ships grew from 20 to 200, and the production of larger surface ships, including support ships for ocean-going operations, increased. The Navy also began development of nuclear-powered attack submarines (SSN) and nuclear-powered ballistic missile submarines (SSBN).

In the 1980s the Navy was developing into a regional naval power with some blue-water capabilities. Naval construction continued at a level somewhat below the 1970s rate. Modernization efforts encompassed higher educational and technical standards for personnel; reformulation of the traditional coastal defense doctrine and force structure in favor of more blue-water operations; and training in naval combined-arms operations involving submarine, surface, naval aviation, and coastal defense forces. Examples of the expansion of China's blue-water naval capabilities were the 1980 recovery of an intercontinental ballistic missile (ICBM) in the Western Pacific by a twenty-ship fleet, extended naval operations in the South China Sea in 1984 and 1985, and the visit of two naval ships to three South Asian nations in 1985. In 1982 the Navy conducted a successful test of an underwater-launched ballistic missile; in 1986 the Navy's order of battle included two Xia-class SSBNs armed with twelve CSS-NX-4 missiles and three Han-class SSNs armed with six SY-2 cruise missiles. The Navy also had some success in developing a variety of ship-to-ship, ship-to-shore, shore-to-ship, and air-to-ship missiles. In the late 1980s, major deficiencies reportedly remained in antisubmarine warfare, mine warfare, naval electronics (including electronic countermeasures equipment), and naval aviation capabilities.

Nuclear Forces

In the late 1980s, China was the world's third-largest nuclear power, possessing a small but credible nuclear deterrent force of 225 to 300 nuclear weapons. Beginning in the late 1970s, China deployed a full range of nuclear forces and acquired an incipient nuclear second-strike capability. The nuclear forces were operated by the 100,000-person Strategic Missile Force, which was controlled directly by the General Staff Department.

China began developing nuclear weapons in the late 1950s with substantial Soviet assistance. When Sino-Soviet relations cooled in the late 1950s and early 1960s, the Soviet Union withheld plans and data for an atomic bomb, abrogated the agreement on transferring defense technology, and began the withdrawal of Soviet advisers in 1960. Despite the termination of Soviet assistance, China committed itself to continue nuclear weapons development to break "the superpowers' monopoly on nuclear weapons," to ensure Chinese security against the Soviet and United States threats, and to increase Chinese prestige and power internationally.

China made remarkable progress in the 1960s in developing nuclear weapons. In a thirty-two-month period, China successfully exploded its first atomic bomb (October 16, 1964), launched its first nuclear missile (October 25, 1966), and detonated its first hydrogen bomb (June 14, 1967). Deployment of the Dongfeng-1 conventionally armed short-range ballistic missile and the Dongfeng-2 (CSS-1) medium-range ballistic missile (MRBM) occurred in the 1960s. The Dongfeng-3 (CCS-2) intermediate-range ballistic missile (IRBM) was successfully tested in 1969. Although the Cultural Revolution disrupted the strategic weapons program less than other scientific and educational sectors in China, there was a slowdown in succeeding years.

In the 1970s the nuclear weapons program saw the development of MRBM, IRBM, and ICBM capabilities and marked the beginning of a minimum deterrent force. China continued MRBM deployment, began deploying the Dongfeng-3 IRBM, and successfully tested and commenced deployment of the Dongfeng-4 (CSS-3) limited-range ICBM.

By 1980 China had overcome the slowdown in nuclear development caused by the Cultural Revolution and had some spectacular successes in its strategic weapons program. In 1980 China successfully test launched its full-range ICBM, the Dongfeng-5 (CSS-4); the missile flew from central China to the Western Pacific, where it was recovered by a naval task force. The Dongfeng-5 possessed the capability to hit targets in the western Soviet Union and the United States. In 1981 China launched three satellites into space orbit from a single booster, indicating that China might possess the technology to develop multiple, independently targetable reentry vehicles (MIRVs). China also launched the Xia-class SSBN in 1981, and the next year it conducted its first successful test launch of the CSS-NX-4 submarine-launched ballistic missile. In addition to the development of a sea-based nuclear force, China began considering the development of tactical nuclear weapons. PLA exercises featured the simulated use of tactical nuclear weapons in offensive and defensive situations beginning in 1982. Reports of

Surface-to-air missiles in transit
Courtesy Xinhua News Agency

Chinese possession of tactical nuclear weapons remained unconfirmed in 1987.

In 1986 China possessed a credible minimum deterrent force with land, sea, and air elements. Land-based forces included ICBMs, IRBMs, and MRBMs. The sea-based strategic force consisted of SSBNs. The Air Force's bombers were capable of delivering nuclear bombs but would be unlikely to penetrate the sophisticated air defenses of modern military powers such as the Soviet Union.

China's nuclear forces, in combination with the PLA's conventional forces, served to deter both nuclear and conventional attack. Chinese leaders repeatedly have pledged never to be the first to use nuclear weapons, and they have accompanied the no-first-use pledge with a promise of certain nuclear counterattack if nuclear weapons are used against China. China envisioned retaliation against strategic and tactical attacks and would probably strike countervalue rather than counterforce targets. The combination of China's few nuclear weapons and technological factors such as range, accuracy, and response time might further limit the effectiveness of nuclear strikes against counterforce targets. China is seeking to increase the credibility of its nuclear retaliatory capability by dispersing and concealing its nuclear forces in difficult terrain, improving their mobility, and hardening its missile silos.

Paramilitary Forces

Militia

The role of the militia and the degree of party and PLA control over it have varied over the years. During the 1940s the militia served primarily as a PLA support force. After 1949 the party consolidated control over the country and gradually used the militia to maintain order and help the PLA with defense of the borders and coast. In the mid-1950s Minister of National Defense Peng Dehuai attempted to build a reserve system incorporating the militia. Peng's efforts were thwarted when the party expanded the militia, assigning it duties as a production force and internal security force during the Great Leap Forward. Lin Biao reduced the size of the militia and reemphasized military training in the early 1960s. The militia was fragmented during the early years of the Cultural Revolution, but in the 1970s it was rebuilt and redirected to support the PLA. The Gang of Four attempted to build up the urban militia as an alternative to the PLA, but the urban militia failed to support the Gang of Four in 1976, when Hua Guofeng and moderate military leaders deposed them. The militia's logistical support of the PLA was essential during the Sino-Vietnamese border war of 1979. In the 1980s Chinese leaders undertook to improve the militia's military capabilities by reducing its size and its economic tasks.

In 1987 the militia was controlled by the PLA at the military district level and by people's armed forces departments, which devolved to civilian control at the county and city levels as part of the reduction in force. The militia was a smaller force than previously, consisting of 4.3 million basic or primary—armed—militia, and the 6-million-strong general or ordinary militia. The basic militia was comprised of men and women aged eighteen to twenty-eight who had served or were expected to serve in the PLA and who received thirty to forty days of military training per year. The basic militia included naval militia, which operated armed fishing trawlers and coastal defense units, as well as specialized detachments, such as air defense, artillery, communications, antichemical, reconnaissance, and engineering units, which served the PLA. The ordinary militia included men aged eighteen to thirty-five who met the criteria for military service; they received some basic military training but generally were unarmed. The ordinary militia had some air defense duties and included the urban militia. Efforts were made to streamline militia organization and upgrade militia weaponry. By 1986 militia training bases had been established in over half the counties and cities in the nation.

The militia's principal tasks in the 1980s were to assist in production, to undergo military training, and to defend China's frontiers in peacetime. In wartime, the militia would supply reserves for mobilization, provide logistical support to the PLA, and conduct guerrilla operations behind enemy lines.

Reserve Service System

The 1984 Military Service Law stipulated the combination of the militia and the reserve service system. Military training for senior middle-school and college and university students commenced in 1984 as China sought to provide additional qualified reserve-service officers. The reserve force consisted primarily of the militia and was organized into reserve-service divisions and regiments. In 1987 China began to make reference to the National Defense Reserve Force, which apparently consisted of reserve soldiers (including all militia, demobilized soldiers, and specialized technical personnel registered for reserve service) and reserve officers (including demobilized officers and soldiers assigned to reserve officer service, college and university graduates, and civilian cadres and specialized technicians).

An air-defense shelter in Beijing is turned into an underground inn.
Courtesy
China Reconstructs

Production and Construction Corps

Before the Cultural Revolution, the Production and Construction Corps was a paramilitary organization of 3 to 4 million people under joint government, party, and PLA control. The Production and Construction Corps was used in remote and unproductive areas to build roads, reclaim land, construct defense and water works, and operate mines, state farms, and industrial plants. A secondary role was border defense, and some units were armed with light infantry weapons. All received basic military training. Unlike the militia, Production and Construction Corps personnel were full time and uniformed. The PLA took over the Production and Construction Corps during the Cultural Revolution, then civilianized it in the 1970s. In the 1980s the corps appeared to have been abolished except in Xinjiang-Uygur Autonomous Region. There it operated under regional party and government organizations, the Xinjiang Military District, and the Ministry of Agriculture, Animal Husbandry, and Fishery.

People's Armed Police Force

The People's Armed Police Force was formed in 1983 when the PLA transferred its internal security and border defense units to the Ministry of Public Security (see Public Security Forces, ch. 13). In wartime, the armed police, as part of China's armed forces, presumably would perform border defense and support functions in assisting the PLA.

Accomplishments and Prospects

Beginning in the late 1970s, China's military modernization program achieved success in increasing China's status as a regional power. The PLA disengaged itself from politics and concentrated its attention on military tasks. Reforms in organization, doctrine, education and training, and personnel practices brought the PLA much closer to its objective of molding a modern combat force capable of waging combined-arms warfare. Defense science and industry became more closely integrated with their civilian counterparts and began producing more civilian goods in addition to modernizing PLA weaponry with foreign technology. Nevertheless, PLA capabilities still lagged behind advanced world levels, and the presence of potent adversaries on China's borders meant that defense modernization would be a long-term program, probably lasting well into the next century.

* * *

Beginning in the late 1970s, the volume of information published on the Chinese military increased greatly. Ellis Joffe's *The Chinese Army After Mao* provides a good introduction to military modernization and changes in the PLA in the 1980s. The role of politics in PLA development is delineated in Harlan W. Jencks' *From Muskets to Missiles*; Harvey W. Nelsen's *The Chinese Military System*; and Monte R. Bullard's *China's Political-Military Evolution*. The Jencks and Nelsen books also contain valuable information on PLA organization and force structure in the early 1980s. The United States Defense Intelligence Agency's 1984 *Handbook of the Chinese People's Liberation Army* is another good source on PLA organization, equipment, and tactics. Various aspects of military reforms in defense policy, doctrine, training and education, defense industry, weapons modernization, and force structure are dealt with in *The Chinese Defense Establishment*, edited by Paul H. B. Godwin; *Chinese Defence Policy*, edited by Gerald Segal and William T. Tow; and *China's Military Reforms*, edited by Charles D. Lovejoy and Bruce W. Watson. These books also deal with the international implications of Chinese military power. China's involvement in foreign conflicts is covered in Segal's *Defending China*. Chinese military assistance and arms sales are treated in *China and the Arms Trade* by Anne Gilks and Segal. *China as a Maritime Power* by David G.

Muller, and *Eighth Voyage of the Dragon* by Bruce Swanson provide good overviews of the PLA Navy.

Articles on the Chinese military appear in the general, scholarly, and military periodical literature. *Far Eastern Economic Review* and *Asiaweek* offer the most articles among weekly news publications. *China Quarterly*, *Asian Survey*, and *Problems of Communism* feature occasional articles on the PLA. Useful military publications include *Jane's Defence Weekly*, *Asian Defence Journal*, *International Defense Review*, *Aviation Week and Space Technology*, and *Flight International*. (For further information and complete citations, see Bibliography.)

Appendix A

Table

1 Metric Conversion Coefficients and Factors
2 Provincial-Level Units and Selected Urban Centers, Pinyin Form and Wade-Giles Form
3 Selected Place-Names, Pinyin Form and Conventional Form
4 Climatic Statistics for Twenty Selected Stations
5 Age Structure, 1982 Census
6 Population, 1953–87. Reconstructed Data Model
7 Estimated Distribution of Population by Region, 1987
8 Cities with Populations over 1 Million, 1982
9 Size and Distribution of Minority Nationalities, 1982
10 Number of Schools and Students, Selected Years, 1957–85
11 Composition of Gross Value of Agricultural Output, Selected Years, 1955–85
12 Manufactured Agricultural Inputs, Selected Years, 1955–85
13 Grain Production and Per Capita Consumption of Selected Products, Selected Years, 1955–85
14 Agricultural Exports and Imports, 1985
15 Production, Use, and Import of Major Commodities, Selected Years, 1952–85
16 Gross Value of Industrial Output, by Region, 1952, 1957, and 1983
17 Composition of Trade, Selected Years, 1970–85
18 Major Trading Partners, 1986

Table 1. Metric Conversion Coefficients and Factors

When you know	Multiply by	To find
Millimeters	0.04	inches
Centimeters	0.39	inches
Meters	3.3	feet
Kilometers	0.62	miles
Hectares (10,000 m^2)	2.47	acres
Square kilometers	0.39	square miles
Cubic meters	35.3	cubic feet
Liters	0.26	gallons
Kilograms	2.2	pounds
Metric tons	0.98	long tons
	1.1	short tons
	2,204	pounds
Degrees Celsius (Centigrade)	9 divide by 5 and add 32	degrees Fahrenheit

Table 2. Provincial-Level Units and Selected Urban Centers, Pinyin Form and Wade-Giles Form

Pinyin	to Wade-Giles	Wade-Giles	to Pinyin
Provincial-Level Units			
Anhui	An-hui	An-hui	Anhui
Beijing	Pei-ching	Che-chiang	Zhejiang
Fujian	Fu-chien	Chiang-hsi	Jiangxi
Gansu	Kan-su	Chiang-su	Jiangsu
Guangdong	Kuang-tung	Chi-lin	Jilin
Guangxi-Zhuang	Kuang-hsi-Chuang	Ch'ing-hai	Qinghai
Guizhou	Kui-chou	Fu-chien	Fujian
Hebei	Ho-pei	Hei-lung-chiang	Heilongjiang
Heilongjiang	Hei-lung-chiang	Ho-nan	Henan
Henan	Ho-nan	Ho-pei	Hebei
Hubei	Hupei	Hsin-chiang-Wei-wu-erh	Xinjiang Uygur
Hunan	Hu-nan	Hsi-tsang	Xizang
Jiangsu	Chiang-su	Hu-nan	Hunan
Jiangxi	Chiang-hsi	Hupei	Hubei
Jilin	Chi-lin	Kan-su	Gansu
Liaoning	Liao-ning	Kuang-hsi-Chuang	Guangxi-Zhuang
Nei Monggol	Nei-meng-ku	Kuang-tung	Guangdong
Ningxia-Hui	Ning-hsia-Hui	Kui-chou	Guizhou
Qinghai	Ch'ing-hai	Liao-ning	Liaoning
Shaanxi	Shen-hsi	Nei-meng-ku	Nei Monggol
Shandong	Shan-tung	Ning-hsia-Hui	Ningxia-Hui
Shanghai	Shang-hai	Pei-ching	Beijing
Shanxi	Shan-hsi	Shang-hai	Shanghai
Sichuan	Ssu-ch'uan	Shan-hsi	Shanxi
Tianjin	Tien-chin	Shan-tung	Shandong
Xinjiang-Uygur	Hsin-chiang-Wei-wu-erh	Shen-hsi	Shaanxi
Xizang	Hsi-tsang	Ssu-ch'uan	Sichuan
Yunnan	Yun-nan	Tien-chin	Tianjin
Zhejiang	Che-chiang	Yun-nan	Yunnan
Selected Urban Centers			
Changchun	Ch'ang-ch'un	Ch'ang-ch'un	Changchun
Chengdu	Ch'eng-tu	Ch'eng-tu	Chengdu
Chongqing	Ch'ung-ch'ing	Ch'ing-tao	Qingdao
Dalian	Ta-lien	Ch'ung-ch'ing	Chongqing
Guangzhou	Kuang-chou	Ha-erh-pin	Harbin
Harbin	Ha-erh-pin	Hsi-an	Xi'an
Lüda*	Lü-Ta	Kuang-chou	Guangzhou
Nanjing	Nan-ching	Lü-Ta*	Lüda
Qingdao	Ch'ing-tao	Nan-ching	Nanjing
Shenyang	Shen-yang	Shen-yang	Shenyang
Taiyuan	T'ai-yuan	T'ai-yuan	Taiyuan
Wuhan	Wu-han	Ta-lien	Dalian
Ürümqi	Wu-lu-mu-ch'i	Wu-han	Wuhan
Xi'an	Hsi-an	Wu-lu-mu-ch'i	Ürümqi
Yan'an	Yen-an	Yen-an	Yan'an

* Lüda/Lü-Ta comprises the twin cities of Lüshun/Lü-shun (variant: Port Arthur) and Dalian/Ta-lien (variant: Dairen).

Source: Based on information from United States Department of Interior, Board on Geographic Names, *Gazetteer of the People's Republic of China: Pinyin to Wade-Giles, Wade-Giles to Pinyin*, Washington, July 1979.

Table 3. Selected Place-Names, Pinyin Form and Conventional Form

Pinyin*	to Conventional Form	Conventional Form	to Pinyin*
Beijing	Peking	Amoy	Xiamen
Chang Jiang	Yangtze River	Amur River	Heilong Jiang
Da Hinggan Ling	Greater Khingan Range	Argun River	Ergun He
Dongbei Pingyuan	Manchurian Plain	Brahmaputra River	Yarlung Zangbo Jiang
Ergun He	Argun River	Canton	Guangzhou
Gangdise Shan	Kailas Range	China, People's Republic of	Zhonghua Renmin Gongheguo
Guangzhou	Canton	Dzungarian Basin	Junggar Pendi
Guangxi-Zhuang Zizhiqu	Kwangsi-Chuang Autonomous Region	Great Wall	Wanli Changcheng
Heilong Jiang	Amur River	Greater Khingan Range	Da Hinggan Ling
Huang He	Yellow River	Hainan Strait	Qiongzhou Haixa
Junggar Pendi	Dzungarian Basin	Inner Mongolian Autonomous Region (Inner Mongolia)	Nei Monggol Zizhiqu
Karakorum Shankou	Karakoram Pass	Kailas Range	Gangdise Shan
Kunlun Shan	Kunlun Mountains	Karakoram Pass	Karakorum Shankou
Lancang Jiang	Mekong River	Kashgar	Kashi
Mu Us Shamo	Ordos Desert	Koko Nor	Qinghai Hu
Nei Monggol Zizhiqu	Inner Mongolian Autonomous Region (Inner Mongolia	Kunlun Mountains	Kunlun Shan
Ningxia-Hui Zizhiqu	Ninghsia-Hui Autonomous Region	Kwangsi-Chuang Autonomous Region	Guangxi-Zhuang Zizhiqu
Nu Jiang	Salween River	Lesser Khingan Range	Xiao Hinggan Ling
Qaidam Pendi	Tsaidam Basin	Manchurian Plain	Dongbei Pingyuan
Qingdao	Tsingtao	Mekong River	Lancang Jiang
Qinghai Hu	Koko Nor	Ninghsia-Hui Autonomous Region	Ningxia-Hui Zizhiqu
Qing-Zang Gaoyuan	Tibet, Plateau of	Ordos Desert	Mu Us Shamo
Qin Ling	Tsinling Mountains	Pearl River	Zhu Jiang
Qiongzhou Haixia	Hainan Strait	Peking	Beijing
Shantou	Swatow	Red River	Yuan Jiang
Sichuan Pendi	Szechwan Basin	Salween River	Nu Jiang
Songhua Hu	Sungari Reservoir	Sinkiang-Uighur Autonomous Region	Xinjiang-Uygur Zizhiqu
Songhua Jiang	Sungari River	Sungari Reservoir	Songhua Hu
Taklimakan Shamo	Takla Makan Desert	Sungari River	Songhua Jiang
Tarim He	Tarim River	Swatow	Shantou
Tarim Pendi	Tarim Basin	Szechwan Basin	Sichuan Pendi
Tianjin	Tientsin	Takla Makan Desert	Taklimakan Shamo
Tian Shan	Tien Shan	Tarim Basin	Tarim Pendi
Tumen Jiang	Tumen River		
Turpan Pendi	Turfan Depression		
Wanli Changcheng	Great Wall		
Wusuli Jiang	Ussuri River		
Xiamen	Amoy		

Table 3.—Continued.

Pinyin*	to Conventional Form
Xiao Hinggan Ling	Lesser Khingan Range
Xinjiang-Uygur Zizhiqu	Sinkiang Uighur Autonomous Region
Xizang Zizhiqu	Tibetan Autonomous Region (Tibet)
Yalu Jiang	Yalu River
Yarlung Zangbo Jiang	Brahmaputra River
Yuan Jiang	Red River
Zhonghua Renmin Gongheguo	China, People's Republic of
Zhu Jiang	Pearl River

Conventional Form	to Pinyin*
Tarim River	Tarim He
Tibetan Autonomous Region (Tibet)	Xizang Zizhiqu
Tibet, Plateau of	Qing-Zang Gaoyuan
Tien Shan	Tian Shan
Tientsin	Tianjin
Tsaidam Basin	Qaidam Pendi
Tsingtao	Qingdao
Tsinling Mountains	Qin Ling
Tumen River	Tumen Jiang
Turfan Depression	Turpan Pendi
Ussuri River	Wusuli Jiang
Yalu River	Yalu Jiang
Yangtze River	Chang Jiang
Yellow River	Huang He

*Including generic parts of Chinese place-names.

Source: Based on information from United States Department of Interior, Board on Geographic Names, *Gazetteer of the People's Republic of China, Pinyin to Wade-Giles, Wade-Giles to Pinyin*, Washington, July 1979, 915–16.

Table 4. Climatic Statistics for Twenty Selected Stations

Station	Temperature (in degrees Celsius)			Humidity (in percentage)			Precipitation (in millimeters)			Sunshine (in percentage)		
	January	July	Annual	January	July	Annual	January	July	Annual	January	July	Annual
Beijing	-4.7	26.0	11.6	44	77	59	2.6	196.6	682.9	69	62	63
Chengdu	5.6	25.8	16.3	79	85	82	5.0	223.9	976.0	24	39	28
Golmud	-11.8	17.6	3.7	42	36	34	0.8	6.9	38.3	n.a.	n.a.	n.a.
Guangzhou	13.4	28.3	21.8	69	84	78	39.1	219.6	1680.5	42	56	44
Haikou	17.1	28.4	23.8	85	82	85	26.4	188.6	1689.6	n.a.	n.a.	n.a.
Hami	-12.3	27.7	9.9	66	32	40	1.6	6.4	33.4	72	72	76
Harbin	-19.7	22.7	3.6	73	77	67	4.3	176.5	553.5	61	51	59
Hohhot	-13.5	21.8	5.6	57	64	56	2.4	104.4	426.1	70	60	67
Hotan	-5.7	25.5	12.1	52	41	42	1.6	3.4	35.0	n.a.	n.a.	n.a.
Kunming	7.8	19.7	14.8	68	83	72	10.0	216.4	991.7	73	36	57
Lanzhou	-7.3	22.4	9.1	59	60	59	1.4	59.3	331.9	63	58	60
Lhasa	-2.3	14.9	7.5	28	67	45	0.2	141.7	453.9	78	51	68
Qingdao	-2.6	24.7	11.9	67	88	74	7.6	209.7	777.4	63	43	58
Shanghai	3.3	27.9	15.7	74	83	80	44.2	142.4	1128.5	45	57	46
Shenyang	-12.7	24.6	7.7	65	78	65	8.5	217.7	755.4	59	48	58
Taipei	14.6	28.6	22.3	84	78	82	100.0	255.4	2047.5	n.a.	n.a.	n.a.
Wuhan	2.8	29.0	16.3	76	79	79	35.5	179.0	1260.1	40	61	47
Xi'an	-1.3	26.7	13.3	66	71	71	7.5	105.9	604.2	48	51	46
Xisha Islands	22.8	28.6	26.4	78	84	82	19.0	231.3	1392.2	n.a.	n.a.	n.a.
Yinchuan	-9.2	23.5	8.5	60	64	59	1.0	38.2	205.5	76	64	68

n.a.—not available

Source: Based on information from *Physical Geography of China*, Beijing, 1986, 206–209.

Table 5. Age Structure, 1982 Census

Age-Group	Population (in thousands)*	Percentage of total*
0-4	94,704	9.43
5-9	110,736	11.03
10-14	131,811	13.13
15-19	125,366	12.49
20-24	74,363	7.41
25-29	92,564	9.22
30-34	72,958	7.27
35-39	54,222	5.40
40-44	48,438	4.82
45-49	47,403	4.72
50-54	40,816	4.07
55-59	33,894	3.38
60-64	27,362	2.73
65-69	21,260	2.12
70-74	14,348	1.43
75-79	8,617	0.86
80-84	3,705	0.37
85-89	1,088	0.11
90 and over	257	0.03
TOTAL	1,003,912	100.02

*Approximate because of rounding.

Source: Based on information from *Zhongguo 1982 Nian Renkou Pucha Ziliao (Dianzi Jisuanji Huizong)* [1982 Population Census of China (Results of Computer Tabulation)], Beijing, March 1985, 272-81.

*Table 6. Population, 1953–87. Reconstructed Data Model**

Year	Midyear Population (thousands)	Crude Birth Rate (per thousand)	Crude Death Rate (per thousand)	Rate of Natural Increase (per thousand)	Total Fertility Rate (per thousand)	Life Expectancy at Birth	Infant Mortality Rate (per thousand)
1953	584,191	42.24	25.77	16.47	6.05	40.25	175
1954	594,725	43.44	24.20	19.24	6.28	42.36	164
1955	606,730	43.04	22.33	20.71	6.26	44.60	154
1956	619,136	39.89	20.11	19.78	5.86	46.99	143
1957	633,215	43.25	18.12	25.13	6.40	49.54	132
1958	646,703	37.76	20.65	17.11	5.68	45.82	146
1959	654,349	28.53	22.06	6.47	4.31	42.46	160
1960	650,661	26.76	44.60	-17.84	4.02	24.56	284
1961	644,670	22.43	23.01	-0.58	3.29	38.44	183
1962	653,302	41.02	14.02	27.00	6.03	53.00	89
1963	674,249	49.79	13.81	35.98	7.51	54.91	87
1964	696,065	40.29	12.45	27.84	6.18	57.08	86
1965	715,546	38.98	11.61	27.37	6.07	57.81	84
1966	735,904	39.83	11.12	28.71	6.26	58.59	83
1967	755,320	33.91	10.47	23.44	5.32	59.41	82
1968	776,153	40.96	10.08	30.88	6.45	60.29	81
1969	798,641	36.22	9.91	26.31	5.73	60.84	76
1970	820,403	36.98	9.54	27.44	5.82	61.41	70
1971	842,456	34.87	9.24	25.63	5.45	61.98	65
1972	863,439	32.45	8.85	23.60	4.99	62.55	60
1973	883,020	29.85	8.58	21.27	4.54	62.96	56
1974	901,318	28.08	8.32	19.76	4.17	63.37	52
1975	917,899	24.79	8.07	16.72	3.58	63.79	49
1976	932,671	23.05	7.84	15.21	3.23	64.21	45
1977	946,100	21.04	7.65	13.39	2.85	64.63	41
1978	958,766	20.73	7.52	13.21	2.72	65.06	37
1979	971,786	21.37	7.61	13.76	2.75	64.98	39
1980	983,379	17.63	7.65	9.98	2.24	64.89	42
1981	994,905	21.04	7.73	13.31	2.69	64.80	44
1982	1,008,175	21.09	7.89	13.20	2.71	64.72	46
1983	1,020,722	18.66	7.93	10.73	2.28	65.05	42
1984	1,032,814	17.52	7.79	9.73	2.11	65.46	40
1985	1,043,203	17.82	7.72	10.10	2.12	65.75	39
1986	1,053,716	17.43	7.69	9.74	2.03	65.99	38
1987	1,064,147	17.38	7.65	9.73	2.00	66.24	37

*Data in this table may vary from officially reported statistics.

Source: Based on information from computer reconstruction provided by Judith Banister, China Branch, Center for International Research, U.S. Bureau of the Census, January 1987.

Table 7. Estimated Distribution of Population by Region, 1987

Region* Provincial-Level Unit	Population (in thousands)	Area (in square kilometers)	Density (people per square kilometer)
Northeast			
Heilongjiang	33,945	460,000	74
Jilin	23,230	180,000	129
Liaoning	37,203	140,000	266
North			
Beijing	10,200	16,807	607
Hebei	56,364	180,000	313
Nei Monggol	20,689	1,200,000	17
Shanxi	26,724	150,000	178
Tianjin	8,396	11,305	743
East			
Anhui	52,225	130,000	402
Fujian	27,708	120,000	231
Jiangsu	62,622	100,000	626
Jiangxi	35,135	160,000	220
Shandong	78,231	150,000	521
Shanghai	12,323	6,185	1,992
Zhejiang	40,695	100,000	407
Central-South			
Guangdong	63,987	210,000	305
Guangxi	39,928	230,000	174
Henan	78,440	160,000	490
Hubei	49,802	180,000	277
Hunan	57,229	210,000	272
Southwest			
Guizhou	30,102	170,000	177
Sichuan	103,201	570,000	181
Xizang	2,062	1,200,000	2
Yunnan	34,728	390,000	89
Northwest			
Gansu	20,875	450,000	46
Ningxia	4,266	60,000	71
Qinghai	4,237	720,000	6
Shaanxi	30,277	190,000	159
Xinjiang	14,108	1,600,000	9

*Regional divisions are for descriptive purposes only and have no official administrative significance.

Source: Based on information from China Handbook Editorial Committee, *China Handbook Series: Geography*, Beijing, 1983, 131-253.

Table 8. Cities with Population over 1 Million, 1982

City	Provincial-Level Unit	Total Population (in thousands)*	Population of City Districts (in thousands)*	Suburban Population (in thousands)*
Shanghai	Shanghai	6,321	6,321	0
Beijing	Beijing	5,598	2,418	3,180
Tianjin	Tianjin	5,143	3,943	1,999
Shenyang	Liaoning	4,003	2,658	1,345
Wuhan	Hubei	3,252	2,624	628
Guangzhou	Guangdong	3,148	1,943	1,205
Chongqing	Sichuan	2,634	456	2,179
Harbin	Heilongjiang	2,543	2,543	0
Chengdu	Sichuan	2,467	1,238	1,229
Zibo	Shandong	2,232	2,232	0
Xi'an	Shaanxi	2,197	1,227	969
Nanjing	Jiangsu	2,134	1,206	928
Liupanshui	Guizhou	2,090	2,090	0
Taiyuan	Shanxi	1,775	1,240	534
Changchun	Jilin	1,757	1,307	450
Dalian	Liaoning	1,479	967	512
Zhengzhou	Henan	1,428	900	527
Kunming	Yunnan	1,426	581	845
Lanzhou	Gansu	1,416	1,183	234
Jinan	Shandong	1,338	876	462
Tangshan	Hebei	1,338	1,338	0
Guiyang	Guizhou	1,319	740	579
Taian	Shandong	1,270	1,270	0
Zaozhuang	-do-	1,238	1,238	0
Pingxiang	Jiangxi	1,225	265	960
Qiqihar	Heilongjiang	1,224	1,224	0
Anshan	Liaoning	1,214	888	326
Fushun	-do-	1,193	1,050	142
Hangzhou	Zhejiang	1,192	1,192	0
Qingdao	Shandong	1,174	1,174	0
Fuzhou	Fujian	1,129	787	342
Shaoxing	Zhejiang	1,107	134	973
Jilin	Jilin	1,079	804	275
Changsha	Hunan	1,076	834	243
Baotou	Nei Monggol	1,070	1,070	0
Shijiazhuang	Hebei	1,066	1,066	0
Nanchang	Jiangxi	1,061	832	230
Huainan	Anhui	1,025	1,025	0

d.o.—ditto
*Approximate because of rounding.

Source: Based on information from *Zhongguo 1982 Nian Renkou Pucha Ziliao (Dianzi Jisuanji Huizong)* [1982 Population Census of China (Results of Computer Tabulation)], Beijing, March 1985, 64–85.

Table 9. Size and Distribution of Minority Nationalities, 1982

Minority Nationality	Approximate Population	Major Areas of Distribution
Zhuang	13,400,000	Guangxi-Zhuang Autonomous Region; Yunnan, Guangdong, Guizhou provinces
Hui	7,200,000	Ningxia-Hui Autonomous Region; Gansu, Henan, Qinghai, Yunnan, Hebei, Shandong provinces; Xinjiang-Uygur Autonomous Region
Uygur	6,000,000	Xinjiang-Uygur Autonomous Region; Hunan Province
Yi	5,500,000	Yunnan, Sichuan, Guizhou provinces; Guangxi-Zhuang Autonomous Region
Miao	5,000,000	Guizhou, Hunan, Yunnan, Sichuan provinces; Guangxi-Zhuang Autonomous Region
Manchu	4,300,000	Liaoning, Heilongjiang, Jilin, Hebei provinces; Nei Monggol Autonomous Region; Beijing Municipality
Zang (Tibetan)	3,800,000	Xizang Autonomous Region; Sichuan, Qinghai, Gansu provinces
Mongolian	3,400,000	Nei Monggol Autonomous Region; Liaoning Province; Xinjiang-Uygur Autonomous Region
Tujia	2,800,000	Hubei, Hunan, Sichuan provinces
Buyi	2,100,000	Guizhou Province
Korean	1,800,000	Jilin, Heilongjiang, Liaoning provinces
Dong	1,400,000	Guizhou, Hunan provinces; Guangxi-Zhuang Autonomous Region
Yao	1,400,000	Guangxi-Zhuang Autonomous Region; Hunan, Yunnan, Guangdong provinces
Bai	1,100,000	Yunnan Province
Hani	1,100,000	-do-
Kazak	900,000	Xinjiang-Uygur Autonomous Region
Li	890,000	Guangdong, Guizhou provinces
Dai	840,000	Yunnan Province
Lisu	480,000	-do-
She	370,000	Fujian, Zhejiang provinces
Lahu	300,000	Yunnan Province
Va	300,000	-do-
Shui	290,000	Guizhou Province
Dongxiang	280,000	Gansu Province; Xinjiang-Uygur Autonomous Region
Naxi	250,000	Yunnan Province
Tu	160,000	Qinghai Province
Kirgiz	114,000	Xinjiang-Uygur Autonomous Region
Qiang	100,000	Sichuan Province
Daur	95,000	Nei Monggol Autonomous Region; Heilongjiang Province
Jingpo	93,000	Yunnan Province
Mulao	90,000	Guangxi-Zhuang Autonomous Region
Xibe	84,000	Liaoning Province; Xinjiang-Uygur Autonomous Region

Table 9.—Continued.

Minority Nationality	Population	Approximate Major Areas of Distribution
Salar	69,000	Qinghai, Gansu provinces
Bulang	58,000	Yunnan Province
Gelao	54,000	Guizhou Province
Maonan	38,000	Guangxi-Zhuang Autonomous Region
Tajik	27,000	Xinjiang-Uygur Autonomous Region
Pumi	24,000	Yunnan Province
Nu	23,000	-do-
Achang	20,000	-do-
Ewenki	19,000	Nei Monggol Autonomous Region; Heilongjiang Province
Jing	13,000	Guangxi-Zhuang Autonomous Region; Guizhou, Guangdong provinces
Benglong	12,000	Yunnan Province
Uzbek	12,000	Xinjiang-Uygur Autonomous Region
Jinuo	12,000	Yunnan Province
Yugur	11,000	Gansu Province
Baoan	9,000	-do-
Drung	4,600	Yunnan Province
Tartar	4,100	Xinjiang-Uygur Autonomous Region
Oroqen	4,100	Nei Monggol Autonomous Region; Heilongjiang Province
Russian	2,900	Xinjiang-Uygur Autonomous Region
Gaoshan	1,700	Fujian, Guizhou provinces
Hezhe	1,500	Heilongjiang Province
Moinba	1,140	Xizang Autonomous Region
Lhoba	1,100	-do-
Other	800,000	Guizhou, Yunnan provinces

d.o.—ditto

Source: Based on information from *Zhongguo 1982 Nian Renkou Pucha Ziliao (Dianzi Jisuanji Huizong)* [1982 Population Census of China (Results of Computer Tabulation)], Beijing, March 1985, 218–31.

Table 10. Number of Schools and Students, Selected Years, 1957–85

Kind of School	1957	1965	1975	1985
Number of schools				
Institutions of higher learning [1]	229	434	387	1,016
Secondary schools				
Regular	11,096	18,102	123,505	93,221
Technical	728	871	1,326	2,529
Teacher training	592	394	887	1,028
Agricultural and vocational	n.a.	61,626	n.a.	28,070
Total secondary schools	12,474 [2]	80,993	125,718	104,848
Primary schools	547,306	1,681,939	1,093,317	832,309
Kindergartens	16,420	19,226	171,749	172,262
Schools for blind and for deaf students	66	266	246	350
Number of students [3]				
Institutions of higher learning [1]	44.1	67.4	50.1	170.3
Secondary schools				
Regular	628.1	933.8	4,466.1	4,706.0
Technical	48.2	39.2	40.5	101.3
Teacher training	29.6	15.5	30.2	55.8
Agricultural and vocational	n.a.	443.3	n.a.	229.5
Total secondary schools	708.1 [2]	1,431.8	4,536.8	5,092.6
Primary schools	6,428.3	11,620.9	15,094.1	13,370.2
Kindergartens	108.8	171.3	620.0	1,479.7
Schools for blind and for deaf students	0.8	2.3	2.7	3.8

n.a.—not available.

[1] Institutions of higher learning include colleges and universities, professional colleges, and scientific research institutions. They do not include adult education, spare-time colleges, or correspondence schools.

[2] Total as provided in original source.

[3] Tens of thousands.

Source: Based on information from China, State Statistical Bureau, *Statistical Yearbook of China, 1986*. Oxford, New York, Tokyo: Oxford University Press, 1986, 623, 626.

Table 11. Composition of Gross Value of Agricultural Output, Selected Years, 1955–85
(in percentage)

Sector	1955	1965	1975	1985
Crops	81.8	75.8	72.5	49.8
Livestock	12.2	14.0	14.0	14.5
Forestry	1.2	2.0	2.9	3.8
Fishery	0.4	1.7	1.5	1.8
Sideline production	4.4	6.5	9.1	30.1
TOTAL	100.0	100.0	100.0	100.0

Source: Based on information from China, State Statistical Bureau, *Zhongguo Tongji Nianjian* (China Statistical Yearbook), Beijing, 1985 and 1986, various pages.

Table 12. Manufactured Agricultural Inputs, Selected Years, 1955–85

Item	Unit	1955	1965	1975	1985
Chemical Fertilizer					
Production	thousands of tons	255	1,726	5,247	13,350
Use	thousands of tons	200	1,942	5,369	17,758
Tractors					
Large	thousands	5	73	345	864
Small	thousands	- - -	4	599	3,810
Rural electrical power consumption	millions of kilowatt hours	104	3,710	18,310	51,200
Chemical pesticides production	thousands of tons	26	193	422	205

- - - means negligible.

Source: Based on information from United States, Department of Agriculture, Economic Research Service, *Agricultural Statistics of the People's Republic of China, 1949–82*, Statistical Bulletin No. 714, October 1984, 29–34; and China, State Statistical Bureau, *Zhongguo Tongji Nianjian* (China Statistical Yearbook), Beijing, 1986, 147–49.

Table 13. Grain Production and Per Capita Consumption of Selected Products, Selected Years, 1955–85

	1955 [1]	1965	1975	1985
Grain Production [2]				
Wheat	22,965	25,220	45,310	85,810
Rice	78,025	87,720	125,560	168,857
Corn	20,320	23,660	47,220	63,830
Sorghum	9,529	7,100	10,750	5,610
Millet	10,276	6,200	7,150	5,980
Potatoes	15,120	19,860	28,570	26,040
Soybeans	9,120	6,140	7,240	10,509
Other	18,580	18,625	12,765	12,474
Total grain production	183,935	194,525	284,565	379,110
Per capita consumption [3]				
Grain	195.0	183.0	190.0	254.0
Edible oil	2.2	1.7	1.7	5.1
Pork	4.9	6.3	7.6	14.0
Beef and mutton	1.0	1.0	0.7	1.3
Poultry	0.5	0.4	0.4	1.6
Eggs	1.2	1.4	1.6	5.0
Aquatic products	4.0	3.3	3.3	4.9
Sugar	1.1	1.7	2.3	5.6
Total per capita consumption	274.7	198.8	209.6	291.5

[1] Estimate.
[2] Thousands of tons.
[3] Kilograms.

Source: Based on information from China, State Statistical Bureau, *Zhongguo Tongji Nianjian* (China Statistical Yearbook), Beijing, 1986.

Table 14. Agricultural Exports and Imports, 1985
(in millions of United States dollars)

	Value
Exports	
Textile fibers	1,163
Fresh and frozen meat	987
Fruits and vegetables	984
Grain	782
Coffee, tea, and spices	524
Oilseed and nuts	502
Crude animal and vegetable materials	494
Live animals	329
Other	747
Total exports	6,512
Imports	
Textile fibers	1,576
Grain	1,050
Wood	647
Crude rubber	315
Sugar	216
Tobacco	201
Other	655
Total imports	4,660

Source: Based on information from United States Central Intelligence Agency, *China: International Trade, Fourth Quarter, 1985*, Research Paper, No. EA CIT 86-001, July 1986, 8-11.

Table 15. Production, Use, and Import of Major Commodities, Selected Years, 1952-85
(in millions of tons)

Year	Grain Output	Cotton Output	Chemical Fertilizer Use	Grain Imports
1952	161	1.3	0.078	0.0
1957	191	1.6	0.373	0.2
1965	195	2.1	1.942	6.4
1970	240	2.3	4.266*	5.4
1975	275	2.4	5.369	3.7
1980	321	2.7	12.694	13.4
1985	379	4.2	17.758	5.7

*Estimate.

Source: Based on information from China, State Statistical Bureau, *Zhongguo Tongji Nianjian* (China Statistical Yearbook), Beijing, 1981-86, various pages; and *Zhongguo Nongye Nianjian* (China Agricultural Yearbook), Beijing, 1980-86, various pages.

Table 16. Gross Value of Industrial Output, by Region, 1952, 1957, and 1983
(in millions of 1952 yuan) [1]

Region [2] Provincial-Level Unit	1952	1957	1983 [3]	1983 [4]
Northeast				
Heilongjiang	1,189	3,930	34,406	28,850
Jilin	1,102	2,378	24,704	16,507
Liaoning	4,523	11,710	71,549	51,664
Total northeast	6,814	18,018	130,659	97,021
North				
Beijing	825	2,300	39,954	25,060
Hebei	1,342	2,805	33,660	25,269
Nei Monggol	192	757	9,195	7,534
Shanxi	643	1,832	19,055	15,187
Tianjin	1,836	4,300	34,830	22,920
Total north	4,838	11,994	136,694	95,970
East				
Anhui	628	1,501	20,348	16,069
Fujian	414	1,224	13,276	9,581
Jiangsu	2,584	4,553	81,970	56,945
Jiangxi	575	1,173	13,945	10,620
Shandong	2,091	4,068	53,625	40,558
Shanghai	6,510	12,969	102,629	67,858
Zhejiang	1,099	2,374	37,783	26,811
Total east	13,901	27,862	323,576	228,442
Central-South				
Henan	881	1,705	31,033	23,664
Hubei	955	2,799	43,268	31,266
Hunan	770	1,819	28,574	29,586
Guangdong	1,745	3,812	44,016	30,594
Guangxi	343	798	12,585	9,488
Total central-south	4,694	10,933	159,476	124,598

Table 16.—Continued.

Region [2] Provincial-Level Unit	1952	1957	1983 [3]	1983 [4]
Southwest				
Guizhou	269	605	8,569	6,223
Sichuan	1,649	4,873	46,706	33,997
Xizang	- - -	10	154	130
Yunnan	333	1,101	11,270	8,916
Total southwest	2,251	6,589	66,699	49,266
Northwest				
Gansu	230	560	12,132	8,811
Ningxia	10	25	2,145	1,612
Qinghai	837	101	1,928	1,427
Shaanxi	381	1,263	18,538	12,945
Xinjiang	175	446	5,947	5,349
Total northwest	1,633	2,395	40,690	30,144
Total	34,031	77,791	857,797	599,232

- - - means negligible.

[1] For value of yuan—see Glossary.

[2] Regional divisions are for descriptive purposes only and have no official administrative significance.

[3] Actual.

[4] To make the shares of output comparable and the output indexes measure real growth, the data for 1983 are converted from 1980 prices to 1952 prices by deflating the output of industrial branches of industry within each provincial-level unit by the national price indexes for the respective branches.

Source: Based on information from Robert Michael Field, "China: The Changing Structure of Industry," pages 526–27, in United States Congress, 99th, 2d Session, Joint Economic Committee, ed., *China's Economy Looks Toward the Year 2000, 1: The Four Modernizations*, Washington, 1986.

Table 17. Composition of Trade, Selected Years, 1970–85 [1]
(in percentage)

	1970	1975	1980	1985
Exports				
Food and live animals	30.6	28.7	17.0	12.5
Beverages and tobacco	0.9	1.1	0.6	0.4
Crude materials (including textiles, fibers, and wastes)	17.6	11.8	9.6	9.4
Petroleum and petroleum products	2.8	14.4	23.3	23.0
Edible oils	1.2	0.8	0.4	4.2
Chemicals	5.3	5.0	6.2	5.1
Manufactured goods (including finished textiles and iron and steel products)	27.4	23.1	23.3	19.8
Machinery and transport equipment	3.5	3.6	3.2	3.8
Miscellaneous manufactures	10.4	11.2	15.9	21.3
Other	0.2	0.4	0.3	4.2
Total exports [2]	99.9	100.1	99.8	103.7
Imports				
Food and live animals	16.1	11.9	14.8	4.1
Crude materials (excluding fuels)	11.5	10.7	17.2	8.4
Petroleum and petroleum products	2.0	1.9	0.9	1.3
Edible oils	0.2	0.6	0.9	1.3
Chemicals	15.2	11.9	11.3	9.3
Manufactured goods (including iron and steel products)	33.7	32.1	23.7	27.5
Machinery and transportation equipment	19.8	29.4	27.7	41.5
Miscellaneous manufactures	1.2	1.1	2.5	6.2
Other	- - -	0.4	0.9	1.5
Total imports [2]	97.7	100.0	99.9	101.1

- - - means negligible.
[1] Free on board.
[2] Totals do not add to 100 percent because of rounding.

Source: Based on information from United States Central Intelligence Agency, *Handbook of Economic Statistics, 1986*, September 1986, 106–107.

Table 18. Major Trading Partners, 1986

	Percentage of Trade
Exports	
Hong Kong	31.6
Japan	15.3
United States	8.5
United Kingdom	4.6
Soviet Union	4.0
Singapore	3.9
Jordan	3.4
West Germany	3.3
Netherlands	1.5
Poland	1.5
Other	22.4
Total exports	100.0
Imports	
Japan	28.9
Hong Kong	13.1
United States	10.8
West Germany	8.4
Soviet Union	3.4
Australia	3.2
Italy	2.6
United Kingdom	2.3
Canada	2.3
France	1.7
Other	23.3
Total imports	100.0

Source: Based on information from China, General Administration of Customs, *Chinese Customs Statistics, No. 1 (1987)* [Hong Kong], April 1987, table 4, in *Business China* [Hong Kong], June 22, 1987, 92.

Appendix B

Chronology and Lists

1 Chronology of Chinese Communist Party National Party Congresses and Plenums, 1921–87
2 Selected Foreign-Trade Corporations and Enterprises, 1987
3 Government Organizations, 1987
4 Diplomatic Relations, 1949–87

Appendix B

Table 1. Chronology of Chinese National Party Congresses and Plenums, 1921–87

Congress Location	Plenum	Date	Significance
First			
Shanghai	First	July 1921	Attended by thirteen representatives; elected general secretary and three-man Central Bureau; developed general political program. Mao Zedong recording secretary. Chinese Communist Party (CCP) had fifty-seven members.
Second			
Shanghai	First	July 1922	Adopted concept of democratic centralism (see Glossary), elected Central Executive Committee (in 1927 shortened to Central Committee), and decided to join Comintern (see Glossary). Accepted united front with Guomindang, although opposed by some, as temporary expedient to combat warlords and foreign imperialism. Party grew to 123 members.
Third			
Guangzhou	First	June 1923	Under Comintern pressure, formally sanctioned united-front policy made CCP members concurrently Guomindang members. Tension built as CCP attempted to fulfill conflicting goals of national and social revolutions. Party had 432 members in 1923.

Table 1.—Continued.

Congress Location	Plenum	Date	Significance
Fourth			
Shanghai	First	January 1925	CCP's activist role in labor and peasant circles augmented by explosive anti-imperialist social movements. Growing CCP influence increased strains in united front. Secretariat established to handle documentation and communications. Party had 950 members by 1925.
Beijing	Second	October 1925	
Beijing	Third	July 1926	
Fifth			
Wuhan	First	April–May 1927	Elected CCP's first Political Bureau. Tensions mounted within party over concessions to maintain united front. After abandonment of united front policy in mid-July, the August 7 Emergency Conference elected new party leadership, emphasized tight organization and party discipline, and called for armed struggle against Guomindang. Over 10,000 party members on rolls.

Table 1.—Continued.

Congress Location	Plenum	Date	Significance
Sixth			
Moscow	First	June-July 1928	Conflict arose among leaders concerning proper course for the Chinese revolution: revolutionary movement responsive to local—mainly rural—conditions; urban revolution; or strict adherence to Moscow's instructions. Mao Zedong, a leader in rural-oriented group, emerged dominant by 1935, bolstered by his military skill during the Long March (1934–35). Mao Zedong Thought formally adopted at the Seventh Plenum. The Sino-Japanese War (1937–45) and the concomitant second united front with Guomindang against Japan became sources of inner-party tension. Party grew from 40,000 in 1928 to 1.2 million by 1945.
Shanghai	Second	November 1929	
Shanghai	Third	September 1930	
Shanghai	Fourth	January 1931	
Ruijin	Fifth	January 1934	
Yan'an	Sixth	October 1938	
Yan'an	Seventh	April 1945	
Seventh			
Yan'an	First	April-June 1945	Party Constitution of 1945 stressed greater centralism. After defeat of the Guomindang and establishment of the People's Republic of China in October 1949, party emphasis on indoctrination, rectification, and mass campaigns was supplemented with economic recovery and consolidation programs. Focus of party work shifted from countryside to cities. Party membership totaled 10.2 million by 1956.
Xibaipo	Second	March 1949	
Beijing	Third	June 1950	
Beijing	Fourth	February 1954	
Beijing	Fifth	April 1955	
Beijing	Sixth	October 1955	
Beijing	Seventh	September 1956	

Table 1.—Continued.

Congress Location	Plenum	Date	Significance
Eighth [First Session]		September 1956	
Beijing	First	September 1956	Mao advocated "struggle" between the two opposing lines—rapid communization and continuing revolution, which he favored, and central planning, reliance on party organizations, and limited individual incentives. The failure of the Great Leap Forward (1956-60) led to a temporary ascendancy of Liu Shaoqi, Deng Xiaoping, and others who stressed planned development. In response, Mao turned to Lin Biao who was building a People's Liberation Army (PLA) power base, and reverted to factionalism, calling his opponents "revisionists." The ensuing Cultural Revolution (1966-76) eventually required the PLA to restore stability because party and state organizations had been disrupted. CCP membership reached 20 million by 1966.
Beijing	Second	November 1956	
Beijing	Third	September-October 1957	
Beijing	Fourth	May 1958	
[Second Session]		May 1958	
Beijing	Fifth	May 1958	
Wuchang	Sixth	November-December 1958	
Shanghai	Seventh	April 1959	
Lushan	Eighth	August 1959	
Beijing	Ninth	January 1961	
Beijing	Tenth	September 1962	
Beijing	Eleventh	August 1966	
Beijing	Twelfth	October 1968	

Table 1.—Continued.

Congress Location	Plenum	Date	Significance
Ninth			
Beijing	First	April 1969	Party constitution of 1969 named Lin Biao as Mao's successor. Mao continued as chairman with Lin as vice chairman. Mao Zedong Thought extolled. New Central Committee included 45 percent military representation (27 percent on the Eighth Central Committee). Political outcome was to empower three factions: the Maoists; administrators around Zhou Enlai; and the PLA around Lin Biao. After Lin's 1971 attempted coup, PLA influence was reduced. Party membership was 28 million by 1973.
Lushan	Second	September 1970	
Tenth			
Beijing	First	August 1973	Zhou's Enlai's policies strengthened with rehabilitation of purged leaders, notably Deng Xiaoping. After Zhou's death (January 1976), tensions increased. Mao's death in September 1976 precipitated open confrontation. Hua Guofeng, Mao's successor, arrested the Gang of Four and attempted to consolidate his position. But by July 1977, Hua faced a challenge from Deng Xiaoping, who regained all his posts at the Third Plenum. Party members increased to 35 million in 1977.
Beijing	Second	January 1975	
Beijing	Third	July 1977	

Table 1.—Continued.

Congress Location	Plenum	Date	Significance
Eleventh			
Beijing	First	August 1977	Hua Guofeng continued party chairman. New party constitution of 1977 approved. Deng Xiaoping confirmed as party vice chairman, giving him a platform from which to advocate reform. Hua's links to the Maoist legacy undercut his ability to lead, and at the Third Plenum, Deng's practical approach set the CCP on a course of reform instead of class struggle. Deng's forces assumed command with the rise of Zhao Ziyang and Hu Yaobang; reassessment of Mao's role preserved Mao Zedong Thought but condemned his mistakes in later years. Hua's resignation as party chairman was accepted and Hu Yaobang became chairman, as well as secretary general of the restored Secretariat. Party ranks increased to 40 million by 1981.
Beijing	Second	February 1978	
Beijing	Third	December 1978	
Beijing	Fourth	September 1979	
Beijing	Fifth	February 1980	
Beijing	Sixth	June 1981	

Table 1.—Continued.

Congress Location	Plenum	Date	Significance
Twelfth			
Beijing	First	September 1982	With emphasis on collective leadership, the new party constitution of 1982 abolished the post of party chairman. Deng further consolidated the reform leadership's position with high-level appointments and retirements of party veterans to new Central Advisory Commission. Party rectification and key urban economic reforms initiated. Additional elderly leaders retired and younger, better educated ones elevated at September 18–23, 1985 National Conference of Party Delegates. Hu Yaobang demoted at enlarged Political Bureau meeting in January 1987 for failing to control student demonstrations and thereby undermining party discipline and predominance. Party membership reached 46 million by 1987.
Beijing	Second	October 1983	
Beijing	Third	October 1984	
Beijing	Fourth	September 1985	
Beijing	Fifth	September 1985	
Beijing	Sixth	September 1986	

Table 2. Selected Foreign-Trade Corporations and Enterprises, 1987

Corporation	Subordinate to
China Electronics Import and Export Corporation (CEIEC)	Ministry of Electronics Industry
China Light Industrial Corporation for Foreign Economic and Technical Cooperation (LIGHTIND)	Ministry of Light Industry
China National Aero-Technology Import and Export Corporation (CATIC)	Ministry of Astronautics
China National Agricultural Machinery Import and Export Corporation (AGRIMEX)	State Machine-Building Industry Commission
China National Arts and Crafts Import and Export Corporation (ARTCHINA)	Ministry of Foreign Economic Relations and Trade
China National Cereals, Oils, and Foodstuffs Import and Export Corporation (CEROILFOOD)	Ministry of Foreign Economic Relations and Trade
China National Chemicals Import and Export Corporation (SINOCHEM)	Ministry of Foreign Economic Relations and Trade
China National Foreign Trade Transportation Import and Export Corporation (SINOTRANS)	Ministry of Foreign Economic Relations and Trade
China National Import and Export Corporation of Medical Health Products (MEHECO)	Ministry of Foreign Economic Relations and Trade
China National Instrument Import and Export Corporation (INSTRIMPEX)	Ministry of Foreign Relations and Trade
China National Light Industrial Products Import and Export Corporation (INDUSTRY)	Ministry of Foreign Economic Relations and Trade
China National Machinery and Equipment Import and Export Corporation (EQUIMPEX)	State Machine-Building Industry Commission
China National Machinery Import and Export Corporation (MACHIMPEX)	Ministry of Foreign Economic Relations and Trade
China National Metallurgical Import and Export Corporation (CMIEC)	Ministry of Metallurgical Industry
China National Metals and Minerals Import and Export Corporation (MINMETALS)	Ministry of Foreign Economic Relations and Trade
China National Native Produce and Animal Byproducts Import and Export Corporation (CHINATUHSU)	Ministry of Foreign Economic Relations and Trade

Table 2.—Continued.

Corporation	Subordinate to
China National Offshore Oil Corporation (CNOOC)	Ministry of Petroleum Industry
China National Packaging Import and Export Corporation (CHINAPACK)	Ministry of Foreign Economic Relations and Trade
China National Publications Import and Export Corporation (PUBIMPORT)	State Science and Technology Commission
China National Seed Corporation (CNSC)	Ministry of Agriculture, Animal Husbandry, and Fishery
China National Technical Import and Export Corporation (TECHIMPORT)	Ministry of Foreign Economic Relations and Trade
China National Textiles Import and Export Corporation (CHINATEX)	Ministry of Foreign Economic Relations and Trade
China Northern Industrial Corporation (NORINCO)	State Machine-Building Industry Commission
China Nuclear Energy Industry Corporation (CNIEC)	Ministry of Nuclear Industry
China Ocean Shipping Company (COSCO) . .	Ministry of Communications
China Oriental Scientific Instruments Import and Export Corporation (ASCHI)	Chinese Academy of Sciences
China Petrochemical Corporation (SINOPEC)	State Council
China Scientific Instruments and Materials Corporation (CSMIC)	State Science and Technology Commission
China State Shipbuilding Corporation (CSSC)	State Council
Great Wall Industrial Corporation (GWIC) . . .	Ministry of Astronautics

*Table 3. Government Organizations, 1987**

Leading Groups

Central Job Titles Reform
Commodity Prices
Electronics Industry Invigoration
Enterprise Consolidation
Foreign Funds and Management
General Survey of China's Industry
Nationwide "Safety Month" Activities
Nuclear Power Plants
Rural Energy Development
Science and Technology
Sea, Land, and Air Ports

Ministries

Aeronautics
Agriculture, Animal Husbandry, and Fishery
Astronautics
Chemical Industry
Civil Affairs
Coal Industry
Commerce
Communications
Culture
Electronics Industry
Finance
Foreign Affairs
Foreign Economic Relations and Trade
Forestry
Geology and Minerals
Justice
Labor and Personnel
Light Industry
Metallurgical Industry
National Defense
Nuclear Industry
Petroleum Industry
Posts and Telecommunications
Public Health
Public Security
Radio, Cinema, and Television
Railways
State Security
Supervision
Textile Industry
Urban and Rural Construction and Environmental Protection
Water Resources and Electric Power

Commissions

National Defense Science, Technology, and Industry
State Economic
State Education
State Family Planning
State Machine-Building Industry
State Nationalities
State Planning
State Physical Culture and Sports
State Restructuring of Economic System
State Science and Technology

Table 3.—Continued.

Agencies	
Auditing Administration	State Environmental Protection Bureau
China Council for the Promotion of International Trade	State Import and Export Commodities Inspection Administration
China Shipping Inspection Bureau	State Materials and Equipment Bureau
China Travel and Tourism Bureau	State Meteorological Administration
China Welfare Fund	State Oceanography Bureau
Foreign Experts Bureau	State Patent Bureau
General Administration of Civil Aviation	State Pharmaceutical Administration
General Administration of Customs	State Seismological Administration
Nuclear Safety Administration	State Standardization Bureau
Press and Publications Administration	State Statistical Bureau
Religious Affairs Administration	State Supplies Bureau
State Administration of Exchange Control	State Tobacco Monopoly Administration
State Archives Bureau	State Weights and Measures Bureau
State Building Materials Industry Administration	Trade Mark Bureau
State Commodities Prices General Administration	Xinhua (New China) News Agency

Offices	
Central Greening Commission	Hong Kong and Macao Affairs Office
China Rural Development Research Center	Media and Publications Office
Chinese Olympic Committee	National Academic Degree Committee
Counselors Office	National Antarctic Survey Committee
Economic Legislation Research Center	Northeastern Economic Zone Planning Office
Economic, Technological, and Social Development Research Center	Special Economic Zones Office
Environmental Protection Commission	State Commission for Guiding the Examination of Economic Management Cadres
Government Offices Administrative Bureau	State Language Work Committee

Banks	
Agricultural Bank	Communications Bank
Bank of China	People's Bank of China
China Industrial and Commercial Bank	People's Construction Bank
China Investment Bank	People's Insurance Company of China

*The organizations in this list are subordinate to the State Council.

Table 4. Diplomatic Relations, 1949–87 [1]

Country	Year Established [2]	Country	Year Established [2]
Afghanistan	1955	Guyana	1972
Albania	1949	Hungary	1949
Algeria [3]	1958	Iceland	1971
Angola	1983	India	1950
Antigua and Barbuda	1983	Indonesia [6]	1950
Argentina	1972	Iran	1971
Australia	1972	Iraq	1958
Austria	1971	Ireland	1979
Bangladesh	1975	Italy	1970
Barbados	1977	Jamaica	1972
Belgium	1971	Japan	1972
Belize	1987	Jordan	1977
Benin [4]	1964	Kenya	1963
Bolivia	1985	Kiribati	1980
Botswana	1975	Korea, North	1949
Brazil	1974	Kuwait	1971
Bulgaria	1949	Laos	1962
Burkina Faso	1973	Lebanon	1971
Burma	1950	Lesotho	1983
Burundi [4]	1963	Liberia	1977
Cambodia [5]	1958	Libya	1978
Cameroon	1971	Luxembourg	1972
Canada	1970	Madagascar	1972
Cape Verde	1976	Malaysia	1974
Central African Republic [4]	1964	Maldives	1972
		Mali	1960
Chad	1972	Malta	1972
Chile	1970	Mauritania	1965
Colombia	1980	Mauritius	1972
Comoros	1975	Mexico	1972
Congo	1964	Mongolia	1949
Côte d'Ivoire	1983	Morocco	1958
Cuba	1960	Mozambique	1975
Cyprus	1972	Nepal	1955
Czechoslovakia	1949	Netherlands [7]	1954
Denmark	1950	New Zealand	1972
Djibouti	1979	Nicaragua	1985
Ecuador	1980	Niger	1974
Egypt	1956	Nigeria	1971
Equatorial Guinea	1970	Norway	1954
Ethiopia	1970	Oman	1978
Fiji	1975	Pakistan	1951
Finland	1950	Papua New Guinea	1976
France	1964	Peru	1971
Gabon	1974	Philippines	1975
Gambia	1974	Poland	1949
Germany, East	1949	Portugal	1979
Germany, West	1972	Romania	1949
Ghana [4]	1960	Rwanda	1971
Greece	1972	San Marino [8]	1971
Grenada	1985	Sao Tomé and Principe	1975
Guinea	1959	Senegal	1971
Guinea-Bissau	1974	Seychelles	1976

Table 4.—Continued.

Country	Year Established [2]	Country	Year Established [2]
Sierra Leone	1971	Turkey	1971
Somalia	1960	Uganda	1962
Soviet Union	1949	United Arab Emirates	1984
Spain	1973	United Kingdom [7]	1954
Sri Lanka	1957	United States	1979
Sudan	1959	Vanuatu	1982
Suriname	1976	Venezuela	1974
Sweden	1950	Vietnam	1950
Switzerland	1950	Western Samoa	1975
Syria	1956	Yemen, North	1956
Tanzania	1964	Yemen, South	1968
Thailand	1975	Yugoslavia	1955
Togo	1972	Zaire [4]	1961
Trinidad and Tobago	1974	Zambia	1964
Tunisia [4]	1964	Zimbabwe	1980

[1] Israel (1950) and Bhutan (1971) have recognized China, but diplomatic relations have not been established. China and Singapore have exchanged commercial representative offices since 1981, but have no formal diplomatic ties.

[2] When a discrepancy exists between the year of recognition and the year in which full diplomatic relations went into effect, the latter date is given.

[3] China established diplomatic relations with the provisional government of Algeria in 1958 before Algerian independence in 1962.

[4] China's relations with six African nations were broken off in the 1960s and reestablished in the 1970s: Benin (broken off, 1966, resumed, 1972), Burundi (broken off, 1965, resumed, 1971), Central African Republic (broken off, 1966, resumed, 1976), Ghana (broken off, 1966, resumed, 1972), Tunisia (broken off, 1964, resumed 1971), and Zaire (broken off, 1961, resumed, 1972). The Chinese embassy in Zaire closed soon after it opened in 1961.

[5] Beijing recognizes the exiled Coalition Government of Democratic Kampuchea led by Prince Norodom Sihanouk.

[6] Beijing's ties with Jakarta were broken off in 1967 after Indonesian accusations of Chinese involvement in a coup attempt. Diplomatic relations had not been restored as of mid-1987.

[7] China's relations with the Netherlands and the United Kingdom were at the chargé d'affaires level from 1954 until 1972, when they were upgraded to the ambassadorial level. In 1981 China reduced its level of representation in the Netherlands to chargé d'affaires to protest the sale of Dutch submarines to Taiwan. Ambassadorial relations were reestablished in 1984.

[8] Consular relations only.

Appendix C

THE PEOPLE'S LIBERATION ARMY AT A GLANCE

Ground Forces

Strength: 2,110,000

Group armies (main forces)

35 armies, comprising:
- 118 infantry divisions
- 13 armored divisions
- 17 artillery divisions
- 16 antiaircraft artillery divisions
- At least 71 independent regiments and 21 independent battalions (artillery, antiaircraft artillery, signal, antichemical warfare, reconnaissance, and engineer)

Regional forces

73 divisions
140 independent regiments

Major weapons systems

Armor
- Type 80 main battle tank—105mm gun, 38 tons, had not yet entered production in 1987
- Type 69 main battle tank—105mm gun, 36 tons, improved Type 59 tank
- Type 59 main battle tank—100mm gun, 36 tons, improved copy of Soviet T-54 tank
- Type 63 light tank—85mm gun, 18 tons, improved version of Soviet PT-76 amphibious light tank
- Type 62 light tank—85mm gun, 21 tons, reconnaissance version of Type 59 tank
- T-34 main battle tank—85mm gun, 32 tons, Soviet manufacture, may be given to regional forces
- M-1984 armored personnel carrier—6 x 6 wheeled type with 23mm gun
- M-1974 armored personnel carrier—2 crew, 20 passengers, 12.7mm machine gun, tracked, amphibious
- M-1967 armored personnel carrier—4 crew, 10 passengers, tracked, amphibious

Artillery
- 152mm gun—Type 83, entered service in 1980s
- 152mm self-propelled howitzer—Type 83, entered service in 1980s
- 152mm gun/howitzer—Type 66, towed, copy of Soviet D-20
- 152mm howitzer—copy of Soviet M-1943
- 130mm field gun—Type 59-1, towed, same chassis as 122mm gun
- 122mm gun/howitzer—Type 83, copy of Soviet D-30
- 122mm gun—Type 60, towed, copy of Soviet D-74
- 122mm howitzer—Type 54, towed, copy of Soviet M-1938
- 122mm self-propelled howitzer—Type 54 howitzer mounted on M-1967 armored personnel carrier
- 85mm antitank gun—Type 55, towed, copy of Soviet D-44
- 130mm rocket launcher—Type 70, 19-tube, armored-personnel-carrier-mounted
- 130mm rocket launcher—Type 63, 19-tube, truck-mounted
- 122mm rocket launcher—Chinese version of Soviet BM-21
- 107mm rocket launcher—Type 63-1, 12-tube, towed
- M-1979 antitank minelaying rocket launcher—10 tubes

Antiaircraft artillery
- 100mm antiaircraft gun—Type 59, radar, towed, copy of Soviet KS-19
- 85mm antiaircraft gun—radar, towed, copy of Soviet KS18
- 57mm antiaircraft gun—Type 59, radar or optic, towed, copy of Soviet S-60
- 37mm antiaircraft gun—Type 65, optic, towed, twin-barrel
- 37mm antiaircraft gun—Type 55, optic, towed, copy of Soviet M-1939
- 14.5mm antiaircraft machine gun—Type 58, optic, towed, 4-barrel copy of Soviet ZPU-2
- 14.5mm antiaircraft machine gun—Type 56, optic, towed, twin-barrel copy of Soviet ZPU-4

* * * * *

Air Force

Strength: 390,000, including 220,000 air defense personnel
Combat elements organized in group armies of varying numbers of air divisions

Weapons

100 surface-to-air missile sites
16,000 antiaircraft guns

Aircraft

30 F–8/Finback fighters (indigenous model derived from Soviet designs)
200 F–7/Fishbed fighters (copy of MiG-21)
3,000 F–6/Farmer fighters (copy of MiG-19)
400 F–5/Fresco fighters (copy of MiG-17)
500 F–4/Fagot (copy of MiG-15) and A–5/Fantan (derived from F–6) ground attack fighters
120 B–6/Badger bombers (copy of Tu-16 intermediate-range bomber)
500 B–5/Beagle bombers (copy of Il-28 medium-range bomber)
550 transports (Y–5, Y–7, Y–8, Il-14, Il-18, Tridents, etc.)
400 helicopters (Z–5/6, Z–9, Alouette, Super Frelon, Bell, Super Puma, and Sikorsky)

* * * * *

Navy

Strength: 350,000 including Coastal Defense Forces, Naval Air Force, and Marine Corps

Ships and boats

Submarines

2 Xia-class nuclear-powered ballistic missile submarines (SSBN) (See Strategic Missile Force)
3 Han-class nuclear-powered attack submarines (SSN)
1 Golf-class ballistic missile submarine (SSB) (trials)
90 Romeo-class diesel attack submarines (SS)
20 Whiskey-class diesel attack submarines (SS)
2 Ming-class training submarines (SS)

Surface combatants

11 Lüda-class destroyers
4 Anshan-class destroyers
20 Jianghu-class frigates
2 Jiangdong-class frigates
4 Chengdu-class frigates
5 Jiangnan-class frigates

14 patrol combatants
181 patrol craft—large and river/coastal
877 fast-attack craft (gun, missile, or torpedo)
33 mine warfare ships
613 amphibious warfare ships and craft
49 support ships

Naval Air Force
50 B-6/Badger bombers
130 B-5/Beagle bombers
600 fighters, including F-4, F-5, F-6, and F-7

* * * * *

Strategic Missile Force

Strength: 100,000 in 6 or 7 divisions

Nuclear warheads: estimated between 225 and 300

Missiles
50 Dongfeng-2 (CSS-1) medium-range ballistic missiles (MRBM) (650nm)
60 Dongfeng-3 (CSS-2) intermediate-range ballistic missiles (IRBM) (1,620nm)
4 Dongfeng-4 (CSS-3) limited-range intercontinental ballistic missiles (ICBM) (3,780nm)
2 Dongfeng-5 (CSS-4) full-range intercontinental ballistic missiles (ICBM) (8,100nm)

Submarines
2 Xia-class nuclear-powered ballistic missile submarines (SSBN), each with 12 CSS-NX-4 IRBMs (1,190nm to 1,620nm)

Source: Based on information from United States Defense Intelligence Agency, *Handbook of the People's Liberation Army*, Washington, 1984, various pages; and International Institute for Strategic Studies, *The Military Balance, 1986–87*, London, 1986, 140–45.

Bibliography

Chapter 1

Barnett, A. Doak. "Ten Years after Mao," *Foreign Affairs*, 65, No. 1, Fall 1986, 37–65.

______. *Uncertain Passage: China's Transition to the Post-Mao Era*. Washington: Brookings Institution, 1974.

Baum, Richard. *Prelude to Revolution: Mao, the Party, and the Peasant Question*. New York: Columbia University Press, 1975.

Bedeski, Robert E. "The Evolution of the Modern State in China: National and Communist Continuities," *World Politics*, 27, No. 4, July 1975, 541–68.

Bianco, Lucien. "People's China: 25 Years. 'Fu-chiang' and Red Fervor," *Problems of Communism*, 23, No. 5, September–October 1974, 2–9.

Boorman, Howard L., and Richard C. Howard (eds.). *Biographic Dictionary of Republican China*. 5 vols. New York: Columbia University Press, 1967–79.

Bridgham, Philip. "The Fall of Lin Piao," *China Quarterly* [London], No. 55, July–September 1973, 427–49.

Brodsgaard, Kjeld Erik. "The Democracy Movement in China, 1978–1979: Opposition Movements, Wall Poster Campaigns, and Underground Journals," *Asian Survey*, 21, No. 7, July 1981, 747–74.

Buhite, Russell D. *Decisions at Yalta: An Appraisal of Summit Diplomacy*. Wilmington, Delaware: Scholarly Resources, 1986.

Burns, John P. "Reforming China's Bureaucracy, 1979–82," *Asian Survey*, 23, No. 6, June 1983, 692–722.

Burns, John P., and Stanley Rosen (eds.). *Policy Conflicts in Post-Mao China: A Documentary Survey, with Analysis*. Armonk, New York: Sharpe, 1986.

Chang, Chun-shu. *The Making of China: Main Themes in Premodern Chinese History*. Englewood Cliffs: Prentice-Hall, 1975.

Chang, Parris H. "Chinese Politics: Deng's Turbulent Quest," *Problems of Communism*, 30, No. 1, January–February 1981, 1–21.

______. *Power and Policy in China*. University Park: Pennsylvania State University Press, 1975.

Chen, Yung-fa. *Making Revolution: The Communist Movement in Eastern and Central China, 1937–1945*. Berkeley and Los Angeles: University of California Press, 1986.

Cheng, Te-k'un. *Studies in Chinese Archaeology*. Hong Kong: Chinese University of Hong Kong Press, 1982.

Cheng Dalin. *The Great Wall of China*. Hong Kong: South China Morning Post, 1984.

Chesneaux, Jean. *China: The People's Republic, 1949–1976*. (Trans., Paul Aster and Lydia Davis.) New York: Pantheon, 1979.

Chi, Wen-shun. *Ideological Conflicts in Modern China: Democracy and Authoritarianism*. New Brunswick, New Jersey: Transaction Books, 1986.

China Handbook Editorial Committee. *China Handbook Series: History*. (Trans., Dun J. Li.) Beijing: Foreign Languages Press, 1982.

China Official Annual Report. Hong Kong: Kingsway International, 1981–83.

Coye, Molly Joel, and Jon Livingston (eds.). *China Yesterday and Today*. (2d ed.) New York: Bantam Books, 1979.

Cranmer-Byng, John. "The Chinese View of Their Place in the World: An Historical Perspective," *China Quarterly* [London], No. 53, January-March 1973, 67–79.

deBary, Wm. Theodore, et al. *Sources of Chinese Tradition*. New York: Columbia University Press, 1960.

Dien, Albert E., et al. (eds.). *Chinese Archaeological Abstracts. 2. Prehistoric to Western Zhou*. (Monumenta Archaeologica, vol. 9.) Los Angeles: Institute of Archaeology, University of California at Los Angeles, 1985.

Dittmer, Lowell. "Bases of Power in Chinese Politics: A Theory and an Analysis of the Fall of the 'Gang of Four'," *World Politics*, 30, No. 4, October 1978, 26–60.

______. "Death and Transfiguration: Liu Shaoqi's Rehabilitation and Contemporary Chinese Politics," *Journal of Asian Studies*, 40, No. 3, May 1981, 455–80.

______. *Liu Shao-ch'i and the Chinese Cultural Revolution: The Politics of Mass Criticism*. Berkeley and Los Angeles: University of California Press, 1974.

Domes, Jürgen. *The Internal Politics of China, 1949–1972*. (Trans., Rudiger Machetzki.) New York: Praeger, 1973.

______. *China after the Cultural Revolution: Politics Between Two Party Congresses*. (With a contribution by Marie-Luise Näth.) Berkeley and Los Angeles: University of California Press, 1977.

______. *The Government and Politics of the PRC: A Time of Transition*. Boulder: Westview Press, 1985.

Dreyer, June Teufel. "China's Quest for a Socialist Solution," *Problems of Communism*, 24, No. 5, September–October 1975, 49–62.

Eberhard, Wolfram. *A History of China*. (4th ed.) Berkeley and Los Angeles: University of California Press, 1977.

Egashira, K. "Chinese-Style Socialism: Some Aspects of Its Origin and Structure," *Asian Survey*, 15, No. 11, November 1975, 981-95.

Elisseeff, Daniel, and Vadime Elisseeff. (Trans., Larry Lockwood.) *New Discoveries in China: Encountering History Through Archaeology*. Fribourg, Switzerland: Chartwell Books, 1983.

Elvin, Mark. *The Pattern of the Chinese Past*. Stanford: Stanford University Press, 1973.

Fairbank, John King. *The Great Chinese Revolution, 1800–1985*. New York: Harper & Row, 1986.

Fairbank, John K., and Edwin O. Reischauer. *China: Tradition & Transformation*. Boston: Houghton Mifflin, 1978.

Fairbank, John K., Edwin O. Reischauer, and Albert Craig. *East Asia: The Modern Transformation*. Boston: Houghton Mifflin, 1965.

Fontana, Dorothy Grouse. "Background to the Fall of Hua Guofeng," *Asian Survey*, 22, No. 3, March 1982, 237–60.

Gayn, Mark. "People's China: 25 Years. A View from the Village," *Problems of Communism*, 23, No. 5, September–October 1974, 10–15.

Gittings, John. "New Light on Mao: His View of the World," *China Quarterly* [London], No. 60, October–December 1974, 750–66.

______. *The World and China, 1922–1972*. New York: Harper & Row, 1974.

Goodman, David S. G. "China: The Politics of Succession," *World Today* [London], 33, No. 4, April 1977, 131–40.

______. "The Provincial Revolutionary Committee in the People's Republic of China, 1967–79: An Obituary," *China Quarterly* [London], No. 85, March 1981, 49–79.

Goodrich, L. Carrington. *A Short History of the Chinese People*. London: Allen & Unwin, 1969.

Grieder, Jerome B. *Intellectuals and the State in Modern China: A Narrative History*. (Transformation of Modern China series.) New York: Free Press, 1981.

Han, Suyin. *The Morning Deluge: Mao Tse-tung and the Chinese Revolution, 1893–1953*. London: Jonathan Cape, 1972.

______. *Wind in the Tower: Mao Tsetung and the Chinese Revolution, 1949–1975*. Boston: Little, Brown, 1976.

Harding, Harry, Jr. "Asian Communism in Flux: China after Mao," *Problems of Communism*, 26, No. 2, March–April 1977, 1–18.

______. "China: The 1st Year Without Mao," *Contemporary China*, No. 2, Spring 1978, 81–98.

______. *China: The Uncertain Future.* (Headline series, No. 223.) New York: Foreign Policy Association, December 1974.

Hearn, Maxwell K. "An Ancient Chinese Army Rises from Underground Sentinel Duty," *Smithsonian*, 10, No. 8, November 1979, 38–51.

Hiniker, Paul J. "The Cultural Revolution Revisited: Dissonance Reduction or Power Maximization," *China Quarterly* [London], No. 94, June 1983, 282-303.

Hinton, Harold C. (ed.). *The People's Republic of China: A Handbook.* Boulder: Westview Press, 1979.

Ho, Ping-ti. "The Paleoenvironment of North China—A Review Article," *Journal of Asian Studies*, 43, No. 4, August 1984, 723–34.

Hsieh, Chiao-min. *Atlas of China.* New York: McGraw-Hill, 1973.

Hsiung, James C. *Ideology and Practice: The Evolution of Chinese Communism.* New York: Praeger, 1970.

Hsu, Cho-yun. "Early Chinese History: The State of the Field," *Journal of Asian Studies*, 38, No. 3, May 1979, 453–75.

Hsü, Immanuel C.Y. *The Rise of Modern China.* (3d ed.) New York: Oxford University Press, 1984.

Hu Sheng, et al. *The 1911 Revolution: A Retrospective after 70 Years.* (China Studies series.) Beijing: New World Press, 1983.

Hucker, Charles O. *China to 1850: A Short History.* Stanford: Stanford University Press, 1978.

Johnson, Chalmers (ed.). *Ideology and Politics in Contemporary China.* Seattle: University of Washington Press, 1973.

Johnson, David, et al. (eds.). *Popular Culture in Late Imperial China.* (Studies on China series.) Berkeley and Los Angeles: University of California Press, 1985.

Keightley, David N. "Shang China Is Coming of Age—A Review Article," *Journal of Asian Studies*, 41, No. 3, May 1982, 549–57.

Kim, Ilpyong J. *The Politics of Chinese Communism: Kiangsi under the Soviets.* Berkeley and Los Angeles: University of California Press, 1974.

Klein, Donald W., and Anne B. Clark. *Biographic Dictionary of Chinese Communism, 1921–1965.* 2 vols. Cambridge: Harvard University Press, 1971.

La Dany, L. "People's China: 25 Years. Shrinking Political Life," *Problems of Communism*, 23, No. 5, September–October 1974, 25–28.

Lee, Shao Chang. "China's Cultural Development." (Wall chart) East Lansing, Michigan, 1964.

Levenson, Joseph R., and Franz Schurmann. *China: An Interpretative History from the Beginnings to the Fall of Han.* Berkeley and Los Angeles: University of California Press, 1969.

Li, Dun J. *The Ageless Chinese: A History*. New York: Charles Scribner's Sons, 1971.

Li Xueqin. *Eastern Zhou and Qin Civilization*. (Trans., K.C. Chang.) New Haven: Yale University Press, 1985.

Lieberthal, Kenneth. "China in 1975: The Internal Political Scene," *Problems of Communism*, 24, No. 3, May–June 1975, 1–11.

Lindsay, Michael. "Analysis of the People's Republic of China," *Asia Quarterly* [Brussels], 2, 1975, 153–74.

______. "The Chinese Communist Party: History and Doctrines." Pages 123–96 in Yuan-li Wu (ed.), *China: A Handbook*. New York: Praeger, 1973.

Liu, James T. C. *Political Institutions in Traditional China: Major Issues*. New York: John Wiley and Sons, 1974.

Loewe, Michael. *Imperial China: The Historical Background to the Modern Age*. New York: Praeger, 1966.

MacFarquhar, Roderick. "China after the 10th Congress," *World Today* [London], 29, No. 12, December 1973, 514–26.

Mancall, Mark. *China at the Center: 300 Years of Foreign Policy*. (Transformation of Modern China series.) New York: Free Press, 1984.

Meisner, Maurice. *Mao's China and After: A History of the People's Republic*. (rev. ed.) (Transformation of Modern China series.) New York: Free Press, 1986.

Michael, Franz. "China after the Cultural Revolution: The Unresolved Succession Crisis," *Orbis*, 17, No. 2, Summer 1973, 315–33.

Oksenberg, Michel. "Mao's Policy Commitments, 1921–1976," *Problems of Communism*, 25, No. 6, November–December 1979, 1–26.

Oksenberg, Michel, and Steven Goldstein. "The Chinese Political Spectrum," *Problems of Communism*, 23, No. 2, March–April 1974, 1–13.

Onate, Andres D. *Chairman Mao and the Chinese Communist Party*. Chicago: Nelson-Hall, 1979.

People's Republic of China Year Book. Beijing: Xinhua Publishing House, 1983–85.

Pirazzoli-t'Serstevens, Michèle. *The Han Dynasty*. (Trans., Janet Seligman.) New York: Rizzoli, 1982.

Pong, David, and Edmund S.K. Fung (eds.). *Ideal and Reality: Social and Political Changes in Modern China, 1860–1949*. Lanham, Maryland: University Press of America, 1985.

Pye, Lucian W. "Mao Tse-tung's Leadership Style," *Political Science Quarterly*, 91, No. 2, Summer 1976, 219–36.

Qi Wen. *China: A General Survey*. Beijing: Foreign Languages Press, 1979.

Reischauer, Edwin O. "The Sinic World in Perspective," *Foreign Affairs*, 52, No. 2, January 1974, 341-48.

Rice, Edward E. *Mao's Way*. Berkeley and Los Angeles: University of California Press, 1972.

______. "People's China: 25 Years. A Radical Break with the Past," *Problems of Communism*, 23, No. 5, September-October 1974, 16-20.

Ristaino, Marcia R. *China's Art of Revolution: The Mobilization of Discontent, 1927 and 1928*. Durham: Duke University Press, 1987.

Rossabi, Morris (ed.). *China among Equals: The Middle Kingdom and Its Neighbors, 10th-14th Centuries*. Berkeley and Los Angeles: University of California Press, 1983.

Salisbury, Harrison E. *The Long March: The Untold Story*. Franklin Center, Pennsylvania: Franklin Library, 1985.

Sandschneider, Eberhard. "Political Succession in the People's Republic of China: Rule by Purge," *Asian Survey*, 25, No. 6, June 1985, 638-58.

Schram, Stuart R. "To Utopia and Back: A Cycle in the History of Chinese Communist Party," *China Quarterly* [London], No. 87, September 1981, 407-39.

Schurmann, Franz, and Orville Schell (eds.). *Communist China: Revolutionary Reconstruction and International Confrontation, 1949 to the Present* (China readings, 3). Harmondsworth: Penguin, 1968.

Schwarcz, Vera. *The Chinese Enlightenment: Intellectuals and the Legacy of the May Fourth Movement of 1919*. Berkeley and Los Angeles: University of California Press, 1986.

Service, John S. "Edgar Snow: Some Personal Reminiscences," *China Quarterly* [London], No. 50, April-June 1972, 209-19.

Smith, Richard J. *China's Cultural Heritage: The Ch'ing Dynasty, 1644-1912*. Boulder: Westview Press, 1983.

Solomon, Richard H. *Mao's Revolution and the Chinese Political Culture*. Berkeley and Los Angeles: University of California Press, 1971.

Somers, Robert M. "Time, Space, and Structure in the Consolidation of the T'ang Dynasty (A.D. 617-700)," *Journal of Asian Studies*, 45, No. 5, November 1986, 971-94.

Starr, John Bryan. "Chinese Politics, 1973-76: From the 10th Party Congress to the Premiership of Hua Kuo-feng: The Significance of the Colour of the Cat," *China Quarterly* [London], No. 67, September 1976, 457-88.

Sullivan, Lawrence R. "The Role of the Control Organs in the CCP, 1977-83," *Asian Survey*, 24, No. 6, June 1984, 597-619.

Tang Tsou. *The Cultural Revolution and Post-Mao Reforms: A Historical Perspective*. Chicago: University of Chicago Press, 1986.

Teiwes, Frederick C. "Reports from China: Before and after the Cultural Revolution," *China Quarterly* [London], No. 58, April–May 1974, 332–48.

Terrill, Ross. "China in the 1980s," *Foreign Affairs*, 58, No. 4, Spring 1980, 920–35.

______. *800,000,000: The Real China*. Boston: Little, Brown, 1972.

Terrill, Ross (ed.). *The China Difference*. New York: Harper & Row, 1979.

Thaxton, Ralph. "On Peasant Revolution and National Resistance: Toward a Theory of Peasant Mobilization and Revolutionary War with Special Reference to Modern China," *World Politics*, 30, No. 1, October 1977, 24–57.

Thornton, Richard C. *China: A Political History, 1917–1980*. Boulder: Westview Press, 1982.

Townsend, James R., and Brantly Womack. *Politics in China*. (3d ed.) (Series in Comparative Politics: A Country Study.) Boston: Little, Brown, 1986.

Tung Chi-ming (comp.). *An Outline History of China*. (Originally published in People's Republic of China by Foreign Languages Press in 1958 and 1959.) Hong Kong: Joint Publishing, 1979.

Uhalley, Stephen, Jr. *Mao Tse-tung: A Critical Biography*. New York: New Viewpoints, 1975.

Wakeman, Frederic E., Jr. *The Fall of Imperial China*. (Transformation of Modern China series.) New York: Free Press, 1975.

Walder, Andrew G. "Methodological Note: Press Accounts and the Study of Chinese Society," *China Quarterly* [London], No. 79, September 1979, 568–92.

Wang, Ting. "The Succession Problem," *Problems of Communism*, 22, No. 3, May–June 1973, 13–24.

Whiting, Allen S. "New Light on Mao. Quemoy 1958: Mao's Miscalculations," *China Quarterly* [London], No. 62, June 1975, 263–70.

Whitson, William W. *Chinese Military and Political Leaders and the Distribution of Power in China, 1956–1971*. (R–1091–DOS/ARPA June 1973.) (Report prepared for Defense Advanced Research Projects Agency and Department of State.) Santa Monica: Rand, June 1973.

Wich, Richard. "The Tenth Party Congress: The Power Structure and the Succession Question," *China Quarterly* [London], No. 58, April–May 1974, 231–48.

Wilson, Dick (ed.). *Mao Tse-tung in the Scales of History*. (Preliminary assessment organized by *China Quarterly*.) London: Cambridge University Press, 1977.

Womack, Brantly. "Modernization and Democratic Reforms in China," *Journal of Asian Studies*, 43, No. 3, May 1984, 417-40.

Wu, Yuan-li (ed.). *China: A Handbook*. New York: Praeger, 1973.

Yang, Benjamin. "The Zunyi Conference as One Step in Mao's Rise to Power: A Survey of Historical Studies of the Chinese Communist Party," *China Quarterly* [London], No. 106, June 1986, 235-71.

(Various issues of the following publications were also used in the preparation of this chapter: *Beijing Review* [Beijing]; *Bibliography of Asian Studies*; *China News Analysis* [Hong Kong]; *China Quarterly* [London]; *Chinese Studies in History*; Foreign Broadcast Information Service, *Daily Report: China*; Joint Publications Research Service, *China Report: Political, Sociological, and Military Affairs*, and *Journal of Asian Studies*.)

Chapter 2

Aird, John S. "Fertility Decline in China." Pages 119-227 in Nicholas Eberstadt (ed.), *Fertility Decline in the Less Developed Countries*. New York: Praeger, 1981.

______. "The Preliminary Results of China's 1982 Census," *China Quarterly* [London], No. 96, December 1983, 613-40.

Arnold, Fred, and Liu Zhaoxiang. "Sex Preference, Fertility, and Family Planning in China," *Population and Development Review*, 12, No. 2, June 1986, 221-46.

Banister, Judith. "An Analysis of Recent Data on the Population of China," *Population and Development Review*, 10, No. 2, June 1984, 241-71.

______. *China's Changing Population*. Stanford: Stanford University Press, 1987.

______. "Urban-Rural Population Projections for China." Bureau of the Census, Center for International Research, Washington: March 1986.

Banister, Judith, and Kim Woodward. "A Tale of New Cities," *China Business Review*, 14, No. 2, March-April 1987, 12-21.

Bianco, Lucien. "Family Planning Programs and Fertility Decline in Taiwan and Mainland China: A Comparison," *Issues & Studies* [Taipei], 21, No. 11, November 1985, 53-95.

Bongaarts, John, and Susan Greenhalgh. "An Alternative to the One-Child Policy in China." (Working Papers, No. 115.) New York: Center for Policy Studies, Population Council, October 1985.

Burns, John P., and Stanley Rosen (eds.). *Policy Conflicts in Post-Mao China: A Documentary Survey, with Analysis*. Armonk, New York: Sharpe, 1986.

Chan, Kam Wing, and Xu Xueqiang. "Urban Population Growth and Urbanization in China since 1949: Reconstructing a Baseline," *China Quarterly* [London], No. 104, December 1985, 583–613.

Chang, Luke T. *China's Boundary Treaties and Frontier Disputes*. London: Oceana, 1982.

Chang, Sen-dou. "Trends in Internal Migration and Urbanization in China." (Paper presented at China Population Analysis Conference, University of Hawaii, East-West Center, May 19–23, 1980.) Honolulu: 1980.

Chao, Kang. *Man and Land in Chinese History: An Economic Analysis*. Stanford: Stanford University Press, 1986.

Chen Haifeng. *Modern Chinese Medicine, III: Chinese Health Care*. Beijing: MTP Press, 1984.

Chen, Xiangming. "The One-Child Population Policy, Modernization, and the Extended Chinese Family," *Journal of Marriage and the Family*, 47, No. 1, February 1985, 193–202.

China. State Statistical Bureau. *China: Urban Statistics, 1985*. Essex, United Kingdom: Longman Group, 1985.

China Handbook Editorial Committee. *China Handbook Series: Economy*. Beijing: Foreign Languages Press, 1984.

______. *China Handbook Series: Geography*. Beijing: Foreign Languages Press, 1983.

Chung Chi. *An Outline of Chinese Geography*. Beijing: Foreign Languages Press, 1978.

Cressy, George Babcock. *Land of the 500 Million*. New York: McGraw-Hill, 1955.

Croizier, Ralph. *Traditional Medicine in Modern China*. Cambridge: Harvard University Press, 1968.

Croll, Elisabeth J. *China's One-Child Family Policy*. New York: St. Martin's Press, 1985.

______. "Production Versus Reproduction: A Threat to China's Development Strategy," *World Development* [Oxford], 11, No. 6, June 1983, 467–81.

Davin, Delia. "The Single-child Family Policy in the Countryside." Pages 37–45 in Elisabeth Croll (ed.), *China's One-Child Family Policy*. New York: St. Martin's Press, 1985.

Dreyer, June Teufel. *China's Forty Millions: Minority Nationalities and National Integration in the People's Republic of China*. Cambridge: Harvard University Press, 1976.

Editorial Committee of the China Official Yearbook. *China Official Yearbook, 1983-84*, Hong Kong: Dragon Pearl, 1983.

Edward, Mike. "China's Born-Again Giant Shanghai," *National Geographic*, 158, No. 1, July 1980, 15-43.

Emerson, John Philip. *The Growth of the Chinese Labor Force, 1957-1979*. Washington: Department of Commerce, 1981.

Fang Chun-ie. *1981/2 China Official Annual Report*. Hong Kong: Kingsway International, 1981.

Fei Hsiao Tung. *Toward a People's Anthropology*. Beijing: New World Press, 1981.

Geelan, P.J.M., and D.C. Twitchett (eds.). *Times Atlas of China*. London: Times Newspapers, 1974.

Goldstein, Sydney, and Alice Goldstein. "China on the Move: New Responsibilities, New Challenges," Pages 59-71 in Jane Vanderlind and William Barrows (eds.), *Proceedings of the Eighteenth Annual Conference*. New York: Association for Population/Family Planning Libraries and Information Centers, International, 1986.

______. *Population Mobility in the People's Republic of China*. (Papers of the East-West Population Institute, No. 95, East-West Center.) University of Hawaii: Honolulu, 1985.

Goyer, Doreen. *Workshop in Census Population*. Pages 41-56 in Jane Vanderlind and William Barrows (eds.), *Proceedings of the Eighteenth Annual Conference*. New York: Association for Population/Family Planning Libraries and Information Centers, International, 1986.

"Greenery to Be Accelerated," *Beijing Review* [Beijing], 27, No. 12, March 19, 1984, 10.

Hoffman, Charles. "Employment in the People's Republic of China," *Asian Thought and Society*, 7, No. 20, July 1982, 156-75.

Hsiao, William C. "Transformation of Health Care in China," *New England Journal of Medicine*, 310, No. 14, April 5, 1984, 932-36.

Hsieh, Chiao-min. *Atlas of China*. New York: McGraw-Hill, 1973.

Jamison, Dean T. *China: The Health Sector*. (World Bank Country Study, No. 84-13150). Washington: World Bank, 1984.

Kallgren, Joyce K. "Family Planning in China," *Current History*, 85, No. 512, September 1986, 269-72, 281, 304.

Kaplan, Fredric M., Julian M. Sobin, and Stephen Andors (eds.). *Encyclopedia of China Today*. Fair Lawn, New Jersey: Eurasia Press, 1979.

Keyfitz, Nathan. "The Population of China," *Scientific American*, 250, No. 2, February 1984, 38-47.

Kirkby, Richard J.R. *Urbanization in China: Town and Country in a Developing Economy, 1949-2000 AD*. New York: Columbia University Press, 1985.

Lampton, David M. *The Politics of Medicine in China*. (Westview Special Studies on China and East Asia.) Boulder: Westview Press, 1977.

Li Chengrui (ed.). *A Census of One Billion People: Papers of the International Seminar on China's 1982 Census*. Boulder: Westview Press, 1987.

Li Shengqi. "The Kazak: A Nationality on Horseback," *New China Quarterly* [Hong Kong], No. 1, July 1986, 92-95.

Liu, Alan P.L. *How China Is Ruled*. Englewood Cliffs: Prentice-Hall, 1986.

Lu Guangtian. "A Review of Demographic Studies of China's National Minorities," *Social Sciences in China* [Beijing], No. 3, September 1986, 89-110.

Ma, Laurence J.C. "Preliminary Results of the 1982 Census," *Geographical Review*, 73, No. 2, April 1983, 198-210.

Moser, Leo J. *The Chinese Mosaic: The Peoples and Provinces of China*. (Westview Special Studies on East Asia, No. 9.) Boulder: Westview Press, 1985.

Mosher, Steven. "Thinking Clear: Forced Abortions and Infanticide in Communist China," *Human Life Review*, 11, No. 3, Summer 1985, 7-34.

Orleans, Leo A. *Every Fifth Child: The Population of China*. Stanford: Stanford University Press, 1972.

______. *Health Policies and Services in China*. (United States Congress, 93d, 2d Session, Senate, Committee on Labor and Public Welfare, Subcommittee on Health.) Washington: GPO, 1974.

Orleans, Leo A., and Ly Burnham. "The Enigma of China's Urban Population," *Asian Survey*, 24, No. 7, July 1984, 788-804.

Pannell, Clifton W., and Laurence J.C. Ma. *China: The Geography of Development and Modernization*. Washington: Winston and Sons, 1983.

Parish, William L., and Martin King Whyte. *Village and Family Life in Contemporary China*. Chicago: University of Chicago Press, 1978.

Physical Geography of China. Beijing, 1986.

Platte, Erika. "China's Fertility Transition: The One-Child Campaign," *Pacific Affairs* [Vancouver], 57, No. 4, Winter 1984-85, 646-71.

Prescott, J.R.V. *The Maritime Boundaries of the World*. New York: Methuen, 1985.

Qi Wen. *China: A General Survey*. Beijing: Foreign Languages Press, 1979.

"Reforming the Public Security Forces," *China News Analysis* [Hong Kong], No. 1318, September 15, 1986, 1-9.

Rosenthal, Marilynn M. *Health Care in the People's Republic of China: Moving Toward Modernization*. (Westview Special Studies on China.) Boulder: Westview Press, 1986.

Schwarz, Henry G. *The Minorities of Northern China: A Survey*. Bellingham, Washington: Center for East Asian Studies, Western Washington University, 1984.

Shabad, Theodore. *China's Changing Map*. New York: Praeger, 1972.

Shan Fang. "Mainland China's Rural Surplus Labor," *Issues & Studies*, [Taipei], 22, No. 4, April 1986, 51-68.

Taylor, Jeffrey R. *Employment and Unemployment in China: Results from 10-Percent Sample Tabulation of 1982 Population Census*. (Foreign Economic Report, No. 23.) Washington: Department of Commerce, Bureau of the Census, September 1985.

Tien, H. Yuan. "China: Demographic Billionaire," *Population Bulletin*, 38, No. 2, April 1983, 1-43.

______. "Redirection of the Chinese Family: Ramifications of Minimal Reproduction."(Michigan State University Working Papers, Women in International Development series, No. 67.) East Lansing: Michigan State University, October 1984.

Ting, Tin-yu, and Chen Hsin-mu. "Involuntary Family Size: An Evaluation of Mainland China's One-Child Family Policy," *Issues & Studies* [Taipei], 22, No. 2, February 1986, 45-63.

Treagear, T.R. *An Economic Geography of China*. New York: American Elsevier, 1970.

United States. Department of Agriculture. Economic Research Service. *China: Review of Agriculture in 1981 and Outlook for 1982*, Washington, August 1982.

United States. Department of Interior. Board on Geographic Names. *Gazetteer of the People's Republic of China: Pinyin to Wade-Giles, Wade-Giles to Pinyin*, Washington, July 1979.

United States. Congress. 99th, 1st Session. Senate. Committee on Finance. *MFN Status for Hungary, Romania, China, and Afghanistan*. Washington: GPO, 1986.

United States. Congress. 99th, 2d Session. Joint Economic Committee (ed.) *China's Economy Looks Toward the Year 2000, 1: The Four Modernizations*. Washington: GPO, 1986.

Warner, Denis. "The Bear Across the Chinese Border," *Pacific Defence Reporter* [Victoria, Australia] 13, No. 3, September 1986, 31-33.

Wu Yiming. *People's Republic of China Year-Book, 1984*. Beijing: Xinhua Publishing House, 1984.

Yang, Zunyi. *The Geology of China*. New York: Oxford University Press, 1986.

Yue, Guangzhao. "Employment, Wages and Social Security in China," *International Labor Review* [Montreal] 124, No. 4, July–August 1985, 411–22.

Zhao Songqiao. *Physical Geography of China*. Beijing: Science Press, 1986.

Zheng Zhensun. *People's Republic of China Year Book, 1985*, Beijing: Xinhua Publishing House, 1985.

Zhongguo 1982 Nian Renkou Pucha Ziliao (Dianzi Jisuanji Huizong) [1982 Population Census of China] (Results of Computer Tabulation), Beijing, March 1985.

(Various issues of the following publications were also used in the preparation of this chapter: *Beijing Review* [Beijing]; British Broadcasting Corporation, *Summary of World Broadcasts: Far East Report* [Caversham Park, United Kingdom]; *China Daily* [Beijing]; *China Reconstructs* [Beijing]; *Far Eastern Economic Review* [Hong Kong]; Foreign Broadcast Information Service, *Daily Report: China*; Joint Publications Research Service, *China Report: Political, Sociological, and Military Affairs*; and *Ta Kung Pao Weekly Supplement* [Hong Kong].)

Chapter 3

"As We Reform the Party, We Must Oppose the Art of Using Connections," *Study and Research* [Beijing], May 5, 1985, 43–46.

Bernstein, Thomas. *Up to the Mountains and Down to the Villages: The Transfer of Youth from Urban to Rural China*. New Haven: Yale University Press, 1977.

Blecher, Mark. "Balance and Cleavage in Urban-Rural Relations." Pages 219–45 in William L. Parish (ed.), *Chinese Rural Development: The Great Transformation*. Armonk, New York: Sharpe, 1985.

Bodde, Derk. *China's Cultural Tradition: What and Whither?* New York: Rinehart, 1957.

Brown, G. Thompson. *Christianity in the People's Republic of China*. (rev. ed.) Atlanta: John Knox Press, 1986.

Chan, Anita. *Children of Mao: Personality Development and Political Activism in the Red Guard Generation*. Seattle: University of Washington Press, 1985.

Chan, Anita, and Jonathan Unger. "Grey and Black: The Hidden Economy of Rural China," *Pacific Affairs* [Vancouver], 55, No. 3, Fall 1982, 452-71.

Chan, Anita, Richard Madsen, and Jonathan Unger. *Chen Village: The Recent History of a Peasant Community in Mao's China.* Berkeley and Los Angeles: University of California Press, 1984.

Chao Yuen Ren. *Aspects of Chinese Sociolinguistics.* Stanford: Stanford University Press, 1976.

Chesneaux, Jean. *Popular Movements and Secret Societies in China.* Stanford: Stanford University Press, 1977.

China. State Statistical Bureau. *Statistical Yearbook of China, 1986.* Hong Kong: Economic Information & Agency, 1986.

Croll, Elisabeth. "Marriage Choice and Status Groups in Contemporary China." Pages 175-97 in James L. Watson (ed.), *Class and Social Stratification in Post-Revolution China.* New York: Cambridge University Press, 1984.

Davin, Delia. *Woman-Work: Women and the Party in Revolutionary China.* New York: Oxford University Press, 1976.

DeGlopper, Donald R. "Recent Changes in Chinese Society," *Annals of the American Academy of Political and Social Sciences*, 402, July 1972, 15-25.

Diamond, Norma. "Taitou Revisited: State Policies and Social Change." Pages 246-70 in William L. Parish (ed.), *Chinese Rural Development.* Armonk, New York: Sharpe, 1985.

"Educated Women Groan under Housework," *Beijing Review* [Beijing], 29, No. 49, December 8, 1986, 20.

Edwards, R. Randle. "Civil and Social Rights: Theory and Practice in Chinese Law Today." Pages 41-69 in R. Randle Edwards, Louis Henkin, and Andrew J. Nathan (eds.), *Human Rights in Contemporary China.* New York: Columbia University Press, 1986.

Fewsmith, Joseph. "Rural Reform in China: Stage Two," *Problems of Communism*, 34, No. 4, July-August 1985, 48-55.

Gold, Thomas. "After Comradeship: Personal Relations in China since the Cultural Revolution," *China Quarterly* [London], No. 104, December 1985, 657-75.

Graham, A.C. *Two Chinese Philosophers: Cheng Ming-tao and Cheng Yi-chuan.* London: Lund Humphries, 1958.

Henderson, Gail. *The Chinese Hospital.* New Haven: Yale University Press, 1984.

Hinton, William. *Hundred Day War: The Cultural Revolution in Tsinghua University.* New York: Monthly Review Press, 1972.

Hsiao Kung-ch'üan. *Rural China: Imperial Control in the Nineteenth Century.* Seattle: University of Washington Press, 1960.

Kirkby, Richard J.R. *Urbanization in China: Town and Country in a Developing Economy, 1949–2000 AD*. New York: Columbia University Press, 1985.

Leong, S.T. "The Hakka Chinese of Lingnan: Ethnicity and Social Change in Modern Times." Pages 287–326 in David Pong and Edmund S.K. Fung (eds.), *Ideal and Reality: Social and Political Change in Modern China, 1860–1949*. Lanham, Maryland: University Press of America, 1985.

Levenson, Joseph R. *Confucian China and Its Modern Fate*. Berkeley and Los Angeles: University of California Press, 1968.

Lewis, John Wilson (ed.). *The City in Communist China*. Stanford: Stanford University Press, 1971. .

Liang Heng, and Judith Shapiro. *Son of the Revolution*. New York: Vintage Books, 1984.

Lieberthal, Kenneth. "The Future of Reform in China," *AEI Foreign Policy and Defense Review*, 6, No. 3, August 1986, 3–10.

"'Love Corner' Gone in Shanghai," *Beijing Review* [Beijing], 29, No. 46, November 17, 1986, 8–9.

Madsen, Richard. *Morality and Power in a Chinese Village*. Berkeley and Los Angeles: University of California Press, 1984.

Moser, Leo J. *The Chinese Mosaic: The Peoples and Provinces of China*. (Westview Special Studies on East Asia, No. 9.) Boulder: Westview Press, 1985.

Nivison, David (ed.). *Confucianism in Action*. Stanford: Stanford University Press, 1959.

Oi, Jean C. "Commercializing China's Rural Cadres," *Problems of Communism*, 35, No. 5, September–October 1986, 1–15.

______. "Peasant Grain Marketing and State Procurement: China's Grain Contracting System," *China Quarterly* [London], No. 106, June 1986, 272–90.

Pannell, Clifton W., and Laurence J.C. Ma. *China: The Geography of Development and Modernization*. Washington: V.H. Winston, 1983.

Parish, William L. "Introduction: Historical Background and Current Issues." Pages 3–32 in William L. Parish (ed.), *Chinese Rural Development: The Great Transformation*. Armonk, New York: Sharpe, 1985.

Parish, William L., and Martin K. Whyte. *Village and Family in Contemporary China*. Chicago: University of Chicago Press, 1978.

Peck, Graham. *Two Kinds of Time*. (2d ed.). Boston: Houghton Mifflin, 1967.

Perry, Elizabeth J. "Rural Violence in Socialist China," *China Quarterly* [London], No. 103, September 1985, 414–40.

Pruitt, Ida. *A Daughter of the Han: The Autobiography of a Chinese Working Woman*. Stanford: Stanford University Press, 1967.

Rawski, Evelyn S. (ed.). *Popular Culture in Late Imperial China*. Berkeley and Los Angeles: University of California Press, 1985.

Rosen, Stanley. *Red Guard Factionalism and the Cultural Revolution in Guangzhou*. Boulder: Westview Press, 1982.

Schurmann, Franz. *Ideology and Organization in Communist China* (2d ed.) Berkeley and Los Angeles: University of California Press, 1968.

Sheng Huochu, and Liu Hongfa. "Resurvey of Workers' Living Standards in Tianjin," *China Reconstructs* [Beijing], 35, No. 12, December 1986, 29-32.

Shirk, Susan. *Competitive Comrades: Career Incentives and Student Strategies in China*. Berkeley and Los Angeles: University of California Press, 1982.

Skinner, G. William. "Mobility Strategies in Late Imperial China." Pages 83-126 in Carol A. Smith (ed.), *Regional Analysis*, 1. New York: Academic Press, 1976.

______. "Rural Marketing in China: Repression and Revival," *China Quarterly* [London], No. 103, September 1985, 393-413.

Skinner, G. William (ed.). *The City in Late Imperial China*. Stanford: Stanford University Press, 1977.

Smith, Arthur H. *Chinese Characteristics*. New York: Revell, 1894.

______. *Village Life in China*. New York: Revell, 1899.

Stacey, Judith. *Patriarchy and Socialist Revolution in China*. Berkeley and Los Angeles: University of California Press, 1983.

Tai Houying. *Stones of the Wall*. (Trans., Frances Wood.) New York: St. Martin's Press, 1985.

Thurston, Anne F., and Burton Pasternak (eds.). *The Social Sciences and Fieldwork in China: Views from the Field*. Boulder: Westview Press for the American Association for the Advancement of Science, 1983.

Unger, Jonathan. "The Class System in Rural China: A Case Study." Pages 121-41 in James L. Watson (ed.), *Class and Social Stratification in Post-Revolution China*. New York: Cambridge University Press, 1984.

Vogel, Ezra F. *Canton under Communism*. Cambridge: Harvard University Press, 1969.

Walder, Andrew G. *Communist Neo-Traditionalism: Work and Authority in Chinese Industry*. Berkeley and Los Angeles: University of California Press, 1986.

Ward, Barbara E. "Varieties of the Conscious Model: The Fishermen of South China." Pages 37-71 in M.E. Banton (ed.), *The*

Relevance of Models for Social Anthropology. London: Tavistock Press, 1968.

Watson, James L. (ed.). *Class and Social Stratification in Post-Revolution China*. New York: Cambridge University Press, 1984.

White, Lynn T., III. *Careers in Shanghai: The Social Guidance of Personal Energies in a Developing Chinese City, 1949–1966*. Berkeley and Los Angeles: University of California Press, 1978.

Whyte, Martin King. *Small Groups and Political Rituals in China*. Berkeley and Los Angeles: University of California Press, 1974.

______. "Social Trends in China: The Triumph of Inequality?" Pages 103–23 in A. Doak Barnett and Ralph N. Clough (eds.), *Modernizing China: Post-Mao Reform and Development*. Boulder: Westview Press, 1986.

Whyte, Martin King, and William L. Parish. *Urban Life in Contemporary China*. Chicago: University of Chicago Press, 1984.

Wolf, Margery. *Revolution Postponed: Women in Contemporary China*. Stanford: Stanford University Press, 1985.

Wolf, Margery, and Roxane Witke. *Women in Chinese Society*. Stanford: Stanford University Press, 1975.

Yang, C.K. *A Chinese Village in Early Communist Transition*. Cambridge: MIT Press, 1959.

______. *Religion in Chinese Society*. Berkeley and Los Angeles: University of California Press, 1961.

Yue Daiyu and Carolyn Wakeman. *To the Storm*. Berkeley and Los Angeles: University of California Press, 1985.

Zhou Qiren. "The Rediscovery of Household Management: On Changes in the Agricultural Management Organization Due to the Contract System," *Social Sciences in China* [Beijing], No. 2, June 1986, 93–112.

Zweig, David. "Prosperity and Conflict in Post-Mao Rural China," *China Quarterly* [London], No. 105, March 1986, 1–18.

(Various issues of the following publications were also used in the preparation of this chapter: *Beijing Review* [Beijing]; *China Daily* [Beijing]; Foreign Broadcast Information Service, *Daily Report: China*, and Joint Publications Research Service series *China Report: Economic Affairs* and *China Report: Political, Sociological, and Military Affairs*.)

Chapter 4

Bai Hua. "Ku Lian" (Bitter Love), *Cheng Ming* (Contending) [Hong Kong], No. 44, June 1981, 82–98.

Bao Zhenxi. ''Fazhan Zhong de Zhongguo Tushuguan Shiye'' (China's Developing Library Service), *Liaowang Zhoukan* (Outlook Weekly) [Hong Kong], No. 44, November 3, 1986, 32–33.

Bastid, Marianne. ''Educational Necessity and Political Ideals in Educational Reform During the Cultural Revolution,'' *China Quarterly* [London], No. 42, April–June 1970, 16–45.

Burns, John P., and Stanley Rosen (eds.). *Policy Conflicts in Post-Mao China: A Documentary Survey, with Analysis*. Armonk, New York: Sharpe, 1986.

Ch'en, Shou-yi. *Chinese Literature: A Historical Introduction*. New York: Ronald Press, 1961.

Chen, Theodore. *The Maoist Educational Revolution*. New York: Praeger, 1974.

China ABC. Beijing: New World Press, 1985.

Ci Hai. Shanghai: Shanghai Cishu Chubanshe (Shanghai Dictionary Publishers), 1979.

Cleverley, John. *The Schooling of China*. Sydney: Allen & Unwin, 1985.

Croizier, Ralph C. *China's Cultural Legacy and Communism*. New York: Praeger, 1970.

Delfs, Robert. ''Contending Thoughts: Party Liberals Push for Free Academic Debate,'' *Far Eastern Economic Review* [Hong Kong], June 19, 1986, 49–50.

Dietrich, Craig. *People's China: A Brief History*. New York: Oxford University Press, 1986.

Duke, Michael S. *Blooming and Contending: Chinese Literature in the Post-Mao Era*. Bloomington: Indiana University Press, 1985.

''Educational Developments,'' *China Exchange News*, 14, No. 3, September 1986, 28–29.

Feldman, Gayle. ''Field Note: The Organization of Publishing in China,'' *China Quarterly* [London], No. 107, July–September 1986, 519–29.

Glassman, Joel. *Centralized Planning—Decentralized Administration: Community Control in Chinese Communist Education*. (Proceedings of 30th International Congress of Human Sciences in Asia and North Africa.) Mexico City: December 1976.

______. ''Educational Reform and Manpower Policy in China, 1955–58,'' *Modern China*, 3, No. 3, 1977, 259–90.

______. ''The Political Experience of Primary School Teachers in the People's Republic of China,'' *Comparative Education* [Oxford], 15, No. 2, June 1979, 159–73.

Goldman, Merle. *China's Intellectuals: Advise and Dissent*. Cambridge: Harvard University Press, 1981.

Gunn, Edward M. (cd.). *Twentieth-Century Chinese Drama: An Anthology*. Bloomington: Indiana University Press, 1983.

Hamrin, Carol Lee, and Timothy Cheek (eds.). *China's Establishment Intellectuals*. Armonk, New York: Sharpe, 1986.

Hawkins, John N. *Education and Social Change in the People's Republic of China*. New York: Praeger, 1983.

Hayhoe, Ruth. *Contemporary Chinese Education*. Armonk, New York: Sharpe, 1984.

Hightower, James Robert. *Topics in Chinese Literature: Outlines and Bibliographies*. (rev. ed.) (Harvard-Yenching Institute Studies.) Cambridge: Harvard University Press, 1966.

Ho, Ping-ti. *The Ladder of Success in Imperial China*. New York: Columbia University Press, 1962.

Hsia, C.T. *A History of Modern Chinese Fiction*. (2d ed.) New Haven: Yale University Press, 1971.

Hsu, Kai-yu. *Literature of the People's Republic of China*. Bloomington: University of Indiana Press, 1980.

Kaplan, Fredric M., and Arne J. de Keijzer. *The China Guidebook*. New York: Eurasia Press, 1984.

Kaplan, Fredric M., Julian M. Sobin, and Stephen Andors (eds.). *Encyclopedia of China Today*. New York: Harper & Row, 1979.

Kinkley, Jeffrey C. (ed.). *After Mao: Chinese Literature and Society, 1978–1981*. Cambridge: MIT Press, 1985.

Lampton, David M. *A Relationship Restored: Trends in U.S.-Chinese Educational Exchanges, 1978–1984*. Washington: National Academy Press, 1986.

Legge, James. *The Chinese Classics*. Hong Kong: Hong Kong University Press, 1960.

Leyda, Jay. *Dianying: An Account of Films and the Film Audience in China*. Cambridge: MIT Press, 1972.

Link, Perry (ed.). *Roses and Thorns: The Second Blooming of the Hundred Flowers in Chinese Fiction, 1979–1980*. Berkeley and Los Angeles: University of California Press, 1984.

Liu, Alan P.L. *How China Is Ruled*. Englewood Cliffs: Prentice-Hall, 1986.

Liu Wu-chi. *An Introduction to Chinese Literature*. Bloomington: Indiana University Press, 1966.

McDougall, Bonnie S., and Hu Liuyu (trans.). *Literature and the Arts*. (China Handbook series.) Beijing: Foreign Language Press, 1983.

Montaperto, Ronald N., and Jay Henderson (eds.). *China's Schools in Flux*. White Plains: Sharpe, 1979.

Munro, Donald J. "Egalitarian Ideal and Educational Fact in Communist China." Pages 256–301 in John Lindbeck (ed.), *China:*

Management of a Revolutionary Society. Seattle: University of Washington Press, 1971.

Orleans, Leo A. *Manpower for Science and Engineering in China*. (Science and Technology in the People's Republic of China, Background Study, No. 4.) (Prepared for United States Congress, 96th, 2d Session, House of Representatives, Committee on Science and Technology, Subcommittee on Science.) Washington: GPO, 1980.

______. *Professional Manpower and Education in Communist China*. Washington: National Science Foundation, 1961.

Parker, Franklin, and Betty June Parker. *Education in the People's Republic of China, Past and Present: An Annotated Bibliography*. New York: Garland, 1986.

Pepper, Suzanne. "Chinese Education after Mao: Two Steps Forward, Two Steps Back, and Begin Again?" *China Quarterly* [London], No. 81, March 1980, 1-65.

Rosen, Stanley. "Chinese Education in Transition," *Current History*, 82, September 1983, 254-58, 277-78.

Schram, Stuart (ed.). *Authority, Participation, and Cultural Change in China*. London: Cambridge University Press, 1973.

Seifman, Eli. "China: The Decision on the Reform of the Education System," *Asian Thought and Society*, 11, No. 31, March 1986, 37-42.

Seto, May. "Modernization and the Media: China's TV, Radio, and Publications Experience: A Renaissance," *China Business Review*, 12, No. 5, September-October 1985, 10-13.

Seybolt, Peter. *Revolutionary Education in China: Documents and Commentary*. White Plains: International Arts and Science Press, 1973.

______. "The Yenan Revolution in Mass Education," *China Quarterly* [London], No. 48, October-December 1971, 641-69.

Shirk, Susan L. "Educational Reform and Political Backlash: Recent Changes in Chinese Educational Policy," *Comparative Education Review*, 23, No. 2, June 1979, 183-217.

Sullivan, Michael. *The Arts of China*. Berkeley and Los Angeles: University of California Press, 1978.

______. *A Short History of Chinese Art*. Berkeley and Los Angeles: University of California Press, 1967.

"A Time to Speak Out," *Asiaweek* [Hong Kong], June 22, 1986. 47-48, 53-56.

Townsend, James R., and Brantly Womack. *Politics in China*. (3d ed.) (Series in Comparative Politics: A Country Study.) Boston: Little, Brown, 1986.

Tung, Constantine, and Colin Mackerras. *Drama in the People's Republic of China*. Albany: State University of New York Press, 1987.

Unger, Jonathan. "The Chinese Controversy over Higher Education," *Pacific Affairs* [Vancouver], 53, No. 1, Spring 1980, 29–47.

Wang, Chi. "An Overview of Libraries in the People's Republic of China," *China Exchange News*, 12, No. 3, September 1984, 1–5.

Wang, Shu-shin. "The Rise and Fall of the Campaign Against Spiritual Pollution in the People's Republic of China," *Asian Affairs: An American Review*, 13, No. 1, Spring 1986, 47–62.

Wei Liming. "Criticism: Key to Flourishing Culture," *Beijing Review* [Beijing], 29, No. 27, July 7, 1986, 14–19.

World Bank. *China: Issues and Prospects in Education, Annex 1*. Washington: 1985.

Wyman, Molly E. "An Industry Struggles to Meet Demand: The Lure of Television," *China Business Review*, September–October 1985, 14–21.

Zheng Zhensun. *People's Republic of China Year Book, 1985*. Beijing: Xinhua Publishing House, 1985.

Zhongguo Dianying Nianjian, 1983 (Chinese Motion Picture Yearbook, 1983). Beijing: Zhongguo Dianying Chubanshe (China Motion Picture Publishing House), 1984.

(Various issues of the following publications were also used in the preparation of this chapter: *Beijing Review* [Beijing]; *China Daily* [Beijing]; *China Exchange News; China News Analysis* [Hong Kong]; *China Reconstructs* [Beijing]; Foreign Broadcast Information Service, *Daily Report: China*; Joint Publications Research Service, *China Report: Political, Sociological, and Military Affairs*; and *Zhongguo Chuban Nianjian* (Chinese Publishing Yearbook) [Beijing].)

Chapter 5

Barker, Randolph, and Radha Sinha, (eds.), with Beth Rose. *The Chinese Agricultural Economy*. (Westview Special Studies on China and East Asia.) Boulder: Westview Press, 1982.

Byrd, William A. *China's Financial System: The Changing Role of Banks*. Boulder: Westview Press, 1983.

Chen, Nai-Ruenn. *Chinese Economic Statistics*. Chicago: Aldine, 1967.

Chen, Nai-Ruenn, and Walter Galenson. *The Chinese Economy under Communism*. Chicago: Aldine, 1969.

China. State Statistical Bureau, *Statistical Yearbook of China, 1986*. Hong Kong: Economic Information & Agency, 1986.

Chinese Woodcutters' Association (comp.). *Woodcuts of Wartime China, 1937–1945*. Shanghai: Kaiming, 1946.

Chow, Gregory C. *The Chinese Economy*. New York: Harper & Row, 1985.

Congressional Quarterly. *China: U.S. Policy since 1945*. Washington: 1980.

Crook, Frederick W. "The Commune System in the People's Republic of China, 1963-1974." Pages 366-410 in United States Congress, 94th, 1st Session, Joint Economic Committee (ed.), *China: A Reassessment of the Economy*. Washington: GPO, 1975.

Dernberger, Robert F. (ed.). *China's Development Experience in Comparative Perspective*. (Harvard East Asian Series, No. 93.) Cambridge: Harvard University Press, 1980.

Donnithorne, Audrey. *China's Economic System*. London: Allen & Unwin, 1967.

Eckstein, Alexander. *China's Economic Revolution*. New York: Cambridge University Press, 1977.

Eckstein, Alexander (ed.). *Quantitative Measures of China's Economic Output*. Ann Arbor: University of Michigan Press, 1980.

Elvin, Mark. *The Pattern of the Chinese Past*. Stanford: Stanford University Press, 1973.

Feuerwerker, Albert. *The Chinese Economy, ca. 1870-1911*, V. (Michigan Papers in Chinese Studies.) Ann Arbor: Center for Chinese Studies, University of Michigan, 1969.

______. *Economic Trends in the Republic of China, 1912-1949*, XXI. (Michigan Papers in Chinese Studies.) Ann Arbor: Center for Chinese Studies, University of Michigan, 1977.

Gurley, John G. *China's Economy and the Maoist Strategy*. New York: Monthly Review Press, 1976.

Howe, Christopher. *China's Economy: A Basic Guide*. New York: Basic Books, 1978.

______. *Employment and Economic Growth in Urban China, 1949-1957*. London: Cambridge University Press, 1971.

Hsiao, Katherine H. *Money and Monetary Policy in Communist China*. New York: Columbia University Press, 1971.

Hsu, Robert C. *Food for One Billion: China's Agriculture since 1949*. Boulder: Westview Press, 1983.

Lardy, Nicholas R. *Agriculture in China's Modern Economic Development*. Cambridge: Cambridge University Press, 1983.

______. *Economic Growth and Distribution in China*. New York: Cambridge University Press, 1978.

Liu, Ta-Chung, and Kung-Chia Yeh. *The Economy of the Chinese Mainland*. Princeton: Princeton University Press, 1965.

Myers, Ramon H. *The Chinese Economy Past and Present*. Belmont, California: Wadsworth, 1980.

Perkins, Dwight H. *Agricultural Development in China, 1368–1968.* Chicago: Aldine, 1969.

______. *Market Control and Planning in Communist China.* (Harvard Economic Studies.) Cambridge: Harvard University Press, 1966.

Perkins, Dwight H. (ed.). *China's Modern Economy in Historical Perspective.* Stanford: Stanford University Press, 1975.

Perry, Elizabeth J., and Christine Wong (eds.). *The Political Economy of Reform in Post-Mao China.* Cambridge: Harvard University Press, 1985.

Rawski, Thomas G. *Economic Growth and Employment in China.* (World Bank Research Publication.) New York: Oxford University Press, 1979.

Riskin, Carl. *China's Political Economy: The Quest for Development since 1949.* Oxford: Oxford University Press, 1986.

United States. Central Intelligence Agency. *People's Republic of China Atlas.* Washington: GPO, 1971.

______. National Foreign Assessment Center. *China: A Statistical Compendium.* (Research Paper, No. ER 79-10374.) Washington: July 1979.

______. *China: Demand for Foreign Grain.* (Research Paper, No. ER 79-10073.) Washington: January 1979.

______. *China: The Continuing Search for a Modernization Strategy.* (Research Paper, No. ER 80-10248.) Washington: April 1980.

______. *Handbook of Economic Statistics, 1979.* (Research Aid, No. ER 79-10274.) Washington: 1979.

United States. Congress. 90th, 1st Session. Joint Economic Committee (ed.). *An Economic Profile of Mainland China.* Washington: GPO, 1967.

United States. Congress. 92d, 2d Session. Joint Economic Committee (ed.). *People's Republic of China: An Economic Assessment.* Washington: GPO, 1972.

United States. Congress. 94th, 1st Session. Joint Economic Committee (ed.). *China: A Reassessment of the Economy.* Washington: GPO, 1975.

United States. Congress. 95th, 2d Session. Joint Economic Committee (ed.). *Chinese Economy Post-Mao.* Washington: GPO, 1978.

United States. Congress. 96th, 1st Session. Joint Economic Committee (ed.). Subcommittee on Priorities and Economy in Government. *Allocation of Resources in the Soviet Union and China, 1979*, Pt. 5. (Hearings June 26 and July 9, 1979.) Washington: GPO, 1980.

United States. Congress. 97th, 2d Session. Joint Economic Committee (ed.). *China under the Four Modernizations*, Pts. 1 and 2. Washington: GPO, 1982.

United States. Congress. 99th, 2d Session. Joint Economic Committee (ed.). *China's Economy Looks Toward the Year 2000*, 2 vols. Washington: GPO, 1986.

World Bank. *World Development Report, 1986*. New York: Oxford University Press, 1986.

(Various issues of the following publications were also used in the preparation of this chapter: *Beijing Review* [Beijing]; *China Daily* [Beijing]; *China Quarterly* [London]; *China Reconstructs* [Beijing]; and *The Economist* [London].)

Chapter 6

American Plant Studies Delegation. *Plant Studies in the People's Republic of China*. Washington: National Academy of Sciences, 1975.

Barker, Randolph, and Radha Sinha, (eds.), with Beth Rose. *The Chinese Agricultural Economy*. Boulder: Westview Press, 1982.

Buck, John L. *Land Utilization in China*. Nanjing: University of Nanking, 1937.

Chinese Woodcutters' Association (comp.). *Woodcuts of Wartime China, 1937–1945*. Shanghai: Kaiming, 1946.

Crook, Frederick W. "The Commune System in the People's Republic of China, 1963–1974." Pages 366–410 in United States Congress, 94th, 1st Session, Joint Economic Committee (ed.), *China: A Reassessment of the Economy*. Washington: GPO, 1975.

______. "The Reform of the Commune System and the Rise of the Township-Collective-Household System." Pages 354–375 in United States Congress, 99th, 2d Session, Joint Economic Committee (ed.), *China's Economy Looks Toward the Year 2000, 1: The Four Modernizations*. Washington: GPO, 1986.

Erisman, Alva L. "China: Agriculture in the 1970s." Pages 324–49 in United States Congress, 94th, 1st Session, Joint Economic Committee (ed.), *China: A Reassessment of the Economy*. Washington: GPO, 1975.

Groen, Henry J. and James A. Kilpatrick. "China's Agricultural Production." Pages 607–52 in United States Congress, 95th, 2d Session, Joint Economic Committee (ed.), *Chinese Economy Post-Mao, 1: Policy and Performance*. Washington: GPO, 1978.

Howe, Christopher. *China's Economy: A Basic Guide*. New York: Basic Books, 1978.

International Rice Research Institute. *Rice Research and Production in China*. Los Baños, Philippines: 1978.

Lardy, Nicholas R. *Agriculture in China's Modern Economic Development*. Cambridge: Cambridge University Press, 1983.

Myers, Ramon H. *The Chinese Economy Past and Present*. Belmont, California: Wadsworth, 1980.

______. *The Chinese Peasant Economy*. Cambridge: Harvard University Press, 1970.

Parish, William L., and Martin K. Whyte. *Village and Family in Contemporary China*. Chicago: University of Chicago Press, 1978.

Perkins, Dwight H. *Agricultural Development in China, 1368–1968*. Chicago: Aldine, 1969.

Schran, Peter. *The Development of Chinese Agriculture*. Urbana: University of Illinois Press, 1970.

Shen, T.H. *Agricultural Resources of China*. Ithaca: Cornell University Press, 1951.

Shue, Vivienne. *Peasant China in Transition*. Berkeley and Los Angeles: University of California Press, 1980.

Stavis, Benedict. *People's Communes and Rural Development in China*. Ithaca, New York: Rural Development Committee, Center for International Studies, Cornell University, 1977.

Surls, Frederic M., and Francis Tuan. "China's Agriculture in the Eighties." Pages 419–48 in United States Congress, 97th, 2d Session, Joint Economic Committee (ed.), *China under the Four Modernizations, 1: The Four Modernizations*. Washington: GPO, 1982.

Tang, Anthony M., and Bruce Stone. *Food Production in the People's Republic of China*. Washington: International Food Policy Research Institute, 1980.

Tuan, Francis C., and Frederick W. Crook. *Planning and Statistical Systems in China's Agriculture*. (Economic Research Service, No. FAER-181.) Washington: Department of Agriculture, April 1983.

United States. Central Intelligence Agency. *China: International Trade Fourth Quarter, 1985*. (Research Paper, No. EA CIT 86-001.) Washington: July 1986.

______. *People's Republic of China Atlas*. Washington: GPO, 1971.

United States. Department of Agriculture. Economic Research Service. *Agricultural Statistics of the People's Republic of China, 1949–82*. Statistical Bulletin, No. 714, October 1984.

______. *China: Situation and Outlook Report*. (No. RS-86-8.) Washington, July 1986.

Walker, Kenneth R. *Food Grain Procurement and Consumption in China*. Cambridge: Cambridge University Press, 1984.

______. *Planning in Chinese Agriculture: Socialization and the Private Sector*. Chicago: Aldine, 1965.

(Various issues of the following publications were also used in the preparation of this chapter: *China Daily* [Beijing]; *China Quarterly*

[London]; *Nongye Nianjian* (Agricultural Yearbook) [Beijing]; and *Zhongguo Tongji Nianjian* (Statistical Yearbook of China) [Beijing].)

Chapter 7

Bohnet, Armin, and Güntner Jaehne. ''China's New Economic Policy,'' *Intereconomics* [Hamburg], 20, No. 1, January–February 1985, 43–51.

British Columbia. Ministry of International Trade and Investment. *China: Economic Overview, A British Columbia Perspective*. Victoria, British Columbia: 1986.

Burns, John P., and Stanley Rosen (eds.). *Policy Conflicts in Post-Mao China: A Documentary Survey, with Analysis*. Armonk, New York: Sharpe, 1986.

Chang, John K. *Industrial Development in Pre-Communist China*. Chicago: Aldine, 1969.

Cheng, Chu-yuan. *China's Economic Development: Growth and Structural Change*. Boulder: Westview Press, 1982.

Ch'en Te-sheng. ''The Development of Town and Township Enterprises in Mainland China since 1979,'' *Issues & Studies* [Taipei], 22, No. 10, October 1986, 67–88.

China. State Statistical Bureau. *Statistical Yearbook of China, 1984*. Hong Kong: Economic Information & Agency, December 1984.

China Handbook Editorial Committe. *China Handbook Series: Economy*. Beijing: Foreign Languages Press, 1984.

Chow, Gregory C. *The Chinese Economy*. New York: Harper & Row, 1985.

Clark, Allen L., James P. Dorian, and Powfoong Fan. ''An Estimate of the Mineral Resources of China,'' *Resources Policy* [Guildford, United Kingdom], 13, No. 1, March 1987, 68–84.

Conroy, Richard. ''Technological Innovation in China's Recent Industrialization,'' *China Quarterly* [London], No. 97, March 1984, 1–23.

Field, Robert Michael. ''Changes in Chinese Industry since 1978,'' *China Quarterly* [London], No. 100, December 1984, 742–61.

Henley, John S., and Mee-Kau Nyau. ''Reforming Chinese Industrial Management,'' *Euro-Asia Business Review* [Chichester, United Kingdom], 5, No. 3, July 1986, 10–15.

Howe, Christopher. *China's Economy: A Basic Guide*. New York: Basic Books, 1978.

Khanna, Anupam. *Issues in the Technological Development of China's Electronic Sector*. (World Bank Staff Working Papers, No. 762.) Washington: World Bank, 1986.

Klenner, Wolfgang. "Economic Reforms in the Industrial Sector of the Peoples Republic of China," *Intereconomics* [Hamburg], 18, No. 5, September–October 1983, 245–50.

Lim, Edwin, et al. *China: Long-Term Development Issues and Options: The Report of a Mission Sent to China by the World Bank.* (World Bank Country Economic Report.) Baltimore: Johns Hopkins University Press, 1985.

Pollack, Jonathan D. *The R&D Process and Technological Innovation in the Chinese Industrial System.* (R–3284.) Santa Monica: Rand, 1985.

Prybyla, Jan S. "China's Economic Experiment: From Mao to Market," *Problems of Communism*, 35, No. 1, January–February 1986, 21–38.

Rawski, Thomas G. *China's Transition to Industrialism.* Ann Arbor: University of Michigan Press, 1980.

Riva, Joseph P., Jr. "The Petroleum Endowment of China," *Congressional Research Service Review*, 7, No. 6, June 1986, 19–22.

Simon, Denis Fred. "The Challenge of Modernizing Industrial Technology in China," *Asian Survey*, 26, No. 4, April 1986, 420–39.

Solinger, Dorothy J. "China's New Economic Policies and the Local Industrial Political Process: The Case of Wuhan," *Comparative Politics*, 18, No. 1, July 1986, 379–99.

Tidrick, Gene. *Productivity, Growth, and Technological Change in Chinese Industry.* (World Bank Staff Working Papers, No. 761.) Washington: World Bank, 1986.

United States. Central Intelligence Agency. *Handbook of Economic Statistics, 1986.* (Reference Aid, No. CPAS 86–10002.) Washington: September 1986.

United States. Congress. 98th, 2d Session. House of Representatives. Committee on Energy and Commerce. Special Subcommittee on United States Trade with China. *China's Offshore Oil Development and the Energy Security of the Pacific Rim.* (Hearings February 28, 1984.) Washington: GPO, 1984.

United States. Congress. 99th, 2d Session. Joint Economic Committee (ed.). *China's Economy Looks Toward the Year 2000.* 2 vols. Washington: GPO, 1986.

Walder, Andrew G. "China Turns to Industry Reform," *Challenge*, 28, No. 1, March–April 1985, 42–47.

Warwick, Graham. "China: Rebuilding an Industry," *Flight International* [London], June 28, 1986, 28–29.

Woodward, Dennis. "China's Industrial Reform Policy," *Australian Journal of Chinese Affairs* [Canberra], No. 14, July 1985, 85–104.

World Bank. *China: Long-Term Development Issues and Options, Annex 3: China: The Energy Sector*. (World Bank Country Study.) Washington, 1983.

______. *China: Long-Term Development Issues and Options, Annex 5: China: Economic Structure in International Perspective*. (World Bank Country Study.) Washington, 1985.

______. *China: Socialist Economic Development*, 1 and 2. (World Bank Country Study.) Washington: 1983.

Yeh, K.C. *Industrial Innovation in China with Special Reference to the Metallurgical Industry*. (Rand Notes, N-2307.) Santa Monica: Rand, 1985.

(Various issues of the following publications were also used in the preparation of this chapter: *Asian Business* [Hong Kong]; *Asian Wall Street Journal* [Hong Kong]; *Beijing Review* [Beijing]; *Business China* [Hong Kong]; *China Business Review*; *China Daily* [Beijing]; *China News Analysis* [Hong Kong]; *China Reconstructs* [Beijing]; *China's Foreign Trade* [Beijing]; *China Trade Report* [Hong Kong]; *Country Report: China, North Korea* [London]; *Far Eastern Economic Review* [Hong Kong]; Foreign Broadcast Information Service, *Daily Report: China*; Foreign Broadcast Information Service, *Press Note*; Joint Publications Research Service, *China: Economic Affairs*; *Quarterly Economic Review of China, North Korea* [London]; *Sino-British Trade Review* [London]; and *Ta Kung Pao Weekly Supplement* [Hong Kong].)

Chapter 8

Almanac of China's Economy. Beijing: Beijing Economic Management Press, 1985.

"Aviation and Airport Development," *China Transport* [Hong Kong], 2, No. 2, Summer 1986, 72-74.

Batsavage, Richard E., and John L. Davie. "China's International Trade and Finance." Pages 707-41 in United States Congress, 95th, 2d Session, Joint Economic Committee (ed.), *Chinese Economy Post-Mao*. Washington: GPO, 1978.

Bernstein, Thomas P. "Reforming Chinese Agriculture," *China Business Review*, 12, No. 2, March-April 1985, 45-49.

Chao Yu-sen. "Promotion of Lateral Economic Ties on Chinese Mainland," *Issues & Studies* [Taipei], 22, No. 7, July 1986, 5-9.

Chen, Nai-Ruenn. "China's Foreign Trade, 1950-74." Pages 617-52 in United States Congress, 94th, 1st Session, Joint Economic Committee (ed.), *China: A Reassessment of the Economy*. Washington: GPO, 1975.

Chen, Nai-Ruenn, and Jeffrey Lee. *China's Economy and Foreign Trade, 1981-85*. Washington: Department of Commerce, International Trade Administration, 1984.

Chen Muhua. "Major Reform of China's Foreign Trade System," *PRC Quarterly* [Beijing] No. 4, January 1985, 86-88.

China. General Administration of Customs. *Chinese Customs Statistics, No. 1 (1987)* [Hong Kong], April 1987, table 4, 92, *Business China* [Hong Kong], June 22, 1987.

China. State Statistical Bureau. *Statistical Yearbook of China, 1984*. Hong Kong: Economic Information & Agency, 1984.

China's Economic Construction: 100 Projects. Beijing: China Pictorial, 1984.

"China's Rural Reforms," *New China Quarterly* [Hong Kong], No. 1, July 1986, 57, 60-61.

China Urban Statistics, 1985. Beijing: Longman Group and China Statistical Information and Consultancy Service, 1985.

Craig, Jack. "China: Domestic and International Telecommunications, 1949-74." Pages 289-310 in United States Congress, 94th, 1st Session, Joint Economic Committee (ed.), *China: A Reassessment of the Economy*. Washington: GPO, 1975.

Draper, Rosemary. "Uncertain Course for Inland Waterways," *China Business Review*, 13, No. 4, July-August 1986, 20-26.

"Eat from the Great Bowl or 'Insure Yourself'," *China News Analysis* [Hong Kong], No. 1322, November 15, 1986, 1-9.

Eckstein, Alexander. *China's Economic Revolution*. New York: Cambridge, University Press, 1977.

______. *Communist China's Economic Growth and Foreign Trade*. New York: McGraw-Hill, 1966.

Editorial Committee of the China Official Yearbook. *The China Official Yearbook, 1985/6*. Hong Kong: Salem International Publications, 1985.

Ellman, Michael. "Economic Reform in China," *International Affairs* [London], 62, No. 3, Summer 1986, 423-42.

Engle, Tom. "CITIC: Pacesetting Corporation," *China Business Review*, 12, No. 4, July-August 1985, 6-10.

Frankenstein, John. "Understanding Chinese Trade," *Current History*, 85, No. 512, September 1986, 257-60, 274-75.

Gold, Thomas B. "China's Private Entrepreneurs," *China Business Review*, 12, No. 6, November-December 1985, 46-50.

"The Highways Bureau," *China Transport* [Beijing], 2, No. 2, Summer 1986, 66-68.

International Monetary Fund. *International Financial Statistics Yearbook, 1986*. Washington; 1986.

Kueh, Y.Y., and Christopher Howe. "China's International Trade: Policy and Organizational Change and Their Place in the 'Economic Readjustment'," *China Quarterly* [London], No. 100, December 1984, 813-48.

LoPinto, Beverly. "Airport Development," *China Business Review*, 13, No. 4, July-August 1986, 43-48.

Mah, Feng-hwa. *The Foreign Trade of Mainland China*. Chicago: Aldine-Atherton, 1971.

Nakajima, Seiichi. "Transport and the 7th Five-Year Plan," *China Newsletter* [Tokyo], No. 61, March-April 1986, 12-16.

"A New Look at Communications," *China Transport* [Beijing], 2, No. 2, Summer 1986, 58-61.

Oi, Jean C. "Peasant Grain Marketing and State Procurement: China's Grain Contracting System," *China Quarterly* [London], No. 106, June 1986, 272-90.

People's Republic of China Year Book, 1986. Beijing: Xinhua Publishing House, 1986.

"Railway Growth—the Details," *China Transport* [Beijing], 2, No. 2, Summer 1986, 69-70.

Ross, Madelyn C. "Civil Aviation," *China Business Review*, 11, No. 3, May-June 1984, 50-55.

"Satellite Network Goes on Line," *Beijing Review* [Beijing], 29, No. 29, July 21, 1986, 29.

Seto, May. "Modernization and the Media: China's TV, Radio, and Publications Experience: A Renaissance," *China Business Review*, 12, No. 5, September-October 1985, 10-13.

Shi Hao. "Yijiubawu Nian de Zhonggong Jiaotong" (The Chinese Communist Communications in 1985), *Studies on Chinese Communism* [Taipei], 20, No. 2, February 15, 1986, 44-58.

Skinner, G. William. "Rural Marketing in China: Repression and Revival," *China Quarterly* [London], No. 103, September 1985, 393-413.

Theroux, Eugene A. "Legal and Practical Problems in the China Trade." Pages 539-99 in United States Congress, 94th, 1st Session, Joint Economic Committee (ed.), *China: A Reassessment of the Economy*. Washington: GPO, 1975.

Thoburn, John. "China's Special Economic Zones Revisited," *Euro-Asia Business Review* [Chichester, United Kingdom], 5, No. 4, October 1986, 44-49.

United States. Central Intelligence Agency. *Central Government Organizations of the People's Republic of China*. (Reference Aid CR 86-11028.) Washington: 1986.

______. *China: International Trade Fourth Quarter, 1984.* (Reference Aid EA CIT 85-002.) Washington: 1985.

______. *Handbook of Economic Statistics, 1986.* (Reference Aid CPAS 86-10002.) Washington: 1986.

______. *Major Foreign Trade Organizations of the People's Republic of China.* (Reference Aid CR 86-11030.) Washington: 1985.

______. *The World Factbook, Nineteen Hundred and Eighty-Six.* (CRWF 86-001.) Washington: 1986.

United States. Congress. 99th, 2d Session. Joint Economic Committee (ed.). *China's Economy Looks Toward the Year 2000.* 2 vols. Washington: GPO, 1986.

Venny, Jacques, and Lily V. Uy. *Transport in China.* Washington: World Bank, 1985.

Vetterling, Philip W., and James J. Wagg. "The Transportation Sector, 1950-1971." Pages 147-77 in United States Congress, 92d, 2d Session, Joint Economic Committee (ed.), *People's Republic of China: An Economic Assessment.* Washington: GPO, 1972.

Weil, Martin. "The Two Faces of Chinese Rail Technology," *China Business Review,* 11, No. 5, September-October 1984, 24-35.

World Bank. *Long-Term Development Issues and Options, Annex 6: China: The Transport Sector.* (World Bank Country Study.) Washington, 1985.

Wyman, Molly E. "The Lure of Television," *China Business Review,* 12, No. 5, September-October 1985, 14-25.

Yearbook on Chinese Communism, 1986. Taipei: Institute for the Study of Chinese Communist Problems, 1986.

Yenny, Jacques. "Modernizing China's Transport System," *China Business Review,* 13, No. 4, July-August 1986, 20-23.

Yoshida, Hiroshi. "China's Telecommunications Services." *China Newsletter* [Tokyo], No. 61, March-April 1986, 8-11.

Zhao Yutian. "Tourism in China Opens Up to Bright Prospects," *New China Quarterly* [Hong Kong], No. 1, July 1986, 18-21.

Zheng Zhensun. *People's Republic of China Year Book, 1985.* Beijing: Xinhua Publishing House, 1985.

(Various issues of the following publications were also used in the preparation of this chapter: *Asiaweek* [Hong Kong]; *Beijing Review* [Beijing]; *China Business Review*; *China Daily* [Beijing]; *China Trade Report* [Hong Kong]; *China Transport* [Beijing]; *Far Eastern Economic Review* [Hong Kong]; and Foreign Broadcast Information Service, *Daily Report: China.*)

Chapter 9

Baark, Erik. "Information Infrastructures in India and China." Pages 86–141 in Erik Baark and Andrew Jamison (eds.), *Technological Development in China, India, and Japan: Cross-Cultural Perspectives*. New York: St. Martin's Press, 1986.

______. "Putting Domestic Technology to Work," *China Business Review*, 14, No. 3, May–June 1987, 53–55.

Battat, Joseph Y. *Management in Post-Mao China: An Insider's View*. Ann Arbor: UMI Research Press, 1986.

Bauer, Eugene E. *China Takes Off: Technology Transfer and Modernization*. Seattle: University of Washington Press, 1986.

Baum, Richard (ed.). *China's Four Modernizations: The New Technological Revolution*. Boulder: Westview Press, 1980.

Cheng, Chu-yuan. *Scientific and Engineering Manpower in Communist China, 1949–1963*. Washington: National Science Foundation, 1965.

Fischer, William A. "China's Scientific and Technological Policy: An Assessment." Pages 1–15 in Pierre M. Perrolle and Denis F. Simon (eds.), *China's Scientific and Technological Modernization: Domestic and International Implications*. (Occasional Paper, No. 11) Washington: East Asia Program, Wilson Center, 1982.

______. "Scientific and Technical Planning in the People's Republic of China," *Technological Forecasting and Social Change*, No. 25, May 1984, 189–207.

Goldman, Merle. *China's Intellectuals: Advise and Dissent*. Cambridge: Harvard University Press, 1981.

Grow, Roy F. "How Factories Choose Technology," *China Business Review*, 14, No. 3, May–June 1987, 35–39.

Heymann, Hans. "Acquisition and Diffusion of Technology in China." Pages 685–709 in United States Congress, 94th, 1st Session, Joint Economic Committee (eds.), *China: A Reassessment of the Economy*. Washington: GPO, 1975.

Khanna, Anupam. *Issues in the Technological Development of China's Electronic Sector*. (World Bank Staff Working Papers, No. 762.) Washington: World Bank, 1986.

Needham, Joseph. *Science and Civilisation in China*, 1–6. Cambridge: Cambridge University Press, 1954–86.

Orleans, Leo A. "Chinese Students and Technology Transfer," *Journal of Northeast Asian Studies*, 4, No. 4, Winter 1985, 3–25.

______. *Professional Manpower and Education in Communist China*. Washington: National Science Foundation, 1961.

______. "Science, Elitism, and Economic Readjustment." Pages 475–88 in United States Congress, 97th, 2d Session, Joint

Economic Committee (ed.), *China under the Four Modernizations*, Pt. 1. Washington: GPO, 1982.

______. *The Training and Utilization of Scientific and Engineering Manpower in the People's Republic of China.* United States Congress, 98th, 1st Session, House of Representatives, Committee on Science and Technology, Subcommittee on Science, Research, and Technology. Washington: GPO, 1983.

Orleans, Leo A. (ed.). *Science in Contemporary China.* Stanford: Stanford University Press, 1980.

Pollack, Jonathan D. *The Chinese Electronics Industry in Transition.* (Rand Notes, N-2306.) Santa Monica: Rand, 1985.

Ridley, Charles P. *China's Scientific Policies: Implications for International Cooperation.* (AEI-Hoover Policy Studies.) Washington: American Enterprise Institute for Public Policy Research, 1976.

Simon, Denis Fred. "China's Capacity to Assimilate Foreign Technology: An Assessment." Pages 514-52 in United States Congress, 97th, 2d Session, Joint Economic Committee (ed.), *China under the Four Modernizations*, Pt. 1. Washington: GPO, 1982.

______. "China's S&T Intellectuals in the Post-Mao Era: A Retrospective and Prospective Glimpse," *Journal of Northeast Asian Studies*, 4, No. 2, Summer 1985, 57-82.

______. "Chinese-Style S&T Modernization: A Comparison of PRC and Taiwan Approaches," *Studies in Comparative Communism*, 17, No. 2, Summer 1984, 87-109.

______. "The Evolving Role of Technology Transfer in China's Modernization." Pages 254-86 in United States Congress, 99th, 2d Session, Joint Economic Committee (ed.), *China's Economy Looks Toward the Year 2000, 2: Economic Openness in Modernizing China.* Washington: GPO, 1986.

______. "Rethinking R&D," *China Business Review*, 10, No. 4, July-August 1983, 25-31.

Suttmeier, Richard P. "The Institutional Structure for Industrial Research and Development in China." Pages 125-49 in Richard Baum (ed.), *China's Four Modernizations: The New Technological Revolution.* Boulder: Westview Press, 1980.

______. "Overview: Science and Technology under Reform." Pages 199-215 in United States Congress, 99th, 2d Session, Joint Economic Committee (ed.), *China's Economy Looks Toward the Year 2000, 2: Economic Openness in Modernizing China.* Washington: GPO, 1986.

______. *Research and Revolution: Science Policy and Societal Change in China.* Lexington, Massachusetts: Heath, 1974.

______. "Research, Innovation, and the Chinese Political Economy," Pages 489-513 in United States Congress, 97th,

2d Session, Joint Economic Committee (ed.), *China under the Four Modernizations*, Pt. 1. Washington: GPO, 1982.

Tang, Tong B. *Science and Technology in China*. London: Longman, 1984.

Tidrick, Gene. *Productivity, Growth, and Technological Change in Chinese Industry*. (World Bank Staff Working Papers, No. 761.) Washington: World Bank, 1986.

Tow, William T. "Science and Technology in China's Defense," *Problems of Communism*, 34, No. 4, July–August 1985, 15–31.

United States. Congress. 98th, 1st Session. House of Representatives. Committee on Energy and Commerce. Special Subcommittee on United States Trade with China. *Science and Technology: Cooperation Between the United States and China*. Washington: GPO, 1983.

United States. Congress. Office of Technology Assessment. *Technology Transfer to China*. (OTA–ISC–340.) Washington: GPO, July 1987.

Volti, Rudi. *Technology, Politics, and Society in China*. (Westview Special Studies on China and East Asia.) Boulder: Westview Press, 1982.

Wei Liming. "China's Scientists Vindicate Their Vocation," *Beijing Review* [Beijing], 29, No. 41, October 13, 1986, 14–19.

World Bank. *China: Long-Term Development Issues and Options*. Baltimore: John Hopkins University Press, 1985.

Wu, Yuan-li, and Robert B. Sheeks. *The Organization and Support of Scientific Research and Development in Mainland China*. New York: Praeger, 1970.

Xu Liangying and Fan Dainian. Pierre M. Perrolle (ed.). *Science and Socialist Construction in China*. (Trans., John C.S. Hsu.) Armonk, New York: Sharpe, 1982.

Yeh, K.C. *Industrial Innovation in China with Special Reference to the Metallurgical Industry*. (Rand Notes, N–2307.) Santa Monica: Rand, 1985.

(Various issues of the following publications were also used in the preparation of this chapter: *Asian Survey*; *Beijing Review* [Beijing]; *China Business Review*; *China Daily* [Beijing]; *China Exchange News*; *China Trade Report* [Hong Kong]; *Comparative Communism*; Foreign Broadcast Information Service, *Daily Report: China*; Joint Publications Research Service, *China Report: Science and Technology*; and *Technological Forecasting and Social Change*.

Chapter 10

Ahn, Byung-joon. *Chinese Politics and the Cultural Revolution: Dynamics of Policy Processes*. Seattle: University of Washington Press, 1977.

Barnett, A. Doak. *Cadres, Bureaucracy, and Political Power in Communist China*. New York: Columbia University Press, 1967.

Barnett, A. Doak, and Ralph N. Clough (eds.). *Modernizing China: Post-Mao Reform and Development*. Boulder: Westview Press, 1986.

Baum, Richard. "Modernization and Legal Reform in Post-Mao China: The Rebirth of Socialist Legality," *Studies in Comparative Communism*, 19, No. 2, Summer 1986, 69–103.

Bedeski, Robert E. "The Concept of the State: Sun Yat-sen and Mao Tse-tung," *China Quarterly* [London], No. 70, June 1977, 338–54.

Burns, John P., and Stanley Rosen (eds.). *Policy Conflicts in Post-Mao China: A Documentary Survey, with Analysis*. Armonk, New York: Sharpe, 1986.

Chan, Steve. "Chinese Conflict Calculus and Behavior: Assessment from a Perspective of Conflict Management," *World Politics*, 30, No. 3, April 1978, 391–410.

Chang, David W. *Zhou Enlai and Deng Xiaoping in the Chinese Leadership Succession Crisis*. Lanham, Maryland: University Press of America, 1984.

Chang, Parris H. *Elite Conflict in the Post-Mao China*. (Occasional Papers/Reprints Series in Contemporary Asian Studies, No. 2, 1983 [55].) Baltimore: School of Law, University of Maryland, 1983.

______. *Radicals and Radical Ideology in China's Cultural Revolution*. New York: Research Institute on Communist Affairs, Columbia University, 1973.

______. "The Tensions Behind the Peking Congress," *Christian Science Monitor*, August 29, 1980, 23.

China. "Constitution of the Communist Party of China," *Beijing Review* [Beijing], 25, No. 38, September 20, 1982, 8–21.

______. "Constitution of the People's Republic of China," *Beijing Review* [Beijing], 21, No. 11, March 17, 1978, 5–14.

______. "Constitution of the People's Republic of China," *Beijing Review* [Beijing], 25, No. 52, December 27, 1982, 10–29.

Chiu, Hungdah. *The 1982 Constitution and the Rule of Law*. (Occasional Papers/Reprints Series in Contemporary Asian Studies, No. 4, 1985 [69].) Baltimore: School of Law, University of Maryland, 1985.

Chiu, Hungdah, and Shao-chuan Leng (eds.). *China: Seventy Years after the 1911 Hsin-Hai Revolution*. Charlottesville: University Press of Virginia, 1984.

Deng Xiaoping. *Selected Works of Deng Xiaoping*. Beijing: Foreign Languages Press, 1984.

Domes, Jürgen. *The Government and Politics of the PRC: A Time of Transition*. Boulder: Westview Press, 1985.

Epstein, Edward. "The Law Leaps Ahead," *Far Eastern Economic Review* [Hong Kong], April 17, 1986, 52.

Falkenheim, Victor C. "County Administration in Fukien," *China Quarterly* [London], No. 59, July-September 1974, 518-43.

______. *Chinese Politics and the Succession to Mao*. New York: Holmes and Meier, 1982.

Godwin, Paul H.B. "The PLA and Political Control in China's Provinces: A Structural Analysis," *Comparative Politics*, 9, No. 1, October 1976, 1-20.

Goodman, David S.G. "The National CCP Conference of September 1985 and China's Leadership Changes," *China Quarterly* [London], No. 105, March 1986, 123-30.

Hinton, Harold C. (ed.). *The People's Republic of China, 1979-84: A Documentary Survey*. Wilmington, Delaware: Scholarly Resources, 1986.

Houn, Franklin W. "Constitution and Government." Pages 221-39 in Yuan-li Wu (ed.), *China: A Handbook*. New York: Praeger, 1973.

Howkins, John. *China Media Industry Report*. New York: Nord Media, 1980.

Jacobson, Harald W. "The Political System." Pages 99-173 in Harold C. Hinton (ed.), *The People's Republic of China: A Handbook*. Boulder: Westview Press, 1979.

Kallgren, Joyce K. "China in 1978: The New Long March," *Asian Survey*, 19, No. 1, January 1979, 1-19.

______. "China 1979: On Turning Thirty," *Asian Survey*, 20, No. 1, January 1980, 1-18.

______. "The Chinese Communist Party: Structure, Membership, and Mass Organization." Pages 197-220 in Yuan-li Wu (ed.), *China: A Handbook*. New York: Praeger, 1973.

Lee, Ching Hua. *Deng Xiaoping: The Marxist Road to the Forbidden City*. Princeton: Kingston Press, 1985.

Lee, Hong Yung. *The Politics of the Chinese Cultural Revolution: A Case Study*. Berkeley and Los Angeles: University of California Press, 1973.

Lieberthal, Kenneth. "The Politics of Modernization in the PRC," *Problems of Communism*, 27, No. 3, May-June 1978, 1-17.

Liu, Alan P.L. *Communications and National Integration in Communist China*. Berkeley and Los Angeles: University of California Press, 1971.

______. *How China Is Ruled*. Englewood Cliffs: Prentice-Hall, 1986.

Lubman, Stanley B. "On Understanding Chinese Law and Legal Institutions," *American Bar Association Journal*, 62, May 1976, 596–99.

Manion, Melanie. "The Cadre Management System Post-Mao: The Appointment, Promotion, Transfer, and Removal of Party and State Leaders," *China Quarterly* [London], No. 102, June 1985, 203–33.

Meisner, Maurice. *Mao's China and After: A History of the People's Republic*. (rev ed.) (Transformation of Modern China series.) New York: Free Press, 1986.

Mills, William deB. "Leadership Change in China's Provinces," *Problems of Communism*, 34, No. 3, May–June 1985, 24–40.

Montaperto, Ronald N. "Political Socialization: Two Paths—the Maoist Approach," *Problems of Communism*, 22, No. 5, September–October 1973, 51–63.

Nathan, Andrew J. *Chinese Democracy*. Berkeley and Los Angeles: University of California Press, 1986.

______. "A Factionalism Model for CCP Politics," *China Quarterly* [London], No. 53, January–March 1973, 34–66.

______. "Policy Oscillations in the People's Republic of China: A Critique," *China Quarterly* [London], No. 68, December 1976, 720–33.

Nelsen, Harvey. "Military Forces in the Cultural Revolution," *China Quarterly* [London], No. 51, January–March 1972, 444–74.

Ogden, Suzanne. "The Approach of the Chinese Communists to the Study of International Law, State Sovereignty, and the International System," *China Quarterly* [London], No. 70, June 1977, 315–37.

Oksenberg, Michel. "Methods of Communication Within the Chinese Bureaucracy," *China Quarterly* [London], No. 57, January–March 1974, 1–39.

Oksenberg, Michel (ed.). *China's Developmental Experience*. New York: Praeger, 1973.

Perrolle, Pierre M. (ed.). *Fundamentals of the Chinese Communist Party*. (China Book Project.) White Plains: International Arts and Sciences Press, 1976.

Qi Wen. *China: A General Survey*. Beijing: Foreign Languages Press, 1979.

Qi Xin, et al. *China's New Democracy—with Full Texts of the Three Constitutions of the People's Republic of China*. Hong Kong: Cosmos Books, 1979.

Raddock, David M. "Between Generations: Activist Chinese Youth in Pursuit of a Political Role in the San-fan and in the Cultural

Revolution,'' *China Quarterly* [London], No. 79, September 1979, 511-28.

Rice, Edward E. ''Chinese Politics, 1973-76: The Second Rise and Fall of Teng Hsiao-p'ing,'' *China Quarterly* [London], No. 67, September 1976, 494-500.

Scalapino, Robert A. (ed.). *Elites in the People's Republic of China*. Seattle: University of Washington Press, 1972.

Schram, Stuart R. (ed.). *The Scope of State Power in China*. London: School of Oriental and African Studies, University of London, 1985.

Schurmann, Franz. *Ideology and Organization in Communist China*. Berkeley and Los Angeles: University of California Press, 1966.

Shambaugh, David L. *The Making of a Premier: Zhao Ziyang's Provincial Career*. Boulder: Westview Press, 1984.

Starr, John Bryan. *Continuing Revolution: The Political Thought of Mao*. Princeton: Princeton University Press, 1979.

Stepanek, James B. ''China's SEZs,'' *China Business Review*, 9, No. 2, March-April 1982, 38-40.

Terrill, Ross. ''China in the 1980s,'' *Foreign Affairs*, 58, No. 4, Spring 1980, 920-35.

Tien, Hung-mao. *The Communist Party of China: Party Powers and Group Politics from the Third Plenum to the Twelfth Party Congress*. (Occasional Papers/Reprints Series in Contemporary Asian Studies, No. 2, 1984 [61].) Baltimore: School of Law, University of Maryland, 1984.

Townsend, James R., and Brantly Womack. *Politics in China*. (3d ed.) (Series in Comparative Politics: A Country Study.) Boston: Little, Brown, 1986.

United States. Central Intelligence Agency. National Foreign Assessment Center. *China: The Continuing Search for a Modernization Strategy*. (Research Paper, No. ER 80-10248.) Washington: April 1980.

United States. Congress. 99th, 2d Session. Joint Economic Committee (ed.). *China's Economy Looks Toward the Year 2000, 1: The Four Modernizations*. Washington: GPO, 1986.

Wang, James C.F. *Contemporary Chinese Politics: An Introduction to Political Institutions and Processes*. Englewood Cliffs: Prentice-Hall, 1980.

Weng, Byron S.J. (ed.). ''Studies on the Constitutional Law of the People's Republic of China,'' *Chinese Law and Government*, 16, Nos. 2-3, Summer-Fall 1983, 3-192.

Zheng Zhensun. *People's Republic of China Year Book, 1985*. Beijing: Xinhua Publishing House, 1985.

(Various issues of the following publications were also used in the preparation of this chapter: *China Daily* [Beijing]; *China News Analysis* [Hong Kong]; *Christian Science Monitor*; Foreign Broadcast Information Service, *Daily Report: China*; Joint Publications Research Service, *China Report: Political, Sociological, and Military Affairs*; and *Washington Post*.)

Chapter 11

Barnett, A. Doak. *Cadres, Bureaucracy, and Political Power in Communist China*. New York: Columbia University Press, 1967.

______. "Ten Years after Mao," *Foreign Affairs*, 65, No. 1, Fall 1986, 37–65.

Barnett, A. Doak and Ralph N. Clough (eds.). *Modernizing China: Post-Mao Reform and Development*. Boulder, Colorado: Westview Press, 1986.

Baum, Richard (ed.). *China's Four Modernizations: The New Technological Revolution*. Boulder: Westview Press, 1980.

Brugger, Bill (ed.). *Chinese Marxism in Flux, 1978–84*. Armonk, New York: Sharpe, 1985.

Chang, David W. *Zhou Enlai and Deng Xiaoping in the Chinese Leadership Succession Crisis*. Lanham, Maryland: University Press of America, 1984.

Chang, Parris H. *Power and Policy in China*. University Park: Pennsylvania State University Press, 1975.

______. "The Rise of Wang Tung-hsing: Head of China's Security Apparatus," *China Quarterly* [London], No. 73, March 1978, 122–37.

Chen, Jerome (ed.). *Mao*. Englewood Cliffs: Prentice-Hall, 1969.

Chen, Yung-fa. *Making Revolution: The Communist Movement in Eastern and Central China, 1937–1945*. Berkeley and Los Angeles: University of California Press, 1986.

Chi Hsin (pseud. for research group in Hong Kong). *The Case of the Gang of Four*. Hong Kong: Cosmos Books, 1977.

______. *Teng Hsiao-ping: A Political Biography*. Hong Kong: Cosmos Books, 1978.

Chi, Wen-shun. *Ideological Conflicts in Modern China: Democracy and Authoritarianism*. New Brunswick, New Jersey: Transaction Books, 1986.

Ching, Frank. "The Current Political Scene in China," *China Quarterly* [London], No. 80, December 1979, 691–715.

Clarke, Christopher M. "Reorganization and Modernization in Post-Mao China." Pages 90–109 in United States Congress,

99th, 2d Session, Joint Economic Committee. *China's Economy Looks Toward the Year 2000, 1: The Four Modernizations*. Washington: GPO, 1986.

Dittmer, Lowell. "The Legacy of Mao Zedong," *Asian Survey*, 20, No. 5, May 1980, 552-73.

Domes, Jürgen. "China in 1977: Reversal of Verdicts," *Asian Survey*, 18, No. 1, January 1978, 1-16.

Falkenheim, Victor C. "Administrative Reform and Modernization in Post-Mao China," *Pacific Affairs* [Vancouver], 53, No. 1, Spring 1980, 5-28.

Gardner, John. *China under Deng*. (Conflict Studies, No. 197.) London: Centre for Security and Conflict Studies, 1987.

______. *Chinese Politics and the Succession to Mao*. New York: Holmes & Meier, 1982.

Goodman, David S.G. (ed.). *Groups and Politics in the People's Republic of China*. Armonk, New York: Sharpe, 1984.

______. "The National CCP Conference of September 1985 and China's Leadership Changes," *China Quarterly* [London], No. 105, March 1985, 123-30.

______. "The Second Plenary Session of the 12th CCP Central Committee: Rectification and Reform," *China Quarterly* [London], No. 97, March 1984, 84-90.

______. "State Reforms in the People's Republic of China since 1976: A Historical Perspective." Pages 116-32 in Stephen White and Daniel Nelson (eds.), *Communist Politics: A Reader*. New York: New York University Press, 1986.

Gottschalk, Marie. "The Politics of Change in China," *Nation*, 242, No. 4, February 1, 1986, 105-109.

Hamrin, Carol Lee. "Competing Political-Economic Strategies." Pages 72-89 in United States Congress, 99th, 2d Session, Joint Economic Committee (ed.), *China's Economy Looks Toward the Year 2000, 1: The Four Modernizations*. Washington: GPO, 1986.

Harding, Harry. "Competing Models of the Chinese Communist Policy Process: Toward a Sorting and Evaluation," *Issues & Studies* [Taipei], 20, No. 2, February 1984, 13-36.

______. "Political Development in Post-Mao China." Pages 13-37 in A. Doak Barnett and Ralph N. Clough (eds.), *Modernizing China: Post-Mao Reform and Development*. Boulder: Westview Press, 1986.

______. "Political Stability and Succession." Pages 49-71 in United States Congress, 99th, 2d Session, Joint Economic Committee (ed.), *China's Economy Looks Toward the Year 2000, 1: The Four Modernizations*. Washington: GPO, 1986.

Hinton, Harold C. (ed.). *The People's Republic of China, 1979–84: A Documentary Survey*. Wilmington, Delaware: Scholarly Resources, 1986.

Joseph, William A. "China's Modernization of Mao," *Current History*, 85, September 1986, 265–81.

Kallgren, Joyce. "China in 1983: The Turmoil of Modernization," *Asian Survey*, 24, No. 1, January 1984, 60–80.

______. "China 1979: On Turning Thirty," *Asian Survey*, 20, No. 1, January 1980, 1–18.

Leys, Simon. "The End of Peking's Spring," *Encounter* [London], 54, No. 3, November 1979, 31–42.

Lieberthal, Kenneth. *Central Documents and Politburo Politics in China*. (Michigan Papers in Chinese Studies, No. 33.) Ann Arbor: University of Michigan Press, 1978.

Lin, Yi. "Achievements of the CCP Secretariat since Its Foundation," *Tung Hsiang* (Trends) [Hong Kong], No. 22, July 16, 1980, 16–17.

Mackerras, Colin. "'Party Consolidation' and the Attack on 'Spiritual Pollution'," *Australian Journal of Chinese Affairs* [Canberra], No. 11, January 1984, 175–85.

Manion, Melanie. "The Cadre Management System, Post-Mao: The Appointment, Promotion, Transfer and Removal of Party and State Leaders," *China Quarterly* [London], No. 102, June 1985, 203–33.

Meisner, Maurice. *Mao's China and After: A History of the People's Republic*. New York: The Free Press, 1986.

Moody, Peter R., Jr. *Chinese Politics after Mao: Development and Liberalization, 1976 to 1983*. New York: Praeger, 1983.

Nathan, Andrew J. *Chinese Democracy*. Berkeley and Los Angeles: University of California Press, 1986.

Oi, Jean C. "Commercializing China's Rural Cadres," *Problems of Communism*, 35, No. 5, September-October 1986, 1–15.

Oksenberg, Michel. "The Exit Pattern from Chinese Politics," *China Quarterly* [London], No. 67, September 1976, 501–18.

Oksenberg, Michel, and Richard Bush. "China's Political Evolution: 1972–1982," *Problems of Communism*, 31, No. 5, September-October 1982, 1–19.

Oksenberg, Michel, and Sai-chang Yeung. "Hua Kuo-feng's Pre-Cultural Revolution Hunan Years, 1949–66: The Making of a Political Generalist," *China Quarterly* [London], No. 69, March 1977, 1–53.

Onate, Andres D. "Hua Kuo-feng and the Arrest of the 'Gang of Four'," *China Quarterly* [London], No. 75, September 1978, 540–65.

Pye, Lucian W. *Asian Power and Politics: The Cultural Dimensions of Authority*. Cambridge: Harvard University Press, 1985.

______. *The Dynamics of Factions and Consensus in Chinese Politics: A Model and Some Propositions*. (R-2566-AF.) Santa Monica: Rand, 1980.

______. "On Chinese Pragmatism in the 1980s," *China Quarterly* [London], No. 106, June 1986, 207-34.

Rice, Edward E. "The Second Rise and Fall of Teng Hsiao-ping," *China Quarterly* [London], No. 67, September 1976, 494-500.

Rosen, Stanley. "China in 1986: A Year of Consolidation," *Asian Survey*, 27, No. 1, January 1987, 35-55.

Schram, Stuart R. "'Economics in Command?' Ideology and Policy since the Third Plenum, 1978-84," *China Quarterly* [London], No. 99, September 1984, 417-61.

______. *Mao Tse-tung*. New York: Simon and Schuster, 1967.

Schurmann, Franz. *Ideology and Organization in Communist China*. Berkeley and Los Angeles: University of California Press, 1966.

Schwarcz, Vera. *The Chinese Enlightenment: Intellectuals and the Legacy of the May Fourth Movement of 1919*. Berkeley and Los Angeles: University of California Press, 1986.

Selden, Mark, and Victor Lippit (eds.). *The Transition to Socialism in China*. Armonk, New York: Sharpe, 1982.

Shaw, Yu-ming (ed.). *Power and Policy in the PRC*. Boulder: Westview Press, 1985.

Solomon, Richard H. *Mao's Revolution and the Chinese Political Culture*. Berkeley and Los Angeles: University of California Press, 1971.

Stacey, Judith. *Patriarchy and Socialist Revolution in China*. Berkeley and Los Angeles: University of California Press, 1983.

Teiwes, Frederick C. *Politics and Purges in China*. White Plains: Sharpe, 1979.

______. "'Rules of the Game' in Chinese Politics," *Problems of Communism*, 28, Nos. 5-6, September-December 1979, 67-76.

Townsend, James R., and Brantly Womack. *Politics in China*. (3d ed.) (Series in Comparative Politics: A Country Study.) Boston: Little, Brown, 1986.

Wang, Ting. "A Concise Biography of Hua Kuo-feng," *Chinese Law and Government*, 11, No. 1, Spring 1978, 1-71.

Wilson, Dick. *Chou: The Story of Zhou Enlai, 1898-1976*. London: Hutchinson, 1984.

Wilson, Dick (ed.). *Mao Tse-tung in the Scales of History: A Preliminary Assessment*. London: Cambridge University Press, 1977.

Womack, Brantly. "Politics and Epistemology in China since Mao," *China Quarterly* [London], No. 80, December 1979, 768-92.

(Various issues of the following publications were also used in the preparation of this chapter: Foreign Broadcast Information Service, *Daily Report: China*, and Joint Publications Research Service, *China Report: Political, Sociological, and Military Affairs*.)

Chapter 12

Abidi, A.H.H. *China, Iran, and the Persian Gulf*. Atlantic Highlands, New Jersey: Humanities Press, 1982.

Asia 1985 Yearbook. Hong Kong: Far Eastern Economic Review, 1985.

Barnett, A. Doak. *China and the Major Powers in East Asia*. Washington: Brookings Institution, 1977.

______. *The Making of Foreign Policy in China: Structure and Process*. (SAIS Papers in International Affairs, No. 9.) Boulder: Westview Press, 1985.

Bedeski, Robert E. *The Fragile Entente: The 1978 Japan-China Peace Treaty in a Global Context*. Boulder: Westview Press, 1983.

Behbehani, Hashim S.H. *China's Foreign Policy in the Arab World, 1955–75: Three Case Studies*. Boston: Kegan Paul International, 1981.

Burns, John P. "The Process of Assimilation of Hong Kong (1997) and Implications for Taiwan," *AEI Foreign Policy and Defense Review*, 6, No. 3, March 1986, 19–26.

Camilleri, Joseph. *Chinese Foreign Policy: The Maoist Era and Its Aftermath*. Seattle: University of Washington Press, 1980.

Chang, Luke T. *China's Boundary Treaties and Frontier Disputes*. London: Oceana, 1982.

Chang, Pao-min. "Sino-Vietnamese Territorial Dispute," *Asia Pacific Community* [Tokyo], No. 28, Spring 1985, 74–87.

Chang, Parris H. "US-China Relations: From Hostility to Euphoria to Realism," *Annals of the American Academy of Political and Social Science*, 476, November 1984, 156–70.

Chavan, R.S. *Chinese Foreign Policy: The Chou Enlai Era*. New Delhi: Sterling, 1979.

Chen, King C. (ed.). *China and the Three Worlds: A Foreign Policy Reader*. White Plains: Sharpe, 1979.

Cheng, Joseph Y.S. "Sino-Soviet Relations in the 1980s," *Asia Pacific Community* [Tokyo], No. 27, Winter 1985, 44–62.

"Chinese Foreign Relations: Adaptation, a Sign of Continuity," *China News Analysis* [Hong Kong], No. 1309, May 1, 1986, 1–10.

Choudhury, G.W. *China in World Affairs: The Foreign Policy of the PRC since 1970*. Boulder: Westview Press, 1982.

Clough, Ralph H. "Recent Trends in Chinese Foreign Policy." Pages 293-307 in Claude A. Buss and W. Glenn Campbell (eds.), *National Security Interests in the Pacific Basin*. Stanford: Stanford University Press, 1985.

Cloughley, B.W. "Sino-Indian Border: Talks Scheduled but Conflict Possible," *Pacific Defence Reporter* [Victoria, Australia], 13, No. 9, March 1987, 38-40.

Culley, Harriet (ed.). "US-China Relations," *GIST* (Department of State), April 1987, 1-2.

Duiker, William J. *China and Vietnam: The Roots of Conflict*. (Indochina Research Monograph.) Berkeley: Institute of East Asian Studies, University of California, 1986.

Dumbaugh, Kerry B., and Richard F. Grimmett. "Arms Sales to China: The Limits to US-Chinese Military Cooperation," *Washington Quarterly*, 9, No. 3, Summer 1986, 89-99.

Ellison, Herbert J. (ed.). *The Sino-Soviet Conflict: A Global Perspective*. Seattle: University of Washington Press, 1982.

Fairbank, John K. *China Perceived: Images and Policies in Chinese-American Relations*. New York: Knopf, 1974.

______. *The United States and China*. (4th ed.) Cambridge: Harvard University Press, 1983.

Feeney, William R. "Chinese Policy in Multilateral Financial Institutions." Pages 266-92 in Samuel S. Kim (ed.), *China and the World: Chinese Foreign Policy in the Post-Mao Era*. Boulder: Westview Press, 1984.

______. *The Participation of the PRC in the United Nations*. (Asian Studies: Occasional Papers series, No. 11.) Edwardsville: Southern Illinois University at Edwardsville, 1974.

Fewsmith, Joseph. "China among the Three Worlds." Pages 315-34 in Robert W. Clawson (ed.), *East-West Rivalry in the Third World: Security Issues and Regional Perspectives*. Wilmington, Delaware: Scholarly Resources, 1986.

Gardner, John. *China under Deng*. (Conflict Studies, No. 197.) London: Centre for Security and Conflict Studies, 1987.

Garrett, Banning N., and Bonnie S. Glaser. *War and Peace: The Views from Moscow and Beijing*. (Policy Papers in International Affairs.) Berkeley: Institute of International Studies, University of California, 1984.

Gelman, Harry. *The Soviet Far East Buildup and Soviet Risk-Taking Against China*. (R-2943-AF.) Santa Monica: Rand, 1982.

Gittings, John. *The World and China, 1922-1972*. New York: Harper & Row, 1974.

Gold, Thomas B. "The Status Quo Is Not Static: Mainland-Taiwan Relations," *Asian Survey*, 27, No. 3, March 1987, 300-15.

Green, Elizabeth E. "China and Mongolia: Recurring Trends and Prospects for Change," *Asian Survey*, 26, No. 12, December 1986, 1337–63.

Gregor, A. James. *The China Connection: US Policy and the People's Republic of China*. Stanford: Stanford University Press, 1986.

Griffith, William E. "China and Europe: 'Weak and Far Away'." Pages 159–77 in Richard H. Solomon (ed.), *The China Factor: Sino-American Relations and the Global Scene*. Englewood Cliffs: Prentice-Hall, 1981.

______. "Sino-Soviet Rapprochement?" *Problems of Communism*, 32, No. 2, March–April 1983, 20–29.

Gurtov, Melvin, and Byong-Moo Hwang. *China under Threat: The Politics of Strategy and Diplomacy*. Baltimore: Johns Hopkins University Press, 1980.

Hamrin, Carol Lee. "Emergence of an 'Independent' Chinese Foreign Policy and Shifts in Sino-US Relations." Pages 63–84 in James C. Hsiung (ed.), *US-Asian Relations: The National Security Paradox*. New York: Praeger, 1983.

Harding, Harry. "Change and Continuity in Chinese Foreign Policy," *Problems of Communism*, 32, No. 2, March–April 1983, 1–29.

______. "China and the Third World: From Revolution to Containment." Pages 257–95 in Richard H. Solomon (ed.), *The China Factor: Sino-American Relations and the Global Scene*. Englewood Cliffs: Prentice-Hall, 1981.

______. "China's Changing Role in the Contemporary World." Pages 177–223 in Harry Harding (ed.), *China's Foreign Relations in the 1980s*. New Haven: Yale University Press, 1984.

______. (ed.). *China's Foreign Relations in the 1980s*. New Haven: Yale University Press, 1984.

Harris, Lillian Craig. "China's Islamic Connection," *Asian Affairs*, 8, No. 5, May–June 1981, 362–72.

Harris, Lillian Craig, and Robert L. Worden (eds.). *China and the Third World: Champion or Challenger?* Dover, Massachusetts: Auburn House, 1986.

Hartland-Thunberg, Penelope. "China's Modernization: A Challenge for the GATT," *Washington Quarterly*, 10, No. 2, Spring 1987, 81–97.

Heaton, William R. "America and China: The Coming Decade," *Air University Review*, 35, No. 2, January–February 1984, 18–29.

Hinton, Harold C. "Interpretations of Mainland China's Recent Foreign Policy." Pages 649–60 in Yu-ming Shaw (ed.), *Mainland China: Politics, Economics, and Reform*. Boulder: Westview Press, 1986.

———. "The People's Republic of China and the World, 1949-1981." Pages 490-523 in Hungdah Chiu and Shao-chuan Leng (eds.), *China: Seventy Years after the 1911 Hsin-Hai Revolution*. Charlottesville: University Press of Virginia, 1984.

Hiramatsu, Shigeo. "A Chinese Perspective on Sino-Soviet Relations," *Journal of Northeast Asian Studies*, 2, No. 3, September 1983, 51-65.

Hsiung, James C. "Soviet-Chinese Detente," *Current History*, 84, No. 573, October 1985, 329-33.

Hsüeh, Chün-tu (ed.). *China's Foreign Relations: New Perspectives*. New York: Praeger, 1982.

Hunt, Michael H. "Chinese Foreign Relations in Historical Perspective." Pages 1-42 in Harry Harding (ed.), *China's Foreign Relations in the 1980s*. New Haven: Yale University Press, 1984.

"International Relations Studies," *China Exchange News*, 13, No. 2, June 1985, 1-17.

Ismael, Tareq Y. "The People's Republic of China and the Middle East." Pages 199-226 in Tareq Y. Ismael (ed.), *International Relations of the Contemporary Middle East*. Syracuse: Syracuse University Press, 1986.

Johnson, U. Alexis, George R. Packard, and Alfred D. Wilhelm (eds.). *China Policy for the Next Decade: Report of the Atlantic Council's Committee on China Policy*. Washington: Atlantic Council of the United States, 1983.

Jones, Peter, and Sian Kevill. *China and the Soviet Union, 1949-84*. New York: Facts on File, 1985.

Kihl, Young Whan, and Lawrence E. Grinter. *Asian-Pacific Security: Emerging Challenges and Responses*. Boulder: Lynne Rienner, 1986.

Kim, Hong N., and Jack L. Hammersmith. "US-China Relations in the Post-Normalization Era, 1979-1985," *Pacific Affairs* [Vancouver], 59, No. 1, Spring 1986, 69-91.

Kim, Samuel S. "China and the Third World: In Search of a Neorealist World Policy." Pages 178-211 in Samuel S. Kim (ed.), *China and the World: Chinese Foreign Policy in the Post-Mao Era*. Boulder: Westview Press, 1984.

———. *China, the United Nations, and World Order*. Princeton: Princeton University Press, 1979.

Kim, Samuel S. (ed.). *China and the World: Chinese Foreign Policy in the Post-Mao Era*. Boulder: Westview Press, 1984.

Klein, Donald W. "China and the Second World." Pages 161-77 in Samuel S. Kim (ed.), *China and the World: Chinese Foreign Policy in the Post-Mao Era*. Boulder: Westview Press, 1984.

Larkin, Bruce D. "China and the Third World in Global Perspective." Pages 63-84 in James C. Hsiung and Samuel S. Kim (eds.), *China in the Global Community*. New York: Praeger, 1980.

Levine, Steven I. "The End of Sino-Soviet Estrangement," *Current History*, 85, No. 512, September 1986, 245-48, 279-80.

Li Huichuan. "The Crux of the Sino-Soviet Boundary Question," (Pt. 1), *Beijing Review* [Beijing], 24, No. 30, July 27, 1981, 12-17.

______. "The Crux of the Sino-Soviet Boundary Question," (Pt. 2), *Beijing Review* [Beijing], 24, No. 31, August 3, 1981, 13-16.

Lian Yan. "The CPC's Relations with Other Parties," *Beijing Review* [Beijing], 29, No. 27, July 7, 1986, 22-25.

Liao, Kuang-sheng. *Antiforeignism and Modernization in China, 1860-1980.* New York: St. Martin's Press, 1984.

Mancall, Mark. *China at the Center: 300 Years of Foreign Policy.* (Transformation of Modern China series.) New York: Free Press, 1984.

Manning, Robert. "The Third World Looks at China." Pages 139-54 in Lillian Craig Harris and Robert L. Worden (eds.), *China and the Third World: Champion or Challenger?* Dover, Massachusetts: Auburn House, 1986.

Mao Zedong. *Report to the Second Plenary Session of the Seventh Central Committee of the Communist Party of China*. Beijing: Foreign Languages Press, 1968.

Melman, Yossi, and Ruth Sinai. "Israeli-Chinese Relations and Their Future Prospects: From Shadow to Sunlight," *Asian Survey*, 27, No. 4, April 1987, 395-407.

Nanto, Richard K., and Hong N. Kim. "The Development of Sino-Japanese Relations," *Current History*, 85, No. 512, September 1986, 253-77.

North, Robert C. *The Foreign Relations of China*. (2d ed.) (Comparative Foreign Relations series.) Encino, California: Dickenson, 1974.

Oksenberg, Michel. "China's Confident Nationalism," *Foreign Affairs*, 65, No. 3, Fall 1987, 501-23.

Oksenberg, Michel, and Robert B. Oxnam. *Dragon and Eagle: United States-China Relations, Past and Future*. New York: Basic Books, 1978.

O'Leary, Greg. "Chinese Foreign Policy—From 'Anti-Imperialism' to 'Anti-Hegemonism'." Pages 203-52 in Bill Brugger (ed.), *China: The Impact of the Cultural Revolution*. New York: Barnes & Noble, 1978.

Pollack, Jonathan D. *The Lessons of Coalition Politics: Sino-American Security Relations*. (R-3133-AF.) Santa Monica: Rand, 1984.

———. *Security, Strategy, and the Logic of Chinese Foreign Policy.* (Research Papers and Policy Studies, No. 5.) Berkeley: Institute of East Asian Studies, University of California, 1981.

———. *The Sino-Soviet Rivalry and Chinese Security Debate.* (R-2907-AF.) Santa Monica: Rand, 1982.

Robinson, Thomas W. "The United States and China in the New Balance of Power," *Current History*, 84, No. 503, September 1985, 241-44, 281.

Ross, Robert S. "International Bargaining and Domestic Politics: US-China Relations since 1972," *World Politics*, 38, No. 2, January 1986, 255-87.

Scalapino, Robert A. "China and Northeast Asia." Pages 178-215 in Richard H. Solomon (ed.), *The China Factor: Sino-American Relations and the Global Scene.* Englewood Cliffs: Prentice-Hall, 1981.

Segal, Gerald. "China and Afghanistan," *Asian Survey*, 21, No. 11, November 1981, 1158-74.

———. *Sino-Soviet Relations after Mao.* London: International Institute for Strategic Studies, 1985.

Seth, S.P. "Sino-Indian Relations: Problems and Prospects," *Asia Pacific Community* [Tokyo], No. 26, Fall 1984, 66-85.

Shaw, Yu-ming (ed.). *Power and Policy in the PRC.* Boulder: Westview Press, 1985.

Shen Shouyuan. "Sino-European Relations in the Global Context: Increased Parallels in an Increasingly Plural World," *Asian Survey*, 26, No. 11, November 1986, 1164-83.

Shichor, Yitzhak. "The Middle East." Pages 263-78 in Gerald Segal and William T. Tow (eds.), *Chinese Defence Policy.* Urbana: University of Illinois Press, 1984.

Simon, Sheldon W. "The Two Southeast Asias and China: Security Perspectives," *Asian Survey*, 24, No. 5, May 1984, 519-33.

Sobell, Vladimir. "The Reconciliation Between China and Eastern Europe," *Washington Quarterly*, 10, No. 2, Spring 1987, 99-109.

Solomon, Richard H. "The China Factor in America's Foreign Relations: Perceptions and Policy Choices." Pages 1-47 in Richard H. Solomon (ed.), *The China Factor: Sino-American Relations and the Global Scene.* Englewood Cliffs: Prentice-Hall, 1981.

Starr, John Bryan. "Sino-American Relations: Policies in Tandem," *Current History*, 85, No. 512, September 1986, 241-44, 277-78.

Stuart, Douglas. "Western Europe." Pages 209-21 in Gerald Segal and William T. Tow (eds.), *Chinese Defence Policy.* Urbana: University of Illinois Press, 1984.

Sutter, Robert G. *The China Quandary: Domestic Determinants of U.S. China Policy, 1972–1982*. (Westview Special Studies in International Relations.) Boulder: Westview Press, 1983.

______. *Chinese Foreign Policy after the Cultural Revolution, 1966–1977*. (Westview Special Studies on China and East Asia.) Boulder: Westview Press, 1978.

______. *Chinese Foreign Policy: Developments after Mao*. New York: Praeger, 1986.

______. "North Korea: The Fourth 'Obstacle' in Sino-Soviet Relations?" *Korea and World Affairs* [Seoul], 10, No. 2, Summer 1986, 370–403.

______. "The Strategic Consequences of Nuclear Proliferation in South Asia for China," *Journal of Strategic Studies* [London], 8, No. 4, December 1985, 49–56.

Townsend, James R., and Brantly Womack. *Politics in China*. (3d ed.) (Series in Comparative Politics: A Country Study.) Boston: Little, Brown, 1986.

United States. Central Intelligence Agency. *Directory of Chinese Officials and Organizations: A Reference Aid*. Washington: 1986.

United States. Congress. 98th, 2d Session. Senate. Committee on Foreign Relations. *United States-China Relations: Today's Realities and Prospects for the Future*. (Hearing.) Washington: GPO, 1984.

United States. Department of State. Bureau of Intelligence and Research. *Chinese Communist World Outlook*. (Department of State Publication, Far Eastern series, 112.) Washington: GPO, 1962.

Van Ness, Peter. "Three Lines in Chinese Foreign Relations, 1950–1983: The Development Imperative." Pages 113–42 in Dorothy Solinger (ed.), *Three Visions of Chinese Socialism*. Boulder: Westview Press, 1984.

Vertzberger, Yaacov. "Afghanistan in China's Policy," *Problems of Communism*, 31, No. 3, May–June 1982, 1–23.

______. *The Enduring Entente: Sino-Pakistani Relations, 1960–1980*. (Washington Papers, 10, No. 95.) New York: Praeger, 1982.

______. "South Asia." Pages 247–62 in Gerald Segal and William T. Tow (eds.), *Chinese Defence Policy*. Urbana: University of Illinois Press, 1984.

Vohra, Ranbir. *China's Path to Modernization*. Englewood Cliffs: Prentice-Hall, 1987.

Wang, Gungwu. *China and the World since 1949: The Impact of Independence, Modernity, and Revolution*. (The Making of the 20th Century.) New York: St. Martin's Press, 1977.

Whiting, Allen S. "Assertive Nationalism in Chinese Foreign Policy," *Asian Survey*, 23, No. 8, August 1983, 913–33.

______. "China and the World." Pages 15-75 in Allen S. Whiting and Robert F. Dernberger (eds.), *China's Future: Foreign Policy and Economic Development in the Past-Mao Era.* New York: McGraw-Hill, 1977.

______. *China Crosses the Yalu: The Decision to Enter the Korean War.* Stanford: Stanford University Press, 1968.

______. *Chinese Domestic Politics and Foreign Policy in the 1970s.* Ann Arbor: Center for Chinese Studies, University of Michigan, 1979.

______. "Foreign Policy of China." Pages 246-89 in Roy C. Macridis (ed.), *Foreign Policy in World Politics.* Englewood Cliffs: Prentice-Hall, 1985.

Worden, Robert L. "International Organizations: China's Third World Policy in Practice." Pages 75-99 in Lillian Craig Harris and Robert L. Worden (eds.), *China and the Third World: Champion or Challenger?* Dover, Massachusetts: Auburn House, 1986.

Yahuda, Michael B. "China's New Outlook: The End of Isolationism?" *World Today* [London], 35, No. 5, May 1979, 180-88.

______. *China's Role in World Affairs.* London: Croom Helm, 1978.

______. "The Ministry of Foreign Affairs of the People's Republic of China." Pages 154-61 in Zara Steiner (ed.), *The Times Survey of Foreign Ministries of the World.* London: Times Books, 1982.

______. *Towards the End of Isolationism: China's Foreign Policy after Mao.* New York: St. Martin's Press, 1983.

Yearbook of International Organizations, 1984-85. Brussels: Union of International Organizations, 1984.

Yin, Ch'ing-yao. "The Evolution of Communist China's Foreign Policy." Pages 499-525 in Yu-ming Shaw (ed.), *Mainland China: Politics, Economics, and Reform.* Boulder: Westview Press, 1986.

Zhang Jia-lin. "Assessing United States-China Relations," *Current History*, 84, No. 503, September 1985, 245-47, 304.

(Various issues of the following publications were used in the preparation of this chapter: *Asian Wall Street Journal* [Hong Kong]; *Asiaweek* [Hong Kong]; *Beijing Review* [Beijing]; *China Quarterly* [London]; *Christian Science Monitor*; *Far Eastern Economic Review* [Hong Kong]; Foreign Broadcast Information Service, *Daily Report: China*; *Issues & Studies* [Taipei]; Joint Publications Research Service, *China Report: Political, Sociological, and Military Affairs*; and *Washington Post.*)

Chapter 13

Baker, Beverly G. "Chinese Law in the Eighties: The Lawyer and the Criminal Process," *Albany Law Review*, 46, No. 3, Spring 1982, 751-75.

Berney, Karen A. "China's New Revolution Introduces Democracy," *China Business Review*, 4, No. 5, September-October 1979, 45-49.

Blaustein, Albert O. (ed.). *Fundamental Legal Documents of Communist China*. South Hackensack, New Jersey: Rothman, 1962.

Bodde, Derk, and Clarence Morris. *Law in Imperial China*. Cambridge: Harvard University Press, 1967.

Bowden, Tom, and David S.G. Goodman. "The Heroes of Tien An Men: Public Security in China," *Journal of the Royal United Services Institute for Defence Studies* [London], 121, No. 4, December 1976, 20-26.

Braybrooke, George. "Recent Developments in Chinese Social Science, 1977-79," *China Quarterly* [London], No. 79, September 1979, 593-606.

Chang Gong. "Renmin Sifa Gongzuo de Hao Zhangcheng" (A Good Guideline for Administering People's Justice), *Faxue Yanjiu* (Studies in Law) [Beijing], April 1979, 34-37.

Chen, Phillip M. *Law and Justice: The Legal System in China, 2400 B.C. to 1960 A.D.* New York: Dunellen, 1973.

Chen Shouyi, Liu Shengping, and Zhao Zhenping. "Wo Guo Fazhi Jianshe Sanshi Nian" (Thirty Years of Our Country's Legal System), *Faxue Yanjiu* (Studies in Law) [Beijing], April 1979, 1-8.

China. New China News Agency. "Completely Smash the Feudal, Capitalist, and Revisionist Legal System," *Chinese Law and Government*, 2, No. 4, Winter 1969-70, 7-11.

Ch'ü, T'ung-tsu. *Law and Society in Traditional China*. (no. 4 of Le Monde d'outre-ma, passe et present. 1. Series, etudes.) Paris: Mouton, 1965.

Cohen, Jerome Alan. "China's Changing Constitution," *China Quarterly* [London], No. 76, December 1978, 794-841.

______. "Chinese Law: At the Crossroads," *China Quarterly* [London], No. 53, January-March 1973, 139-43.

______. *The Criminal Process in the People's Republic of China, 1949-1963*. Cambridge: Harvard University Press, 1968.

______. "Drafting People's Mediation Rules." Pages 29-50 in John Wilson Lewis (ed.), *The City in Communist China*. Stanford: Stanford University Press, 1971.

Cohen, Jerome Alan, and Hungdah Chiu. *People's China and International Law: A Documentary Study*, I and II (Studies in East Asian Law series.) Princeton: Princeton University Press, 1974.

Eberhard, Wolfram. *A History of China*. (4th ed.) Berkeley and Los Angeles: University of California Press, 1977.

Edwards, R. Randle. "Formal Law Begins a Comeback in Post-Mao China," *Contemporary China*, 2, No. 2, Summer 1978, 92-102.

Epstein, Edward J. "The Evolution of China's General Principles of Civil Law," *American Journal of Comparative Law*, 34, No. 4, Fall 1986, 705-14.

Fairbank, John King, Edwin O. Reischauer, and Albert M. Craig. *East Asia: Tradition and Transformation*. Boston: Houghton Mifflin, 1987.

Fan Fenglin. "Tan Tan Rending Fanzui de Jige Jiben Wenti" (Discussing Some Basic Problems in Determining Guilt), *Faxue Yanjiu* (Studies in Law) [Beijing], April 1979, 29-33, 41.

Gardner, John. "The Chinese Constitution of 1975," *Government and Opposition* [London], 11, No. 2, Spring 1976, 212-23.

Gelhorn, Ernest. "The Developing Role of Law and Lawyers in China: Introduction," *Albany Law Review*, 46, No. 3, Spring 1982, 687-90.

Herman, Richard A. "The Education of China's Lawyers," *Albany Law Review*, 46, No. 3, Spring 1982, 789-804.

Hiramatsu, Shigeo, and Koichiro Takahashi. "Chugoku Jinmin Buso Keisatsu Budai no Sosetsu" (The Founding of the Chinese People's Armed Police Force), *Kokubo* (National Defense) [Tokyo], February 1984, 8-28.

Hsia, Tao-tai, and Kathryn A. Haun. *The 1975 Revised Constitution of the People's Republic of China*. Washington: Law Library, Library of Congress, 1975.

______. *Peking's Minister of Public Security on Strengthening the Legal System*. Washington: Law Library, Library of Congress, August 1979.

______. *The Re-Emergence of the Procuratorial System in the People's Republic of China*. Washington: Law Library, Library of Congress, 1978.

Hsia, Tao-tai, and Constance Axinn Johnson. *Law Making in the People's Republic of China: Terms, Procedures, Hierarchy, and Interpretation*. Washington: Law Library, Library of Congress, 1986.

______. *The Chinese Communist Party Constitution of 1982: Deng Xiaoping's Program for Modernization*. Washington: Law Library, Library of Congress, 1984.

Hsia, Tao-tai, Charlotte A. Hambley, and Constance A. Johnson. "Introduction to the State Secrets Laws of the People's Republic of China," *China Law Reporter*, 2, No. 4, Fall 1983, 267-78.

Hsü, Immanuel C.Y. *The Rise of Modern China*. (3d ed.) New York: Oxford University Press, 1983.

Hsüeh, Chün-tu. "China in 1975: The New Constitution," *Problems of Communism*, 14, No. 3, May-June 1975, 11-19.

Hucker, Charles O. *China's Imperial Past*. Stanford: Stanford University Press, 1975.

Itatsu, Sogi. "Chugoku-han no KGB no Sosetsu" (Chinese KGB Established), *Gunji Kenkyu* (Japan Military Review) [Tokyo], November 1983, 194-204.

Keith, Ronald C. "Transcript of Discussions with Wu Daying and Zhang Zhonglin Concerning Legal Change," *China Quarterly* [London], No. 81, March 1980, 111-21.

Koeltl, John G. "Civil Rights and Liberties in China," *Albany Law Review*, 46, No. 3, Spring 1982, 740-50.

Lamb, Franklin P. "An Interview with Chinese Legal Officials," *China Quarterly* [London], No. 66, June 1976, 323-27.

Lan Quanpu. *Sanshi Nian Lai Wo Guo Fagui Yange Gaikuang* (Thirty Years of Legal Reform in Our Country). Beijing: Qunzhong Chubanshe (The Masses Publishing House), 1980.

Latourette, Kenneth Scott. *The Chinese: Their History and Culture.* New York: Macmillan, 1972.

"Laymen Learn about the Law," *China Reconstructs* [Beijing], 36, No. 3, March 1987, 64.

Leng, Shao-chuan. "Crime and Punishment in Post-Mao China," *China Law Reporter*, 2, No. 1, Spring 1982, 5-33.

______. *Justice in Communist China*. Dobbs Ferry: Oceana, 1967.

Leng, Shao-chuan, and Hungdah Chiu. *Criminal Justice in Post-Mao China: Analysis and Documents*. Albany: State University of New York Press, 1985.

Li, Victor H. "The Evolution and Development of the Chinese Legal System." Pages 221-55 in John M.H. Lindbeck (ed.), *China: Management of a Revolutionary Society*. Seattle: University of Washington Press, 1971.

______. *Law Without Lawyers*. Stanford: Stanford University Press, 1977.

______. "The Public Security Bureau and Political-Legal Work in Hui-yang, 1952-64." Pages 51-74 in John Wilson Lewis (ed.), *The City in Communist China*. Stanford: Stanford University Press, 1971.

Li Xunzhou. "Xin Zujiande Zhongguo Renmin Wuzhuang Jingcha Budui" (The Newly Organized Chinese People's Armed Police Force), *Jiefangjun Huabao* (Liberation Army Pictorial) [Beijing], May 1983, 1-3.

Lieberthal, Kenneth. "The Politics of Modernization in the PRC," *Problems of Communism*, 27, No. 3, May-June 1978, 1-17.

Lin, Fu-shun. *Chinese Law Past and Present*. New York: Columbia University Press, 1966.

Lindsay, Michael. *The New Constitution of Communist China: Comparative Analysis*. Taipei: Institute of International Relations, 1976.

Lubman, Stanley B. "Emerging Functions of Formal Legal Institutions in China's Modernization," *China Law Reporter*, 2, No. 4, Fall 1983, 195-266.

______. "Form and Function in Chinese Criminal Process," *Columbia Law Review*, 69, No. 4, April 1969, 536-75.

Meijer, M.J. "The New Criminal Law of the People's Republic of China," *Review of Socialist Law* [Alphen aan den Rijn, Netherlands], 6, No. 1, March 1980, 125-39.

Michael, Franz. "The Role of Law in Traditional China." Pages 57-66 in William T. Liu (ed.), *Chinese Society under Communism*. New York: John Wiley and Sons, 1967.

Milton, David, Nancy Milton, and Franz Schurmann. "People's China: The New Constitution (1975)," *China Quarterly* [London], No. 62, June 1975, 345-50.

Ning, Han-Lin. "Voluntary Confession in the Criminal Law of the People's Republic of China," *Chinese Law and Government*, 2, No. 2, Spring 1969, 16-37.

Pheffer, Richard M. "Crime and Punishment: China and the U.S." Pages 261-81 in Jerome Alan Cohen (ed.), *Contemporary Chinese Law*. Cambridge: Harvard University Press, 1970.

Pinard, Jeanette L. *The People's Republic of China: A Bibliography of Selected English-Language Legal Materials*. Washington: Law Library, Library of Congress, 1983.

Qiao Wei. "The Status of the Studies of Chinese Legal Systems in Chinese Legal Education," *Asian Thought and Society: An International Review*, 11, Nos. 32-33, July-November, 1986, 193-214.

Rickett, Allyn, and Adele Rickett. *Prisoners of Liberation*. New York: Anchor, 1973.

Ruge, Gerd. "An Interview with Chinese Legal Officials," *China Quarterly* [London], No. 61, March 1975, 118-26.

Schurmann, Franz. *Ideology and Organization in Communist China*. (2d ed.) Berkeley and Los Angeles: University of California Press, 1968.

Schurmann, Franz, and Orville Schell (eds.). *Communist China: Revolutionary Reconstruction and International Confrontation, 1949 to the Present* (China readings, 3.) Harmondsworth: Penguin, 1968.

______. *Imperial China: The Eighteenth and Nineteenth Centuries* (China readings, 1.) Harmondsworth: Penguin, 1967.

______. *Republican China: Nationalism, War and the Rise of Communism 1911-1949* (China readings, 2.) Harmondsworth: Penguin, 1968.

Shi Changchun. "Studying Sociology from a Prison Cell," *China Reconstructs* [Beijing], 36, March 1987, 46-47.

Singer, Floyd L. *Control of the Population of China and Vietnam: The Pao Chia System Past and Present*. (Weapons Planning Group,

NOTS Technical Publication, No. 3680.) China Lake, California: United States Naval Ordnance Test Station, November 1964.

Tang, Peter S.H. "A Revolutionary Charter: The 1975 Constitution of the People's Republic of China," *Asian Thought and Society*, 1, No. 1, April 1976, 33–41.

Tao, Lung-Sheng. "Politics and Law Enforcement in China," *American Journal of Comparative Law*, 22, No. 4, Fall 1974, 713–56.

Van Der Sprenkel, Sybille. *Legal Institutions in Manchu China*. London: Athlone Press, 1962.

______. "The Role of Law in the Changing Society." Pages 225–67 in Jack Grey (ed.), *Modern China's Search for a Political Form*. London: Athlone Press, 1969.

Vogel, Ezra F. "Preserving Order in the Cities." Pages 75–93 in John Wilson Lewis (ed.), *The City in Communist China*. Stanford: Stanford University Press, 1971.

Wang Gangyi. "Long Arm of the Law Flexes New Muscle," *China Daily* [Beijing], 5, No. 1352, November 1985, 1.

Wang Zhigang. "Zhongguo Jianyu Tanmi: Ji Bei Dahuang Baoanzhao Laogai Nongchang" (Exploring the Secrets of a Chinese Prison: Report on Baoanzhao, a Labor Reform Farm in the Great Northern Wasteland), *Liaowang Zhoukan* (Outlook Weekly), 45, November 10, 1986, 16–17.

Zheng, Henry R. "China's New Civil Law," *American Journal of Comparative Law*, 34, No. 4, Fall 1986, 669–704.

(Various issues of the following publications were also used in the preparation of this chapter: *Beijing Review* [Beijing]; *China News Analysis* [Hong Kong]; Foreign Broadcast Information Service, *Daily Report: China*; and Joint Publications Research Service, *China Report: Political, Sociological, and Military Affairs*.)

Chapter 14

Bonds, Ray (ed.). *The Chinese War Machine*. New York: Crescent Books, 1979.

Bullard, Monte R. *China's Political-Military Evolution*. Boulder: Westview Press, 1985.

Bullard, Monte R., and Edward C. O'Dowd. "Defining the Role of the PLA in the Post-Mao Era," *Asian Survey*, 26, No. 6, June 1986, 706–20.

Chen, King C. *China's War Against Vietnam, 1979: A Military Analysis*. (Occasional Papers/Reprints Series in Contemporary Asian Studies, No. 5, 1983 [58].) Baltimore: School of Law, University of Maryland, 1983.

Cheng, Chester J. (ed.). *The Politics of the Chinese Red Army: A Translation of the Bulletin of Activities of the PLA*. Stanford: Hoover Institute, 1966.

Cheung, Tai Ming. "China Switches from Defence to Development," *Pacific Defence Reporter* [Victoria, Australia], 13, No. 5, November 1986, 27–28.

_____. "Ready for Modern War," *Far Eastern Economic Review* [Hong Kong], 133, No. 32, August 7, 1986, 22–23.

Chu, Wellington. "Increased Military Sales to China: Problems and Prospects," *Journal of International Affairs*, Winter 1986, 133–47.

Connor, G. G. "Defence Procurement Procedures in the People's Republic of China," *Jane's Defence Weekly* [London], 4, No. 5, August 3, 1985, 218–19, 221.

Copper, John F. "China's Military Assistance." Pages 96–134 in John F. Copper and Daniel S. Papp (eds.), *Communist Nations' Military Assistance*. Boulder: Westview Press, 1983.

Corr, Gerard H. *The Chinese Red Army*. Reading, Berskhire, United Kingdom: Osprey, 1974.

Daniel, Donald C., and Harlan W. Jencks. "Soviet Military Confrontation with China: Options for the USSR, the PRC, and the United States," *Conflict*, 5, No. 1, 1983, 57–87.

Dreyer, June Teufel. "China's Military in the 1980's," *Current History*, 83, No. 494, September 1984, 269–71, 276–78.

_____. "China's Military Modernization," *Orbis*, 27, No. 4, Winter 1984, 1011–26.

_____. "Civil-Military Relations in the People's Republic of China," *Comparative Strategy*, 5, No. 1, 1985, 27–49.

_____. "The Role of the Armed Forces in Contemporary China." Pages 25–54 in Edward A. Olsen and Stephen Jurika, Jr. (eds.), *The Armed Forces in Contemporary Asian Societies*. Boulder: Westview Press, 1986.

Frankenstein, John. "Military Cuts in China," *Problems of Communism*, 34, No. 4, July–August 1985, 56–68.

Fraser, Angus M. *The People's Liberation Army*. New York: Crane, Russak, 1973.

Frieman, Wendy. "Foreign Technology and Chinese Modernization." Pages 51–68 in Charles D. Lovejoy, Jr. and Bruce W. Watson (eds.), *China's Military Reforms: International and Domestic Implications*. Boulder: Westview Press, 1986.

Ghosh, S.K. "China Military Modernization Programme," *China Report* [New Delhi], 14, No. 4, July–August 1978, 66–77.

Gilks, Anne, and Gerald Segal. *China and the Arms Trade*. New York: St. Martin's Press, 1985.

Girling, J.L.S. *People's War*. London: Allen & Unwin, 1969.

Gittings, John. *The Role of the Chinese Army*. London: Oxford University Press, 1967.

Godwin, Paul H.B. *The Chinese Defense Establishment: Continuity and Change in the 1980s*. Boulder: Westview Press, 1983.

______. "The Chinese Defense Establishment in Transition: The Passing of a Revolutionary Army?" Pages 63–80 in A. Doak Barnett and Ralph N. Clough (eds.), *Modernizing China: Post-Mao Reform and Development*. Boulder: Westview Press, 1986.

______. "People's War Revised: Military Doctrine, Strategy, and Operations." Pages 1–13 in Charles D. Lovejoy, Jr. and Bruce W. Watson (eds.), *China's Military Reforms: International and Domestic Implications*. Boulder: Westview Press, 1986.

Griffith, Samuel B. *The Chinese People's Liberation Army*. (United States and China in World Affairs.) New York: Prentice-Hall, 1967.

______. *Peking and People's War*. New York: Praeger, 1966.

Griffith, Samuel B. (trans.). *Mao Tse-tung on Guerrilla Warfare*. New York: Praeger, 1961.

Guillermaz, Jacques. *The Chinese Communist Party in Power, 1949–1976*. Boulder: Westview Press, 1976.

______. *A History of the Chinese Communist Party, 1921–1949*. New York: Random House, 1972.

Haggerly, J.J. "The Chinese-Vietnamese Border War of 1979," *Army Quarterly and Defence Journal* [Tavistock, United Kingdom], 109, No. 3, July 1979, 265–72.

Hahn, Bradley. "China's Emerging Sea Power," United States Naval Institute. *Proceedings*, 111, No. 3, March 1985, 102–107.

Henning, Stanley E. "Chinese Defense Strategy: A Historical Approach," *Military Review*, 59, No. 5, May 1979, 60–67.

Hsieh, Alice Langley. *Communist China's Strategy in the Nuclear Era*. New York: Prentice-Hall, 1962.

Huck, Arthur. *The Security of China: Chinese Approaches to Problems of War and Strategy*. New York: Columbia University Press, 1970.

International Institute for Strategic Studies. *The Military Balance, 1986–1987*. London: 1986.

Jencks, Harlan W. "China's 'Punitive' War on Vietnam: A Military Assessment," *Asian Survey*, 19, No. 8, August 1979, 801–15.

______. *From Muskets to Missiles: Politics and Professionalism in the Chinese Army, 1945–1981*. Boulder: Westview Press, 1982.

______. " 'People's War under Modern Conditions': Wishful Thinking, National Suicide, or Effective Deterrent?" *China Quarterly* [London], No. 98, June 1984, 305–319.

Joffe, Ellis. *The Chinese Army after Mao*. Cambridge: Harvard University Press, 1987.

______. "Civil-Military Relations." Pages 18–35 in Gerald Segal and William T. Tow (eds.), *Chinese Defence Policy*. Urbana: University of Illinois Press, 1984.

______. *Party and Army: Professionalism and Political Control in the Chinese Officer Corps, 1949–1964*. Cambridge: East Asia Research Center, Harvard University, 1965.

______. "Party and Military in China: Professionalism in Command?" *Problems of Communism*, 32, No. 5, September–October 1983, 48–63.

Joffe, Ellis, and Gerald Segal. "The Chinese Army and Professionalism," *Problems of Communism*, 27, No. 6, November–December 1978, 1–19.

______. "The PLA under Modern Conditions," *Survival* [London], 27, No. 4, July–August 1985, 145–57.

Johnson, Chalmers. *Autopsy on People's War*. Berkeley and Los Angeles: University of California Press, 1973.

Johnston, Alastair I. "Changing Army-Party Relations in China, 1979–1984," *Asian Survey*, 24, No. 10, October 1984, 1012–39.

Kau, Ying-mao. *The People's Liberation Army and China's Nation-Building*. White Plains: International Arts and Sciences Press, 1973.

Kierman, Frank A., Jr., and John K. Fairbank (eds.). *Chinese Ways in Warfare*. Cambridge: Harvard University Press, 1974.

Kux, Ernst. "Reforming China's Army," *Swiss Review of World Affairs* [Zurich], 36, No. 6, September 1986, 29, 31.

Latham, Richard J. "The People's Republic of China: Profits, Consumerism, and Arms Sales." Pages 187–202 in James Everett Katz (ed.), *The Implications of Third World Military Industrialization*. Lexington, Massachusetts: Lexington Books, 1986.

Li Chaochen. "Some Modern Army Women," *China Reconstructs* [Beijing], 34, No. 3, March 1985, 25–27.

Liu, Leo Yuen-Yun. *China as a Nuclear Power in World Politics*. London: Macmillan, 1972.

Lovejoy, Charles D., Jr., and Bruce W. Watson (eds.). *China's Military Reforms: International and Domestic Implications*. Boulder, Colorado: Westview Press, 1986.

Maxwell, Neville. *India's China War*. Bombay: Jaico, 1970.

"Military Situation Surrounding Japan." Pages 23–41 in Japan, Defense Agency (ed.), *Defense of Japan, 1985*. Tokyo: Japan Times, 1985.

Muller, David G., Jr. *China as a Maritime Power*. Boulder: Westview Press, 1983.

______. "A Chinese Blockade of Taiwan," United States Naval Institute. *Proceedings*, 110, No. 9, September 1984, 50–55.

Unnikrishnan, Nandan. "Rapid Modernization of China's Airforce," *Patriot* [New Delhi], October 15, 1986, 4.

Nelsen, Harvey W. *The Chinese Military System: An Organizational Study of the Chinese People's Liberation Army*. (2d ed.) Boulder: Westview Press, 1981.

______. "Internal Management in the Armed Forces: Confucian Anachronism or Model?" Pages 139–54 in Paul H.B. Godwin (ed.), *The Chinese Defense Establishment: Continuity and Change in the 1980s*. Boulder: Westview Press, 1983.

"A New Army for a New Society," *China News Analysis* [Hong Kong], No. 1303, February 1, 1986, 1–8.

"New Blood for the Army," *Asiaweek* [Hong Kong], 11, No. 26, June 28, 1985, 13.

Ng-Quinn, Michael. "The Chinese Military: Political Demands and Control," *Armed Forces and Society*, 12, No. 2, Winter 1986, 253–86.

Parris, Ed. "Chinese Defense Expenditures, 1967–83." Pages 148–68 in United States Congress, 99th, 2d Session, Joint Economic Committee (ed.), *China's Economy Looks Toward the Year 2000, 2: Economic Openness in Modernizing China*. Washington: GPO, 1986.

Robinson, Thomas W. "Chinese Military Modernization in the 1980s," *China Quarterly* [London], No. 90, June 1982, 231–52.

Schofield, Carolyn. "China's Defence Procurement and Production Organizations," *Sino-British Trade Review* [London], No. 265, October 1986, 1–5.

Segal, Gerald. "China." Pages 16–34 in Martin Edmonds (ed.), *Central Organizations of Defense*. Boulder: Westview Press, 1985.

______. *Defending China*. London: Oxford University Press, 1985.

Segal, Gerald, and William T. Tow (eds.). *Chinese Defence Policy*. Urbana: University of Illinois Press, 1984.

Shambaugh, David L. "China's Defense Industries: Indigenous and Foreign Procurement." Pages 43–88 in Paul H.B. Godwin (ed.), *The Chinese Defense Establishment: Continuity and Changes in the 1980s*. Boulder: Westview Press, 1983.

Snow, Edgar. *Red Star Over China*. New York: Grove Press, 1938.

Swanson, Bruce. "Air Forces." Pages 71–84 in Gerald Segal and William T. Tow (eds.), *Chinese Defence Policy*. Urbana: University of Illinois Press, 1984.

______. *Eighth Voyage of the Dragon*. Annapolis: United States Naval Institute Press, 1982.

"The Tiger Grows New Teeth: The Chinese Army and Its Reforms," *China News Analysis* [Hong Kong], No. 1274, November 19, 1984, 1–8.

Tretiak, Daniel. "China's Vietnam War and Its Consequences," *China Quarterly* [London], No. 79, December 1979, 740-67.

United States. Arms Control and Disarmament Agency. *World Military Expenditures and Arms Transfers, 1985*. Washington: GPO, 1985.

United States. Central Intelligence Agency. *Military Organizations of the People's Republic of China*. (CR85-15193.) Washington: 1985.

______. National Foreign Assessment Center. *Chinese Defense Spending, 1965-79*. (Research Paper, No. SR 80-100091.) Washington: July 1980.

United States. Congress. 96th, 1st Session. Joint Economic Committee (ed.). Subcommittee on Priorities and Economy in Government. Allocation of Resources in the Soviet Union and China, 1979, Pt. 5. (Hearings June 26 and July 9, 1979.) Washington: GPO, 1980.

United States. Defense Intelligence Agency. *Handbook of the Chinese People's Liberation Army*. Washington: 1984.

Waller, Thomas G., Jr. "The Inferno of People's War," *Air University Review*, 35, No. 3, March-April 1984, 56-70.

Wang, Robert S. "China's Evolving Strategic Doctrine," *Asian Survey*, 24, No. 10, October 1984, 1040-55.

Weiss, Kenneth G. "Dragon at Sea: China's Navy in Strategy and Diplomacy." Pages 381-407 in James L. George (ed.), *The Soviet and Other Communist Navies: The View from the mid-1980s*. Annapolis: United States Naval Institute Press, 1986.

Whiting, Allen S. *China Crosses the Yalu*. New York: Macmillan, 1960.

______. *The Chinese Calculus of Deterrence: India and Indochina*. Ann Arbor: University of Michigan Press, 1975.

Whitson, William W. *The Chinese High Command*. New York: Praeger, 1974.

Whitson, William W. (ed.). *The Military and Political Power in China in the 1970s*. New York: Praeger, 1972.

Wilson, Dick. *The Long March*. New York: Avon Books, 1971.

Xu Xiaocun. "The Chinese People's Liberation Army and World Peace," *Voice of Friendship* [Beijing], No. 20, December 1986, 29-32.

Yee, Herbert S. "The Sino-Vietnamese Border War: China's Motives, Calculations, and Strategies," *China Report* [New Delhi], 16, No. 1, January-February 1980, 15-32.

Young, P. Lewis. "China and the South China Sea," *Asian Defence Journal* [Kuala Lumpur], July 1986, 22, 26, 28-31.

Yu Yu-lin. "Politics in Teng Hsiao-p'ing's Army-Building Strategy (1977–1984)," *Issues & Studies* [Taipei], 21, No. 10, October 1985, 34–57.

(Various issues of the following publications were also used in the preparation of this chapter: *Asiaweek* [Hong Kong]; *Asian Defence Journal* [Kuala Lumpur]; *Aviation Week and Space Technology*; *Beijing Review* [Beijing]; *China Business Review*; *China Daily* [Beijing]; *Defense and Foreign Affairs Weekly*; *The Economist* [London]; *Far Eastern Economic Review* [Hong Kong]; *Flight International* [London]; Foreign Broadcast Information Service, *Daily Report: China*; *International Defense Review* [Geneva]; *Issues & Studies* [Taipei]; *Jane's Defence Weekly* [London]; Joint Publications Research Service, *China Report: Political, Sociological, and Military Affairs*; and *Pacific Defence Reporter* [Victoria, Australia].)

Glossary

barefoot doctor—Especially during the Cultural Revolution (*q.v.*), a paramedical worker possessing minimal formal training who provided part-time medical service, primarily in rural areas. Promoted basic hygiene, preventive health care, and family planning, and treated common illnesses. Acted as a primary health-care provider at the grass-roots level.

big-character posters (*dazibao*)—Posters, limited-circulation newspapers, excerpted press articles, pamphlets, and blackboard news using large-sized ideographs and mounted on walls as a popular form of communication. Used in China since imperial times but more commonly since literacy increased after the 1911 revolution. Used more frequently after 1949 to publicize party programs and as a means of protest. Became ubiquitous during the Cultural Revolution (*q.v.*); guaranteed as one of the "four big rights" in the 1975 state constitution.

cadre—Person who holds any responsible position (usually in administrative work) in either the party or the governmental apparatus throughout the nation. Term often denotes, in a more restricted sense, a person who has been fully indoctrinated in party ideology and methods and uses this training in his or her work.

China Proper—Used broadly to mean China within the Great Wall, with its eighteen historic provinces. Divisible into two major, sharply contrasting regions, north China and south China. The dependencies on the north and west—Manchuria (now usually referred to as northeast China), Mongolia, Xizang (Tibet), and Xinjiang or Chinese Turkestan—were known in the imperial era as Outer China.

Chinese People's Political Consultative Conference (CPPCC)—A quasi-constitutional united front (*q.v.*) organization that provides an institutional framework for interaction between party and state leaders and representatives of mass groups and democratic parties (*q.v.*). Members include distinguished scholars, educators, and intellectuals, key representatives of religious and minority nationality groups, and leading members of political parties loyal to the Chinese Communist Party during the anti-Guomindang years. The first CPPCC convened in 1949, the second in 1954, the third in 1959, the fourth in 1964, the fifth in 1978, and the sixth in 1983, the seventh was scheduled for 1988. The CPPCC's 1949 Common Program served as the law of the land until superseded by the 1954 state constitution.

class struggle—In Marxist terms, the conflict waged by the masses of the workers and the oppressed under the leadership of the communist party against the privileged, oppressive, and property-owning ruling class. Until late 1978, class struggle was the official line of the Chinese Communist Party.

Comintern—Short form for Communist International or the Third International, which was founded in Moscow in 1919 to coordinate the world communist movement. Officially disbanded in 1943, the Comintern was revived as the Cominform (Communist Information Bureau) from 1947 to 1956.

county (*xian*)—Rural administrative unit below the provincial level.

Cultural Revolution—A slogan introduced by Mao Zedong in 1940, noted again by Liu Shaoqi in 1958, and used more frequently in connection with leftist attacks on the "cultural front" in late 1965 and early 1966. The expression was used to denote the Great Proletarian Cultural Revolution, a political campaign officially inaugurated in August 1966 to rekindle revolutionary fervor of the masses outside formal party organizations. The Cultural Revolution decade (1966–76) can be divided into three periods: 1966–69, from the militant Red Guard (*q.v.*) phase to the Ninth National Party Congress; 1969–71, the period of the zenith and demise of Lin Biao; and 1971–76, the period of Mao's declining health and the ascendancy of the Gang of Four (*q.v.*). At the August 1977 Eleventh National Party Congress, the Cultural Revolution was declared officially to have ended with the arrest in October 1976 of the Gang of Four.

danwei (work unit)—The basic-level organization through which party and government officials control social, political, and economic behavior of residents. The *danwei* typically controls the allocation of housing, grain, edible oil, and cotton rations; the issuance of permits to travel, to marry, and to bear or adopt children; and permission to enter the army, party, and university, and to change employment.

"Democracy Wall"—A wall in the Xidan district in Beijing where, beginning in December 1978, in line with the party's policy of "seeking truth from facts," activists in the democracy movement recorded news and ideas, often in the form of big-character posters (*q.v.*). These activists were encouraged to criticize the Gang of Four and previous (failed) government policies, but the wall was closed in December 1979 when the leadership and the communist party system were being criticized along with past mistakes and leaders. The shutdown coincided with suppression of political dissent.

democratic centralism—A system through which the people influence the policies of the government and party members influence the policies of the party; the government and party maintain centralized administrative power to carry out the policies demanded by their constituents. Within both representative and executive organizations, the minority must abide by the decisions of the majority, and lower bodies must obey the orders of the higher level organizations. The concept, derived from the organizing principles of the Communist Party of the Soviet Union, was called for as early as 1928 by Mao Zedong.

democratic parties—Eight political parties that have been loyal to the communist government since 1949. They are China Association for Promoting Democracy, China Democratic League, China Democratic National Construction Association, China Zhi Gong Dang (Party for Public Interest), Chinese Peasants' and Workers' Democratic Party, Jiusan (September Third) Society, Guomindang Revolutionary Committee, and Taiwan Democratic Self-Government League.

"expert"—Term usually juxtaposed with "red" (*q.v.*). Denotes special knowledge or skills, or both, relating to economic management, science, and technology. Cadres are required to be both red and expert, the emphasis on one or the other depending on the current political milieu.

fiscal year (FY)—January 1 to December 31.

Five Principles of Peaceful Coexistence—Mutual respect for each other's territorial integrity and sovereignty; mutual nonaggression; mutual noninterference in each other's internal affairs; equality and mutual benefit; and peaceful coexistence. Originated with a 1954 agreement between Zhou Enlai and India's Jawaharlal Nehru.

four cardinal principles—Socialism; dictatorship of the proletariat; supporting the party leadership; and Marxism-Leninism-Mao Zedong Thought. In vogue in China since 1979.

Four Modernizations—The core of a development strategy aimed at turning the country into a relatively advanced industrialized nation by the year 2000. The modernizations are those of agriculture, industry, science and technology, and national defense. The concept was embodied first in the Third Five-Year Plan (1966–70), launched in earnest by Zhou Enlai at the Fourth National People's Congress (1975), and adopted as the official party line at the Third Plenum of the Eleventh Central Committee (December 1978).

Gang of Four—Term used by the post-Mao leadership to denote the four leading radical figures—Jiang Qing (Mao's fourth wife), Zhang Chunqiao, Yao Wenyuan, and Wang Hongwen—who played a dominant political role during the Cultural Revolution (*q.v.*) decade (1966–76) until Mao's death in September 1976 and their arrest several weeks later. Their "antiparty" deeds are often linked with Lin Biao, an early leader of the Cultural Revolution, who also has been discredited.

Great Leap Forward—A drive to increase industrial and agricultural production following the suspension of Soviet aid and the desire to catch up with the advanced nations of the world. The campaign was conceived by Mao Zedong in late 1957, adopted by the National People's Congress (*q.v.*) in 1958; it continued through 1960. Emphasis was placed on accelerated collectivization of agriculture, national self-sufficiency, and labor-intensive methods. The campaign resulted in widespread waste of resources and was partially responsible for famine in 1960 and 1961.

Great Proletarian Cultural Revolution—*See* Cultural Revolution.

gross national product (GNP)—The total value of final goods and services produced in the economy. The "estimated GNP" figures used in the text are estimates by United States government analysts of Chinese GNP according to the U.S. definition, which includes personal consumption, gross investment, all government expenditures, and net exports. Through mid-1987, Chinese calculations of national income excluded government and personal services, passenger transportation, and depreciation investment.

Han—Also Han Chinese. Term used to designate the ethnic majority, which constitutes 93 percent of the population. The fifty-five minority nationalities make up the remainder.

Hundred Flowers Campaign—Also Double Hundred Campaign. Party-sponsored initiative to permit greater intellectual and artistic freedom. Introduced first into drama and other arts in the spring of 1956 under the official slogan "Let a hundred flowers bloom, let the hundred schools of thought contend." With Mao's encouragement in January 1957, the campaign was extended to intellectual expression and, by early May 1957, was being interpreted as permission for intellectuals to criticize political institutions of the regime. The effect was the large-scale exposure and purge of intellectuals critical of party and government policies.

"iron rice bowl"—A Chinese idiom referring to the system of guaranteed lifetime employment in state enterprises, in which the tenure and level of wages are not related to job performance.

Long March—The 12,500-kilometer-long trek made by the Red Army in the face of the Guomindang's "annihilation campaigns." Began in October 1934 in Jiangxi Province and ended in October 1935 in Shaanxi Province. Some 100,000 persons left the communist base area in Jiangxi but only about 28,000 arrived in Yan'an, Chinese Communist Party headquarters for the next decade. It was during the Long March that Mao Zedong gained his preeminent role in the party.

Mao Zedong Thought—Sayings and writings of Mao that served as a major source of national ideology until his death in 1976 and since then have undergone a cautious but critical reappraisal. By 1980 the meaning of the term had expanded to include the collective thoughts of all key party leaders.

"mass line"—Term for party policy aimed at broadening and cultivating contacts with the masses of the people and to accentuate the leadership role of the Chinese Communist Party.

mass movement—Derived from the concept of "mass line" (*q.v.*). Party-directed campaign designed to mobilize the masses in support or execution of major policies. Such movements were characteristic of the 1950s through the 1970s and were controlled and coordinated by permanent mass organizations.

National People's Congress—Highest organ of the state, elected in accordance with the principles of democratic centralism (*q.v.*). As of 1987, six congresses had been held, the first (1954), second (1959), third (1965), fourth (1975), fifth (1978), and sixth (1982), the seventh was scheduled for 1988; annual sessions were held most years except during the Cultural Revolution (*q.v.*). The Standing Committee is the permanent organ of the National People's Congress and functions between annual sessions.

neighborhood—Term in general use in China for the urban administrative unit usually found immediately below the district level, although an intermediate, subdistrict level exists in some cities. Neighborhoods encompass 2,000 to 10,000 families. Within neighborhoods, families are grouped into smaller residential units of 100 to 600 families and supervised by a residents' committee; these are subdivided into residents' small groups of fifteen to forty families.

New Culture Movement—Refers to the period between 1917 and 1923, which was marked by student and intellectual ferment and protests against the warlord government. Culminated in the May Fourth Movement of 1919.

one country, two systems—A policy originating in the early 1980s that promotes reunification of Hong Kong, Macao,and Taiwan with the mainland and offers them a high degree of autonomy as special administrative regions of China. Through separate agreements with Britain and Portugal, Hong Kong and Macao are to revert to Chinese control in 1997 and 1999, respectively.

overseas Chinese—Term usually used to refer to any person of Chinese origin living abroad on a permanent basis, without regard to his or her current citizenship. Overseas Chinese minorities are concentrated principally in Southeast Asia but are also found in other parts of Asia, the Middle East, Europe, North America, South America, and the Caribbean. Overseas Chinese have long been important to the government in power in China as a source of business contacts and of financial and moral support from abroad. The majority of foreign investment in China is by overseas Chinese, and more than 90 percent of all foreign tourists who visit China are overseas Chinese. Also used in China to refer to persons living in China who have returned from sojourns abroad.

people's commune—Formerly the highest of three administrative levels in rural areas in the period from 1958 to 1982–85, when they were replaced by townships (*q.v.*). Communes, the largest collective units, were divided in turn into production brigades and production teams (*q.v.*). The communes had governmental, political, and economic functions.

production brigade—Formerly the intermediate administrative level in the people's commune system, the organizational structure of the collective sector in agriculture. The highest level was the commune; the lowest, the production team. Most brigades were transformed into townships or villages in the period from 1982 to 1985. (*See also* people's commune, production team, townships, villages.)

production team—Formerly the basic accounting and farm production unit in the people's commune system. Production teams were largely disbanded during the agricultural reforms of 1982–85. In the administrative hierarchy, the team was the lowest level, the next higher levels being the production brigade and people's commune. Typically the team owned most of the land and was responsible for income distribution. Since 1984 most teams have been replaced by villages. (*See also* people's commune, production brigade, village.)

putonghua—The common spoken language; also called *guoyu* (national language). The official spoken language of China, used in its various forms by more than 70 percent of the population. The People's Republic government started promoting *putonghua* in 1956 for use in schools, the cultural arena, and daily life as a means of bringing about the standardization of the language used by the Han (*q.v.*) nationality. *Putonghua* is based on the northern dialect, and uses Beijing pronunciations as its standard.

"red"—A term referring to political and ideological attitudes prescribed by Maoist doctrine. Usually juxtaposed with "expert" (*q.v.*), the term was seldom used in the 1980s.

Red Guards—Generally used to refer to young people—primarily students—in their teens and twenties who began in May 1966 to support the leftist intraparty struggle then emerging against Liu Shaoqi and others. They made world famous the "little red book," *Quotations from Chairman Mao*, and were known for their use of big-character posters (*q.v.*) during the Cultural Revolution (*q.v.*). Acting under the leadership of Mao and his radical adherents, Red Guards were the "soldiers" and the vanguard of the Cultural Revolution. The term Red Guard was derived from the early days of the Chinese Communist Party's armed struggle.

rehabilitation—A practice dating from the early years of the Chinese Communist Party. Denotes the reinstatement in positions of responsibility of former government and party officials and military personnel who had been accused of wrongdoing. Rehabilitations sometimes take place posthumously to clear a former leader's name and reputation.

responsibility system—A practice, first adopted in agriculture in 1981 and later extended to other sectors of the economy, by which local managers are held responsible for the profits and losses of the enterprise. This system partially supplanted the egalitarian distribution method, whereby the state assumed all profits and losses.

revisionism—As used by communists, term refers to political, economic, and social tendencies that stray to the right of orthodox Marxism-Leninism. The Chinese communists long insisted that these tendencies were counterrevolutionary and that internal and external enemies (such as the Soviet Union) were infected by this negative phenomenon.

Socialist Education Movement—Inaugurated in September 1962 at the Tenth Plenum of the Eighth National Party Congress Central Committee as a mass ideological campaign for both party cadre and the general population. The movement was patterned along the lines of the Yan'an rectification campaign of 1942–45 and was intended to increase ideological "correctness" and consciousness, especially in regard to reversing "capitalist" and "revisionist" tendencies perceived in social and economic life. The Socialist Education Movement, which continued at least until 1965, is considered a precursor of the Cultural Revolution (*q.v.*).

special economic zones—Small coastal areas established beginning in 1979 to promote economic development and introduction of advanced technology through foreign investment. Special preferential terms and facilities are offered to outside investors in taxation, land-use fees, and entry and exit control for joint ventures, cooperative ventures, and enterprises with sole foreign investment. Special economic zones have greater decision-making power in economic activities than provincial-level units. Market regulation is primary.

township (*xiang*)—The basic government administrative unit below the county level in rural areas. Townships existed before people's communes were organized in 1958 and were reconstituted when production brigades and communes were disbanded during the period 1982–85. Each township has a people's congress and an elected chairman. In the mid-1980s, townships were about the same size as the communes they had replaced. (*See also* county, people's communes, production brigades.)

united front—Chinese Communist Party strategy that attempts to utilize an organization or movement for the purpose of building a consensus and an organized following for party-supported programs and goals. Historically, the term is associated with the Guomindang-Chinese Communist Party first united front (1923–27) and second united front (1937–45).

village (*nong cun*)—Replaced production brigades (*q.v.*) from 1982 to 1985 as the lowest-level semiofficial government entity. They provide bureaucratic coordination and welfare payments and settle disputes. Party branches are usually organized at the village level.

yuan (¥)—China's monetary unit, which in mid-1987 had an exchange rate of US$1 to ¥3.72, or ¥1 to US$.269. The yuan is divided into 100 fen, and 10 fen constitute 1 jiao. The currency is known as *renminbi* (RMB), meaning the people's currency. The inscription *renminbi* (or *renminbiao*) appears on bank notes as well as yuan, and the terms *renminbi* and *yuan* are used synonymously in quoting exchange rates. In transactions the terms are universally replaced by the word *kuai* (piece). Beginning in the early 1980s, the standard currency was paralleled by a special currency called Foreign Exchange Certificates, which were issued in exchange for ''hard'' foreign currencies.

Index

Academia Sinica, 376, 377
acupuncture, 95, 382
Afghanistan, 64; boundary issues, 477; foreign policy, 480; Soviet invasion of, 490, 491, 576
Africa (*see also* under names of individual countries): military cooperation, 580; alleged subversive activities in, 480, 496
Agrarian Reform Law of June 28, 1950, 41, 271-72
Agricultural Bank, 243, 244, 245, 351; policy role, 278
agriculture, (*see also* communes; grain; land reform), xxiii-xxiv, 61, 267-97; advanced producers' cooperatives, 215, 272; ancient period, 5-7; animal husbandry, 291-92; collectivization, 41, 42, 125, 208; communes, 44, 217, 231-32, 272-73; contract responsibility system, 126, 207, 224, 225, 231, 232, 275-76, 337-38, 455; cotton, 277, 289-90; credit arrangements, 244, 280; crops, 267, 268-70, 281, 286-91; domestic trade, 212, 337-40; economic organization, 231-34, 278-81; fertilizers, 274, 281-82; fisheries, 292; foreign trade, 294-97; forestry, 292; government role, 127-28, 218-19, 230, 271-81; and gross national product (GNP), 231, 268; investments in, 216, 271, 272, 276-77; irrigation, 2, 216, 270, 274, 284; labor force, 90, 208, 231, 234, 268, 270-71; land ownership, 126, 208, 234; marketing organization, 225-26, 277, 279-80; mechanization, 231, 281, 282-83; pest control, 284-85; pricing policies, 219, 224, 248, 277, 280; private plots, 219, 232; production, 216, 219, 221, 223-24, 277, 286-94; regional disparities, 212-13; research and training, 285-86; seed varieties, 285; shortage of arable land, xxiii, 260, 268; "specialized households," 224, 232, 258; state farms, 234, 272, 278; state procurement system, 337, 338; taxation, 242
air force, 544, 560, 569; campaigns, 584; manpower, 546, 562; rank system, 568; Soviet assistance, 584; structure and equipment, xxvii, 583-85; terms of service, 566; training, 584-85; uniforms, 568
airports and aviation, xxv, 237, 356, 363-64; aircraft production, 316; passenger traffic, 357
Aksai Chin, 45-46, 65, 578
Albania, 501, 580
Alexandria, 12
All-China Federation of Industry and Commerce, 418, 421
All-China Federation of Literary and Art Circles, 421
All-China Federation of Trade Unions, 418, 420
All-China Federation of Youth, 421
All-China Students' Federation, 421
All-China Women's Federation, 418, 421
Altai Mountains, 67
Altun Shan, 67
Amur River. *See* Heilong Jiang
Analects (*Lunyu*), 186
ancestor worship, 132, 146
Andropov, Yuriy, 491
Anhui Province, 343, 362, 388, 461; industry, 325
Annam (*see also* Vietnam), 26
Anshan, 305; iron and steel complex, 308, 310, 313, 316, 392
Anti-Rightist Campaign, 42, 181; legal profession, 514; police domination, 515
Antioch, 12
Anyang, 5, 6
Aomen. *See* Macao
Argentina, 295
Argun River. *See* Ergun He
armed forces (*see also* defense industry; national defense; police), xxvii-xxviii, xxxvi-xxxvii, 543-75; air force, 544, 546, 560, 562, 569, 584; Central Military Commissions, 424-25, 557-59; and the Chinese Communist Party, 116, 416, 548; civil-military relations, 548, 555-57; civilianization of activities, 551, 561, 575; conditions of service, 122, 566-68; contacts with foreign countries, 544; courts, 524-25; defense

expenditures, xxviii, 569; doctrine, strategy and tactics, 553, 562-63; education and training, 564-65, 575; equipment, xxvii, xxxvii, 582-90; foreign technology, 544, 570, 572-73; ground forces, 544, 582-83; historical development, 24, 29, 545-47; manpower, 546, 562; military regions, 547, 550, 561; Military Service Law, 553, 557, 565, 566, 567; militia, xxviii, 544, 590-91; modernization programs, 464, 543-44, 547-49, 551-55; navy, 544, 546, 566, 585-87; nuclear capabilities, 560, 563, 587-90; organization of, 557-62; paramilitary forces, xxviii, 544, 562, 590-93; people's war principles, 546, 562-63; political education, 548, 556; Production and Construction Corps, 592; promotion, 567; public attitudes towards, 108, 115-16, 557; ranks, 567-68; recruitment, 565-66; reductions in force, 561-62; reserve service system, 591; retirement, 567; self-reliance policies, 548; Soviet model, 547-48; Strategic Missile Force, 544, 587; training, 548, 553, 584-85; uniforms, 568

Asian countries (*see also* under names of individual countries): foreign relations, 480; military cooperation, 580

Asian Development Bank, 348

Australia, 581; foreign relations, 498; trade with, 295, 324, 499

Austria, 330

automotive industry, 315, 360-61

Autumn Harvest Uprising, 34, 35, 545

Ba Jin, 188

Baghdad, 12

Bai Hua, 182-83

Bai Juyi, 187

Bangladesh, 580, 582

Bank of China, xxiv, 230, 243, 244, 348, 351, 483

bankruptcy laws, 458

banks and banking, 243-46; agricultural sector, 280; foreign exchange, 230, 244, 347; investment loans, 226, 242; nationalization, 42, 214, 243; personal savings accounts, 246

bao jia (tithing), 525, 526

baogan (household production responsibility), 275-76

Baohuang Hui (Protect the Emperor Society), 28

Baoshan, 313, 500

Baotou, 306

Bay of Hangzhou, 71

Beijing, xxi, 48, 52, 61, 81, 177, 199, 431, 440; import-export companies, 349; industry, 235, 314, 315, 319; international airport, xxv; machinery centers, 314; military region, 561; population, 82; shopping, 343-44; university, xxii, 201; visitor regulations, 80; during Yuan dynasty, 17

Beijing Foreign Languages Institute, 484

Beijing Institute for International Strategic Studies, 485

Beijing Research Academy, 377

Beijing Research Laboratory, 377

Beijing Review, 184, 185

Beijing-Tianjin-Tangshan Economic Zone, xxiii, 342

Beiping (*see also* Beijing), 28

Bhutan, U.S. forces in, 65

bicycles, 301, 322

Bo Hai Gulf, 68, 69; oil reserves, 327

Bo Yibo, 46

Book of Changes (*Yijing*), 185-86

border disputes: with Burma, 65; with India, 45, 65, 477, 496, 544, 578; settlements, 477; with Soviet Union, 21-22, 49, 64-65, 477, 489-90, 491, 492, 576; with Vietnam, 55, 477, 496, 544, 552-53, 577

Borodin, Mikhail, 33

Boxer Uprising, 28-29

Brahmaputra River, 65

Brezhnev, Leonid, 491

Brunei, 65

Buddhism. *See* religion

budget, 242-43

bureaucracy. *See* cadre system

Burma, 26, 65; military ties with, 580

cadre system (*see also* government), 53, 238, 434-37; abolishment of tenure, 410, 434, 436; accountability of, 464; centralization, 11, 15; examination system, 106, 107-8, 180; imperial period, 11-12, 14, 15, 106-8; job assignments, 143; legal cadres, 510-11, 513; and

mass organizations, 418; personnel reform, 436-37; prestige, 115-16; in public security, 527-28; "red" and "expert" criteria, 436; reorganization of, 410, 445, 446, 463-64; retirement, 122, 436; rural areas, 127-28; wages and benefits, 114-15, 122
calligraphy. *See* cultural developments
Cambodia, 480; and France, 26; invasion of, 577, 578; military cooperation, 580
"Cambulac," 17. *See also* Beijing
Canada: technical assistance, 330; trade with, 295, 499
Cankao Xiaoxi (Reference News), 200, 439
Cankao Ziliao (Reference Information), 200, 439
Canton. *See* Guangzhou
Cao Yu, 192
Capital Construction Engineering Corps, 561, 575
census. *See* population
Central Advisory Commission, 411, 416, 451; establishment of, 452
Central Commission for Discipline Inspection, 449, 451
Central Committee, 50; economic planning, 239; foreign policy role, 482; membership, 413, 556; staff reductions, 435; United Front Work Department, 418
Central Military Commissions: and foreign policy, 482; party, 415; State, 424-25
Central People's Broadcasting Station, 366, 368, 440
Central Radio and Television University, 178
Chang Jiang, xxii, 6, 68, 237, 245, 284, 328, 330, 355; freight traffic, xxv, 361-62
Chang Jiang Basin, 289
Chang Jiang Delta, 69
Chang Jiang Valley, 37, 119, 269; agricultural crops, 288, 289; forestry products, 292; industry, 235; population, 78
Chang'an (*see also* Xi'an), 11, 14
Changchun, 159, 314
Changsha, 34
chemicals industry, 221, 317-18
Chen Boda, 48, 56
Chen Duxiu, 188
Chen Junsheng, xxxix
Chen Xilian, 55
Chen Xitong, xxxix
Chen Yun, xxxv, xxxvii-xxxviii, 46, 54, 413, 449, 456, 458; opposition of, 462
Chengdu, 314, 561
Chernenko, Konstantin, 490
Chiang Ching-kuo, xl
Chiang Kai-shek, xxxii, 33, 37, 39, 419, 478, 509, 526; Northern Expedition, 33-34
Chin-men. *See* Jinmen
China Association for Promoting Democracy, 419
China Association of Science and Technology, 394-95, 396
China Central Television (CCTV), 366, 368, 440
China Council for the Promotion of International Trade (CCPIT), 351-52, 483
China Daily, 200
China Democratic League, 419
China Democratic National Construction Association, 419
China Electronics Import and Export Corporation, 574
China Industrial and Commercial Bank, 243, 351; education loans, 173
China International Economic Consultants Corporation, 350
China International Trust and Investment Corporation, 351
China Investment Bank, 243, 351
China Merchant Steam Navigation Company, 433
China National Aero-Technology Import and Export Corporation (CATIC), 573
China National Offshore Oil Corporation, 327
China National Seed Company, 285
China News Service (Zhongguo Xinwenshe), 199, 440
China Northern Industrial Corporation (NORINCO), 350, 573
China Ocean Shipping Company (COSCO), 356
China Precision Import and Export Corporation, 573
China Proper, 6, 11, 69, 268; population density, 78
China Publishing House (Zhonghua Shuju), 198, 199
China Shipbuilding Trading Corporation, 574

China Shipping Inspection Bureau, 362
China State Shipbuilding Corporation, 570
China Travel and Tourism Bureau, 229, 351
China Xinshidai Corporation, 570, 573
China Xinxing Corporation, 574
China Zhi Gong Dang (Party for Public Interest), 419
Chinese Academy of Sciences, 387-88; emphasis on basic research, 388; export companies of, 401; founding of, 377; membership, 388; privileged position of, 393; Soviet cooperation, 378, 396
Chinese Academy of Social Sciences, 5; Law Institute, 518
Chinese Communist Party (CCP) (*see also* government), 4, 39, 409-21; attitude towards religion, 145; Central Advisory Commission, 411, 416; Central Commission for Discipline Inspection, 416; Central Committee, 50, 239, 413; Central Military Commission, 57, 391, 415, 451, 485, 551, 555; constitution, xxxvii-xxxviii, 411-12, 422; control of the People's Liberation Army, 556-57; and the Cultural Revolution, 49, 57; decentralization of authority, 411; discipline, 416, 436, 456; economic goals, 213, 230, 412; and education, xxxviii, 156; elections, 417; "four cardinal principles," 154; and government, 460-61; and the Great Leap Forward, 217; and the Guomindang, 34, 37, 38-39; intellectuals and, 42; job assignments, 143; judicial role, 515, 519; land reform, 271-72; and the mass media, 438; and mass organizations, 418-21; membership, 116-17, 417; and the military, 116, 416, 548, 556; minority nationalities, 88; Party Congresses, 50, 51-52, 53, 57, 412-13; party rectification program, 417-18, 436-37, 456-57; Political Bureau, xxvi, xxxvii-xxxviii, 36, 50, 54, 413-14; political realignments, 447-50; populist-style leadership, 46-47; prestige, 117; Propaganda Department, 54, 185, 366; purges, 42, 55; reevaluation of party history, 450; retirement of senior leaders, xxxvii-xxxviii, 452-53; role in modernization, 463-64; rural areas, 279, 416; Secretariat, 409, 415; Soviet support, 32-33; ties with foreign parties, 481, 482, 490; and work units, 116-17, 120-21
Chinese Peasants' and Workers' Democratic Party, 419
Chinese People's Association for Friendship with Foreign Countries, 421, 485-86
Chinese People's Institute of Foreign Affairs, 486
Chinese People's Political Consultative Conference (CPPCC), xxxviii, 418-19; constitutional framework, 422; membership, 418; minority nationalities, 100; science policy, 377
Chinese People's Volunteers, 547
Chinese Turkestan. *See* Xinjiang-Uygur Autonomous Region
Chinese University of Science and Technology, 388
Chongqing, 199, 245; industry, 305, 314, 318
Chuci (Songs of Chu), 186
Chun Qiu (Spring and Autumn), 186
Ci Xi, 25, 28
Cihuai Canal, 362
CITIC Group, 351
civil aviation. *See* airports and aviation
civil bureaucracy. *See* cadre system
civil law. *See* judicial system
civil rights: abolishment of the "four big rights," 422-23; constitutional developments, 513, 516, 518, 519, 521; imperial period, 508-9
civil wars and dissension, 13, 30-31; ancient period, 11, 14; Civil War, xxxii, 240, 302, 310, 448, 546; against Japan, 32; Lhasa riots, xxxix; 19th century, 21, 23-24; post-World War II, 38-39; Republican Revolution of 1911, 29-30; student demonstrations, xxxv, 461; Taiping Rebellion, 23-24
Classic of Documents (*Shujing*), 186
Classic of Poetry (*Shijing*), 186
climate, xxii, 61, 71
coal, 301, 324; reserves, 309
Cochin China. *See* Republic of Vietnam
collectives: agriculture, 41, 42, 125, 208, 234; benefits, 115, 122; constitutional rights, 423; industry, 235-36; public works responsibilities, 234
College of International Relations, 484
colleges. *See* universities and colleges
Comintern, 33, 34, 36

Commercial Press (Shangwu Yinshuguan), 198, 199
communes, 44–45, 112; agriculture, 125, 217, 231–32, 272–73; dissolution of, xxxiii, 164, 207, 225, 275; family planning activities, 76–77; and household unit, 125, 130; income distribution, 232; non-agricultural, 44; public order responsibilities, 535; social consequences of, 133–34; structure of, 46, 217, 231–32; and upward mobility, 125
communications, xxv–xxvi, 35, 209, 212, 304, 366–69; facsimile and computer services, 368; foreign broadcasting, 196, 200, 369, 439–40; foreign circulation, 438–39; historical development, 365–66; Intelsat membership, 367; international network, 366; labor force, 236; limits on criticism, 438; newspapers, 199–200, 438–39; post World War II, 214; radio, 196, 368, 440; restricted publications, 439; satellites, 367, 439–40; services for minority groups, 368; telecommunications, 365–69, 439; telegraph, 367–68; telephone services, 366–67; television, 196, 368–69, 440; use as propaganda tool, 438
Communications Bank, 243
Communist Youth League, 418, 420–21; and armed forces involvement, 531, 561; membership, 420
computers. *See* electronics industry
Confucianism, 145; and the civil service, 11–12, 17; classics, 8, 16, 104, 185; influence on intellectuals, 376; and social control, 508; values of, 104–6
Confucius, 5, 8, 10; shrine, 146; writings of, 186
constitutional developments (*see also* State Constitution of 1982): civil rights, 422–23, 513, 516; Common Program, 511; to facilitate modernization, xxxviii, 409, 421; "four big rights," 49, 516; influence of Mao Zedong Thought, 515; party constitution, 411–12, 451; State Constitution of 1954, 42, 512–15; State Constitution of 1975, 515–17; State Constitution of 1978, 517–21
construction industry, 318–19; funding, 14, 244, 323, 575; housing, 254–55, 322–23
consumer goods and services: availability, 228, 301–2; bicycles, 136, 322; household goods, 254, 322; inflation, xxxvi, 249–50; prices, 246–49; processed food, 321–22; rationing, 120, 230, 252, 344; retail sales, 343–44; rural areas, 277, 344; service sector, 237–38; televisions, 136, 322, 368–69; urban-rural differences, 258, 344; and work units, 122
Council for Mutual Economic Assistance (Comecon), 501, 577
courts (*see also* procuratorates), 522–25; adjudication committees, 523; military, 524–25; Organic Law, 519, 523; Supreme People's Court, 513, 515–16, 517, 523
crime and punishment (*see also* judicial system), 207, 228, 262, 515, 516; categories of offenses, 537–38; for counterrevolutionary activities, 520; crime rate, 456–57, 539; death penalty, 507, 521, 538; juveniles, 539; mediation committees, 536–37; mutual surveillance, 526–27; penal system, 507, 539; penalties, 538
crops. *See* agriculture; grain
Cuba, 295
cultural developments (*see also* Confucianism; society), 185–202; ancient period, 6, 12, 14, 16, 17; Beijing Opera, 190–92; and the Cultural Revolution, 188–96; drama, 190–92; folk and variety arts, 197–98; foreign influences, 189–90, 192, 193–94; libraries and archives, 200–2; literature, 185–88, 188–90; "the literature of the wounded," 189; motion pictures, 195–96; music, 192–94; newspapers, 199–200; painting and calligraphy, 194–95; post-Mao, 154, 189–90; publishing, 198–99; radio and television, 196; socialist realism, 188–89, 195; Soviet influences, 188, 193, 195
Cultural Revolution, xxxiii, 47–53, 99; army role, 549–51; attitude towards intellectuals, 181, 379, 383; cultural activity during, 188–96; economic effects, 220–21, 239, 303; educational policies, 141–42, 153, 163; elimination of service sector, 237; foreign policy repercussions, 474, 480–81, 484, 490, 492, 496; impact on science and technology, 373, 374, 380, 386; internal migration during, 79; labor force effects, 220, 309, 514; Mao's "four big rights," 49; political effects, 445;

reassessment of, 4, 55, 57, 422, 447, 450; and religion, 145-46; role of youth in, 48-49; wage equality, 115
currency, 7, 214
Czechoslovakia, Soviet invasion of, 490, 492, 550, 576

Dagang, 326
Dalai Lama, xxxix-xl, 45
Dalian, xxv, 228, 309, 348
Damanskiy Island. *See* Zhenbao Island
danwei (work units), 114-16, 120-24, 128; economic limitations of, 148, 149; permission to marry, 139; organizational structure, 120, 147-48; research institutes as, 387; social responsibilities, 115, 120; specialization of, 147; wages and benefits, 121-22
dao (Way), 10
Daoism. *See* Taoism
Daqing, 326, 328
Datong, 324
Daya Bay, 331
Dazhai, 274
defense industry (*see also* armed forces), 375, 390-91; accomplishments, 391; arms sales, 573-74; budget, 569; civilianization of, 570-71; concentration of skilled personnel, 387; equipment production, 332, 571-72; funding reform, 400; integration with civilian industries, 332, 544, 553, 568-69, 574; privileged position of, 393; research and development, 569-70; selective importation of foreign technology, 572-73; trading corporations, 573-74
democratic centralism, xxvi, 411, 426, 454, 461, 520; and local administration, 429
Democratic People's Republic of Korea (*see also* Korea): arms sales to, 573; boundary issues, 477; exports to, 295; foreign relations, 498; military cooperation, 580
Democratic Republic of Vietnam (*see also* Republic of Vietnam; Vietnam), 580
demography. *See* population
Deng Liqun, 183, 460, 461
Deng Xiaoping, xxxi, xxxiii, xxxiv, xxxviii, 42, 46, 52, 55, 181, 304, 413, 416; agricultural reforms, 79; background, 448; *Building Socialism with Chinese Characteristics,* 465; and the Chinese Communist Party, 46-47, 52, 53, 448; civil bureaucracy reforms, 434-35; and the constitution, 421; cult of personality, 465; and the Cultural Revolution, 48, 49; economic policies, 51, 208, 213, 222, 225, 346, 445, 447, 449; education policies, 154-56, 167; foreign policy, 477, 481, 486; leadership style, 449, 454, 466; Mao's ideology and, 47, 448; and military modernization, 464, 551, 552, 553, 555; and minority nationalities, 88; political reforms, 460-61; purged from power, 49, 52, 222; rehabilitation, 53, 447-48, 552; and religion, 146; resignation from Political Bureau, xxxvii; science and technology policy, 373, 374, 382-83; The Selected Works of Deng Xiaoping, 465; "spiritual pollution" campaign, 183-84, 457; use of ideology, xxxiv, 466, 468; visit to United States, 493
Deng Yingchao, 449
development plans: 1953-57, 41, 215-16, 240, 301, 302, 306, 346; 1958-62, 43, 216, 240; 1966-70, 240; 1971-75, 240, 303; 1976-80, 240; 1981-85, 240; 1986-90, 153, 166, 240, 304, 310, 315, 316, 323, 356-57, 415; annual plans, 240-41; regional plans, 342; target allocations, 240-41
Deyang, 315
dissension. *See* civil wars and dissension
domestic trade. *See* internal trade
Dongbei Plain, 68
Double Hundred Campaign. *See* Hundred Flowers Campaign
down to the countryside movement (*xiafang*), 43-44, 47-48
Dream of the Red Chamber. *See Hong Lou Meng*
Du Fu, 187
dynasties (*see also* names of individual dynasties), history: ancient period, 5-10; Han, 10, 11-13; Jin, 13; Ming, 18; Qin, 11; Qing, 18-20; Shang, 5-6; Song, 14-15; Sui, 13-14; Tang, 14; Three Kingdoms, 13; Xia, 5; Yuan, 16-17; Zhou, 6-7, 10

East China Sea, 69, 71
Eastern Europe (*see also* under names of individual countries): foreign relations,

500–1; scientific cooperation, 396; trade with, 501
Eastern Zhou dynasty, 7, 11, 185
economy (*see also* agriculture; industry), xxiii–xxiv, 207–62; budget, 242–43; capital investments, 210–11; capitalism, xxxiv, 224; centrally planned economy, 207, 208; Civil Code stipulations, 427–28; control mechanisms, 223, 229–30, 232; development planning, 215–16, 238–42; development zones, 226, 228, 342–43; Four Modernizations program, 54–58; gross national product, 208; inflation, 207, 214, 228, 249–50; market exchanges, 124, 149; 19th century, 21; policies, 207, 213–28, 223; post-Mao, 222–23; post-World War II, 37–38, 213–14; pricing policies, xxxvi, 209, 246–49, 302; reduction of central planning, 223, 242; reform programs, xxxv–xxxvi, 149, 207, 209, 222–28, 454–55; Soviet model, 215–16, 301; statistical data, 109–10; structure of, 228–50; subsidies to minorities, 86, 101; urban reforms, 458–59
education (*see also* universities and colleges), xxii, 153–80; administration of, 155–56, 157, 158; adult, 177–79; compulsory, 153, 155, 157–59, 160; and Confucianism, 104; and the Cultural Revolution, 141–42; enrollment rates, 160, 161–62, 164, 165, 166; examination system, 142, 143; foreign language study, 161; foreign training, 62, 83, 154, 173, 375; funding of, 159, 160, 174; key schools, 159; labor force, 176, 177, 238; and literacy, 179–80; Maoist policies, 141–42; National Conference on Education (1985), 156–57; "nonformal" courses, 177–79; parental involvement, 140; policies, 154–56; political and moral training, 161; preschool, 162; primary, 160–62; productive labor requirements, 161; reform of, xxxvi, 47– 48, 153, 156–57; rural-urban distinctions, 119, 259, 270; school systems, 156–67; science and technology, 153, 154; secondary, 163–66; spare-time schools, 178; special schools, 163; teacher training, 176–77; and upward mobility, 110, 112; via television, 178– 79; vocational and technical, 163, 164–66
Egypt, military ties with, 573, 580
elections, 461; Party, 417; procuratorates, 520; state, 410
electronics industry: computers, 306, 332; consumer products, 317; labor force, 317; limitations of, 308; research, 392
elite groups. *See* intellectuals; society
emigration, 38, 62, 83; labor force exports, 83; Tibetan refugees, 45
energy, xxiv; coal, 310; consumption, 209, 283; electricity, 283, 330; foreign assistance, 330; hydroelectricity, 260, 302, 328, 329–30; nuclear power, 302, 330–31; oil and natural gas, 326–28; power shortages, 310, 328; thermal power plants, 329
Engineering Corps, 575
Enlightenment Daily. *See Guangming Ribao*
Ergun He, 64
ethnic groups. *See* Han Chinese; minority nationalities
Europe. *See* Eastern Europe; under names of individual countries; Western Europe
exports, xxiv, 223, 297; agricultural products, 270, 295, 321, 346; alcoholic beverages, 322; crude oil and petroleum, 326, 352–53; manufactured goods, 352; military equipment, 332; rare metals, 309; tea and silk, 290; textiles, 320, 353

fa (School of Law), 8, 10, 508
family life: ancestor worship, 132, 146; birth control programs, 62, 75–78; effect of communes on, 44; kinship principles, 131–32; marriage, 131, 132, 139; and nonstandard family forms, 130, 131; role of the household, 126–27, 130–32, 138, 139–40; rural society, 130–32; size, 130, 138; and social stratification, 109–10; urban areas, 138–40
Fan Memorial Biological Institute, 377
Fang Yi, 384, 394
Federal Republic of Germany. *See* West Germany
feudalism, 6–7
film industry, 195–96
First Workers' and Peasants' Army. *See* Red Army
fisheries, 292
"five anti" movement. *See* "wu fan" movement
Five Principles of Peaceful Coexistence, 45, 480–81; and Third World relations, 497

five-year plans. *See* development plans
food (*see also* grain): consumption, 209, 251-52, 288; and internal migration, 79-80; post-World War II, 214; production, 321-22; rationing system, 118; shortages, 44, 210, 218, 273
Foreign Affairs College, 484
Foreign Affairs Small Group, 482, 486, 488
foreign debts, 348
foreign exchange, 209; administration of, 230, 244, 351; credit card for, 245; reserves, 347
Foreign Investment and Control Commission, 349
foreign investments, 221; categories of, 348; and the Civil Code, 427-28; constitutional framework, 424; government policy, 218; industry loans and credit, 309; joint ventures, xxxiii, 207, 226, 260, 309, 433; legalization of, 226; special economic zones for, 226, 228
foreign policy, xxvii, xl-xli, 473-503; Chinese nationalism and, 476-78; constitutional framework, 424; decision-making processes, 481-88; developed nations, 498-501; diplomatic relations, xli, 473; economic modernization as basis, 473; embassies and consulates, 484; Europe, 500-1; Five Principles of Peaceful Coexistence, 45, 480-81, 497; influence of ideology, 478-81; international organizations, 501-3; Japan, 499-500; Mao's Theory of the Three Worlds, 497; opening up policy, xxxvi, 455; opposition to imperialism, 479; organizations involved in, 482-88; "people-to-people" diplomacy, 485-86; pragmatic shifts in, 480; Soviet Union, xl, 46, 488-91; special administrative regions, 434; support for worldwide revolution, 479-80; Taiwan, xl, 45; territorial cessions, 26; territorial integrity goals, 477; Third World, 495-98; training of personnel, 484; United States, xli, 45, 51, 492-95; with the West, 51
foreign technology. *See* scientific and technological developments
foreign trade, xxiv, 21, 22, 209, 344-54; ancient period, 12-13, 17, 18, 345; banking structure for, 351; corporations and enterprises, 349, 350, 351-52; decentralization of, 349-50; expansion of, 224-25, 226, 346; export-import patterns, 352-53; and gross national product (GNP), xxiv, 345-46; historical overview, xxxii, 344-47; "open cities," 348; opening up policy, 346-47; organization, 349-52; policy, 230, 347-48; post-Mao, 222; reform policies, 454-55; special economic zones, 348; trade deficits, 347; trading partners, 353-54; world ranking, 347
foreigners, 3, 476; campaigns against, 28-29, 40-41; early assimilation of, xxxii, 3; rejection of Western philosophies, 375-76; traditional view of, 4, 475; unequal treaties with, xxxii, 476
forestry, 292
Four Modernizations, xxxiii-xxxvii, 54-58, 62, 221, 275, 409; economic policies, 222-23; education policies, 153-54, 168-69; effect on local administration, 430; historical antecedents, xxxi; ideological basis, xxxiv; industry, 304; labor force changes, 409; national defense, 552; politics of, xxxv, 445, 446, 454, 462-65; and population growth, 76; role of intellectuals, 182, 409; science and technology policy, 308, 373, 382-83
France, 21, 330, 501; exports from, 295; military ties with, 581; and Vietnam, 26
Freedom Land (Kalayaan), 65
Fu Xi, 186
Fujian Province, 226, 234, 269, 433, 579; agricultural crops, 290; import-export companies, 349
Fushun, 305, 324

Gang of Four, 53, 55, 57, 88, 142, 190, 213, 240, 383, 507, 518; arrest of, 551; control of militia, 528; economic goals, 221-22, 239; effect on industry, 303-4; trial of, 56, 522
Gangdise Shan, 67
Gansu Corridor, 68
Gansu Province, 11, 68, 213; industry, 325; population, 78; rural incomes, 258
Gao Gang, 42
General Administration of Civil Aviation of China (CAAC), xxv, 229, 356, 363-64

General Administration of Customs, 230, 350, 351
General Agreement on Tariffs and Trade (GATT), 348, 502
geography, xxi, 62–71; boundaries, 64–65; size, xxi, 64; terrain and drainage, 65–71; territorial waters, 69, 71
Germany, war with, 32 (*see also* West Germany)
Gongren Ribao (Workers' Daily), 184, 185
Gorbachev, Mikhail S., xl, 491; on border disputes, 64–65
government (*see also* cadre system; Chinese Communist Party (CCP); local administration; National People's Congress (NPC); State Council), xxvi, 39– 41, 409–10, 421–34; administrative structure, xxvi, 81, 88, 100–1; agricultural role, 127–28, 271–81; Central Military Commission, 424–25, 485, 553, 556; and Confucianism, 17; decentralization of authority, 411; economic role, 228–31; elections, 410; establishment of the People's Republic, xxxii, 39–40; establishment of the republic, xxxii; international recognition, 40; judicial system, 427–28; Legalism doctrine, 8, 10; under Mao, 39–53; and minority nationalities, 86–88; under the Nationalists, 34–39; post-Mao, 53–54
grain (*see also* agriculture): consumption rates, 251; corn, 288–89; hybrid rice, 285; imports, 273, 288; pricing policy, 246, 248–49, 277; production, 251, 272, 286–90; rice, 268, 288; soybeans, 289; wheat, 269, 270, 288, 295
Grand Canal, 14, 17, 18, 68
Great Britain, 21, 501; and Burma, 26; and Hong Kong, 26, 434, 477–78; military ties with, 581; trade with, 22–23; and Xizang, 31
Great Leap Forward, xxxii–xxxiii, 43–46, 99, 216–18, 240; and agriculture, 44; economic management, 216–18, 239; economic repercussions, 44–45, 272–73, 465; education policies, 153; effects on science and technology, 373, 380; industry, 44, 302–3, 312; and judicial system, 514–15; literary restrictions, 188–89; political consequences, xxxii–xxxiii, 45; Soviet reactions to, 489
Great Proletarian Cultural Revolution. *See* Cultural Revolution
Great Wall, 11, 14, 36, 68
Great Wall Card, 245
Great Wall Industrial Corporation, 350, 573
Greater Hinggan Range, xxii, 66, 68
Group of 77, 502
Guangdong Province, xxxix, 71, 226, 234, 269, 355, 433; agricultural crops, 290; economic growth, 128, 149; forestry products, 292; import-export companies, 349; standard of living, 119; textile production, 320
Guangming Ribao (Enlightenment Daily), 199, 438
Guangxi-Zhuang Autonomous Region, 355; agricultural crops, 290; economic subsidies, 86; population, 84, 85; textiles, 320
Guangxu, 28
Guangzhou, 228, 245, 348; industry, 318; military region, 561; as seat of government, 32, 33, 34; textiles, 321; trade, 21, 22
Guizhou Province, 24; agricultural crops, 290; economic subsidies, 86; population settlement, 84, 85; textile production, 320
Gulf of Tonkin (Beibu Wan), 327
Guo Moruo, 188
Guomindang, xxxii, 30, 31, 32–33, 34–35; and Chiang Kai-shek, 33–34; and the Chinese Communist Party (CCP), 37, 38–39; and intellectuals, 180; legal system, 509; public policing, 526; Red Army support, 545; Revolutionary Committee, 419; scientific policy, 376–77; suppression of warlords, 509
Guowuyuan Gongbao (State Council Bulletin), 439

Hai He, 69
Hainan Island, xxi, 71, 81, 84, 328, 579; change in status of, xxxix; PLA seizure of, 546
Han Chinese (*see also* minority nationalities), 12, 24, 84; attitudes towards minorities, 87, 99–100; diversity and unity of, 101–3
Han Dynasty, xxxi, 10, 11–13, 14, 525; cultural developments, 186–87, 197; legal system, 508
Han Fei, 8, 10

Han Yu, 187
Hangzhou, 198
Hao, 6
Hao Jianxiu, 420
Harbin, 61; industry, 314, 315, 316, 319
health care, xxii, 62, 90-96; AIDS programs, 92; barefoot doctor system, 91, 94-95; facilities, 94; personnel, 92, 238; preventive measures, 91; rural areas, 91, 94-95, 259; traditional medicine, 95-96; urban areas, 259
Heavenly Kingdom of Great Peace (*see also* Taiping Rebellion), 24
Hebei Province, 52; industry, 324; textiles, 320
Hefei, 388
Heilong Jiang, xxi, 21, 26, 64, 71, 576
Heilongjiang Province, xxi, 11, 64, 71, 81, 234; agricultural crops, 290; mining industry, 324
Henan Province, 5, 7, 69, 343, 396; agricultural crops, 290
Himalayas, 65, 66, 67
historiography, 12; Marxist model, 4; post-Mao Zedong, 4-5
Honduras, 498
Hong Kong, 23, 418, 500; arrangements for return of, 477-78; Joint Declaration on, 434; joint ventures with, 331, 348; migration to, 83; trade relationship, xxiv, 353
Hong Lou Meng (Dream of the Red Chamber), 187-88
Hong Xiuquan, 23-24
Hongqi (Red Flag), 439
Hongshui He, 330
household production responsibility. *See baogan*
housing: construction, 254; egalitarian standards, 136; income subsidies, 256; investments in, 276-77, 322-23; living space, 254-255, 322; private ownership, 255; shortage, 136; urban society, 135, 136-38; and work units, 122
Hu Qiaomu, 183, 462
Hu Qili, xxxvii, 184
Hu Shi, 188
Hu Yaobang, xxxvii, 53, 54, 56, 185, 192, 409, 413, 415, 438, 449, 453, 454; as chairman, 57; political reforms, 461; resignation of, xxxv, 228, 262, 446, 462
Hua Guofeng, 52, 53, 55, 240, 447, 551, 590; economic policies, 222; judicial reforms, 516; removal of, 449, 450; resignation as chairman, 57; science policy, 384
Huabei, 327
Huai He, 69, 362
Huai He Plain, 362
Huaihai Economic Zone, 343
Huang Hai, 68, 71
Huang He, xxii, 3, 64, 68, 330; embankment concerns, 68
Huang He Valley, 5
Huang Xing, 29
Huangpu, xxv; military academy (*see also* Whampoa), 33
Hubei Province, 30; industry, 306, 325; textiles, 320
Hunan Province, 24, 34, 35, 545
Hundred Days' Reform, 28-29
Hundred Flowers Campaign, 42-43, 181, 513-14; cultural developments, 190; and scientists, 379
Hundred Schools of Thought, 7-10; contributions to literature, 186
Huolinhe, 575

immigration, 83-84
Imperial China, 11-13; civil bureaucracy, 106-8; civil rights, 508-9; dynastic governments, 11-30; foreign policy, 476, 479; legal system, 508-9, 525-26; mutual aid groups, 526; tributary system, 13
Import-Export Control Commission, 349
imports, xxiv; aircraft, 316; barley, 295; chemical fertilizer, 282; chemicals, 318; 18th century, 22-23; food, 352; grains, 210, 218, 288, 295; iron and steel, 312, 313, 352; machinery and equipment, 219, 221, 222, 352, 403; metals, 309; minerals, 326; opium, 22-23; pulp and paper, 320; raw cotton, 289; sugar, 290, 295; textiles, 352
income, 255-59; agricultural, 226, 257-58; benefits and subsidies, 235, 255-56; bonus system, 224; collectively owned industries, 236; disparities, 119, 207, 228, 257-58, 262; equalization goals, 115, 213; and family size, 130-31; growth rate, 216; minority areas, 86; nonagricultural rural enterprises, 258-59; private sector, 256-57; rural areas, 126, 277; state-owned industries,

235, 255; urban society, 135, 256; work units, 121–22
India, 14; border dispute, 45–46; foreign relations, 496, 498; People's Liberation Army activities in, 549; as security threat, 578; Tibetan refugees in, 45
Indonesia, 498, 580; alleged subversive activities in, 480, 496
industry (*see also* defense industry), xxiii, 301–33; chemical fertilizer plants, 282; collective ownership, 235–36, 305; construction, 322–23; economic reforms, 119, 224, 226, 301; energy, 326–31; energy shortages, 302, 310; geographical distribution, 234–35, 305–6, 307; government policies, 215, 304, 306; and gross national income, 234; handicrafts, 215; heavy, deemphasis of, 223–24, 225, 301; historical trends, 302–4; internal trade, 340–42; investments in, 118, 135, 216–17, 226, 303, 304, 308–9; "iron rice bowl" system, 302; labor force, 234–36, 309; manufacturing, 310–22; market forces, 301, 304; mining, 324–26; nationalization, 42, 112, 114, 214; organization of, 305; ownership of, 235, 305; post-World War II, 302; pricing policies, 248; production rates, 216, 219, 221, 222–23, 302–4; raw materials, 309–10; research and development, 306–8; resource allocation system, 229–30; rural, 331–32; "rural economic unions," 236; service, 304; small-scale, 219; sources of capital, 308–9; Soviet influence, 41; state ownership, 235, 305; taxation, 242; technology level, 208, 261, 306–8
inflation, 207, 214, 228, 249–50
Inner Mongolia (*see also* Nei Monggol Autonomous Region), 32
Institute of Criminal Police, 533
intellectuals; "antibourgeois liberalization," 182–83; campaigns against, 4, 41, 182–83; and the Chinese Communist Party, 42, 116; Confucian influences, xxxi, 376; and the Cultural Revolution, 181; exodus of, 180; under Four Modernizations, 181, 409, 447; government policy towards, 180–85; and the Hundred Flowers Campaign, 181; limits on free expression, 184; manual labor, 47–48, 115; post-Mao encouragement of, 154, 182–85, 383; "spiritual pollution" campaign, 183–84, 457
Intelsat, 367
internal migration, xxxiii, 78–81, 117–18, 271; frontier regions, 81; limitations, 80; political expulsions, 79
internal security, 47, 525–37; citizen's involvement in, 527, 534–37; counterintelligence operations, 533–34; grassroots organizations, 534–37; mediation committees, 536–37; militia units, 527, 528; mutual surveillance, 534; revolutionary committees, 527; security system, 529–33
internal trade, 209, 337–44; agricultural goods, 337–40; commercial departments, 214, 338; economic zones, 342–43; free-market activities, 228, 338, 340; industrial goods, 340–42; lateral economic cooperation, 342–43; nationalization, 42; pricing policies, 338, 340, 342; rationing, 338; retail sales, 343–44; state distribution system, 340, 342
International Atomic Energy Agency (IAEA), 502
International Monetary Fund (IMF), 497; membership, 347–48, 502
International Olympic Committee, 502
Iran, military exports to, xli, 332, 573
Iraq; arms sales to, 573; labor force requests, 83
iron and steel industry, 310–13; reserves, 309
"iron rice bowl," xxxiii, 392; system, 302
irrigation, 216, 270, 274, 284; origins, 7
Israel, xli, 498
Italy, military ties with, 581

Jammu, 65
Japan, 3, 16, 18, 26; Chinese students in, 375; foreign relations, xxvii, 474, 498; influences of, 29; invasion of China, 499; joint ventures with, 348; and Manchuria, 36; peace treaty with, 499–500; scientific cooperation, 396; and Taiwan, 499, 500; technology exports from, 308, 330; trade with, 219, 295, 313, 326, 353, 500; unequal trade treaties, 345; wars with, xxxii, 31–32, 36–38, 180, 448
Ji Dengkui, 55
Jiamusi Airport, 364

Jiang Jieshi. *See* Chiang Kai-shek
Jiang Qing, 48, 50, 53, 56, 57, 189, 190, 528
Jiangnan, 308, 376
Jiangsu Province, 343; economic growth, 128, 149; industry, 308, 327; textiles, 320, 321
Jiangxi Province, 35, 36, 45, 234, 417, 545
Jianyang, 198
Jiefangjun Bao (Liberation Army Daily), 182, 183, 199, 438
Jiefangjun Wenyi (Liberation Army Literature and Art), 182
Jieziyuan Huazhuan (Manual of the Mustard Seed Garden), 195
Jilin Province, 81, 234; agricultural crops, 290; industry, 318
Jin dynasty, 13
Jinan, 561
Jinggang Mountains, 545
Jinmen, 45
Jinxi, 318
Jiulong. *See* Kowloon
Jiusan (September Third) Society, 419-20
Journal of Radio and Television (*Wuxiandian Yu Dianshi*), 196
judicial system, xxvi-xxvii, 427-28, 507-40; Civil Code, 427-28; civil rights, 513, 516, 518; Common Program, 511; courts, 427, 522-25; criminal code, 508, 513; ideological basis, 509-11; law enforcement, 525-37; legal profession, 510-11, 521-22; legal statutes, 518-21, 537-38; legal training, 507, 513, 539; local level, 507; Organic Law, 427, 431; penal system, 537-40; procuratorates, xxvii, 507, 511, 518, 519-20, 529; public education, 511; reforms, xxxvi, 507-8, 512, 516-17; Soviet model, 510, 512; under the State Constitution, 515-22
Junggar Basin, 67, 327
junzi (ruler's son, gentleman), 8

Kaifeng, 198
Kailas Range, 66
Kailuan, 312, 324
Kalayaan (Freedom Land), 65
Kang Sheng, 50, 56
Kang Youwei, 28
Kashi Airport, 364
Kashmir, 65
Kazaks, 84, 86, 88
Kexue (Science), 376
Khmer Rouge, support for, 580
Khrushchev, Nikita, 45, 489
Kinmen. *See* Jinmen
Kissinger, Henry A., 493
Kong Zi. *See* Confucius
Korea, 3, 13, 14, 16; and Japan, 26; Koreans in China, 86
Korean War, 499, 502, 584; Chinese involvement in, 40, 489; PLA deficiencies in, 547; trade repercussions, 501; Unites States stance on, 492
Kosygin, Aleksey, 490
Kowloon, 26
Kublai Khan, 16
Kunlun Mountains, 65, 66, 67, 68, 69
Kuomintang (KMT). *See* Guomindang
Kuwait, 330

labor force (*see also* cadre system; income; "iron rice bowl"; scientific and technical personnel), 88-90; age breakdown, 90; agriculture, xxiii, 90, 208, 231, 268, 270-71; building materials industry, 319; and the Chinese Communist Party, 116-17, 148; contract system, 458-59; educational level, 90; electronics industry, 317; hereditary job transmission, 142-43; industrial sector, xxiii, 234-36, 309; job assignments, 140-42, 172-73, 398; job mobility, 148; lawyers, 508; nonagricultural rural enterprises, 234, 259, 271; private sector, 256; productivity, 210; rural unemployment, 80, 81; service sector, 135, 136, 138, 238; shortage of skilled workers, 209, 221, 261-62, 309; state farms, 234; state vs. collective employment, 115-16; trade and transportation sectors, 337; trade unions, 420; urban unemployment, 309; women, 74, 135, 144-45; work units (*danwei*), 114-16
lakes, salt, 68
land reform, 41, 55, 112, 214, 267; administrative structure, 127-28; Agrarian Reform Law of 1950, 41, 271-72; collectivization, 124-25, 272; and corruption, 128; decollectivization, 125-26, 127-28, 134; establishment of state farms, 272; goals of, 124-25,

271–72; mutual aid system, 214, 272; social consequences of, 112, 133–34
language, 35; Han Chinese, 101; minority, 87; pinyin, 179; *putonghua* (common spoken language), 161, 179; reform plan, 179; spoken, 102; telegraph transmission of, 367; written, 102, 179
Lanzhou, 561; industry, 314
Lao Zi (Old Master), 10
Laos, military ties with, 580
leadership, 413, 415; ancient kings, 6; collective, 411, 450–52, 463; constitutional framework, 423; cult of personality, 451; need for central control, 462–63; prohibition of cults, 411; succession issue, 465; *tianming* doctrine, 6
Leading Group for Science and Technology, 394
League of Left-Wing Writers, 188
League of Nations, 36
Legal Affairs Commission, 519
legal statutes: civil cases, 521; counterrevolutionary activities, 537; criminal, 518, 520–21, 537; Electoral Law, 519; of limitation, 520; Organic Law, 519
Legalism. *See* School of Law (*fa*)
Legation Quarter, 29
Lhasa: airport, 364; riots, xxxix
li (propriety), 508
Li Bai, 187
Li Guixian, xxxix
Li Hongzhang, 25
Li Peng, xxxvii, xxxix
Li Si, 10
Li Teng-hui, xl
Li Xiannian, xxxvii, xxxviii, 53, 413, 462; visit to United States, 495
Liang Qichao, 28
Liaohe, 327
Liaohe Basin, 326
Liaoning Province, 81, 234, 245, 309, 392; industry, xxiii, 308, 310, 324; textiles, 320
Liberation Army Daily. *See Jiefangjun Bao*
Liberation Army Literature and Art. *See Jiefangjun Wenyi*
libraries and archives, 200–2; foreign access to, 202
Liji (Record of Rites), 186
Lin Biao, 45, 47, 48, 50, 57, 181, 213, 586, 590; death of, 51; "Long Live the Victory of People's War," 480, 496; military coup by, 448; military policies, 51, 548; political involvement of, 549, 550; trial of associates, 56; "war preparations" campaign, 550
Lin Zexu, 22
Linyi, 328
literacy, 110; adult classes, 178; rate, 179; rural areas, 159, 270
Literary Gazette. *See Wenyibao*
Liu Shaoqi, 42, 46, 57, 448; chairman, 45; and the Cultural Revolution, 48, 49; economic policies, 213; Mao's ideology and, 47; reinstatement of, 56
livestock, xxiv; dairy and poultry sector, 291; draft animals, 291; feed mills, 291–92; hogs, 291
local administration (*see also* government), 428–34; constitutional provisions, 428, 432; decision-making authority of, 429, 430–31; elections, 431; mass organizations, 432; people's congresses, 429–30; reforms, 431–34, 436–37; special economic zones, 433; staffing reorganization, 435; standing committees, 429, 430; *xiang* (administrative towns), 429, 432
Long March, 416, 448, 545
Lu Xun, 188
Lüda, 328; industry, 318; Soviet Union naval base at, 489
Lunyu (Analects), 186
Luo Ruiqing, 527
Luoyang, 7, 13, 396; industry, 314, 319
Lushan, 45

Ma Ding. *See* Song Longxian
Ma-tsu. *See* Mazu
Macao, 21, 418, 500; arrangements for return of, 477–78; Joint Declaration on, 434
machine-building industry, 313–17; electric power equipment, 315; electronics equipment, 317; machine tools, 314–15; metallurgical equipment, 316; modernization efforts, 314–15; plants, 314; technological limitations, 313; transportation equipment, 315–16
Malaysia: military cooperation, 580; sovereignty claims, 65
Manchukuo, 36
Manchuria, 21; and Japan, 32; secession of, 26; Soviet troops in, 26, 38
Manchurian Plain, 68

Manchus, 18–20, 29; and Hundred Days' Reform opposition, 28; invasion of China, 4; and Russia, 21
"mandate of heaven." *See tianming*
Manual of the Mustard Seed Garden (*Jieziyuan Huazhuan*), 195
manufacturing industry: building materials, 318–19; chemicals, 317–18; consumer goods, 322; food processing, 321–22; iron and steel, 310–13; machine building, 313–17; pulp and paper, 319–20; textiles, 320–21
Mao Dun, 188
Mao Zedong, xxxii, 4, 5, 34, 167, 213, 215, 304, 445; agricultural policies, 277; as chairman, 42; and the Chinese Communist Party (CCP), 37, 39, 47; condemnation for Cultural Revolution, 57; death of, xxxiii, 52–53; earthquake prediction interest, 382; and the economy, 216; education policies, 47–48, 141–42; foreign policy, 477, 480, 481, 497; Great Leap Forward program, 44, 45; ideology, 446–47, 465–66; military strategy, 545–46, 548; mobilization of peasantry, 35–36; "On the Correct Handling of Contradictions among the People," 181, 514; opposition to legal system, 510, 514; personal security force, 528; political style, 466; population growth policies, 75–76; *Quotations from Chairman Mao*, 49; reassessment of, 56, 409, 422, 447, 466; science and technology policies, 378; self reliance policies, 455; and the Socialist Education Movement, 47; and Soviet relations, 488–89; "Yan'an Talks on Literature and Art," 188
Mao Zedong Thought, xxvi, 37, 54, 410; and constitutional developments, 515; and foreign policy, 478–81; reassessment of, 446–47, 465–69; social values, 468
maritime shipping. *See* ports and shipping
Marshall, George C., 39
Marxism-Leninism, xxvi, 410, 456; and foreign policy, 478–81; under Mao Zedong, 37; reassessment of, 446–47, 465–69
mass organizations (*see also* under names of organizations), 418–21; constitutional framework, 422; local level, 432; mobilization of, 43; origins of, 114; support for modernization program, 420, 421
Master Kong. *See* Confucius
May Fourth Movement, 32, 35, 198
Mazu, 45
media. *See* communications
Meishan, 198
Mencius, 8, 186
Meng Zi. *See* Mencius
metallurgical industry. *See* mining industry
Miao people, 85
Middle East, 14, 16
Middle Kingdom, xxxi, 4, 475, 476
migration. *See* emigration; immigration; internal migration
military technology. *See* defense industry
minerals. *See* mining industry
Ming dynasty, 18, 476; cultural developments, 195; science and technology, 374–75
mining industry, 6, 324–26; coal, 260, 324; equipment production, 316; exports, 309; iron and iron ore, 7, 260, 324–25; mechanization level, 324; resources, xxiii, 67, 325–26; technological innovations, 308; transportation, 324; uranium, 326
ministerial portfolios, xxxviii–xxxix; agriculture, animal husbandry, and fishery, 229, 278, 592; astronautics, 570, 574; coal industry, 390; communications, 356, 433; culture, 183, 198, 484; education, 157, 539; electronics industry, 390, 570; finance, 229, 243, 390, 483; foreign affairs, 483–84, 486; foreign economic relations, xxiv, 224, 230, 349, 350, 351, 483, 484, 488; foreign trade, 224, 349; justice, 523; machine-building industry, 313; metallurgical industry, 313; national defense, 483, 484–85, 524, 547, 555, 559; nuclear industry, 570; ordnance industry, 350, 570, 574; posts and telecommunications, 364, 366; public health, 75, 90–91; public security, xxviii, 525, 529, 531, 592; radio, cinema, and television, 178, 196, 366; 440; railways, 316, 356; state security, 525, 533–34; supervision, 410, 427; water resources and electric power, 229, 284, 330
minority nationalities (*see also* Han Chinese), xxii; armed forces involvement, 566; assimilationist policies,

87–88, 99–100; and border security, 86; economic assistance to, 86; education system, 159; government policy towards, 87–88, 100–1, 430; and Han dominance, 101; Kazaks, 84, 86, 88; Korean, 86; Miao, 85; Mongol, 86; radio services, 368; settlement patterns, 61, 84–86; Shan, 86; Tibetans, xxii, xxxix, 84, 85, 88; Uygurs, 84, 86; Yao, 86; Yi, 85; Zhuang, 85
Mo Zi (Mo Di), 10, 186
modernization movements (*see also* Four Modernizations; Great Leap Forward); effect of traditional attitudes, 105–6; Hundred Days' Reform, 28–29; role of education, 155–56; Self-Strengthening Movement, 24–26
Moism, 10
monetary system. *See* currency
Mongolian People's Republic, xl, 20; autonomy of, 31; boundary issues, 477, Chinese control of, 477; Chinese recognition of, 477
Mongols, 18, 86; invasion of China, 3–4, 16–17
Multi-Fiber Agreement, 348
Muslim Rebellion, 24
mythology, 3

Nan Ling, 69
Nanchang, 34; uprising, 545, 568
Nanjing, 13, 18, 24, 30, 34, 328; chemical industry, 318; military region, 561; research laboratory, 376; treaty of, 23; university, 184
Nanjing Regional Economic Cooperation Association, 343
Nanning, 319
Nansha Islands, xl, 65, 576, 579
National Book Coordination Act of 1957, 200
National Conference of Party Delegates (1985), 413, 415
national defense (*see also* armed forces), xxvii–xxviii, xxxvi–xxxvii, 543–93; foreign cooperation, 579–82; foreign port calls, 581–82; India and, 578; security threats, 575–76; Soviet Union and, 576–77; Taiwan and, 579; Vietnam and, 577–78
National Defense Council, 547
National Defense Industries Office, 391
National Defense Science, Technology, and Industry Commission (NDSTIC), 305, 400; responsibilities, 390–91, 559, 569–70
National Defense University, 564
National Library of China, 201
National Natural Science Foundation, 399, 400
National Party Congress, xxvi, 50, 51–52, 53, 57, 412–13; eleventh, 409, 412; twelfth, 412, 452, 465; thirteenth, xxxiv, xxxvii
National People's Congress (NPC), 42, 45, 421, 424–26; committees, 410, 425; economic planning, 229, 239; elections, 410; Foreign Affairs Committee, 482; foreign policy role, 482, 482–83; fourth, 52, 221; fifth, 54, 56, 57–58, 222; functions, 424; judicial role, 512–13, 518; local-level congresses, 429–30; membership, 425; minority representation, 88; Organic Law of, 519; reduction of power, 515; sixth, 159; seventh, xxxviii; Standing Committee, 425, 482
National People's Party. *See* Guomindang
National Revolutionary Army, 33
National Science Conference, 383–84, 384
nationalism (*see also* Guomindang), 33, 108, 180; and foreign policy, 476–78
natural disasters, 68
natural resources, xxxiii, 260, 309–10, 325–26
navy (*see also* armed forces), 544, 560; blue-water capabilities, 587; defense expenditures, 569; force structure and equipment, xxvii, 585–87; manpower, 546, 562; Naval Academy, 586; rank system, 568; South China Sea activities, 579; Soviet assistance, 586; terms of service, 566; uniforms, 568
NDSTIC. *See* National Defense Science, Technology, and Industry Commission
Nehru, Jawaharlal, 496
Nei Monggol Autonomous Region (*see also* Inner Mongolia), xxiv, 64, 71, 213, 234, 269, 270, 429; agricultural crops, 270, 290; economic subsidies, 86; housing conditions, 255; industry, 306, 318, 325; population, 78, 84, 85; supported migration to, 81
Nei Monggol Plateau, 68
Nepal, 477

Netherlands, 501
New China Booksellers (Xinhua Shudian), 198
New China (Xinhua) News Agency, 199, 439
New Culture Movement, 32, 188; influence of Western music, 193; Western painting techniques, 195
"New Long March," 384
New Territories (*see* Kowloon)
New Zealand, 498
newspapers, 199-200
Nian Rebellion, 24
Ningxia-Hui Autonomous Region, 68, 86
Nixon, Richard M., 499; visit to China, 51, 367, 493
Nonaligned Movement, 502
North Atlantic Treaty Organization, 501
North China Plain, 66, 68, 69, 283; agricultural crops, 270, 288, 289; irrigation needs, 284; population, 78
North Korea. *See* Democratic People's Republic of Korea
Northeastern Economic Zone, 342
Northern Song dynasty, 15
Norway, 330
NPC. *See* National People's Congress (NPC)
nuclear science, 330, 391; industry applications, 330-31; Soviet weapons agreement, 46; weapons production, 301, 306, 587-88

Office of the Science, Technology, and Armaments Commission, 391
oil and natural gas: exports, 326; foreign explorations, 327; offshore exploration, 327, 328; pipelines, 328; refineries, 328; reserves, 310, 326, 327, 328; South China Sea, 579
Opium War, 22-23, 345
Organization of Petroleum Exporting Countries, 502
Outer Mongolia. *See* Mongolian People's Republic
overseas Chinese, 419; radio broadcasts to, 368; support for 1911 revolution, 29-30; United Front Work Department, 482

Pakistan, 64; boundary issues, 477; foreign relations, 498; military ties with, 573, 580, 582
Palestine Liberation Organization, support for, 480
Pamir Mountains, xxi, 64, 67
Pangu, 5
paper industry, 319-20
PAPF. *See* People's Armed Police Force (PAPF)
Paracel Islands. *See* Xisha Islands
Paraguay, 498
Pearl River. *See* Zhu Jiang
peasants (*see also* rural areas), xxxiii, 108-9; and the Chinese Communist Party, 42; community structure, 133- 34; family life, 130-32, 139; mobilization of, 35-36, 43-44; settlement patterns, 61; "spiritual pollution" campaign, 183-84, 457; stratification, 109
penal system. *See* crime and punishment
Peng Dehuai, 45, 54, 57, 548, 590
Peng Zhen, 46, 425, 429, 460, 462, 520; judicial reforms, 519
Penghu Islands, 26
People's Armed Police Force (PAPF), 533, 544, 561, 562, 592-93
People's Bank of China, xxxix, 214, 243, 351, 483; economic planning role, 229, 240, 244
People's Communes. *See* communes
People's Construction Bank, 243, 244, 351
People's Daily (*Renmin Ribao*), 199, 431, 438
People's Insurance Company of China, 243, 352
People's Liberation Army (PLA) (*see also* armed forces), xxvii, 39, 220, 415; campaigns, 549, 551; and the Chinese Communist Party (CCP), 543; Chinese People's Volunteers, 40; civilian attitudes towards, 557; Cultural Revolution and, 48, 49, 549-51; discord in, 50-51; 8341 Unit, 528; General Logistics Department, 556, 559, 561; General Political Department, 555, 559, 560-61; General Staff Department, 555, 559, 560; law enforcement responsibilities, 516-17, 527; manpower, 544, 562; newspaper, 199, 438, 560; origins, 545; promotion of professionalism, 51; rank system, 567-68; revolutionary committees, 550; role in politics and government, 464, 550-51, 555-56; Sino-Indian border deployments, 578;

Sino-Soviet border deployments, 577; uniforms and insignia, 568; weapons production, 571
People's Literature Publishing House, 199
People's Publishing House, 199
petroleum, 260
Philippines: imports from, 295; military cooperation, 580; sovereignty claims, 65
philosophical developments (*see also* Confucianism): Hundred Schools of Thought, 7-10; Neo-Confucianism, 16, 20
PLA. *See* People's Liberation Army (PLA)
police, xxviii, 507; Anti-Rightist Campaign mandate, 515; auxiliary units, 528; People's Armed Police Force, 533, 544, 561, 562, 592-93; powers and responsibilities, 511, 515, 527, 529-32; recruitment, 532-33; residential control, 530-31; secret police, 531; Soviet model, 527; training, 533; use of weapons and force, 532
Political Bureau, xxxvii-xxxviii; foreign policy role, 482; membership, xxxvii, 413, 556; Standing Committee, 413, 451
political developments (*see also* Chinese Communist Party (CCP); government), xxvi, 445-69; cadre system, 434-37, 463-64; campaign against "bourgeois liberalization," 461-62; centralization, 42; collective leadership, 450-52, 463; decentralization of power, 445, 459-60; democratic centralism principle, 411, 426, 454, 461, 520; direct elections, 461; economic emphasis, 54, 447; imperialism, 11-30; Marxism-Leninism-Mao Zedong Thought, 410, 446, 447, 456, 465-66; militarization of, 463, 464, 543; opening up policy, 454-55; political consciousness, 213; political parties, 419- 20, 422; public participation, 418-21, 461, 463; reforms, 450-52, 453-55, 460-62; republicanism, 29-31, 39-40, 509; role of ideology, 466-69; "spiritual pollution" campaign, 457; stability vs. revolution, 447; transition to socialism, 41-43
Polo, Marco, 17
population, xxii, xxxiii, 61-62, 72-88; birth control programs, 75-78, 131; birth rates, 74-75; density and distribution, 78-84, 231; growth rates, 261; infant mortality rates, 209; life expectancy, xxii, 90, 209, 240; minority groups, 61; mortality rates, 74, 94; 1982 census, 61-62, 72-74; 1953 census, 41; urbanization, 81-83
ports and shipping, xxv, 21; construction projects, 357; container ship fleet, 362; inadequacies, 356, 362-63
Portugal, 21; and Macao, 434, 477-78
postal services, 364-65; labor force, 236
procuratorates (*see also* judicial system), xxvii, 518; elections, 520; functions, 511, 529; Organic Law of, 519-20
Production and Construction Corps, 575
Propaganda Department, 482
Protect the Emperor Society. *See* Baohuang Hui
Protocol of 1901, 29
public order. *See* internal security
publishing industry, 198-99; nationalization, 198; restrictions, 198
Puyi, 30, 36

Qaidam Basin, 67, 327
Qiao Shi, xxxvii
Qilian Shan, 67
Qin dynasty, 11, 13, 508, 525; cultural developments, 193
Qin Jianxian, 185
Qin Ling, 69, 268
Qing dynasty, xxxi, xxxii, 18-30, 365, 475, 509; cultural developments, 190; legal system, 525-26; science and technology, 374-75
Qing Zang Plateau, xxii, 65, 66, 68, 69, 71
Qingdao, xxv; industry, 305; textiles, 321
Qinghai Province, 65, 328; chemical industry, 318; economic subsidies, 86; minority riots, xxxix; population, 78, 85; supported migration to, 81
Qinghai-Tibet Plateau. *See* Qing Zang Plateau
Qinghua University, xxii, 172
Qinhuangdao, xxv, 319, 328
Qinshan, 331
Qu Yuan, 186
Quemoy. *See* Jinmen

radio and television. *See* communications
Radio Beijing, 366, 368; foreign language broadcasting, 368
railroads, xxv, 236, 357-58; imported technology, 316; investments in, 315-16, 358; passengers, 357
Railway Engineering Corps, 561, 575
rainfall, 71, 268
Rao Shushi, 42
Reagan, Ronald, 495
Record of Rites (*Liji*), 186
Red Army (*see also* People's Liberation Army (PLA)), 37; Long March, 36, 545; political alignments, 545; theatrical productions, 192
Red Flag. *See Hongqi*
Red Guards, 166, 220, 527, 550; Mao Zedong and, 48-49; origins, 48
Reference Information. *See Cankao Ziliao*
Reference News. *See Cankao Xiaoxi*
reform movements. *See* modernization movements
religion, 145-46; anti-Christian campaigns, 28-29, 40-41; Buddhism, xxxii, 13, 14, 16, 145, 146; Christianity, 146; and Confucianism, 104; and the Cultural Revolution, 101; Islam, 17; Jesuits in China, 22; Lamaism (Tibetan Buddhism), 17; Nestorians, 17; political organizations, 421; Protestants, 145; rituals, 146; Roman Catholicism, 17, 22, 145; Taoism, 145, 146
Renmin Ribao (People's Daily), 199, 431, 438
Republic of Korea, 498
Republic of Vietnam (*see also* Democratic Republic of Vietnam; Vietnam); and France, 26; PLA actions, 551
research (*see also* scientific and technological developments): agriculture, 285-86; Chinese Communist Party role, 308, 382; colleges and universities, 391-92; duplication of, 387; emphasis on applied work, 382, 384; funding, 392; industry, 306-8; institutes, 387, 387-92; military sector, 390-91; peasants mobilization for, 382; planning, 392-93; in productive enterprises, 392
roads, xxv, 237, 357, 360
Roman Empire, 13
Romania, 501, 580
ru (School of Literati), 8
Ruijin, 36
rulers. *See* leadership
rural areas (*see also* agriculture; peasants): cadres, 127-28; class labelling, 125; community structure, 133-34; consumer services, 344; corruption, 128; education, 160, 162, 164; family organization, 126-27, 130-32; household investments, 276-77; incomes, 257-59; industrial enterprises, 331-32; marketing system, 277; marriage, 132; nonagricultural concerns, 232, 234, 278, 292, 294; regional inequalities, 455; and religion, 146; township governments, 279
Russia (*see also* Soviet Union): imperialist actions, 26; and Outer Mongolia, 31; trade with, 21; unequal treaties with, 490

san fan ("three anti") movement, 41, 512
san min zhuyi (Three Principles of the People), 29-30
satellites, 301, 306, 332, 366, 367, 390; ground stations, 367
Saudi Arabia, 498; military exports to, xli
School of Law (*fa*), 8, 10, 508
School of Literati (*ru*), xxxi, 8
Science Society of China, 376
scientific and technical personnel, 386-87, 401-3; consulting work, 402; emigration of, 377; employment rewards, 398, 399; exchanges with Soviet Union, 378; job assignment system, 398, 402; job mobility, 401-3; lowering of professional standards, 380; misemployment of, 398; overseas training and research, 395, 396; professional bodies, 394-95; "reds" versus "experts," xxxiii-xxxiv, 379-82; shortages, 386, 404
scientific and technological developments (*see also* research), xxvi, 373-404; achievements, 373; in agriculture, 211, 231; ancient period, 12, 13, 14; applications to industry, 377-78, 398; commercialization of, 398-99, 400; coordinating bodies, 393-95; emphasis on practical benefits, 385; exchange agreements and joint projects, 384, 396-97, 400-1, 403-4; funding, 398-99, 400; historical developments, 374-86; in industry, 211, 306-8; institutions, 376-77, 387-92;

international ties, 384, 395–97; Joint Commissions, 378, 396; under Mongol rule, 17; organization/administration of, 379, 387–95; planning, 378, 384–85, 392–93; popularization of, 376, 395; pre-1949, 374–77; reforms, xxxvi, 382–86, 397–403, 447; role of politics, 383; 1950's, 377–79; separation of research from production, 378; Soviet influences, 377–79, 385, 491; technology markets, 400–1; technology transfer, xxiii, 378, 403–4; Western influences, 24–25
Second Artillery Corps. *See* Strategic Missile Force
"second revolution." *See* Four Modernizations
Secretariat, 409; foreign policy, 482; functions, 451; International Liaison Department, 482; membership, 415; reestablishment of, 415, 451, 463
Self-Strengthening Movement, 24–26; scientific developments, 375
Sha Yexin, 192
Shaanxi Province, 6, 36, 68, 213, 274, 357, 417; industry, 325
Shan people, 86
Shandong Province, 146, 270, 328, 343; agricultural crops, 277, 290; industry, 325; and Japan, 31–32; textiles, 320
Shang dynasty, 5–6
Shanghai, 33, 52, 61, 81, 195, 199, 228, 237, 245, 348; aircraft production plants, 316; education system, 159; import-export companies, 349; incomes, 258; industry, xxiii, 235, 305, 314, 315, 318; population, 82; textiles, 320, 321
Shanghai Communiqué, 493
Shanghai Economic Zone, 342
Shanghai Municipal Library, 201
Shanghai People's Art Theater, 192
Shangwu Yinshuguan (Commercial Press), 198, 199
Shantou, 34, 226, 348, 433
Shekou, 433
Shengli, 326, 327, 575
Shenyang, 159, 199, 245; industry, 305, 314, 316, 318; military region, 561; population, 78, 82
Shenzhen, 159, 226, 348, 433
Shijie Jingji Daobao (World Economic Journal), 185
Shijing (Classic of Poetry), 186
shipbuilding, 316
Shuihu Zhuan (Water Margin), 546
Shujing (Classic of Documents), 186
Siberia, 21
Sichuan Basin, 69, 269; population, 78
Sichuan Province: agricultural crops, 290; industry, 306, 315, 318, 324; natural gas reserves, 327; textiles, 320
Signal Corps, 575
Sima Qian, 12
Sino-Burmese Boundary Treaty, 65
sinocentrism, 4, 6, 13, 475; and foreign policy, 475–76
socialism. *See* political developments
Socialist Education Movement, 47, 153
society (*see also* cultural developments; family life; Han Chinese; income; minority nationalities; religion; standard of living), xxii, 99–150; attitudes towards government, 105–6; class structure, 15, 39; and communist party membership, 116–17; and Confucianism, 104–6; elite groups, 106, 107; ethnic tension, 101; government control, 112–14; *guanxi* (personal connections) system, 122–24; inequalities, 147, 149; language, 101; moral deterioration, 228; 1950's transformation of, 112–14; organizational units, 114–16; partible inheritance system, 106; political life, 121; reeducation of, post-Mao, 445; role of women, 143; rural, 124–34; social stratification, xxxi–xxxii, 108–10; "spiritual pollution" campaign, 183–84, 457; traditional culture, 103–12; upward mobility, 109, 110, 112, 117, 120, 125; urban, 134–43; urban-rural distinctions, 117–19, 212, 231; welfare programs, 115, 122; and work units, 120–24
Society of Righteousness and Harmony, 28–29
Somalia, 573, 580
Song Defu, 420
Song dynasty, xxxi, 14–16, 525; cultural developments, 187, 194
Song Jiaoren, 30
Song Longxian, 184–85
Song Yu, 186
Songs of Chu (*Chuci*), 186
Songhua Jiang, 326
South Africa, 498

South China Sea, 71, 544, 551, 576; oil reserves, 327; strategic importance of, 579
Southern Song dynasty, 15
Southwestern Economic Zone, 342
Soviet Union (*see also* Russia), 64; border disputes, 21-22, 49, 64-65, 477, 489-90, 491, 492, 576; and Chinese warlords, 32-33; economic assistance, 215; foreign relations, xxvii, 46, 474, 488-91; ideological differences, 489-90; industrial assistance, 215, 302; invasion of Czechoslovakia, 49; labor force requests, 83; and Manchuria, 38; military cooperation, 547, 580; normalization of relations, 491; nuclear energy assistance, 330; political support, 32-33; scientific and technical assistance, 306, 377-79, 396; as security threat, 490, 544, 575-77; and Sino-Indian border dispute, 46; suspension of aid from, 46; and Taiwan, 46; trade with, 44, 295, 346, 353, 491; war reparations, 214
Spain, 21, 498
Special Economic Zones Office, 351
"spiritual pollution" campaign, 183-84, 457
Spratly Islands. *See* Nansha Islands
Spring and Autumn (*Chun Qiu*), 186
Spring and Autumn Period, 7-10
Sri Lanka, military ties with, 580, 582
standard of living, 209, 250-59; clothing, 252, 254; cost of living, 257; food consumption, 251-52; government services, 136; and increased expectations, 147; minority areas, 86; regional variations, 117-18, 119, 259; rural society, 126-27; urban society, 117-18, 259
State Administration of Exchange Control, 351
State Administrative Council (*see also* State Council), 39
State Capital Construction Commission, 240
State Constitution of 1982 (*see also* constitutional developments), 421-24; articles of, 422-24; civil rights, 521; economic provisions, 228-29; foreign policy provisions, 434; legal reforms, 521-22; local administration provisions, 428
State Council, xxvi, 42, 426; birth control activities, 75; economic role, 229, 239; Foreign Affairs Coordination Point, 486, 488; foreign policy role, 482, 483; foreign trade organizations, 349, 351; Hong Kong and Macao Affairs Office, 426, 434; and industry organization, 305; job contract system, 148; membership, 426, 427, 452; restructuring of, xxxviii; role in decision making, 451-52; science and technology responsibilities, 388; Special Economic Zones Office, 426; task forces, 426-27
State Council Bulletin. *See Guowuyuan Gongbao*
State Economic Commission, 229, 240, 278, 392; foreign trade role, 351; science policy role, 390
State Education Commission, 153, 155, 157, 166, 176, 178, 484; research funding, 392
state farms, 234, 272, 278
State Import and Export Commodities Inspection Administration, 351
State Machine-Building Industry Commission, 229, 305, 570
state-owned enterprises: farms, 234, 272, 278; income, 235, 255; industry, 235, 305; labor force, 309
State Planning Commission, 350, 392; agriculture and, 278; economy and, 229, 240; foreign trade planning, 351; science policy role, 390
State Science and Technology Commission, 385, 388, 402; responsibilities, 388, 390, 392; science policy role, 303, 390
State Statistical Bureau, 209; agriculture and, 278; economy and, 229, 240; labor force statistics, 90, 386
stock exchanges, 245, 458
Strategic Missile Force (Second Artillery Corps), 544; equipment, xxvii; expenditures, 569; manpower, 562; nuclear forces, 587-90
subway system, 358, 360
Sudan, military ties with, 573, 580
Suez Canal Authority, 362
Sui dynasty, 13-14
Sun Yat-sen, 29, 30, 32-33
Sun Yixian. *See* Sun Yat-sen
Sun Zi, 545
Sungari River. *See* Songhua Jiang
Supreme People's Court, xxvi, 513, 515-16, 517, 523; military trial responsibilities, 524-25

Taihang Shan, 66
Taipei, 39
Taiping Rebellion, 23-24, 25, 546
Taiwan, xxxii, 39, 45, 416, 418, 498, 544; and Chinese national defense, 579; and Japan, 26, 499, 500; reunification goal, xl, 478; as security threat, 576; sovereignty claims, 65; Soviet stance on, 489; United States assistance to, 492
Taiwan Democratic Self-Government League, 420
Taiyuan, 305, 314, 318
Talas, 14
Tanaka, Kakuei, 367
Tang dynasty, 14, 476; cultural developments, 187, 194
Tangshan, 52, 68; earthquake, 222, 304, 312, 324; industry, 235, 312
Tanzania, 580
Taoism, 10; cultural influences, 187; Mongol persecution, 17
Tarim Basin, 12, 67, 327
taxation, xxxvi, 242; revenue sharing, 243
technological developments. *See* research; scientific and technological developments
technology transfer. *See* scientific and technological developments
telecommunications. *See* communications
Television University, 369
televisions. *See* communications; consumer goods and services
textiles, 301, 304; cotton, 320-21; production, 320, 321; silk, 320, 321
Thailand, 295, 580
Third World (*see also* under names of individual countries): arms sales to, 573; Bandung conference, 495, 496; China/Soviet Union competition in, 490; Chinese militancy in, 496; cultural ties with, 497; foreign relations, 495-98; military ties with, 332, 544, 580; trade with, 354, 498
"three anti" *san fan* movement, 41, 512
Three Kingdoms (Wei, Shu, and Wu), 13
Three Principles of the People (*san min zhuyi*), 29-30
Tian Jiyun, xxxix
Tian Shan, 67
Tiananmen Square, 53, 54; demonstrations, 52, 516, 528
Tianjin, xxv, 24, 29, 38, 81, 228, 348; education system, 159; import-export companies, 349; industry, 235, 305, 314, 318; population, 82; textiles, 321
tianming ("mandate of heaven"), 6, 8, 52
Tibet. *See* Xizang Autonomous Region
Tibetan people, 84, 85, 88
tithing. *See bao jia*
Tongmeng Hui (United League), 29-30
Tongzhi Restoration, 25
topography, xxii
tourism, xxiv, 17, 354; travel restrictions, xxxix
trade. *See* foreign trade; internal trade
trade unions, 420; strike rights, 422-23
transportation, xxv, 209, 212, 236-37, 354-64; aircraft production, 316; automotive industry, 315; bridges, 361; civil aviation, 363-64; development projects, 304, 356-57; disruptions during Cultural Revolution, 220; freight traffic, 355-56; inadequacies, 119, 354; inland waterways, 355, 361-62; investments in, 356; labor force, 236; maritime shipping, 316, 356, 362-63; non-motorized vehicles, 361; ownership and control, 356; passenger traffic, 356; post-World War II, 214; railroads, 315-16, 355, 357-58; roads, 355-56, 360-61; subways, 355, 358, 360
Treaty of Friendship, Alliance, and Mutual Assistance, 40, 50, 489, 547; termination of, 55, 576
Treaty of Kiakhta, 21
Treaty of Nanjing, 23
Treaty of Nerchinsk, 21, 26
Treaty of Shimonoseki, 26
Triad Society, 21
tributary system, 13
Twenty-One Demands, 31-32

Ulanhu, 88
unemployment. *See* labor force
United Front Work Department, 482
United Kingdom. *See* Great Britain
United League (Tongmeng Hui), 29-30
United Nations (UN): economic and technical assistance from, 502; and the Korean War, 40; membership of, 481, 497, 502; scientific activities, 396
United States: aid to Nationalist government, 38-39; Chinese students in, 83, 173, 375, 386; diplomatic recognition by, 55; emigration policies, 83; foreign

relations with, xxvii, xli, 492-95; joint ventures with, 348; military ties with, 544, 581; normalization of relations, 51, 474, 490, 492, 493; nuclear energy agreement, 494; "open door" Chinese policy, 26, 28; scientific and technological cooperation, 308, 330, 396; security ties, 494; technology transfer limitations, 495; Three Mile Island incident, 330; trade with, xxiv, 295, 353-54, 494, 495; troops in China, 38
universities and colleges (*see also* education), 166-67, 376; administration of, 168; admission rates, 170; adult students, 171; during Cultural Revolution, 221, 380; enrollment plans and policies, 167, 169-73; funding of, 168-69; institutions, 171; minority groups, 170, 171; political criteria for admission, 167; prestige, 169, 174; radio and television services, 440; research, 391-92; scholarship and loan system, 173; staffing, 172; student exchanges, 222; study abroad, 173-74
University of Police Officers, 533
University of Public Security, 533
urban areas: administrative barriers, 118; ancient period, 15; cost of living, 257; decentralization of power, 459-60; economic subsidies, 136; education system, 162; family life, 138-40; household registers, 134-35; housing, 135, 136-38; reforms, 458-59; service sector shortages, 136, 138
Uruguay, 498; diplomatic relations with, xli
Ussuri River. *See* Wusuli Jiang
Uygurs, 84, 86

Vavilov, Sergei I., 378
Vietnam (*see also* Democratic Republic of Vietnam; Republic of Vietnam), xl, 3, 13, 16, 18; border wars with, 55, 552-53; as security threat, 577-78; sovereignty claims, 65; War, 492

Wan Li, xxxix
wan xi shao campaign, 74
Wang Dongxing, 53, 55
Wang Hongwen, 50, 56
Wang Mang, 13
Wang Meng, 185
Wang Zhen, 449
warlords, xxxii, 13, 31, 509; opposition to, 32-34
Warring States Period, 7, 186, 508; philosophical developments, 7-10
Water Margin (*Shuihu Zhuan*), 546
waterways, xxv, 69, 236-37; freight traffic, 361-62
Way (*dao*), 10
Wei Valley, 6
welfare programs. *See* society
Wenyibao (Literary Gazette), 183
the West (*see also* under names of individual countries), 20; adoption of Western technology, 24-25; attitudes towards, 4, 51; cultural contamination, 455, 456; cultural influences, 207; trade relationship, 21, 22; travel in China, 17
West Germany: foreign relations, 498; labor force requests, 83; technology imports from, 308; trade relationship, xxiv, 354
Western Europe (*see also* under names of individual countries): Chinese students in, 375; foreign relations, 500-1; military ties with, 544, 581; scientific cooperation, 396; trade relationship, 219, 354
Western Han dynasty, 344-45
Western Zhou dynasty, 7
Whampoa Military Academy, 33
White Lotus, 21
wildlife, 71-72
women, 143-45; armed forces, 565, 566; discrimination, 144-45; education, 143, 144; labor force, 74, 135, 144-45; status, 143-44, 513
work units. *See danwei* (work units)
World Bank, 160, 209, 314, 351, 373, 497; membership, 347, 502; research assistance, 392
World Economic Journal. *See Shijie Jingji Daobao*
World Intellectual Property Organization, 502
World War I, 31-32
writing system, 3, 6
Wu De, 55
Wu Di, 12, 193
wu fan ("five anti") movement, 41, 512
Wu Han, 48
Wu Xueqian, xxxix, xli

Wuchang, 30
Wuhan, 34, 199, 245; industry, xxiii, 305, 306, 313, 314, 319; revolt, 586
Wusuli Jiang, 26, 49, 64, 576
Wuxi, 308
Wuxiandian Yu Dianshi (Journal of Radio and Television), 196

xenophobia, effects of, 221
Xia dynasty, 5
xiafang (down to the countryside), 43–44; and school reform, 47–48
Xiamen, 159, 226, 348, 433
Xiamen Construction and Development Corporation, 433
Xi'an (*see also* Chang'an), 6, 37, 199, 245; industry, 314, 316
Xianggang. *See* Hong Kong
Xie Fuzhi, 50, 56
Xinhua (New China) News Agency, 199, 439
Xinhua Shudian (New China Booksellers), 198
Xinjiang Military District, 592
Xinjiang-Uygur Autonomous Region, xxii, 12, 26, 71, 234, 270, 328, 592; agricultural crops, 290; economic subsidies, 86; ethnic tensions, 88, 101; housing conditions, 255; population, 78, 84; strategic importance of, 578; supported migration to, 81
Xisha Islands, 65, 576, 579; PLA actions, 551
Xizang Autonomous Region, xxii, 20, 40, 45, 65, 270; alleged human rights violations, xli; autonomy of, 31; control of, 477; economic subsidies, 86; ethnic tensions, 101; housing conditions, 255; minority discontent, xxxix, 88; PLA activities, 546, 549; population, 78, 84; strategic importance of, 578
Xun Zi, 8

Yalü Jiang River, 40
Yalta Conference, 38
Yan'an, 36, 37
Yan'an Forum on Literature and Art, 193
Yang Dezhi, 552
Yang Shangkun, xxxviii
Yangtze River. *See* Chang Jiang
Yangzhou, 69
Yanshan, 392
Yao people, 86
Yao Wenyuan, 48, 50, 56
Yao Yilin, xxxvii, xxxix
Yarlung Zangbo Jiang. *See* Brahmaputra River
Ye Jianying, 53, 55, 413, 551, 557
Yellow River. *See* Huang He
Yellow Sea. *See* Huang Hai
Yi people, 85
Yihetuan (Society of Righteousness and Harmony), 28–29
Yijing (Book of Changes), 185–86
Yin dynasty. *See* Shang dynasty
Yin Shan, 68
yin-yang philosophy, 10
Ying He, 362
Yining Airport, 364
young people: armed forces involvement, 531, 561; and crime, 539; and the Cultural Revolution, 48–49; mass organizations, 161, 418, 420–21; support for Deng Xiaoping, 54
Young Pioneers, 161, 421
Yuan dynasty, 16–17, 475; cultural developments, 190
Yuan Shikai, 28, 30–31
Yugoslavia, 501, 580
Yunnan-Guizhou Plateau, 66, 69; standard of living, 119
Yunnan Province: agricultural crops, 290; economic subsidies, 86; industry, 325; population settlement, 84, 85

Zaire, 580
Zambia, 580
Zeng Guofan, 24
Zengmu Shoal, xxi
Zhang Chunqiao, 50, 56, 551
Zhanjiang, 575
Zhao Ziyang, xxxv, xxxvii, xxxviii, 56, 409, 413, 450, 451; background, 450; and Chinese Communist Party, 461; civil bureaucracy reforms, 434–35; economic policies, 450; foreign policy, 503; premier, 56, 450; science policy, 394, 397; "spiritual pollution" campaign, 457; visit to United States, 495
Zhejiang Province, 332; industry, 327; textiles, 320, 321
Zhenbao Island, 49, 490
Zhongguo. *See* Middle Kingdom

Zhongguo Xinwenshe (China News Service), 199, 440
Zhonghua Shuju (China Publishing House), 198, 199
Zhonghua Xinwenshe. *See* China News Service
Zhongyuan Basin, 328
Zhou dynasty, 6-7, 10; cultural developments, 193
Zhou Enlai, xxxi, 39, 50, 57, 181, 215, 221, 304, 448, 545, 551; and the Cultural Revolution, 48; death of, 52, 222, 445; economic policies, 51, 213, 221, 222; foreign policy, 481, 483-84, 490, 496; Four Modernizations program, 52; nuclear energy policy, 330; and the People's Liberation Army, 50-51; premier, 42; scientific policy, 382-83; trade policy, 346
Zhou Weizhi, 182
Zhu De, 35, 57, 545; death of, 52
Zhu Houze, 185
Zhu Jiang, xxv, 69, 355
Zhu Jiang Basin, 330
Zhu Jiang Delta, 327, 343; population, 78
Zhu Xi, 16
Zhuang people, 85
Zhuang Zi, 10, 186
Zhuhai, 226, 348, 433
Zuo Zongtang, 25

Published Country Studies

(Area Handbook Series)

550-65	Afghanistan	550-174	Guinea
550-98	Albania	550-82	Guyana
550-44	Algeria	550-151	Honduras
550-59	Angola	550-165	Hungary
550-73	Argentina	550-21	India
550-169	Australia	550-154	Indian Ocean
550-176	Austria	550-39	Indonesia
550-175	Bangladesh	550-68	Iran
550-170	Belgium	550-31	Iraq
550-66	Bolivia	550-25	Israel
550-20	Brazil	550-182	Italy
550-168	Bulgaria	550-69	Ivory Coast
550-61	Burma	550-30	Japan
550-50	Cambodia	550-34	Jordan
550-166	Cameroon	550-56	Kenya
550-159	Chad	550-81	Korea, North
550-77	Chile	550-41	Korea, South
550-60	China	550-58	Laos
550-26	Colombia	550-24	Lebanon
550-33	Commonwealth Caribbean, Islands of the	550-38	Liberia
550-91	Congo	550-85	Libya
550-90	Costa Rica	550-172	Malawi
550-152	Cuba	550-45	Malaysia
550-22	Cyprus	550-161	Mauritania
550-158	Czechoslovakia	550-79	Mexico
550-52	Ecuador	550-49	Morocco
550-43	Egypt	550-64	Mozambique
550-150	El Salvador	550-88	Nicaragua
550-28	Ethiopia	550-157	Nigeria
550-167	Finland	550-94	Oceania
550-155	Germany, East	550-48	Pakistan
550-173	Germany, Fed. Rep. of	550-46	Panama
550-153	Ghana	550-156	Paraguay
550-87	Greece	550-185	Persian Gulf States
550-78	Guatemala	550-42	Peru

550–72	Philippines	550–62	Tanzania
550–162	Poland	550–53	Thailand
550–181	Portugal	550–89	Tunisia
550–160	Romania	550–80	Turkey
550–51	Saudi Arabia	550–74	Uganda
550–70	Senegal	550–97	Uruguay
550–180	Sierra Leone	550–71	Venezuela
550–184	Singapore	550–32	Vietnam
550–86	Somalia	550–183	Yemens, The
550–93	South Africa	550–99	Yugoslavia
550–95	Soviet Union	550–67	Zaire
550–179	Spain	550–75	Zambia
550–96	Sri Lanka	550–171	Zimbabwe
550–27	Sudan		
550–47	Syria		

☆U.S. GOVERNMENT PRINTING OFFICE: 1989 -0- 242-444 00001